Pathway

Teachers' Manual

Einführungsphase
Sekundarstufe II

Herausgegeben von:
Iris Edelbrock

Erarbeitet von:
Iris Edelbrock
Alexandra Peschel
Elin Arbin
Andrew Lesh
Ronnie Halligan

Sprachliche Betreuung:
Elin Arbin
Ronnie Halligan

Schöningh
westermann

Die Begleitmaterialien zu „Pathway" können über den Buchhandel oder direkt beim Verlag bezogen werden:

- **Students' Book**
  Best.-Nr. 040175

- **Audio-CDs**
  Hörtexte und Songs
  Best.-Nr. 062531

- **Grammar and Skills Trainer**
  Best.-Nr. 040176

- **Differenzierungsmaterial**
  Kopiervorlagen
  Best.-Nr. 040177

- **Comprehension: Reading – Listening – Viewing**
  Kopiervorlagen mit standartisierten Aufgabenformaten
  Best.-Nr. 040168

- **Mündliche Prüfung**
  Kopiervorlagen
  Best.-Nr. 040156

Weitere Informationen finden Sie unter www.westermann.de.

Acknowledgements

Images

|Condé Nast, New York: © David Sipress/The New Yorker Collection/The Cartoon Bank 7. |Domke, Franz-Josef, Hannover: 59, 94, 96, 100, 105, 139, 272.

Wir arbeiten sehr sorgfältig daran, für alle verwendeten Abbildungen die Rechteinhaberinnen und Rechteinhaber zu ermitteln. Sollte uns dies im Einzelfall nicht vollständig gelungen sein, werden berechtigte Ansprüche selbstverständlich im Rahmen der üblichen Vereinbarungen abgegolten.

westermann GRUPPE

Druck A[4] / Jahr 2019
Alle Drucke der Serie A sind im Unterricht parallel verwendbar.

Umschlaggestaltung: Nora Krull, Bielefeld; Fotos: © Frans Lemmens/Corbis (vorn); Oote Boe/OKAPIA (hinten)
Druck und Bindung: Westermann Druck GmbH, Braunschweig

ISBN 978-3-14-**040178**-4

Contents

Vorwort 7

Kompetenzorientiert unterrichten mit *Pathway* 8

Die Kombination von Aufgabenformaten / Klausurformate 18

Stoffverteilungspläne 18

Additional tasks for differentiation available *(Pathway Differenzierungsmaterial)*

M Mediation between German and English

Film viewing tasks

Listening comprehension

Who Am I? ... Who Are You? – Challenges in Teenage Life

Start-up Activities

●●○ Leland Bobbé: The Two Sides of a Coin (photo) 28

●○○ Sting: Tomorrow We'll See (song) 28

Who Am I? ... Who Are You? – Role Models and Gender Roles

●●○ Joel Stein: The Me Me Me Generation (magazine article, cover, cartoons) 30

●●● John Irving: Owen Meany – Being Attractive to Girls (novel, photos) 37

●●○ Male Attractiveness: Abs-Olutely Fabulous (magazine article, cartoon) 40

●●○ 'Superficial Nightmare': Feminists Take Aim at Barbie Dreamhouse (magazine article, photos) 45

●●○ Colin Higgins: Harold and Maude (play, film stills) 50

What's Love Got to Do with It? – Family and Teenage Pregnancy

●○○ P!nk: Family Portrait (song, photo) 54

●○○ Eric Bogosian: No Problems (play, statistics) 57

M ●●○ Jens Jessen: Über Coolness (German magazine article) 62

●●● Ron Koertge: But Baseball and Sex? (poem, book cover) 65

●○○ Diablo Cody: Juno – Breaking the Big News (screenplay, film stills, cartoon, visuals) 68

Focus on Facts: Teenage Birthrates

●●● A High School Teacher Talks About Teenage Pregnancy (interview) 73

Big & Beautiful or Slim & Sexy? – Living with Your Body

●●● Robin Givhan: Why Skinny Young Models Persist on the Spring Runways (magazine article, photo) 77

●●○ Patrick Hickey Jr.: Artist Creates Healthy, "Normal" Barbie (online article, photo) 80

●○○ Jeremy Laurance: Hundreds of Websites Urging Girls to "Starve for Perfection" (newspaper article, photo) 81

●●○ Mirror, Mirror on the Wall ... Who Is the Fairest One of All? (photo page) 84

●●○ Disfigured – Learning to Accept Your Body (film) 86

People, Places, Perspectives – Mapping out Your Future

Start-up Activities

Rise up!! (photo) 90
Po Bronson: Why Teenagers Are Growing up So Slowly Today (magazine article/blog) 91

School's Out – What Next? – Crossroads, Choices & Careers ...

Fields of Learning and Their Components (mind map) 92
John Green: Looking for Alaska (novel, cartoon) 93
Gossip: Get a Job (song, photo) 101
Jane Goodall: Roots & Shoots (visual, website information, photo) 105
– Volunteer (website information) 108
– Testimonials (Internet testimonials/blogs) 108
– Role Cards (writing an email) 108
Focus on Facts: **Volunteerism in the USA**
Job Offers ... (job adverts) 109
Being Interviewed on the Phone (interview questions, role cards) 114
Recruiting Interns – All Work and No Pay? (magazine article, cartoons) 119
EU Migration to Germany – *Sprechen Sie Job?* (magazine article, cartoons) 123

Professional Communication & Correspondence

Planning for Your Graduation Ball (project) 127
Finding out About Interesting Products and Services – Making an Enquiry (telephoning, role cards) 128
When Customers Are Unhappy ... Making a Complaint (telephoning, role cards) 131

Life: A Box of Chocolates ...? – Coming to Grips with Reality

Start-up Activities

Mel Bochner: Oh Well (painting) 136
Teen Spirit: What's It Really Like to Be a Teenager (letters to the editor) 136

Between Paradise and the "End of the World"? – How Children Live ... and Survive ...

Moya Irvine: Child Labour – No School or Play for Millions of Young Workers (newspaper article, visual) 138
UNICEF: Child Deprivation Rates in Rich Countries (statistics) 138
Lucy Alibar: Juicy and Delicious – It's the End of the World, Y'All (play, painting) 142
Bruno Bettelheim: The Uses of Enchantment (lecture) 142
Lucy Alibar, Benh Zeitlin: Beasts of the Southern Wild (screenplay, cartoon, film still, film) 148
John Irving: Trying to Save Piggy Sneed (short story, photo) 153
Sarah O'Connor: London's Rail Stations Still Attract Vulnerable Runaways (newspaper article, website information) 161

Youth in Crisis – Broken Dreams and Lost Hopes

Generation Jobless (magazine article, statistics, cartoons) 164
Hillary Clinton: Remarks on Youth (political speech) 168
Christopher Dickey: Kill Zone (magazine article, statistics) 172
Moms Demand Action on Gun Laws (adverts) 176

Common Grounds and Cultural Clashes?! – Living Together in the 21st Century

Start-up Activities

- Applying for U.S. Citizenship (cartoon) 182
- The Global Village Project (online article, visual) 182

Are You with Us? – Cultural Clashes and Common Grounds

- Eric Bogosian: subUrbia (play, book cover, cartoon) 184
- Marike Frick: Tanz mit mir (German newspaper interview, cartoon) 192
- David Cameron: Speech on the Government's Immigration Policy (political speech, visual, cartoon) 195
- Marilyn Chin: How I Got That Name – An Essay on Assimilation (poem, photo) 202

Let's Come Together?! – Migrants, Minorities, Majorities

- David Cameron: The Doctrine of Multiculturalism Has Failed (political speech) 206
- Sunny Hundal: Multiculturalism Has Won the Day. Let's Move On (newspaper article) 207
- Khola Hasan: Mr. Cameron, British Multiculturalism Is Doing Fine (newspaper article) 207
- Fareed Zakaria: Broken and Obsolete (magazine article, cartoon, statistics) 215
- Sandra Cisneros: No Speak English (novel, magazine cover) 220
- **Focus on Facts: Great Britain: Immigration and Minorities**
- **Focus on Facts: The United States: Immigration and Minorities**
- Jhumpa Lahiri: The Namesake (novel, film, film stills) 226

The Global Village – The World in a Nutshell?!

Start-up Activities

- David J. Smith, Shelagh Armstrong: If the World Were a Village (children's book, visual) 233
- Living in the Global Community (cartoon) 233

Message in a Bottle? – Plastic, Pollution & Progress

- Greenpeace: The Trash Vortex (photo, online article, documentary, role cards, visual, cartoon) 236
- **Focus on Facts: Plastics**
- **Focus on Facts: Environmental and Ecological Movements**
- Clemens Höges: The Children of Sodom and Gomorrah – How Europe's Discarded Computers Are Poisoning Africa's Kids (magazine article, photo) 242

Getting Active & Being Responsible

- Lenny Kravitz: What Did I Do with My Life? (song) 248
- Katrin Zeug: Mit Biodiesel zur Party (German newspaper article, photo) 249
- Global Giving – The Girl Effect (Internet website, visuals) 253
- Malala Yousafzai: Speech at the United Nations (honorary address) 257
- HOKISA – Homes for Kids in South Africa (report, photos) 262
- Derek Markham: Recycled Orchestra Turns Trash Into Music (Internet article, photos) 267
- **Focus on Facts: Technology, Progress & Responsibility in a Global World**

Fashion, Fabrics & Fabs – How Expensive Is Cheap Fashion?

- Hasnain Kazim, Nils Klawitter, Wieland Wagner: The High Human Price of Cheap T-Shirts (magazine article, photos, statistics) 271
- How Expensive Is Cheap Fashion? – The Best Eco-Fashion Brands and Eco-Criteria (photo page) 276
- Made in Germany: Eco-Fashion – Save the Planet and Look Good (Internet report, cartoons) 279
- Brita Belli: The Eco-Fashion Revolution – You Are What You Wear (Internet article, photos, visual) 282

Virtual Communities and Social Networks – Living in the Digital Age

Start-up Activities

- Blue Man Group: GiPad (photo) 290
- Digital Lifestyle (cartoon, statistics) 290

It's a Digital World – Connections & Disconnections

- Matt Richtel: Wasting Time Is New Divide in Digital Era (newspaper article, statistics, cartoons) 292
- Mehr Lehm (German newspaper article, photo) 292
- Tablet Teachers – Digital Education in Kenya (magazine article, photo) 297
- Vivian Yee: A School Distanced from Technology Faces Its Intrusion (newspaper article, photo) 303
- **Focus on Facts: Key Qualifications and Soft Skills**
- Robert Waugh: TXT BAD 4 UR BRAIN? Text Messaging Can Dent Your Reading Abilities Say Scientists (newspaper article, cartoon) 306
- **Focus on Facts: The Media**

Chat Room or Conference Room? – Meeting People in Formal and Informal Situations

- James Poniewozik: Serial Killing (magazine article, visual) 309
- Spaces and Spectres – Living Multimedia-Based (cartoon strips) 313
- Chat Rooms – Opportunities and Risks (cartoon, statistics, screenshot, visual) 316
- Charlie Rose: Exclusive Interview with Facebook Leadership Mark Zuckerberg and Sheryl Sandberg (interview) 320

Sending You an SMS ... – Youth Culture & Digital Lifestyle

- Adam Sorensen: Cats, Bears and Bacon. How to Build a Web-Comic Phenomenon (magazine article, cartoon strip) 323
- Rosemary Bennett: Why Facebook Friends Click When They Meet in the Flesh (newspaper article, cartoon) 325

Für Nutzer des Pathway-Lehrerbandes bieten wir **6 Klausuren zum kostenlosen Download** über unsere Homepage an.

Sie finden die **Klausuren inklusive Bewertungsbögen als editierbare Word-Dokumente** unter folgendem Link: www.schoeningh-schulbuch.de**/040178**

Vorwort

Liebe Kolleginnen und Kollegen,

das Lehrerhandbuch für das in der Neubearbeitung vorliegende „Pathway" möchte Ihnen Ihre Arbeit erleichtern und Sie darin unterstützen, einen schülerorientierten, methodisch vielfältigen und fachkompetenten Unterricht im Rahmen der Vorgaben des neuen Kernlehrplans zu gestalten.
Es bietet neben den Lösungen zu den Aufgabenapparaten des Schülerbuches eine Vielzahl von weiteren methodischen Vorschlägen und folgt der Chronologie des Schülerbuches.
Im Einzelnen enthält das Lehrerbuch folgende Elemente:

1. Eine einführende Tabelle zu Beginn jedes Kapitels gibt eine **Gesamtübersicht** über
- die Materialien des Schüler- und Lehrerhandbuches,
- weitere Übungen im *Grammar and Skills Trainer (GaST)*,
- weitere binnendifferenzierende Lern- und Arbeitsformen sowie Aufgabenstellungen im Differenzierungsmaterial,
- halb offene und geschlossene Aufgaben im Comprehension-Material in Ergänzung der Comprehension-Aufgaben des Schülerbuches,
- den inhaltlichen Bezug des Materials (Topic) sowie
- die mit dem Material verbundenen Kompetenzen (Skills).

2. Jeder Text/jedes Material des Schülerbuches wird im Lehrerbuch zunächst in Form einer **Übersichtstabelle** vorgestellt. Sie enthält Informationen zum Autor, Hintergrundinformationen über den Text oder das Werk, den Schwierigkeitsgrad des Textes sowie Hinweise auf Übungen in den Pathway-Begleitmaterialien.

3. Der sich anschließende **didaktisch-methodische Kommentar** bietet Ihnen in Ergänzung zu den Aufgabenstellungen im Schülerbuch weitere methodische Hinweise z.B. zum motivierenden Einstieg in eine neue Unterrichtsreihe oder zum Umgang mit einem neuen Material/Text. Der Kommentar gibt Anregungen für mögliche Sozialformen und/oder Sozialformwechsel und enthält darüber hinaus Beispiele für **Tafelbilder, z.B. zur Ergebnissicherung**.

4. Die sich anschließenden **Solutions** folgen der Chronologie der Aufgaben des Schülerbuches und werden zur Orientierung am Rand durch die auch im Schülerbuch verwendeten Symbole gekennzeichnet. Zu vielen Materialien/Texten finden sich im Anschluss an die *Solutions* weitere Aufgabenangebote (*Additional Tasks*) mit dazugehörenden Lösungen.

5. Zu jedem Kapitel finden sich unter dem Webcode **SNG-40175-031** auf der Seite www.westermann.de umfangreiche kopierfähige **Vokabellisten** (*Focus on Vocab*) zum eigenständigen Lernen oder für eine Überprüfung des thematischen Wortschatzes.

6. **Klausurvorschläge**, die in ihrer Struktur den **neuen Aufgabenformaten (Schreiben-Leseverstehen; Sprachmittlung; Hör-/Hörsehverstehen)** des Kernlehrplans sowie des Zentralabiturs entsprechen, stehen unter https://www.westermann.de/artikel/978-3-14-040178-4/Pathway-Lese-und-Arbeitsbuch-Englisch-zur-Einfuehrung-in-die-gymnasiale-Oberstufe-Neubearbeitung-Teachers-Manual#Ergaenzende_Materialien zum Download zur Verfügung. Zu jeder Klausur gibt es einen Erwartungshorizont.

7. Darüber hinaus geben **konkretisierte Unterrichtsvorhaben im Rahmen eines schulinternen Lehrplans für die gymnasiale Oberstufe** (Einführungsphase NRW) einen tabellarischen Überblick über mögliche Sequenzen und Unterrichtsreihen (S. 18).

Einen motivierenden, erfolgreichen und freudenreichen Unterricht wünscht Ihnen

das Pathway-Team

"There's nothing to be scared of, Mrs. Miller, it's just another teaching tool!"

Kompetenzorientiert unterrichten mit *Pathway*

Die Neuerungen des Kernlehrplans

1. Soziokulturelles Orientierungswissen

Einführungsphase
Oberthema: Alltagswirklichkeiten und Zukunftsperspektiven junger Erwachsener
• (Sprachen-)Lernen, Leben und Arbeiten im englischsprachigen Ausland
Oberthema: Politische, soziale und kulturelle Wirklichkeiten
• Zusammenleben, Kommunikation und Identitätsfindung im digitalen Zeitalter
Oberthema: Globale Herausforderungen und Zukunftsvisionen
• Wertorientierung und Zukunftsentwürfe im „*global village*“

2. Kompetenzen in Verbindung mit Kompetenzbereichen

<table>
<tr><td rowspan="3">Sprachlernkompetenz
(language learning awareness)</td><td>Interkulturelle kommunikative Kompetenz
Verstehen Handeln
Wissen Einstellungen Bewusstheit</td><td rowspan="3">Sprachbewusstheit
(language awareness)</td></tr>
<tr><td>Funktionale kommunikative Kompetenz
Hör-/Hörsehverstehen
Leseverstehen
Schreiben
Sprechen
Sprachmittlung
Verfügen über sprachliche Mittel und kommunikative Strategien</td></tr>
<tr><td>Text- und Medienkompetenz
mündlich schriftlich medial</td></tr>
</table>

3. Verknüpfung von Einzelkompetenzen
4. Vernetzung von Inhalten und Kompetenzen
5. Neue Klausurformate: Verknüpfung von Einzelkompetenzen (s. Übersicht, S. 18)
6. Neue standardisierte Aufgabenformate
   → Kombination von Aufgabenformaten und Einzelkompetenzen
   → geschlossene, halboffene, offene Aufgabenformate
7. Kooperative und individualisierende Arbeitsformen
   → Erweitertes Repertoire von Strategien und Techniken des selbstständigen und kooperativen Lernens
8. Individuelle Förderung und Differenzierung
   → Stärkeorientierung
9. Erweiterung der kulturellen Handlungsfähigkeit in anspruchsvollen anwendungsbezogenen Lernarrangements
10. Nutzung kreativer Arbeitsformen des Sprachenlernens

Die *Pathway*-Materialien im Überblick

- **Schülerband**
  mit Filmanalyse-Software auf CD-ROM
  Best.-Nr. 040175
- **Grammar and Skills Trainer**
  Best.-Nr. 040176
- **Differenzierungsmaterial**
  Best.-Nr. 040177
- **Ordner Teachers' Manual**
  Best.-Nr. 040179
- **Audio-CDs**
  Hörtexte und Songs, Doppel-CD, 2 x 74 Min.
  Best.-Nr. 062531
- **Comprehension: Reading – Listening – Viewing**
  Best.-Nr. 040168
- **Teachers' Manual**
  Best.-Nr. 040178

Pathway
Schülerbuch

Pathway
Comprehension
Reading • Listening • Viewing

- Training von standardisierten, geschlossenen und halboffenen Aufgabenformaten
- das Schülerbuch ergänzende Kopiervorlagen zum Einüben der standardisierten Aufgabenformate und Klausuraufgaben
- *multiple choice, matching, true-false, note-taking, short answers, paraphrasing, corrections, proof-reading, true-false-not given, gapped texts, sequencing*

Pathway
Grammar and Skills Trainer

- selbstständiges Arbeiten mit Texten und Materialien, die die Materialien des Schülerbuches ergänzen und vertiefen
- kombinierte Textformate
- standardisierte Aufgabenformate zu allen Anforderungsbereichen
- step-by-step Anleitungen zum gezielten Methoden- und Kompetenzerwerb
- zusätzliche, kontextualisierte Sprach- und Grammatikübungen

Pathway
Differenzierung

- die Aufgabenapparate des Schülerbuches ergänzende, leistungsdifferenzierende Aufgaben
- ergänzende Worksheets (Kopiervorlagen)
  - zur Binnendifferenzierung von heterogenen Gruppen
  - zur Förderung kooperativer Arbeitsformen
  - für die individuelle Förderung von Schülern
- didaktisch-methodischer Kommentar für den Lehrer
- Focus on Diff-Seiten

Die Kombination von Aufgabenformaten in *Pathway* und im Begleitmaterial zum Lehrwerk

Schülerbuch

Message in a Bottle? – Plastic, Pollution & Progress

Greenpeace

The Trash Vortex[1]

AWARENESS

It is hard to imagine the modern world without plastics … cars, computers, cell phones, kitchen utensils, textiles … even food … made of or wrapped in plastic are part of everyday life and plastic appears to be irreplaceable.
In a Pyramid Discussion (→ FoM, p. 272), exchange your views on whether plastics are a blessing or rather a curse of life today.

Chris Jordan, *Midway: Message from the Gyre*[2] (2009)

Tips on vocab
albatross ▪ skeletonized ▪ to decay (*verfallen*) ▪ dishevelled/hackly (*zerrupft, zerzaust*) ▪ plumage (*Federkleid*) ▪ intestines (*Innereien*) ▪ plastic items ▪ husk (*Hülse*) ▪ bottle cap

The very thing that makes plastic items useful to consumers, their durability[3] and stability, also makes them a problem in marine environments. Around 100 million tonnes of plastic are produced each year of which about 10 percent ends up in the sea. About 20 percent of this is from ships and platforms, the rest from land.

Take a walk along any beach anywhere in the world and washed ashore will be many polythene[4] plastic bags, bottles and containers, plastic drums, expanded polystyrene[5] packing, polyurethane foam[6] pieces, pieces of polypropylene[7] fishing net and discarded[8] lengths of rope. Together with traffic cones[9], disposable lighters,

[1] **vortex** *Wirbel* – [2] **gyre** [ˈdʒaɪə(r)] *Wirbel* – [3] **durability** *Strapazierfähigkeit* – [4] **polythene** [ˈpɒlɪθiːn] *Polyethylen, PE* – [5] **polystyrene** [ˈpɒlɪstriːn] *Polystyren* – [6] **polyurethane foam** [ˌpɒliˈjʊərəθeɪn fəʊm] *Polyurethan-Schaum* – [7] **polypropylen** [ˌpɒliˈprəʊpəliːn] *Polypropylen* – [8] **to discard sth.** *etw. achtlos wegwerfen* – [9] **traffic cones** *Verkehrskegel, Baustellenwarnhüte*

vehicle tyres[10] and toothbrushes, these items have been casually thrown away on land and at sea and have been carried ashore by wind and tide[11].
These larger items are the visible signs of a much larger problem. These big items do not degrade like natural materials. At sea and on shore under the influence of sunlight, wave action and mechanical abrasion[12] they simply break down slowly into ever smaller particles.
A single one litre bottle could break down into enough small fragments to put one on every mile of beach in the entire world. These smaller particles are joined by the small pellets[13] of plastic which are the form in which many new plastics are marketed and which can be lost at sea by the drum[14] load or even a whole container load. These modern day "marine tumbleweeds[15]" have been thrown into sharp focus, not only by the huge quantities removed from beaches by dedicated[16] volunteers, but by the fact that they have been found to accumulate[17] in sea areas where winds and currents[18] are weak.
The North Pacific sub-tropical gyre covers a large area of the Pacific in which the water circulates clockwise[19] in a slow spiral. Winds are light. The currents tend to force any floating[20] material into the low energy central area of the gyre. There are few islands on which the floating material can beach. So it stays there in the gyre, in astounding[21] quantities estimated at six kilos of plastic for every kilo of naturally occurring[22] plankton. The equivalent of an area the size of Texas swirling slowly around like a clock. This gyre has also been dubbed[23] "the Asian Trash Trail" the "Trash Vortex" or the "Eastern Garbage Patch[24]".
This perhaps wouldn't be too much of a problem if the plastic had no ill effects. The larger items, however, are consumed by seabirds and other animals which mistake them for prey[25]. Many seabirds and their chicks have been found dead, their stomachs filled with medium sized plastic items such as bottle tops, lighters and balloons. A turtle found dead in Hawaii had over a thousand pieces of plastic in its stomach and intestines[26]. It has been estimated that over a million sea-birds and one hundred thousand marine mammals[27] and sea turtles are killed each year by ingestion[28] of plastics or entanglement[29]. Animals can become entangled in discarded netting and line. Even tiny jelly-fish like creatures become entangled in lengths of plastic filament[30] or eat the small plastic particles floating in the water.

www.greenpeace.org/international/en/campaigns/oceans/pollution/trash-vortex [30.06.2013]

COMPREHENSION

1. **Before reading or listening** to one of the texts, have a closer look at the photo above the text. Describe the photo using the words and phrases from the vocab box. Then relate the photo to the title of this chapter – what is its "message in a bottle"?
→ Focus on Skills, Analysis of Visuals, p. 262

2. Divide the class into groups of 3–4 students each. The groups have a choice here:
a) you can **either read** the Greenpeace text about the Pacific Trash Vortex **or**
b) you can **listen** to the Planet100 audio text on the same topic.

Whatever material you choose, take notes while reading/listening and try to answer the questions/tasks below.
Be careful: not all the questions refer to both materials – thus you cannot answer all the questions/tasks at once.
- What is the meaning of the term "Pacific Trash Vortex"?
- Where does all the trash come from?
- What kind of garbage is discarded into the ocean?

[10] **tyre** [ˈtaɪə(r)] *Reifen* – [11] **tide** [taɪd] *Gezeiten* – [12] **abrasion** *Abnutzung* – [13] **pellet** a small hard ball of any substance – [14] **drum** a large container for oil or chemicals – [15] **tumbleweed** *Steppenläufer (Pflanze, die vom Wind ins Rollen gebracht wird)* – [16] **dedicated** *engagiert* – [17] **to accumulate** to gradually get more and more – [18] **current** *Strömung* – [19] **clockwise** *im Uhrzeigersinn* – [20] **to float** *treiben* – [21] **astounding** astonishing; *erstaunlich* – [22] **naturally occurring** *natürlich vorkommend* – [23] **to dub** *titulieren* – [24] **patch** area – [25] **prey** *Beute* – [26] **intestines** *Eingeweide* – [27] **mammal** *Säugetier* – [28] **ingestion** [ɪnˈdʒestʃən] *Nahrungsaufnahme* – [29] **entanglement** *Verwicklung* – [30] **filament** [ˈfɪləmənt] *Draht*

Kombination von ***reading and listening comprehension***

Worksheets aus dem *Differenzierungsmaterial* zum differenzierenden Arbeiten sowie zum Einüben der neuen (halboffenen) Aufgabenformate:

Differenzierungsmaterial

No. 1 Worksheet

Greenpeace

The Trash Vortex (Reading Comprehension)

Read the text about the Pacific Trash Vortex and decide whether the statements below are true or false. Tick the appropriate box and indicate the line where you found the respective information. Make corrections to the incorrect statements.

	True	False
1. Plastic items are useful to customers because they can be so easily disposed of.	☐	☐
2. 25% of the 100 million tons of plastic discarded each year ends up in the sea.	☐	☐
3. The majority of plastic items that have been thrown away are plastic toys, plastic textiles, polystyrene packaging and polyurethane foam pieces.	☐	☐
4. The influence of sunlight, wave action and mechanical abrasion cause the plastic items to decompose.	☐	☐
5. Small plastic pellets are transported across the oceans in huge containers.	☐	☐
6. Modern-day "marine tumbleweeds" are removed from beaches by dedicated volunteers.	☐	☐
7. The North Pacific sub-tropical gyre circulates about six kilos of plastic for every kilo of natural plankton.	☐	☐
8. The Trash Vortex covers an area twice the size of Texas.	☐	☐
9. Over a million seabirds and one hundred thousand marine mammals and sea turtles are killed each year by digestion of plastics or entanglement.	☐	☐
10. Only tiny jelly-fish like creatures are safe from small plastic particles.	☐	☐

No. 2 Worksheet

Greenpeace

The Trash Vortex (Listening Comprehension)

Listen to the Planet 100 special episode about the pacific Trash Vortex. Then read the statements below. After a second listening decide whether the following statements are true or false. Make corrections to the false statements.

	True	False
1. The Pacific Trash Vortex is a huge soup of trash.	☐	☐
2. The Pacific Trash Vortex is four times as large as Texas.	☐	☐
3. 50 percent of this trash is plastic, 80 percent of which comes from land and 20 percent from ships and oil platforms.	☐	☐
4. The Pacific Trash Vortex consists of three large separate vortexes.	☐	☐
5. There is the Eastern garbage patch between Hawaii and California and the Western garbage patch between Japan and Hawaii.	☐	☐
6. The developing world and China in particular are responsible for this trash.	☐	☐
7. Plastic has been around for about 200 years.	☐	☐
8. Every piece of plastic ever made still exists.	☐	☐
9. The world is turning out about 100 million tons of plastic annually.	☐	☐
10. The Pacific Trash Vortex is one of five huge trash vortexes which cover about 60 percent of the world's oceans.	☐	☐
11. Each inhabitant on earth disposes of 185 pounds of plastics every year.	☐	☐
12. Reducing, reusing and recycling would reduce the waste stream by at least 50 percent.	☐	☐

Role cards zum kreativen und anwendungs- und handlungsorientierten Arbeiten mit dem Material:

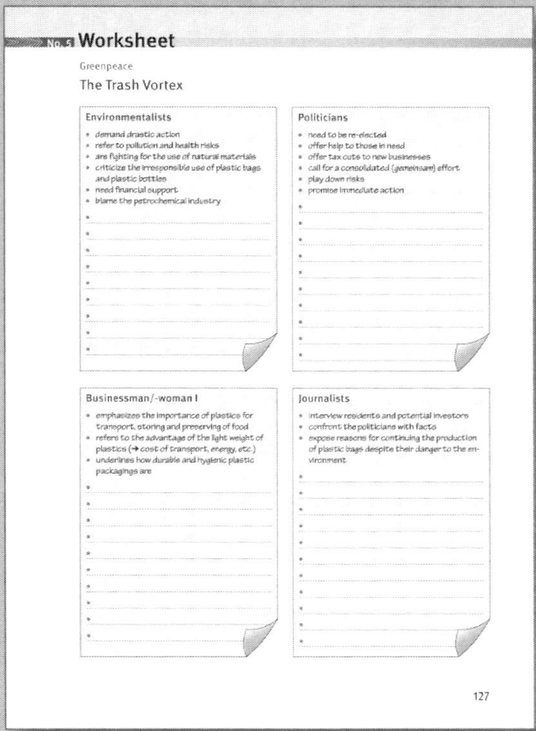
No. 5 Worksheet

Greenpeace

The Trash Vortex

Environmentalists
- demand drastic action
- refer to pollution and health risks
- are fighting for the use of natural materials
- criticize the irresponsible use of plastic bags and plastic bottles
- need financial support
- blame the petrochemical industry

Politicians
- need to be re-elected
- offer help to those in need
- offer tax cuts to new businesses
- call for a consolidated (gemeinsam) effort
- play down risks
- promise immediate action

Businessman/-woman I
- emphasizes the importance of plastics for transport, storing and preserving of food
- refers to the advantage of the light weight of plastics (→ cost of transport, energy etc.)
- underlines how durable and hygienic plastic packagings are

Journalists
- interview residents and potential investors
- confront the politicians with facts
- expose reasons for continuing the production of plastic bags despite their danger to the environment

127

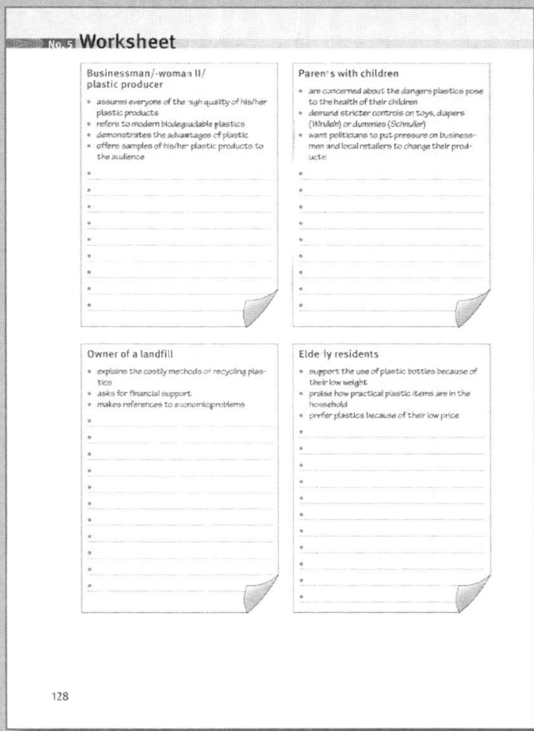
No. 5 Worksheet

Businessman/-woman II/ plastic producer
- assures everyone of the high quality of his/her plastic products
- refers to modern biodegradable plastics
- demonstrates the advantages of plastic
- offers samples of his/her plastic products to the audience

Parents with children
- are concerned about the dangers plastics pose to the health of their children
- demand stricter controls on toys, diapers (Windeln) or dummies (Schnuller)
- want politicians to put pressure on businessmen and local retailers to change their products

Owner of a landfill
- explains the costly methods of recycling plastics
- asks for financial support
- makes references to economic problems

Elderly residents
- support the use of plastic bottles because of their low weight
- praise how practical plastic items are in the household
- prefer plastics because of their low price

128

Differenzierungsmaterial

Unterstützung des selbstständigen Arbeitens und der anwendungsorientierten Entwicklung von Fähigkeiten und Fertigkeiten durch weitere, das Material ergänzende und unterstützende Aufgaben und Materialien im ***Grammar and Skills Trainer***:

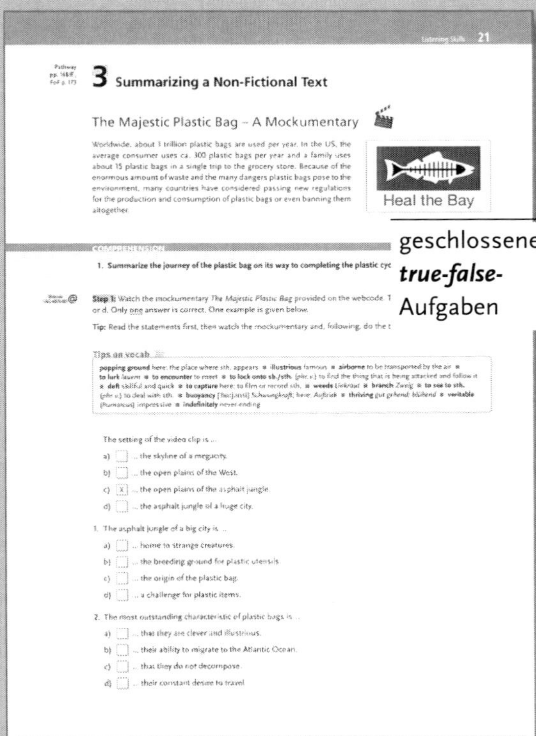
Listening Skills 21

3 Summarizing a Non-Fictional Text

The Majestic Plastic Bag – A Mockumentary

Worldwide, about 1 trillion plastic bags are used per year. In the US, the average consumer uses ca. 300 plastic bags per year and a family uses about 15 plastic bags in a single trip to the grocery store. Because of the enormous amount of waste and the many dangers plastic bags pose to the environment, many countries have considered passing new regulations for the production and consumption of plastic bags or even banning them altogether.

Heal the Bay

COMPREHENSION

1. Summarize the journey of the plastic bag on its way to completing the plastic cyc…

Step 1: Watch the mockumentary The Majestic Plastic Bag provided on the webcode. … or d. Only one answer is correct. One example is given below.

Tip: Read the statements first, then watch the mockumentary and, following, do the t…

Tips on vocab

The setting of the video clip is …
a) … the skyline of a megacity.
b) … the open plains of the West.
c) [x] … the open plains of the asphalt jungle.
d) … the asphalt jungle of a huge city.

1. The asphalt jungle of a big city is …
a) … home to strange creatures.
b) … the breeding ground for plastic utensils.
c) … the origin of the plastic bag.
d) … a challenge for plastic items.

2. The most outstanding characteristic of plastic bags is …
a) … that they are clever and illustrious.
b) … their ability to migrate to the Atlantic Ocean.
c) … that they do not decompose.
d) … their constant desire to travel.

geschlossene
true-false-
Aufgaben

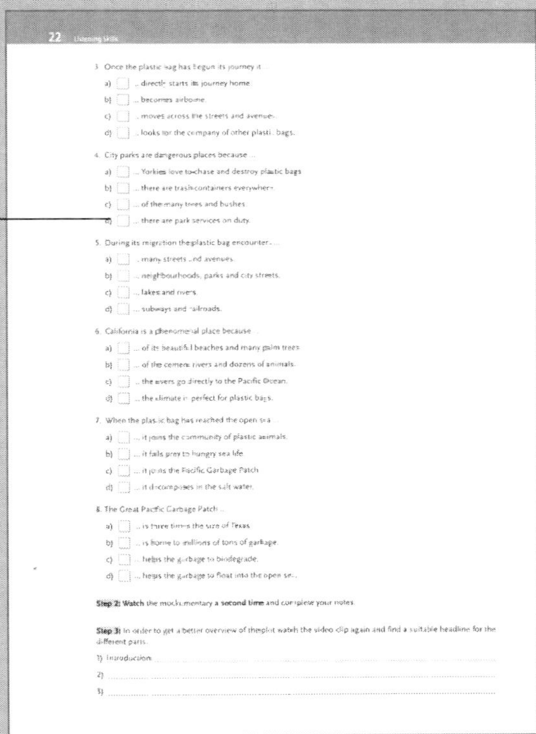
22 Listening Skills

3. Once the plastic bag has begun its journey it …
a) … directly starts its journey home.
b) … becomes airborne.
c) … moves across the streets and avenues.
d) … looks for the company of other plastic bags.

4. City parks are dangerous places because …
a) … Yorkies love to chase and destroy plastic bags.
b) … there are trash containers everywhere.
c) … of the many trees and bushes.
d) … there are park services on duty.

5. During its migration the plastic bag encounters …
a) … many streets and avenues.
b) … neighbourhoods, parks and city streets.
c) … lakes and rivers.
d) … subways and railroads.

6. California is a phenomenal place because …
a) … of its beautiful beaches and many palm trees.
b) … of the cement rivers and dozens of animals.
c) … the rivers go directly to the Pacific Ocean.
d) … the climate is perfect for plastic bags.

7. When the plastic bag has reached the open sea …
a) … it joins the community of plastic animals.
b) … it falls prey to hungry sea life.
c) … it joins the Pacific Garbage Patch.
d) … it decomposes in the salt water.

8. The Great Pacific Garbage Patch …
a) … is three times the size of Texas.
b) … is home to millions of tons of garbage.
c) … helps the garbage to biodegrade.
d) … helps the garbage to float into the open sea.

Step 2: Watch the mockumentary a second time and complete your notes.

Step 3: In order to get a better overview of the plot watch the video clip again and find a suitable headline for the different parts.
1) Introduction
2) …
3) …

Grammar and Skills Trainer

Audio-visuelle Textgrundlage zum Themenbereich *trash vortex, plastic, pollution* in Ergänzung zum Material des Schülerbuches (geschlossene sowie halboffene Aufgabenformate)

Ein **deutscher Zeitungsartikel** zum Thema in Verbindung mit einem offenen **Mediationsschreibauftrag** bietet eine weitere Kombinationsmöglichkeit von Textsorten und Aufgabenformaten in Verbindung mit der **Kombination verschiedener Einzelkompetenzen**.

Grammar and Skills Trainer

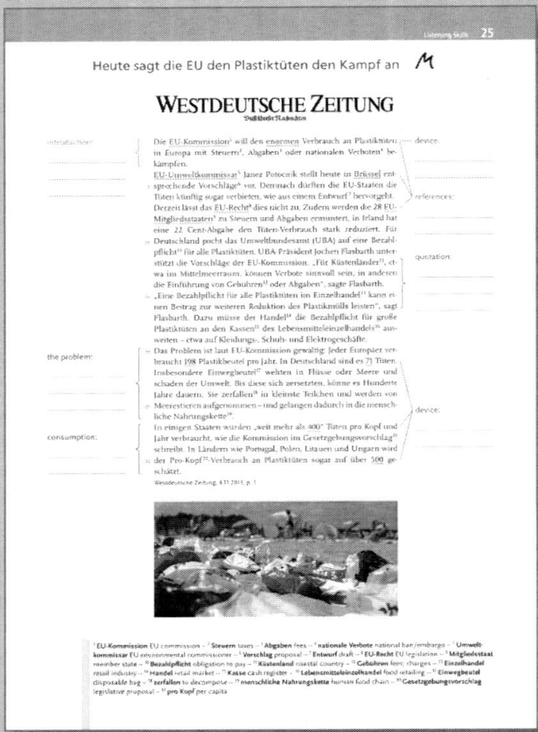

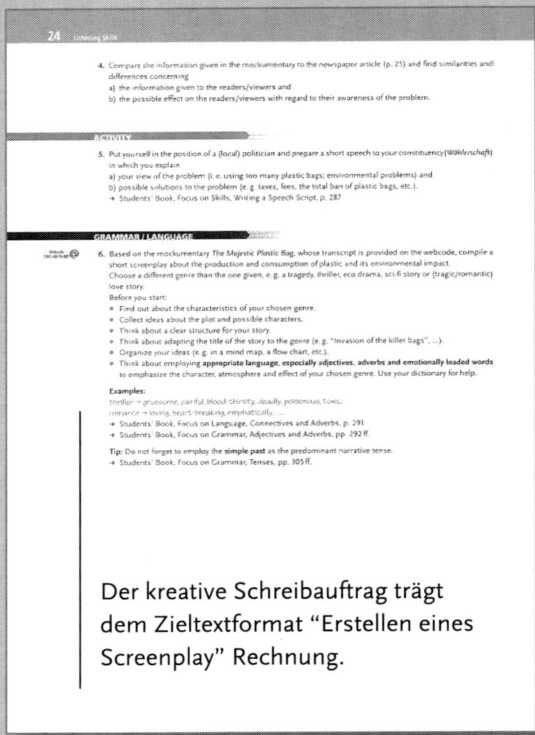

Der kreative Schreibauftrag trägt dem Zieltextformat “Erstellen eines Screenplay” Rechnung.

Zum vertiefenden Einüben der neuen, *kombinierten Klausurformate* (hier: isolierte *Listening-Comprehension* mit *Reading/Writing*) bietet der ***Grammar and Skills Trainer*** Übungsklausuren mit Lösungen:

Grammar and Skills Trainer

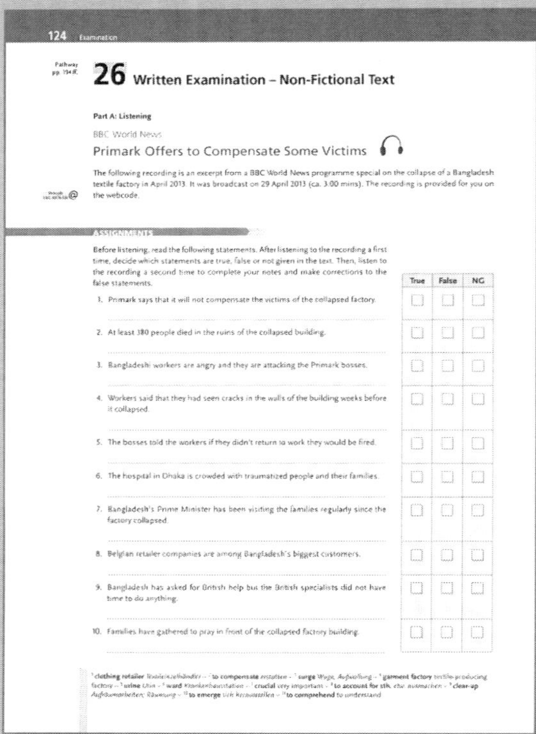

Strategien und Techniken des selbstständigen und kooperativen Lernens in *Pathway*

Das ***Differenzierungsmaterial*** bietet methodische Hilfen für kooperative und selbstständige Arbeitsformen im Umgang mit den Materialien des Schülerbuches.

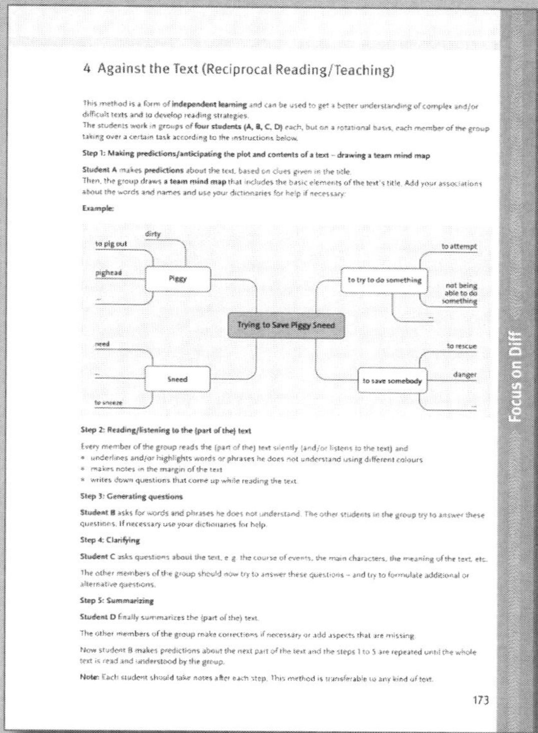

4 Against the Text (Reciprocal Reading/Teaching)

Step 1: Making predictions/anticipating the plot and contents of a text – drawing a team mind map

Example:

Trying to Save Piggy Sneed

Step 2: Reading/listening to the (part of the) text

Step 3: Generating questions

Step 4: Clarifying

Step 5: Summarizing

173

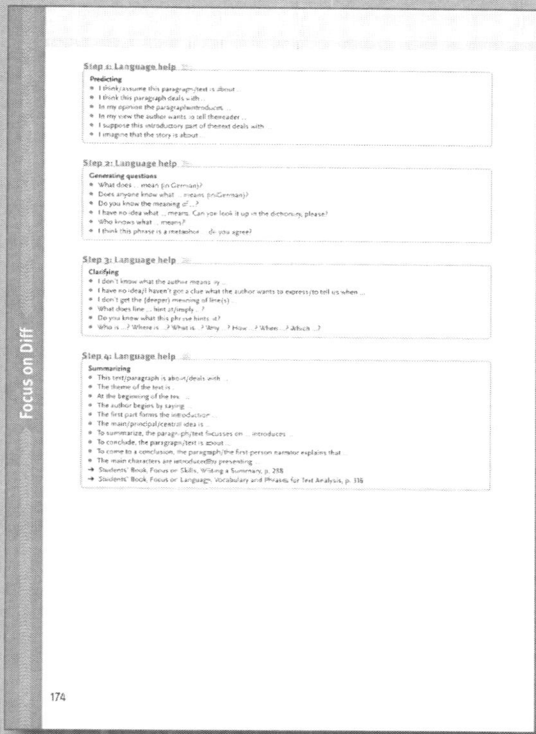

Step 1: Language help

Step 2: Language help

Step 3: Language help

Step 4: Language help

174

Differenzierungsmaterial

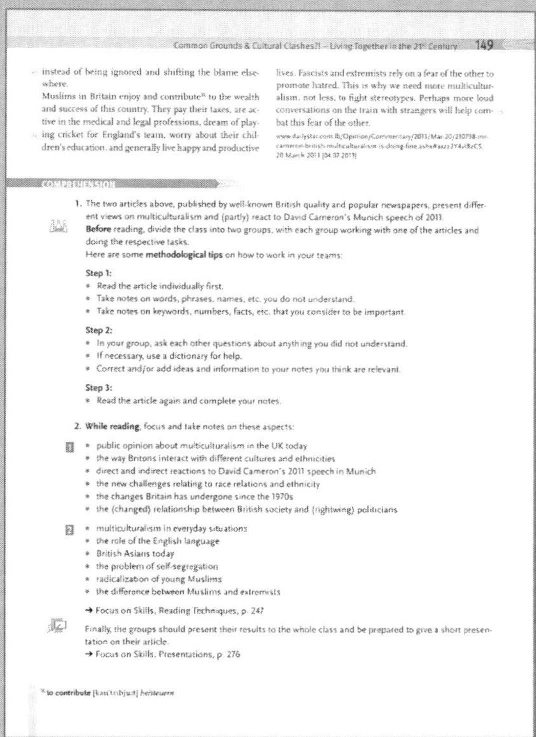

Common Grounds & Cultural Clashes?! – Living Together in the 21st Century 149

COMPREHENSION

Step 1:

Step 2:

Step 3:

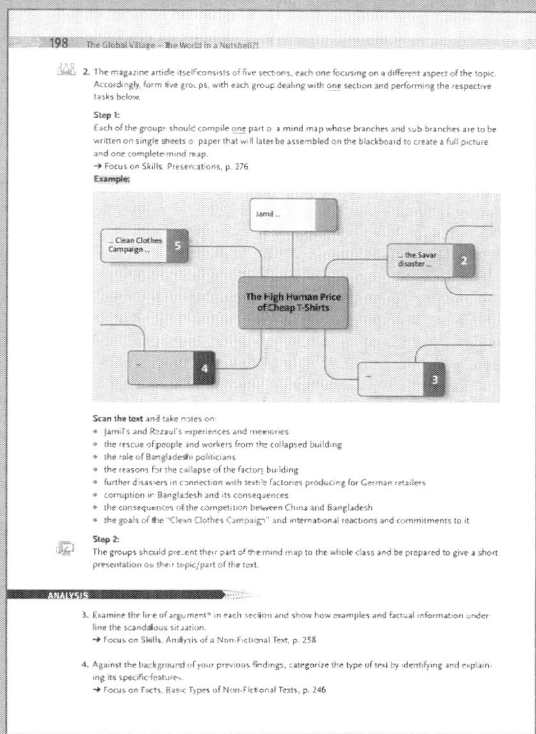

198 The Global Village – The World in a Nutshell?!

Step 1:

Example:

The High Human Price of Cheap T-Shirts

Step 2:

ANALYSIS

Schülerbuch

Geschlossene und halboffene Aufgabenformate in *Pathway*

Das neu entwickelte ***Comprehension***-Material bietet eine Vielzahl von das Schülerbuch ergänzenden Aufgaben in den neuen Formaten.

Comprehension

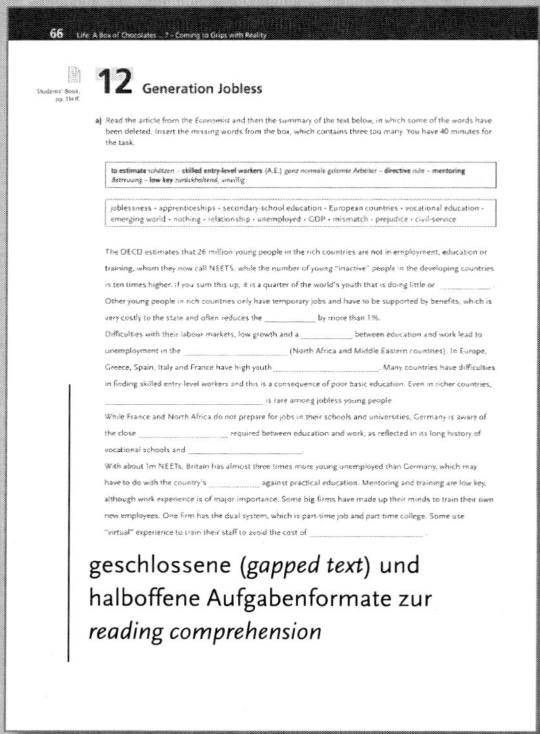

geschlossene (*gapped text*) und halboffene Aufgabenformate zur *reading comprehension*

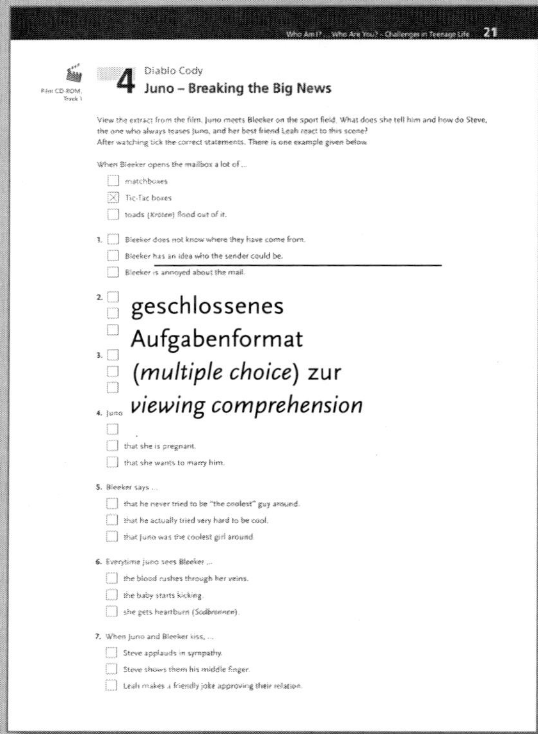

geschlossenes Aufgabenformat (*multiple choice*) zur *viewing comprehension*

Comprehension

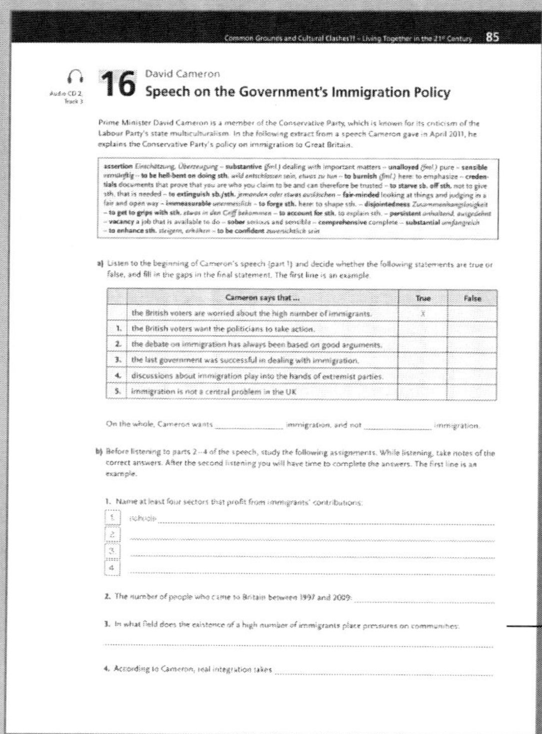

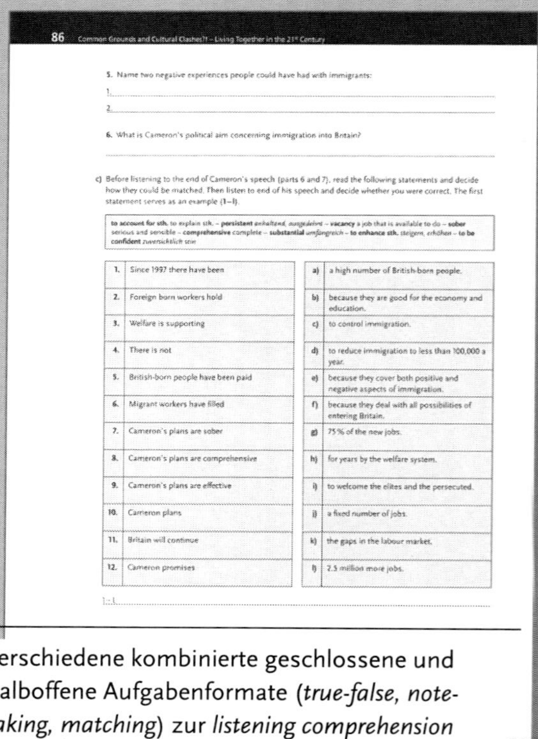

verschiedene kombinierte geschlossene und halboffene Aufgabenformate (*true-false, note-taking, matching*) zur *listening comprehension*

Selbstständiges Arbeiten unter *step-by-step* Anleitung in *Pathway*

Der ***Grammar and Skills Trainer*** bietet vielfältige Materialien und Aufgabenformate zur selbstständigen Erarbeitung in Ergänzung zum Schülerbuch. Umfassende *solutions* dienen der Selbstkontrolle der Schüler.

Common Grounds & Cultural Clashes?! – Living Together in the 21st Century 159

Jhumpa Lahiri

The Namesake[1]

AWARENESS

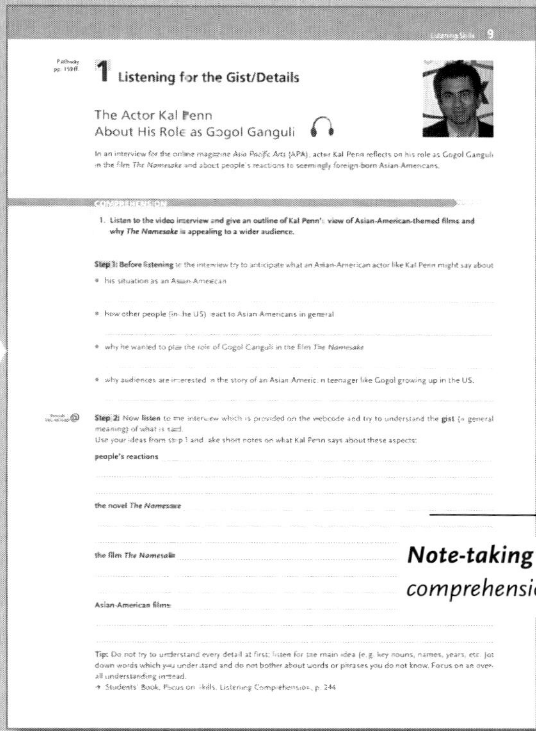

Listening Skills 9

1 Listening for the Gist/Details

The Actor Kal Penn About His Role as Gogol Ganguli

COMPREHENSION

Note-taking und *listening comprehension*

geschlossene ***true-false*** Aufgabenformate

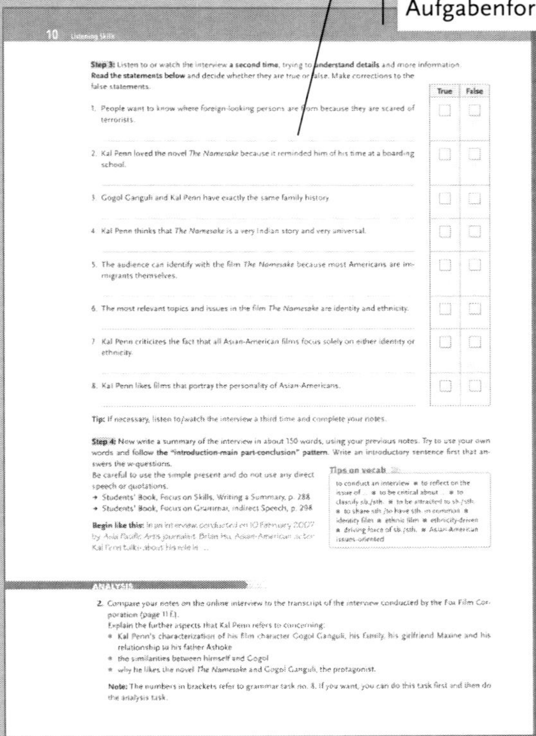

10 Listening Skills

ANALYSIS

detaillierte und umfassende Lösungen dienen der Selbstkontrolle

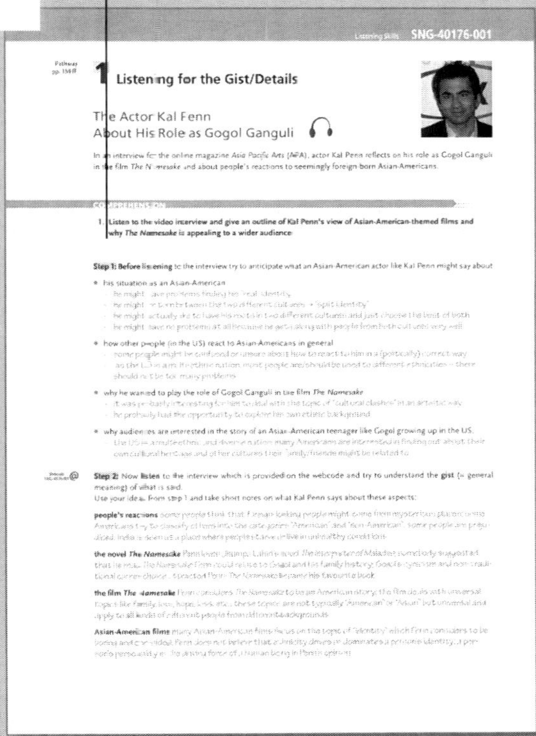

Listening Skills SNG-40176-001

1 Listening for the Gist/Details

The Actor Kal Penn About His Role as Gogol Ganguli

COMPREHENSION

Grammar and Skills Trainer

Themen- und unitübergreifendes Lernen und Arbeiten mit *Pathway* – Vernetzung von Themen, Textsorten und Skills

Um das in den neuen Kernlehrplänen geforderte Transfer- und „Querdenken" der Schüler zu fördern und zu vertiefen, lassen sich viele Themen des Schülerbuches, aber auch der darüber hinaus gehenden Materialien des *Pathway*-Produktkranzes miteinander verbinden.

Ergänzend zum Schülerbuch bieten
- der ***Grammar and Skills Trainer***
- das ***Differenzierungsmaterial*** sowie
- das ***Comprehension***-Material

eine große Vielfalt weiterer Aufgaben und Aufgabenformate, unterschiedliche Textsorten sowie audio- und audio-visuelle Materialien.
Vor allem leitmotivisches Arbeiten bietet hier lohnende Verknüpfungen, die zum Transferdenken und der inhaltlichen Verbindung von inhaltlichen und thematischen Aspekten anregen.

Im Folgenden finden Sie eine Auswahl an Leitmotiven:

Mögliche Leitmotive:

- **childhood**
  Owen Meany (19ff.), Why Teenagers Are Growing up So Slowly Today (61), The Children of Sodom and Gomorrah (175ff.), Kill Zone (119ff.), Malala Yousafzai speech (185f.)
- **role models**
  Harold and Maude (26ff.), Superficial Nightmare (23ff.), Skinny Young Models (48ff.)
- **society**
  The Trash Vortex (168ff.), The Girl Effect (183ff.), HOKISA (187ff.), Vulnerable Runaways (111ff.), The Global Village Project (129)
- **beauty**
  Skinny Young Models (48ff.), Mirror, Mirror on the Wall (53)
- **work / career**
  The Me Me Me Generation (14ff.). Get a Job (66f.)
- **tolerance**
  Tomorrow We'll See (13), Piggy Sneed (106ff.), suburbia (130ff.), The Government's Immigration Policy (137ff.)
- **poverty**
  Child Labour (94ff.), Juicy and Delicious (97f.)
- **phantasy and imagination**
  Beasts of the Southern Wild (102ff.), No Problems (33ff.)
- **stereotypes / clichés**
  Piggy Sneed (106ff.), Kill Zone (119ff.), The Namesake (159ff.)
- **being connected and disconnected**
  Sprechen Sie Job? (80ff.), The Uses of Enchantment (101), Generation Jobless (114ff.)
- **being "in" and "out"**
  But Baseball and Sex (38f.), A School Distanced from Technology (220ff.), The Eco-Fashion Revolution (204ff.), Generation Jobless (114ff.)
- **real and unreal worlds**
  Hundreds of Websites Urging Girls to Starve for Perfection (51ff.), Serial Killing (227ff.)
- **qualifications and skills**
  Why Teenagers Are Growing up So Slowly Today (61) Fields of Learning (62), Applying for U.S. Citizenship (128)
- **loneliness**
  Piggy Sneed (106ff.), Looking for Alaska (106ff.), No Speak English (153ff.)
- **temptations**
  Serial Killing (227ff.), Disfigured (54f.), Harold and Maude (26ff.)
- **responsibility**
  The Girl Effect (183ff.), Cheap T-Shirts (194ff.), Roots & Shoots (68ff.)

Binnendifferenzierung und individuelle Förderung

Der neue Kernlehrplan weist in besonderer Weise auf die Verpflichtung zur individuellen Förderung von Schülern hin. Damit verbunden ist im Unterrichtszusammenhang in der Regel die Binnendifferenzierung und die Initiierung von differenzierenden Arbeits- und Sozialformen sowie die Bereitstellung von Arbeitsmaterialien und Aufgabenstellungen, die heterogenen Schülergruppen Rechnung tragen.
Das *Pathway* Schülerbuch bietet im Zusammenklang mit den Begleitmaterialien einen umfassenden Pool an sowohl in Umfang wie in Anspruchsniveau unterschiedlich anspruchsvollen Texten. Das Anspruchsniveau der Materialien wird durch ein Punktesystem ausgewiesen (basic ●○○ intermediate ●●○ advanced level ●●●).

Schülerbuch

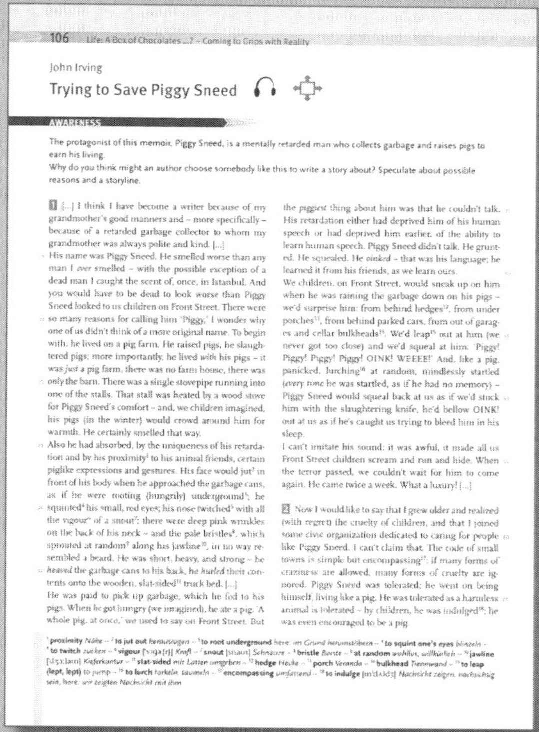

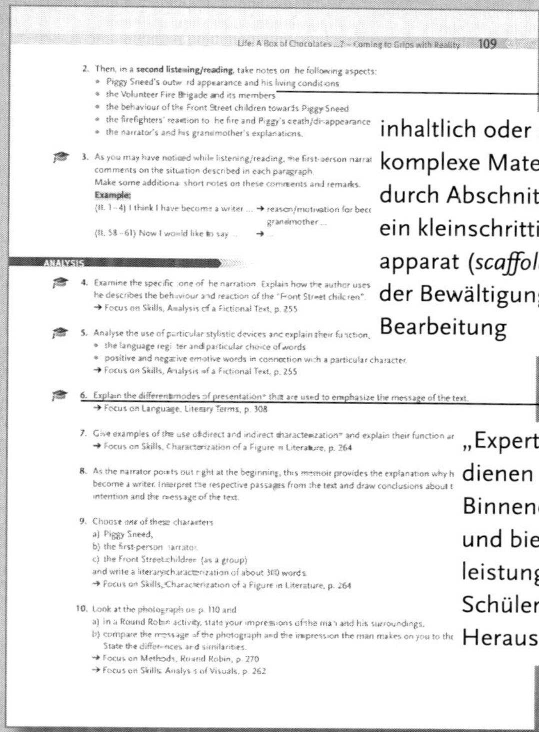

inhaltlich oder sprachlich komplexe Materialen werden durch Abschnitte „portioniert"; ein kleinschrittiger Aufgabenapparat (*scaffolding*) hilft bei der Bewältigung der Bearbeitung

„Expertenaufgaben" dienen der Binnendifferenzierung und bieten leistungsstärkeren Schülern zusätzliche Herausforderungen

Differenzierungsmaterial

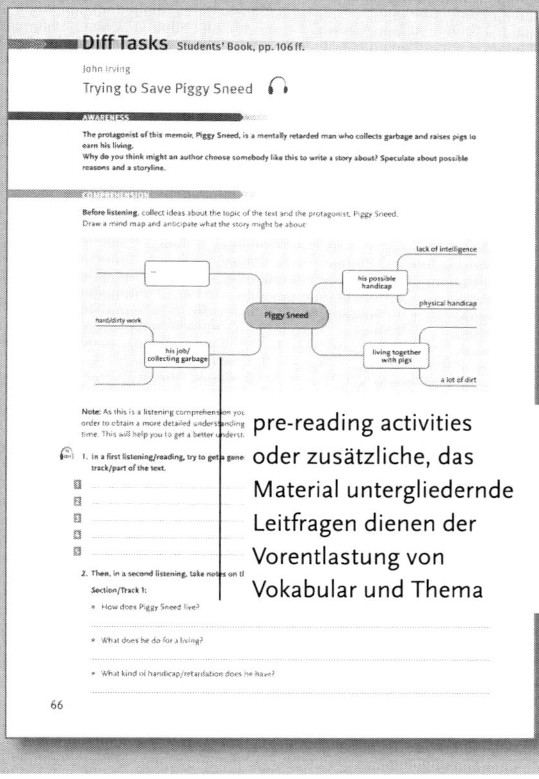

pre-reading activities oder zusätzliche, das Material untergliedernde Leitfragen dienen der Vorentlastung von Vokabular und Thema

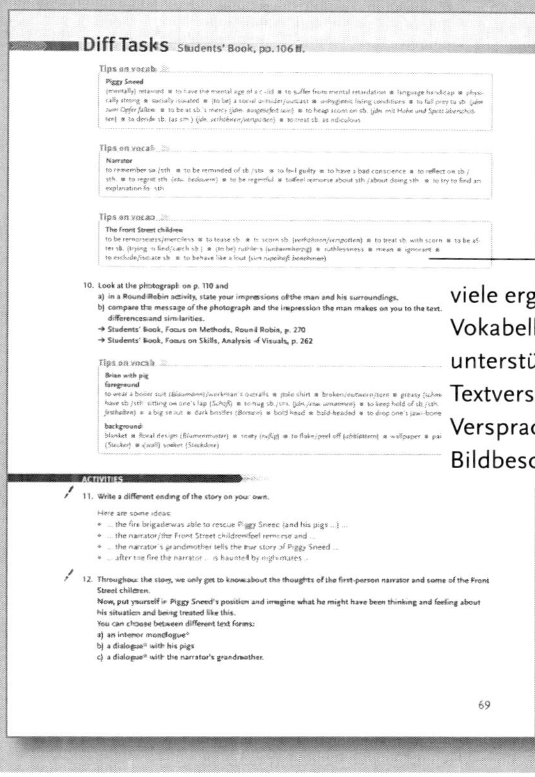

viele ergänzende Vokabelhilfen unterstützen das Textverständnis und die Versprachlichung von Bildbeschreibungen etc.

Die Kombination von Aufgabenformaten / Klausurformate

Die neuen Klausurformate verlangen in jeder Klausur die verbindliche Überprüfung von insgesamt drei Einzelkompetenzen:

Aufgabentyp 1: Schreiben mit einer weiteren integrierten Teilkompetenz, i. d. R. Leseverstehen (Klausurteil A). Eine weitere Teilkompetenz in *isolierter* Überprüfung (Klausurteil B).

Klausurteil A	Klausurteil B
Schreiben – Leseverstehen (70%) • *comprehension – analysis – evaluation/ re-creation of text*	Sprachmittlung / Mediation (30%) • situativ eingebettete Sprachmittlung
Schreiben – Leseverstehen (80%) • *comprehension – analysis – evaluation/ re-creation of text*	Hör-Hörsehverstehen (20%) • geschlossene oder halboffene Teilaufgabe
Schreiben – Leseverstehen (100%)	Sprechen (wird durch mündl. Prüfungen ersetzt)
Schreiben – Hör-Hörsehverstehen (80%) • *comprehension – analysis – evaluation* (z. B. in Bezug auf Klausurteile A und B)	Leseverstehen (20%) • geschlossene *Comprehension*-Aufgaben

Aufgabentyp 2: Schreiben mit zwei weiteren *integrierten* Teilkompetenzen.

Schreiben – Leseverstehen – Hör-/Hörsehverstehen
- *Comprehension (listening)*
- *Comprehension (reading) + analysis + evaluation*

Aufgabentyp 3: Schreiben sowie zwei weitere Teilkompetenzen in *isolierter* Überprüfung.

Klausurteil A (50%)	Klausurteil B (50%)
Visueller Impuls (z. B. Cartoon, Foto, etc.) • *analysis – comment/evaluation*	1. Schriftlicher englischer Text z. B. *political speech* (USA, UK) • *comprehension* (geschlossen) 2. Schriftlicher deutscher Text z. B. Zeitungsartikel (Reaktion auf die o. g.Rede) • situativ eingebettete Sprachmittlung

Stoffverteilungspläne

Konkretisierte Unterrichtsvorhaben im Rahmen eines schulinternen Lehrplans für die gymnasiale Oberstufe (Einführungsphase NRW)

Die folgenden sechs Stoffverteilungspläne folgen zum einen den sechs Units des Schülerbuches, andererseits bilden sie die vier Quartale eines Schuljahres ab. Sie umfassen jeweils ein Stundenkontingent von 18-20 Stunden, was ungefähr 6-7 Wochen Unterricht entspricht, d.h. circa einem Quartal. Themen und Units können daher je Bedarf und schulinternem Curriculum individuell kombiniert und gestaltet und z.B. mit der Lektüre einer Ganzschrift oder einem Projekt verknüpft werden. Für das 2. und 4. Quartal des Schuljahres wird optional jeweils eine alternative Unterrichtsreihe vorgeschlagen. Die Stoffverteilungspläne bieten in Verknüpfung mit den Vorgaben des Kernlehrplans folgende Schwerpunkte für die Einführungsphase (EF):

1. Quartal: Who Am I? ... Who Are You? – Challenges in Teenage Life

2. Quartal: People, Places, Perspectives – Mapping out Your Future
2. Quartal: Life – A Box of Chocolates ...? (alternative Unterrichtsreihe)

3. Quartal: Common Grounds and Cultural Clashes?! – Living Together in the 21st Century

4. Quartal: The Global Village – The World in a Nutshell?!
4. Quartal: Virtual Communities and Social Networks – Living in the Digital Age (alternative Unterrichtsreihe)

EF 1.1: 1. Quartal
Kompetenzstufe B1 des GeR
Who Am I? ... Who Are You? – Challenges in Teenage Life

Das Unterrichtsvorhaben dient der intensiven Auseinandersetzung mit dem Rollenverständnis und dem Schönheitsideal Jugendlicher sowie der Auseinandersetzung mit schwierigen Entscheidungssituationen (Schwangerschaft). Beim Eintritt in die gymnasiale Oberstufe sollen sich die SuS ihre Sprachlernerfahrung bewusst machen und systematisch mit einer Bestandsaufnahme ihrer funktionalen kommunikativen und interkulturellen Kompetenzen beginnen. Dabei erweitern sie ihre kommunikativen Kompetenzen im rezeptiven Bereich (Leseverstehen: *magazine articles*, Hörverstehen: *songs*, Hör-/Sehverstehen: *excerpts from films*) und im produktiven Bereich (Schreiben: *writing dialogues, acrostics, letter to the editor*).

Gesamtstundenkontingent: ca. 18-20 Std.

Sprachlernkompetenz

- die eigene sprachliche Kompetenz einschätzen, den Lernprozess beobachten und planen, kontinuierlich eigene Fehlerschwerpunkte bearbeiten und diese Ergebnisse dokumentieren

Interkulturelle kommunikative Kompetenz

- **Orientierungswissen**: Kennenlernen von fiktionalen und nicht fiktionalen Beispielen für die Identitäts- und Rollenfindung (z.B. Leland Bobbé: *The Two Sides of a Coin*) sowie das Agieren in Konfliktsituationen (z.B. wie ungewollter Schwangerschaft, *Juno*) und auch Wissen über das Ausmaß dieser Probleme (FoF *Teenage Birthrates*, p. 46; Interview: *A High School Teacher Talks About Teenage Pregnancy*)
- **Einstellungen und Bewusstheit**: eigene Wertmaßstäbe kritisch reflektieren und mit denen anderer Menschen unterschiedlicher kultureller und sozialer Herkunft vergleichen
- **Verstehen und Handeln:** Toleranz gegenüber anderen Orientierungen entwickeln, mit Konflikten umgehen und sie im sozialen Zusammenhang bewältigen lernen

Funktionale kommunikative Kompetenz

- **Hör-/Hör-Sehverstehen**: authentischen Hörtexten (Songs: *Tomorrow We'll See, Family Portrait*) und Filmausschnitten wichtige – auch implizite – Informationen entnehmen, textexternes Vorwissen zum Aufbau eines Textverständnisses verknüpfen lernen
- **Leseverstehen:** nicht fiktionalen (z.B. *The Me, Me, Me Generation*) und fiktionalen Texten (z.B. J. Irving, *Owen Meany*) Hauptaussagen und Einzelinformationen entnehmen und dabei auch implizite Informationen erschließen
- **Sprechen – an Gesprächen teilnehmen**: Ergebnisse präsentieren, in Dialogen verschiedene Rollen annehmen und dabei Vorurteile und Klischees thematisieren
- **Schreiben**: kreatives Schreiben (*acrostics etc.*), unter Beachtung wesentlicher Textmerkmale Sachtexte verfassen (z.B. *letter to the editor, comment*) und dabei Standpunkte begründen
- **Sprachmittlung**: in Begegnungssituationen Aussagen in die Zielsprache mündlich übertragen (J. Jessen, Über Coolness)

Verfügen über sprachliche Mittel

- **Wortschatz**: erweiterter thematischer Wortschatz zu *Role models, Teenage Pregnancy, Health & Beauty* FoV, pp. 56 ff.; Metawortschatz zu dem Bereich ‚sprachliche Mittel', FoS *Analysis of a Fictional Text*, p. 255; FoS *Analysis of a Non-Fictional Text*, p. 258; *Analysis of Statistical Data*, p. 261; Filmanalyse: *Analysis of a Screenplay/Film Scene*
- **Grammatische Strukturen**: Festigung *comparative forms; conditional clauses, indirect speech, use of simple present – present progressive*
- **Aussprache und Intonation**: Entwicklung eines Repertoires an typischen Intonationsmustern

Text- und Medienkompetenz

- **analytisch-interpretierend**: medial vermittelte Texte (*songs, film excerpts* aus *Juno, Disfigured*) in Bezug auf Aussageabsicht, Darstellungsform und Wirkung deuten und dabei Wechselbeziehungen zwischen sprachlichen und filmischen Mitteln berücksichtigen
- **produktions- und anwendungsorientiert**: unterschiedliche Darstellungsformen (*writing a one-act comedy*, Task 7, p. 22) nutzen, um eigene mündliche und schriftliche Texte adressatengerecht zu stützen

Sprachbewusstheit

- Sprachgebrauch angemessen an Kommunikationssituationen anpassen

Texte und Medien

- **Sach- und Gebrauchstexte**: Texte der öffentlichen Kommunikation und internationalen Presse (Artikel aus Time, Die Zeit, online articles etc. wie Joel Stein: *The Me Me Me Generation*)
- **medial vermittelte Texte**: Auszüge aus Spielfilmen (*Disfigured, Juno*), Songs (Sting: *Tomorrow We'll See; P!nk: Family Portrait*), interview: *A High School Teacher talks about Teenage Pregnancy*
- **literarische Texte**: Novel: John Irving: *Owen Meany – Being Attractive to Girls*; play: Colin Higgins: *Harold and Maude*; screenplay: *Juno*
- **diskontinuierliche Texte**: Photo: Leland Bobbé: *The Two Sides of the Coin*; Cover (z.B. Die Zeit, p. 14, p. 19); Cartoons (z.B. p. 23)

Projektvorhaben

- **Standortbestimmung/Lernbedarfsanalyse**: *Learning a language – ways to express your identity*
- **Extensives Lesen**: z. B. Sharon M. Draper: *November Blues*, New York 2007

Lernerfolgsüberprüfungen

- **schriftliche Arbeit (Klausur)**: Schreiben mit Leseverstehen (integriert), z.B. Ausschnitt aus einem *Newspaper Article*, Hörverstehen (isoliert), z.B. Ausschnitt aus einem Play

EF 1.2: 1. – 2. Quartal
Kompetenzstufe B1 des GeR
People, Places, Perspectives – Mapping out Your Future

Das Unterrichtsvorhaben dient dem Bewusstmachen von Faktoren des sozialen Umfelds für das Erwachsenwerden und die Berufswahl, der Auseinandersetzung mit Ausbildung und Chancen des Arbeitens und Sozialengagements im englischsprachigen Ausland. Die Schülerinnen und Schüler erweitern ihre funktionalen und interkulturellen Kompetenzen im rezeptiven (z.B. Stellenanzeigen online und in Zeitungen/*job interviews*) und produktiven Bereich (Bewerbungsschreiben, CV, *job interviews*).
Gesamtstundenkontingent: ca.16 - 18 Std.

Sprachlernkompetenz
- Techniken für die Planung und Realisierung eigener Redebeiträge nutzen und adressatengerecht anwenden; intentions- und adressatengerechte Präsentation

Interkulturelle kommunikative Kompetenz
- **Orientierungswissen**: die Schüler erweitern ihr Wissen in Bezug auf sozio-kulturelle Faktoren des Erwachsenwerdens und Findens des Berufsweges (z.B. Po Bronson: *Why Teenagers Are Growing up so Slowly Today*, John Green: *Looking for Alaska, Recruiting Interns/The Economist*) und die Möglichkeiten von Praktika und freiwilligem sozialen Engagement (z.B. Jane Goodall: *Roots and Shoots*)
- **Einstellungen und Bewusstheit**: die Schüler erfahren, dass es verschiedene Wege zum Erreichen des Berufswunsches gibt (p. 62), machen sich in englischsprachigen Kommunikationssituationen mit Normen und Verhaltensweisen der Arbeitswelt vertraut (pp. 77-78)
- **Verstehen und Handeln**: Sprachhandeln bedarfsgerecht planen (*Being Interviewed on the Phone*, p. 76; *Making an Enquiry*, p. 85, *Making a Complaint*, p. 87); mögliche sprach- und kulturbedingte Missverständnisse antizipieren und eigenständig Lösungsansätze entwickeln (*Planning for Your Graduation Ball*, p. 83)

Funktionale kommunikative Kompetenz
- **Hör-/Hör-Sehverstehen:** authentischen Situationen (z.B. *Being Interviewed on the Phone*, p. 76; *Making an Enquiry*, p. 85) wichtige Informationen entnehmen und wesentliche Aussagen des/der Sprechenden erfassen; Variationen des Englischen erfassen und dekodieren
- **Leseverstehen**: Sachtexten (z.B. *Recruiting Interns*) und literarischen Texten (z.B. *Looking for Alaska*) wesentliche implizite Informationen entnehmen und mit textexternen Informationen verbinden
- Sprechen – an Gesprächen teilnehmen: an Gesprächen teilnehmen; eigene Redebeiträge planen und realisieren (z.B. p. 88 *Role Play: Telephone Conversation*)/ FoL *Conversation and Discussion/Communicative Strategies/Job Interview*
- **Schreiben**: unter Beachtung wesentlicher Textsortenmerkmale (Bewerbungsschreiben, CV, Letter of Complaint) Texte für die private und berufliche Kommunikation verfassen und adressatengerecht gestalten (FoS *Writing a Formal Letter/Writing an Email/Writing a CV and a Letter of Application*)
- **Sprachmittlung**: in informellen und formellen Begegnungssituationen wesentliche Aussagen und wichtige Details in die Zielsprache mündlich sprachmittelnd übertragen (*Job Interview/Making an Enquiry*); die Darstellung von Sachverhalten in die Zielsprache sprachmittelnd verschriftlichen (z.B. p. 84, Step 5: *Write a Letter of Complaint*)

Verfügen über sprachliche Mittel
- **Wortschatz**: thematischer Wortschatz zum Themenfeld ‚Arbeitswelt' (*Youth, Volunteering, Career, Professional Communication*, FoV, p. 89) sowie situationsangemessen formelle und informelle Ausdrücke in verschiedenen Kommunikationssituationen (z.B. Small Talk) ausbauen
- **Grammatische Strukturen**: Verfeinerung und Festigung des Gebrauches von *Adverbs and Adjectives, Use of Modal Auxiliaries, Superlatives and Comparatives*
- **Aussprache und Intonation**: Repertoire gängiger Intonationsmuster festigen

Text- und Medienkompetenz
- **analytisch-interpretierend**: Texte vor dem Hintergrund ihres spezifischen kommunikativen Kontextes verstehen (z.B. Job Adverts, p. 74)
- **produktions- und anwendungsorientiert**: eigene schriftliche und mündliche Texte adressatenorientiert verfassen (*Formal Letters, CV, Formal and Informal Conversations*)

Sprachbewusstheit
- Beziehungen zwischen Sprach- und Kulturphänomenen reflektieren; Sprachgebrauch an Kommunikationssituationen anpassen (z.B. Telephoning); Sprachhandeln bedarfsgerecht planen

Texte und Medien
- **Sach- und Gebrauchstexte**: *Texts from various magazines, e.g. The Economist, Job Adverts, CV*
- **medial vermittelte Texte**: Song (Gossip, *Get a Job*), Websites (Jane Goodall, *Roots & Shoots*)

Projektvorhaben
- **Standortbestimmung/Lernbedarfsanalyse**: *Planning for Your Graduation Ball; Research on the Chances of the European Programme Erasmus*

Lernerfolgsüberprüfungen
- **schriftliche Arbeit (Klausur)**: Mediation (isoliert); Schreiben mit Hörverstehen integriert (z.B. *Telephone Call*)

EF 1.3: 2. Quartal
Kompetenzstufe B1 des GeR
Life – A Box of Chocolates ...?

Das Unterrichtsvorhaben dient der intensiven Auseinandersetzung der Herausforderungen und Gefahren, denen sich Kinder und Jugendliche ausgesetzt sehen. Dabei soll Orientierungswissen über Lebensverhältnisse global und im englischsprachigen Raum vermittelt werden. Die Schülerinnen und Schüler sollen dabei systematisch ihre funktionalen und interkulturellen Kompetenzen erweitern – rezeptiv in Bezug auf Hör-/Sehverstehen (Spielfilmszenen), Leseverstehen/Hörverstehen (Romanauszug, Auszug aus politischer Rede) und produktiv (*Writing a different ending, dialogues, an interior monologue*).

Gesamtstundenkontingent: ca. 18-20 Std.

Sprachlernkompetenz		Sprachbewusstheit
• den eigenen Lernprozess beobachten und zunehmend gezielt Fehlerschwerpunkte angehen	**Interkulturelle kommunikative Kompetenz** • **Orientierungswissen**: Wissen in Bezug auf Faktoren wie Gewalt, unsichere soziale Verhältnisse und Perspektivlosigkeit, der viele Kinder ebenso weltweit wie auch im englischsprachigen Raum ausgesetzt sind (z.B. Moya Irvine: *Child Labour – No School or Play*), erweitern • **Einstellungen und Bewusstheit**: sich der Vielfältigkeit der Probleme von innerer und äußerer Gewalt und Hilflosigkeit bewusst werden und die Konsequenzen dieser Faktoren für das spätere Leben antizipieren • **Verstehen und Handeln**: die wechselseitigen Wirkungen negativer und positiver sozialer Faktoren verstehen und die eigene mögliche Rolle bei der Lösung dieser Probleme skizzieren **Funktionale kommunikative Kompetenz** • **Hör-/Hör-Sehverstehen**: Gesamtaussage, Hauptaussagen und Einzelinformationen aus auditiven (z.B. Hillary Clinton: *Remarks on Youth*; John Irving: *Trying to Save Piggy Sneed*) und audiovisuellen Texten (Lucy Alibar: *Beasts of the Southern Wild*) entnehmen • **Leseverstehen**: Sach- und Gebrauchstexten (z.B. *Bruno Bettelheim: The Uses of Enchantment; Cristopher Dickey: Kill Zone; The Economist: Generation Jobless*) Hauptaussagen und Einzelinformationen entnehmen und dabei auch implizite Informationen erschließen • **Sprechen – an Gesprächen teilnehmen**: Ergebnisse von Recherchen präsentieren (z.B. p. 122); FoS *Presentations*, p. 276 • **Schreiben**: Sachtexte (z.B. *Generation Jobless, Kill Zone*) und literarische Texte (Screenplay *Beasts of the Southern Wild*; John Irving: *Piggy Sneed*) analytisch-interpretierend in Bezug auf Aussageabsicht, Form und Wirkung deuten **Verfügen über sprachliche Mittel** • **Wortschatz**: Erweiterung des thematischen Wortschatzes (z.B. *Youth in Crisis, Unemployment, Violence*, FoV, p. 126) sowie des Meta-Wortschatzes (*Film Analysis, Literary Terms; Films/Movies*, FoL p. 314; *Analysis of a Film Scene*, FoS, p. 256, und *Analysis of Statistical Data*, FoS, p. 261; *Characterization of a Figure in Literature*, FoS, p. 264) • **Grammatische Strukturen**: Festigung der *Indirect Speech, Use of Simple Present* **Text- und Medienkompetenz** • **analytisch-interpretierend**: literarische und audiovisuell/auditiv vermittelte Texte analysieren und dabei auffällige Wechselbeziehungen zwischen sprachlichen und filmischen Mitteln berücksichtigen; wesentliche Merkmale der relevanten Textsorte beachten: z.B. John Irving: *Trying to Save Piggy Sneed* (Erzählweise, Erzählperspektive, Charakterisierung); Sachtexte bezüglich des Standpunktes des Autors und journalistischer Ausgewogenheit untersuchen (z.B. Christopher Dickey: *Kill Zone*; FoS *Analysis of a Non-Fictional Text*, p. 258) • **produktions- und anwendungsorientiert**: sich der Wirkung von Texten (Rede: Hillary Clinton: *Remarks on Youth*), Sachtexten (z.B. Christopher Dickey: *Kill Zone*) und diskontinuierlichen Texten (*statistics, placards*) durch die Entwicklung eigener kreativer Texte annähern	• sich Normabweichungen von Sprache bewusst werden (z.B. Beasts of the Southern Wild) und sich zunehmend der Bedeutung von Sprachanalyse bewusst werden

Texte und Medien

- **Sach- und Gebrauchstexte**: Christopher Dickey: *Kill Zone*; Economist: *Generation Jobless*; S. O'Connor: London Rail Stations
- **medial vermittelte Texte**: auditiv: H. Clinton: *Remarks on Youth*; Lucy Alibar: *Beasts of the Southern Wild*
- **diskontinuierliche Texte**: *Caricatures* (z.B. p. 117), *statistics* (pp. 114, 116, 120, 122), *photos/paintings*: Mel Bochner: *Oh Well; Cave Painting; Placards* (pp. 123f.)
- **literarische Texte**: Romanauszug (John Irving: *Trying to Saving Piggy Sneed*)

Projektvorhaben

- *Make a video clip about children's dreams and nightmares*

Lernerfolgsüberprüfungen

- **Schriftliche Arbeit (Klausur)**: Schreiben (z.B. Analyse eines Romanauszuges) mit integriertem Leseverstehen; Hörverstehen (isoliert) (z.B. Auszug einer politischen Rede zum gleichen Thema)
- **Alternativ**: Mündliche Prüfung: 1. Prüfungsteil (Sprechen – zusammenhängendes Sprechen): Vorstellen eines literarischen Charakters (behandelter Film-/Romanausschnitt); 2. Prüfungsteil: (Sprechen – an Gesprächen teilnehmen): *Children's Dreams and Nightmares – And What You Can Do About It*

EF 1.4: 3. Quartal
Kompetenzstufe B1 des GeR
Common Grounds and Cultural Clashes?! – Living Together in the 21st Century

Das Unterrichtsvorhaben dient der intensiven Auseinandersetzung mit Problemen und Chancen von Migration speziell in Großbritannien und den USA. Soziokulturelles Orientierungswissen soll durch die intensive Beschäftigung mit Texten, Statistiken und Reden vermittelt werden. Dabei kann auch die Möglichkeit des fächerübergreifenden Unterrichtes genutzt werden, um textexternes Wissen zunehmend mit textinternen Informationen zu verknüpfen sowie deutschsprachige Texte aus anderen Sachfächern sprachmittelnd heranzuziehen. Dabei erweitern die Schülerinnen und Schüler zunehmend ihre funktionalen kommunikativen Kompetenzen im rezeptiven Bereich des Hör-Sehverständnisses (politische Rede, Film).
Gesamtstundenkontingent: ca. 20 Std.

Sprachlernkompetenz

- Techniken für die Planung und Realisierung eigener Redebeiträge nutzen und adressatengerecht anwenden; intentions- und adressatengerechte Präsentation

Interkulturelle kommunikative Kompetenz

- **Orientierungswissen**: aktuelle Entwicklungen von Migrationsbewegungen und Migrationspolitik in GB und den USA kennenlernen; Kenntnisse über politische, kulturelle, sprachliche und andere Probleme von Migranten der 1. und der 2. Generation erwerben und mit Vorwissen verknüpfen (FoF *Great Britain: Immigration and Minorities*; p. 156; FoF *The United States: Immigration and Minorities*, p.158)
- **Einstellungen und Bewusstheit**: Toleranz entwickeln in Bezug auf andere gesellschaftliche Normen; sich zunehmend z.B. der sprachlichen Schwierigkeiten von Migranten bewusst werden (z.B. in Konfliktsituationen)
- **Verstehen und Handeln**: differenziert Empathie/kritische Distanz entwickeln; lernen, sensible Dialoge zu führen (FoL *Conversation and Discussion*, p. 266f.; FoF *Communicative Strategies*, p. 268)

Funktionale kommunikative Kompetenz

- **Hör-/Hör-Sehverstehen**: Gesamtaussage, Hauptaussagen und Einzelinformationen aus audiovisuellen Texten (J. Lahiri: *The Namesake*) und auditiven Texten (z.B. E. Bogosian: *subUrbia*; David Cameron: *Speech on the Government's Immigration Policy*) entnehmen und dabei Unterschiede in Aussprache/Dialekt/Register und deren Wirkung beschreiben können
- **Leseverstehen**: Sach- und Gebrauchstexten Hauptaussagen und Einzelinformationen entnehmen und die z.B. ironische/kritische/ernsthafte Haltung des jeweiligen Autors erfassen (David Cameron: *The Doctrine of Multiculturalism Has Failed* im Kontrast zu Sunny Hundal und K. Hasan
- **Sprechen – an Gesprächen teilnehmen**: Interviews/Befragungen durchführen (z.B. *Hot Seat*, task 6, p. 142) und dabei Perspektivwechsel durch unterschiedliche Rollen einnehmen
- **Schreiben**: kreativ: Verfassen von formellen Briefen (z.B. *Letter to the Editor*, task 6, p. 150; FoS *Writing a Letter to the Editor*, p. 290), Kreieren von Plakaten, Broschüren, Flyern etc. unter Beachtung wesentlicher Textmerkmale (z.B. Task 7, p. 153, FoS *Creating an Advert*, p. 278)
- **Sprachmittlung**: anhand des Textes M. Frick: *Tanz mit mir* sprachmittelnd die unterschiedlichen Verhaltensweisen und Ausdrücke in Geschäftsbeziehungen erklären, Probleme der Sprachmittlung antizipieren und Strategien, um Missverständnisse zu vermeiden, entwickeln (task 3, p. 136, FoS *Mediation*, p. 265)

Verfügen über sprachliche Mittel

- **Wortschatz**: den thematischen Wortschatz zu *Migration, Multiculturalism, Cultural Clashes*, p. 163ff. sowie den Funktions- und Interpretationswortschatz zur Analyse rhetorischer Mittel erweitern (FoL *Literary Terms, Non-Fictional Texts*, p. 311)
- **Grammatische Strukturen**: Sensibilisierung für *appropriate/formal* und *informal/everyday* English; *adverbs and adverbials*

Text- und Medienkompetenz

- **analytisch-interpretierend**: Reden und Artikel der internationalen Presse in Hinsicht auf Aussageabsicht, Darstellungsform und Wirkung deuten, dabei Struktur und sprachliche Mittel als Mittel der Manipulation von Lesern/Zuhörern berücksichtigen (FoS *Analysis of a Political Speech*, p. 260, FoS *Analysis of a Non-Fictional Text*, p. 258)
- **produktions- und anwendungsorientiert**: unterschiedliche Medien (*blogs, articles, placards* etc.) und Darstellungsformen (*Hot Seat*) nutzen, um kooperativ verschiedene Perspektiven zu erarbeiten

Sprachbewusstheit

- Beziehungen zwischen Sprach- und Kulturphänomenen reflektieren; Sprachgebrauch an Kommunikationssituationen anpassen (z.B. Telephoning); Sprachhandeln bedarfsgerecht planen

Texte und Medien

- **Sach- und Gebrauchstexte**: aktuelle meinungsbildende Artikel der internationalen Presse: z.B. Khola Hasan: *Mr. Cameron, British Multiculturalism Is Doing Fine; Fareed Zakaria: Broken and Obsolete; Marike Frick: Tanz mit mir*
- **medial vermittelte Texte**: David Cameron: *Speech on Government's Immigration Policy*; J. Lahiri: *The Namesake* (film)
- **literarische Texte**: Jhumpa Lahiri: *The Namesake* (novel), E. Bogosian, *subUrbia* (play), S. Cisneros, *No Speak English* (novel)
- **diskontinuierliche Texte**: Cover (z.B. p. 154), Cartoons (z.B. pp. 152f.)

Projektvorhaben

- Ausarbeitung einer Kampagne, um junge Leute zu bewegen, in die USA zu immigrieren

Lernerfolgsüberprüfungen

- **schriftliche Arbeit (Klausur)**: Schreiben mit Hörverstehen (integriert), z.B. politische Rede und Sprachmittlung (isoliert), z.B. deutscher Zeitungsartikelausschnitt

EF 1.5: 3 – 4. Quartal
Kompetenzstufe B1 des GeR
The Global Village – The World in a Nutshell?!

Das Unterrichtsvorhaben dient der Auseinandersetzung mit dem Problem der globalen Verantwortung des Einzelnen. Der Umgang mit Plastikartikeln, Müll, Mode, aber auch der Bedeutung des Zugangs zu Erziehung und Information soll differenziert erarbeitet werden und Orientierungswissen erlangt werden. Die funktionalen kommunikativen Kompetenzen sollen rezeptiv im Bereich Hörverstehen (Song, Rede, Greenpeace-Text) und produktiv in Bezug auf Sprechen (*Pyramid Discussion*) und Schreiben (*Comment, Writing Personal Letters, Transforming of Text Type/Factual Text – Feature Story*) gestärkt werden.

Gesamtstundenkontingent: ca. 16 – 18 Std.

Sprachlernkompetenz

- Arbeitsergebnisse intentions- und adressatengerecht präsentieren

Interkulturelle kommunikative Kompetenz

- **Orientierungswissen**: Wissen um globale Probleme, die durch Verbraucherverhalten in Bezug auf Plastik, Müll und Mode verursacht werden (FoF *Plastics*, p. 173, FoF *Technology, Progress & Responsibility in a Global World*, p. 193), sowie Kennenlernen internationaler Organisationen, die sich dem Schutz der Umwelt und Biodiversität verschrieben haben (FoF *Environmental and Ecological Movements*, p. 174); Erweiterung des Wissens um die Bedeutung des Zugangs zu Wissen und Erziehung (z.B. *Global Giving – The Girl Effect*; *HOKISA – Homes for Kids in South Africa*)
- **Einstellungen und Bewusstheit**: sich des eigenen Verhaltens in Bezug auf Umwelt und Mode bewusst werden; erkennen, dass Zugang zu Bildung für die gesamte globale Gemeinschaft Konsequenzen hat
- **Verstehen und Handeln**: verstehen, dass man z.B. durch sein eigenes Kaufverhalten wichtige Änderungen herbeiführen kann; dass man durch seine Reaktion auf Aktionen, die Bildung unterstützen (z.B. durch E-Mails), und Zivilcourage (Malala Yousafzai) Umdenken anstoßen kann

Funktionale kommunikative Kompetenz

- **Hör-/Hör-Sehverstehen**: Gesamtaussage, Hauptaussagen und Einzelinformationen aus auditiven Texten entnehmen (Song: L. Kravitz: *What Did I Do with My Life?*; Malala Yousafzai, *Speech at the United Nations*; Greenpeace, *The Trash Vortex*, Internet report: *Made in Germany*)
- **Leseverstehen**: Sach-und Gebrauchstexten Hauptaussagen und Einzelinformationen entnehmen und mit textexternen Informationen verbinden (z.B. *The Trash Vortex* mit Abbildung *Garbage at Sea*, p. 172, sowie FoF *Plastics*, p. 173)
- **Sprechen – an Gesprächen teilnehmen**: an Diskussionen partizipieren (z.B. task 1, p. 181, oder *Pyramid Discussion*, task 4, p. 182; FoL *Conversation and Discussion*, p. 266), wobei die Vorbereitung einer Diskussion möglichst durchgängig in der Zielsprache erfolgen sollte; in Rollenspielen spezifische Rollen sprachlich adäquat vertreten (Task 9, p. 171)
- **Schreiben**: unter Beachtung wesentlicher Textsortenmerkmale Kommentare (FoS *Writing a Comment or A Review*, p. 279), Briefe/E-Mails offiziell oder persönlich (FoS *Writing an E-Mail*, p. 284, *Writing a Formal Letter*, p. 282) verfassen; sich der sprachlichen Mittel anderer Zieltextformate bewusst sein und diese beim Umschreiben in ein anderes Zieltextformat anwenden (z.B. *Speech – Newspaper Article*)
- **Sprachmittlung**: Karin Zeug, *Mit Biodiesel zur Party* sprachmittelnd in Form eines Interviews in die Zielsprache übertragen

Verfügen über sprachliche Mittel

- **Wortschatz**: thematisches Vokabular: *Plastic, Pollution, Environment, Technology and Responsibility*, pp. 207ff., Metawortschatz zu *Text Analysis*, pp. 316ff., festigen
- **Grammatische Strukturen**: *Simple Present, Passive Voice, Indirect Speech, Connectives* (FoG Tenses, p. 305, Passive, p. 303)

Text- und Medienkompetenz

- **analytisch-interpretierend**: Rede, Song und Sachtexte in Bezug auf Aussageabsicht, Darstellung und Wirkung untersuchen und deuten
- **produktions- und anwendungsorientiert**: eine Differenziertheit von Aussagen und Meinungen erreichen, indem in Interviews und Diskussionen die Möglichkeit gegeben wird, andere Sichtweisen anzunehmen und zu vertreten

Sprachbewusstheit

- die Anwendung technischen Vokabulars als Möglichkeit begreifen, sich international über gemeinsame Probleme austauschen zu können

Texte und Medien

- **Sach- und Gebrauchstexte**: Auszug aus Sachbuch (Lutz van Dijk, *African Kids*), Artikel der internationalen Presse, auch online (z.B. *Die Zeit, Spiegel online international*)
- **medial vermittelte Texte**: Rede (Malala Yousafzai)
- **literarische Texte**: Song (Lenny Kravitz: *What Did I Do with My Life*)
- **diskontinuierliche Texte**: Cartoons (z.B. Haderer, *Das Weihnachtsgeschäft boomt*, p. 203), Graphs (z.B. *German Companies*, p. 199), Screenshots (*The Girl Effect*, pp. 183-184)

Projektvorhaben

- Living Without Plastic – A Project to Save the Seas

Lernerfolgsüberprüfungen

- **schriftliche Arbeit (Klausur)**: Sprachmittlung isoliert (z.B. den Inhalt einer Homepage einer deutschen Umweltorganisation sinngemäß übertragen), Schreiben mit Leseverstehen integriert (z.B. Online-Artikel)

EF 1.6: 4. Quartal
Kompetenzstufe B1 des GeR
Virtual Communities and Social Networks – Living in the Digital Age

Das Unterrichtsvorhaben dient der Auseinandersetzung mit den Chancen und Risiken einer zunehmenden Digitalisierung und Technisierung unseres Lebens. Hierbei soll nicht nur das Orientierungswissen über digitale Medien erweitert werden, sondern auch Regeln für das adäquate Verhalten in der virtuellen Welt thematisiert werden. Die Schülerinnen und Schüler erweitern ihre funktionalen kommunikativen Kompetenzen im rezeptiven (Hör- und Leseverstehen von Sachtexten und medial vermittelten Texten, z.B. Interview mit Sheryl Sandberg und Mark Zuckerberg) und im produktiven Bereich (mündlich: *Diskussionen/Panel Discussion*, Interviews; schriftlich: *creating cartoons*).
Gesamtstundenkontingent: ca. 16 - 18 Std.

Sprachlernkompetenz
- zunehmend unterschiedliche Textformate sinngemäß sprachmittelnd übertragen

Interkulturelle kommunikative Kompetenz

- **Orientierungswissen**: die Schüler erweitern ihr Wissen über die Chancen (z.B. *Digital Education in Kenia*) und Risiken (z.B. *TXT Bad 4 UR BRAIN?*) vor allem digitaler Medien (FoF *The Media*, p. 226/ Cartoons), der Auswirkung auf ihren Lebensstil und des adäquaten Verhaltens z.B. in Chatrooms (z.B. *Safebook*, p. 234) oder die Bedeutung von Kernkompetenzen für die Kommunikation (FoF *Key Qualifications and Soft Skills*, p. 223)
- **Einstellungen und Bewusstheit**: sich bewusst werden, dass die digitalen Medien die Chance bereithalten, das Problem des Zugangs zu Bildung und sozialem Aufstieg gerade in den Entwicklungsländern zu lösen, und zudem eine Plattform bieten, sich kreativ zu entfalten; ein Risiko aber darin besteht, dass man im Netz evtl. Missbrauch ausgesetzt ist und als Individuum im ‚main stream' untergeht; sich bewusst machen, dass ein bestimmtes Regelwerk sinnvoll ist, um sich respektvoll zu begegnen
- **Verstehen und Handeln**: Vorsichtsmaßnahmen beachten, um sich nicht selbst oder seine Daten in Gefahr zu bringen; offen mit den Möglichkeiten der internationalen Kommunikation umgehen (z.B. Kontaktaufnahme über E-Twinning)

Funktionale kommunikative Kompetenz

- **Hör-/Hör-Sehverstehen**: authentischen Hörtexten (z.B. Charlie Rose: *Exclusive Interview with Facebook Leadership Mark Zuckerberg and Sheryl Sandberg*) wichtige implizite Informationen entnehmen und mit externem Vorwissen verbinden
- **Leseverstehen**: Sach- und Gebrauchstexten (z.B. Vivian Yee: *A School Distanced from Technology Faces Its Intrusion*; Matt Ritchel: *Wasting Time Is New Divide in the Digital Era*) Hauptaussagen und Einzelinformationen entnehmen und mit textexternen Informationen verbinden
- **Sprechen – an Gesprächen teilnehmen**: Kontroverse Standpunkte bei Diskussionen einnehmen und dabei Persuasionsstrategien entwickeln (z.B. task 9, p. 219), Präsentieren und Evaluieren von Ergebnissen (z.B. ‚*Simplify your life*', task 7, p. 222)
- **Schreiben**: unter Beachtung wesentlicher Textsortenmerkmale Sachtexte (*comments, letters*) sowie Texte für Cartoons verfassen
- **Sprachmittlung**: Zeitungsartikel wie ‚*Mehr Lehm*', Statistiken wie ‚*Digital Lifestyle*' und das Video ‚*Wo ist Klaus?*' sprachmittelnd sinngemäß übertragen

Verfügen über sprachliche Mittel

- **Wortschatz**: thematischer Wortschatz zu *Digital Life(style)*, *Education*, *(Social) Media, Youth Culture*, FoV, pp. 240ff., Metawortschatz zu Analysis of Statistical Data, FoS p. 261
- Grammatische Strukturen: If-clauses type I, II, III

Text- und Medienkompetenz

- **analytisch-interpretierend**: unter Bezugnahme auf ihr eigenes Orientierungswissen Sach- und Gebrauchstexte interpretieren und begründet Stellung nehmen
- **produktions- und anwendungsorientiert**: eigene Ideen (z.B. *cartoons, websites*, Projekt: *Simplify your life*) adressatengerecht präsentieren und reflektieren

Sprachbewusstheit
- Sprachgebrauch in der virtuellen Welt und beim Verfassen von Nachrichten reflektieren

Texte und Medien

- **Sach- und Gebrauchstexte**: Texte der internationalen Presse (z.B. James Poniewozik: *Serial Killing, Time*)
- **medial vermittelte Texte**: Interview (mit Facebook Leadership)
- **diskontinuierliche Texte**: Fotos (z.B. Blue Man Group: GiPad), Cartoons (z.B. pp. 238f.)

Projektvorhaben

- Verabredung über Skype oder E-Twinning mit einer anderen Schule in der Zielsprache Englisch
- Kreieren einer Website, die Schule, Ort oder z.B. ein humanitäres Projekt vorstellt

Lernerfolgsüberprüfungen

- **schriftliche Arbeit (Klausur)**: Hör-Sehverstehen mit Schreiben integriert (z.B. Interview, Youtube Video), Sprachmittlung isoliert (z.B. Auszug aus deutschem Internetblog)

Who Am I? ... Who Are You? – Challenges in Teenage Life

TM [1]	SB [2]	Author: Title of text	Type of text	Topic	Competences	Audio CD	Film CD-ROM	GaST [3]	Diff [4]	Comp [5]
Start-up Activities										
28	12	Leland Bobbé: The Two Sides of a Coin	photo	typical feature of men and women	• describing and analysing a visual			no. 16		
28	13	Sting: Tomorrow We'll See	song	the life of a prostitute seen from different perspectives	• listening comprehension • making a comment	CD 1, 1		no. 17		no. 1
Who Am I? ... Who Are You? – Role Models and Gender Roles										
30	14	Joel Stein: The Me Me Me Generation	magazine article, cover, cartoons	the millenials – description of a generation	• analysing the contents and language of a text • analysing visuals • visualizing statistics • creative writing • carrying out a hot seat discussion					no. 2
37	19	John Irving: Owen Meany – Being Attractive to Girls	novel, photos	growing up in a working class area in the late 1950s changes and developments in teenagers	• listening comprehension • analysing the style of a text • analysing visuals • creative working with visuals • grammar: using and comparing adjectives	CD 1, 2		no. 11, 12, 13	6	no. 3
40	21	Male Attractiveness: Abs-Olutely Fabulous	magazine article, cartoon	physical characteristics that make men attractive to women other factors that add to male attractiveness	• analysing the contents of a text • describing a visual • examining the vocabulary of a text • creative writing • grammar: conditional clauses			no. 13, 19		

1 TM = page in Teachers' Manual
2 SB = page in Students' Book
3 GaST = material in Grammar and Skills Trainer
4 Diff = page in Differenzierungsmaterial
5 Comp = material in Comprehension: Reading – Listening – Viewing

TM [1]	SB [2]	Author: Title of text	Type of text	Topic	Competences	Audio CD	Film CD-ROM	GaST [3]	Diff [4]	Comp [5]
45	23	'Superficial Nightmare': Feminists Take Aim at Barbie Dreamhouse	magazine article, photos	reactions to the opening of the first "Barbie Dreamhouse Experience" in Europe by the press and various protest groups the aspects criticised	• describing visuals • analysing the contents and language of a text • creative writing • giving a speech			no. 16		
50	26	Colin Higgins: Harold and Maude	play, film stills	different views of life	• listening comprehension • analysing the contents and style of a text • creative writing • grammar: indirect speech	CD 1, 3		no. 12, 18		
What's Love Got to Do with It? – Family and Teenage Pregnancy										
54	30	P!nk: Family Portrait	song, photo	child-parent relationship in broken families	• listening comprehension • analysing stylistic devices • creative writing	CD 1, 4				
57	33	Eric Bogosian: No Problems	play, statistics	a person talking about the ideal life he lives	• listening comprehension • analysing the language of a text • analysing statistical data • characterizing a fictional person • creative writing • role play • internet research	CD 1, 5				
62	36	Jens Jessen: Über Coolness	German magazine article	the relationship between a teenage daughter and her movie star father the meaning of coolness	• mediation • examining the vocabulary • creative writing • grammar: different language registers					
65	38	Ron Koertge: But Baseball and Sex?	poem, book cover	poem: sexual behaviour of teenagers	• discussing a given topic • listening comprehension • analysing a poem • analysing a visual • creative writing: poem	CD 1, 6		no. 11	14	

TM [1]	SB [2]	Author: Title of text	Type of text	Topic	Competences	Audio CD	Film CD-ROM	CaST [3]	Diff [4]	Comp [5]
68	40	Diablo Cody: Juno – Breaking the Big News	screenplay, film stills, cartoon, visuals	teenage pregnancy	• finding information in a text • discussing the problems/topics mentioned in the text • analysing the stylistic and cinematic devices • doing internet research • writing and acting a scene • analysing visuals • analysing a film • grammar: present and future tenses, conditional forms		1, 2			no. 4
	46	Teenage Birthrates	Focus on Facts							
73	47	A High School Teacher Talks About Teenage Pregnancy	interview	reasons and effects of teenage pregnancy	• listening comprehension • analysing statistics • doing internet research • creative writing	CD 1, 7			22	
Big & Beautiful or Slim & Sexy? – Living with Your Body										
77	48	Robin Givhan: Why Skinny Young Models Persist on the Spring Runways	magazine article, photo	the fashion industry and teenage models fashion causing dissatisfaction fashion: a commodity or an art form?	• analysing the contents and style of a text • holding a discussion • doing internet research				31	
80	50	Patrick Hickey Jr.: Artist Creates Healthy, "Normal" Barbie	online article, photo	the creation of a "normal size" barby doll	• designing an advert • grammar: collecting vocabulary on a certain subject • creating and acting out a role play					
81	51	Jeremy Laurance: Hundreds of Websites Urging Girls to "Starve for Perfection"	newspaper article, photo	websites about the experiences of anorexic girls and the effect they have on their readers	• analysing the contents and style of a text • creative writing					no. 5
84	53	Mirror, Mirror on the Wall … Who Is the Fairest One of All?	photo page	different definitions of beauty	• describing pictures • analysing different concepts of beauty • doing Internet research			no. 15, 19		
86	54	Disfigured – Learning to Accept Your Body	film	meeting and ensuing friendship of two very different young women	• analysing film scenes • finding slogans for a given topic • holding a discussion		3, 4			no. 6
	56	Thematic Vocabulary	Focus on Vocab							

Start-up (pp. 12–13)

About the artists	Leland Bobbé is an American photographer centered in New York City. His photos are both considered commercial and fine art, focusing on beneath the surface ideas. His collection, Half-Drag, centers around people with half of their face in drag while the other half is without any make-up or alteration in appearance.	Sting is an English musician known as an instrumentalist, singer, songwriter, activist, actor. He is known both for his solo career and for his career as the lead singer of the rock band The Police.
About the photo **About the song**	The photo comes from the Half-Drag collection in which half of the model's face is in drag and the other half is unaltered.	The song was influence by Sting thinking about a transsexual prostitute. He wrote this after thinking that he was very comfortable writing about heterosexual life and wanted to go out of that comfort zone with a transsexual muse.
Level	● ● ○	● ○ ○
Additional material	• GaST: no. 16	• Audio CD 1, 1 • GaST: no. 17 • Comprehension: no. 1

- Da die Grenze zwischen typischen Merkmalen bzw. Verhaltensmustern einer Person und stereoptypen Vorstellungen davon fließend ist, sollte der Unterschied im Vorfeld der Beschäftigung mit Bobbés Fotografie geklärt werden. Während typische Merkmale und Verhaltensmuster biologisch und entwicklungsgeschichtlich bestimmt sind, werden Stereotypen zwar auf der Grundlage dieser typischen Muster gebildet, verselbstständigen sich jedoch zu Wunsch- oder Standardvorstellungen, die auf das einzelne Erscheinungsbild projiziert werden.
- Im Anschluss an die **Erarbeitungsphase** (Aufg. 1) können die einzelnen von den Schülern genannten Aspekte noch einmal auf diesen Unterschied hin **überprüft** werden.
- Aufgabe zwei kann als **individueller Schreibauftrag** erledigt werden. Danach können die Ergebnisse in **Kleingruppen** ausgetauscht und anhand der entsprechenden Focus on Skills-Seite (SB, S. 262) **evaluiert** werden.

SOLUTIONS START-UP ACTIVITIES

1. **What is typical of women and men? Try to find this out by writing your ideas on the subject on different cards. Then fix all the cards on the board and compare the different thoughts. Are there cards that apply to both sexes? Did you really reach the core of the matter or did you write down stereotypes?**

   What is typical:

   Women:
   - Physically often described as beautiful (long hair, make-up, wearing dresses/skirts, high voices); empathetic; sensitive; nurturing; home-makers/family oriented; dramatic; catty.

   Men:
   - Physically often described as handsome (short hair, muscular, wearing long pants/shirts, deep voices); restricted emotions; strength; aggression; pursuit of achievement and status.

   Are there cards that apply to both sexes?
   - Yes. Women and men often share these attributes and cross categories, some men having more feminine traits than masculine and vice versa, begging the question whether these descriptions are accurate?

Did you really reach the core of the matter or did you write down stereotypes?

- The attributes listed in each category are stereotyped. Often, the descriptors that we use to identify men and women are separate sets of attributes, behaviours, roles, and physical characteristics generally associated with either gender. These descriptive terms may be more socially constructed than biologically-created, contributing to stereotyped, socially defined gender roles. These constructs stretch across history and culture.

2. Now describe the person in Leland Bobbé's photo and relate your previous findings to the description.
→ Focus on Skills, Analysis of Visuals, p. 262

- The photo captures the femininity and masculinity of one person. The person's right side signifies a woman through the use of make-up (eye shadow, lipstick, blush), long hair, and jewelry. The left side signifies a man through the use of short hair, an unshaven face, and without make-up.
- The photo poses questions such as:
  - Whether men and women ought to be classified into gendered groups based on self made physical alterations (make-up, hairstyle, etc.)?
  - Might we know if this image was a man or a woman if his/her entire face was made up to look feminine or masculine?
  - Why does society and culture place such great significance on the gender divide? If someone wants to look a certain way, whether it be masculine or feminine, why might they be judged if they choose an image outside their classified gender?

CD 1 1

3. Listen to Sting's song twice. In order to get a better understanding of the song, form groups, each group focusing on one or two of the following aspects:
○ the setting of the scene, ○ the singer: his outward appearance, his body language, how he speaks to attract customers, ○ the singer's friend and his destiny, ○ the singer's customers: their social status, their lives, their attitude, ○ the singer's view of the present and the future.
In a second listening, find out about the relationship between the singer and the addressee.

- The singer is a prostitute, selling sex for money. His use of the word "tawdry" is interesting, defined as "cheap, gaudy, showy, of poor quality", it is used to set the scene, the way the lights hit the street at a certain point of the night. These descriptors, however, are often used to describe prostitutes.
- The relationship between the singer and the addressee is one of capitalism, supply and demand, even if the service is illegal. The singer represents the prostitute, selling his/her body for sex, while the addressee is a man looking to buy love or an opportunity to have an emotional release or human connection, even if he must pay for it.
- The singer explains that she/he is not remorseful, her/his choice to sell her/his body is one of necessity – in order to make a living – and the addressee is a willing customer.
- The song makes us question the circumstances of the singer – what led him/her to this lifestyle? He/she explains this life is a matter of chance and could have happened to anyone. She/he acknowledges it is a dangerous lifestyle, having had a friend who was apparently murdered while working the street, and the lonesomeness, while no one cared as the body was simply taken away and another person took her/his place. However, the song also suggests that the addressee, the customer, is also lonesome and takes dangerous risks by the fact that he is purchasing this type of physical connection from a stranger.

Webcode SNG-40175-001 @

4. Now, watch Sting's introduction to the song sung at a live concert in Berlin on the video clip. What does he say about the creation of the song and why he did not shy away from this topic? Do you think the singer's words "Don't judge me ..." have some truth? Make a comment.

In the process of creation, Sting said 'finish the music first'. He composed the music before the lyrics and while listening to the music alone, Sting thought of a transsexual. Not thinking that he could delve into that world, he walked away from the music for a while but that changed. He felt that he was being judgemental. Writing songs like *Roxanne* came natural to him in a heterosexual world but he shied away from trying to put himself in a transsexual mind-set. Sting himself was judging that world. The words "Don't judge me..." come from his own thoughts.

Who Am I? ... Who Are You? – Role Models and Gender Roles

Joel Stein

The Me Me Me Generation (pp. 14–18)

About the author	Joel Stein (born July 23, 1971) is an American journalist who wrote for the *Los Angeles Times* and is a regular contributor to *Time*. (cf. en.wikipedia.org/wiki/Joel_Stein)
About the text	In May 2013, Stein penned a *Time* cover story entitled "The Me Generation" about the narcissistic and immature tendencies of millennials, but how they will also "save us all." Stein's piece was criticized in *The New Republic*, *The Atlantic*, *New York*, and *The Nation*, among others, for selective use of evidence, for making sweeping generalizations about the behaviour of millennials, and for repeating claims that prior generations had made about the young people in their times. (cf. en.wikipedia.org/wiki/Joel_Stein) In arguing Stein might be wrong, Noah Fitzgerel, Senior Class President, Annandale High School, argues in a *Huffington Post* article: "We are just as passionate, informed and inquiring as our parents. In fact, our ostensible propensity to over-extend ourselves in the digital world often means that we learn of important news stories before our parents. ... So, are we the 'Me, Me, Me Generation?' In the sense that we use ourselves as vehicles for positive and impactful change, this label might be apt. But, regarding Stein's use of the expression, I think Jay Gatsby would have to shrug and say, "You're wrong, old sport."" (cf. Noah Fitzgerel, Huffington Post, What Would Jay Gatsby Say to Joel Stein and His 'Me, Me, Me Generation'?, 5 March 2013, www.huffingtonpost.com/noah-fitzgerel/joel-stein-me-generation_b_3304383.html)
Level	● ● ○
Additional material	• Comprehension: no. 2

- Der **Narzissmythos** ist zumindest einem Teil der Schülerinnen und Schüler aus dem Latein- oder Geschichtsunterricht bekannt. Daher sollte eine kurze Besprechung der **Awareness-Aufgabe** ohne weiteren Rechercheauftrag zu Beginn der Beschäftigung mit dem Thema möglich sein.
- Für die die **zweimalige Lektüre** des recht umfangreichen Textes einschließende Bearbeitung von **Aufgabe 1** müssen je nach Leistungsstand der Klasse zwischen **30 und 40 Minuten** veranschlagt werden. Aus Gründen der **Zeitökonomie** kann daher Aufgabe 1 als die Arbeit mit dem Text **vorbereitende Hausaufgabe** erteilt werden. In diesem Fall kann jedoch nicht sichergestellt werden, dass die Schülerinnen und Schüler die Aufgabe tatsächlich als **scanning exercise** bearbeiten.
- Wird die Aufgabe im Unterricht bearbeitet, so kann sie dadurch **zeitlich entlastet** werden, dass die Schülerinnen und Schüler ein **Arbeitsblatt** erhalten, auf dem sie die Aufgaben sowie Platz für ihre Notizen finden. Außerdem kann die Aufgabe als arbeitsteilige **Partnerarbeit** gestaltet werden, wobei die Partner die Ergebnisse des anderen übernehmen, sodass am Ende das gesamte Arbeitsblatt ausgefüllt ist.
- **Aufgabe 2** wird ebenfalls in **Partnerarbeit** erledigt. Im Anschluss können die Ergebnisse mit einer **weiteren Zweiergruppe** verglichen werden. Eine abschließende kurze **Diskussion** im **Plenum** ermöglicht eine weitere Vereinheitlichung der Ergebnisse, falls dies gewünscht ist.
- **Aufgabe 3** wird **individuell** bearbeitet. Die Schülerinnen und Schüler erhalten den Auftrag, einen Cartoon **auszuwählen** und in einem kurzen Text **schriftlich** zu analysieren. Dazu können sie ggf. auf die angegebene **Focus on Skills-Seite** (SB, S. 262) verwiesen werden. Nach der Erarbeitungsphase werden die Ergebnisse in **Kleingruppen** ausgetauscht und diskutiert. Einige Texte können zum Abschluss vorgelesen werden.
- **Aufgabe 4** kann als den ersten Teil der Textarbeit abschließende **Hausaufgabe** erteilt werden.
- Die Bearbeitung von **Aufgabe 5** kann in **Partnerarbeit** stattfinden. Die Ergebnisse können nach der Erarbeitungsphase im **Plenum** besprochen und an der **Tafel** gesichert werden:

Joel Stein, The Me Me Me Generation

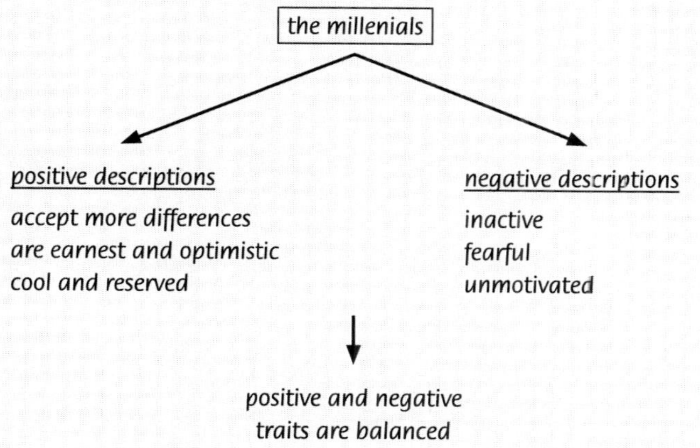

- Zur Bearbeitung von **Aufgabe 6** sollten die Schülerinnen und Schüler Zugang zu **Computerarbeitsplätzen** haben. Die grafischen Darstellungen werden in Gruppen erarbeitet. Die Ergebnisse der Beschäftigung mit der Aufgabenstellung werden auf **Flipchartbögen** visualisiert und durch die jeweiligen Gruppen **präsentiert**.
- **Aufgabe 7** wird in **Partnerarbeit** bearbeitet. Die Ergebnisse werden im Plenum diskutiert und auf **Folie** gesichert. Die Folie kann im Anschluss für die gesamte Klasse **kopiert** werden.
- **Aufgabe 8** wird als **Hausaufgabe** erledigt. Die angegebene **Focus on Skills-Seite** (SB, S. 290) sollte im Unterricht kurz mit der Lerngruppe besprochen werden.
- Zur Vorbereitung der **Hot Seat Discussion (Aufg. 9)** werden die Schülerinnen und Schüler aufgefordert, sich noch einmal mit der *Me Me Me* Generation und ihren Eigenheiten vertraut zu machen und vor diesem Hintergrund **stichwortartig** Fragen an den Autor zu notieren. Ein oder zwei Schüler bereiten die Rolle des Autors vor. Sie können ihren Mitschülern entweder gleichzeitig oder nacheinander Rede und Antwort stehen. Bei großen Lerngruppen kann ein Teil der Schüler die Diskussion als **Beobachter** begleiten und im Anschluss ein **Feedback** bezüglich Sprache und Inhalt geben.

SOLUTION AWARENESS

Have you ever heard of Narcissus, a figure in Greek mythology? Find out who he was and what psychiatrists mean when they talk of a narcissistic personality. Then guess what is meant by the "Me Me Me Generation" and what the visual below wants to express.

Who was Narcissus?

The myth of Narcissus is well-known for its moral tale. It has two versions: one Greek, by the writer Conon, and the other Roman, by the poet Ovid. In both versions, Narcissus sees his reflection in a lake or pond and is amazed and entranced by the beauty of his reflection. When he realizes he cannot obtain the object of his desire because it is merely an image, he kills himself or dies from his sorrow. Narcissus is the origin of the term narcissism, a fixation with oneself. (cf. "The Myth of Narcissus", web article, published on Greek Myths & Greek Mythology. www.greekmyths-greekmythology.com/narcissus-myth-echo, [20 March 2014]; cf. entry on "Narcissus," Wikipedia, en.wikipedia.org/wiki/Narcissus_(mythology)#cite_note-greekmyths-greekmythology.com-1 [20 March 2014])

What is Narcissism?

Narcissism is a term used to describe one who gains gratification from vanity or admiration of one's own physical or mental attributes, deriving from arrogant pride. (cf. entry on "Narcissism" en.wikipedia.org/wiki/Narcissism, [20 March 2014])

In psychology, Narcissistic Personality Disorder involves arrogant behaviour, a lack of empathy for other people, and a need for admiration. Individuals with this disorder generally believe that the world revolves around them and desire to keep the focus on themselves at all times. People who are narcissistic are frequently described as cocky, self-centered, manipulative, and demanding. Narcissism is a less extreme version of Narcissistic Personality Disorder. Narcissism involves cockiness, manipulativeness, selfishness, power motives, and vanity. (cf. entry on "Narcissistic Personality Disorder," Psychology Today: Diagnosis Dictionary, www.psychologytoday.com/conditions/narcissistic-personality-disorder [20 March 2014])

- Marc Tracy, a self-proclaimed millennial, wonders if members of his generation are "stunted" – i.e., not leaving their parents' house, getting married, or having kids – because older generations left them with a shattered economy.
- The problem with these stories, says Reeve, is that everyone, in every generation, is kind of lost and navel-gazing in their 20s. "Basically, it's not that people born after 1980 are narcissists, it's that young people are narcissists, and they get over themselves as they get older."
- Stein balances negative traits associated with millennials (narcissistic, lazy, stunted) with positive ones (resourceful, optimistic, adaptable).

The 5 best reactions to the TIME cover story on millennials. By Keith Wagstaff. The Week. May 9, 2013 theweek.com/article/index/244017/5-best-reactions-to-the-time-cover-story-on-millennials, [20 March 2014]

"The most recent Time cover story calls the generation of young adults known as millennials "lazy, entitled narcissists." Writer Joel Stein points out, "The incidence of narcissistic personality disorder is nearly three times as high for people in their 20s as for the generation that's now 65 or older, according to the National Institutes of Health; 58 percent more college students scored higher on a narcissism scale in 2009 than in 1982." ("Let Me Tell You All About My Narcissism" by Emma Roller, www.slate.com/articles/health_and_science/explainer/2013/05/time_magazine_millennials_me_me_me_generation_by_joel_stein_how_do_researchers.html, last updated 14 May 2013 [20 March 2014])

"In their new book, 'The Narcissism Epidemic', psychologists Jean M. Twenge and W. Keith Campbell explore the rise of narcissism in American culture and explain how this can lead to aggression, materialism and shallow values." (Today Books, www.today.com/id/30312181/ns/today-today_books/t/me-me-me-americas-narcissism-epidemic/#.UysiSK1dVxs, last updated 20 April 2009 [20 March 2014])

1. Point out the author's main ideas about the "Me Me Me generation". In order to find out what his main ideas really are, read the text twice. In a first reading take notes on the following points:

1	□ **what the author says about older people's opinions of younger ones** □ **what he states about the reliability of his own statements** • Older people often find the younger generations lazy, entitled, selfish and shallow. • He states that his opinions are valid because he has proof in the form of statistics and quotes from respected academics.
2	**what data prove the rise of narcissistic personality disorder** • The occurrence of narcissistic personality disorder is nearly three times as high for people in their 20s as for the generation that's now 65 or older. • 58% more college students scored higher on a narcissism scale in 2009 than in 1982.
	how the new generation sees/assesses their chances of making a career and • The article suggests that millennials believe they should be promoted in the workplace based on years served rather than accomplishment, due to the fact many millenials were recognized for mere participation in youth activities and sports. • Many millennials strive professionally for assistant jobs over those of executives, indicating desire for success in the workplace is unusually low.
	why they believe they make the right assumptions • 60% of millennials who trust their instinct when contemplating moral questions suggests millennials have misplaced self-confidence.
	what information is given about where and with whom the millennials live • Millenials' maturity is stunted, evidenced by the fact that a larger number live with their parents.
	what attitude to work they show • Millennials are lazy and underachieving – a smaller number of millennials who dream of having jobs with greater responsibility actually reach this achievement. • Due to technological advancements, millennials did not have to learn complex mathematics or theory, leaving them less able to comprehend and analyse complicated situations and problems.

3	□ **the data about date of birth and number of millennials** • Millennials are categorized as people born from 1980 to 2000 and are mostly teens and 20-somethings today. • About 80 million millennials exist, making them the largest age group in American history.
	□ **what globalization and the new media have to do with the generation's characteristic traits** • Because globalization has helped to connect today's millennials, through social networking such as facebook and youtube, the exportation of Western culture, and the speed of information exchange and change, worldwide, today's millennials are more similar than older generations within their nations.
	□ **in what way the Industrial Revolution and the information revolution changed people's lives** • The Industrial Revolution provided individuals with more power – it was easier to travel, start businesses, and organize people. • The information revolution has provided individuals with easy access to technology, allowing them to compete with and be heard by large corporations, newspapers, and even nation states. • The article suggests millennials are over-confident and self-involved.
4	□ **what is pointed out about children and their education and social life in 1910** • In 1910, not many teenagers went to high school, so the majority of most young adult interaction was with other adults in their family or at work.
	□ **how cell phones influence what group determines children's behaviour** • Cell phones allow teenagers to socialize at any moment and are constantly being influenced by their peers.
	□ **why older people and not people the same age are more important for the development of children and teenagers** • Interacting with people of many different ages exposes people to different degrees of maturity and social awareness; this diverse interaction is important for intellectual development.
	□ **what effect it has when teenagers read about the successes of others on Facebook** • Facebook encourages users to inflate or exaggerate their experiences to gain social approval. This false embellishment encourages insincere communication and distorted self-image.
5	□ **why millennials are more tolerant than older generations** • Millennials are nicer and more accepting of differences than older generations. Because there are so many countercultures, there is no norm; the us-vs.-them mentality no longer exists.
	□ **what other positive characteristic traits of millennials the author mentions** • Millennials are earnest, showing intense conviction; they are optimistic; they embrace systems. • Millennials are idealists, hoping for a better world; they are tinkerers, understanding how to use a breadth of new-age technology; they are dreamers and life hackers.
	□ **to what extent some of their attitudes appear to be paradoxical** • While idealism would suggest an aptitude for creating social change, millennials rarely revolt because their world view includes few leaders and discredits large institutions; they are dispassionate. • Although millennials are extremely accepting, they seek constant approval from their peers and fear missing out. • While the article suggests millennials are narcissistic, self-involved, and seeking affirmation, this generation has less debt than previous generations; they are more pro-business and less materialistic.

2. In a second reading, complete your notes and decide on the main ideas. Then arrange them in a logical order.

- There is statistical evidence supporting the rise in young people who believe they deserve more success with less work.
- People commonly believe they are entitled to career advancement whether or not they earned it.
- Millennials are information inundated with the ease of access sometimes making them overwhelmed.

3. Describe the two cartoons on p. 17 and show what image of the young generation is created here.
→ Focus on Skills, Analysis of Visuals, p. 262

Young people do not appreciate what it takes to be successful. They have acquired an entitlement mentality. Often, this creates situations where even highly educated individuals are not qualified or prepared to do a job available in the workplace.

SOLUTIONS ANALYSIS

4. Find headlines for each section and explain what line of argument the author uses.
→ Focus on Skills, Analysis of a Non-Fictional Text, p. 258
Example: Section 1: The I, I, I author ... ironical, funny, introductory statements

Section 2: You can make sweeping generalizations based on isolated statistics. Instead of looking at broad based evidence, the author uses statistics to support an opinion already embraced.

Section 3: Describing millennials, and how globalization and the information revolution has influenced their identity. The author uses both facts and comparisons to other generations to prove his point.

Section 4: The increase of peer communication and interaction has reduced the opportunity for young people to mature adequately. The author uses comparison, statistics, and arguments based on the effects of social media to prove his point.

Section 5: Millennials have many good qualities too, despite the fact they still fall short. The argument uses a list of positive traits: they are less judgemental of individual differences, making them nicer than generations past; they are optimistic, they are spiritual but not religious, and cool but often passionless.

5. Examine how the author's statement that millennials are "lazy, entitled, selfish and shallow" is replaced by a more differentiated picture. Filling in the grid might help you.

positive descriptions	negative descriptions
• accept more differences	• inactive
• are earnest and optimistic	• fearful
• cool and reserved	• unmotivated

Although the author indicates that millennials have many negative traits, he does describe how these shortfalls are balanced against many positive characteristics.

6. Visualize the given statistical data by for example making bar charts and examine whether the data really prove the author's statements.
→ Focus on Skills, Analysis of Statistical Data, p. 261

The data does not prove the author's statements but rather leads the reader in a direction that would support the narcissistic opinion of the millennials despite the fact that there is little proof in the data.

7. Analyse the linguistic devices and structure of the text to show whether the article should be taken seriously or whether it is just a commonplace complaint of older generations about the young.
Example: I am about to do ..., but I have statistics! ... I have proof ...
□ Use of personal pronoun "I" to emphasize that a personal opinion is given.
□ Use of conjunction "but" to introduce that the author introduces a contrast/the opposite; here: that the statement is not only emotional but well-founded. This is underpinned by employing anaphora/parallelism of "I have ..."

Paragraph 1: Use of exclamation points make the article seem uneducated. Exclamatory remarks, though they have their place, make writing in general less formal and less likely to be taken seriously.

Paragraph 2: Using the phrase fame-obsessed does not necessarily work for this argument. Saying you want to be a personal assistant to a famous person does not mean you yourself will be famous but you are assisting that famous person. Using that example and comparing it to a senator, who is by his own right

famous, makes the argument fall out. Someone wanting fame would much rather become a Senator than an assistant. In addition to that, the complaining nature of some of the words chosen makes this article seem less serious.
Examples: "Here's the cold, hard data" (ll. 13f.) – Unless you are writing about data on ice or metal and want to use some kind of pun, this phrase comes off in a negative, and non-academic way.
"Participation trophies ..." (l. 22). This comes off as an insult. The way it is used makes the author sound like he is saying that all millennials deserve nothing, even though some of those 'participating' have done great work. By using 'participation', Stein is grouping all millennials into one pot and neglecting those who have done their fair share.
"Their development is stunted" (ll. 33f.) – This phrase has quite a bit of negative connotation.
The last line of the paragraph is a great use of timing and structure in sentencing, "... 80% of people under 23 wanted to one day have a job with greater responsibility; 10 years later, only 60% did." That line shows great use of withholding information to make a point. Using data showing a better side of millennials was a good way to rope the reader in before making a perfectly backed up point to his greater theme.

Paragraph 3: "Ghetto-fabulous" – if someone is trying to be taken seriously, they should not use this type of slang even when using it as an insult, especially against an already maligned portion of the community, the poor.
Admission of fear – When trying to write on a serious topic that you are critiquing, do not admit you fear that topic. "That's why we're scared of them." This type of admission pokes holes in an argument for those reading. The thought of course would go something like this, "So, you are only complaining about this group because you are terrified of them," and then you lose your ethos.

Paragraph 4: By starting this portion with backing data on peer pressure (ll. 73-86) the author does great work to make his point believable before bringing up the narcissistic use of 'embellishment' (l. 97) as a way of building oneself up to one's peers.

Paragraph 5: Backhanded compliments – Stein begins his last paragraph with a bunch of seemingly genuine compliments about how millennials are very accepting to everyone. This lures the audience into a sense of security in the writing, escaping from the 'millennial-bashing' from the previous chunks. That is all turned on its head when Stein uses this compliments to fuel his last insult, saying that "Their world is so flat that they have no leaders" (ll. 119-120). Because of this, I would argue that this is more a complaint about the new generation. Being filled with insulting commentary and negatively toned comments along with backhanded compliments with little truly supporting data, this essay comes off as a complaint.

SOLUTIONS ACTIVITIES

8. Comment on the author's statement: "Millennials don't need us. That's why we are scared of them." Write a letter to the editor in which you refute some of the allegations the author has made as to your generation being lazy and self-centered.
→ Focus on Skills, Writing a Letter to the Editor, p. 290

The fact that older generations may feel less worthy or useful based on the fact that millenials do not need them suggests that older generations equate their self-worth with being needed by others. Perhaps this is flawed reasoning.

Melissa Lesh
932 Oakland St.
South Bend, Indiana 46615
USA
Mwibbs@gmail.com
Re: Why "The Me Me Me Generation" has it all wrong

Dear Editor/Sir/Madam,

I am writing in response to the article "The Me Me Me Generation" by Joel Stein. While the article suggests that my generation, millennials, are lazy and self-centered, I have to adamantly disagree.

The article indicates we are lazy because a smaller percentage of young people who dream about having a job with greater responsibility one day actually achieve it. This does not support the fact that we are lazy at all. In fact, many different reasons for this outcome are possible. Perhaps, less jobs with more responsibility are available, maybe when our generation grows older they realize that the responsibilities of family and personal life require balance and do not allow for a job with more responsibility, and why would a job with more responsibility suggest that a person is any more lazier than a person whose job is labour intensive or time consuming but requires the same amount of responsibility as their previous jobs?

In addition, the article suggests we are self-centered because we have scored higher on a narcissism scale than youth in the past, we have been given more participation trophies growing up, and have unlimited access to technology and peer to peer interaction. I would argue that these supporting facts do not weigh in favour of self-centeredness but instead support the idea that the millennial generation has greater self-awareness, self-esteem, and optimism than previous generations who were raised in a more fear-based society. Millennials have more self-confidence and may define success in a different way than older generations, but, this suggests that they have a different outlook on life – not that they are lazy and entitled.

Sincerely,
Melissa Lesh

9. It's show time: Joel Stein is invited to take the Hot Seat and is questioned and criticized by members of the Me Me Me generation.

→ Focus on Methods, Hot Seat, p. 270

Step into the character's shoes – what is he thinking:
Perhaps Mr. Stein is thinking about his own youth and how differently he and his peers acted. Maybe he is romanticizing his childhood and thinks they worked harder because he is looking at the world through rose-coloured glasses.

Questions for the author:

- How do you think major historic events have played a role in how we perceive various generations, e. g., the hippie movement, industrial revolution, war, etc.?
- What affect do you think today's narcissism will have on tomorrow's generation?
- What criticism did the older generation have of yours when you were young?

What have you learned:

- Often a person's perspective is jaded based on the generation in which they grew up.
- Criticism is sometimes important and can be constructive, giving the reader food for thought and perhaps might caution one's actions.
- Judgement is rarely fair.

John Irving

Owen Meany – Being Attractive to Girls (pp. 19–21)

About the author	John Irving is an American novelist and screenwriter. His novels include *The World According to Garp* and *A Widow for One Year*. Some of his other novels have also been turned into successful films: *The Cider House Rules* and *A Prayer for Owen Meany* (Film adaptation: Simon Birch).
About the text	This text is an excerpt from the novel *A Prayer for Owen Meany* (1989). The story is narrated by John Wheelwright, who is looking back at his life. He tells stories about growing up with his best friend, Owen Meany. Owen is unusually small for his age and has problems with his voice, which is abnormally high-pitched.
Level	● ● ●
Additional material	• Audio CD 1, 2 • Differenzierungsmaterial, p. 6 • GaST: no. 11, 12, 13 • Comprehension: no. 3

- Die Frage nach den Faktoren, die eine Person attraktiv erscheinen lassen (**Awareness-Aufgabe**), kann in einem kurzen **Unterrichtsgespräch** geklärt werden. Um den Schülerinnen und Schülern einen unvoreingenommenen Zugang zu diesem Thema zu ermöglichen, sollte dies bei **geschlossenen Büchern** geschehen.
- Bei in der Technik des **Hörverstehens** (**Aufg. 1**) ungeübten Lerngruppen sollten die Hinweise auf der entsprechenden **Focus on Skills-Seite** (SB, S. 244) im Unterrichtsgespräch erläutert werden.
  Zur Vorbereitung der Hörverstehensübung werden die Schülerinnen und Schüler zunächst aufgefordert, die vorgegebenen Fragen, wo nötig, auf wenige **Stichwörter** zu **reduzieren**, um eine Konzentration auf die wesentlichen Informationen im Text zu ermöglichen.
  Folgende **Lösungsmöglichkeiten** sind denkbar:
  1) Owen's childhood
  2) physical/mental changes – age 16
  3) effect of work on development
  4) attributes – adult

  Die Schülerinnen und Schüler machen sich beim ersten Hördurchgang Notizen zu den einzelnen Themen, die sie beim zweiten Durchgang ergänzen.
  Nach der zweiten Präsentation des Textes erhalten die Schüler Zeit, ihre Notizen zu vervollständigen. Die **Ergebnisse** können im **Unterrichtsgespräch** verglichen und gebündelt werden. Alternativ dazu können die Schülerinnen und Schüler dazu aufgefordert werden, ihre individuellen Ergebnisse anhand des **vorliegenden Textes selbst zu überprüfen** und gegebenenfalls zu korrigieren.
- Aufgabe 3 kann zunächst textbezogen und danach allgemein diskutiert werden. Folgende **Impulsfragen** können in diesem Zusammenhang eingesetzt werden:
  - Do men have to have muscles?
  - Do muscles make men attractive?
  - Do girls go for men with muscles?
  - How important is it in our society to look young and healthy?
  - How do people attain that look?
  - Should girls have muscles, too?

  Nach der Einführung der Begriffe „scenic presentation“ und „panoramic presentation“ (SB, S. 309, s.v. „mode of presentation“) kann **Aufgabe 4** im **Unterrichtsgespräch** bearbeitet werden. Die Ergebnissicherung erfolgt in einem **informellen Tafelanschrieb**.
- Bei der Bearbeitung von **Aufgabe 5** werden die Schülerinnen und Schüler zunächst dazu aufgefordert, die auf der Titelseite abgebildete Person zu **beschreiben**. In einem zweiten Schritt werden die so erarbeiteten männlichen Schönheitsideale mit dem im Text formulierten **verglichen**.
  Dies kann in einem **informellen Unterrichtsgespräch** geschehen. Es mag in diesem Zusammenhang lohnenswert sein, der Frage nachzugehen, ob Jungen und Mädchen dieselben Merkmale an Männern attraktiv finden.

Die **Ergebnissicherung** erfolgt in einem **informellen Tafelanschrieb** und ist die Grundlage für die Gestaltung der Titelseite zum „sexiest man alive“ (Aufg. 6).

- Aufgabe 7 wird in **Gruppenarbeit** erledigt. Für die in der Aufgabenstellung geforderte Bildbearbeitung sind der Zugang zu **Computern** und die Kenntnis von **Bildbearbeitungsprogrammen** unerlässlich. Ggf. kann hier **fächerübergreifend** mit dem Fach ITG gearbeitet werden.
- Aufgabe 8 kann als **Wiederholung** der Steigerung von Adjektiven im Englischen genutzt werden. Hierzu wird das **Vorwissen** der Schülerinnen und Schüler in einer kurzen **Brainstorming-Phase** reaktiviert. Die Schülerbeiträge werden zunächst ungeordnet an der Tafel gesammelt. In einer anschließenden **Gruppenarbeitsphase** (Gruppen zu jeweils 4 Schülern) erhalten die Schülerinnen und Schüler den Auftrag, mithilfe der Grammatikzusammenfassung (SB, S. 292) und der Ergebnisse des Brainstormings einen **Grammatikaufschrieb** zum Thema „The Comparison of Adjectives“ zu erarbeiten. Die Ergebnisse werden auf **Folie** festgehalten und im Plenum **präsentiert**. Die gelungensten Arbeiten werden im Anschluss für die gesamte Lerngruppe **kopiert**.
  Vor dem Formulieren der Vergleichssätze können die von den Schülerinnen und Schülern erarbeiteten Adjektive in einer kurzen **mündlichen Übungsphase** gesteigert werden. Die Erarbeitung der Vergleichssätze kann als **Hausaufgabe** erledigt werden.

SOLUTIONS AWARENESS

What makes a person appear mature and grown-up – and attractive to others? Without reading along, simply listen to the text first (cf. No. 1).

For example:
Physical appearance: height, muscles, developed breasts and hips (for women), facial hair (for men). A look of **sovereignty and confidence** can often be seen in one's face and body language, which are usually associated with maturity and are very attractive qualities. **The way someone talks** also says a lot about how grown-up they are: they sound serious, smart, **act courteously**, and do not giggle or act silly.

SOLUTIONS COMPREHENSION

CD 1 2 **1. First of all, just listen to the text *Being Attractive to Girls* without reading it. While listening, take notes on what you get to know about:**

- **Owen's childhood**
  - unusually small, was made fun of by his friends and other children (ll. 13 – 15)

- **the physical and mental changes he went through at the age of 16**
  - suddenly became very in command and confident, which attracted girls (ll. 15 – 21)
  - developed manly-looking muscles (ll. 22 – 30)
  - growing facial hair (ll. 60 – 63)
  - "his face had a permanent adult quality" (l. 74)

- **the effect work has had on Owen's development**
  - gave him big muscles (ll. 29 – 30)
  - spent a lot of time working with older men and learning a lot about quarrying and acting like a man (ll. 32 – 43)

- **the attributes that mark him as an adult**
  - muscles (see above)
  - working knowledge and experience (see above)
  - smoking cigarettes (ll. 73 – 74)
  - speaking in a "worldly" way (l. 76)

2. Listen again, and complete your notes.

./.

SOLUTIONS ANALYSIS

3. Explain whether physical work is a key to masculinity.

Owen becomes much more masculine thanks to physical work for two reasons. First, physical labour makes him stronger, developing his muscles and making him more manly-looking (ll. 24 – 30). Second, he spends a lot of time with the workmen, and as a result takes up more mature, masculine ways of behaving, such as smoking (l. 73), boasting about his skills at work (ll. 56 – 60), and sounding confident when talking about girls (ll. 75 – 83). Owen starts working before the other boys and changes significantly while the other boys do not develop as quickly, which underlines that Owen's growing masculinity is due to the work he did in the summer.

4. Examine the text concerning the mode of presentation* and its function and effect. In what passages has the author employed scenic* or panoramic presentation*?

Scenic presentation:
- direct quotation of Owen talking about working in the quarries, as he said it in real time (ll. 56 – 60)
- the narrator presents Owen talking about girls, recalling his exact words and facial expressions (ll. 75 – 85)

Panoramic presentation:
- "Even though girls ignored us that summer, that was when I noticed that Owen was attractive to women – not only to my mother" (ll. 1 – 3) – a period of a whole summer
- the narrator describes how he and Owen had grown up together since childhood, i. e. a period of many years (ll. 11 – 15)

5. Look at the magazine cover (p. 19): Discuss to what extent it corresponds to the narrator's idea of being manly – and attractive to women.

- Brad Pitt and Hugh Jackman have facial hair ("fuzz ... on his upper lip", l. 61)
- the men on the covers look "in command" and confident, similar to Owen (l. 16). They are looking directly into the camera, which suggests confidence.
- Though it is not easy to tell on the covers, all three men are known for being tall, physically fit and muscular.
- Their muscles correspond with Owen's manliness (ll. 24 – 25). Owen is attractive to women, but the author implies that he is attractive despite his short height ("he was tiny, but he was fiercely strong", l. 25; "I had derided his smallness as surely as the other children had – and yet ... he appeared *in command*", ll. 14 – 16).

SOLUTIONS ACTIVITIES

6. Against the background of your previous discussion (task 5), create your own front page for a magazine presenting the "sexiest man alive". You can use photoshop or a similar programme to alter a photo of somebody "normal" and make him more attractive. Then present your covers in class, explaining why you enhanced certain features.

Individual solutions

SOLUTIONS GRAMMAR/LANGUAGE

7. In a first step, collect adjectives that describe and characterize Owen's outward appearance, attitude, views and behaviour. Second, compare Owen to "the rest of us" (l. 17) and say in what way he is different. Use comparisons/comparative forms for your descriptions.

Example:
a) adjectives: attractive, muscular, manly, physically strong, etc.

smart, mature, grown-up, adult, in command, rational, experienced, worldly, shy, awkward, small, lean, etc.

b) comparison: Owen was a better student and a better driver than the others. (ll. 9 ff.)
Owen was more muscular than the other boys ... (ll. 24 ff.)

- Owen was a much better student and a better driver than the others. (ll. 9ff.)
- Owen was more muscular than the other boys. (ll. 24ff.)
- Owen was more attractive to women than the others. (ll. 2f.)
- Owen was physically much smaller than the other boys his age. (ll. 14f.)
- Owen was more in command of himself than the other 16-year-old boys. (ll. 16ff.)
- Owen appeared more adult and mature than the others because of his physical strength. (ll. 24ff.)

Male Attractiveness: Abs-Olutely Fabulous (pp. 21–23)

About the author	*The Economist* is a weekly, English language newspaper based in London. Formed in 1843, *The Economist* is a liberally aligned news outlet that aims to "take part in a severe contest between intelligence, which presses forward, and an unworthy, timid ignorance obstructing our progress".
About the text	The text describes a study done by a doctor, Brian Mautz, wherein he asks 105 heterosexual women what they find attractive in a series of digitally created men. The points of attractiveness he inquires about are: height, shoulder-to-waist-ratio, and flaccid penis size. After describing the results, the author digresses from the results to analyse how women would be entitled to a more selective process when choosing a mate.
Level	● ● ○
Additional material	• GaST: no. 13, 19

- Die **Awareness-Aufgabe** wird zunächst **individuell** bearbeitet. Die Schülerinnen und Schüler erhalten eine bestimmte Anzahl von **Moderationskarten** (rot für die Beschreibung der perfekten Partnerin und blau für die Beschreibung des perfekten Partners), auf die sie ihre Vorstellungen schreiben. Für das anschließende **Ranking** ist es wichtig, dass pro Karte jeweils nur ein Stichwort verzeichnet wird. Im Anschluss daran werden die Karten verdeckt eingesammelt und nach Aspekten geordnet an eine **Moderationswand** geheftet. In einem weiteren Schritt erfolgen die **Diskussion** der einzelnen Aspekte und das **Ranking**. Die Moderationswand kann für die Dauer der Behandlung des Themas im Klassenzimmer verbleiben.
- Die **Comprehension-Aufgaben** (**Aufg. 1-3**) können **arbeitsteilig** erledigt werden, d.h., die Klasse wird in drei Gruppen eingeteilt, von denen jede eine Aufgabe in **Stichworten** bearbeitet. Die Ergebnisse werden im **Plenum** diskutiert und in folgendem **Tafelbild** gesichert:

Male Attractiveness

women	*look for*	***men***
– *have limited reproduction capability* – *look for a partner with the best genes to pass on to their offspring (survival of the fittest)*		– *with broad shoulders* – *with a narrow waist*

The study does not take into effect social status, country, time, personal beliefs, education, etc.

- **Aufgabe 4** wird individuell bearbeitet. Zur Schulung der **mündlichen Sprachkompetenz** notieren sich die Schülerinnen und Schüler lediglich **Stichwörter**, die sie in einem **Kurzvortrag** elaborieren.
- Da sich gerade jüngere Schülerinnen und Schüler mit der sprachlichen Analyse von Texten oft schwertun, empfiehlt es sich, bei der Bearbeitung von **Aufgabe 5 Kategorien** (s. Lösungsvorschlag) **vorzugeben**, für die dann in **Partnerarbeit** Beispiele aus dem Text gesucht werden. Die **Ergebnissicherung** erfolgt im anschließenden **Unterrichtsgespräch**. Alternativ dazu kann die Aufgabe gemeinsam mit der gesamten Lerngruppe gelöst werden. Die Ergebnisse werden in diesem Fall **informell** an der **Tafel** gesichert.

- **Aufgabe 6** kann mündlich im **Plenum** diskutiert werden.
- Die **Aufgaben 7 und 8** können **alternativ** als eine die Beschäftigung mit dem Text begleitende **Wochenaufgabe** erteilt werden, wobei sich für **Aufgabe 7** die Sozialform der Partnerarbeit anbietet. Die Ergebnisse werden in der Abschlussstunde im **Plenum** präsentiert.
- **Aufgabe 9** kann in **häuslicher Arbeit** erledigt werden, sollte jedoch im Unterricht mithilfe der angegebenen **Focus on Grammar-Seite** (SB, S. 296) vorbereitet werden. Die wichtigsten Aspekte können in folgendem **Tafelanschrieb** zusammengefasst werden:

Conditional Sentences

type	*if-clause*	*main clause*	*meaning*	German
I	*simple present*	*will/modal auxiliary + infinitive; imperative*	*fulfilment possible and likely*	Indikativ
II	*simple past*	*would + infinitive*	*fulfilment possible but less likely*	*würde*
III	*past perfect*	*would + infinitive perfect*	*fulfilment impossible*	*wäre/hätte*

No will/would in the if-clause!
if: conditional
when: temporal

SOLUTIONS AWARENESS

Today there are all kinds of organizations matching people via the Internet. They boast that they can find your perfect partner if expectations coincide. So try to set up criteria for your perfect partner in terms of outward appearance, social status, profession, hobbies, etc. Make a ranking stating what is more or less important to you and discuss the matter in class.

Criteria ranked from most important to least important:
- smart
- funny
- kind
- athletic
- involved in student government
- musician
- alternative
- spiritual but not religious

1. Present how Brian Mautz set up his experiment to find out what women really want and the results he obtained.

Dr. Mautz showed 105 heterosexual Australian women a series of digitally generated pictures of men in which three bodily characteristics were varied – height, shoulder-to-waist-ratio and flaccid penis size. The women were asked to rate the men as sexual partners.

His study found that women thought that the combination of broad shoulders and a narrow waist was the most important combination for attractiveness, surprising some that the answer was not tied to height or a larger penis.

2. State why the study is not perfect.

The study does not take into effect social status. All of the subjects come from a single country, making it more difficult to separate the effects of nurture versus nature. The study does not take into account variations of accountability over time. The sample size did not include an individual's fundamental beliefs, education level, occupation, personality, or interests, making it less realistic in terms of the overriding question of what a woman wants in a partner, overall, not just what she might be looking for physically.

3. Define the meaning of "evolutionary reasons" as depicted in the text.

The text explains that throughout history, women have been much pickier than men for evolutionary reasons. Because women have limited reproduction capability, they must choose a partner with the best genes to pass on to their offspring in order to produce the strongest/most attractive/most intelligent lineage as possible. Survival of the fittest is an important concept in evolution, which is supported in this example. Men, on the other hand, have nearly unlimited reproductive capacity and are able to spread their genes with as many women as possible, making them less picky when picking a partner.

4. Describe the cartoon on page 23 and reflect on how the man and the woman see themselves.
→ Focus on Skills, Analysis of Visuals, p. 262

Author and source:
- title: Untitled
- artist: Rick Enright
- publisher information: Not listed

Descriptive level:
- people, objects, setting: A man looking in the mirror, seemingly flexing his muscles, which look much bigger in the reflection. A woman looking in the mirror, seemingly negatively judging her weight as she sees a drumstick in the place of her toothbrush.
- action: It describes the different way men and women see their own reflection.
- issue: This is a social issue regarding the differences in gender, self-image/self-esteem, and how one perceives the opposite sex.

Symbolic figurative level:
- tools used to convey the message: The blunt captions emphasizing gender – What men see versus what women see when they look in the mirror, juxtaposed with the positive self-image a man sees and the negative self-image the woman sees conveys the message that men are often overly self-confident and women are often overly self-conscious.
- person/group on which the cartoon focuses: The cartoon focuses on a wide section of individuals, although it depicts a middle aged white man and woman. Because any woman or man can relate to the gender and the message, it is able to raise the question of self-awareness among men and women across generations and ethnicity.

SOLUTIONS ANALYSIS

5. Examine the vocabulary that is used to show the scientific approach of researchers.
Example: three bodily characteristics were varied (ll. 11f.) a matter-of-fact, thought-out approach using different criteria ... studies have linked (l. 24) → comparison of data
→ Focus on Skills, Analysis of a Non-Fictional Text, p. 258

- Three bodily characteristics were varied (ll. 11f.) – This vocabulary summarizes the criteria used in the study. Instead of saying women were asked to judge three differing physical characteristics of males, the terminology (bodily, characteristics, varied) emphasizes the scientific nature of the study, dehumanizing the question and making it appear less subjective.
- Experimental data (l. 6) – Using the word data in the place of results or findings gives strength to the text, making the study seem more scientifically accurate.
- The latest evidence (l. 7) – This terminology gives the text more importance or weight, suggesting that the "latest evidence" was correctly studied, is accurate, and up to date.
- Shoulder-to-waist-ratio (l. 12) –The study used a mathematical comparison when indicating one aspect of a male physique, which is used as one of the three bodily characteristics observed.
- Three-quarters of the variation in attractiveness (ll. 21-22) – Using fractions helps describe results in studies.
- Weak predictor (l. 23) – This terminology helps explain one result of the study – that height was surprisingly not as important to women when judging attractiveness.
- Diminishing returns (ll. 26-27) – The use of this phrase more succinctly describes an observation in the study that increases in height or size became less and less important with each extra centimeter.

6. Explain why preferences for slimmer or curvier persons have changed during the centuries. Relate your findings to the photo page "Mirror, Mirror on the Wall ..." (p. 53).

Modern and western culture prefers slimmer persons over those who are curvier, a significant change from the 15th – 19th centuries during which curvier persons were depicted as most beautiful in sculpture and paintings. Perhaps this is because a thicker stature in the past was indicative of social status and/or wealth, making them more attractive, whereas today this is not the case. Additionally, today, the media depicts under-weight images of women as beautiful, warping the opinions of what others find beautiful.

SOLUTIONS ACTIVITIES

7. Write a one-act comedy where two women or two men have just read the article ending with "Back to the sit-ups, boys".

Two boys sitting at lunch in the school cafeteria, one who is tall and athletic and arrogant (Ben) and one who is shorter, fuller, and kind (Doug), finish reading the article "Male Attractiveness: Abs-Olutely Fabulous" for class and look up at each other, laughing.
Ben: I knew my sit-ups would pay off!
Doug: What are you talking about, Ben? When is the last time you had a date?
Ben: Well, I don't know, Doug. I could get any girl I wanted. Why don't you point one out and I'll prove it.
Doug: [Doug gazes across the room and points out an attractive girl their age.] I pick her.
Ben: [Ben calls her over to the table.] Hey sweetheart! How are you doing? How about I make it your lucky day and offer to take you out this weekend?
[The girl smirks, rolls her eyes, and leans over pecking Doug on the cheek and walks away peering at Doug over her shoulder putting her hand to her ear signaling he should call her some time.]
Doug: Oh man! That's what I thought! Ha-ha. Nice always beats jerk!
Ben: [Ben grabs his books and gets up from the table.] I've got more sit-ups to do! [Ben marches away, shaking his head.]

8. Write a letter to Dr Mautz in which you criticize the sloppiness of his research and make propositions how he could improve his experiments.

→ Focus on Skills, Writing a Comment and a Review, p. 279

Dear Dr Mautz,

I recently read an article describing one of your recent studies which sought to better understand what women want in the opposite sex. Why does this study fail to account for non-physical characteristics like intelligence, personality, and social status and only use three bodily characteristics – height, flaccid penis size, and shoulder-to-waist ratio when identifying types of men that women find attractive?

By failing to include non-physical characteristics, this study does not accurately depict what women want but only what physically might appear more attractive. Moreover, by failing to take into account ethnicity, hair/eye colour, smile, hygiene, etc., the study fails to accurately depict what women might find most attractive. It seems to me that your study only takes into account what size of a person is most attractive. Additionally, a person is not able to tell the size of another's flaccid penis without seeing that person naked which is unlikely to happen unless a woman has already found a man attractive. So, taking this into account in your study at the beginning seems flawed.

I urge you to redefine the purpose of your study since others reading your findings will likely find it unhelpful and not realistic. Personally, I believe many more factors go into deciding what a woman might find is attractive in a man and this is difficult to quantify since so many non-physical characteristics come into play when forming an opinion. Moreover, what I, as a woman, find most attractive may not be what I want in the end if the man lacks intelligence, a kind disposition, or a funny personality. In the end, I think your study falls short when trying to identify what women want in the opposite sex.

Sincerely,
A Critical Reader

SOLUTIONS GRAMMAR/LANGUAGE

9. Use conditional clauses to point out the conditions that have to be fulfilled by a man/woman who you would choose as a partner.

→ Focus on Grammar, Conditional Sentences (If-Clauses), p. 296

For example:
- If he had tons of money, I would instantly marry him.
- I would not consider meeting him/her, if he/she was really unattractive.
- I would not mind if he/she was not that attractive. After all, it is the character that counts.
- If a man/woman is not reliable and honest, I do not want to have a relationship with him/her.
- etc.

'Superficial Nightmare': Feminists Take Aim at Barbie Dreamhouse (pp. 23–26)

About the author	Spiegel Online (SPON) is the online sibling of Germany's print weekly *Der Spiegel*. It was launched in 1994[2] and is one of the most visited German language news websites. en.wikipedia.org/wiki/Spiegel_Online [5 March 2014]
About the text	The article, 'Superficial Nightmare': Feminists Take Aim at Barbie Dreamhouse, describes and criticizes the life-size "Barbie Dreamhouse Experience" opening in Berlin. Critics and protestors are calling attention to how Barbie is a sexist role model propagating a negative perception of women and gendered social conditions which support women placing importance on materiality, how they look, and what they ought to be doing: cooking and cleaning.
Level	● ● ○
Additional material	• GaST: no. 16

- Die Auseinandersetzung mit einer bestimmten Art von Spielzeug (**Awareness-Aufgabe**) kann dadurch intensiviert werden, dass die Schülerinnen und Schüler dazu aufgefordert werden, ihre alten **Spielsachen** von zu Hause mitzubringen und zu erklären, welche Bedeutung diese hatten oder vielleicht immer noch haben.
- **Aufgabe 1** kann als Übung zur Stärkung der **Kommunikationskompetenz** eingesetzt werden. Die Schülerinnen und Schüler arbeiten **paarweise** und beschreiben und interpretieren gemeinsam das angegebene Foto. Dazu können ihnen folgende **Vokabelhilfen** als **Kopie** oder auf **Folie** an die Hand gegeben werden, die ggf. noch erweitert werden:

Helpful phrases:

Describing a picture:
in the foreground/background
in the centre
in the bottom/top righthand/lefthand corner

Discussing a picture:
the picture shows/depicts
the artist wants to express/emphasise
I agree/disagree
I do not think you are right because
on the one hand/on the other hand
in my opinion

- Die **Comprehension-Aufgaben** (Aufg. 2 und 3) können **individuell** bearbeitet werden, wobei sich die Schülerinnen und Schüler **Stichwörter** notieren. Die Ergebnisse werden im Anschluss an die Erarbeitungsphase im **Plenum** diskutiert und fließen in folgendes **Tafelbild** ein.

"Superficial Nightmare": Feminists take Aim at Barbie Dreamhouse

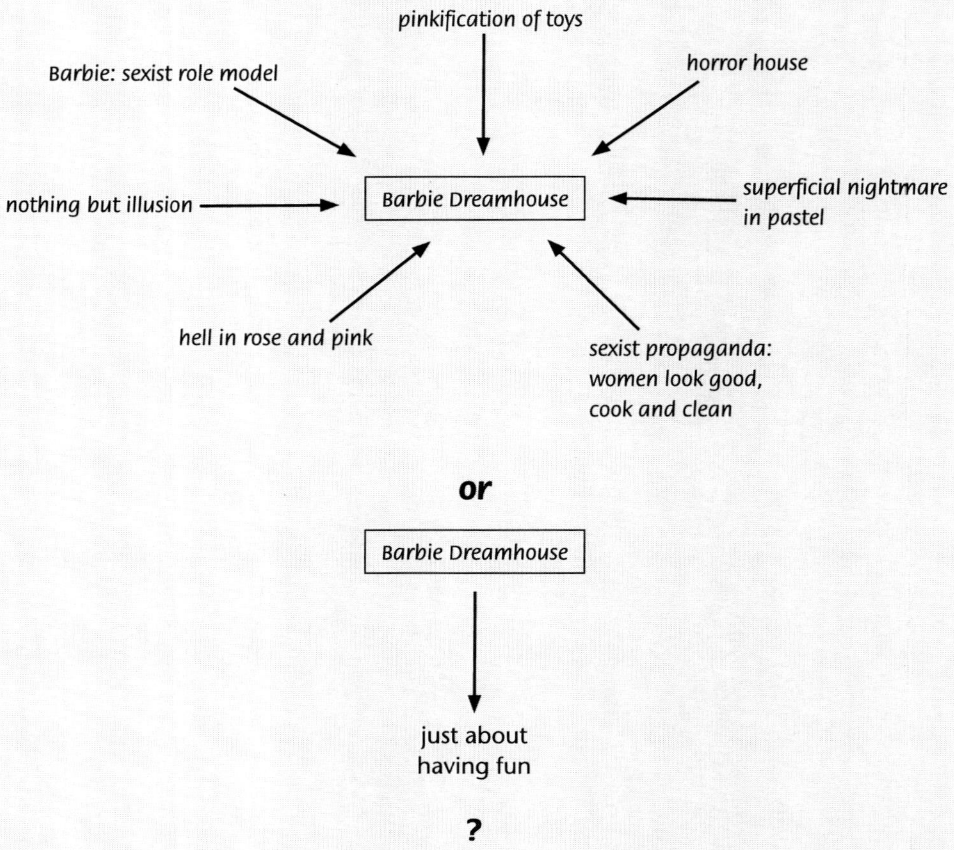

- **Aufgabe 4** kann in **Einzel- oder Partnerarbeit** bearbeitet werden. Die Ergebnisse werden im **Unterrichtsgespräch** gebündelt und in **Tabellenform** (s. Lösungsvorschlag unten) an der **Tafel** oder auf **Folie** gesichert.
- **Aufgabe 5** kann ebenfalls in **Einzel- oder Partnerarbeit** bearbeitet werden. Die Ergebnisse der sprachlichen Untersuchung können in **Stichwörtern** informell an der **Tafel** gesichert werden.
  Der Aufbau des Textes kann in folgendem **Tafelbild** visualisiert werden:

"Superficial Nightmare"

- *description of the dreamhouse*
  protestors against the dreamhouse
  positive evaluation of the protests
- *protestors as heroes*
- *Mattel's reaction*

➔ *The article shows both sides of the argument and covers any interpretation.*

- **Aufgabe 6** wird in **Partnerarbeit** bearbeitet. Alternativ zur in der Aufgabenstellung geforderten Ausformulierung des Dialogs können die Schülerinnen und Schüler auch Rollenkarten erstellen, auf denen sie **stichwortartig** verzeichnen, was die beiden Personen sagen könnten. Dies ermöglicht eine authentischere Präsentation des Dialogs, erfordert jedoch auch die Möglichkeit, den Dialog vor der Präsentation einzuüben. Für die Bearbeitung der Aufgabe und die Präsentation sollte eine Doppelstunde veranschlagt werden.
- Der Dialog kann zunächst in **Gruppen** zu sechs Mitgliedern (drei Dialoge) präsentiert werden. Die Mitglieder der Kleingruppen wählen den jeweils **besten Dialog** aus, der dann noch einmal im **Plenum** vorgetragen wird. So kann innerhalb eines vertretbaren Zeitrahmens jeder Schüler vier unterschiedliche Ausarbeitungen kennenlernen.

- **Aufgabe 7** kann nach der Lektüre und Besprechung der **Focus on Skills-Seite** (SB, S. 275) als **Hausaufgabe** erledigt werden.

SOLUTIONS AWARENESS

Have you ever played with Barbie, Ken or action figures? What did you experience when you played with these dolls and to what extent did you identify with them? Form groups and in a Think! Pair! Share! Activity (→ FoM, p. 273), present your results in class.

I have played with Barbie, Ken and action figures. As a girl, when playing with Barbie dolls, it was difficult to relate to them because their body shape is very unrealistic and they encourage materialism. When playing with action figures, it was also difficult to relate because these are mostly masculine and the few that are depicted as female are often physically objectified.

SOLUTIONS COMPREHENSION

1. Describe the photo on p. 24 (the activists).

This picture depicts a protest and the woman is dressed up like a Barbie in order to question the gendered rolls the doll encourages among kids. Drawing even more attention and, perhaps, for a shock-factor, she is topless. The pink Barbie house is in the background. The image of the burning cross is quite dramatic and questions the morality of the Barbie empire. People in the background appear to be walking past, basically ignoring the protestor and going along with their day.

2. Point out the reasons why feminists and other protest groups are so opposed to the Barbie Dreamhouse Experience.

The protest groups and feminists are frustrated with the image that Barbie encourages. It sends the message to young girls that physical appearance is what is most important, above morality, intelligence, courage or honour, etc.

3. State how U.S. toymaker Mattel and Dreamhouse creator Koschitzki responded to this criticism.

Koschitzki called the protests "totally unnecessary" (ll. 92-93) and indicated the Barbie Dreamhouse Experience is "just about having fun." (l. 92) Mattel is used to criticism and indicated that Barbie has been used as a means to advance other groups and organization's agendas (ll. 98-99).

SOLUTIONS ANALYSIS

4. Compare what the *Berliner Zeitung* said of the exhibition to the photos on pp. 24 – 45.

The article does not state exactly what was happening at or during the protests so there is not a direct comparison from the *Berliner Zeitung* (read ll. 24-30). Mention of a topless woman with a burning cross was neglected in the article's summation of that newspaper excerpt, something that would come across as a major problem for those in the audience. If the text was truly trying to dissuade someone from going to the Barbie Dreamhouse Experience then there would have been more information regarding what was happening at the protests rather than description of the pink kitchen where one can bake cookies with Barbie.

***Berliner Zeitung* about the exhibition**	**the photos and their messages**
"Glitz, Glamour, Ghastliness" Superficial Nightmare horror house in overwhelming pink a pink-coloured, sparkling world of beautiful illusion	topless woman (photo 1) burning cross (photo 1) angry protesters out front (photo 1) child looking at cooking supplies (photo 2) pink kitchen (photo 2) ➔ the child's leaning posture, looking like a type of longing (photo 2) ➔ the first photo's message is clear: people are not entirely happy about the Barbie Dream-house's message to little girls ➔ the second photo's message is a little harder to perceive: Though the child's pose looks cute – leaning right over the kitchen counter, adoring what the Dreamhouse holds – the photo in combination with the story has an ulterior message; little girls are impressionable and the Dreamhouse can cause problems in their self-image.

5. **Examine the choice of words and structure of the text to determine the author's stance on the matter, paying special attention to the last sentence.**
➔ Focus on Skills, Analysis of a Non-Fictional Text, p. 258

Much of the article was written in a way that is acceptable in journalism today. Descriptions of the events ("culminating weeks of criticism", ll. 11), quotations of other people (e.g. using the phrase "pinkification" ll. 14, 73, 75f.), headlines of other newspapers (ll. 24-33); most of the information is coming secondhand so *Spiegel* does not sound like it has an agenda. In description of the Dreamhouse, *Spiegel* used these other newspaper outlets (*Berliner Zeitung*, ll. 24-30 and *Süddeutsche Zeitung*, ll. 31-33) to portray the dream house in a very negative light. "Horror house", "superficial nightmare in pastel", "hell in rose pink", were a few of these phrases. This is just the beginning of the article en route to describing the more negative aspects of everything the Dreamhouse has to offer.
After the description of the attraction itself, the article shifts its focus to the protesters. Whereas the information regarding the Dreamhouse was negative, the article is almost protective of the protesters. By writing about the good these demonstrators are doing ("Don't want young girls exposed", l. 57, not targeting parents or children but the perception ..., ll. 60-67), the article is showing these protesters as heroes, fighting against the negative perception of women that is being propagated by the Barbie Dreamhouse.
Again, by using a quotation from a Mattel spokesperson, "Barbie has again become a tool for some to advance their own agenda" (ll. 98f.), the article strays away from advancing any of its own opinions and stays true to journalistic writing. This final touch gives the impression that the author may stand with Mattel, against the protesters, in favour of Barbie just being a simple toy without a "pinkification" pathway. This writing style shows that the journalist writing the article is aware that there will always be two sides to any argument, protest, even war, and by using the last line to show favour with Mattel, the writer covers any interpretation that any reader may have.

SOLUTIONS ACTIVITIES

6. **Imagine you are the godmother or godfather to a little 5-year-old girl whose only wish is to go and see the exhibition accompanied by its own Barbie-doll. How do you react after having read all the articles about the Dreamhouse project? Write a dialogue and act it out in class.**

Me: Honey, I'm not sure we should be going to this Dreamhouse. Some of the stuff I've read ... well ... it just might not be that fun.
5YOG: But you promised we could! I wanted to go to the big closet and the bakery and see all the pink!
Me: It just might not be a good idea for someone your age to get mixed in with all that's going on down there.

5YOG: But it's Barbie. I even put on her new clothes so she can come with me.
Me: You do know that Barbie's Dreamhouse is not a real home? You need to know that people don't live in giant pink mansions. It's something that just doesn't happen.
5YOG: It will for me!
Me: Sweetheart, once you see it, you may not want a pink house. Besides, what do you really want to do when you grow up?
5YOG: I want to be Barbie!
Me: But I thought you wanted to help animals when you grow up?
5YOG: I do.
Me: Well, Barbie has never helped animals. All she does is wear clothes that she can't even put on herself and sit in a car she can't even drive. Wouldn't you rather help animals than not be able to put on your own clothes?
5YOG: Yeah.
Me: Then how about we do this. Instead of going to the pink house, we take Barbie to the zoo where she can meet all the animals you are going to help when you grow up?
5YOG: Okay!

7. For firms sales figures are important. As a CEO of Mattel you give a speech pointing out that "pink" was a colour boys wore in the Middle Ages and up to the 19th century signifying the power of blood and that you really cannot understand the protesters. However, there is someone on the board of directors who takes the allegations seriously and gives a speech reconsidering the policy of the firm.
→ Focus on Skills, Giving a Speech, p. 275

Speech 1:
I cannot understand why they continuously protest the colour pink. Saying things, "pinkification", and talking about how girls become addicted to "pink life"; the colour is not just about clothes and the high life, it is all about power.
Both men and boys in the Middle Ages wore the colour to signify their power and strength. Pink was all about blood and warfare. That meaning makes everything these protesters are saying meaningless. Pink is not just cute, pink is power.

Speech 2:
With the knowledge that pink signifies blood, alongside everything that the protesters are arguing, I believe we should take another look at the policy. We should reconsider using the colour pink for everything Barbie.
The protesters say it is a colour that makes our audience strive for lofty ideals, a Barbie lifestyle that is unreachable with the colour pink attracting all of these young girls to something they can never attain. They say it is sexist, only playing for the attention of these little girls and completely neglecting half of the world's population. In addition, our own CEO has made it clear that the colour pink is a symbol for the blood of warfare. Is that the type of thing we want to sell to children, vulnerable and impressionable children who already live in a world of violence? Is that the type of business we want to be a part of? Or do we want to do things right?
I propose we change the pink policy. Use more androgynous colours. Use greens and blues and yellows, denim jeans and gender-unbiased t-shirts replacing pink jumpers and pink dresses. With those types of changes, I believe that Mattel can reach out to a larger audience and, hopefully, create a new line of toy that is acceptable to everyone without a need for protests.

Colin Higgins

Harold and Maude (pp. 26–29)

About the author	Colin Higgins wrote the screenplay to the film 1971 *Harold and Maude*. Higgins was an American screenwriter, director and producer. Some of his other screenplays include *Silver Streak*, *Nine to Five* and *The Best Little Whorehouse in Texas*. He died ir 1988.
About the text	*Harold and Maude* was released in 1971 and starred Bud Cort as Harold and Ruth Gordon as Maude.
Level	● ● ○
Additional material	• Audio CD 1, 3 • GaST: no. 12, 18

- Nach der Diskussion der **Awareness-Frage** im **Unterrichtsgespräch** bei **geschlossenen Büchern** kann zum ersten Hördurchgang übergegangen werden (**Aufg. 1**). Dabei erhalten die Schülerinnen und Schüler lediglich den Auftrag, die Atmosphäre der Szene und die Art der Beziehung zwischen den beiden Protagonisten zu erläutern. Dies kann in einem **informellen Gespräch** erfolgen.
- Beim zweiten Hördurchgang konzentrieren sich die Schülerinnen und Schüler auf die in **Aufgabe 2** formulierten Aspekte und notieren sich **Stichwörter**. Diese werden im **Unterrichtsgespräch** kurz diskutiert und münden in folgendes **Tafelbild**:

Harold and Maude	
– *enjoys people's attention when they think he has attempted suicide*	– *fought for liberty, rights, justice* – *took part in violent rallies and demonstrations* – *tries not to be too moral* – *embraces and appreciates life* – *takes risks*
↓	↓
"I decided then I enjoyed being dead"	*"And this too shall pass away"*

- **Aufgabe 3** greift noch einmal die in **Aufgabe 1** bereits thematisierten Aspekte vertiefend auf. Sie wird in **Einzelarbeit** gelöst. Die Ergebnisse werden informell an der **Tafel** gesichert.
- **Aufgabe 4** kann in Partnerarbeit bearbeitet werden. Die Schülerinnen und Schüler vergleichen beide Versionen des Textes und füllen dazu eine **Tabelle** aus:

Colin Higgins, "Harold and Maude"

audio version	***text***
the spoken text makes it easier to understand the character's moods	*stage directions give information on what happens*
tone and inflection enable the audience to empathise with the characters' emotions	*stage directions give information on how the characters react emotionally*
tonal changes and pauses tell about the persons' feelings	

↓

Both ways of presenting a text have advantages and disadvantages.

- Zur Vorbereitung von Aufgabe 5 sollten die Begriffe „**panoramic**" und „**scenic presentation**" (Focus on Skills, SB, S. 255) erläutert werden.

- Aufgabe 6 kann in **Partnerarbeit** erledigt werden. Vor der Bearbeitung der Aufgabe erhalten die Schülerinnen und Schüler zunächst den Auftrag, anhand der entsprechenden Focus on Facts-Seite (SB, S. 254) die wichtigsten **Elemente des Dramas** zu erarbeiten und diese in einem zweiten Schritt auf den vorliegenden Dramenauszug anzuwenden.
- Die **Aufgaben 8 und 9** können **alternativ** gestellt werden, die Schülerinnen und Schüler entscheiden selbst, welche Form der kreativen Auseinandersetzung mit dem Thema sie wählen. Aufgabe 8 wird in Einzelarbeit, der Dialog wird in **Partnerarbeit** erarbeitet.
- Beim Erarbeiten des **Dialogs** betrachten die Schülerinnen und Schüler zunächst das Bild und beschreiben die Situation: Die sehr viel ältere Maud fährt Motorrad oder Motorroller, während der junge Harold hinter ihr sitzt. Maud blickt auf die Straße, erweckt aber auch den Eindruck, dass sie sich auf etwas anderes konzentriert. Harold hält eine Schaufel in der Hand.
  Aus dieser Situation sowie dem, was sie über beide Charaktere im Lauf der Diskussion des Textauszugs erfahren haben, entwickeln die Schüler nun ihren Dialog.
  Die Dialoge werden zunächst in **Partnerarbeit** eingeübt. Danach können sich **Gruppen** von 4 oder 6 Schülern bilden, die sich ihre Dialoge gegenseitig vorspielen. In einer Art **Gruppenpyramide** können dann die jeweils besten Dialoge ermittelt werden. Diese werden noch einmal im **Plenum** vorgetragen.
- **Aufgabe 9** kann als abschließende **Hausaufgabe** eingesetzt werden. Die Bildung der **indirekten Rede** im Englischen sollte an dieser Stelle mithilfe der angegebenen **Focus on Grammar-Seite** (SB, S. 298) wiederholt werden. Auf den Gebrauch des -s in der 3. Person Singular Simple Present sollte ebenfalls hingewiesen werden.
  Die wichtigsten Aspekte der Bildung der indirekten Rede im Englischen kann in folgendem **Tafelanschrieb** zusammengefasst werden:

Indirect Speech

We form the indirect speech by backshifting the predicate.

direct speech	***indirect speech***
present tense	*past tense*
present perfect	*past perfect*
past tense	*past perfect*
past perfect	*past perfect*
will	*would*
is/are going to	*was/were going to*
can	*could*
may	*might*

!
- *there is no backshifting if the introductory sentence is in the present tense*
- *the aspect of the verb is not changed*
- *pronouns and adverbials have to be changed according to the logic of the sentence*

SOLUTIONS AWARENESS

In the given scene, Harold visits Maude in her little house; they are talking about what really matters in life. What are the things in life that matter most to people in different phases in life? – Discuss in class.

When people are younger, they tend to think more about material wealth and having fun. As they get older, family becomes more important as does living "meaningfully" ...

SOLUTIONS COMPREHENSION

CD 1 3 **1. In a first listening, try to get an impression of the overall atmosphere and the relationship between Harold and Maude.**

In the first listening, Maude seems like that "wise old mentor" to Harold. She is telling the stories like they are fond memories of a long time ago, somewhere Harold wants to go. While reminiscing, Maude's mood changes to become more somber and more serious, almost as if she truly misses her younger days, younger days which Harold comes to embody.

2. In a second listening, take notes and try to answer the following questions:
- **What has Maude fought for in life?**
- **What is her philosophy of life?**
- **Why does Harold stage fake suicides?**

Maude fought for "big issues. Liberty. Rights. Justice" (l. 27). The specific issues are not named, but she had taken part in many violent rallies and demonstrations when she was young (ll. 21 – 25).
Maude mentions several life mottos which she lives by:
- She tries not to be too moral so she can live life more fully (ll. 61 – 64).
- "And this too shall pass away" – everything is temporary; everything changes and dies (l . 79 – 81).
- She embraces and appreciates life. She is not afraid of making mistakes and taking risks because they are a part of life and part of living fully, and they make life interesting (ll. 129 – 133).

Harold seems to enjoy the attention he receives and the dramatic reaction he gets when people think he is dead. He describes the very emotional, dramatic reaction of his mother the first time she thought he was dead: "I decided then I enjoyed being dead." (ll. 123f.)

3. Now, take a closer look at the text and specifically at the stage directions.
Point out the atmosphere that is created, the mood the characters are in, as well as the behaviour and reactions of the characters in relation to each other.

- In the beginning of the scene, the atmosphere is described as being "warm and cozy" (ll. 4 f.). Maude shows off her kimono to Harold, which establishes that they are getting to know one another and show each other new things.
- There are many stages directions which simply reveal reactions or movements (e.g. "laughing", l. 16; "SHE takes it down", l. 21; etc.). This helps the flow of the scene by revealing their moods and non-verbal behaviour. Some of these directions contain an adjective to emphasize the characters' feelings, for example: "HE looks at Maude **intently**" (ll. 68 – 69), "HAROLD takes a **thoughtful** drag" (l. 82), etc.
- "HAROLD looks at her not knowing what to say. SHE seems suddenly very small and fragile" (ll. 42 f.): denotes a shift in the mood from light to more thoughtful and somewhat awkward as Maude temporarily gets lost in the past.

SOLUTIONS ANALYSIS

4. Compare the audio version and the text from the play: which similarities and differences concerning the rendering of for example the stage directions can you detect?

The audio version of the play makes understanding the character's moods so much easier. By listening to tone and inflection, the audience is able to empathise with the character's emotions in a way that simple reading could never do. Hearing tonal changes and listening to how long one pauses in between thoughts and sentences is a great tell for how each person is feeling while they are speaking. These shifts in tone and slight laughs between lines can signify the happiness of the speakers. Though there are stage directions that allow a reader to understand when someone laughs (e.g. ll. 16, 87) or how they are supposed to be acting (ll. 42), without hearing a professional actor/actress actually speak, reading can only go so far in creating an empathetic feeling between reader and writing.
This is a double-edged sword though. Without the stage directions within the audio, the audience cannot be aware of what is happening in the scene or the emotive responses both characters have on their faces while the conversation is taking place. Stage directions are used in a way that a novel employs physical description. By using the direction "She smiles and gazes softly into the fire" (ll. 40-41), the audience, readership, knows that Maude is remembering fondly what she had done in the past. Softly gazing signifies reminiscing while that smile gives away the fondness of that memory. These smiles and laughs come up again and again in the stage directions in just this scene (ll. 16, 24, 40, 50, 59, 66, 79, 83, 87, 93, 135, 137). This type of imagery is an impossible thing when listening to an audio version.

5. In this scene, the author employs various narrative techniques*. What modes of presentation* are used in Maude's and Harold's narratives?
➔ Focus on Skills, Analysis of a Fictional Text, p. 255

panoramic presentation:
- Maude talks about her involvement in political demonstrations and rallies which presumably went on for several years (ll. 21 – 25).
- Maude talks about changing times: "Kings died and kingdoms fell" (l. 28).

- Harold explains that he faked his own death 17 times, which probably took place over a period of several months or years ("Died. Seventeen times", l. 86).

scenic presentation:

- Maude tells about how she met Frederick: "That's how we met. I knocked off his hat. With a snowball in the Volksgarten" (ll. 38 – 40).
- Maude describes reading the pin that Frederick brought to her in a hotel room in Persia (ll. 77 ff.).
- Harold describes his first staged suicide (ll. 93 – 115).

6. Create a list of the typical features of drama* that are employed in this scene.
→ Focus on Facts, Drama and Theatre, p. 254

- This excerpt shows the **act** and **scene** numbers from the entire play (ll. 1 – 2).
- The text employs **stage directions** throughout which describe the setting, the characters' actions, feelings, and reactions.
- Most of the text consists of **dialogue** between Harold and Maude as well as longer monologues in which the characters tell longer stories.
- **Dramatic tension** is achieved via the two different characters from different backgrounds (Harold is young, male, inexperienced, and obsessed with death, while Maude is old, female, has a lot of life experience, and embraces life fully).
- **Comic relief** is provided in the scenes where Harold giggles from smoking the hookah pipe or when Maude acts like a silly cheerleader.

SOLUTIONS ACTIVITIES

7. The film still on p. 27 shows Harold and Maude smoking marijuana.
Comment on taking this way out of possible problems.

Regardless of one's views on this particular drug, it seems clear that smoking is no way to get out of real problems. It may be OK to smoke occasionally to relieve stress and relax, but if "real" problems exist they must be addressed and dealt with directly.

8. Write an interior monologue* that might have sprung to Harold's mind in response to Maude's memoirs of the past.

Wow, she really is old! It reminds me of what Grandpa used to talk about ... But he used to complain about the protesters. I wonder what he would say to Maude now if he were still alive. No matter, I'm glad he's not here now. She's been through so much. I hope she doesn't think I'm a naïve little boy ... Frederick? Oh yeah ... Weird, why do I suddenly feel jealous? Why is she staring at the fire like that? Oh, poor Maude ... I don't know what to do, I should say something! But what? I don't want to say anything stupid. ...

9. Take a close look at the film still on p. 27.
What might they be talking about? Write that dialogue and act it out in class.

Individual answers

SOLUTIONS GRAMMAR/LANGUAGE

10. Write a summary of the scene in about 150 words. Use the simple present and remember that you must not use direct speech in a summary. Therefore use indirect speech to depict what the characters are talking about.
Example: ll. 9 f.: Maude explains that the kimono she is wearing was made for her in Yokohama.
→ Focus on Grammar, Indirect Speech, p. 298

Harold and Maude have just finished a Japanese type dinner in Maude's little house. She explains to him that she fought for big issues like liberty and justice when she was young. She reflects on her youth in Vienna back when there were still kings and remembers the time she was taken to the palace for a party, where she met her first love. She tells Harold that she does not fight anymore but tries to make friends with people and make good things happen. In contrast to Maude's interesting and diversified life and experiences, Harold's only hobby is performing fake suicides, which he describes in detail. Maude's advice to him is to enjoy life and have as many experiences as possible so that he will have some good memories in his old age. (134 words)

What's Love Got to Do with It? – Family and-Teenage Pregnancy

P!nk

Family Portrait (pp. 30–32)

About the author	P!nk (or "Pink") is an American singer and actress. Her birthname is Alecia Moore. She is known for her collaboration on the cover of *Lady Marmelade* as well as many hits as a solo artist, including *You Make Me Sick*, *Get the Party Started*, *So What* and *Try*. Her parents divorced when she was 7 years old.
About the text	This song was written by P!nk about her early family life; it appeared on her second album, *Missundaztood* (2001).
Level	● ○ ○
Additional material	• Audio CD 1, 4

- Vor der Bearbeitung der Hörverstehens-Aufgabe sollten die Schülerinnen und Schüler die **Leitfragen**, auf die sie achten sollen, ins Heft notieren und jeweils genügend Raum für **Notizen** lassen. Alternativ dazu und aus Gründen der Zeitersparnis kann ein entsprechendes Arbeitsblatt ausgeteilt werden. Vor der Präsentation der CD sollen die Schüler wichtige Stichwörter in den vier Fragen unterstreichen.
  z. B.: Frage 1: speaker – hear – bed – night
  Frage 2: promises – parents – fix situation
  Frage 3: consequences – parents' divorce
  Frage 4: family portrait – restore
- Die Ergebnisse der Bearbeitung von Aufgabe 2 können als Tabelle gesichert werden (s. Lösungsvorschlag auf S. 55).
- Vor der Bearbeitung von Aufgabe 4 sollten die Schülerinnen und Schüler auf bestimmte Merkmale moderner Poesie wie freie Verse (free verse) und freie Rhythmen (free rhythm) aufmerksam gemacht werden, da die Gattung Lyrik sehr häufig grundsätzlich mit Reim und Metrum in Verbindung gebracht wird, was die Kreativität der Schüler oftmals stark einschränkt (cf. Literary Terms, p. 310).
- Neben der angegebenen Focus on Grammar-Seite (S. 298) kann zur Erläuterung der indirekten Rede im Vorfeld der Bearbeitung von Aufgabe 7 auch auf die entsprechenden Ausführungen auf S. 50ff. rekurriert werden.

SOLUTIONS AWARENESS

What is (a perfect) family in your eyes?

I do not think there is such thing as a "perfect" family, but families that stick together and love and support each other are probably happier than families that only fight and separate ...

SOLUTIONS COMPREHENSION

CD 1 4 **1. Listen to the song and take notes on the following questions:**

What does the speaker hear when he/she sits up in bed at night?

Momma crying, l. 2
sound of pain, ll. 2/3
glasses breaking, l. 4
fighting about money, l. 7
Daddy yellin, l. 18
Mama cryin, l. 19
noise, l. 24

What are the promises he/she makes to his/her parents to fix the situation?

she promises to "be better" and that she will "do anything", l. 14

What are the consequences he/she will have to face once his/her parents are divorced?

spend holidays at two different places, have two addresses, and after her mother remarries she will have a step-brother and her mother will change her last name, ll. 39 – 43

What is shown in the family portrait, and how does the speaker want to restore it?

the family looks happy and normal, and the speaker wants to restore it by acting that way again, ll. 44ff.

Compare your findings in class and complete your notes.
→ Focus on Skills, Listening Comprehension, p. 244

SOLUTIONS ANALYSIS

2. What are the linguistic devices employed to show the speaker's despair and her desperate wish to save the family?
→ Focus on Skills, Analysis of Poetry and Lyrics, p. 259

Rhetorical questions: answer is obviously "no", underlines hopeless situation for speaker	Can we work it out? Can we be a family?	l. 13 & throughout song
Anaphora: underlines speaker's desperation for things to return to normal	No ... no ... Can we ... Can we ... Let's ... let's	l. 26, l. 13 & throughout l. 37
Repetition: emphasizes speaker's fear and desperation	Ran ... ran ... ran	l. 24
Allusion/hyperbole: shows how scary and all-consuming situation is for speaker	World War III	ll. 9, 27

3. Find and list colloquial and slang expressions and rewrite them in Standard English.
→ Focus on Language, The Language Register of English, p. 315

colloquial/slang expression	Standard English
• deep shit (l. 1)	→ big trouble, a serious matter
• it's tearin' me down (l. 3)	→ it makes me sad, depressed; tearing
• 'bout (l. 7)	→ about
• ain't (l. 9)	→ isn't
• yellin' (l. 18)	→ yelling
• cryin' (l. 19)	→ crying
• cuz (l. 19)	→ because
• wanna (l. 25)	→ want to
• growin' (l. 27)	→ growing
• knowin' (l. 28)	→ knowing

SOLUTIONS ACTIVITIES

4. The song seems to create a portrait of a "modern" family by referring to divorce, remarriage and further problems.
Imagine either a different family or a historical portrait of your own family, showing, for example, your grandparents. Write a poem or song about them, their problems and the hardships they had to face, e.g. coping with war, separation, etc.

Different family aspects might include:
- same-sex parents
- adopted children
- step-families
- death in family/missing family member
- abuse/alcoholism/addiction

Historical family:
- war
- woman at home, man earning the money
- poverty, disease
- marrying out of necessity and not out of choice/love
- no possibility of divorce

5. Two years after the birth of her daughter Willow Sage, P!nk reappears on stage.
Against the background of the lyrics that express her rather sad family experience, can you understand her decision to have a baby herself, even as a very busy working mom?

Individual answers, e. g.:
Yes, she might be determined to give her daughter the happy childhood that she never had. ...
No, I think that celebrities have especially stressful lives, and since P!nk herself did not have a good childhood, it might be especially difficult for her to balance work and family life. ...

SOLUTIONS GRAMMAR/LANGUAGE

6. In addition, you can do acrostics on certain keywords related to "family" – here are some examples:

F
A
M
I
Love
Y

M
O
M

D
A
D
D
Y

Dispute
Isolation
V
O
Row
C
E

Write your acrostics on little posters and display them in class; discuss their respective focal points with the whole group.

Individual answers

7. Imagine you are a journalist from a newspaper and are asked to write about the problems and domestic quarrels the family in the song is dealing with. Based on the information given by the speaker ("I"), write an article that portrays the situation.
Use indirect speech to report what the speaker described and expressed. Be careful to use the correct tense(s) and change the language register where necessary.
Example: The speaker expressed her concern about the serious problems her family was facing. She told me that she had begged her mother to stop crying because she had not been able to stand ...

→ Focus on Grammar, Indirect Speech, p. 298
→ Focus on Language, The Language Register of English, p. 315

The speaker expressed her concern about the serious problems her family was facing. She told me that she had begged her mother to stop crying because she had not been able to stand the sound. She explained that her parents had been arguing about financial issues and about how to raise her and her brother.

She begged her mother to stop yelling and her father not to leave the family and asked herself whether they could be a family (again). The speaker even blamed herself, promising her mother she would be better and that she would do anything in order to get her family back together. Looking at her happy family portrait, she realized that it was only pretense and did not show reality. The speaker was concerned about having to split her holidays between two homes if her parents divorce. She expressed that she did not want to have a step-family and a step-brother. She repeatedly underlined her desire to keep the family together and keep up the appearance of being a happy family like in the portrait (again).

Eric Bogosian

No Problems (pp. 33–35)

About the author	Eric Bogosian is an American actor, playwright, monologuist, and novelist. He is well-known for his plays *Talk Radio* and *subUrbia* along with numerous one-man shows. Bogosian has performed on Broadway and has won three Obie Awards for his solo shows. As a Guggenheim Fellow, he is considered one of the most exceptional creative artists in the field of theatre.
About the text	The text is a monologue that portrays the "typical" American family. No problems, a well-paying job, a happy family, and perfect health are all parts of the typical American lifestyle as portrayed in the reading. The character in question elaborates on how he has no problems of his own though he has concerns on the world's troubles. As soon as those troubles are brought to the surface however, the character again begins speaking on how he as a great life.
Level	● ○ ○
Additional material	• Audio CD 1, 5

- Die **Awareness-Aufgabe** wird in Gruppenarbeit (Gruppen mit vier Mitgliedern) bearbeitet. Das Nachschlagen der vorgegebenen Begriffe kann als **vorbereitende Hausaufgabe** erledigt werden.
- Die Schülerinnen und Schüler erhalten zunächst den Auftrag, in einem **Brainstorming** mögliche Probleme zu notieren, die ein Mensch im Alltag haben kann. In einem zweiten Schritt werden die Ideen der Gruppenmitglieder verglichen und kurz diskutiert. Danach müssen **Großkategorien** gefunden werden, unter denen sich die gefundenen Begriffe subsumieren lassen. Die **Mindmaps** werden auf **Folie** geschrieben und im **Plenum** präsentiert und diskutiert. Gelungene Exemplare können für die gesamte Lerngruppe **kopiert** werden.
- Die Ergebnisse der beiden Hördurchgänge (**Aufg. 1 und 2**) werden **stichwortartig** notiert und im **Unterrichtsgespräch** diskutiert.
- Nach der Einstimmung auf das Thema durch die **Hörverstehensübung** wird **Aufgabe 3** zunächst in **Einzelarbeit** bearbeitet und danach im **Unterrichtsgespräch** diskutiert. Dabei ist es wichtig, die Diskrepanz zwischen dem nach außen gezeigten Idealbild der amerikanischen Mittelklassefamilie, wie es durch den Text und die Fotografie transportiert wird, und der Realität, die durch das Zahlenmaterial belegt wird, aufzuzeigen und zu verdeutlichen. Es mag lohnenswert sein, in diesem Zusammenhang der Frage nach den Gründen für das Aufbauen und Erhalten des schönen Scheins der heilen und sorgenfreien Familie nachzugehen.
- **Aufgabe 4** wird zunächst in **Einzelarbeit** erledigt. Die Ergebnisse werden im **Unterrichtsgespräch** gesammelt und in folgendem **Tafelbild** gesichert:

Eric Bogosian, "No Problems"

adjectives/intensifying adverbs	use
perfect, completely clean, great	*positively describing his health (ll.7-12)*
good, very well, semi-creative	*positively describing his job (ll. 13-18)*
loving, very supporting, great, lovely, very well, precocious, very pretty, no "mother-in-law" stuff, golden, very proud	*positively describing familial life (ll. 19-38)*
happy, healthy, very nice, good	*positively describing his friends (ll. 39-52)*
safe, clean, excellent, important, top rated, good, new, nothing wrong, running smoothly	*positively describing environment (ll. 53-60)*
concerned, disturbing	*negatively describing the rest of the world (ll. 63-66)*

→ The speaker uses positive adjectives and intensifying adverbs to describe his own surroundings and negative ones to describe the rest of the world.

- Nach der ausführlichen Beschäftigung mit dem Gebrauch von Adjektiven und Adverbien in der vorangehenden Aufgabe kann Aufgabe 5 mündlich im Unterrichtsgespräch bearbeitet werden. Das Ergebnis kann informell an der Tafel gesichert werden.
- Aufgabe 6 kann in Einzel- oder Partnerarbeit bearbeitet werden. Die Schülerinnen und Schüler erhalten den Auftrag, eine Tabelle zu erstellen (s. Lösungsvorschlag unten).
- Aufgabe 7 kann als die Beschäftigung mit dem Text abschließende Hausaufgabe eingesetzt werden. Dazu sollte im Unterricht die angegebene Focus on Skills-Seite (SB, S. 264) besprochen werden.
- Die Aufgaben 8 und 9 können als die Beschäftigung mit dem Text begleitende Wochenaufgabe oder im Unterricht bearbeitet werden. Für die Bearbeitung im Unterricht ist eine, für die Präsentation der Ergebnisse eine weitere Doppelstunde zu veranschlagen. Während Aufgabe 8 in Partnerarbeit erledigt wird, wird Aufgabe 9 in Gruppenarbeit bearbeitet.
  Für die Gestaltung des Interviews (Aufg. 8) können folgende Internetadressen hilfreich sein:
  www.nerdwallet.com/blog/credit-card-data/average-credit-card-debt-household
  www.statisticsbrain.com/american-family-financial-statistics/
  quickfacts.census.gov/qfd/states/00000.html
  www.oecdbetterlifeindex.org/countries/united-states/

SOLUTIONS AWARENESS

The monologue below is taken from a collection of rather experimental "monodramas" which usually portray one character. Everything the audience views on stage is portrayed from the mental state of the protagonist. In the scene at hand, the protagonist is the "typical" average American who is reflecting on his life and family.
What is the difference between "no problem", "it's not my problem" or "what's your problem?" Look this up in a dictionary first as to how the meaning changes with intonation. Then make a mind map of problems people might be confronted with in their everyday lives. In a final step link the expressions above to the problems laid out in the mind map. Which expression would you choose if confronted with one of the problems?

No Problem = used to express agreement or acquiescence
It's not my problem = used to show lack of care for another person's issue
What's your problem = used to suggest a difficulty in someone else's mental state, usually responding to an unprovoked statement or inappropriate action

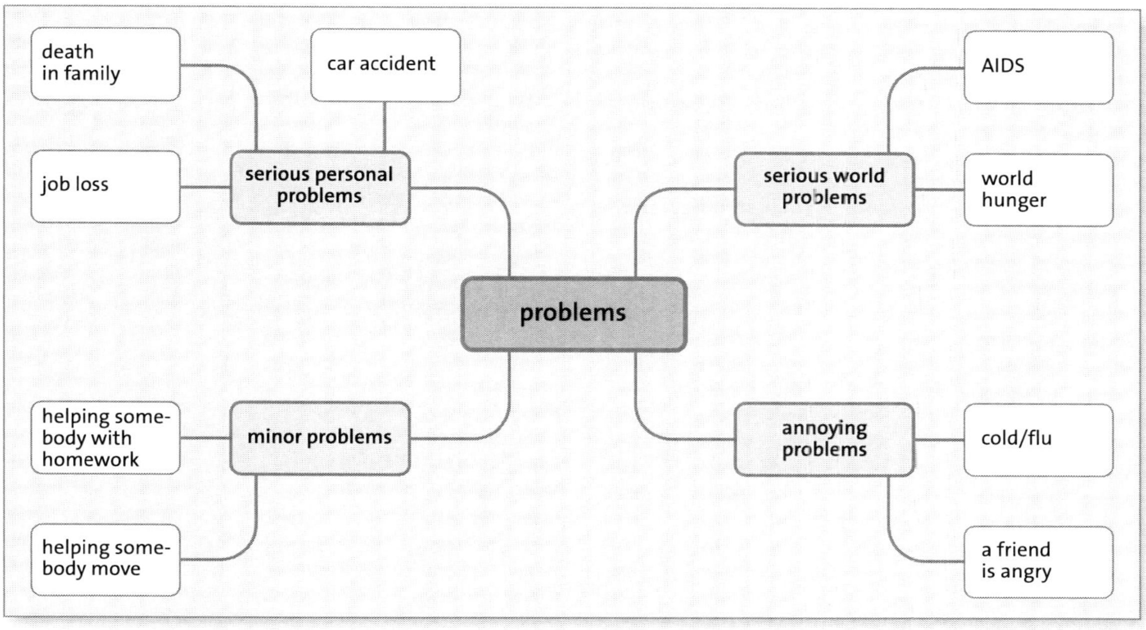

Expressions and problems

AIDS, Warfare, Hunger: Many would say 'It's not my problem'. Though probably not malicious in intent, the larger world problems are usually put to the back of the typical person's mind.

Death: Different answers depending on the individual. Someone may ask 'What's your problem' with a caring intonation in an attempt to provide comfort. Some may say 'Not my problem' having not known the person who passed away.

Job Loss: Some could say 'no problem' either to be glad of the job loss or for the opportunity to find a better position. Others might say 'not my problem' when confronted with a homeless person, either out of disinterest or lack of knowledge of the unemployed's situation.

Car Accident: 'No problem' could come from someone willing to help. 'Not my problem' would come from someone just passing by.

Car breakdown: Again, 'no problem' would be the response from someone willing to help though 'not my problem' would be just as likely from passersby. Depending on the situation, 'What's your problem' could also be given when the breakdown occurred due to lack of action on the driver's part.

Cold/flu: Intonation is a factor here. 'What's your problem' with a caring tone could come from someone trying to get information about the sickness.

Angry friend: Tone is a key factor here again because a spiteful 'what's your problem' would be the likely response and would most likely set off an argument.

Homework/moving/milk: Although all are minor inconveniences, the usual response here is 'no problem' as, most likely, a person would be willing to help in these situations.

SOLUTIONS COMPREHENSION

CD 1 5 **1. Listen to Eric Bogosian's "No Problems". In a first listening take notes on the following aspects: What information does he provide about**
- **himself,**
- **his family,**
- **his friends,**
- **his environment?**

Himself
Perfect health, good job (ll. 7-18)
Family
Solid marriage, great sex life, child is well-rounded and well-liked, both sets of grandparents are alive and well with retirement plans fully worked out (ll. 19-38)
Friends
Sees them once a week, they go bowling, go to dinner, see movies and plays, and they are all very nice (ll. 39-52)
Environment
Safe and clean, excellent town council and school committee, top rated fire department and police force, the house is in excellent condition (ll. 53-61)

2. In a second listening, focus on what the speaker is concerned about.

The speaker is concerned about all the trouble going on in the world. He feels that the news is disturbing but it is his duty to watch the news for the more unfortunate people's sake. (ll. 62-68)

3. Describe the visual "Meet the Average American Family" and point out whether the figures match the impression the family makes on the onlooker.
→ Focus on Skills, Analysis of Visuals, p. 262

The visual shows a set of three Caucasians, smiling parents and their young, smiling girl. The picture itself seems to show that the average American family is well-off and is more than ready for what life can bring their way, good or bad, and will always be content in their new home. The figures tell a dramatically different story. The monetary issues that an average American family faces would not equate to a smiling trio in front of their brand new house.

SOLUTIONS ANALYSIS

4. Examine the author's choice of adjectives and intensifying adverbs.
→ Focus on Skills, Analysis of a Fictional Text, p. 255
Example: intensifying adverbs: completely, very → an emphasis of perfection and extraordinariness adjectives: clean, attractive → positively connoted words

Perfect, completely clean, great: all positively describing his health (ll. 7-12)
Good, very well, semi-creative: all positively describing his job (ll. 13-18)
Loving, very supporting, great, lovely, very well, precocious, very pretty, no 'mother-in-law' stuff, golden, very proud: all positively describing familial life (ll. 19-38)
Happy, healthy, very nice, good: all positively describing his friends (ll. 39-52)
Safe, clean, excellent, important, top rated, good, new, nothing wrong, running smoothly: all positively describing environment (ll. 53-60)
Concerned, disturbing: negatively describing the rest of the world (ll. 63-68)

5. Analyse whether all the positive expressions are really meant positively and show what some of these expressions actually imply.
Example: semi-creative job, very little pressure to perform (ll. 14 f.) → a not very demanding, boring

- Semi-creative job – very little pressure to perform (ll. 14 f.) → not very demanding, boring. Using the phrase semi-creative is a tell that his job is in no way perfect. That just means that he does not have to work exceptionally hard. Although the pay may be decent, saying 'good' as opposed to great and then saying 'like' as opposed to love is a way to see that the job is anything but perfect.
- Description of his wife as a steak – meaning she is more attractive than most women (l. 24). This phrase, although well-intended, may come off as slightly insulting. Referring to one's wife as a piece of meat does not always go well with said wife. Treating her as a slice of steak and comparing her to the hamburgers out on the street is not very complimentary.
- Precocious – Although this means 'developing abilities at an earlier than usual age' (l. 30), the word is often used as an insult, meaning 'know-it-all-little-brat'. Once again, this is probably not the intended use but in many cases there is a negative connotation that goes along with the word.

- 'Mother-in Law' stuff (l. 33) – This means having an intrusive and rude mother-in law. The preconceived notion coming into marriage is that the mother-in law will be a problem to both parties in the marriage. There is a lot of negative connotation with the phrase 'Mother-in law stuff' because of the negative outlook on mother-in laws in the United States.
- (And that's important!) (l. 55) –The phrasing in this is very sarcastic. Use of the exclamation point for emphasis and the parentheses to denote an aside, the reader of the text knows that this is intended to be insulting as the speaker does not truly believe that 'an activist school committee' is important.

6. Compare the figures from the infographic and the Info box (p. 34) with the statements made in the monologue.
→ Focus on Skills, Analysis of Statistical Data, p. 261

The figures from the infographic and the Info box completely contradict what was said in the monologue. The average American family does not have a great job and great retirement options and most definitely does not lack in problems. The figure serves as a guide to what the reality of the "Average American Family" is like while the monologue can be looked at as a type of satire to what most Americans believe.

infographic	monologue/text
$3800 in the bank no retirement account in 50 % of homes no mutual funds, stocks, bonds family owes $95,000 for the house Americans cannot pay off a $2200 credit card debt	well-paying job (ll. 13-18) retired and enjoying saved money (ll. 35-37) pension fund, insurance, some stock (l. 80) house paid in ten years (ll. 75-76) buying a condo on the water and the pension fund (ll. 75-80)

7. Characterize the protagonist by analysing his choice of words and manner of speaking.
→ Focus on Skills, Characterization of a Figure in Literature, p. 264

Using this small sampling of the protagonist's 'life', one could say that he is foolish to think that his life is so perfect. His description of his job (semi-creative) comes off as a euphemism for saying it is boring (l. 14). In addition to his employment, the protagonist's portrayal of his wife, "My wife's very attractive", combined with his tone make for the audience to interpret the description as a possible lie (ll. 21ff.). The entire audio track is told in a tone that makes the protagonist seem unenthused and unconvinced of his own words. The manner of speaking, in a way, makes the entire text seem like it was sarcastic, unreal, and somewhat unbelievable.

SOLUTIONS ACTIVITIES

8. As a journalist who wants to do a portrait of a "normal" American family for a TV channel, you want to interview the protagonist. However, before you do the interview, you do research on the Internet. Is the protagonist a mere parody of the "normal American" or not? Act out the interview and portrait in class or videotape them. If you do the latter, work out a storyboard first.
→ Focus on Skills, Writing an Interview, p. 285
→ Focus on Facts, Screenplays and Storyboards, p. 249

"Good afternoon, I am _______ and I would like to welcome you here today to answer a few questions I have about the 'normal American.'"
"Would you say that you live a 'normal American' life?" Follow up with "What would you say the 'normal American life entails?"
"What do you believe the average American salary in the United States to be?"
"What do you believe the average American credit card debt to be?"
"What percentage of American families do you believe to have saved money for retirement?"
"What percentage do you believe to be working for retirement right now?"
"Those are all of our questions for today. We thank you for your time and your responses have been recorded."

9. Imagine: It is Christmas, a time when the best and worst in family life can happen. The protagonist's family meets for dinner. He has recently lost his job. Very likely there is some tension in the air and it is time to tell each other some truths. Write a scene and act it out in class.

Pro: Honey, I have some bad news for everyone.
Wife: What is it dear? We're here to help.
Grandpa: Yeah son, you know we're here for you.
Pro: Well ... I was laid off last week.
Wife: Oh no, right at Christmas time? How are we going to be able to get everything done? The presents? The Christmas party? Our yearly donation?
Pro: We have a little save. We're just going to have to try to get by.
Grandpa: You still have bills to pay too. You can't get too far behind on the house payments.
Pro: Thanks dad, I know that.
Grandpa: I'm just trying to keep it in perspective here. You have to focus on the big things before the small ones. Have you looked into any other jobs around here?
Pro: I've tried but you know how the economy is. People just aren't hiring like they used to.
Grandpa: Well what are you going to do?
Pro: I'll figure something out.
Wife: Well it has to be soon. You know my teaching salary isn't enough to get by on.
Pro: I'm pretty sure of all the people in this room I know that the best.
Wife: At least I didn't get fired.
Pro: ... I need some air. I'm going to meet the guys over at the pub.
Wife: You shouldn't be drinking right now.
Pro: Well what else can I do!

Door slams, protagonist leaves as wife bursts into tears.

Jens Jessen

Über Coolness (pp. 36–37)

About the author	Jens Jessen is a German journalist that writes for *Zeit Magazin*. The magazine itself is a national, weekly magazine that is well-regarded for its journalistic quality and the periodical as a whole is considered to be aligned with the social-liberal political movement.
About the text	This text taken from *Zeit Magazin* was written in 2013 and is a small study on the subject of "coolness" reflecting on aspects of the relationship between film star Johnny Depp and his 14-year-old daughter Lily Rose.
Level	●●○

- Die **Awareness-Aufgabe** kann als **vorbereitende Hausaufgabe** eingesetzt werden, wobei die Schülerinnen und Schüler genügend Zeit haben sollten, entsprechende Bilder zu suchen und den Zeitstrahl fertigzustellen.
- **Aufgabe 1** wird in **Kleingruppen** bearbeitet. Zur Vorbereitung der Beschäftigung mit der Aufgabe erhält jede Gruppe den Auftrag, eine kurze **Definition** des Begriffes „Coolness" zu verschriftlichen. Die Ergebnisse der Gruppenarbeit werden im **Plenum** kurz präsentiert und gegebenenfalls diskutiert.
- Für die **Mediationsaufgabe** (**Aufg. 2**), die in **Einzel- oder Partnerarbeit** erledigt werden kann, sollte der Text in Kopie ausgeteilt werden, damit die Schülerinnen und Schüler die für die Übertragung ins Englische wichtigen Passagen markieren und, wo nötig, weitere Notizen anbringen können. Ist die Lerngruppe mit dieser Art von Aufgabe noch nicht oder nur wenig vertraut, sollte im Vorfeld die angegebene **Focus on Skills-Seite** (SB, S. 265) besprochen werden.
  Beim anschließenden Vergleich der Ergebnisse sollte zunächst besprochen werden, welche Passagen aus der Textvorlage ins Englische übertragen werden sollten. Danach können einzelne Arbeiten vorgelesen und kommentiert bzw. korrigiert werden. Für eine gründliche Besprechung der Texte erscheint das individuelle Korrigieren der Schülerarbeiten, ggf. auf freiwilliger Basis, sinnvoll.

- **Aufgabe 3** kann gemeinsam im Unterricht bearbeitet werden, wobei die Ergebnisse auf **Folie** geschrieben werden. Die Schülerinnen und Schüler übernehmen den Folienaufschrieb in ihre Hefte. Um Zeit zu sparen, kann die Folie auch einfach für die Klasse **kopiert** werden.
- Aufgabe 4 wird in **Einzelarbeit** erledigt. Die Schülerinnen und Schüler lesen sich ihre Ergebnisse im Rahmen einer **„Milling Around“ Aktivität** gegenseitig vor.
- Aufgabe 5 kann als abschließende **Hausaufgabe** erteilt werden.

SOLUTIONS AWARENESS

Leaf through your family albums and find out what your grandparents and parents thought was cool when they were your age. Illustrate a timeline and present your findings in class.

After leafing through my parents' albums, I came up with a few things that they thought were cool.

1. fast cars, hot rods
2. psychedelic colours
3. long hair on guys, medium length on girls
4. tight pants, loose shirts
5. tall and skinny

SOLUTIONS COMPREHENSION

1. Describe the teenagers in the photo and state if they look cool or not.

I would argue that the girl on the left (Lily Rose Depp) looks 'cooler' than the girl on the right. Lily Rose has a clean-cut look with clothes that I would deem cooler than the wearing of a 'Sex Pistols' shirt. The physical appearance of Lily Rose Depp is also a little softer, making her seem prettier, which equates to 'cool'. In addition, the girl on the right is wearing braces and has multiple piercings, both of which can come across as 'not cool'.

2. Mediate the text by focusing on the following aspects:
- **the roles of a famous father and child when they appear in public**
- **why teenagers accompany/do not accompany their parents to concerts**
- **whether it is normal to find one's father "uncool" and not share his taste of music**
- **in what sense Lily Rose is a well brought-up and loving daughter**

→ Focus on Skills, Mediation, p. 265

Tip: Do not simply translate the text word by word but focus on the tasks given in No. 2.

- The famous father's job is to be just what he is, a big star, beaming and confident, the centre of attention. The child of the famous father is frequently more concerned with his or her own image and whether he or she comes across to everyone as being cool or not.
- Cool teenagers tend not to accompany their celebrity parents to concerts because they do not want to come across as leading an opportunistic, parasitical existence, bathing in their parents' glory. If, however, the father or mother were a despised outsider, a subject of ridicule, cutting a sad figure, biting their fingernails, clumsy and nervous, then the cool teenagers would take sides with them and accompany them everywhere and take them along to parties.
- It is not unusual for children to find their father "uncool" – especially, in this case, when the rest of the world finds him cool. Children have their own minds and form their own opinions. And time moves on. Tastes change.
- Lily Rose Depp is a well brought-up, loving daughter in the sense that she honours her father while not wishing to profit from his status. If her father were really out of place, she would probably stand by him.

SOLUTIONS ANALYSIS

3. Examine the choice of words that underpin the relationship between parent and juvenile.
Example:

German	English	function
legen ihren ganzen Stolz dahinein, sich ein eigenes Urteil zu bilden	to take pride in forming one's own opinion	➔ growing emancipation of children (positively connoted)
Es ist keine Haupteigenschaft von Töchern, ihre Väter cool zu finden	Finding their fathers cool is not one of the main characteristics of daughters	➔ daughters are independent beings, aware of the dictates of their times
Lily Rose ist weit davon entfernt, ungezogen oder undankbar zu sein, ist also in Wahrheit eine sehr wohlgeratene und liebevolle Tochter, die ihren Vater ehrt	Lily Rose is far from being ill-mannered or thankless and is, in truth, a well brought-up and loving daughter who honours her father	➔ lists some of the typical qualities, both positive and negative, associated with the successful or unsuccessful raising of a child

➔ **Focus on Skills, Analysis of a Non-Fictional Text, p. 258**

SOLUTIONS ACTIVITIES

4. As a father/mother you have just accompanied your daughter/son to a concert of your child's liking (e.g. Heavy Metal). You write a letter to the editor describing your experiences there and the comments of your son/daughter on your being cool/uncool.
➔ **Focus on Skills, Writing a Letter to the Editor, p. 290**

Dear Editor,
I am just returning from a concert which I accompanied my son to. The band playing was called 'Taking Back Sunday'. The only previous knowledge I had about the band was that they were my son's favourite music, something I see him listening to on his iPod throughout the day, something that I would never hear if I didn't have a son listening to it.
I was half expecting to walk in and see a bunch of young people wearing black and having chains dangling around their wrists and legs, but I was pleasantly surprised to see a bunch of people just wearing jeans and an assortment of t-shirts. It was a good thing I didn't bring up those reservations to my son, he'd have thought I was too old to be going to the concert. The music itself was a little different than I thought too. Coming in, I thought that the band might have just screamed the entirety of the songs. It turned out that, although 'Taking Back Sunday' did have some moments of screaming, most of the songs were sung with both power and exceptional skill, many even having a storytelling aspect to go alongside the rock soundtrack.
The most gratifying part of the night was on the way home. After seeing mosh pits and jumping circles, then watching the lead singer swing his microphone around like some medieval weapon, it was nice to hear my son thank me for going with him. He knew all too well that I wasn't familiar with the music, but he thought it was really cool for me to go and watch his favourite band perform.

CoolConcertDad

SOLUTIONS GRAMMAR/LANGUAGE

5. In different contexts you use different registers of English. With your classmates you often speak slang or use informal expressions. On formal occasions you would rather choose standard or formal English. You are asked to characterize one of your grandparents/relatives or close friends. Find informal and formal expressions.
Example:

Informal	Formal
• He/she is a real sweetie.	• He/she is very likable, very gentle and kind.
• He/she is really hot.	• He/she is very attractive.
• My friend is a real ace in football.	• My friend is an excellent football player.
• Granddad is quite a back number.	• My grandfather is quite old-fashioned and conservative.
• My friend Tom sometimes behaves like a real bumpkin.	• My friend Tom sometimes is quite heavyhanded and clumsy.
• etc.	• etc.

Ron Koertge

But Baseball and Sex? (pp. 38–39)

About the author	Ron Koertge [rɒn ˈkɜːtʃɪ] is an American author and poet who has published many novels for young readers, including *The Arizona Kid*, *Boy Girl Boy* and *Stoner and Spaz*. In addition to his work as an author, he taught English and Creative Writing at Pasadena City College in California from 1965 – 2001.
About the text	In this poem, sex is compared to the game of baseball. It shows how boys view sexually active girls and how rumours and gossip about sexual activity are spread.
Level	● ● ●
Additional material	• Audio CD 1, 6 • Differenzierungsmaterial, p. 14 • GaST: no. 11

- Das Gedicht selbst sollte den Schülerinnen und Schülern **erst nach der Bearbeitung** der Hörverstehensaufgabe (Aufgabe 2) präsentiert werden.
- In der Einstiegsübung (Stille Post) sollten die Schülerinnen und Schüler über die Reflexion des Spiels – ein Satz verändert sich im Laufe der Flüsterkette, weil er nicht korrekt gehört und daher nicht korrekt weitergegeben wurde – zu einer Analyse der **Wirkungsweise von Gerüchten** herangeführt werden.
- Die anschließende Diskussion (Aufgabe 1) stimmt die Schülerinnen und Schüler inhaltlich auf das Gedicht ein. Wichtige Diskussionsergebnisse können in Form von **Definitionen** an der Tafel festgehalten werden.
  Z. B.: Having sexual encounters is just like a game of sports because there is the same excitement and suspense./Having sexual encounters is just like a game of sports because there are no winners or losers. Sex is not a competition.
- Vor der Bearbeitung von Aufgabe 2 kann, falls die Schülerinnen und Schüler mit der Vorgehensweise bei Hörverstehensaufgaben nicht vertraut sind, auf die entsprechenden Ausführungen im Schülerbuch (Focus on Skills, **Listening Comprehension**, S. 244) eingegangen werden. Sinnvoll erscheint in diesem Fall das Erstellen einer „**checklist**", in der die wichtigsten Arbeitsschritte zusammengefasst werden.
- Die Aufgaben 3, 5 und 7 thematisieren die unterschiedlichen Haltungen von Jungen und Mädchen in Bezug auf Beziehungen und sexuelle Aktivitäten. In diesem Zusammenhang könnte es lohnenswert sein, die Schülerantworten nach Geschlechtern getrennt zu sammeln und deutlich werdende **Gemeinsamkeiten bzw. Unterschiede** zu thematisieren.
- Aufgabe 4 kann im **Unterrichtsgespräch** bearbeitet werden. Zunächst werden die Schülerinnen und Schüler dazu aufgefordert, die **Metaphorik** des Gedichts anhand des annotierten Vokabulars zu erläutern. Danach wird der Frage nachgegangen, weshalb der Autor diese Metaphern benutzt. Die Ergebnisse werden informell an der **Tafel** gesichert.
- Aufgabe 6 kann dahingehend erweitert werden, dass die Schülerinnen und Schüler in Kleingruppen alternative Illustrationen des Gedichts in Form von **Standbildern** entwickeln und diskutieren.
- Zur Vorbereitung der *additional task* sollte die im Gedicht verwendete **Metaphorik** und ihre Wirkung thematisiert werden. Dazu kann auf die Ergebnisse von Aufgabe 1 zurückgegriffen werden.

SOLUTIONS AWARENESS

Most people know the game *Telephone* or *Chinese Whispers*. Although it is a game that is usually played by children, it is often considered a metaphor for ever-increasing error, especially regarding the way rumours or gossip spread, or for the general unreliability of human recollection.
Start with a short sentence – and pass it on to your neighbour. What is the outcome?

James and Julie went shopping for new shoes and then ate Mexican food.
Julie went shopping for new shoes and then ate Mexican food.
Julie bought new shoes and then ate Mexican food.
Julia bought new shoes and went to a Mexican restaurant.
Julia went shopping and then went to a restaurant.
The sentence changes because people do not hear or repeat it correctly. The information gets changed or omitted, or people invent new, false information. The more people retell it, the more the sentence changes. This shows how rumours change as they spread, eventually having very little to do with the truth.

SOLUTIONS COMPREHENSION

1. Discuss: Is having sexual encounters just like a game of sports as the title of the poem hints?

Yes: The physical pleasure in sexual counters is similar to the excitement and suspense of a sporting event. In some relationships, sex is the main objective/goal. For some men (but also for some women), having a sexual encounter with someone is like winning a prize and gives them a sense of accomplishment, power and prestige, similar to "winning" a sports game.
No: It implies that there is a winner and a loser, and that sex is a competition. Sexual encounters should be mutually enjoyable and about love. ...

CD 1 6 **2. While listening to the audio-version of the poem, take notes on the following questions:**
a) What happens to Dori Soretsky's reputation in the course of the poem?

Her reputation becomes damaged because going to "second base" is associated with a girl being "easy"/a slut (ll. 8 – 10, l. 19).

b) What are the boys' primary concerns when it comes to girls, as suggested in the poem?
→ Focus on Skills, Listening Comprehension, p. 244

They are primarily concerned with how far a girl will go with them sexually (ll. 5 – 6). According to Greg and Fabian, it is not important whether the girl actually likes them, only whether she will let them touch/have sex with her (ll. 14 – 19).

3. Speculate on what kind of girl Dori is.

She might be a girl who is very sexual and lets "anybody" go to second base with her, as the boys think. On the other hand, she may or may not have "gone to second base" with her boyfriend, and the rumours are false. Someone might have just started those rumours as a joke or to harass Dori.

SOLUTIONS ANALYSIS

4. Examine the reasons why first sexual encounters are not spoken about openly but hidden behind the expressions associated with a game.
→ Focus on Skills, Analysis of Poetry and Lyrics, p. 259

Sex in general is a rather taboo topic that is not talked about openly and explicitly. Therefore, people rely on euphemisms to refer to sex (e. g. making love, going all the way, doing it, etc.). This is especially true for young people talking about their first sexual encounters because they are inexperienced and may lack the maturity, confidence and vocabulary to talk about it with their friends. Referring to sexual acts using "safe" vocabulary (such as "first base", "home run", etc.) makes this new, unknown and sometimes scary topic less intimidating. It may help young people to play down their fear and anxiety with regard to their sexual experiences and how they measure up compared to what their friends have done. By using euphemistic terms, they can be more vague about what they have/have not experienced.

5. Explain whether there is any truth in the cliché that boys have fun in hunting down their prey, whereas girls are looking for love.

In my experience, this cliché is usually true. Boys are more interested in trying to "win" a girl's affection or just trying to sleep with her, but there are also many counter-examples of boys who are faithful and looking for love, and girls who are interested in sex but not in a serious relationship. ...

6. Examine and analyse the body language of the girl and the boy on the film poster. Could this be a good illustration for the poem? Explain your opinion.

The boy looks bewildered and confused. His slouchy posture and his scratching his head show that he is not very self-confident. It implies that he does not understand how the girl got pregnant (scratching one's head is usually associated with bewilderment). The girl seems a bit sad but has a more confident, almost defiant posture, like maybe she is challenging the people who are judging her for getting pregnant.

I think this illustrates the poem well, because the pregnancy and the body language of the boy and the girl reflect what can happen when young people have sex before they are ready. The resulting teen pregnancy shows that sex is not just a fun "game" (like baseball, as implied in the poem), but that it also has serious consequences.

SOLUTIONS ACTIVITIES

7. Do you think Greg is right? Is he only being a wise guy – or is he speaking from experience?

Greg probably does not know the truth about Dori because he has not been out with her yet. He may only be bluffing to make himself seem confident, knowledgeable and sexually experienced. ("... every guy talks like/he wants to .../But I don't think he does", ll. 5 – 7).

8. Comment on whether being sexually active is good or bad for a girl's/boy's reputation.

Individual solutions, for example:
I generally agree with the poem: It is OK for boys to sleep around (ll. 5 – 6), but not OK for girls to do the same thing (ll. 8 – 10). If a boy sleeps with many different girls, it means that he is attractive and desirable, but if a girl sleeps around she is a "slut." This is an unfair double standard.
On the other hand, boys who sleep around are seen as "players" and may be avoided by girls who are interested in a loving, long-term relationship.

SOLUTIONS GRAMMAR/LANGUAGE

9. Compose a poem about friendship, love, sex and/or the rumours or gossip about these topics. Here is the "recipe" for a Diamond Poem that you can use for a start:
Line 1: The name of an emotion/a colour/a person
Line 2: Two adjectives that describe that emotion/colour/person
Line 3: Three actions that you associate with that emotion/colour/person
Line 4: Four things (nouns) that you associate with that emotion/colour/person
Line 5: Three participles that indicate a change/a new beginning
Line 6: Two adjectives that describe the changed emotion/colour/person
Line 7: The name of your second (opposite) emotion/colour/person
→ two opposites should change into each other
Present your poems to your class and exchange your ideas.

For example:

happy
joyful excited
smile shine love
friends laughter celebration success
doubting shaming blaming
quiet lonely
sad

Individual answers

ADDITIONAL TASK

Write a German version of the poem on p. 38. Use a similar imagery.

For example:

Jungs fragen immer: „Hast du's mit ihr bis zur
Mittellinie geschafft?"
Jungs sind also die Spieler und Mädchen sind
was, der Ball?
Was noch merkwürdiger ist, ist, dass jeder Junge immer so tut,
als wollten sie jedes Mal einen Treffer landen.
Aber ich glaube das nicht, nicht wirklich.
Und Mädchen sollen sicherlich nicht einfach so einen
Treffer zulassen. Die Elfmeter-Linie ist
irgendwie o.k., aber nicht das Tor.
Dori Soretsky hat Eric Altheim bis zur
Elfmeter-Linie kommen lassen. Jetzt erwartet jeder Typ,
der mit Dori geht, er kann gleich bis zur Straflinie durchmarschieren.
Max und Fabian redeten darüber,
dass sie gerne mit Dori gehen würden.
Fabian sagte: „Vielleicht würde sie
nicht jeden ranlassen. Vielleicht ließ sie nur Eric,
weil sie ihn mochte."
Max sagte: „Nein, die würde jetzt jeden ranlassen."

Diablo Cody

Juno – Breaking the Big News (pp. 40–45)

About the author	Diablo Cody is an American writer who was born in 1978. She wrote the screenplay for the movie *Juno* as well as for the television series *The United States of Tara*. She is also a journalist, novelist, blogger, and former stripper. The name "Diablo Cody" is a pen name; her real name is Brook Busey-Hunt.
About the text	This text is an excerpt from the screenplay of the 2007 film *Juno* starring Ellen Page and Michael Cera.
Level	● ○ ○
Additional material	• Film CD-ROM, 1 + 2 • Comprehension: no. 4

- Die in der Awareness-Aufgabe behandelte Thematik erfordert u.U. eine sehr intensive Lenkung des Gesprächs, da es für viele Schülerinnen und Schüler sicherlich nicht einfach ist, sich mit dem Thema Schwangerschaft auseinanderzusetzen und sich in der Klasse dazu zu äußern. Eine Alternative zur Diskussion im Klassenverband ist das anonyme Verschriftlichen der Antworten auf die Impulsfragen auf Moderationskarten. Diese können dann vom Lehrer/der Lehrerin vorgelesen und inhaltlich gebündelt werden. Daran kann sich eine Diskussion der verschiedenen Lösungsvorschläge anschließen.

- Die Comprehension-Aufgaben 1 – 3 können im Unterrichtsgespräch diskutiert werden. Die Ergebnisse können informell an der Tafel gesichert werden.
- In den Analyse-Aufgaben 4 – 6 beschäftigen sich die Schülerinnen und Schüler noch einmal intensiv mit dem Text und setzen sich mit der Situation der schwangeren Hauptperson auseinander. Die so gewonnenen Informationen fließen in die in Aufgabe 7 vorgeschlagene Diskussion ein. Diese kann als **Hot Seat** durchgeführt werden. Dazu bereiten die Schülerinnen und Schüler Fragen bezüglich der von Juno intendierten Adoption vor. Eine Schülerin oder ein Schüler stellt sich als Juno den Fragen der Mitschüler. Die Ergebnisse dieser Diskussion können in einem informellen Tafelanschrieb gebündelt werden.
- Im Zusammenhang mit Aufgabe 9 können die Begriffe „**text**" (tatsächlicher Textkörper) und „**subtext**" (Bühnen- und Regieanweisungen) eingeführt werden. Um die Bedeutung des Subtexts für die Handlung zu unterstreichen, können die Schülerinnen und Schüler aufgefordert werden, die einzelnen Regieanweisungen in Standbildern darzustellen und im Anschluss daran weitere Textstellen mit passenden Regieanweisungen zu versehen.
- Aufgabe 10 kann als die diese Sequenz der Diskussion des Textes abschließende Hausaufgabe gestellt werden.
- Bei der in Aufgabe 12 vorgeschlagenen Diskussion kann ggf. auf die Aktionen am Welt-AIDS-Tag eingegangen werden, die vielerorts an Schulen durch die SMV unterstützt werden.
- Aufgabe 13 sollte als **Gruppenarbeit** organisiert werden. Gruppen zu je vier Schülern erhalten den Auftrag, zu einer der im Schülerbuch vorgeschlagenen Möglichkeiten eine kurze Szene zu schreiben.
- Folgender Arbeitsauftrag kann über **Folie** oder als **Tafelanschrieb** präsentiert werden:

Role-play

- *work in groups of 4*
- *determine a time-keeper*
- *agree on one of the suggestions for a role-play*
- *find a storyline*
- *divide the characters among your group*
- *each member prepares a role card with keywords for their character (do not write down the complete text as you do not have time to memorize it)*

➔ *rehearse your scene*

- Vor der Bearbeitung der Aufgaben 14 und 15 sollte der Gebrauch der entsprechenden Tempora im Englischen wiederholt werden. Dies kann mithilfe der **Focus on Grammar-Seiten** (SB, S. 305, S. 296) geschehen. Während der Gebrauch des *simple present* und des *present progressive* die Schülerinnen und Schüler kaum vor Probleme stellen dürfte (auf das anzufügende –s in der 3. Person Singular sei sicherheitshalber hingewiesen), sollten die verschiedenen Möglichkeiten, Zukunft auszudrücken, sowie die Bildung des *conditional* ausführlicher besprochen und ggf. in einem kurzen Tafelanschrieb gesichert werden.
  Beide Aufgaben eignen sich zur häuslichen Bearbeitung.

SOLUTIONS AWARENESS

Juno is sixteen years old and has only recently found out that she is pregnant. In this scene, she is about to tell her parents about her pregnancy. Her best friend Leah has accompanied her to give her "moral support". (How) would you confess to your parents that you are pregnant or that your girlfriend is? What do you imagine their reaction would be?

For example:
I would be afraid of my parents' reaction, so I would tell them with a friend or someone else from outside the family present, or I would tell them in a public place so that they would not become too emotional. I imagine my parents would become very angry; my mother might cry and scream.

SOLUTIONS COMPREHENSION

1. Describe the parents' expectations when Juno says that she has to make a confession.

They guess that she got expelled from school, she needs money or legal counsel (she did something illegal), or was in a car accident (ll. 8 – 23), or that she was into hard drugs or was caught driving drunk (ll. 166 – 170).

2. How do the parents react to Juno's decision to have the baby (and not get an abortion)?

Bren reacts positively, calling Juno "brave" (ll. 111 – 113). This shows that she supports Juno's decision. Mac does not react directly to Juno's not having an abortion, but he is suspicious of his daughter's plans to give her baby up for adoption (ll. 129 – 132).

3. Point out the parents' view of Paulie Bleeker's role in the unwanted pregnancy.

Mac wants to blame Paulie for what happened and "punch [him] in the wiener" (ll. 170 – 172), while Bren believes that Paulie is a "sweet kid" and that "it wasn't his idea" (ll. 174 – 175), i. e. she holds Juno (equally) accountable.

SOLUTIONS ANALYSIS

4. Explain the parents' biggest concerns about the situation.

- They are concerned about the emotional toll the situation will take on Juno (ll. 96 – 97).
- They are worried about the adoptive parents Juno found and are afraid they might try to take advantage of her (l. 89, ll. 129 – 132).
- They are concerned that Juno is not ready to be a mother (ll. 101 – 102), and they are not ready to be grandparents (l. 156).
- They feel like Juno's pregnancy means they did something wrong as parents (ll. 148 – 149).

5. Illustrate how they assess Juno's maturity and capability of raising a child.

Mac reasons that Juno is not ready to be a mother because she cannot even remember to give her stepsister, Liberty Bell, her medicine (ll. 101 – 102). They question her judgment about finding adoptive parents (ll. 129 – 132) and hint that Juno does not have a realistic idea of how hard pregnancy and adoption will be (ll. 96 – 97), which suggests that they do not think she is very mature.

6. What are the alternatives for Juno to being a mother, as suggested by the others? Are they given serious consideration by anyone involved in the discussion?

Bren mentions only one alternative, referring to it only as "the alternative" (l. 106) – implying an abortion. Bren only asks whether Juno has considered this option, and it is not discussed again.

7. Discuss Juno's idea of giving the child up for adoption. On the surface, it sounds like a wonderful alternative.
Nevertheless, what difficulties will she probably have to face?

She will have to cope with her **changing, pregnant body** until the birth, which will affect her everyday life as a teenager. When she becomes noticeably pregnant, she will probably face a lot of **criticism, curiosity, and other reactions from people** at school and in her town. The pregnancy might **affect her relationship** with **Paulie** and her relationships with **family and friends**. Although she is not ready to become a mother, she may still have strong feelings about/for the baby and it may be **difficult for her to give it up**. She might also mourn the loss of the baby after its adoption.

8. The scene portrays a serious matter dealt with in a humorous and entertaining way. Analyse the stylistic devices (e.g. use of language*, situational comedy*, alternation of tension* vs. comic relief*, etc.) that create the comic effect* of the scene.
Example: ll. 53 – 61 ("Who is the kid?" … "The baby?" … "No, I mean the father!" …) → situational comedy; misunderstanding

→ Focus on Skills, Analysis of a Screenplay, p. 257

Use of language:

- Mac and Bren's use of childish or colloquial expressions when they are angry instead of using profanity, which one would expect in a tense situation: "Damn skippy" (l. 101), "Pop-pop" (l. 156), "wiener" (l. 171), "frigging" (l. 161)
- Juno's parents discussing a serious, adult issue with her and then calling her by her childhood nicknames: "You're a little Viking!" (l. 113), "Junebug" (l. 96, 152)

Situational comedy:

- Juno mentioning her heartburn and constipation (ll. 45 – 48); talking about Paulie's sexual performance and that they had sex in a chair (ll. 78 – 79)
- Juno found adoptive parents in the Penny Saver (l. 35, ll. 87 – 88)

Alternation of tension vs. comic relief:

- Use of colloquial expressions within serious registers is shocking and humorous: "Somebody is going to find a precious blessing from Jesus in this garbage dump of a situation" (ll. 159 – 161), "crap it out" in reference to Juno's delivery (ll. 122 – 127)
- Focusing on superficial or unimportant issues in a tense situation: Bren is interested in the unimportant detail that the foetus has fingernails (l. 59); laughing because Paulie doesn't look "virile" (ll. 64 – 73); Bren mentioning that prenatal vitamins will make your fingernails look beautiful (ll. 118 – 120)
- The above-mentioned use of humorous language and situational comedy also provides comic relief in this tense situation.

9. Look at the technical directions employed in the screenplay.
To what extent do the director's instructions clarify the state the different characters are in?
How do they convey the emotional rollercoaster ride (Achterbahnfahrt) that the characters find themselves on?
➔ Focus on Facts, Screenplays and Storyboards, p. 249

The author uses descriptive words to reveal how the characters are feeling: Juno paces nervously (l. 3); Juno cringes (l. 52), shocked laughter (l. 64), indignant (l. 77), looks alarmed (l. 89)

10. Explain the behaviour of the parents in the cartoon and compare their reactions to Juno's parents' reactions.
➔ Focus on Skills, Analysis of Visuals, p. 262

In the cartoon, the parents are accepting of the children being gay and getting piercings. At first they seem genuinely understanding and supportive, but it is implied that they are putting their true negative feelings aside (third panel: "Er ...", "Honest"). In the last panel they react in an extreme way, wanting to disown their child for wanting to be a banker.
In contrast, Juno's parents are upset but remain rational and want to help her ("we have to move on from here and help her figure it out", ll. 153 – 154). All in all, Juno's parents seem genuinely supportive in this scene despite the difficult situation, whereas the parents in the cartoon try to be supportive but ultimately end up judging and reacting in an unsupportive way.

SOLUTIONS ACTIVITIES

M @ **11. Collect information about the financial aid and other help you can get in Germany when you are pregnant (e. g. www.profamilia.de, www.donumvitae.org) and write about this to your pen pal in America.**

www.profamilia.de

- encourages pregnant teens to seek help as soon as possible
- offers a contact list of medical and information centres all over Germany where teens can seek advice or help
- offers information on the "morning after pill" to prevent pregnancy after unprotected sex

www.donumvitae.org

- also offers a list of information centres throughout Germany
- offers psychological and financial aid for pregnant women
- a Christian/Catholic-based organization that is open to people of all faiths

12. Preventing pregnancies: Do you think that campaigns like in the advert (below and on p. 45) are helpful? Discuss what effect they might have on juveniles.

→ Focus on Language, Conversation and Discussion, p. 266

On juveniles, these advertisements are helpful. By making condoms/contraceptives look like fun, young people would be more willing to use them. Coloured and comical, the advertisement is supposed to elicit a feeling of enjoyment for someone looking on. When regarding sex, enjoyment is, more often than not, the goal for juveniles. By making the condoms look enjoyable, the goal is to create a sense that they would be enjoyable to use.

13. In a role play, act out different alternatives for Juno's pregnancy and how to deal with it. Imagine that
a) Juno wants an abortion,
b) Juno wants to keep the child,
c) Juno's parents are so upset about Juno being pregnant that they are about to throw her out ...

a) Juno: I am not ready to be a mother or go through a pregnancy. I want to get an abortion.
Bren: Oh honey, this is a decision you will have to live with for the rest of your life. You need to think about this carefully. Does Paulie know? How does he feel about it? ...

b) Juno: I know this is a bad time for me, but Paulie and I are really in love. I can't bear to give up this child. I know it will be hard, but I know I love this child already and I want to keep it.
Mac: You bet your bippy it's a bad time! And how do you plan to support the child? Where will you live? Here?! Paulie has already accepted a scholarship for track, do you think he will just give that up so he can get some low-paying job to buy diapers? What about you and your college plans? ...

c) Juno: I'm pregnant. (tense silence, Mac and Bren are breathing hard, their faces turn red in anger)
Juno: I know this is –
Bren: I can't believe this!
(Mac picks up a family portrait and smashes it into the wall, glass shattering.) HAVE YOU LOST YOUR MIND? How could you be so stupid?!
Bren: (screaming) I can't even look at you, I can't even think straight. Get out of here, I can't deal with this.

SOLUTIONS GRAMMAR/LANGUAGE

14. Look at the film still No. 1 on page 41 and

a) describe it by paying attention to details, e.g. the (camera) perspective, the arrangement of the persons in the room, the people's facial expressions, etc.
Use the simple present or the present progressive for your description.
Example: The given film still presents Juno standing in the middle of a hallway. She seems to be lost in thought ... whereas the other students are standing ...

→ Focus on Facts, Camera Operations, p. 252
→ Focus on Grammar, Tenses, p. 305

The given film still presents Juno standing in the middle of a hallway. She seems to be lost in thought. Her facial expression reveals that she is concerned or even sad about something. In the background one can see the other students standing below big posters announcing the upcoming Junior Prom. Most of them are looking at Juno, but they do not seem to be saying anything to her. The chosen camera perspective is a long shot that emphasizes the arrangement of the people and shows the spatial (and emotional) distance between Juno and the other students.

b) anticipate Juno's attitude toward the upcoming Junior Prom, using future tenses.
Example: Judging from Juno's facial expression and the reaction/behaviour of the other students, Juno will not participate in the Junior Prom ...

Judging from Juno's facial expression and the reaction/behaviour of the other students, Juno will not participate in the Junior Prom. Possibly there will be a lot of gossip about Juno's pregnancy and Juno will not have anybody to talk to or dance with at the prom. In addition to this, she will almost certainly not be able to find a formal prom dress to fit her pregnant body. Most likely she will stay at home in order to avoid being isolated and having to see Paulie Bleeker dance with another girl.

c) Now, evaluate your findings after working with the Scene *Spring* on the CD-ROM.

Individual solutions

15. Judging from the film still No. 2 on p. 42,

a) speculate on the development of Juno and Paulie Bleeker's relationship during her pregnancy. Use the future tense as well as conditional forms (would/could/might + infinitive).
Example: Although both of them are looking very friendly and Paulie Bleeker is even holding his hand on Juno's belly, he might feel rather unsure about what to do and how to behave ... Juno might wish that he would ...

➔ Focus on Grammar, Tenses, p. 305
➔ Focus on Grammar, Conditional Sentences (If-Clauses), p. 296

Although both of them are looking very friendly and Paulie Bleeker is even holding his hand on Juno's belly, he might feel rather insecure about what to do and how to behave. Juno might wish that Paulie would be more supportive during her pregnancy. If he helped her with some of her difficult decisions, she would not feel so alone. Paulie might be scared that if he tries to offer his support, Juno will think that he is interfering. ...

b) Finally, characterize their relationship as depicted in the scene *The Coolest* on the CD-ROM.

Juno and Paulie seem to love and respect one another very much. Juno is very thoughtful and gives Paulie lots of his favourite candy mints as a surprise because she knows he likes them. When Paulie sees Juno, he is obviously very pleased and happy because he stops running and smiles as she approaches. She apologizes for her rude behaviour and tells him that she loves him because he is cool, smart and not like everyone else. The fact that he does not stare at Juno's stomach but instead looks at her face shows he respects her. He admits that he loves her too.

ADDITIONAL TASK

Sixteen years later ... Juno's "baby" now is a teenager himself/herself and has been raised by the couple that Juno had chosen. Now, her son/daughter wants to know why Juno gave him/her away for adoption. Write a dialogue in which Juno explains her decision to her son/daughter ...

Juno: It is so amazing to meet you, Mina.
Mina: (coldly) I've been wanting to meet you for some time.
Juno: I guess I owe you an explanation. I know you are looking for answers about your early life and background. As you probably know, I was only 16 when I got pregnant. I knew I couldn't give you the life you deserved, but I knew that I wanted to have you and not have an abortion. I have never felt that abortion was right, at least not for me. ...

A High School Teacher Talks About Teenage Pregnancy (p. 47)

About the author	Catherine Shultz is a high school teacher that has been teaching for ten years. Her speciality is FACS, Family and Consumer Sciences, specializing in early education. Her teaching covers health, recycling, lifestyle choices and much more.
About the text	Catherine Shultz is speaking on teenage pregnancy choices. Whether it concerns wanting a baby, accidental pregnancy, contraceptive use, even rape. She continues to speak on what happens after the pregnancy begins (costs, nutrition, counseling, child care, schooling, repeat pregnancy, student support). The interviewer asks about school support which Shultz responds by saying that most schools are very supportive (child care, leniency in classes, even other students refraining from gossip). This then transitions to questions about class status and pregnancy. Shultz's response is another surprise as she explains that class does not usually determine pregnancy. In the United States, the aid for theses teen mothers changes from state to state, as do the programs within the schools.

Level	●●●
Additional material	• Audio CD 1, 7 • Differenzierungsmaterial, p. 22

- Die **Awareness-Aufgabe** kann in einem kurzen **Unterrichtsgespräch** behandelt werden.
- Zur Vorbereitung der Hörverstehensaufgaben (**Aufg. 1 und 2**) werden die Schülerinnen und Schüler aufgefordert, die angegebenen Aufgaben zu bearbeiten. **Aufgabe 1** gibt bereits Aufschluss über den Inhalt des Interviews (the reasons for and the effects of teenage pregnancy). Die in **Aufgabe 2** verzeichneten Aspekte, über die die Schülerinnen und Schüler weitere Informationen sammeln sollen, müssen **inhaltlich** so **reduziert** werden, dass sie beim Zuhören leicht zu identifizieren sind. Dies geschieht dadurch, dass sich die Schülerinnen und Schüler die wichtigsten **Stichwörter** pro Teilfrage ins Heft notieren. Folgende Lösungen sind denkbar:
  - reasons/consequences of teenage pregnancy
  - problems and dangers
  - attitude of father/parents
  - help/support for future mothers
  - role of grandparents

  Die Ergebnisse können im **Plenum** besprochen und auf **Folie** gesichert werden.
- Die Analyse-Aufgaben (**Aufg. 3-5**) können als Vorbereitung für die Bearbeitung von Aufgabe 6 in **Partnerarbeit** bearbeitet werden. Die Schülerinnen und Schüler wählen eine Aufgabe aus, die sie bearbeiten und im Anschluss daran einer weiteren Zweiergruppe präsentieren. Um sicherzustellen, dass alle Aufgaben bearbeitet werden, kann der Lehrer bzw. die Lehrerin die Aufgaben zuweisen.
- **Aufgabe 6** wird in Gruppen bearbeitet. Jede Gruppe bearbeitet alle drei Aufgaben und visualisiert ihre Ergebnisse auf **Moderationswänden** bzw. **Flipchart-Blättern**. Im Anschluss an die Erarbeitungsphase werden die Gruppenergebnisse **präsentiert**.
  Folgende **Internetseiten** können zur Bearbeitung der Aufgabe hilfreich sein:
  www.nationmaster.com/country-info/stats/Health/Teenage-pregnancy
  www.data.worldbank.org/indicator/SP.ADO.TFRT
- **Aufgabe 7** kann als abschließende **Hausaufgabe** eingesetzt werden.

SOLUTIONS AWARENESS

In the USA, many high schools offer optional lessons on family science and parenting. Explain why you would (not) like to attend such a course.

./.

SOLUTIONS COMPREHENSION

CD 1 7

1. Listen to the interview about the reasons for and the effects of teenage pregnancy, and try to get the gist. The interview is with a teacher of family and consumer sciences at a high school in the Midwest of the USA. These lessons involve the topics of adult roles and responsibilities, interpersonal relationships, human development, family wellness, as well as child development and parenting.

- Catherine Shultz and her job
  has worked as a high school teacher for 10 years; teaches FACS (Family and Consumer Sciences); specializes in Early Childhood Education (vocational course)
- the FACS courses
  Family and Consumer Sciences → basic life skills for teenagers, how to live on one's own
  topics: nutrition, finances, housing, budgeting, getting a job, child development, parenting, health, reproductive issues, how to repair/recycle/reuse materials

2. Take notes while listening for the second time, and pay particular attention to what the teacher explains about

a) the reasons for and the consequences of teenage pregnancies,

Reasons:
- some pregnancies are planned; the girl wants to change her life by having a baby

- some girls are raped and become pregnant
- some girls have sex and do not want to get pregnant, but they either do not use contraception or use it incorrectly

Consequences:

- young mothers find that it is very difficult to raise a child
- judged by some teachers, but generally supported by other students

b) problems or dangers connected with these pregnancies,

lack of support, financial problems, loss of friends, difficulty staying in school, increased chance of repeat pregnancy, malnutrition effects on the child, transportation

c) the attitude of the father, or the parents of the teenage parents,

- most fathers not supportive; attitude of either pride or denial
- fathers cannot offer financial support because they do not work
- grandparents are usually very supportive of their child and grandchild

d) what help/support is given to the future mothers,

varies by state, but many programmes available:

- WIC, Women Infants and Children, help with nutritional needs
- TANF, Temporary Assistance for Needy Families
- free and reduced school lunch program
- free and reduced textbook program
- welfare
- Hoosier Healthwise: medical payment plan
- child care voucher program
- BABE, Beds And Bridges, etc.: clothing and equipment earned through educational vouchers or coupons
- Real Services: utilities and educational support

e) the role of the grandparents.

- grandparents often raise the child, but it is very hard
- mother's parents are often responsible for housing, feeding, medical expenses, transporting their daughter and grandchild everywhere
- paternal grandparents rarely contribute financially

→ Focus on Skills, Listening Comprehension, p. 244

SOLUTIONS ANALYSIS

3. Compare what Miss Shultz says about getting pregnant voluntarily/involuntarily to the data given in the statistics dealing with "Intendedness of Births" (FoF, p. 46, table 2).

intended pregnancy	**unintended pregnancy**
C. Shultz: • some pregnancies are planned; the girl wants to change her life by having a baby statistics: 22 % of births among women aged 15-19 were intended in 2002 23 % of births were intended among the same age group between 2006 and 2010 = a slight rise in the percentage of intended pregnancies	C. Shultz: • some girls are raped and become pregnant – some girls have sex and do not want to get pregnant, but they either do not use contraception or use it incorrectly statistics: 78 % unintended births among 15-to-19-year-olds in 2002 vs. 77 % between 2006 and 2010 = slight decrease in unintended pregnancies

→ there are far more unintended pregnancies than intended pregnancies among teens (about three times as many); this has hardly changed from 2002 to 2006-2010

4. Analyse the statistic on "Teen pregnancy rates" (FoF, p. 46, table 1) by
- **looking at the overall development of pregnancies in the different ethnic groups**
- **the relationship between live births and loss of babies through natural loss and abortion – what does the statistic reveal about the risks of getting pregnant early?**

The bar chart shows the outcomes of teen pregnancies in 2008 among 15-17-year-olds and 18-19-year-olds, with each age group divided according to race (white, black and Hispanic). Among all ages and races, the overall trend is that most of the teens' pregnancies ended in live births, as opposed to natural fatal loss or induced abortion. However, there is a somewhat higher proportion of induced abortion among black teens compared to whites and Hispanics. In both age groups, most pregnancies are among black girls, with white girls having the fewest; the number of pregnancies among Hispanic teens is similar to but slightly lower than the black group. Another striking trend is that there are many more pregnancies among the 18-19-year-old group compared to the younger group, and this holds across all races. The number of overall pregnancies in the older groups is over twice that of the younger groups – and in the case of white teens over three times as many. (160 words)

5. Examine the changes between 2003 and 2009 in teenage fertility rates. What has changed and where?
→ Focus on Skills, Analysis of Statistical Data, p. 261

Small relative increase in fertility between 2003 and 2009	Spain, Belgium, United Kingdom
Large relative increase ...	--
Small decrease ...	Switzerland, Netherlands, Italy, Denmark, Sweden, France, Norway, Finland, Poland, Ireland, United States
Large decrease ...	Germany, Czech Republic, Greece, Austria, Canada, Portugal, Hungary

→ The vast majority of European countries and the United States have seen an overall decrease in the number of teenage births from 2003 and 2009, whereas only Spain, Belgium and the UK show a very slight increase.

SOLUTIONS ACTIVITIES

@ **6. As an additional task you can do research on the Internet finding data about countries that are not included in this chart. What do you expect to find out? Compare the data of your personal research to the data given in the statistics on p. 46. Choose significant material to present in class and point out if your hypothesis matched your actual findings.**
→ Focus on Skills, Presentations, p. 276

./.

7. Statistics only show plain figures; films and novels often have a "happy ending" or only focus on important decisions and events. C. Shultz, however, mentions everyday problems. What do you think a day in your life would be like if you or your girlfriend had a baby? Write a diary entry in which you depict in detail all the tasks you have to perform and the differences in your life now that you have a baby.

./.

Big & Beautiful or Slim & Sexy? – Living with Your Body

Robin Givhan

Why Skinny Young Models Persist on the Spring Runways (pp. 48–50)

About the author	Robin Givhan is a fashion correspondent for *Newsweek* and *The Daily Beast*. Formerly the fashion editor for *The Washington Post*, Givhan was the first fashion critic to win the Pulitzer Prize in 2006. She has contributed to numerous books and also has written a book set to be released in late 2014 to early 2015.
About the text	The article is describing a problem that has been ingrained in the fashion industry for years – impossibly skinny, extremely young models. Many top fashion executives have made pledges to change the image but most have fallen flat on their promises. Surprisingly, the relation between average model size and number of eating disorders has not correlated positively or negatively. The text concludes with a paragraph explaining that the incessant desire for something more is the culprit behind poor self-image, not the fashion industry.
Level	● ● ●
Additional material	• Differenzierungsmaterial, p. 31

- Nach der Einstimmung auf das Thema durch die **Awareness-Aufgabe** werden die **Aufgaben 1 und 2** in **Einzelarbeit** bearbeitet. Die Ergebnisse werden im **Unterrichtsgespräch** diskutiert und auf **Folie** gesichert.
- **Aufgabe 3** kann in **Partnerarbeit** erledigt werden. Die Schülerinnen und Schüler füllen dazu die im Buch vorgegebene **Tabelle** aus. Die **Ergebnissicherung** erfolgt im anschließenden Unterrichtsgespräch mithilfe einer auf **Folie** kopierten Tabelle (s. Lösungsvorschlag unten).
- Bei der Bearbeitung von **Aufgabe 4** wird die Wortwahl des Autors kritisch reflektiert. Dies kann im **Unterrichtsgespräch** geschehen. Die Ergebnisse werden informell gesichert.
- Vor der Bearbeitung von **Aufgabe 5**, die in **Partnerarbeit** bearbeitet werden kann, sollte mit den Schülerinnen und Schülern die angegebene **Focus on Skills-Seite** (SB, S. 258) durchgesprochen werden. Bei in dieser Art von Aufgabe ungeübten Lerngruppen können einige relevante Kategorien der Stilanalyse vorgegeben werden, zu denen die Schülerinnen und Schüler lediglich **Beispiele** aus dem Text suchen müssen.
- Zur Vorbereitung der **Podiumsdiskussion** (**Aufg. 6**) lesen die Schülerinnen und Schüler die angegebene **Focus on Methods-Seite** (SB, S. 270). Die Podiumsdiskussion wird so organisiert, dass zunächst die Rollen verteilt werden. Die Schülerinnen und Schüler erstellen dazu **Rollenkarten**, auf denen sie lediglich **Stichwörter** verzeichnen, um zu vermeiden, dass sie ihre Argumente in der Diskussion ablesen, statt sie spontan zu formulieren. Bei großen Lerngruppen bietet es sich an, die Klasse in **zwei Gruppen** zu teilen, von denen die eine aktiv an der Diskussion teilnimmt, die andere als Zuhörer agiert und den Gesprächsverlauf protokolliert. Im Anschluss an die Diskussion geben die Zuhörer ein **Feedback** zu bestimmten Aspekten. Ein solcher **Feedbackbogen** kann folgendermaßen gestaltet sein:

<u>Feedback on the Panel Discussion</u>

participant	**language**		**arguments**		**manner of speaking**	**additional remarks**
	positive aspects	negative aspects	convincing	less convincing		
designer						
entrepreneur						
critic						
model						
customer						

- Sind die einzelnen Rollen mehrfach besetzt, muss der Feedbackbogen entsprechend erweitert werden. Ggf. kann die Diskussion noch einmal wiederholt werden, wobei die bisherigen Teilnehmer und die Zuschauer die Rollen tauschen.
- Für die Beschaffung von Bildmaterial und Informationen für die Bearbeitung von **Aufgabe 7** eignen sich Modemagazine wie *Elle, Madame, Marie Claire* oder *Vogue* und die entsprechenden Internetauftritte. Beim Herunterladen von Bildmaterial aus dem Internet müssen die geltenden rechtlichen Bestimmungen beachtet werden.
  Folgende **Internetadressen** können in diesem Zusammenhang hilfreich sein:
  www.news.com.au/lifestyle/fashion/skinny-model-debate-hits-mercedes-benz-fashion-week-again
  www.mamamia.com.au/body-image/skinny-models-sydney-fashion-week
  Diese Aufgabe kann als den ersten Teil der Beschäftigung mit dem Text abschließende **Hausaufgabe** eingesetzt werden.

SOLUTIONS AWARENESS

In a Round Robin activity (→ FoM, p. 270), say what you think a fashion failure is. It may help you to look at the photo of 14-year-old Ondria Hardin modeling in a fashion show in 2012.

For example:
- ill-fitting clothes (too large or too small)
- clothes that do not fit the occasion (too formal/informal/sexy/...)
- clothes that make you feel uncomfortable – literally and figuratively
- clothes that are too old-fashioned

SOLUTIONS COMPREHENSION

1. Present the controversy between the fashion industry and its designers and their critics. To make it easier to restructure the text first focus on the following aspects:

1	• **the outward appearance of models in the 2013 fashion shows** impossibly skinny, extremely young
2	• **what the fashion industry sells along with their clothes** idealized images of women • **what kind of harm is thereby inflicted on women** grievous harm (some models have eating disorders; giving readers unhealthy body image) • **the agreement that was approved of by the 19 editors-in-chief** agreed not to use mannequins/models who were younger than 16 or who appeared to have eating disorders • **what the magazines did to show that they took the matter seriously** dedicated issues to promote healthy body images
3	• **who broke the pledge** *Vogue* China and Japan • **why the pledge was broken** skinny young girls are the preferred look in fashion
4	• **what experts found out about the relationship between eating disorders and the size of models** how models look does not affect the number of eating disorders • **what women who see a perfect body become aware of** that they are not pretty, luxurious and glamorous enough; that they are not thin, toned and tight enough
5	• **what activists suggest would make women more comfortable when buying fashion** if fashion showed a diversity of body sizes and designed clothes for all of them • **the unwanted side-effect of being able to buy cheap, trendy fashion** if cheap, trendy fashion is available to all, then no one is exempt – i.e., there is no excuse not to be beautiful/fashionable • **women's conflict between buying what is needed and the dreams they have** they cannot decide whether fashion should be a commodity for everyone, or whether it should be an art form and be elitist/elusive

6	**the kinds of photos *Vogue* showed in its golden years** black and white images of models in exaggerated poses emphasizing lithe physiques; illustrations that reduce the body to simple geometry **the reasons why magazine photos today are criticized** they do not take into account the well-being of models; promote unrealistic body images

→ Focus on Skills, Reading Techniques, p. 247

2. In a second reading, complete your notes and arrange the controversial issues in a logical order.

- The fashion industry uses very young girls who are extremely skinny as models.
- Fashion magazine *Vogue* promised to promote healthier/more realistic body images, but did not uphold this promise.
- Although the fashion industry is being blamed for the growth of eating disorders, studies show that there is no connection. However, unrealistic fashion images make women feel inadequate.
- Making fashion more "democratic" and available to women of all sizes makes women feel better. However, this also means that fashion becomes less of an "art form" and loses its fantasy appeal.

SOLUTIONS ANALYSIS

3. To have a closer look at the author's choice of words, first fill in the grid:

wordfield: war and peace	wordfield: outward appearance	wordfield: fashion's unwanted side-effects
battle	impossibly skinny	to peddle satisfaction
détente	young gazelles	to add to stress
ambassadors	perfectly round derrière	grievous harm
broken the pledge	baby face	brutal, frustrating fantasy
brutal	skinny young girl	psychic battering
battering	waifs, Amazons	exacerbate the occurrence of eating disorders
democracy	pretty, luxurious, glamorous	sin
peace	thin, toned, tight	big-tent conceit
	lithe physiques	
	legs elongated to lines	

4. Examine the author's choice of words and show what this conveys about her stance on the issue.

The author employs many words that refer to war and peace, such as ... This underlines the extent of the controversy and the bad feelings between the public and the fashion industry. This reveals that the author takes a critical stance towards the fashion industry ...
In describing the outer appearance of fashion models, the author utilizes words that emphasize how unrealistic and unattainable models' bodies are ... She also points out the models' very young age. She thus reveals her disapproving view towards these extreme images ...
By underlining the many negative side-effects of the fashion industry, the author shows that she sides with the critics who argue that fashion images are harmful. She achieves this by using negative emotive words such as ... which influence the reader and evoke sympathy. ...

5. Analyse the stylistic devices* used and show what effect they have on the readership.
Example: never quite pretty enough, luxurious enough → dissatisfaction/discontent
→ Focus on Skills, Analysis of a Non-Fictional Text, p. 258

Tip: Do not forget to note the line(s) you refer to in order to prove the accuracy of your analysis.

The author uses several stylistic devices in order to underline the dangers of the fashion industry to the readership. She emphasizes the **harmfulness and ridiculousness** of the extreme images fashion magazines and designers promote by using **alliteration** (e.g. simply ... skinny ..., l. 29, fashion continues ... a ...

frustrating fantasy ..., ll. 30f.), **hyperbole** (impossibly skinny, ll. 2f., extremely young, l. 3) and **contrast** (e.g. baby face – giant fur hat, l. 28, waifs or Amazons, ll. 35f., flesh and blood ... smoke and mirrors, ll. 70f.). These help get the readers' attention and create vivid images. Furthermore, she uses **negative emotive words** to describe fashion's harmful effects and evoke the readers' emotions and draw their sympathy (e.g. ongoing battle, l. 6, grievous harm, l. 8, brutal, frustrating fantasy ... psychic battering, ll. 31f.)
The author also underlines the **credibility and seriousness** of the article by using **formal language** (e.g. détente, l. 10, unapologetically, l. 26) as well as **technical terms** from the fashion industry (e.g. black-and white images, l. 58, editors-in-chief, l. 9), which shows that she is well-informed and the article is well-researched. In addition, she cites **examples and references**, lending further credibility to the article (e.g. ll. 17f., 26ff., 43ff.). All in all, these devices effectively make the readership take a critical view of the fashion industry. (221 words)

SOLUTIONS ACTIVITIES

6. In a panel discussion, designers, entrepreneurs, critics, models and customers of fashion talk about the issue: "Is fashion enriching or destroying our lives? Do we need ethical standards?"

In your group, think about further arguments on the issue and complete the role cards that are provided for you on worksheet no. 2.

Individual solutions

@ **7. You are a journalist and have to review the fashion shows in Paris, Berlin or Milan. Do research on the Internet or in magazines. Arrange a line of photos you comment on, giving background information on how the fashion industry deals with skinny models and normal models.**
→ Focus on Methods, Panel Discussion, p. 270

Individual answers

- As you can see, this Milan fashion show uses a variety of models with a range of body types. This was likely in response to recent protests that claimed ...
- This Berlin fashion show only depicts models who are extremely tall and thin. Notice that these two women in particular have visibly jutting hipbones and ribs, which could be a sign that ...

Patrick Hickey Jr.

Artist Creates Healthy, "Normal" Barbie (pp. 50–51)

About the author	Though more known for his work in sports journalism, Patrick Hickey has ventured into both video games and toys for his NBC Bay Area news outlet. With interviews ranging from professional athletes to musicians to Kabuki voice actors, he has an array of articles in various fields.
About the text	The article summarizes the inception and creation of a new type of Barbie Doll. Instead of the strangely skinny, 'perfectly formed' Barbie of old, this one takes the measurements from an average 19-year-old girl.
Level	●●○

- **Aufgabe 8** kann in **Kleingruppen** bearbeitet werden. Die Ergebnisse werden im Klassenzimmer ausgehängt und im Rahmen eines **Museumsrundgangs** zur Kenntnis genommen und diskutiert.
- **Aufgabe 9** wird in **Partnerarbeit** bearbeitet. Nach der vorbereitenden Vokabelarbeit erstellen die Schülerinnen und Schüler **Rollenkarten** und üben ihre Dialoge ein. Im Anschluss daran werden die Dialoge in **Kleingruppen** (6 Teilnehmer, 3 Dialoge) präsentiert. Während dieser Unterrichtsphase hat der Lehrer bzw. die Lehrerin die Möglichkeit, sich verschiedene Dialoge anzuhören und ggf. inhaltlich oder sprachlich zu korrigieren. Besonders gelungene Dialoge können im Anschluss im Plenum präsentiert werden.

SOLUTIONS ANALYSIS

8. You are the creative director of an advertising agency and you have the task of promoting the normalsized Barbie. Make an advert that is intended to persuade children or their parents to buy this new doll. You may also create a new collection of clothes for the doll.

Individual solutions, e. g.:

"She's pretty. She's well-dressed. She's real."
(insert image of normalsized Barbie)
"For Real Girls."

- She looks beautiful – just like you!
- Average and normal is beautiful!
- Demi Lovato loves the new, healthy Barbie!
- Healthy, happy, and gorgeous!
- Let your daughter know she's beautiful – just the way she is!

SOLUTIONS GRAMMAR/LANGUAGE

9. As a shop assistant in a famous boutique you have to give advice to customers whose figures are frequently far from perfect. You have to be polite and sensitive. Use your dictionaries and collect words and expressions that serve that purpose. Then stage such a conversation.
Example: If I may suggest ..., I think this colour matches your eyes perfectly, I recommend ...

- If I may suggest the larger size – dress pants/slacks are worn casually this season.
- I think this colour perfectly matches your eyes.
- I recommend the dress with the vertical stripes instead of the horizontal ones – they are so much more becoming and make you appear even taller.
- Could I interest you in this beautiful black dress – it is so elegant and exclusive.
- This stylish shirt is the top of the range.

etc.

Jeremy Laurance

Hundreds of Websites Urging Girls to "Starve for Perfection" (pp. 51–52)

About the author	Jeremy Laurance is the former Health Editor of *The Independent* and *The i*. In 2011, Laurance was named Specialist Journalist of the Year by *The British Press*. That speciality is, naturally, health issues.
About the text	The text is about the growing number of websites, available to the public, which are glorifying extreme dieting, anorexia, and ultra-skinny girls. These websites include images of the super-thin, links to obtain laxatives and diet pills, even tips on purging, information on self-harming, and pro-suicide advice. Though the author makes clear that not all of these websites are debasing to the 'average' person, the rising availability of the websites have a correlation with the growing number of eating disorders.
Level	● ○ ○
Additional material	• Comprehension: no. 5

- Mit dem Thema **Magersucht** muss sehr vorsichtig umgegangen werden, da viele Betroffene ihre Essstörungen so verheimlichen können, dass selbst beste Freundinnen und Freunde nichts davon wissen. Ggf. sollte vor der Beschäftigung mit dem Text der **Beratungslehrer bzw. die Beratungslehrerin** der Schule konsultiert werden.
- Die Länge und der Schwierigkeitsgrad des Textes lassen eine parallel zur Lektüre ablaufende Bearbeitung der **Comprehension-Aufgaben** (**Aufg. 1-3**) zu. Um Zeit zu sparen, können diese Aufgaben arbeitsteilig erledigt werden. Dazu wird die Klasse in drei **Gruppen** unterteilt, deren Mitglieder sich individuell mit ihrer entsprechenden Aufgabe beschäftigen. Die Ergebnisse werden im **Unterrichtsgespräch** ausgetauscht und in folgendem **Tafelbild** gesichert:

J. Laurance: Hundreds of Websites Urging Girls to "Starve for Perfection"

pro-anorexia websites

promote diets of merely 400-500 calories a day (average: women: 2,000; men: 2,500)
additionally promote coffee, cigarettes, diet pills, and laxatives
500,000 visitors annually
take celebrities (Keira Knightly, Victoria Beckham) as examples

↓

effects on the readership

↙ ↘

physical/mental problems

under-eating
over-exercising
physical problems
poor self-image
mental instability

danger of abuse

visual representation on the internet
advice on self-harming
suicide sites

- Aufgabe 4 wird in **Partnerarbeit** erledigt. Die Sicherung erfolgt im anschließenden **Unterrichtsgespräch**.
- Aufgabe 5 kann als abschließende **Hausaufgabe** erteilt werden.

SOLUTIONS COMPREHENSION

1. Point out what pro-anorexia websites encourage their visitors to do and why they are successful.

These pro-anorexia websites promote diets of merely 400-500 calories a day (ll. 4ff.). The recommended average for women is 2,000 while for men it is 2,500. That meager ration of calories combined with coffee, cigarettes, diet pills, and laxatives are all promoted by the websites so girls can 'starve for perfection' (ll. 8-11). With over 500,000 people visiting the sites annually, images of ultra-thin celebrities (Keira Knightly, Victoria Beckham), people attach themselves to the diets prescribed though those same celebrities are not promoters of these websites (ll. 12-15).

2. Show what effects are caused once girls are seriously engaged in visiting websites and blogs.

The most prevalent would of course be under-eating. After seeing all of the 'super-skinny' girls on these websites, many others would want to emulate the look and begin under-eating to achieve that image. Outside of the obvious physical problems that can be seen on the websites, mental issues permeate the audience as well. Laurance calls out to a 'goddess-like feeling' for a girl who is seen as an inspiration to many (ll. 26ff.). Because of the feeling of gratification, these types of girls will continue to under-eat, over-exercise, and use supplements to aid in fat loss, which all contribute to greater health problems.
In summation:

- under-eating
- poor self-image
- mental instability
- over-use of dieting supplements

3. State in how far vulnerable girls are abused by communicating via the Internet.

Vulnerable girls are abused not only by person to person communication, but greatest part of their abuse comes from the visual representation of women on the internet. The representations are not a direct means of abuse, but because they are seen by a wide number of vulnerable people, the abuse comes in the form of destroying self-image.

On these websites also comes a more disturbing side than mere skinny pictures: advice on self-harming and links to pro-suicide sites (ll. 67f.). When considering those who are vulnerable, self-mutilation and suicide are very big issues. When there are outlets that glorify these acts, the vulnerable may seek to perform the actions.

SOLUTIONS ANALYSIS

4. Fill in the grid, then examine what register of English is used:

How teenagers experience pro-ana websites	What the websites really do
• lovely, pretty, attractive – seeing these skinny girls makes website goers think they are in perfect shape (ll. 1-15, 62-63)	• create rivalry between ana-buddies – one person wants to become skinnier than their 'friend' (ll. 69-71)
• visualize goals – website goers want to become like these impossibly skinny women, something that just is not possible (ll. 9-12)	• advice on self-harming/suicide – some websites literally give advice on how best to hurt oneself or commit suicide (ll. 67-68)
• sex symbolism – skinny people are seen as the sex symbols in society today and many people want to look just like these symbols (ll. 12-14)	• glorify the unhealthy – by prescribing impossible diets, these websites glorify those who are hurting themselves (ll. 9-12)
• sense of belonging – seeing these websites and interacting with other website users, a person can feel like they are part of a community (ll. 23-24, 63)	• alienate those from non-anorexic – once the website goer has entrenched his/herself in the world, they can become anti-average body weight and only believe that their anorexic world is the norm and appropriate (ll.16-28)
• inspiring – seeing other people starve themselves to perfection 'inspires' others to do the same (ll. 39-42)	• destroy self-image – trying to obtain the unobtainable body weight will hurt someone's self-image. This is what leads to self-harming and suicide. (ll. 14-15, 58-68)

→ Focus on Skills, Analysis of a Non-Fictional Text, p. 258

SOLUTIONS ACTIVITIES

5. You are aware that your best friend is more and more distancing him-/herself from you and really seeming to become addicted to pro-ana websites. You see that your friend is really being seduced into believing that only the person on the blog/Internet can understand him/her. As a means of helping him/her you set up your own blog about beauty, friendship and understanding.

For the website, include images of 'average' superstars whose body weight is not considered over- or underweight (Beyoncé, Padma Lakshmi, Kate Upton). In addition, include links to healthy dieting, dangers of diet pills and purging, and statistical averages on consumption, all to indicate a less drastic form of dieting.

With those forms of communication, alongside self-image boosting quotes and inspirational sayings, one could make a website which those same girls who are ruining themselves could visit in order to become healthy once again.

Mirror, Mirror on the Wall ... Who Is the Fairest One of All? (pp. 53–54)

About the images	These are famous sculptures and paintings that depict the human body in very different ways. They represent a range of eras, from ancient to modern times, as well as different cultures. They were created by artists who were known especially for portraying human bodies.
Level	● ● ○
Additional material	• GaST: no. 15, 19

- Aufgabe 1 kann arbeitsteilig erledigt werden, d. h., jeder Schüler erhält den Auftrag, zwei der auf S. 53 abgebildeten Kunstwerke zu beschreiben. Um die Auswahl etwas besser steuern zu können, kann sie dahingehend modifiziert werden, dass jeder Schüler eine Skulptur und ein Bild beschreiben muss.
- Aufgabe 2 führt inhaltlich zu Aufgabe 3 und kann daher in einem kurzen Unterrichtsgespräch bearbeitet werden. Dabei sollte deutlich werden, dass sich Schönheitsideale nicht nur im Laufe der Zeit verändern, sondern dass sie von den jeweiligen historischen Gegebenheiten beeinflusst werden. Aufgabe 3 vertieft diesen Aspekt.
- Da Aufgabe 4 einen zeitintensiven Rechercheauftrag beinhaltet, kann sie als die Beschäftigung mit dem Thema begleitende Wochenaufgabe erteilt werden. Eine Bearbeitung in Kleingruppen erscheint sinnvoll. Die folgende Internetadresse bietet einen historischen Überblick über die Darstellung des menschlichen Körpers im Laufe der Jahrtausende:
www.arthistoryarchive.com/arthistory/european/European-Ideal-Beauty-of-the-Human-Body-in-Art.html

SOLUTIONS AWARENESS

"Beauty is in the eye of the beholder."
Do you agree with this phrase? – What does physical attractiveness mean to you?

I think this is true. Although there are people and qualities that are generally considered more attractive than others, there is always an element of personal taste about what is "beautiful." Someone's inner qualities also have a huge effect on whether they are perceived as attractive or not. Confidence, kindness, and a sense of humour are attractive qualities that can make someone seem more beautiful on the outside, too. Mothers always think that their baby is the most beautiful, which shows that beauty is subjective.
To me, physical attractiveness combines classic attractive features (big eyes, nice teeth and smile, being well-groomed, clear and glowing skin) with positive inner qualities (kindness, sense of humour). For me, someone who is attractive but not a nice person is not beautiful.

SOLUTIONS COMPREHENSION

1. How are the men and women in the different pictures posed?
Describe their body language and outward appearance.

All the people shown are naked or nearly naked.

Venus of Willendorf: The sculpture shows an obese-looking woman, with enormous sagging breasts, a round belly and large thighs. She looks a bit coy with one leg slightly raised. She has no face/facial expression, but her head is up and body is standing straight, so she looks rather confident.

Evening Shadow: The sculpture is an extremely tall and skinny figure, with feet and legs together, and body straight with arms against the figure's sides, creating one long continuous line. While the body is exaggeratedly elongated, its head is normal and round. The figure is naked and rather androgynous, but the genitalia reveal that it is male.

Venus: This painting is unmistakeably of a female, with long flowing hair. She has a very curvy body with a soft belly, breasts and hips, but she does not look obese. She seems coy and shy, covering her breasts and genitals. One leg is also raised coyly, like the Venus of Willendorf. She has a distant, melancholy look on her face.

David: This sculpture shows a naked, muscular man with a washboard stomach and curly hair. He is looking confidently to the side. Unlike Venus, he is not attempting to conceal his genitals.

Honoré de Balzac: This sculpture also shows a naked man, but unlike David he has a potbelly. His arms are folded above his belly and he is taking a big step forward. He has a confident expression on his face. Although he is very fat, he is also muscular and strong-looking.

Toilet of Venus: The painting depicts a woman wearing only a sheer piece of cloth around her midsection. She seems to be on the fat side, with fat and cellulite on her back and bottom. She has a healthy, attractive appearance, with shiny golden hair and a pink glow in her cheeks. She is wearing earrings and a bracelet on her upper arm. Two servants are helping her get ready, and they seem to be admiring her beauty.

2. How have the idealized shape and contours of the human body changed – as reflected in works of art?

The three women are extremely curvy and voluptuous. This shows that women's beauty used to be associated with softness, curves, large breasts and hips more than it is today. Two of the male sculptures both show muscles and confidence, which are still valued in males today. However, Honoré de Balzac's potbelly is no longer considered an aesthetic ideal today. When the statue was made, a large belly may have signified wealth and power. The exaggerated height and length of Evening Shadow reflects the abstract/distorted form of a long shadow rather than a human body ideal.

SOLUTIONS ANALYSIS

3. Is what you look like only a matter of fashion – or are there other reasons behind the ideal of beauty and a particular conception of the human physique?
Copy the following chart into your notebook and complete it.

work of art	historical epoque	expression of:
Venus of Willendorf	Stone Age	need for fertile women ➔ survival of the tribe
Evening Shadow	Classical period (Greek influence)	height, exaggerated length, androgyny ➔ celebrates the form of the human body as it is changed and distorted by the evening sun
Venus (Sandro Botticelli)	Renaissance	luxury as contrast to poverty ➔ expression of wealth ...
David (Michelangelo)	Renaissance	idealized muscular strength ➔ healthy, strong, powerful men were most successful
Honoré de Balzac (Auguste Rodin)	Impressionism	wealth, strength, power, embracing pleasure and life ➔ honours the man Honoré de Balzac
Toilet of Venus (Peter Paul Rubens)	Baroque	beauty, fertility, wealth ➔ a need for many children for continuation/success of family; beauty for pure pleasure

SOLUTIONS ACTIVITIES

@ **4. The given works of art depict the human body and ideals of beauty in different historical eras. Now, find examples of contemporary art that show the recent ideal(s) of the human body. Do research on the Internet, in your library, at a museum, etc. and collect examples. Then, prepare short presentations in class and explain your findings.**

Individual answers

Disfigured – Learning to Accept Your Body (pp. 54–55)

About the author	The movie *Disfigured* (2008) was written and directed by Glenn Gers. Originally from New York City, Gers has spent many years working as a screenwriter. Some of his other screenplays include *Mad Money*, *My Brother's Keeper* and *The Accountant*.
About the text	*Disfigured* was shot over a period of only 15 days with very minimal costs and was filmed completely in a documentary style with handheld cameras. Lydia is played by Deidra Edwards, and Darcy is played by Staci Lawrence, who is not anorexic in real life.
Level	●●○
Additional material	• Film CD-ROM 3 + 4, • Comprehension: no. 6
Further Research	• Website on the topic of "No diet": www.eskimo.com/~largesse/INND/slogans.html

- Vor dem Einsatz der CD-ROM im Unterricht sollten die Schülerinnen und Schüler darauf hingewiesen werden, dass es sich bei den im Film dargestellten Szenen um **Fiktion** in **Form einer Dokumentation**, nicht etwa um eine solche handelt.
- Bei der Bearbeitung der nicht durch die CD-ROM gestützten Aufgaben 2 und 3 sollte deutlich werden, dass das Akzeptieren des eigenen Körpers und seiner Bedürfnisse vor allem Verantwortung bedeutet, was heißt, dass jede Form von Extremen schädlich ist. Insofern ist sowohl einem durch die Medien und die Modeindustrie geförderten Schlankheits- und Jugendwahn als auch einer uneingeschränkten Genusssucht eine Absage zu erteilen.
- Aufgabe 3 kann in **Partnerarbeit** erledigt werden.
- Zur Vorbereitung der in Aufgabe 5 geforderten Diskussion können die Schülerinnen und Schüler aufgefordert werden, sich Argumente zum Thema zu überlegen und diese stichwortartig zu notieren.

SOLUTIONS AWARENESS

Reflect on the title of the film – what do you associate with the word "disfigured"?

I associate this word with birth defects or the effects of a bad accident or disease: a hunchback, major scarring or mutilation, being born without certain body parts ...

SOLUTIONS ACTIVITIES

1. The members of the Fat Acceptance Group are at first very scornful and disapproving. To acquire a deeper understanding of their reaction to Darcy's suggestion, watch the scene *The First Meeting* on the CD-ROM, and complete the given tasks.

Darcy's suggestion is that the 'Fat Acceptance Group' is about changing the way these people feel about their self-image. Darcy, a recovering anorexic, believes she is fat (Though she is not) and wants to try to find acceptance in her own self-image. All but one person in the group react with scorn and they ask Darcy to leave, no doubt feeling their own reservations about allowing a thin person into the group though their problems with self-image are very similar.

2. After working with the next two scenes, *Lessons?* and *Lessons Begin*, on the CD-ROM, discuss the pros and cons of Lydia's idea in class.

Lydia's idea to start anorexia lessons

Pro's: lose weight, people won't call you fat, possibility to have stronger self-image
Con's: it's an eating disorder so health would fail, mental instability, possibility to end up like Darcy with a poorer self-image

3. On May 6, 1992, the first INDD (International No Diet Day) was established by Mary Evans Young, a recovered anorexic and author of a bestselling book in Britain titled *Diet Breaking*.
Here is the logo and some of the INND slogans:

- Beauty, health and fitness come in ALL sizes
- Born to be WIDE
- Diets kill!
- Do It Anyweigh!
- Fat Power!
- I'm not dying to be thin
- Life is a banquet – why should I starve?
- One size does NOT fit all
- Redefine yourself
- Scales are for fish, not people
- Self-esteem is not a dress size

4. Now create more logos or slogans that support the idea of NO DIET.

Individual answers

5. According to the INDD Website, www.eskimo.com/~largesse/INDD, the most important reason for giving up dieting is "learning to love and accept yourself just as you are". Is this good advice? – Discuss.

For example:
This is bad advice because the most important thing is for people to be healthy. If someone is dangerously obese (or underweight) it could kill them, which is a more serious issue than self-esteem. ...

ADDITIONAL TASK

1. Write a review yourself, based on the scenes of the film *Disfigured* that you have watched (Film CD-ROM, tracks 3, 4 and 5).
Point out what you (dis-)like about the scenes.

Two physical opposites become friends when a struggling anorexic and a woman tired of being overweight begin sharing lessons with one another. Although sometimes funny, the harsh realities of their situations make for moments of uncomfortable awkwardness which can leave the audience in a strange place. The message of course outweighs (no pun intended) the awkward situations. Eating healthy as opposed to starving oneself or gorging is the only way to find the self-image that everyone is looking for. To anyone looking for a docudrama with meaning behind the message, this one is for you.

People, Places, Perspectives – Mapping out Your Future

TM[1]	SB[2]	Author: Title of text	Type of text	Topic	Competences	Audio CD	Film CD-ROM	GaST[3]	Diff[4]	Comp[5]
Start-up Activities										
90	60	Rise Up!!	photo							
90	61	Po Bronson: Why Teenagers Are Growing Up So Slowly Today	magazine article/blog	growing up: school vs. reality	• analysing a photo • holding a discussion • analysing a text			no. 5, 6, 13, 17, 18, 24	40	
School's Out? – What Next? Crossroads, Choices & Careers ...										
92	62	Fields of Learning and Their Components	mind map	necessary things we learn for life	• ranking one's ideas • creating a mind map			no. 17, 21		
93	63	John Green: Looking for Alaska	novel, cartoon	the protagonist's arrival at his new preparatory school his farewell to his parents	• analysing the contents of a text • speculating on the text • analysing a cartoon • creative writing • designing a poster • grammar: indirect speech					no. 7
101	66	Gossip: Get a Job	song, photo	the need to have a job	• talking about statements • listening comprehension • analysing the contents and language of a text • creative writing • grammar: conditional sentences	CD 1, 8		no. 12		no. 8
105	68	Jane Goodall: Roots & Shoots	visual, website information, photo	the guiding principles of the Roots & Shoots program	• analysing the contents and language of a text • doing internet research • designing a display • creative writing			no. 22		

1 TM = page in Teachers' Manual
2 SB = page in Students' Book
3 GaST = material in Grammar and Skills Trainer
4 Diff = page in Differenzierungsmaterial
5 Comp = material in Comprehension: Reading – Listening – Viewing

TM[1]	SB[2]	Author: Title of text	Type of text	Topic	Competences	Audio CD	Film CD-ROM	GaST[3]	Diff[4]	Comp[5]
108	71	Volunteer	website information	the volunteer program of the Jane Goodall Institute	• creative writing					
108	71	Testimonials	Internet testimonials/blogs	young people speak about their experiences as volunteers with Roots & Shoots	• see above					
108	72	Role cards	writing an email	asking for and giving information on volunteer work	• see above					
	73	Volunteerism in the USA	Focus on Facts					no. 22		
109	74	Job Offers ...	job adverts	various job adverts	• analysing the contents and language of a text • mediation • creative writing • creating an advert • grammar: register			no. 21		
114	76	Being Interviewed on the Phone	interview questions, role cards	a young German is being interviewed for a job in English	• preparing for a telephone call in English • listening comprehension • carrying out a job interview • acting out a role play • grammar: working with language	CD 1, 9				
119	78	Recruiting Interns – All Work and No Pay?	magazine article, cartoons	different kinds of internships advantages and disadvantages of internships	• analysing the contents and language of a text • analysing a cartoon • writing and acting out a role play			no. 9, 21	43	
123	80	EU Migration to Germany – *Sprechen Sie Job?*	magazine article, cartoons	young European migrant looking for jobs the problem of language	• analysing the contents and style of a text • analysing a cartoon • creative writing • grammar: modal auxiliaries			no. 17		no. 9
Professional Communication & Correspondence										
127	83	Planning for Your Graduation Ball	project	various tasks in preparing a graduation ball	• doing research preparing and giving a presentation • grammar: superlatives and comparatives					
128	85	Finding out About Interesting Products and Services – Making an Enquiry	telephoning, role cards	organizing the entertainment for a ball	• listening comprehension • creative writing • writing a summary • preparing and acting out a role play	CD 1, 10				

TM[1]	SB[2]	Author: Title of text	Type of text	Topic	Competences	Audio CD	Film CD-ROM	GaST[3]	Diff[4]	Comp[5]
131	87	When Customers Are Unhappy ... Making a Complaint	telephon-ing, role cards	complaining about something	• listening compre-hension • analysing and evaluating a conversation • preparing and acting out a role play	CD 1, 11				
	89	Thematic Vocabulary	Focus on Vocab							

Start-up (pp. 60–61)

About the event **About the author**	"Rise Up!!" – demonstration against youth unemployment in Madrid, Spain. At the time of the photo, youth unemployment was at 43 % and during the protests people stayed for over a week to show their displeasure.	Po Bronson is an American best-selling author and journalist. As a journalist, he has written for *New York Times Magazine*, *Wired*, *TIME*, and others. He is the author of the following books: *Bombardiers* (1995), *The First $20 Million Is Always the Hardest* (1997), *The Nudist on the Late Shift* (1999), *What Should I Do with My Life?* (2002), *Why Do I Love These People?* (2005), *Nurture Shock: New Thinking About Children* (with Ashley Merryman) (2009) and *Top Dog: The Science of Winning and Losing* (2013).
About the photo **About the text**	The photo shows teens demon-strating against the unemploy-ment rate in Spain, some happy to be there and others looking forlorn.	The article excerpt presents research by authors Dr Joe Allen and Dr Claudia Worrell Allen on how to raise teenagers so that they "grow up" successfully and reach their potential as adults.
Level	● ○ ○	● ● ●
Additional material	---	• Differenzierungsmaterial, p. 40 • GaST: no. 5, 6, 13, 17, 18, 24

- Vor der Beschäftigung mit Aufgabe 1 sollte die vorgeschlagene **Arbeitsmethode** anhand der Ausführungen auf der entsprechenden FoM-Seite erläutert werden, um sicherzustellen, dass sich die Schülerinnen und Schüler über die Ergebnisse ihrer Beschäftigung mit der Fotografie austauschen.
- Aufgabe 2 kann sich inhaltlich unmittelbar an die Beschäftigung mit dem Foto anschließen, kann jedoch um andere Themen, die den Schülerinnen und Schülern näherliegen (Schule, Gemeinde), erweitert werden.
- Zur Erledigung von Aufgabe 3 kann die Sozialform der **Partnerarbeit** eingesetzt werden, wobei Partner 1 sich mit den Aspekten beschäftigt, die zum Erwachsenwerden der Teenager beitragen, während Partner 2 Aspekte findet, die dies verzögern bzw. verhindern. Die Ergebnisse können im Anschluss in einer **Tabelle** an der **Tafel** gesichert werden:

Teenagers grow up on time	*Teenagers do not grow up on time*
they need real-life experiences to learn to distinguish between good and bad risks (ll. 43ff.)	*they are protected from real life (ll. 20f.)*
they need real stress and challenges (ll. 51f.)	*they are insulated from adult-like work, relationships, consequences (ll. 22f.)*
they need the possibility to take productive risks (ll. 52f.)	*school and education are considered more important than work (ll. 27ff.)*
	they are given plenty of time to adjust to the biological changes which growing up brings with it (ll. 36f.)
	their brains are not sufficiently developed (ll. 37f.)
	they are not given the chances to take risks that are productive (ll. 52f.)
	they are made passive by their environment (ll. 55f.)

- Nach der Bearbeitung von Aufgabe 3 werden die Schülerinnen und Schüler aufgefordert, individuell oder in Partnerarbeit ihre Einschätzung des Problems in **wenigen Sätzen schriftlich zu formulieren** (Aufg. 4).
- Die Ergebnisse der in Aufgabe 5 vorgeschlagenen Diskussion können informell an der **Tafel** gesichert werden.
- Aufgabe 6 kann als **Hausaufgabe** eingesetzt werden. Jeder Schüler wählt ein Bild aus, für das er vor dem Hintergrund der Aufgabenstellung eine **Kurzpräsentation** erarbeitet. Hierzu können die **Tips on vocab** noch einmal umgewälzt werden. In der Folgestunde werden die Bilder zunächst innerhalb von **Gruppen** von 4-6 Schülern präsentiert und im Anschluss daran im Klassenzimmer ausgehängt, um der Lerngruppe die Möglichkeit zu geben, alle Bilder zu sehen und zu diskutieren. Der Lehrer bzw. die Lehrerin sollte darauf achten, dass die Schüler während der gesamten Unterrichtsphase **in der Fremdsprache kommunizieren**.

SOLUTIONS START-UP ACTIVITIES

1. In a Think! Pair! Share! Activity (→ FoM, p. 273), first describe the photo of the Spanish protesters, then exchange your impression of its message.
→ Focus on Skills, Analysis of Visuals, p. 262

Unlike many pictures of protesters where anger and frustration fuel their thoughts, the trio at the front looks relatively happy to be demonstrating against youth unemployment. Outside of those holding the sign, the young people look a little more morose, more upset by the situation that they are no doubt in.

2. Do you think that "rising up" and protesting for your rights against deplorable states of affairs (= Missstände) can help to bring about a change for the better? Discuss in class.
→ Focus on Language, Conversation and Discussion, p. 266

Yes, it is proven that protesting and strikes can get a message across and can accomplish some semblance of change even in the most dire of situations. By forming a group of likeminded individuals, all with a sense of purpose and intention to create change, the poor states these people are in can be changed for the better. With a goal in mind driving the protesters on, the people responsible for causing that poor state will have to take notice, and, if they want to stop the protesting, change what caused the problems.

3. Read the text on the opposite page and point out what – according to Dr Joe Allan – makes teenagers (not) grow up on time.

Teenagers grow up on time	Teenagers do not grow up on time
they need real-life experiences to learn to distinguish between good and bad risks (ll. 43ff.)	they are protected from real life (ll. 20f.)
they need real stress and challenges (ll. 51f.)	they are insulated from adult-like work, relationships, consequences (ll. 22f.)

Teenagers grow up on time	Teenagers do not grow up on time
they need the possibility to take productive risks (ll. 52f.)	school and education are considered more important than work (ll. 27ff.)
	they are given plenty of time to adjust to the biological changes which growing up brings with it (ll. 36f.)
	their brains are not sufficiently developed (ll. 37f.)
	they are not given the chances to take risks that are productive (ll. 52f.)
	they are made passive by their environment (ll. 56f.)

4. State why it is important to subject teenagers to "real" stress and challenges and make them take "productive risks".

Without the sometimes painful experiences that only real life brings with it, it is not possible to tell the difference between what you should really fear and what not and what risks are worth taking and what not. In real life the harmful effects and the genuine rewards are immediately felt or recognized. There is no substitute for real stress and for real tasks and challenges when it comes to learning. You can only learn "the hard way" and develop a feeling for when it makes sense to take a "productive", calculated risk that in the end turns out to be worth taking.

5. Discuss Dr Allen's thesis that "their environment makes them [teens] passive" and state whether or not you share his view.

Dr Allen believes that we pamper and protect teenagers from real life and its consequences and subject them to an environment which renders it more difficult for them to grow up, slowing down their development. As he sees it, endless monotonous years in education or overly protective parenting styles cocoon young people in a sheltered or artificial, primarily passive state of existence.

There is, I feel, a considerable element of truth in this. Fifty years ago, for example, children left the house to play and their parents had no real idea where they were. Even when playing, they took more risks. And there was no such thing as a mobile phone. People also married earlier and had children earlier. On the other hand, we all live longer now and maybe the different phases of life are all just being stretched out a little more. Certainly society has changed, as societies will always do and we are today living in a very different world from the media point of view – a world with new and different dangers.

6. Collect pictures, adverts or photos from newspapers, brochures or magazines that show teenagers assembling their concerns and discuss their various messages and intentions in class.

Individual answers

School's Out – What Next? Crossroads, Choices & Careers …

Fields of Learning and Their Components (p. 62)

About the material	The material is a mind map concerning different styles of education and learning: academic, personal training, social learning, and professional work.
Level	● ● ○
Additional material	● GaST: no. 17, 21

- Die Awareness-Aufgabe kann mithilfe von **Moderationskarten** bearbeitet werden. Jeder Schüler/jede Schülerin erhält eine bestimmte Anzahl von Karten, auf die die persönlichen Ideen verzeichnet werden. Um die Anzahl der Karten zu verringern, können auch immer zwei Schülerinnen oder Schüler eine bestimmte Anzahl von Karten erhalten, die sie zusammen beschriften.
- Die Karten werden eingesammelt und zunächst ohne bestimmte Reihenfolge an die Tafel geheftet. Doppelte Karten werden aussortiert. Die Schülerinnen und Schüler erhalten pro Person eine bestimmte Anzahl von Klebepunkten, die sie an den entsprechenden Karten anbringen. An der Anzahl der **Klebepunkte** orientiert sich das folgende Ranking. Die Karten werden dabei auf einer **Moderationswand** angebracht oder auf **Flipchartpapier** geklebt, damit sie für die Dauer der Unterrichtseinheit im Klassenzimmer sichtbar bleiben.
- Aufgabe 2 wird anhand der ausführlichen Anweisungen im Schülerbuch bearbeitet.

SOLUTIONS AWARENESS

A Latin proverb says "Non scholae, sed vitae discimus." – "We learn not for school but for life." Accordingly, there are many other aspects that are at least as important as academic learning and studying. Collect ideas about the "things we learn for life" in class and make a ranking concerning their importance and relevance.

1. the ability to navigate intrapersonal relationships
2. personal beliefs as we grow
3. empathy
4. life skills (raising kids, fixing cars, sewing, animal care, etc.)
5. primary schooling skills
6. travel experience
7. professional skills
8. media information
9. politics
10. university education

SOLUTIONS ACTIVITIES

1. **In a Group Puzzle activity (→ FoM, p. 271), describe and discuss the mind map, with each group focusing on one field of learning. Copy your part of the mind map on a poster and complete your field of learning by adding further branches, sub-branches and components. You can use some of the components below, but also consider further aspects. Finally, the groups put all the different fields of learning/posters together and discuss and evaluate the results of the completed mind map with the entire class.**

→ Focus on Language, Conversation and Discussion, p. 266

- academic-University-core classes, specialized classes, electives
- social Learning-gym membership, social club, social meeting place
- professional-Inter-business relationships, work training
- personal-Researching, libraries, personal training

John Green

Looking for Alaska (pp. 63–66)

About the author	John Green is an American author specializing in young adult fiction. His debut novel, *Looking for Alaska*, won the Printz Award and his most recent novel, *The Fault in Our Stars*, debuted at number one on the *New York Times* bestseller list. Green was also included in *Time Magazine's* "100 Most Influential People".
About the text	The text is an excerpt from Green's award winning novel, *Looking for Alaska*. It describes the main character, Miles Halter, and his first moments at his new boarding school in Birmingham, Alabama.
Level	● ● ○
Additional material	• Comprehension: no. 7

- Die **Awareness-Aufgabe** kann in einem lockeren **Unterrichtsgespräch** bearbeitet werden. Alternativ dazu können die Schülerinnen und Schüler dazu aufgefordert werden, reihum ihre Erfahrungen des ersten Schultages in jeweils einen Satz bzw. ein Stichwort zu fassen. Der Lehrer bzw. die Lehrerin kann diese Stichwörter dann bündeln.
- Wird die **Think! Pair! Share! Aktivität** in **Gruppen** zu vier Mitgliedern durchgeführt, so werden die Mindmaps auf Folie geschrieben und im Anschluss an die Erarbeitungsphase **präsentiert**. Bei großen Klassen können auch wenige interessante Mindmaps vom Lehrer bzw. der Lehrerin für die Präsentation ausgewählt werden. Wird die Aktivität mit der gesamten Klasse durchgeführt, so wird die **Mindmap** auf eine mit Papier bezogene **Moderationswand** übertragen. Die Schülerinnen und Schüler heften daran ihre auf **Moderationskarten** geschriebenen Stichwörter an.
- Die Ergebnisse der Bearbeitung von **Aufgabe 2** können im **Unterrichtsgespräch** gebündelt und informell an der **Tafel** gesichert werden.
- **Aufgabe 3** kann in **Partnerarbeit** erledigt werden. Es ist darauf zu achten, dass die Schülerinnen und Schüler die von ihnen gefundenen Abschnitte mit **Zeilenzahlen** versehen.
- **Aufgabe 4** kann arbeitsteilig bearbeitet werden, wobei sich die eine Hälfte der Klasse auf das Zimmer, die andere sich auf den Campus konzentriert. Die Ergebnisse werden im **Unterrichtsgespräch** gebündelt und fließen in folgendes **Tafelbild** ein:

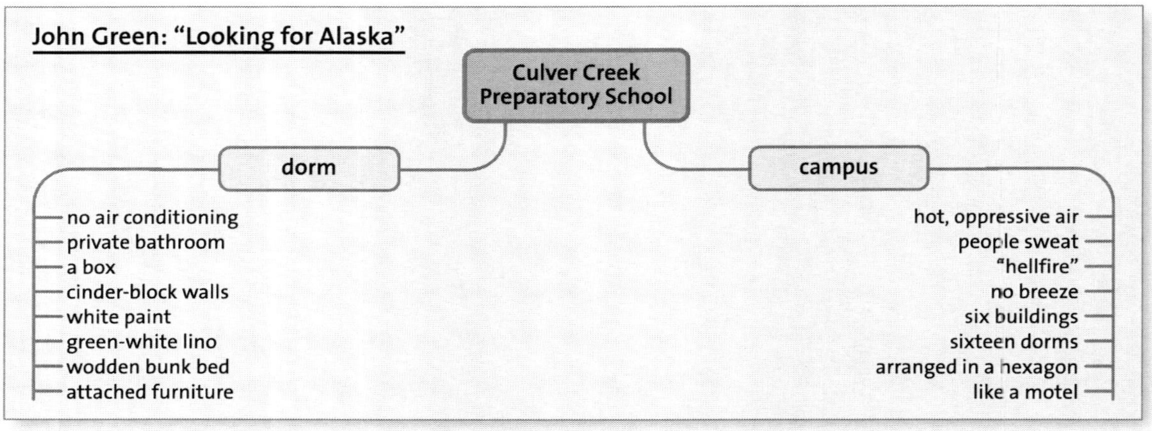

- Bei der Bearbeitung von **Aufgabe 5** werden die Schülerinnen und Schüler aufgefordert, sich Stichwörter zu notieren und die Abschiedsszene in einem kurzen **Statement** mündlich zusammenfassen.
- **Aufgabe 6** kann als die den ersten Teil der Beschäftigung mit dem Text abschließende **Hausaufgabe** eingesetzt werden.
- **Aufgabe 7** wird in **Partnerarbeit** bearbeitet. Die Schülerinnen und Schüler tragen ihre Ergebnisse in eine **Tabelle** ein. Die Ergebnisse werden nach der Erarbeitungsphase besprochen und vom Lehrer in die auf **Folie** kopierte Tabelle eingetragen. Die Schüler korrigieren ggf. ihre Ergebnisse.

Miles and his parents

what they say	***what they mean***
I can unpack, Mom (l. 33)	*Miles is trying to take on more responsibility* *he is ready to be out on his own as soon as they arrive*
Let me at least make your bed (l. 35)	*the mother is not ready to let Miles go yet*
No, really: I can do it. It's okay (l. 36)	*Miles is assuming the mature, adult position* *he is trying to send them along*
God, we'll miss you (l. 40)	*the mother is trying to let go of something she does not want to* *she knows that both her life and the life of her son will change dramatically* *she is not yet ready to let her son go*
I's gonna learn how t'talk right Southern (ll.47f.)	*Miles is releasing the tension with a little comedy because he knows it is difficult for his mother*
No drugs, no drinking, no cigarettes (l. 50)	*the father had gone through the boarding school previously and he knows what can happen while being there* *he is making sure the son comes away with something that can help him at school*
I love you … five pay phones (ll. 57-64)	*the family is telling Miles that they love him* *Miles and the parents want to stay in contact; Miles tells them that he will call every Sunday and the parents made sure he was very close to the pay phones*

- Nach der ausführlichen Bearbeitung von **Aufgabe 7** kann **Aufgabe 8** unter Berücksichtigung der gerade gemachten Beobachtungen in einem informellen **Unterrichtsgespräch** erledigt werden.
  Ggf. müssen die Begriffe *inner monologue* und *comment* im Vorfeld geklärt werden. Dies kann mithilfe der **Focus on Language-Seiten** (SB, S. 309 bzw. S. 311) geschehen.
- Alternativ dazu können die im Lösungsvorschlag unten angegebenen Textstellen vom Lehrer bzw. der Lehrerin vorgegeben und von den Schülerinnen und Schülern kommentiert werden.
- **Aufgabe 9** kann im **Unterrichtsgespräch** bearbeitet werden. Die Ergebnisse können in folgendem **Tafelbild** fixiert werden:

Foreshadowing in „Looking for Alaska"

Culver Creek Preparatory School

future possibilities
parties
streaking through hay fields
drinking
drugs
cigarettes

present situation
morose new living quarters

→ *possible excitement for what is to come in the future*

- **Aufgabe 10** kann im **Unterrichtsgespräch** gelöst werden. Die Ergebnisse der Diskussion können informell an der **Tafel** gesichert werden.
- **Aufgabe 11** wird in **Einzelarbeit** schriftlich bearbeitet. Im Anschluss werden die Ergebnisse in **Vierergruppen** ausgetauscht und besprochen.
- Die Ergebnisse der Bearbeitung von **Aufgabe 12** werden in einer **Gruppenpyramide** evaluiert. Dazu wird die Klasse in **Gruppen** von 4 – 6 Schülern eingeteilt, die dieselbe Person bearbeitet haben. Innerhalb der

Gruppen werden alle Texte der Gruppenmitglieder gelesen und der beste bestimmt. Die jeweiligen Gruppensieger lesen ihre Texte im Anschluss im Plenum vor.

- Zur Vorbereitung der Bearbeitung von **Aufgabe 13** können die Schülerinnen und Schüler Bildmaterial aus Magazinen und Illustrierten mitbringen.
- Für die Bearbeitung von **Aufgabe 14** muss mindestens eine **Doppelstunde** veranschlagt werden. Die Begriffe *scenic presentation* und *panoramic presentation* sollten im Vorfeld anhand der angegebenen **Focus on Language-Seiten** (SB, S. 308) geklärt werden.
- Die Ergebnisse der kreativen Arbeit können in einer **Milling Around Phase** präsentiert werden. Dazu gehen die Schülerinnen und Schüler im Klassenzimmer umher und auf ein Signal des Lehrers bzw. der Lehrerin suchen sie sich einen Partner, dem sie ihren Text vorlesen. Dies kann bis zu dreimal wiederholt werden, sodass jeder Schüler maximal drei verschiedene Versionen zur Kenntnis nehmen kann.
- **Aufgabe 15** kann als abschließende **Hausaufgabe** eingesetzt werden. Im Vorfeld sollte die **entsprechende Focus on Grammar-Seite** (SB, S. 298) besprochen werden. Zu einem möglichen **Tafelanschrieb** vgl. S. 51.

SOLUTIONS AWARENESS

The novel the following excerpt is taken from tells the story of 16-year-old Miles Halter, who leaves home to start his high school junior year at a boarding school. Do you remember what your first day at grammar school was like? What fears and hopes did you have back then?

I struggle remembering exactly what my first day was like in grammar school. If I had to assume, I am sure I was full of anxiety, fearing what the coming months and years would bring in the way of friendships, relationships, academic struggles, and personal experiences. At the forefront of my mind was no doubt the social aspect in school. Would people like me? Would I be 'cool'? Would I find my niche to be amongst a group of real friends? These were no doubt the biggest worries in my mind when I was growing up and it was not until my time at university where academics would really take the lead in my thoughts.

SOLUTIONS COMPREHENSION

1. Speculate about the title: What do you associate with "Alaska"? In a Think! Pair! Share! activity, collect ideas and draw a mind map.
➔ Focus on Methods, Think! Pair! Share!, p. 273

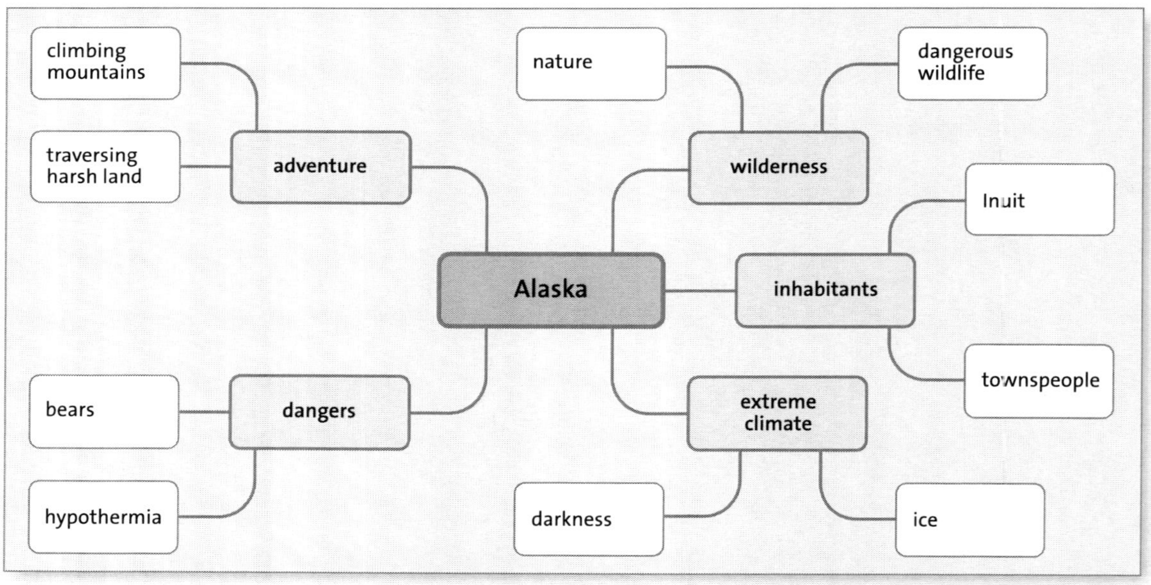

2. Now, together with a partner, try to anticipate what Miles, the protagonist of the novel, might be looking for.

- relief from the harsh weather
- someone to talk to
- something reminding him of home
- an escape

- friends
- acceptance
- new life

3. Divide the text into thematic units and find a suitable headline for each of them.
Tip: Do not only follow the paragraphs and lay-out of the excerpt but pay attention to interruptions and breaks in the course of the narration.

- From "hot to hotter" (ll. 1-29): Comparing Florida to his new school in Alabama, speaking entirely about the environment before speaking about moving stuff in and out. The 'headline' not only includes going from hot Florida to hotter Alabama and then also includes movement from a warm outside environment into an even warmer interior with his new dorm.
- "Unpacking" (ll. 30-64): In keeping with the multiple themes, this portion can mean the literal unpacking of the car, the unpacking of their reservoir of feelings between parents and child, and then also the unpacking ('getting rid of') his parents who seem hesitant to go. This part of the excerpt is all about the changing of things; physical change of both the car and the room, taking items out of one and moving them to the other, emotional change as they both spout out 'I love you's' and pieces of advice, and personal change in the way he begins to strike out on his own, without his parents help.
- "Miles Away" (ll. 65-87): Miles finally has the chance to take in his surroundings as he is sitting outside. The big change from his home in Florida to this new place in Alabama is, of course, literally miles away from one another. Then there is the obvious pun on his name in this headline. As there is a change in Miles' environment, there will also be a change in Miles. He is looking at everything around him and is yearning for some type of connection, connections he already had in his home of Alabama but now needs to find them anew.

4. Describe "Culver Creek Preparatory School" as observed by Miles. What do his new room and the campus look like?

The Dorm: Unair-conditioned, private bathroom, a box, cinder-block walls with thick layers of white paint, green and white checkered linoleum, looked like a hospital, unfinished wooden bunk bed, furniture attached to walls so they cannot be moved. (ll. 16-29)
Campus: The environment is hot, made him sweat, called it hellfire (ll. 1-15) and then the campus lacked a breeze even in the shade of eaves, air was oppressive, six buildings with sixteen dorms a piece arranged in a hexagon, like a motel.

5. Give an outline of the family's farewell.

1. unpacking and setting up the room (Mother trying to be motherly one last time before saying goodbye) (ll. 16-34)
2. Miles trying to (nicely) get his parents going (ll. 36-39)
3. the 'we'll miss you' stage and embracing in a goodbye hug (ll. 40-46)
4. advice and comic relief, parent say 'Don't do anything stupid', 'No drugs. No drinking. No cigarettes ...' and Miles makes a joke about learning to speak with a southern accent to ease the tension (ll. 47-56)
5. the 'I Love You's' and the goodbyes. The family says its final goodbyes with reassurances of love (ll. 57-64)

SOLUTIONS ANALYSIS

6. Collect examples from the text that demonstrate the narrator's* view of
a) his new "home" and
b) saying goodbye to his parents.
Examples:

- **(ll. 13 ff.) ... the sun burned ... into my skin with vicious ferocity ... hellfire → observation of a dangerous and evil place**
- **(ll. 36 ff.) ... you cannot draw out these things forever ... it hurts ... → he assumes the adult position; seems to be mature and detached (= abgeklärt)**

- Home: The environment is hot, made him sweat, he called it hellfire (ll. 1-15)... This obviously is showing that the new environment is much warmer than what Miles is used to. Using a phrase like hellfire has a strong negative connotation in which one can assume Miles is uncomfortable with his new home.

- Unair-conditioned (l. 17) and then back with 'And no air-conditioning' (l. 29). Using this phrasing multiple times is a way to show that there is no relief for Miles, no matter where he goes. He is looking for an escape somewhere but without the air-conditioning, he cannot find one.
- 'Hospital' (l. 24): Calling one's new home hospital-like is a sure sign that the person is very uncomfortable with the place. Hospitals bring with them sickness, injury, and death; three things that would not be welcome in the home. This, more than all else, shows that Miles is not fully comfortable with his new Alabama home.
- Saying goodbye: 'You cannot draw these things out forever ... and then you're relieved' (ll. 36-39): Miles is assuming the mature, adult position. Seeing that it is hard for his mother to leave him Mile takes up the mantle to try and send them along.
  'I knew I ought to cry ... separation seemed overdue'(ll. 44-46): In this statement, the reader can see that Miles does care for his parents. He knows what he should be doing but that chance for freedom is at hand now.
  'I's gonna learn how t'talk right Southern' (ll. 47-48): Miles is releasing the tension with a little comedy. He knows it is difficult for his mother so he tries to get her to laugh a little bit.
  'No drugs ... days were now behind him' (ll. 50-56): This is fatherly advice and an interior monologue from Miles showing that the two are connected. Miles knows about his father's past and his father does not want to see Miles make some of the same mistakes he did.
  'I love you ... five pay phones' (ll. 57-64): These lines literally show the family telling Miles that they love him and they show Miles reciprocating that feeling. Both Miles and the parents want to stay in contact. Miles tells them that he will call every Sunday and the parents made sure he was very close to the pay phones.

7. Examine the dialogue between Miles and his parents and explain in what way it reveals the relationship between the characters.

- 'I can unpack, Mom' (l. 33): This line reveals that Miles is trying to take on more responsibility. He is ready to be out on his own at the boarding school and he wants that opportunity as soon as they arrive.
- 'Let me at least make your bed' (l. 35): The mother is still trying to 'keep her bird in the nest'. She is not ready to let Miles go yet.
- 'No, really: I can do it. It's okay' (l. 36): Miles is assuming the mature, adult position. Seeing that it is hard for his mother to leave him, Mile takes up the mantle to try and send them along.
- 'God, we'll miss you' (l. 40): This is more of the mother trying to let go of something she does not want to. She knows that both her life and the life of her son will change dramatically after time away from one another and she is not yet ready to make that step.
- 'I's gonna learn how t'talk right Southern' (ll. 47-48): Miles is releasing the tension with a little comedy. He knows it is difficult for his mother so he tries to get her to laugh a little bit.
- 'No drugs, no drinking, no cigarettes.' (l. 50): This is fatherly advice. His father had gone through the boarding school previously and he knows what can happen while being there. Giving Miles this small piece of advice, his father is making sure the son comes away with something that can help him at school.
- 'I love you ... five pay phones' (ll. 57-64): These lines literally show the family telling Miles that they love him and they show Miles reciprocating that feeling. Both Miles and the parents want to stay in contact. Miles tells them that he will call every Sunday and the parents made sure he was very close to the pay phones.

8. Show in what way the narrator reacts to his parents' statements by referring to his inner monologues* and comments.

- 'Because you simply cannot draw ... and then you're relieved' (ll. 36-39): Miles is assuming the mature, adult position. Seeing that it is hard for his mother to leave him, Mile takes up the mantle to try and send them along. He is not doing it in a vicious way, but rather endearing. Knowing that his mother struggles with it, he has to be the adult.
- 'I knew I ought to cry ... separation seemed overdue' (ll. 44-46): In this statement, the reader can see that Miles does care for his parents. He knows what he should be doing but that chance for freedom is at hand now and is ready to take that step.
- 'As an alumnus ... days were behind him now' (ll. 50-56): This reaction to his dad's advice shows that Miles knows about his past. He connects with his dad knowing that his father hated the fact that the school used to be all boys. Miles also uses 'badass' as a term of endearment when referring to his dad's past.

9. There are clues given in the text that indirectly foreshadow upcoming (exciting) events (e.g. ll. 52 ff.: secret parties ...). This is contrasted with Miles' rather depressing assessment of his own situation. Explain the intended function and effect of these devices.

→ Focus on Skills, Analysis of a Fictional Text, p. 255

Most of the exciting foreshadowing comes from a couple of lines when speaking about Miles' father (ll. 50-56). The parties, the streaking, the drinking, drugs, and cigarettes, it all foreshadows what Miles could do in his own time at Culver Creek. This, contrasted with the rather morose state of Miles' new home, makes for a build-up of possibilities. Instead of only choosing words and themes in which the reader dreads everything the school had to hold, changing up the manner of speaking and chain of associations allows the audience to get excited for what is to come as opposed to worry about what Miles' future holds.

10. What does the narrator's daydreaming (ll. 78 – 85) reveal about his position and rank in his peer group and emotions?

He needs to be accepted. Miles is making up stories about hypothetical situations in which he is the star. This reveals that he has never really been the 'cool guy' or the person everyone knows. He wants to become that person but, seeing that he cannot walk up to someone and start a conversation, it is unlikely he will ever become that person.

11. Describe the cartoon and compare it to the situation depicted in the excerpt. Which similarities can you detect?

→ Focus on Skills, Analysis of Visuals, p. 262

The cartoon depicts one of two things:

1. A student asking his parents if it is their first time away from home or
2. A student seeing his roommate walk in with his mother, connected by a wire to the wrist.

Either way, there are similarities. Miles is trying to say goodbye to his parents who are at a strange place in their lives, seeing their son at college for the first time. The other one, much more appropriate, would show someone else seeing a Miles-type character walk in with his mother literally attached at the wrist. Both ways, you see the trouble of parents letting go for the first time.

SOLUTIONS ACTIVITIES

12. Work together with a partner and rewrite the excerpt from a different point of view*:

a) the narrator's father or

b) the narrator's mother.

Think about how they might have experienced the situation and what they might have thought.

Father's:

I had to agree with Miles. We were used to being in a hot environment but this was downright oppressive. Alabama heat was different than Florida's. It was humid, unforgiving, sticky, and sweaty whereas Florida's, although hot, was easily handled with the ocean and every building with air-conditioning to fall back on as a reprieve. This was not Florida. This was a humid, sweaty, hellhole that we were moving my son into.

I remember it being a little different from my day. I had the memories of the parties and the late night hayfield runs. I had the memories of seeing the girls from the school down the street and acting like it was God's holiest gift to earth when they walked by. I remember sports and I remember my teammates. I remembered good times. It was different for Miles.

He had no friends here. Just us.

As Miles' things dwindled in the car and rose up in the dorm, I knew it was time for us to get going. Mom was not going to go easy. She was blubbering about how she needed to make his bed and do one more thing for Miles but our son, trying to be independent, wouldn't let her touch it. We just could not keep him forever. He needed to go out on his own eventually and it was finally time for that separation; we had to go.

"God, we'll miss you," mom said suddenly before stepping up and hugging Miles. I joined in as we formed a sort of huddle though we couldn't keep it up with the heat.

"Don't worry," Miles said with a smile, "I's gonna learn how t'talk right Southern." Mom laughed.

"Don't do anything stupid," I said. "Okay? No drugs, no drinking, no cigarettes." I still remember what my time at Culver Creek was like. Secret parties, streaking, a ton of drinking, smoking, and drugs — those days were thankfully behind me now but I didn't want Miles to try the same things.
Mom and I stepped up again and simultaneously we said, "I love you."
Miles grinned, "I love you too. I'll call every Sunday."
We hugged again and that was it. I watched my son and the school fade away into the distance in my rear view mirror and we were gone.

Mother's:
I didn't care that it was so hot here. I just wanted Miles to be happy. If we could make sure he has a great first day then maybe the rest of his year will only get better. Moving things into his dorm, trying to fan him while sweat rolled down his forehead, cleaning his new digs, anything at all to help, that is what I was trying to do for him.
Everything in his room was just too bland. Dormitory bunk beds with an unfinished touch, cinder-block walls painted thick with ancient paint, desks and dressers unable to be moved around; outside of the private bathroom, the room was like some sanatorium's inspiration.
We were running low on things in the car so I just had to find another way to help. "Let me at least make your bed."
"No, really: I can do it. It's okay." Miles responded, really trying to be the adult here.
"God, we'll miss you," I said, feeling tears well up in the corners of my eyes. I stepped over some of the bags like they were mines to get over to Miles and hug him. Once I arrived, we were also greeted by my husband, forming a sort of huddle which only added to the unholy heat that was Alabama. It didn't last too long because of the heat but it seemed enough.
"Don't worry," Miles said with a smile, "I's gonna learn how t'talk right Southern." Mom laughed.
"Don't do anything stupid," Dad said. "Okay? No drugs, no drinking, no cigarettes." I had heard about his time at Culver Creek. Secret parties, streaking, a ton of drinking, smoking, and drugs — those days were thankfully behind him now but I didn't want Miles to try the same things.
I stepped up again to say 'I love you' and was surprised to hear Dad say the same words at the same time.
Miles grinned, "I love you too. I'll call every Sunday."
We hugged again and that was it. I watched my son and the school fade away into the distance in my rear view mirror and we were gone.

13. In the course of the novel it turns out that Alaska is not a place but the name of a girl. Against the background of your findings in task 1 and 2, speculate on what kind of girl Alaska might be or what Miles might be fascinated with. Together with a partner, compile a "Wanted" poster of Alaska.

14. Together with a partner, imagine how the story might go on. Think about further characters, adventures, events, etc. Employ scenic and panoramic presentation* in your texts.
→ Focus on Language, Literary Terms, p. 308
Knowing what we know from Miles' father's past, the likelihood of parties is high. Drugs, drinking, and cigarettes will probably have their place in the novel and, using what we know about the 'wild' Alaska, it would be safe to assume that she would be a factor in Miles' decisions.
Miles will most likely head out into the Alabama backwoods with Alaska and a few of her friends, trying to show that he is just as wild, trying to prove that he deserves acceptance. Those backwoods are where

Alaska and her friends go to partake in the more risqué parts of Culver Creek. They sneak drugs and alcohol out there to use for recreation and Miles, ever-looking for group of friends, will indulge in the activities once or twice before he realizes what he is doing is wrong.
From what we have read on just Miles' relationship with his parents, we can see that he is, at heart, a basically decent young man. With that knowledge, I would think that, after getting into some type of trouble, Miles' parents are called. Seeing them, Miles regrets his decisions and tries to make the others come around too, though never telling the school headmaster which others were with him out in the woods.

SOLUTIONS GRAMMAR/LANGUAGE

15. Later that day Miles writes a letter to a friend back home in Florida about his arrival in Culver Creek and the farewell of his parents. Use indirect speech and pay attention to the correct use of the tenses.
Example:
- **(ll. 33 f.) I told Mom that I could unpack myself ...**
- **(ll. 35 f.) Mom wanted me to let her make the bed ...**

For example:
- (ll. 13ff.) When we arrived the sun almost burnt like hellfire.
- (l. 33) I told Mom that I could unpack myself when she opened the trunk.
- (ll. 35ff.) Mom wanted me to let her make the bed but I thought you should not draw out things forever.
- (ll. 40-43) Mom suddenly said that they would miss me and Mom, Dad and I formed a sort of huddle.
- (ll. 44ff.) I knew that I should have cried but I had lived with my parents for sixteen years.
- (ll. 47f.) I told them not to worry and that I would learn how to talk right Southern.
- (l. 57) They both blurted out simultaneously that they loved me.
- (l. 61) I told them that I loved them too and that I would call them every Sunday.
- etc.

Gossip

Get a Job (pp. 66–68)

About the band	The American Indie band, Gossip, consists of vocalist Beth Ditto, guitarist Brace Paine, and drummer Hannah Blilie. After breaking through with their 2006 album, *Standing in the Way of Control*, they released two more full-length albums, *Music for Men* and *A Joyful Noise*.
About the song	The song, *Get a Job*, comes off of the studio album *A Joyful Noise*. The song is about maturing by literally getting a job and making the right decisions when growing up.
Level	● ○ ○
Additional material	• Audio CD 1, 8 • GaST: no. 12 • Comprehension: no. 8

- Zur Bearbeitung der **Awareness-Aufgabe** können die verschiedenen Statements auf große **Bögen Papier** kopiert werden, die im Klassenzimmer ausgehängt werden. Die Schülerinnen und Schüler notieren die Ergebnisse ihrer Beschäftigung mit den Statements auf folgende **Arbeitsblätter**, die sie unter das entsprechende Statement heften:

Gossip: "Get a Job"

The deeper meaning of my statement is ...

I agree/disagree with this statement because ...

Work means for me ...

Die Ergebnisse werden im Anschluss an die Erarbeitung im Rahmen eines Museumsrundgangs zur Kenntnis genommen und diskutiert.

- Zur Vorbereitung der Hörverstehensaufgabe werden die in Aufgabe 2 aufgeführten Aspekte auf das Wesentliche reduziert ins Heft übertragen. Folgende Ergebnisse sind möglich:
  What – addressee do – when young?
  How – rich girl – spend time?
  What – girl's dealing – money?
  Why – getting job – important?
  Which problems – finding a job?
- Aufgabe 3 kann zunächst in Einzelarbeit erledigt werden. Danach werden die Ergebnisse im Unterrichtsgespräch besprochen und in einer Tabelle (s. Lösungsvorschlag unten) auf Folie gesichert.
- Zur Vorbereitung der Bearbeitung von Aufgabe 4 sollten die Focus on Grammar-Seiten zum Gebrauch der Tempora (SB, S. 305-307) besprochen werden. Die Aufgabe kann in Partnerarbeit bearbeitet werden. Die Ergebnisse werden im Unterrichtsgespräch gebündelt und folgendermaßen an der Tafel gesichert.

"Get a Job" – tenses

simple present	*simple past*	*present progressive*	*going-to-future*	*imperative*
i hear you laughing	*it was adorable when you were in your twenties*	*spending other people's money*	*you never know how it's gonna end up tomorrow*	*you'd better get a job*
I don't think it's funny		*you're sleeping in*		*you gotta try try try*
...	...	...	...	...
→ *the speaker is stating facts about the girl's behaviour*	→ *what the girl did in her twenties*	→ *the girl is still doing these things in her thirties*	→ *the uncertainty of the future makes a job necessary*	→ *the speaker tells the girl to change things*

- Da das Bewusstmachen verschiedener Stilebenen viele Schülerinnen und Schüler schon bezüglich der deutschen Sprache vor Schwierigkeiten stellt und diese in der Fremdsprache erfahrungsgemäß noch größer sind, sollte Aufgabe 5 im Klassenverband bearbeitet werden. Im Vorfeld sollte die angegebene Focus on Language-Seite (SB, S. 315) besprochen und erläutert werden. Die Ergebnisse können informell an der Tafel gesichert werden.
- Vor der Bearbeitung von Aufgabe 6 muss der Begriff *interior monologue* geklärt werden. Dies kann anhand der entsprechenden Focus on Language-Seite (SB, S. 309) geschehen. Die Aufgabe wird individuell bearbeitet, die Ergebnisse können in Gruppen ausgetauscht und evaluiert werden. Einige Exemplare können danach in der Klasse vorgelesen werden.
- Aufgabe 7 kann im Klassengespräch bearbeitet werden.
- Zur Bearbeitung von Aufgabe 8 können an die Schülerinnen und Schüler verschiedenfarbige Moderationskarten ausgeteilt werden, auf denen sie ihre Argumente für und gegen die im Lied vorgebrachte Meinung notieren. Diese Karten können an der Tafel oder an einer Moderationswand gesammelt und im Anschluss diskutiert werden.
- Aufgabe 9 kann als abschließende Hausaufgabe eingesetzt werden. Vor der Bearbeitung sollten die Schülerinnen und Schüler die entsprechende Focus on Grammar-Seiten (SB, S. 296) zur Kenntnis nehmen. Für einen möglichen Grammatikaufschrieb sei auf die Unterrichtshandreichungen auf S. 41 (Text: *Male Attractiveness: Abs-Olutely Fabulous*) verwiesen.

SOLUTIONS AWARENESS

Together with a partner, choose one of the statements about "work" below and
a) explain its deeper meaning,
b) state whether/why you agree or disagree with the statement,
c) try to find your own "definition" of "work".
Finally, exchange and discuss your various results in class.

"Nothing will work unless you do."– Maya Angelou.
a) Unless you put maximum effort into what you are doing, things will not work out in your favour.
b) Agree – unless a person is truly trying their hardest and putting as much work into something as possible 1. It will not be done correctly and 2. It probably will not be done at all.
c) Putting effort and exertion into some task

SOLUTIONS COMPREHENSION

CD 1 8 **1. In a first listening, try to understand the gist of the song and jot it down in five sentences.**

The first verse is about the speaker disagreeing with a friend's lifestyle which, at one time, the speaker thought was cute but now sees that the friend must grow up. This type of intervention style speaking continues into the second verse as the speaker notes on choices that she believes are poor (hair instead of rent, weekend every day, sleeping in, ll. 17-25) and again in the third verse when the singer asks 'who's gonna hire you with lack of experience ... (ll. 38-41). The chorus lines sing a different tune however, one that is more supportive. 'I know it's hard but you never know how it's gonna go, end up tomorrow, you gotta try try try ...': these repeating lines are urging the audience to get a job and work, grow up, mature, and become an adult.

2. In a second listening, focus on details and take notes on the following questions:
- **What did the "you" of the poem, the addressee, do when she was young?**
- **How did the "rich little girl" spend her time?**
- **What are the girl's dealings with money?**
- **Why – according to the speaker – is getting a job of such importance?**
- **Which problems in finding a job does the speaker expect?**

Listen to the song another time and complete your notes.
→ Focus on Skills, Listening Comprehension, p. 244

- 'You' basically did the same thing she's doing now. Didn't have a job in her twenties (ll. 6f.), slept in (l. 25), received inheritance money (l. 41), and partied.
- Rich little girl got her hair done (l. 17), spent every day like a weekend (l. 23) and partied (l. 37)
- She didn't know where her money had gone (l. 20) and receiving in heritance (l. 41)
- Because you never know what life is going to throw your way, 'you never know how it's gonna go, how it's all gonna end up tomorrow' (ll. 46-47)
- Lack of experience and lack of maximum work effort (ll. 39-45)

SOLUTIONS ANALYSIS

3. Examine the relationship between the speaker and "the girl" by collecting and explaining examples from the text.

Example:	• (l. 2) i don't think it's funny – criticism of the girl's silly behaviour
	• (l. 8) not so cute anymore – warning ...
	• (ll. 11) I know it's hard – knowing that the girl is unaware of the difficulties in the real world
	• (ll. 22-23) What kind of life is it when every day's a weekend – criticising how the girl spends every day
	• (l. 37) I'd like to stay and party but ... – The speaker would love to join in on the girl's fun but knows she has prior commitments
	• (ll. 37-41) Who's gonna hire you ... – he speaker is once again criticising the past choices of the girl

4. Analyse the function of the grammatical tenses employed in the song text.

Where the speaker begins 'I hear you laughing' (l. 1), this gives the present tense of the speaker currently watching what the girl is doing, making it known that the girl is still doing it. That present progressive use when calling out 'the girl' continues with 'spending' (l. 4) and 'pushing' (l. 9) which once again shows that 'the girl' is still doing these things in her thirties.
Once the chorus comes up, 'you'd better get a job', this is an obvious imperative which the speaker is urging 'the girl' to get a job, especially when the line 'you never know how it's gonna go' (formalized into how it will go) is a call into the future tense and the uncertainty of how things can happen.
This form continues throughout the song; speaker is present, 'the girl' in present progressive, and then a call to the future tense when the speaker is explaining her position.

5. Illustrate the speaker's use of informal language and explain its effect.
→ Focus on Language, The Language Register of English, p. 315

Informal language: all contractions (don't, it's, you'd, I'm, etc.), combination words (gotta, gonna), shortened words ('cause)
This use of informal language is two-pronged. The most common in the music industry is for relation to a larger audience. The goal for any mainstream artist is to sell their music and sell their brand. By using informal language, Gossip can span the gap between themselves and accomplished songwriters and the masses of people who use informal language at all times during the lives.
The deeper meaning however falls in with the conceit of the song. The song is basically an intervention from one friend to another. With this conceit as a working basis, one could reasonably assume that the informal language is an everyday occurrence between the friends. The informality of the language also comes as a way to endear the speaker to 'the girl'. If the speaker was using high-level language throughout the intervention process, the girl may think that the speaker is being self-centered. By using the informal style, the speaker is more of a friend than an authority figure.

SOLUTIONS ACTIVITIES

6. Put yourself in the position of the "little rich girl". How might she respond to the speaker's criticism and recommendations? Write down her thoughts in an interior monologue*.

What if she's right? I have been living a life without responsibility. What if I can't get a job? I have no experience, my inheritance is running low. I've spent it all on partying and making myself look good. What can I do?
She is right. I don't know how things are going to end up. What happens when my parents die? They can't take care of me forever, it's impossible. Seeing her come home from work, exhausted and angry — I just don't know if I could do it though.
She told me it'll be hard. I know it's going to be. Maybe she can help me through it, help me with finding a job, help me with anything. I know I have to grow up, but I just don't know if I can do it alone.

7. Take a look at the statements about "work" again: which of these statements applies to the situation described in the song? Give reasons for your opinion.

"Hard work spotlights the character of people: some turn up their sleeves, some turn up their noses, and some don't turn up at all."
Sam Ewing's statement illustrates the situation perfectly. The character of the speaker is never put into question as we, as an audience, know that she is working and that she is trying to help her friend. She is a person who 'turned up her sleeves'. She works hard and is also trying to help her friend whereas the 'rich girl' has turned up her nose at work for years. Nearly thirty, one would think she would have grown up a little by then but her character has shown in the way she refuses to work and just parties all day, every day.

8. Why is it better to get a job as the speaker demands in the song? Find arguments for and against this view.

The easiest argument to make for getting a job is an economic one. Having a job pays bills whereas being unemployed does not. In addition to the economic argument, learning the value of work is something that can last a person a lifetime, whether it is working at home in the garden of appreciating retirement when the work has all been done.
Arguments against getting a job fall few and far between. If the girl in question is a trust fund kid who does not need an economic pay-out then one could get by without being employed but that is a rare occurrence in this day and age. Other arguments against getting a job: mental or physical handicaps, religious motives, anti-government leanings.

SOLUTIONS GRAMMAR/LANGUAGE

9. Turn the criticism and recommendations given by the speaker into conditional sentences. Use type I, II and III depending on the grammatical tense used in the song.
Example: If you were still in your twenties you could go on spending other people's money ...
→ Focus on Grammar, Conditional Sentences (If-Clauses), p. 296

For example:
- If you were still in your twenties, you could go on spending other people's money.
- If I were close to thirty, I would start to find a job.
- If you do not try really hard to find a job, the future will be even harder for you.
- If you have enough money to go to the hairdresser, you can also pay your share of the rent.
- If you go on sleeping in while I am working, I will no longer pay the rent for you.
- If you had learned to work for your money, your future would be much easier.
- If I were you, I would stop ignoring everything around me.
- If I had enough money, I would love to stay and party but I have to work.
- If employers get to know about your lack of experience, they will not hire you.
- etc.

Jane Goodall

Roots & Shoots (pp. 68 – 70)

About the program	Roots and Shoots was founded by Dr. Jane Goodall, DBE in 1991, with the goal of bringing together youth from preschool to university age to work on environmental, conservation and humanitarian issues. The organization has local chapters in over 132 countries with over 8000 local groups worldwide that involve nearly 100,000 youth.
About the text	The text explains different facets of the Roots & Shoots program. Starting with an overview, then an explanation of who Jane Goodall is, followed by the fun-filled nature and the global power of the program.
Level	● ● ○
Additional material	• GaST: no. 22

- Die **Awareness-Aufgabe** kann in einem kurzen **Unterrichtsgespräch** bearbeitet werden. Sie kann um die Frage „What do you expect from this organisation?" erweitert werden und damit auf die weitere Beschäftigung mit dem Thema hinführen.
- Die **Comprehension-Aufgaben** (**Aufg. 1-4**) können als Übungen zum **Leseverstehen** eingesetzt werden. Dazu wird der Text (SB, S. 68f.) als **Kopie** ausgeteilt, auf der die Schülerinnen und Schüler die für die einzelnen Aufgaben relevanten Passagen in unterschiedlichen Farben unterstreichen. Die Sicherung der Ergebnisse erfolgt in einem kurzen **Unterrichtsgespräch**. Folgendes **Tafelbild** kann dabei erstellt werden:

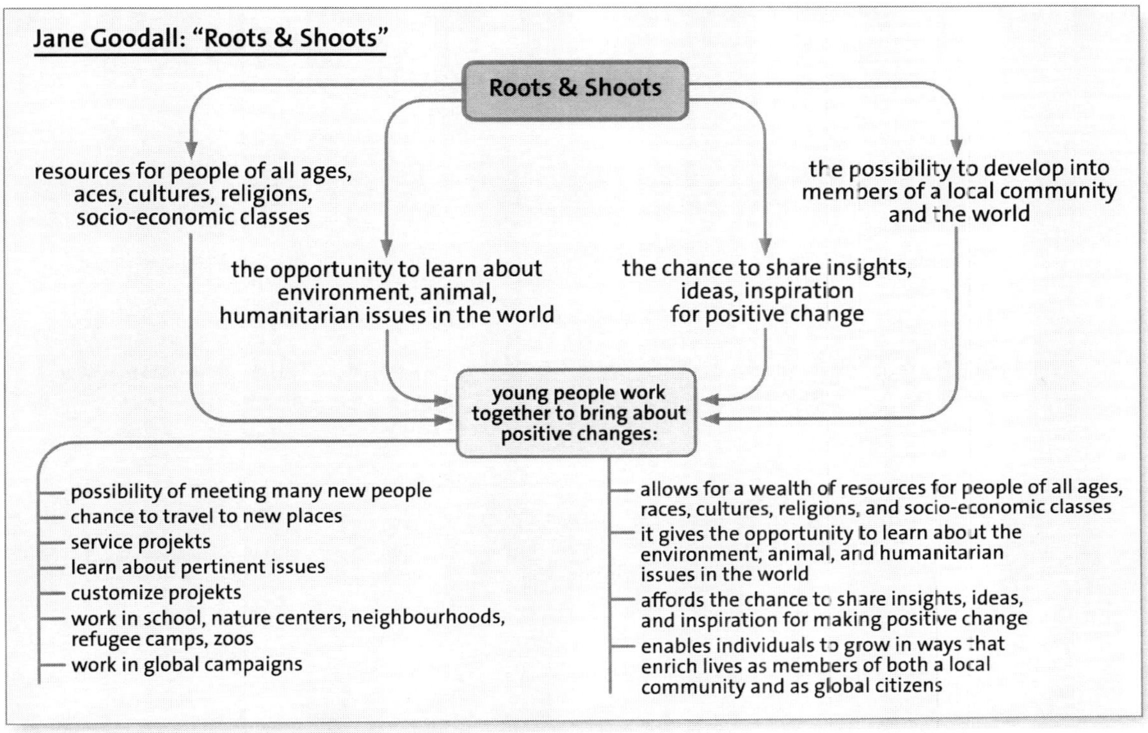

- **Aufgabe 5** kann in einem informellen **Unterrichtsgespräch** bearbeitet werden.
- **Aufgabe 6** wird in **Partnerarbeit** bearbeitet. Die Schülerinnen und Schüler übernehmen dazu die in der Aufgabenstellung vorgegebene **Tabelle** in ihre Hefte und füllen sie aus. Um Zeit zu sparen, kann die **Partnerarbeit** arbeitsteilig organisiert werden, sodass jeder Partner für zwei der vier Kategorien zuständig ist. Die Ergebnissicherung erfolgt im Unterrichtsgespräch über **Folie**.
- Nach der gründlichen Auseinandersetzung mit dem im Text verwendeten Vokabular in der vorigen Aufgabe kann **Aufgabe 7** im **Unterrichtsgespräch** gelöst werden. Die Ergebnisse der Untersuchung können informell an der **Tafel** gesichert werden.
- Die in **Aufgabe 8** geforderte **Internetrecherche** wird in **Kleingruppen** durchgeführt. Dies kann entweder in häuslicher Arbeit oder an der Schule in einem dafür geeigneten Raum geschehen.
  Folgende Adressen können den Schülerinnen und Schülern an die Hand gegeben werden:
  www.janegoodall.org
  www.biography.com/people/jane-goodall-9542363#accomplishments
  www.rootsandshoots.org/
- Die Gruppen evaluieren die Informationen des Ausgangstextes vor dem Hintergrund der in der Internetrecherche gefundenen Seiten und formulieren ein **Statement** zum Thema, das im Anschluss an die Erarbeitungsphase im **Plenum** vorgelesen wird. Eine kurze **Diskussion** der Ergebnisse schließt diese Aufgabe ab.
- Die **Aufgaben 9 und 10** können kombiniert werden, d.h., die Schülerinnen und Schüler erarbeiten ihre **Präsentation**, die sie mithilfe einer **Wandzeitung** bzw. eines **Plakates** visualisieren. Bei der Präsentation ist darauf zu achten, dass alle Gruppenmitglieder teilnehmen.

SOLUTIONS AWARENESS

Look at the screenshot of the website on page 69 and describe its design. What overall atmosphere is created and how does it attract the viewer's attention?

The design is much more image-oriented than text-based. The website-goer is immediately drawn to the picture of two people holding plants which creates an atmosphere that feels as though the website is nature-oriented. Showing the large picture of the plants and two people working together with them makes the audience feel that this program is trying to work together to restore nature. This picture, along with images of well-known humanitarian Jane Goodall, really makes the program's homepage about nature and the natural world as a whole.

SOLUTIONS COMPREHENSION

1. Read the first paragraph in italics and state Jane Goodall's underlying concept of "Roots & Shoots".

Using Roots and Shoots as a metaphor for banding together and breakthrough the problems, Goodall's statement means that young people have the power to band together and right the wrongs of the past. Though seemingly useless and weak individually, much like a root or a shoot, young people together become a strong force that these 'walls' have to contend with.

2. Point out the information given about the "Roots & Shoots" global network.

(ll. 44-59)

- allows for a wealth of resources for people of all ages, races, cultures, religions, and socio-economic classes
- it gives the opportunity to learn about the environmental, animal, and humanitarian issues in the world
- affords the chance to share insights, ideas, and inspiration for making positive change
- enables individuals to grow in ways that enrich lives as members of both a local community and as global citizens
- anyone can become a member

3. Outline the opportunities and possibilities the program offers to young people.

- possibility of meeting many new people (ll. 10-12)
- chance to travel to new places (ll. 10-12)
- service projects (l. 15)
- learn about pertinent issues (l. 27)
- customize projects (l. 33)

- work in schools, nature centers, neighbourhoods, refugee camps, zoos (ll. 36-38)
- work in global campaigns (l. 43)
- allows for a wealth of resources for people of all ages, races, cultures, religions, and socio-economic classes (ll. 45-47)
- it gives the opportunity to learn about the environmental, animal, and humanitarian issues in the world (ll. 51-52)
- affords the chance to share insights, ideas, and inspiration for making positive change (ll. 53-54)
- enables individuals to grow in ways that enrich lives as members of both a local community and as global citizens (ll. 55-57)

4. Who can contribute to the program?

Anyone and everyone

5. Describe the photo and state who or what it appeals to.
→ Focus on Skills, Analysis of Visuals, p. 262

The photo shows Jane Goodall no more than two feet away from a young chimpanzee. She is sitting down so as to be on the same level as the chimp and she is holding a camera, taking a picture of the monkey who is sitting in a nearly identical pose. This would appeal to animal lovers first and foremost but also to all humanitarians and nature lovers. Any person who has ever thought a baby chimpanzee was cute would love this picture and would immediately be drawn to both the animal and the person taking its picture.

SOLUTIONS ANALYSIS

6. The text employs many keywords that refer to elementary principles and fields of volunteering. Collect words and place them in the respective categories of the grid:

environment	work in communities/ social issues	humanitarian aims	effect on the participants
• 'Roots & Shoots'	• identifying problems	• positive change	• connecting youths of all ages
• animals	• service projects	• change the world	• travel
• environment	• youth campaigns	• inspire us all	• inspire
• primatologist	• refugee camps	• make a difference	• learn about issues
• nature	• youth-driven networks	• people come together	• making positive change
• zoos	• global campaigns	• enrich lives	• grow and enrich lives

7. Explain the specific choice of positive emotive words and the use of further stylistic devices that aim at appealing to the reader and making him or her take action.
→ Focus on Skills, Analysis of a Non-Fictional Text, p. 258

- positive change (ll. 8ff.): This is at the very beginning of the text is the first step into Goodall's program. It immediately gets the reader into a positive mindset by literally using the phrase positive change.
- The explanation of the founder, Jane Goodall, is ripe with positively connoted and emotive words; 'guided by', 'extraordinary vision', 'informed and empowered', 'truly make a difference', 'change the world', 'heart of our program', 'powerful message of hope inspires', 'dedicated', 'inspiring', 'lead and implement' – all of these words are focused on how Jane Goodall exemplifies her program. She has done a great deal of good in nature and the world and her vision with the program is/is trying to do the same for young people all over the world.
- 'Possibilities are as varied as young people's imaginations!': This upbeat sentence allows for the audience to feel as though their imaginations can change the world. That, along with the exclamation point, keeps things positive and inspires those reading to take action.
- 'This powerful, youth-driven network fosters a fun, flexible and supportive environment where ...' (ll. 38-43) – This entire sentence is written in a positive way that reinforces all the different ways that someone can enjoy working for the program, making it more and more appealing to the reader.

@ **8. Do further research on Jane Goodall's projects and initiatives and examine the validity and reliability of the information given in the text.**

Currently, the Roots and Shoots program is working with an urban farming initiative and collaborated with a community permaculture garden in the United States. In addition to the American influence, a 'Dance 4 Development' in Tanzania is ongoing as well as a French program called 'Sauvages de ma rue' meaning wildlife on my street. With that information, it is fairly evident that the information given in the text is reliable. Seeing the different ways and the different locales of these programs, one can rightfully assume that there is validity in the program's initiatives. Twitter feeds and Facebook pages add in extra information on Dr. Goodall's works and ongoing projects related to Roots & Shoots.

SOLUTIONS ACTIVITIES

Webcode SNG-40175-003 @ **9. Use the links provided on the webcode and do further research on Jane Goodall and her unique project and prepare a short presentation in class.**
→ Focus on Skills, Presentations, p. 276

Jane Goodall is a British primatologist, ethologist, anthropologist, and UN Messenger of Peace. Considered to be the world's foremost expert on chimpanzees, Goodall is best known for her 45-year study of social and family interactions of wild chimpanzees in Gombe Stream National Park, Tanzania. She is the founder of the Jane Goodall Institute and the Roots & Shoots program, and she has worked extensively on conservation and animal welfare issues. She has served on the board of the Nonhuman Rights Project since its founding in 1996.
Jane Goodall founded the Jane Goodall Institute in 1977 as a global nonprofit that empowers people to make a difference for all living things.
The institute seeks to:
- improve global understanding and treatment of great apes through research, public education and advocacy,
- contribute to the preservation of great apes and their habitats by combining conservation with education and promotion of sustainable livelihoods in local communities,
- create a worldwide network of young people who have learned to care deeply for their human community, for all animals and for the environment, and who will take responsible action to care for them.

In addition to the Institute, she founded the Roots & Shoots in 1991 with the goal of bringing together youth from preschool to university age to work on environmental, conservation and humanitarian issues. With her history as a humanitarian and the establishment of these programs, one can rightfully say that Jane Goodall has done quite a bit of good for all the people she has encountered, ensuring that our planet has a future.

10. In groups, design a wall display using your research results. Employ factual information as well as visuals to flesh out your news sheet.

Individual solutions

Volunteer, Testimonials, Role Cards (pp. 71–72)

About the material	The material comes in three parts: Volunteer Information, Testimonials, and Role Info. The Volunteer Information explains, in minor detail, what one can expect from volunteering with the Jane Goodall Institute. The testimonials are two excerpts from volunteers explaining how they felt about their experience. The role cards are explaining imaginary roles as a volunteer and a prospective volunteer.
Level	● ● ○

- **Aufgabe 11** kann als **Partnerarbeit** organisiert werden, indem ein Partner die Rolle des amerikanischen, der andere die des deutschen Jugendlichen übernimmt. Die Schülerinnen und Schüler erhalten den Auftrag, jeweils zwei E-Mails zu schreiben. Die E-Mails können entweder im Klassenverband **vorgetragen** oder in gedruckter Form im Klassenzimmer **ausgehängt** und gelesen werden. An die Präsentation kann sich eine

Evaluation anschließen, in der die Schülerinnen und Schüler ihren Klassenkameraden ein **Feedback** über Inhalt und Sprache der Mails geben.

- **Aufgabe 12** wird als abschließende **Hausaufgabe** eingesetzt. Im Vorfeld werden die Schülerinnen und Schüler aufgefordert, die entsprechende **Focus on Skills-Seite** (SB, S. 286) und die angegebene **Focus on Grammar-Seite** (SB, S. 292) zur Kenntnis zu nehmen.

SOLUTIONS ACTIVITIES

11. Exchange e-mails with an American friend in which you ask him about his experiences. Use the role cards on p. 72 as well as the information and the testimonials above. As a German student you are interested in doing volunteer work at the Jane Goodall Institute.

American Student:
I absolutely loved the camp experience. I would encourage you to try it out but there are definitely some things you need to do beforehand. First and foremost, make sure you do some practical training in a zoo of some sort because there are a lot of animals around the camps. Some of these animals were orphaned and definitely need some special care as you go through the camp process (there was even a chimpanzee baby that passed away while I was there).
If you need any more advice on the camp I would love to help you out. You could always check the website for information about Roots & Shoots or you'd be welcome to stay over here in the US with me and I can fill you in on my experience. I want to go back so bad but I don't have time to get back to Tanzania until the summer. You'd be welcome to come with me then but the camps are open year round so you can go whenever! All you need are international papers and be eighteen years old before you can go, other than that, everything is good. I would apply early if you're really interested because they have a lot more applicants than spots at the camps.

Good luck!

Andrew

SOLUTIONS GRAMMAR/LANGUAGE

12. After doing research on the Internet on the Roots & Shoots Initiative and the Jane Goodall Institute, write an informative text for your school newspaper in which you depict the concept of the camps as well as the project's background (e.g. Jane Goodall, the founder; the impact of the camps, etc.). In order to flesh out your article and make it more interesting to read, employ adverbs and adjectives where possible.
Example: Jane Goodall's unique project was founded in … and has probably become one of the most successful …
→ Focus on Grammar, Adjectives and Adverbs, p. 292

For example:
Jane Goodall's <u>unique</u> project was founded in <u>1991</u> and has <u>probably</u> become one of the <u>most</u> <u>successful</u> initiatives supporting environmental and humanitarian issues. Jane Goodall, the founder, has gained <u>tremendous</u>, <u>first-hand</u> experience in research into <u>threatened</u> <u>wild</u> animals, <u>particularly</u> chimpanzees, and their habitats. <u>In 1991</u>, a group of <u>deeply</u> <u>concerned</u> <u>local</u> teenagers met Jane Goodall in Dar es Salaam, Tanzania, to discuss matters with her. Jane Goodall was <u>deeply</u> impressed by the passion of these teenagers and promised to support them. The project was carried out <u>totally</u> by the teens <u>at grass-root level</u>. The <u>first</u> Roots & Shoots project involved educating villagers about a <u>more humane</u> treatment of chickens. Etc.

Job Offers (pp. 74–75)

About the material	Three very different kinds of job adverts are shown here.
Level	● ● ○
Additional material	• GaST: no. 21

- Bei der Bearbeitung der **Awareness-Aufgabe** können die Schülerinnen und Schüler dazu aufgefordert werden, ein kurzes **schriftliches oder mündliches Statement** zu verfassen.
- Aufgabe 1 kann in **Einzelarbeit** erledigt werden. Die Ergebnissicherung erfolgt in einem Unterrichtsgespräch nach der Erarbeitungsphase auf **Folie** (s. Lösungsvorschlag). Diese kann im Anschluss für die Lerngruppe **kopiert** werden.
- Zur Vorbereitung der **Mediationsaufgabe** (Aufg. 2) sollten die Schülerinnen und Schüler die der Aufgabenstellung entsprechenden Schwerpunkte im Text **markieren**. Dazu sollte ihnen der Text in **Kopie** zur Verfügung stehen.
- Aufgabe 3 kann in **Partnerarbeit** erledigt werden, wobei jeder Partner drei Aspekte bearbeitet. Es ist darauf zu achten, dass am Ende beide Partner die Ergebnisse des jeweils anderen übernommen haben. Die Sicherung kann im Austausch mit einer anderen Zweiergruppe erfolgen.
- Um Zeit zu sparen, kann Aufgabe 4 arbeitsteilig organisiert werden, d.h., die Klasse wird in drei **Gruppen** eingeteilt, von denen jede zunächst in **Einzelarbeit** einen der drei Artikel analysiert. Nach der Erarbeitungsphase vergleichen Gruppen von je vier Schülern ihre Ergebnisse und fixieren sie **schriftlich**. Diese Ergebnisse werden im Klassenzimmer ausgehängt und im Rahmen eines **Museumsrundgangs** besprochen.
- Die Aufgaben 5 und 6 können als **Hausaufgabe** eingesetzt werden. Zuvor sollte jedoch die angegebene **Focus on Skills-Seite** (SB, S. 289) besprochen werden.
- Aufgabe 7 kann in der Folgestunde in **Gruppenarbeit** bearbeitet werden. Dazu ist es hilfreich, wenn der Unterricht in einem Raum stattfindet, in dem **PCs** zur Gestaltung der Stellenanzeigen zur Verfügung stehen.

SOLUTIONS AWARENESS

Look at the job adverts. Based on your first impression – which of the three is the most eye-catching advert and which one do you find most interesting?

Individual answers

SOLUTIONS COMPREHENSION

1. Read the two adverts written in English first and identify ○ what job is offered, ○ the information given about the respective company, ○ required qualifications, ○ the terms of the job offered.

	Hamleys	"Job description"
what job is offered	• security guard	• sewing jeans and other clothes
information given about the company	• toy store	• makes clothes for Pepe, Guess, Wrangler, Tommy, the Gap and Burton for customers in UK, Ireland, France, Belgium, the Netherlands and the US • factory is owned by Hong Kong company; located in Mauritius
required qualifications	• experience working in retail • in-depth knowledge of P.A.C.E. • smart in appearance (= good-looking) • good references • good eyesight	• young woman • must be willing to work long hours, for low pay, without protective gear • ability to deal with stress • not a member of a union
terms of the offered job	• £8,800 pa (= per annum = per year) plus benefits • working in shifts from 7am–7pm	• work seven days a week, sometimes 24 hours in a row • housing in factory or nearby • low pay

M 2. **Mediate the job advert from the "Verbraucherzentrale Bundesverband e. V." in Germany, emphasizing □ the facts about the organization in general, □ the description of the job and its responsibilities, □ the required qualifications, skills and experience, □ the information concerning the salary.**
Use the "Tips on vocab" box on page 74 for further language help.
→ Focus on Skills, Mediation, p. 265

Consumer Advice Centre – Federal association

The Federal Association of Consumer Advice Centres and Consumer Associations (Verbraucherzentrale Bundesverband e.V. (vzbv)) is the parent/umbrella organization of the sixteen states and 25 other social- and consumer-oriented member organizations and is based in Berlin. The following position (39 hours/ week) is available starting 1 May 2012:

Press relations officer (m/f)

We offer ...
... an exciting, varied/diverse and influential area of responsibility. You are responsible for communicating the corporate identity of the Federal Association of Consumer Advice Centres. Together with the management/executives/directors, you will determine the strategic objective/orientation/focus of Public Relations. You will be responsible for conveying the company's policy to the media and public in a unified/ consistent, effective and serious manner. You will appear publicly as an interview partner and the "voice of the consumers". You work/collaborate on the Federal Association's strategic development of topics and are a link/mediator/liaison to the member organizations in matters of Public Relations. One of the most important strategic communication goals is to continue to increase the Association's visibility and clout/ impact. The focus is on the development and expansion of the Association's online and social media activities.

You offer ...
... a passion for communication and variety, excellent media contacts and a pronounced interest and flair for politics. You possess convincing journalist/ic qualities, you are convincing at the microphone or in front of the camera. You also have a good instinct and intuition for people and topics. Experience working for an association or in consumer protection is an advantage. Leadership qualities and social media experience are also a part of your skillset. In sum, you have:

- completed university studies/higher education
- journalism experience
- work experience in PR
- experience using new media for PR
- excellent knowledge of common Office software
- outstanding English language skills, preferably competence in other foreign languages
- a keen interest in new problems/questions and projects
- experience working with/in charitable/non-profit organizations

Salary/Payment is based on TVÖD EG 15. Send your application by [not until!] 22 March 2012 (post date) to: etc.

SOLUTIONS ANALYSIS

3. **Examine whether the information given in the adverts matches the list of criteria for a well-written job description (see info box below). Copy the grid into your notebook and fill in the information from the adverts.**

Advert	**Hamleys**	**"Job description" (Jeans)**	**Verbraucherzentrale** (Federal Association of Consumer Advice Centres)
identifier	– **action man** – security guard – Personnel Department, Hamleys, 188-196 Regent Street, London W1R 6BT, Telephone: 01-7343161	– no job title – Mauritius – no contact information	– Press relations officer – Berlin – Department of Infrastructure, Andreas Eichhorst, etc.
key responsibilities	– **protection** – preventing toys from being stolen	– sewing jeans and other clothes	– communicating the company's corporate identity – determining the strategic objective of Public Relations – appearing publicly as an interview partner and the "voice of the consumers" – collaborating on the Federal Association's strategic development of topics; being a PR link to the member organizations in questions – increasing the Association's visibility and clout/impact – development and expansion of online and social media activities
qualifications	experience working in retail – in-depth knowledge of P.A.C.E. – smart in appearance (= good-looking) – good references – good eyesight – man or woman	– young woman – ability to deal with stress – not a member of a union	– man or woman – completed university studies/higher education – journalism experience – work experience in PR – experience using new media for PR – excellent knowledge of common Office software – outstanding English language skills, preferably competence in other foreign languages – a keen interest in new problems/questions and projects – experience working with/in charitable/non-profit organizations
Terms	– £8,800 pa (= per annum = per year) plus benefits – working in shifts from 7am–7pm	– work seven days a week, sometimes 24 hours in a row – housing in factory or nearby – low pay (not specified)	– 39 hours/week; starting 1 May 2012 – salary is based on TVÖD EG 15 special requirements
Goals	– uphold Hamleys' reputation as the finest toy store in the world	– output of 500,000 pieces of clothing per month (together with 700 colleagues)	– communication of the corporate image to the media and public should be **unified/consistent, effective and serious** – **passionate** about the work (Spaß am ...)

4. Analyse the specific style of each advert and examine the
□ choice of words, □ the language register, □ use of technical terms, etc.
□ use of keywords, □ use of positive emotive words, □ exaggeration, irony.
Explain how these devices determine the style and the message of the advert.
➔ Focus on Skills, Analysis of a Non-Fictional Text, p. 258

<u>Hamleys</u>

- **choice of words**: action man, Teddy, the forces of evil, Cabbage Patch Kids and Masters of the Universe will keep you on your toes ➔ referring to toys as if they were alive emphasizes the toy store setting, creates humour/light-hearted atmosphere
- **use of keywords**: security guard, shifts, retail environment, busy store, on your toes ➔ gives reader a good idea of the type of job/working environment
- **the language register**: colloquial/humorous (forces of evil, keep you on your toes) and formal (uphold that reputation, experience of working in a retail environment) ➔ gives the advert both a light-hearted as well as professional/serious feel
- **use of positive emotive words**: unique reputation, finest toy store in the world ➔ attracts potential candidates
- **use of expert language/technical terms:** P.A.C.E. ➔ underlines that this is a serious job for specialized/qualified candidates with proper training

➔ style is both humorous/light-hearted and professional

<u>Sewing jeans</u>

- **choice of words**: long hours, low pay, without protective gear, 24 hours in a row, windows that don't open ➔ blunt, shockingly honest and straightforward
- **use of keywords**: protective gear, union activists, sewing, sewing machines, factory ➔ describes job/ideal candidate
- **the language register**: mix of high (ability to deal with, industrial estate, multicultural experience) and low register (sometimes 24 hours in a row, windows that don't open, some who have travelled all the way from China!) ➔ contrast creates humour; although the ad is "trying" to sound serious, it is obviously fake
- **use of positive emotive words**: multicultural experience ➔ makes the work seem interesting/exciting (even though it sounds completely awful otherwise ➔ humour)
- **use of expert language/technical terms**:
- misspelled words (costumers ➔ customers, Wranlger ➔ Wrangler) and irregular use of cursive show a lack of professionalism/credibility
- brand names: Pepe, Guess, Wrangler, etc. ➔ gives the reader an idea of the products that are made
- extremely basic/non-specialized/non-specific equipment: sewing machines, stools ➔ low standards

➔ job advert is not meant to be taken seriously

<u>Verbraucherzentrale</u>

- **choice of words**: a passion for, pronounced interest and flair, convincing journalist qualities, outstanding language skills ➔ underlines the very high standards for this position; company is looking for a very exceptional/special candidate
- **use of keywords**: communication, communicating, responsible, PR, (social/new) media, strategic, experience ➔ underlines the main responsibilities of the job
- **the language register**: very formal/professional (e.g. responsible for conveying the company's policy, communicating the corporate identity, determine the strategic objective) ➔ lends trustworthiness/credibility, attracts educated/serious candidates
- **use of positive emotive words**: exciting, varied/diverse and influential ➔ makes the job sound interesting/attractive
- **use of expert language/technical terms**: parent/umbrella organization, PR, Office software, social media, new media ➔ gives specific information about the ideal candidate's profile

➔ style is completely professional and serious, straightforward

SOLUTIONS ACTIVITIES

5. Traps are not always as obvious as in the jeans advert (p. 74). Scan the newspapers and try to find adverts where you can identify hidden or obvious traps. Use the criteria from the info box.

Individual answers
For example: "Earn up to 1,000€ a week working from home!": coded wording for sex work/escort services …

6. Choose one of the adverts and write
a) a formal letter of application and
b) an informal, more creatively designed letter or ad in which you apply for the job.
→ Focus on Skills, Writing a CV and a Letter of Application, p. 289

a) (return address, address, date, etc.)
Dear Hiring Manager/Dear Sir or Madam,
I am writing to apply for the position of Security Guard. I am enclosing my CV and a list of references.
I have worked for three years as a security guard and have five years' experience working in retail. Furthermore, I am very familiar with P.A.C.E. etc.

b) Individual answers
Hamleys: letters of recommendation "written by" Teddy/toys
Verbraucherzentrale: video in which candidate talks about his/her qualifications and demonstrates competence in front of the camera …

SOLUTIONS GRAMMAR/LANGUAGE

7. Design your own job advert/description (e.g. looking for a summer job, looking for participants in your drama club, a poster, a newspaper ad, etc.).
- **Be careful to choose the appropriate language register that matches the addressee of your ad.**
- **Employ technical terms/phrases and/or specialist language to reflect your professionalism.**

→ Focus on Language, The Language Register of English, p. 315

Individual answers

Being Interviewed on the Phone (pp. 76–78)

About the material	In this dialogue, a young man from Germany calls an employment agency in the UK to inquire about a job he is interested in. The employment agent asks him a series of questions to see whether he is suited and qualified for this particular job.
Level	●●○
Additional material	• Audio CD 1, 9

- Die Awareness-Aufgabe wird anhand der detaillierten Angaben im Schülerbuch gestaltet.
- Für die **Hörverstehensaufgaben** (Aufg. 1 und 2) sollten die Schülerinnen und Schüler in **Einzelarbeit** ein **Raster** vorbereiten, in das sie die entsprechenden Informationen eintragen können. Dazu müssen die vorliegenden Fragen inhaltlich auf die Stichwörter reduziert werden, die die Schülerinnen und Schüler im gesprochenen Text identifizieren können.

Being interviewed on the Phone

1st listening:

who: ______________________________

where: ______________________________

what: ______________________________

when: ______________________________

why: ______________________________

2nd listening:

question	Text
1) How – find – offer?	
2) Who – speaking to?	
3) Job – looking for?	
4) Job offered? Where?	
5) Qualifications?	
6) Motivation for job in UK?	
7) Company's requirements?	
8) Where – send – application to?	
9) Registration number?	
10) Where – headquarters?	
11) When – get reply?	

- Aufgabe 3 wird in **Einzelarbeit** erledigt. Die Sicherung der Ergebnisse erfolgt über **Folie**.
- Die Aufgaben 4 und 5 werden anhand der Erläuterungen im Schülerbuch organisiert.
- Aufgabe 6 kann als abschließende **Hausaufgabe** eingesetzt werden.

SOLUTIONS AWARENESS

Making phone calls in a foreign language, especially for a telephone interview, requires planning. It is especially important to know what to say when making formal or business calls. Prepare your phone call and, in a group, work out a rough draft of

- **the main things you want to say or ask before phoning somebody,**
- **things that the contact person is likely to say or ask,**
- **how to start/end a conversation,**
- **what to say when you need to leave a voice mail.**

→ Focus on Skills, Telephoning, p. 274

Individual answers

SOLUTIONS COMPREHENSION

CD 1 9 **1. Listen to the dialogue/telephone interview on the CD for a first time and try to get the gist of the conversation. Take some notes on the w-questions (who – where – what – when – why).**

who: Diane Kruger (NetJob secretary), Ingo Müller (job applicant), Jane Thompson (recruiter at NetJob)

where: Ingo is in Düsseldorf; NetJob in the UK; apprenticeship at Fosters & Son in Newcastle, company has branches all over UK

what: he calls to find out more about a job opening – apprenticeship at Fosters & Son PR Department

when: present-day; interviews being held 13-14 July

why: Ingo wants to use his foreign language skills and work abroad; Ingo received e-mail about job from NetJob, a job search database; he wants to get a job in Public Relations

2. Now, listen to the interview for a second time, and try to answer these questions:

a) How did Ingo Müller find the job offer?
He registered with NetJob, an online job search database, and received an e-mail from Jane Thompson with a job description.

b) Who is he speaking to?
at first Diane Kruger, the secretary, and then to Jane Thompson, a NetJob recruiter

c) What job is Ingo Müller looking for?
a job where he can use his foreign language skills, preferably in the UK; something related to Public Relations; wants to learn about different branches of a company

d) What kind of job is he offered? Where?
apprenticeship in the PR department of Fosters & Son, in Newcastle, UK

e) What are Ingo Müller's qualifications?
completed Abitur/A-Levels; has spent time in the UK; three months of practical training in Brighton doing PR at a small advertising agency; studied Commercial English at a vocational training college for three years, London Chamber of Commerce and Industry Certificate in English for Business; can use Windows, Word, Excel and graphics programmes Adobe and CorelDraw

f) What is his motivation to look for a job in the UK?
- wants to practice his foreign language skills; he has frequently visited the UK on holidays and already did a three-month training course in Brighton

g) What are the company's requirements concerning the job on offer (e.g. experience, flexibility, etc.)?
- candidate should be flexible and willing to move to the UK
- company will pay for accommodation
- company will offer 500£ for moving expenses
- candidate should have experience in Commercial English and be computer-literate (Windows, Word, Excel)

h) Where does Ingo Müller have to send his application to?
Fosters & Son
Personnel Department
Attn: Mr John Henley
345 South Road
Newcastle, UK

i) What is his registration number?
RHS 7812374

j) Where are the company's headquarters?
Newcastle, UK

k) When can Ingo Müller expect to get a reply?
three weeks after closing date for applications, which is two weeks from now = in five weeks

SOLUTIONS ANALYSIS

3. Listen to the interview for a third time and pay attention to particular keywords that characterize the company's expectations and the applicant's (i. e. Ingo Müller's) qualifications and motivation. Copy the grid into your notebook and complete it, explaining the meaning of certain keywords.

	keywords	→ meaning
Ingo Müller	**independent**	→ **able/willing to move; open to changes**; can move on short notice; does not have to consider a partner/ family when moving
	practical training at small Brighton advertising agency, first insights into PR	→ relevant (but still "beginner-level") work experience in PR; experience working in the UK
	"this sounds like a really interesting and exceptional opportunity"	→ he is enthusiastic
	vocational training college, London ... Certificate in English for Business	→ qualifications from recognized/ legitimate institutions
NetJob/Fosters & Son	**flexible**	→ **able/willing to move; willing to work extra hours**; willing to do different kinds of tasks
	willing to move	→ is not looking to stay at one location, OK with being transferred
	experience in Commercial English	→ able to speak and write formal/ business English
	computer-literate	→ able to use Windows, Word, Excel, the Internet, etc.

SOLUTIONS ACTIVITIES

4. In a Group Puzzle activity, prepare role cards using the interview role cards below and on page 78.

→ Focus on Methods, Group Puzzle, p. 271

Webcode SNG-40175-004 @

Form four/six groups, of which two/three groups will take the role of the German applicant (Michaela/ Thomas Schmitz) and the others will take the part of the British interviewer (Julia/Timothy Robinson). Each group prepares the respective tasks/questions and takes notes. Use your dictionary and/or the vocab pages in your Students' Book to mediate the German applicant's tasks.

→ Focus on Skills, Job Interview, p. 269
→ Focus on Skills, Telephoning, p. 274

- **Then, the groups remix (→ see diagram).**
- **Act out the interviews in class.**
- **During the interviews, the other students should listen and take notes on the performance of the interview partners.**
- **Finally, the class evaluates the job interviews and exchanges ideas for further improvement. You can use the evaluation form on the webcode.**

Sample dialogue:

Role A:

- Hello, this is Michaela/Thomas Schmitz. I'm calling about the apprenticeship position in Sales and Marketing.
- I completed vocational school this past spring. The reason I am interested in working there is because ... apply my English skills ... interested in tourism ... offer a uniquely German perspective ... like to work creatively to develop new products ... spent several holidays in UK and enjoyed it very much ...
- Two years ago, I spent six weeks travelling around England and Ireland with English friends ... I got to really immerse myself in the British way of life ...
- I have developed several prototypes for products. I have a good idea about what is attractive to German tourists because ...
- I have worked with Windows, Word and Excel. In addition to using them regularly for school, I also taught computer literacy to senior citizens as a volunteer ... I also have experience in video production and editing ...

- Yes, I have experience in Business English. I received the highest marks in English every year during vocational school, including last year, when we worked with the book Pathway Professional ...
- I also took the Cambridge English test and received the grade of ...
- I am very flexible and would be able to move to the UK any time after the New Year.
- I love to travel and would be willing to travel as part of the apprenticeship.
- I did a one-month internship last summer working at a German travel agent that specializes in English-speaking countries. There, I was able to learn more about ... language/computer programmes/intercultural awareness ...
- If I were to get the job, would you be able to offer me any temporary accommodations or any other assistance in finding a flat?
- Can you give me an idea of what the salary for this position is? Assuming that the apprenticeship goes well, is there any chance of being hired later on for a full-time position?
- Thank you very much for your time. I am very interested in this position and will send you my written application before the end of the week.
- When can I expect to hear from you?

Role B:
- Hello, this is Julia/Timothy Robinson, how can I help you?
- Yes, we are still taking applications for these positions.
- That's very interesting. Let me tell you more about this job: It is based in the UK. We are looking for candidates who have experience in the tourist business.
- One of the main tasks will be coming up with and developing ideas for merchandise for German tourists who visit the UK.
- What makes you want to apply for this position?
- How well do you know British culture, and what kind of knowledge do you have about the Royal Family?
- Many young people want to work abroad. Why do you want to move to the UK in particular?
- What computer experience do you have? Which programs do you know?
- How soon would you be able to move here and start work?
- Due to the nature of this job, it is essential that our candidates are flexible. How well does this describe you?
- What are your thoughts on travelling for work? Are you an experienced traveller?
- We would offer to pay your travel expenses and have some small company flats available for employees.
- We would ask you to send a complete written application that includes all relevant documents: your CV, testimonials, language certificates, school transcript, etc.
- You can expect to hear from us within the next four weeks.
- It was a pleasure speaking with you; I look forward to receiving your written application. If you have any more questions please don't hesitate to contact me!
- Good-bye!

5. Alternatively, perform a role play for a different job interview. Write role cards with a partner and act out the interview in class. Choose whether you will conduct a telephone or a personal interview.

Individual answers

SOLUTIONS GRAMMAR/LANGUAGE

6. Read the phrases (in the Tips on vocab box) and sort them into the correct category.

starting a conversation	**topics for small talk**	**making plans/ appointments**	**replying/ responding**	**ending a conversation**
Nice to see you (again). How are you doing? Do you mind if I join you? How are you?	Have you seen the new film ... yet? How was your trip? How did you get here? Have you ever been there before? Did you read about ... in the newspaper this morning? Did you see ... on TV ...?	Sorry, I can't manage Wednesday. I'm seeing ... then. If there is a problem, let me know. Friday would suit me better/best. I've got a meeting with ... on ... That's no good. I'm afraid. What about ...?	I couldn't agree more! That's incredible. That's the most interesting aspect.	It was nice talking to you. What a shame, I've got to go. Hope to see you again soon. Have a safe trip home. Please give my warm regards to ...

Recruiting Interns – All Work and No Pay? (pp. 78–80)

About the text	This article explores the topic of internships against the backdrop of the financial crisis and high unemployment and discusses recruitment agencies that place interns with companies.
Level	● ● ●
Additional material	• Differenzierungsmaterial, p. 43 • GaST: no. 9, 21

- Bei der Bearbeitung der **Awareness-Aufgabe** können die Schülerinnen und Schüler auf Erfahrungen, die sie in Praktika, beispielsweise im Rahmen von **Berufsorientierungsprogrammen** wie **Bogy** gemacht haben, zurückgreifen.
- Aufgabe 1 wird in **Einzelarbeit** erledigt, die Ergebnissicherung erfolgt im anschließenden Unterrichtsgespräch.
- Die übrigen **Comprehension-Aufgaben** (Aufg. 2-4) können ebenfalls in **Einzelarbeit** erledigt werden. Um Zeit zu sparen, kann dies **arbeitsteilig** geschehen, d.h., die Klasse wird in drei **Gruppen** eingeteilt, von denen jede eine Aufgabe bearbeitet und die Ergebnisse in jeweils einem kurzen Text fixiert. Alternativ dazu können alle Schülerinnen und Schüler alle Aufgaben bearbeiten, wobei sie zwei Aufgaben auswählen können, die sie lediglich in Stichworten bearbeiten, und zwei, die sie jeweils in einem ausformulierten Text bearbeiten.
- Aufgabe 4 kann zur Stärkung der **mündlichen Sprachkompetenz** eingesetzt werden. Die Schülerinnen und Schüler notieren Stichwörter für ein mündliches **Statement** zum Thema, das sie reihum formulieren.
- Aufgabe 5 kann in **Partnerarbeit** bearbeitet werden. Die Ergebnisse werden in einer **Tabelle** festgehalten und im anschließenden **Unterrichtsgespräch** präsentiert und diskutiert:

Recruiting Interns – All Work and No Pay?

cartoon 1: "work experience"	cartoon 2
young woman holding tray of coffee mugs	**job applicant being interviewed by a man sitting behind a desk**
not learning how to do challenging or specialized work; serving coffee to people who are working	man informs candidate that their part-time unpaid internship might lead to a full-time unpaid internship
doing an internship but not getting anything valuable out of it	interviewer: smiling candidate: worried/concerned look on his face
→ cartoon shows: "unpaid internships are exploitative" (ll. 42f.) → cartoon contradicts: "anything that gives people an opportunity to gain experience is a good thing" (ll. 47f.)	→ cartoon shows: "many internships are unpaid" (ll. 20f.)

- Im Anschluss an die Erarbeitung der Tabelle kann Cartoon 2 näher betrachtet und der Frage nachgegangen werden, ob die Darstellungsweise ironisch oder zynisch ist (Aufg. 6). Dies kann in einer kurzen **Diskussion** geschehen, bei der die Schülerinnen und Schüler noch einmal auf ihre eigenen Erfahrungen bei **Berufspraktika** zurückgreifen können.
- Aufgabe 7 wird in **Partnerarbeit** gelöst. Die Schülerinnen und Schüler füllen dazu eine **Tabelle** aus. Die Sicherung der Ergebnisse erfolgt im anschließenden Unterrichtsgespräch über **Folie**.

Recruiting Interns – All Work and No Pay?

the author's choice of words	**as a reflection of his stance on the issue**
the company wants them to feel transported into a magical new world where they might actually find a job	sarcastic tone, exaggeration, the author implies that finding a job is actually impossible and the company is trying to trick young people for profit
softies, complain, fret	people who are concerned about exploitation are painted as concerned and sympathetic perhaps overreacting?
if an internship is the first rung on the career ladder, the less-affluent will never climb it	descriptive language, underlines the classist/elitist/ divisive nature of unpaid internships
shrugs	headhunter Jim Tapper seems unconcerned about interns being unpaid/exploited; he is painted as dismissive/unsympathetic

- Aufgabe 8 kann im **Unterrichtsgespräch** diskutiert werden.
- Die Aufgaben 9 und 10 können als das Thema abschließende **Gruppenarbeit** eingesetzt werden, wobei die Gruppen bestimmen, welche der beiden Aufgaben sie bearbeiten werden. Die **Dialoge** werden im **Plenum** vorgeführt. Danach sollen die **Zuschauer** jeweils eine kurze **Rückmeldung** zu Sprache, Redestrategien und Inhalt geben.

SOLUTIONS AWARENESS

Have you ever applied for an internship? What were your experiences? Discuss in class.

Individual answers

SOLUTIONS COMPREHENSION

1. Point out why firms and interns might benefit from internships. Copy the grid and complete it:

Due to high unemployment, job seekers want to gain work experience any way they can, and an internship is often the only way to do this. Since many firms are worried about their economic situation and the future, they are especially careful about whom they hire, and offering internships lets them "test out" workers before hiring them permanently (ll. 7-10). Both sides profit by getting to know one another first before committing to each other, and statistics show that employees who first work as interns generally stay at a company longer (ll. 56-63).

2. State what profit the different recruitment agencies make.

Inspiring Interns charges employers £500 per month per intern and takes 10 % of the intern's starting salary if he/she is hired permanently. The agency earned around £1m gross profit last year (ll. 21-25).

Instant Impact Interns has flexible fees and earned £100,000 its first year (ll. 29-32).

3. Present what agencies do to make their clients a better fit for the job market and to increase the interns' chances of getting a permanent job.

Inspiring Interns gives its potential interns personality tests in order to find the best intern-company fit, helps them to improve their interviewing skills and suggests that candidates make a video CV (ll. 18-20).

4. Show why unpaid internships can widen the social gap.

Many internships are unpaid, yet many employers only want to hire people who have internship experience. Only those who come from affluent backgrounds can afford to do unpaid internships, which means that the rich/affluent will be better qualified for jobs while others will have to take unskilled jobs in order to earn money. Thus the rich will become more qualified and richer while the non-affluent will not (ll. 44ff.).

5. Describe cartoons 1 and 2 and relate your findings to the statements in the article.
→ Focus on Skills, Analysis of Visuals, p. 262

1: A young woman is holding a tray of coffee mugs, and the cartoon is titled "work experience". Clearly, she is not learning how to do challenging or specialized work, but is rather serving coffee to people who are working. It is possible that she is doing an internship but is not getting anything valuable out of it. This relates to the quote in the text that "unpaid internships are exploitative" (ll. 42f.), and contradicts the claim that "anything that gives people an opportunity to gain experience is a good thing" (ll. 47f.).

2: A job applicant is being interviewed by a man sitting behind a desk. The man informs the candidate that their part-time unpaid internship might lead to a full-time unpaid internship. The interviewer is smiling but the candidate has a worried/concerned look on his face. This relates to the statement in the text that "many internships are unpaid" (l. 21f.). In contrast to the text, however, this internship does not lead to a full-time (paid) job (cf. ll. 57f.).

SOLUTIONS ANALYSIS

6. Is cartoon 1 ironic or cynical? What is the effect on the readership?
→ Focus on Skills, Analysis of Visuals, p. 262

Cartoon 2 is cynical. It expresses a pessimistic view of the job market. Usually, a part-time/unpaid internship would later lead to a full-time/paid position. Here, there is no hope for the job candidate, and he only has more exploitation to look forward to, i.e. more work for no pay. However, the interviewer is presenting this as a positive thing ("an opportunity to gain even more job experience"). The reader sympathizes with the job candidate's situation and sees the interviewer as being unfair/exploitative.

7. Examine the choice of words* that is used to characterize the job agencies' role in the job market and show in how far it reflects the author's stance on the issue.
Example: l. 2: a wardrobe door → a reference to fantasy; disapproving, criticism
→ Focus on Skills, Analysis of a Non-Fictional Text, p. 258

- the company wants them to feel transported into a magical new world where they might actually find a job (ll.4 ff.) → sarcastic tone, exaggeration; the author implies that finding a job is actually impossible and the company is trying to trick young people for profit
- Softies, complain, fret (ll. 40, 42, 43) → people who are concerned about exploitation are painted as concerned and sympathetic; perhaps overreacting?

- If an internship is the first rung on the career ladder, the less-affluent will never climb it (ll. 44ff.). ➔ descriptive language, underlines the classist/elitist/divisive nature of unpaid internships
- shrugs (l. 48) ➔ headhunter Jim Tapper seems unconcerned about interns being unpaid/exploited; he is painted as dismissive/unsympathetic

8. Analyse how reliable the statements in this article are and why you believe/do not believe them.

Recruiters and intern agencies have an economic self-interest in finding and placing interns and presenting internships as worthwhile. Therefore, they are unlikely to admit that internships are exploitative. The statement by Jim Tapper, the headhunter ("Anything that gives people an opportunity to gain experience is a good thing", ll. 47f.), is thus less reliable.

Conversely, Intern Bridge admits that 77 % of unpaid interns must take second jobs, and that this may negatively impact their job performance at the internship (ll. 37-39). This means that Intern Bridge is genuinely interested in optimizing interns' experience, and therefore seems more reliable.

- Inspiring Interns ... boasts that it can provide ... claims that 65 % of the interns ... (ll. 11-15)

- Ben Rosen ... says it grossed around £1m last year (ll. 23ff.)

- Richard Bottner ... claims to have worked with 80 % of *Fortune 100* firms. (ll. 33ff.)

➔ The author creates distance between himself/herself and these statements. He/she presents these claims as told by others, but does not comment on their validity, thus making them seem somewhat less reliable.

Inspiring Interns: extremely high rate of processing applicants, high fees even though many internships are unpaid, very high profits (ll. 11-25) ➔ seems like they may be driven by profit, possibly exploitative

Instant Impact Interns: more specialized, flexible fees, no unpaid internships, much lower profits (ll. 26-32) ➔ more realistic, less concerned with profit, more concerned with fairness, finding a good fit, etc.

SOLUTIONS ACTIVITIES

9. Imagine: On a social network interns are discussing the changes in employee recruitment and their personal experiences. They also give each other tips on how to avoid being exploited and how to speak to one's superiors if one wants to learn more and become better acquainted with the job profile. Work in groups and present dialogues in class.

Sample dialogue:

#unpaidinternships #nofair #economiccrisisnotover

- If all interns refuse to work for free, employers can no longer exploit us.
- It's not fair, but working for free is better than just sitting at home doing nothing.
- Does anyone else have to empty rubbish bins? Is this normal? This seems rather demeaning to me.
- How much do you earn as an intern?
- Does it cost anything to use an intern agency? Did using one help you find paid work?
- What is your relationship like with your boss? How should I approach her about my problem? ...

10. Imagine: You and several other interns work for a very famous firm. The others have elected you to represent the works council (= Betriebsrat) and want you to convince the boss to change his/her recruitment policy and the way interns are treated. Work out the arguments that might be persuasive and then talk to your boss. The other 'interns' give you feedback on how convincing you were.

Sample dialogue:

intern:
- We are unhappy about the low wages/lack of wages/long working hours ...
- We are qualified, educated workers with university degrees, and we are unhappy that we are expected to perform menial tasks such as serving coffee/cleaning toilets/emptying rubbish bins/etc.
- The average national wage of interns is ☒. Therefore, we expect to be paid at least ☒.
- We are eager to learn skills such as ... and gain more experience in ...
- Instead of hiring interns and paying an agency, it would be better to hire interns directly and pay them better wages.

boss:
- I can understand your concerns. However, due to the state of the economy ...
- Everyone must start at the bottom. Those who work the hardest may later be hired permanently.
- That is an excellent point. That does seem unfair to me.
- I would be happy to bring this up with the general manager.
- It is too costly and time-consuming for us to find our own interns, so we need to go through an agency.

EU Migration to Germany – *Sprechen Sie Job?* (pp. 80–82)

About the text	With unrest in many Southern European countries, unemployment for young people is a large social issue. This text explains the choice of many of the Europeans to move to Germany. Though English is considered the working language for many countries, German is on the rise due to the large number of available jobs and a shortage of qualified applicants. Many qualified foreigners are therefore moving to Germany to find a position.
Level	● ● ○
Additional material	• GaST: no. 17 • Comprehension: no. 9

- Zur Bearbeitung der Awareness-Aufgabe können an die Schülerinnen und Schüler Moderationskarten ausgeteilt werden, auf die sie ihre Statements schreiben. Die Karten werden an die Tafel geheftet, wobei doppelte Karten aussortiert werden. Danach erhalten die Schülerinnen und Schüler pro Person eine bestimmte Anzahl von Klebepunkten, die sie an die Moderationskarten anbringen. Dann werden die Karten anhand der Anzahl der Klebepunkte geordnet.
- Die Comprehension-Aufgaben (Aufg. 1-3) werden in Einzelarbeit erledigt. Die Schülerinnen und Schüler erhalten den Auftrag, die Aufgaben 1 und 2 in Stichwörtern und Aufgabe 3 in einem vollständigen Text zu bearbeiten. Die Ergebnisse werden im Anschluss an die Erarbeitung in Gruppen zu vier Mitgliedern besprochen und ggf. korrigiert.
- Aufgabe 4 wird im Unterrichtsgespräch bearbeitet. Die Ergebnisse werden informell an der Tafel gesichert.
- Aufgabe 5 wird in Partnerarbeit bearbeitet. Zunächst konzentriert sich ein Partner auf das Poster, der andere auf den Cartoon. Danach füllen beide die unten stehende Tabelle aus. Die Ergebnissicherung erfolgt im Austausch mit einer weiteren Zweiergruppe.

EU Migration to Germany – Sprechen Sie Job?

	poster	cartoon
description	– suited men/women turned half-birds flying toward somewhere in unison – they carry briefcases showing their respective countries' flags – the flags represent crisis countries ➔ the workers are migrating to a better work situation to utilize their skills	– there is a large platform coloured in the way of the German flag – this 'platform' is topped by missing puzzle pieces that are coloured in the way of the crisis countries (Greece, Ireland, Spain, and Portugal) – there is a backpacker on top of each one ➔ the migrant workers are moving to Germany in order for work
similarities to text	– migrants go to Germany – they leave the crisis countries – they are in need of work – there are quite a few of these – men and women	
differences from text	– the cartoons look almost sad – Mr. Gomez admits that the German change was difficult but it never sounded as if he was saddened at his state – the images show more nations than the article – Ireland is especially surprising with it being so close to Britain	

- Der Recherche-Auftrag in **Aufgabe 6** kann in **häuslicher Arbeit** erledigt werden. Die mitgebrachten Cartoons werden im Klassenzimmer aufgehängt, zur Kenntnis genommen und in einer informellen **Diskussion** besprochen.
- Eine in diesem Zusammenhang hilfreiche **Internetseite** ist de.toonpool.com/tag_gallery_migration?offest=24.
- Beim Ausdrucken der Cartoons muss auf die Einhaltung geltenden Copyright-Bestimmungen und der Regelungen zur Veröffentlichung von Werken aus dem Internet geachtet werden.
- **Aufgabe 7** wird in **Einzelarbeit** bearbeitet. Nach der Fertigstellung der Texte werden diese in einer **Milling Around Sequenz** vorgelesen. Dazu gehen die Schülerinnen und Schüler im Zimmer umher und suchen auf das Kommando des Lehrers einen Partner bzw. eine Partnerin. Die Partner lesen sich gegenseitig ihre Texte vor.
- Vor der Bearbeitung von **Aufgabe 8** sollte die angegebene **Focus on Grammar-Seite** (SB, S. 301) besprochen werden. Das Thema kann in folgendem **Tafelanschrieb** zusammengefasst werden:

Modal Auxiliaries

modal auxiliary	past tense	all other tenses	German
can	could	to be able to	können
		to be allowed to	dürfen
must		to have to	müssen
may		to be allowed to	dürfen
must not		not to be allowed to	nicht dürfen
need not		not to have to	nicht brauchen nicht müssen

!
- no 3rd person -s
- infinitive without to
- no to do
- should = sollen

SOLUTIONS AWARENESS

In a Round Robin activity (→ FoM, p. 270), first reflect on possible reasons why Germany might be so attractive for migrants from many European countries. Make a ranking in a second step.

With a plethora of job opportunities and a workforce that lacks qualified workers, migrant workers see Germany as a natural landing spot in which they can not only live but also thrive. The country is also on the Euro which makes currency readily available throughout most of Europe and English has become more spoken throughout the workplace allowing for those that do not know German an opportunity.
1) available jobs
2) underqualified workers
3) same currency
4) English speaking workplace

SOLUTIONS COMPREHENSION

1. Give an outline of Daniel Gómez Garcia's education and his experience with the European labour market.
- Spanish Speaker (l. 7)
- passable English (l. 8)
- some German (l. 7)
- four month internship at Spanish Embassy in Berlin (ll. 12-13)
- worked with Excel at a rental firm (ll. 14-15)
- found a way to turn a low-paying job into a full-time accountant gig (ll. 15-16)

2. What does he think about Germany and the Germans?

Mr. Gómez thinks that Germans are challenging, 'always nagging you about recycling or noise or whatever' – but the language is the hardest part. (ll. 33-35)

3. Present the situations of the European labour market as depicted in the article.

Youth unemployment is high in some countries (Spain and Greece) while low in others (Germany) which allows for people to move from crisis countries to more stable environments (ll. 17-23). Migration is up in Germany by 15 % and from those crisis countries the newcomers to Germany are up 53 %from Spain and 78 % from Greece (ll. 24-29). The problem here is the language. With different languages in nearly every country, English has become the more dominate mode of communication but it is still not ubiquitous (ll. 31-41).

SOLUTIONS ANALYSIS

4. Categorize the type of text by examining particular structural and stylistic devices, e. g.:
- **the presentation of factual information**
- **the use of human interest (e. g. emotions)**
- **the use of language (e. g. choice of words, language register, etc.)**

→ Focus on Skills, Analysis of a Non-Fictional Text, p. 258
→ Focus on Skills, Basic Types of Non-Fictional Texts, p. 246

By seeing the text as a story of Mr Gómez' work experience (no jobs in Spain, learning of different languages, taking an unpaid internship, helping with Excel, finding a real job, ll. 1-15) are all using a narrative route to tell a sequence of events, one would say that the text is obviously narrative in nature. Those first sixteen lines definitely use the narrative arch of a story.
This changes in the next few paragraphs however. From ll. 17-55, the text becomes expository. Using a lot of statistics from the unemployment rates and language usage in the EU, the text gives a lot of telling facts about the employment situation in countries of crisis and more stable environment.

5. Describe the cartoon and the poster and compare their messages to the article. Which similarities and differences in their view of migrants (to Germany) can you detect?
→ Focus on Skills, Analysis of Visuals, p. 262

The poster shows a bunch of suited men/women turned half-birds flying toward somewhere in unison while carrying briefcases showing their respective countries' flags. All of these flags are representative of crisis countries; the no doubt interpretation being that these workers are migrating to a better work situation to utilize their skills.
The cartoon shows a large platform coloured in the way of the German flag. This 'platform' is topped by missing puzzle pieces that are coloured in the way of the crisis countries (Greece, Ireland, Spain, and Portugal) with a backpacker on top of each one. This symbolizes the fact that these migrant workers are moving to Germany in order to work.

Similarities: Migrants go to Germany, they leave the crisis countries, they are in need of work, and there are quite a few of these men and women.

Differences: The cartoons look almost sad, though Mr Gómez admits that the German change was difficult, it never sounded like he was saddened at his state. The images also show more nations than the article. Ireland is especially surprising with it being so close to England. The natural assumption is that the Irish would stay in the United Kingdom.

SOLUTIONS ACTIVITIES

@ **6. The poster promotes an international cartoon competition of 2007. Do research on the Internet and collect further cartoons on migration within Europe/to Germany. Display them in class and discuss their different views and messages.**

Individual answers for photos. Though many of the cartoons are depicting a mass exodus to Germany there are a few different views of the worker migrations in Europe. One had a large funnel pouring into the United States while another had British men and women protesting with signs saying 'British jobs for British Workers'. This being the case, it is evident that not everyone is happy that these workers migrate into the country while some countries accept the workers wholeheartedly.

7. Living and working in a foreign country can be an exciting experience – but there are some "challenges" as well. Put yourself in Daniel Gómez' position and write an e-mail to a friend in Spain. What (further) impressions might he have of the Germans and German culture? Which tips and pieces of advice might he give his friend in order to avoid clashes and misunderstandings?

Diego,

Although I love working here, the language is very difficult at some points. All sorts of pronunciation marks and almost guttural words, but I am getting the hang of it ... sort of. I have come to find out that German people are exceptionally straightforward. They don't seem to avoid any issues when speaking and just come right out with what they think. Sometimes this can be a little disconcerting for the unaware but, at the same time, it is refreshing that the culture here is so honest. If you want to avoid any confrontations or misunderstandings, just say what you think. Don't accept less than satisfactory service and never try to be sarcastic. Just be honest and straightforward and you will be able to join the workforce here in no time, well, once you learn a little bit of the language!

Your friend,
Daniel

SOLUTIONS GRAMMAR/LANGUAGE

8. Form groups and compile a "Germany Survival Guide" for foreign students and teenage migrants. Think about useful tips and recommendations that would help foreigners to avoid potential pitfalls. Use modal auxiliaries whenever possible – but be careful not to lecture (= belehren) or moralize.
Example: Germans are very thorough about recycling and sorting trash ... Therefore you should get informed about it ... You can get further information ... Another pitfall you should try to avoid is being noisy after 10 p.m. ...

For example:
Germans are very thorough about recycling and sorting trash. Therefore you should get informed about it. You can get further information at local recycling stations. Another pitfall you should try to avoid is being noisy after 10 p.m. There are quite strict regulations and if you break the law, you can even get fined. Getting fresh food, however, should not be a problem – there are local markets in most towns where you can buy nice fresh fruit and vegetables at affordable prices. Germans can sometimes be quite impatient and brusque. This might appear rude – however, usually they do not mean it that way. You must not take this personally – it is just a matter of habit and is not meant to offend anybody. Etc.

Professional Communication & Correspondence

Planning for Your Graduation Ball (Project) (pp. 83–84)

About the project	The project is simply trying to plan a graduation ball. With thoughts considering invitations, catering, location, flowers, decoration, music, drinks, and entertainment, the project consists of many pieces one has to think about before putting on a celebration.
Level	● ● ○

- Die folgenden Aufgaben können anhand der ausführlichen Anleitungen im Aufgabenapparat durchgeführt werden. Für die Bearbeitung sind zwei Doppelstunden, für die Präsentationen je nach Größe der Klasse eine bis zwei Doppelstunden zu veranschlagen. Während der Arbeit an den Projekten sollten den Schülerinnen und Schülern **Computer** mit **Internetanschluss**, ggf. örtliche Telefonbücher, **Kopierer** und **Moderationsmaterialien** zur Vorbereitung der Präsentationen zur Verfügung stehen. Der Aufgabe kann mehr Authentizität verliehen werden, wenn die von den Schülerinnen und Schülern erarbeiteten Ergebnisse tatsächlich für die Vorbereitungen zu einem Abiball oder Schulfest genutzt werden können.
- Zur Vorbereitung von Aufgabe 2 kann die Steigerung der Adjektive im Englischen wiederholt werden. Hierzu kann folgender Tafelanschrieb erstellt werden:

The comparison of adjectives

monosyllabic adjectives: -er, -est
old – older – oldest
thin – thinner – thinnest
large – larger – largest

disyllabic adjectives (-er, -le, -ow, -y): -er, -est
simple – simpler – simplest (also: more simple – most simple)
narrow – narrower – narrowest
happy – happier - happiest

all other adjectives: more, most
useful – more useful – most useful
beautiful – more beautiful – most beautiful

SOLUTIONS AWARENESS

Activities connected with your class graduation have to be planned a long time in advance and many different aspects and ideas have to be considered. In a Round Robin activity (→ FoM, p. 270), state and exchange your first thoughts and ideas for a graduation ball for your class.

I would think the first thing the planning committee would have to decide on would be the location. After a place is decided upon, the finer details can be hammered out (food, drinks, entertainment, etc.) and then the group can start making invitations and sending them out to the class. This way, no one will be invited until the rest of the evening is planned out and the celebration is fully prepared for.

SOLUTIONS ACTIVITIES

1. This project requires you to work independently as well as together with your group. It is based on the idea of the division of labour (work plan, cf. SB, p. 84).

a) Form groups of 8 – 9 students each. Each group has to develop a complete concept of how to plan and organize the graduation ball, with each of the group members choosing and taking over a particular area of work (e. g. the location, the music, etc.). After working individually (e. g. doing research, making an enquiry/order, etc.) the group finally has to assemble all the different "pieces" and present a complete concept for the graduation ball in class. The class then evaluates the different concepts of the groups and chooses the best idea.

Or:

b) The entire class develops one concept of how to plan and organize a graduation ball. Form groups, with each focusing on one particular area of work and taking all the necessary steps. Finally, the whole class assembles and combines the different results from the group work and works out a complete concept for the graduation ball.

Individual answers

SOLUTIONS GRAMMAR/LANGUAGE

2. In your group, think about catchy slogans to promote your graduation ball. Use superlatives and comparatives to evoke your schoolmates' interest: Example: Do not miss our sensational ball ... Enjoy the best music, entertainment ...

→ Focus on Grammar, Adjectives and Adverbs, p. 292

For example:

- Do not miss our sensational graduation ball.
- Enjoy the best music, entertainment and cocktails.
- Buy four tickets and get one for free!
- Want to spend a most entertaining evening? Come and visit us at ...!
- Get more for your money and join us ...
- etc.

Finding out About Interesting Products and Services – Making an Enquiry (pp. 85–86)

About the material	The recording is a conversation between an agency representative and a customer who is trying to book a band for a graduation ball. The recording illustrates proper etiquette and lines of questioning for a business enquiry.
Level	● ● ○
Additional material	● Audio CD 1, 10

- Zur Vorbereitung der **Hörverstehensübungen** (**Aufg. 1 und 2**) reduzieren die Schülerinnen und Schüler die in Aufgabe 1 aufgelisteten Fragen inhaltlich so, dass sie sich beim Hören auf die notwendigen Informationen konzentrieren können. Bei in dieser Art von Aufgabe noch ungeübten Klassen kann die erste Frage gemeinsam bearbeitet werden. Folgender **Heftaufschrieb** ist denkbar:

Listening Comprehension

a) who – on the other end?
b) position/function – in company?
c) requirement for entertainment?
d) prices?
e) requests – time of playing/breaks?
f) school's address?

- Die Ergebnisse können nach dem zweiten Hördurchgang im Unterrichtsgespräch verglichen werden.
- Die **Aufgaben 3 und 4** können in **Partnerarbeit** bearbeitet werden. Während ein Partner das Memo schreibt, erarbeitet der andere die Zusammenfassung. In beiden Fällen kann auf die Ergebnisse der Hörverstehensaufgabe rekurriert werden. Im Anschluss an die Erarbeitung werden die Ergebnisse mit einer anderen **Zweiergruppe** ausgetauscht und diskutiert.
- **Aufgabe 5** wird nach den Angaben im Aufgabenapparat durchgeführt. Die Präsentation in **Kleingruppen** bietet den Vorteil, dass die Schülerinnen und Schüler in einem geschützteren Raum agieren können. Gerade zurückhaltende oder schwächere Schüler haben hier erfahrungsgemäß weniger Scheu, frei zu reden. Der Lehrer bzw. die Lehrerin hat die Möglichkeit, mehrere Dialoge anzuhören und ggf. inhaltlich oder sprachlich zu korrigieren.
- **Aufgabe 6** kann als abschließende **Hausaufgabe** eingesetzt werden. Im Vorfeld sollten die angegebenen **Focus on Grammar-Seiten** (SB, S. 298 und 296) besprochen werden.

SOLUTIONS AWARENESS

The team responsible for the band and the music has seen an interesting Internet advert in which a British 5-member band performing in Germany and specializing on public events, company parties, etc. offers popular music and neo-classic rock. Larissa Schmidt from your team decides to phone the band to make a first enquiry.

Larissa makes a phone call to the agency, asking about prices, possible musical acts, and any possible discounts on booking someone.

SOLUTIONS COMPREHENSION

CD 1 10

1. Listen to the dialogue for a first time and try to answer the following questions:
a) Who is on the other end of the line?
b) What is the person's position and function in the company?
c) What are the requirements for the musical entertainment?
d) What are the prices offered?
e) Are there any particular requests concerning the time of playing and breaks, etc.?
f) What is the school's address?

→ Focus on Skills, Listening Comprehension, p. 244
→ Focus on Skills, Writing a Formal Letter, p. 282

a) Tommy Evans
b) public relations specialist
c) background music and music that invites people to dance
d) 3000 Euros for one event plus travel expenses and lodging
e) six to seven hours with a 15 minute break every two hours
f) Schiller Gymnasium
Weberstraße 456
45136 Essen
Germany
45136 Essen, Germany

2. Listen to the phone call for a second time and complete your notes.

./.

SOLUTIONS ACTIVITIES

3. As Tommy Evans, write a memo for your band members in which you include the following aspects:
a) What is the event the German students are planning?
b) What relevant data and requirements have to be considered by the band (if you get the order)?
c) What possible discounts or extras can be offered to the German students?
d) Explain why this is an interesting customer for the band.

a) a graduation ball
b) play for 6-7 hours with background music and dance inviting music
c) if they recommend the band to another company or group, they receive a ten percent discount
d) the band is British (not from Germany) and without a huge following, it would be fairly strange to travel to Germany for a small gathering such as this

CD 1 10 **4. As Larissa Schmidt, write a summary of the telephone conversation to present to your graduation ball team.**

I spoke with the public relations representative of the Royal Rockers. Everything he said sounded like they would fit the bill for our graduation ball but let me give you a rundown of what we talked about. Mr Evans said that the band can definitely play the six or seven hours, complete with background and dance music, but they do need a fifteen minute break every two hours. It'll cost around 3,000 euros, plus lodging and travel, but we can get a ten percent discount if we recommend them to another event. So, what do you guys think? Should we put in the order for them?

M **5. Together with a partner, use the role cards on p. 86 (Step 3).**
- **Choose one role and flesh out the given key words and phrases. Use a dictionary, the "Tips on vocab" box on p. 86 and/or the FoS "Writing a Formal Letter" (p. 282) in your Students' Book for further help.**
- **Act out your role play in class/your group.**

Afterwards:

- **Julia/Kai Hofmann: Write a short summary of the dialogue for your graduation ball team.**
- **Annieke/Piet Leuwen: Write a short abstract/summary for your boss in which you sum up the dialogue and make suggestions regarding what kind of offer should be made to the German school or why you think this is an interesting project.**

→ Focus on Skills, Writing a Summary, p. 288

Role Play: Individual Answers
Afterwards: Annieke/Piet: "We had a pretty straightforward conversation. Spoke about prices and I gauged their interest in the band and everything went well. It seems like this would be a good project for us. The German school seems to be very rational and polite, completely understanding of our prices and our break times and such, so I believe we should give them a decent offer, maybe a slight discount in prices, just because they are connected with other schools which they said they would happily recommend us if the band performs well."

SOLUTIONS GRAMMAR/LANGUAGE

6. Report to the group what Mr/Mrs Leuwen said on the phone. Use conditional sentences and indirect speech for your notes. Example: Mr/Mrs Leuwen wanted to know where our group had the Dutch company's name and address from ... he/she stressed that their company offers ...
→ Focus on Grammar, Indirect Speech, p. 298
→ Focus on Grammar, Conditional Sentences (If-Clauses), p. 296

For example:
Mr/Mrs Leuwen wanted to know where our group had the Dutch company's name and address from. He/she stressed that their company offered a wide variety of different entertainment programs, specializing in clowns and stand-up comedians. He/she explained that the company was specialized in public events,

company parties and graduation balls and parties. He/she offered to send us the company's catalogue. He /she apologized for not having any Demo-DVDs – but he/she referred to different show elements and performers that could be watched on the company's website. He/she told me that he/she could send us a price list that included the terms of contract. He/she explained that they could offer discounts if we booked a certain program and a certain number of show elements. She asked if we could offer a changing room for the performers and explained that we had to guarantee a 15-minute break to the performers every two hours. He/she promised she would mail the catalogue right away and thanked us for our interest.

When Customers Are Unhappy … Making a Complaint (pp. 87–88)

About the material	This recording is after the 5-men band performs at the graduation ball. After musical instrument malfunctions and the playing of unrequested music leave a bitter taste in the committee's mouth, Isabel calls the agency and makes a complaint.
Level	● ● ○
Additional material	• Audio CD 1, 11

- Im vorbereitenden Gespräch (**Awareness-Aufgabe**) sollten sich die Schülerinnen und Schüler überlegen, welche Strategien bei einem solchen Telefongespräch zum Erfolg führen könnten. Da vermutlich die wenigsten Schüler Erfahrungen in solchen Gesprächen haben, kann die Aufgabe auch unter Leitung des Lehrers bzw. der Lehrerin bearbeitet werden. Die erarbeiteten Strategien werden an der **Tafel** fixiert.
- Zur Vorbereitung der **Hörverstehensaufgaben** (**Aufg. 1 und 2**) reduzieren die Schülerinnen und Schüler die in Aufgabe 2 aufgeführten Fragen. Folgender **Heftaufschrieb** ist möglich:

Listening Comprehension

Who? ______________________________

Where? ______________________________

What? ______________________________

When? ______________________________

Why? ______________________________

a) reason for complaint?
b) what went wrong?
c) what – customer – order?
d) what – band – perform?
e) consequences for customer?
f) customer's demands?
g) what – agency – offer?

Die Ergebnisse der **Hörverstehensaufgaben** können im **Unterrichtsgespräch** verglichen und korrigiert werden.

- **Aufgabe 3** kann gemeinsam in der Klasse besprochen werden.
- Die bei der Beschäftigung mit **Aufgabe 4** erarbeiteten Ergebnisse können auf Karten geschrieben und im Klassenzimmer aufgehängt werden. Während eines **Museumsrundgangs** können die Schülerinnen und Schüler die Lösungsmöglichkeiten anderer Gruppen zur Kenntnis nehmen und darüber ins Gespräch kommen.
- Vor der Erledigung von **Aufgabe 5** sollten die angegebenen **Focus on Skills-Seiten** (SB, S. 274 und S. 283) zur Kenntnis genommen werden. Zu den verschiedenen Präsentationsmöglichkeiten vgl. LB, S. 134.

SOLUTIONS AWARENESS

Your team is responsible for the music and the band playing at the graduation ball. You wanted musical entertainment that would have met the wishes of the different guests at your party. Therefore you explained to the band that there were certain requirements to be fulfilled concerning the kind of music that you expected them to play. However, during the ball, the band ("The Royal Rockers") had problems with their instruments, and also the kind of music they played did not meet your expectations. Isabel Müller from your team decides to phone the band's agency in England to make a first complaint. In your team, think about possible pitfalls (*Fallstricke*) and how to avoid them. You do not want to be impolite, but you also want to make your point.

Possible pitfalls: losing all money without compensation, possible legal battle, burning a bridge to the agency
How to avoid: do not ask for full compensation, avoid litigation by coming to an understanding over the phone, do not blame the agency for the band's mistakes

SOLUTIONS COMPREHENSION

CD 1 11 **1. Listen to the dialogue for a first time and try to get the gist of the conversation (w-questions: who – where – what – when – why).**

Who: Charles Dougherty and Isabel Müller
Where: Performance at Graduation Ball in Germany or at the Agency in England
What: Performance issues with the band, Müller is making a complaint to Dougherty
When: N/A
Why: The band did not meet expectations due to instrument malfunction and musical cho ces

2. In a second listening pay attention to details and take notes on the following questions:
a) What is the reason for the complaint?
b) What went wrong at the graduation ball?
c) What exactly did the customer order?
d) What did the band perform at the graduation ball?
e) What were/are the consequences for the customer?
f) What are the customer's demands?
g) What does the agency offer?

a) instrument malfunction and poor song selection did not meet expectations
b) the instruments malfunctioned and the guests did not hear the type of music requested
c) 5-member Band "Royal Rockers" in the town hall, wanted them to play popular and neo-classical rock
d) schmaltzy old-fashioned dance hall music
e) people left early because they were disappointed
f) not willing to pay anything, expect some form of compensation
g) try to get a discount or some type of compensation

SOLUTIONS ANALYSIS

3. Taking a closer look at the agency's reaction: How does the man from the agency try to calm down the upset customer? What is his choice of words – and why does the customer get even more upset at first? Analyse and explain the situation.

He at first says he must speak with the band members to find out what 'actually' went wrong. This type of word choice signals that the agency's spokesman may believe the plaintiff is lying about what happened at the ball. He tries to calm her down by apologizing profusely and say that he will contact her but using the term 'actually' made her even more upset than at first. This lack of trust between agency and customer would cause tension and, as a professional, one should never imply that the customer may be bending the truth.

SOLUTIONS ACTIVITIES

4. Together with a partner, evaluate the phone conversation and think about alternative formulations.

- **What possible (further/different) demands could the customer make in order to convey how disastrous the problems with the band were for her and her class's graduation party?**
- **What could the agency's representative do to calm down the customer and create a win-win-situation – so that the company does not lose a new customer and potential future customers?**

a) Expecting full compensation is almost never going to happen. A different solution would be part compensation and a major discount for a future event with a different band as the performers. The customer may also ask for letters of apology to be sent out to all the ball-goers on behalf of the agency.

b) The representative, instead of offering a full compensation, could propose a free event for the customer to try and assuage any tension. That event could be given at the same locale and the agency could send the invitations and cater the event themselves while allowing a different band to play the type of music that was requested in the first place.

5. Together with a partner, first read the role cards given below, then work out a telephone conversation that is based on the given information and phrases.

- **Keep in mind that the roles are difficult here, with a complaining customer who is possibly very upset and frustrated – and the representative of the British company who has to calm down the customer and handle a very difficult situation. He/she does not want to lose a customer, but, of course, he/she also has to limit the costs for the company.**

Act out the conversation in class/your group and discuss the performance.

→ Focus on Skills, Telephoning, p. 274
→ Focus on Skills, Letter of Complaint, p. 283

"My name is Katja Wagner and I placed an order with your company. I have now received delivery but everything has gone wrong and I am not at all happy about the situation."
"What exactly happened?"
"The goods we ordered arrived today in a poor state. The boxes were damaged and had obviously got wet. And to make matters worse, instead of receiving the material on the Royals that we wanted to celebrate passing our exams, we found a lot of stuff – paper palms, shirts and the like – all relating to the topic of Hawaii. These are absolutely useless for our 'Meet the Royals' project. We had ordered garlands, table decoration and paper masks portraying the Royals."
"Oh, I am so sorry for the inconvenience here. I cannot understand why different products were delivered and with such poor care. It may have been a mix-up in the packing or with shipping. If you could email me a list of the wrongly delivered items at MarkKennedy@DecorativeSolutions.com I will make sure to check with the shipping department and to ask about replacement items."
"I will send you the list you need but I would really like to know who is responsible for the incorrect delivery."
"I cannot say at this point."
"We need the articles that we had originally ordered as soon as ever possible since the date for our celebrations is approaching and, of course, this must all be free of any additional charge."
"I will send replacements your way with an invoice tomorrow if possible and I will select a different delivery company but I will have to wait for the insurance company to react before sending it along. Once again, I am sorry for the inconvenience and I will make sure this is quickly and satisfactorily settled."

Life: A Box of Chocolates ...? – Coming to Grips with Reality

TM[1]	SB[2]	Author: Title of text	Type of text	Topic	Competences	Audio CD	Film CD-ROM	GaST[3]	Diff[4]	Comp[5]
Start-up Activities										
136	92	Mel Bochner: Oh Well	painting	the meaning of life from a teenage point of view	• analysing a visual • discussing an issue			no. 5, 19		
136	93	Teen Spirit: What's It Really Like to Be a Teenager	letters to the editor	Teenagers are talking about their lives and what they expect of the future	• discussing a statement			no. 5, 8, 11, 13, 18, 24		
Between Paradise and the "End of the World"? – How Children Live ... and Survive ...										
138	94	Moya Irvine: Child Labour – No School or Play for Millions of Young Workers	newspaper article, visual	child labour – facts and the legal situation the consequences of child labour the family situation attempts to improve the situation	• analysing the contents of a text • analysing statistical data • doing Internet research • creating a poster					
138	96	UNICEF: Child Deprivation Rates in Rich Countries	statistics	child deprivation rates in rich countries	• see above			no. 8		
142	97	Lucy Alibar: Juicy and Delicious – It's the End of the World, Y'All	play, painting	a teacher tells her students about the upcoming end of the world and encourages them to fight for themselves as the cavemen fought the dangerous aurochs the teacher sacrifices herself for her students	• analysing an excerpt from a play • analysing a visual • grammar: indirect speech			no. 4, 6	49	

1 TM = page in Teachers' Manual
2 SB = page in Students' Book
3 GaST = material in Grammar and Skills Trainer
4 Diff = page in Differenzierungsmaterial
5 Comp = material in Comprehension: Reading – Listening – Viewing

TM[1]	SB[2]	Author: Title of text	Type of text	Topic	Competences	Audio CD	Film CD-ROM	GaST[3]	Diff[4]	Comp[5]
142	101	Bruno Bettelheim: The Uses of Enchantment	lecture	typical features of a fairy tale and their effects on children the importance of fairy tales in our times	• see above			no. 13		
148	102	Lucy Alibar, Benh Zeitlin: Beasts of the Southern Wild	screenplay, cartoon, film still, film	Hushpuppy finally encounters the Aurochs they show respect for each other they become friends Wink is dying	• analysing a video • creating a storyboard • writing a summary • analysing a screenplay • analysing a visual • creative writing • doing Internet research • writing a review		5, 6	no. 4	57	no. 10
153	106	John Irving: Trying to Save Piggy Sneed	short story, photo	the mentally retarded Piggy Sneed and his way of earning his living the children's treatment of Piggy the narrator's involvement with the local fire department the fire at Piggy's farm the narrator's attempts to explain Piggy's disappearance his definition of a writer's tasks	• listening/reading comprehension • analysing the contents and style of a narrative • writing a characterization • analysing a photo • creative writing • grammar: thematic vocabulary	CD 1, 12		no. 6, 11	66	no. 11
161	111	Sarah O'Connor: London's Rail Stations Still Attract Vulnerable Runaways	newspaper article, website information	young people hiding in train stations possible dangers the work of Railway Children and New Horizon runaways in the UK	• reading a text • analysing a text • doing Internet research • grammar: the simple present			no. 8		
Youth in Crisis – Broken Dreams and Lost Hopes										
164	114	Generation Jobless	magazine article, statistics, cartoons	unemployment among young people world wide possible reasons the role of education solutions	• reading a text • analysing a text • analysing statistics • analysing visuals • holding a discussion • creative writing			no. 7, 8, 9	77	no. 12

TM[1]	SB[2]	Author: Title of text	Type of text	Topic	Competences	Audio CD	Film CD-ROM	GaST[3]	Diff[4]	Comp[5]
168	118	Hillary Clinton: Remarks on Youth	political speech	then U.S. Secretary of State, Hillary Clinton, talking to young people in Tunesia	• listening comprehension • analysing a speech • analysing the rendering of a speech	CD 2, 1		no. 7, 9, 24		no. 13
172	119	Christopher Dickey: Kill Zone	magazine article, statistics	the story of a 17-year-old African American who has lost family members, among them his mother, in street fights his plans for the future statistics of shootings in American cities the controversy about gun ownership	• analysing the contents and language of a text • analysing a video • analysing statistics • doing Internet research • preparing and giving a presentation • creative writing			no. 7, 8, 27		no. 14
176	123	Moms Demand Action on Gun Laws	adverts	children posing with guns and toys	• analysing visuals • creative writing • designing posters			no. 2, 20, 27		
	126	Thematic Vocabulary	Focus on Vocab							

Start-up (pp. 92–93)

About the artist	Mel Bochner is an American Conceptual artist. After receiving a Bachelor of Fine Arts from Carnegie Mellon University, Bochner began to put on exhibitions where he pioneered ideas such as using the gallery's walls and using photographic snapshots of performance pieces. His work has been featured at Carnegie Mellon, Yale, and the Museum of Modern Art.	- - -
About the picture **About the texts**	The picture is one of Bochner's 'Thesaurus Paintings' where he takes one word or phrase and then uses like terms to create the picture.	The four separate texts are four teens describing what it is like to be a teenager nowadays and the different ways they see the world.
Level	● ● ○	● ● ○
Additional material	GaST: no. 5, 19	GaST: no. 5, 8, 11, 12, 13, 18, 24

- **Aufgabe 1** kann zunächst **individuell** bearbeitet werden, indem jeder Schüler **Stichwörter** notiert, mithilfe derer er das Bild **mündlich** beschreibt. Der Austausch der Ergebnisse findet in **Kleingruppen** statt.

- Bei der Bearbeitung von **Aufgabe 2** werden die Schülerinnen und Schüler dazu aufgefordert, ihre Ideen nach dem Muster „I think the artist wants to express ...“ in wenigen Sätzen zu formulieren. Im Anschluss daran werden die verschiedenen Ideen in **Vierergruppen** diskutiert. Nach einer bestimmten Zeit wird die Diskussion abgebrochen und es finden sich neue Vierergruppen zusammen, die ihre Statements besprechen. Dieser Vorgang kann dreimal wiederholt werden. Dies gibt den Schülerinnen und Schülern die Möglichkeit, eine größere Anzahl verschiedener Meinungen zur Kenntnis zu nehmen.
- Die Bearbeitung der **Aufgaben 3 und 4** wird anhand der Aufgabenstellung organisiert.

SOLUTIONS START-UP ACTIVITIES

1. Describe the painting above using the words and phrases in the vocab box.
→ Focus on Skills, Analysis of Visuals, p. 262

All of these 'figures of speech' are 'catchphrases' that are 'sarcastic' remarks about just allowing life to happen as it will. With this type of downtrodden outlook, the 'colourful', 'bright, and cheery' look of the 'collage' as a whole is a rather ironic choice for colouration. The large lettering, 'use of bold letters', 'complete capitalization', and overall look of the words make this seem like a 'humourous' take on all of these 'synonymous' slogans though, once again, the sayings are more geared toward failings. All these 'words become images' due to the 'verbal jumble' in the 'geometrical shapes', truly a piece of art. (All items in quotations are from the vocab box.)

2. "Oh Well" is one of Bochner's so-called "Thesaurus Paintings" in which figures of speech describe a single idea or feeling. What is the underlying idea or feeling that is expressed here? Discuss in class.

The underlying feeling here is that no one can control what happens in life. The sayings are all about coming to grips with a reality that is uncontrollable and understanding that life will always move on whether or not you come to grips with that.

3. In a Think! Pair! Share! activity (→ FoM, p. 273), state and discuss your personal view of "what it's really like to be a teenager". Write down essential aspects on slips of paper and fix them to the board. Try to sort your statements into categories, e.g. job/work, friends, family, problems, etc.

When I was a teenager I worked in a grocery store. Not exactly the most glamorous of employment opportunities but it gave me the motivation to move on to university and find a better type of job. The big plus about the grocery store is that a lot of my friends worked there alongside me. I had a big group of friends from high school that were with me constantly. Whether it was getting food, going to the movies, playing some type of sport, even getting into trouble; we did everything together.
Unlike a lot of teens, I knew that I had a very good family life. Strong family bonds with my parents both working in high-paying fields – I did not have a lot to complain about when it came to my family life. My big problem as a teen was definitely just wanting to get away from my hometown. It was not my parents. Was not my friends. Wasn't even my school. I wanted to get away from the town because I found it boring. I knew that I was not the first person to want to leave and I know I will not be the last, but as soon as university came calling, I hit the road.

Andrew, South Bend

4. Divide the class into groups, each one dealing with a different statement and compare the views taken by British teenagers to your own findings. Discuss the similarities and disparities in class.

Similarities:
Wanting to be with your friends, text 1 says the 'worst thing is not having the freedom to go to a party' (ll. 9–11) and this obviously connects with my wanting to be with my friends.

Wanting to go to college (l. 14, text 2): 'I can't wait till I'm older, to drive or go to uni' is the same type of feeling I had when I was that age.
Needing to get away, with my home town being so boring, it was fairly easy to connect my wanting to leave with text 1's need for freedom (ll. 9–11).

Differences:
Strong family life: I never told my parents to 'stop stressing' (l. 16, text 2) and was much more in line with text 1 'I'll text her because I respect her' (ll. 14f.) though my parents weren't split up and I lived in a functional familial situation.
Employment feelings: I was not content to 'flip burgers' like in text 3 and I do not think it is easy to get a great job (ll. 12–14).
Political views: The entirety of text 4 is about political issues. When I was sixteen, I did not care about politics. That was a world away for me so it was not something I really looked into.

Between Paradise and the "End of the World"? – How Children Live … and Survive …

Moya Irvine

Child Labour – No School or Play for Millions of Young Workers (pp. 94–96)

and

Child Deprivation Rates in Rich Countries (p. 96)

About the author	Moya Irvine is a contributor to Fachzeitung's *Read On* section which describes some worldwide social issues.	- - -
About the text **About the chart**	The text is describing the situations of child labour throughout the world, highlighting the situation of Sima, a young Afghan brickmaker, and describing the rough lives of child workers throughout the world.	The chart is showing child deprivation rates by percentage in 29 countries. The statistics are determined by verifying children who lack two or more of fourteen categories
Level	●●○	●●○
Additional material	- - -	GaST: no. 8

- Die **Awareness-Aufgabe** wird anhand der Vorgaben im Schülerbuch durchgeführt.
- Die **Comprehension-Aufgaben (Aufg. 1 und 2)** werden in **Partnerarbeit** in **Stichwörtern** bearbeitet. Im Anschluss an die Erarbeitungsphase tauschen zunächst die beiden Partner ihre Ergebnisse aus. Im Anschluss daran diskutierten sie diese mit einer weiteren Zweiergruppe.
- Die **Aufgaben 3 und 4** werden zunächst **individuell** bearbeitet. Die Ergebnisse werden im Unterrichtsgespräch diskutiert und in folgendem **Tafelbild** gesichert:

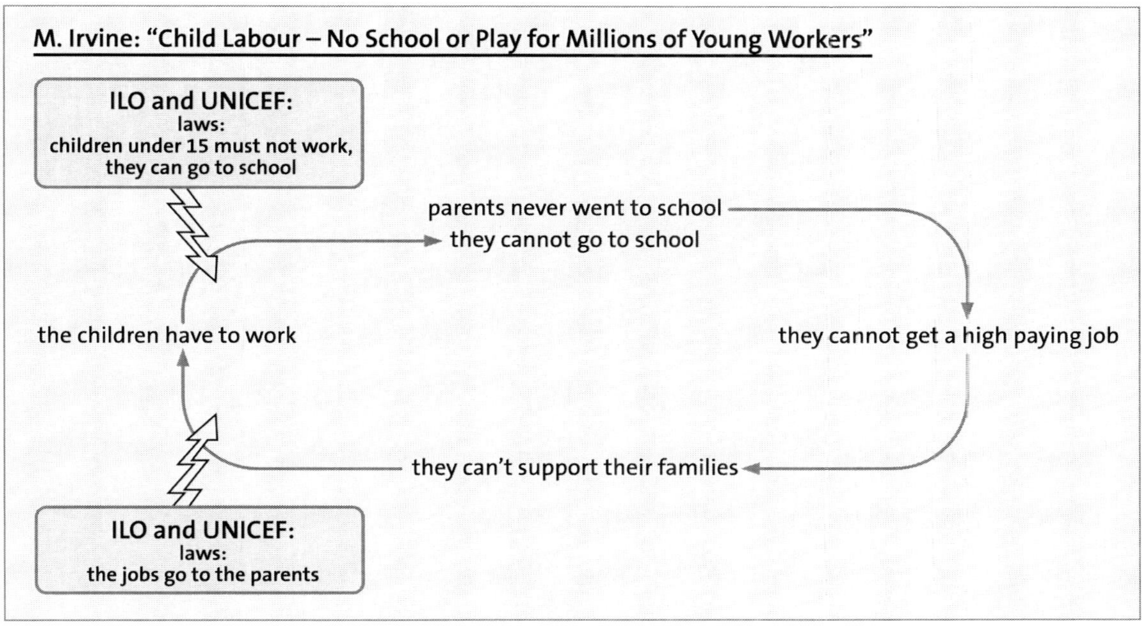

- **Aufgabe 5** kann zur Stärkung der **mündlichen Sprachkompetenz** eingesetzt werden, d.h., die Schülerinnen und Schüler werden aufgefordert, Simas Geschichte mündlich nachzuerzählen und die Situation des Mädchens zu erläutern.
- **Aufgabe 6** kann zunächst individuell gelöst werden. Die Ergebnisse werden im Anschluss im **Unterrichtsgespräch** gebündelt und informell an der **Tafel** gesichert.
- **Aufgabe 7** wird in **Partnerarbeit** bearbeitet, indem die Schülerinnen und Schüler gemeinsam mit ihrem Partner das Diagramm im Hinblick auf die Position Deutschlands beschreiben und interpretieren. Danach erstellen sie **individuell** einen **Text** (120–150 Wörter), der die Ergebnisse ihrer Untersuchung zusammenfasst. Die Texte werden danach im **Plenum** präsentiert.
- **Aufgabe 8** kann vor dem Hintergrund der in Aufgabe 7 erarbeiteten Ergebnisse ebenfalls in **Partnerarbeit** besprochen werden.
- Die in **Aufgabe 9** geforderte **Internetrecherche** kann in **häuslicher Arbeit** erfolgen. Die Diskussion der Ergebnisse findet in der Folgestunde im **Unterrichtsgespräch** statt.
- Für die Bearbeitung von **Aufgabe 10** ist eine Doppelstunde zu veranschlagen, für die **Präsentation** der Ergebnisse je nach Klassengröße eine Einzelstunde oder eine Doppelstunde. Um den Ergebnissen eine nachhaltigere Wirkung zu verschaffen, können die Präsentationen an zentralen Stellen im Schulhaus ausgestellt werden. Eine zeitaufwendigere Variante, die jedoch sicherlich lohnenswert ist, wäre die **Durchführung** einer der ersonnenen Kampagnen.
- **Aufgabe 11** kann als abschließende **Hausaufgabe** eingesetzt werden.

SOLUTIONS AWARENESS

In a Placemat Activity (→ FoM, p. 271), reflect on the question posed in the headline above: Do children (today) grow up "between paradise and the end of the world"?

In many ways, that feeling is not completely off-based. Many children from privileged countries grow up in a place that equates to a type of paradise whereas in the third-world countries and in families without homes and in debt, children may feel like they are living in an apocalyptic situation on a daily basis. There are definitely people who grow up with a niche somewhere in the middle of paradise and world's end, but for the vast majority of kids today, the either-or approach may be better suited than a ladder of bad to good.

SOLUTIONS COMPREHENSION

1. Read the newspaper article and describe the different kinds of work children are forced to do.

Mining and quarry work in which children have to use toxic chemicals, carry heavy loads and stand/dive/squat for hours (ll. 35–50). Brick-making transitions to having poor bone development and lung problems (ll. 48–50). Stitching footballs, shoes, and clothes are other types of work that are generally associated with child labour (l. 72.).

2. How are children protected by the UN Convention globally?

The Convention has allowed for the creation of volunteer programmes to stop children under fourteen from working and they give the jobs to the children's other family members while the kids go to school (ll. 73–78). The convention has also amasses 192 countries' ratifications of a law upping the minimum working age to 15 (ll. 21–30).

3. Sketch out the vicious circle in which children from poor countries find themselves trapped.

The parents of these children never went to school because they had to work. Because of the lack of education, they cannot get a high-paying job and remain poor. Due to the poverty of the family, the kids then have to work and cannot go to school. That all leads to the same situation when the children grow up. (ll. 51–55)

4. What is done to break this circle?

The ILO and UNICEF have made laws to stop children from under 15 from working and have ensure that those jobs will go to the kids' family members in order to pay for school. (ll. 73–78)

SOLUTIONS ANALYSIS

5. Explain the dreadful situation 11-year-old Afghan brickmaker Sima and her family have been forced into.

Sima, an eleven year old Afghani girl, works thirteen hours a day, six days a week for only a few dollars a day. She has been doing this work since she was six years old and stays in a hot, dusty, and dangerous environment (ll. 4–15). She needs to work because her family is quite poor. Due to a lack of education, her family was forced into the same type of job. Now they have no economic backing to send Sima to school so she is forced into the same situation, a reoccurring theme that is all too familiar in countries like Aghanistan (ll. 56–62).

6. Try to identify the author's stance on the matter by examining
- **the structure of the article (e.g. the line of argument*, introduction – main part – conclusion)**
- **her references and examples**
- **her choice of words in connection with the kind of work children have to do and its consequences**
- **the outlook taken at the end of the article.**

→ Focus on Skills, Analysis of a Non-Fictional Text, p. 258

Structure:
The structure is made with a bracketing stance. Irvine begins the essay with an anecdote of Sima, the young Afghani girl (ll. 1–15), then goes through many of the statistics concerning child labour laws throughout the world (ll. 16–62). She then backs these statistics with some of the moves trying to aid these child workers and what can be done in the future (ll. 63–88). The bracketing effect comes at the end however when Irvine ends the passage on a souring note (ll. 89–91). Stating that by 2016, when some of these laws come into effect, it will be too late for a child such as Sima. By taking into account the structure, one can assume that, although Irvine believes these steps are necessary, she thinks that it is going too slowly, leaving children behind.

References and Examples:
Using Sima as an example shows that Irvine obviously cares about what is happening to these children right here and now. Sima is in the situation in the present time, not someone who has come out of it. The references to the statistics show that Irvine is well-read on the subject at hand, knowledgeable of what is going on at a worldwide scale.

Choice of words:
The adjective use and the elaboration on Sima in particular here show that Irvine is quite compassionate about the subject. The description of the work (hot, dusty, dangerous, hard, toxic, slavery-like, ll. 8–13, 39–41) and the passages hitting on Sima's family (ll. 1–15 and 56–62) are written in a way to evoke empathy for the situation.

The outlook:

The final point, as stated previously, shows that Irvine is still unhappy with the efforts currently underway and demonstrates a need to do more.

7. **Analyse the bar chart on p. 96, depicting the child poverty and deprivation rates in (comparatively) rich countries. Although Germany belongs to the richest nations in the world, it only ranks 14th – which is below countries like Spain, Slovenia or the Czech Republic. Can you imagine why?**

→ **Focus on Skills, Analysis of Statistical Data, p. 261**

Though Germany is considered one of the wealthiest nations in the world, there is a possibility that the poorer families are overlooked when concerning wealth. Much like the United States, Germany's wealth could be contained within an elite class while the poor are left with next to nothing. Other possibilities are contained within the data factors. Those fourteen items that are considered in the chart may not necessarily equate to dramatic poverty in Germany if only two possible factors equal child deprivation. That being said, the data could be skewed in a way favouring some countries over others.
The fourteen items are not only including monetary and economic points. If the list was only concerning those types of things, then Germany would be almost entirely off of the list. Some of these items concern leisure time with children (4–7, 13, 14) and if many children do not always get the chance to participate in these types of activities then it may be a familial or cultural move to steer away from them. The items are written in a generalized way that does not necessarily mean that the children are poor. Deprivation, to many kids, may not mean 'only receiving secondhand clothes'. There are families with many children in Germany just as with any country so secondhand clothes may come second nature and a 'quiet' place to study' would be hard to find.

8. **Closely examine the 14 items listed in the box beside the bar chart. Do you agree with the ranking – and do you think this list is complete/exhaustive? If not – which further items would you add or exchange?**

Many, if not all, of the fourteen items are agreeable topics that one could help define child deprivation. This however is in no way exhaustive when concerning things like transportation, more education opportunities, and social opportunities (access to a car or bus, advanced placement opportunities, athletic involvement). The ranking is not necessarily perfect either. The first three are easily agreeable but the other eleven are fairly interchangeable depending upon the judge. I personally would think access to a quiet place for homework and an internet connection are both more important to a child's advancement than indoor games and money for school trips. In addition to that, transportation access is a key figure for most people in the world today and I would think that could replace 7, 8, 13, and 14.

SOLUTIONS ACTIVITIES

Webcode SNG-40175-005 @

9. **The British tour operator *Virgin Holidays* offers sustainable holidays worldwide and is determined to make the business as well as customers contribute to protecting the environment and supporting local communities in holiday destinations. Do research on the initiatives "Helping Youth Shine" and "Our Human Nature Promise" using the links provided on the webcode. Do you consider tourism to be a promising way to support poor people? Discuss.**

Seeing some of the opportunities on the websites, I would say that tourism is a very promising way to aid the poor. Tourism growth promotes more opportunities for employment which would help to alleviate the poverty in many nations. The Caribbean countries in particular use tourism as a main source of income for many of the islands which is a boon on the economy. This type of support can also be used as a source of oppression however, as vendors can employ the poor people for next to nothing and, in many places, have no negative consequence as their profits are off book.

10. **June 12 is the "World Day against Child Labour". In groups, design posters, flyers, etc. in which you inform about child labour and child poverty. Collect ideas and organize a campaign at your school that motivates people to take action and participate in initiatives that support children and help fight child labour and poverty worldwide.**

One way to begin creating awareness for child labour is to have a research competition giving away some type of product made by an anti-child-labour group. By having a great many people do research on companies and countries that are invested in ending child labour, students will gain knowledge on both the economic parties involved and the people afflicted by it. One such topic would be explaining how buying

Toms shoes over Nike or Reebok would support the cause against child labour. Toms not only provides well-made shoes without the use of child labour, but it also gives a free pair of shoes to the needy with every purchase made whereas Adidas and Nike have both been rocked by labour scandals in the past.

Webcode SNG-40175-005 @ **11. Do research on labels and organizations that are dedicated to ending illegal child labour, e. g. GoodWeave International or Rugmark. The links on the webcode provide you with further information.**

GoodWeave International, formerly known as Rugmark, is a network of non-profit organizations dedicated to ending illegal child labour in the rug making industry. Founded in 1994 by children's rights activist Kailash Satyarthi, it provides a certification program that allows companies that pass inspection to attach a logo certifying that their product is made without child labour.
Childfund International is an Indian based program dedicated to ending child labour. They are particularly interested in Indian child labour but their funds and programs reach out globally, most funds go to an education program that starts the children early in order to stop them from going to the workforce.
The Cotton Campaign was established in Uzbekistan in order to end the child labor that runs rampant there. Every year the government of Uzbekistan forcibly mobilizes over a million children, teachers, public servants and employees of private businesses for the manual harvesting of cotton. Because of this, the campaign has publicly renounced the use of children in the cotton fields and called for an ILO investigation of the cotton harvest.

Lucy Alibar

Juicy and Delicious – It's the End of the World, Y'All (pp. 97–100)

and

Bruno Bettelheim

The Uses of Enchantment (p. 101)

About the author	Lucy Alibar lived in relative obscurity, making it pay-check to pay-check and working three jobs until her screenplay, *Beasts of the Southern Wild*, was picked up by the Sundance Institute. Born and raised in rural Florida, she moved to New York before making it big with her Academy Award winning screenplay.	Bruno Bettelheim was an Austrian-born American child psychologist and writer. He gained an international reputation for his work on Freud, psychoanalysis, and emotionally disturbed children.
About the texts	The text is an excerpt from *Beasts of the Southern Wild*. This is a screenplay written by Lucy Alibar and directed/cowritten by Behn Zeitlin who adapted the film from Alibar's one act play. The film centers on six-year old Hushpuppy, who has to navigate her ramshackle bayou community after the icecaps have melted and unleashed an ancient herd of Aurochs.	The text is an excerpt from Bruno Bettelheim's *The Uses of Enchantment*. In this excerpt, Bettelheim is describing how fairy tales offer up a form of escape that not only connects to a child's inner yearnings of security and company, but also proves to be a more mature outlet in which children can escape reality in a mature way that still allows obstacles to be overcome in a realistic way.
Level	●●●	●●○
Additional material	Differenzierungsmaterial, p. 49 GaST: no. 4, 6 GaST: no. 13	

- Das in Aufgabe 1 vorgeschlagene Gruppenpuzzle wird nach den Anweisungen im Schülerbuch durchgeführt.

- Aufgabe 2 kann in Partnerarbeit durchgeführt werden. Die Schülerinnen und Schüler füllen dazu eine Tabelle aus (s. Lösungsvorschlag unten). Die Sicherung der Ergebnisse erfolgt im Unterrichtsgespräch über Folie.
- Vor der Bearbeitung von Aufgabe 3 sollten sich die Schülerinnen und Schüler mit den im Schülerbuch genannten Focus on Facts- und Focus on Language-Seiten (SB, S. 254 und S. 308) vertraut machen.
  Um Bearbeitungszeit zu sparen, kann den Schülerinnen und Schülern ein Arbeitsblatt (s.u.) ausgeteilt werden, auf dem die Regieanweisungen bereits abgedruckt sind. Die Schüler ergänzen die unterschiedliche Wirkung der Anweisungen.

The effect of the stage directions in "Juicy and Delicious"

Stage directions	***How they create tension/build up suspense***
– *Hushpuppy at school. A bunch of scrappy kids who are at the bottom of the food chain.* (ll. 1-2)	
– *MISS BATHSHEBA stands before the picture of an Aurochs.* (ll. 3-4)	
– *We hear the sound of ice cracking – a glacier coming loose and falling into the sea.* (ll. 5-6)	
– *A lemon hits the window. Then several more.*	
– *The sound of cracking ice. Outside, grits fall from the sky. It's kind of scary.* (ll. 39-40)	
– *We hear all kinds of apocalyptic noises. AUROCHS pawing at the door.* (ll. 48-49)	
– *The sounds of animals howling at the door are overwhelming.* (ll. 71-72)	
– *MISS BATHSHEBA pulls out a bucket from behind the desk. The bucket is filled with weapons – lemons, eggs, grits, and flowers. It also contains three beers, which she opens with her teeth.* (ll. 80-83)	
– *She hands the children the weapons. Kisses them all good-bye.* (ll. 87-88)	
– *An AUROCHS bursts through the window and leaps onstage. MISS Bathsheba leaps into its arms.* (ll. 96-97)	
– *The AUROCHS carries MISS BATHSHEBA off.* (l. 100)	

Die Ergebnisse werden ebenfalls im **Unterrichtsgespräch** über **Folie** gesichert.

- **Aufgabe 4** wird zunächst individuell in **Stichwörtern** bearbeitet. Die Ergebnisse werden im **Plenum** diskutiert und können informell an der **Tafel** gesichert werden.
- **Aufgabe 5** kann in Gruppen zu vier Schülerinnen und Schülern bearbeitet werden. Die beiden Leitfragen werden zunächst diskutiert. Die Ergebnisse des in Aufgabenteil b) geforderten Vergleichs werden auf **Folie** in **Tabellenform** (s. Lösungsvorschlag unten) gesichert. Die Folien werden im Anschluss an die Erarbeitungsphase präsentiert. Bei großen Lerngruppen kann der Lehrer bzw. die Lehrerin einige gelungene oder inhaltlich interessante Folien für die Präsentation auswählen.
- **Aufgabe 6** kann im **Unterrichtsgespräch** diskutiert werden.
- **Aufgabe 7** wird als abschließende **Hausaufgabe** eingesetzt. Im Vorfeld sollten die genannten **Focus on Grammar-Seiten** (SB, S. 305, S. 298) besprochen werden. Zu einem möglichen **Grammatikaufschrieb** vgl. LB, S. 51 (Text: *Harold and Maude*).

SOLUTIONS AWARENESS

In groups, look at the prehistoric cave painting which depicts a herd of stampeding prehistoric animals. Try to imagine the atmosphere: Which sounds can you hear, what can you smell – is the light bright or gloomy – what are the predominant colours?

Individual answers

SOLUTIONS COMPREHENSION

1. Before you start reading the excerpt from the play, divide the class into 3 – 6 groups of which 1 – 2 groups focus on one different part. However, all groups should read the introductory lines (ll. 1 – 6). Take notes on:

Introduction:

- **the overall atmosphere in the classroom**
  typical classroom: teacher standing in front of a picture; magical element: sound of glacier and the sea, unclear where it's coming from

- **the description of the children**
  scrappy, bottom of the food chain → dirty, rough, poor

Part I (Lesson One):

- **how Ms Bathsheba introduces her lesson**
  Welcome to Miss Bathsheba's Finishing school! Welcome to the End of the World!

- **her description of the aurochs in the past**
  the world was swarming with aurochs; big, hungry, liked to eat babies

- **the life of the ancient cavemen and their families**
  lived in caves, lived in terror of the aurochs; poor, stupid, small; loved their children

- **the return of the aurochs**
  when the aurochs returned, the cavemen fought them and most cavemen died in the process, but they managed to kill all the aurochs to save their children

- **the collapse of the universe**
  universe is coming unrendered; things are dying ain't supposed to die; fabric of the universe is coming undone

Part 2 (Last Lesson):

- **the apocalyptic scenario of the returning beasts**
  apocalyptic noises, aurochs pawing at the door; end of the world; quantum physical Holocaust, surrounded by a million beasts of the Southern Wild that want to eat the survivors

- **Ms Bathsheba's "last meal"**
  a warm bottle of beer

- **Ms Bathsheba's tricky question about the warm bottle of beer and how long she can wait to drink it**
  she finds a cooler and wants to be able to drink the beer cold before the beasts find and eat her

- **the children's answer to her question**
  Hushpuppy answers 2 hours, Joy answers 11 minutes. Joy is correct and the teacher says she would survive.

Part 3 (The Presents/Weapons):

- **the "stuff" the children have to deal with**
  apocalypse, mercy, aurochs, grace

- **the presents/weapons Ms Bathsheba gives to the children**
  lemons, eggs, grits, flowers, three beers

- **what she wants to do for the children**
  she wants to defend them and show them that someone is taking care of them

- **her final orders and pieces of advice**
  be sweet; take care of each other; don't be ashamed to cry, because most people who live good lives cry a lot

- **how she sacrifices herself.**
  She jumps into the aurochs' arms and lets herself be carried away to save the children.

In a next step, the groups remix (see diagram in SB, p. 99) and exchange their results.

SOLUTIONS ANALYSIS

2. Explain how Ms Bathsheba connects the cavemen of prehistory and the children and their families of today.

Cavemen	Children/families today
• ... couldn't do nothing (l. 20) • ... they were too poor, too stupid, too small (l. 21) • ... a long, painful death (l. 22) • ... but ... (l. 23) • ... cavemen love their children (l. 23) • ... in their ... stupid cavemen way they were going to do something ... (ll. 23ff.) • The cavemen took whatever weapons they could find ... (ll. 26f.) • ... blood, and eyeballs and intestines ... (l. 30) • ... most of the cavemen lay dead (ll. 31f.) → cavemen fight against the Aurochs → most of the cavemen die, but manage to kill the Aurochs → cavemen sacrifice themselves for their children	• Miss Bathsheba's Finishing School (l. 8) • someone was taking care ... (l. 35) • Because they loved you with their whole, huge, breaking, stupid little hearts ... (ll. 37f.) • The universe is coming unrendered ... (l. 43) • Don't be scairt (l. 46) • Miss Bathsheba is gonna teach y'all how to live through it (ll. 46f.) • Here's y'all's last lesson. Imagine ... (ll. 51ff.) • Good girl! You gonna survive! (l. 69) • I'm'll defend y'all. (l. 85) • Bathsheba took care of y'all (l. 86) • Kisses them all good-bye. (ll. 87f.) • Be sweet. Take care of each other. ... don't never be ashamed ... (ll. 91ff.) • ... live a life that's ... good ... (l. 94) → parents are absent → Miss Bathsheba is authority/strong role model → supports and encourages the children → Miss Bathsheba sacrifices herself for the children

3. Take a closer look at the stage directions* and illustrate how they build up tension throughout the scene.
→ Focus on Facts, Drama and Theatre, p. 254
→ Focus on Language, Literary Terms, p. 308

Stage directions	How they create tension/build up suspense
• Hushpuppy at school. A bunch of scrappy kids who are at the bottom of the food chain. (ll. 1f.)	• children appear to be weak, poor and helpless
• MISS BATHSHEBA stands before the picture of an AUROCHS. (ll. 3f.)	• evokes an impression of strength and ancient culture
• We hear the sound of ice cracking – a glacier coming loose and falling into the sea. (ll. 5f.)	• fear of global warming; rising sea levels; people are in danger
• A lemon hits the window. Then several more. (l. 10)	• absurd and grotesque; surprising and unexpected
• The sound of cracking ice. Outside, grits fall from the sky. It's kind of scary. (ll. 39f.)	• absurd situation; apocalyptic scenario
• We hear all kinds of apocalyptic noises. AUROCHS pawing at the door. (ll. 48f.)	• prehistory is reappearing; frightening and absurd scenario
• The sounds of animals howling at the door are overwhelming. (ll. 71f.)	• apocalyptic and dangerous scenario

Stage directions	How they create tension/build up suspense
• MISS BATHSHEBA pulls out a bucket from behind the desk. The bucket is filled with weapons – lemons, eggs, grits, and flowers. It also contains three beers, which she opens with her teeth. (ll. 80ff.)	• grotesque and absurd; combination of contradictory elements: self-defence and humour (beer)
• She hands the children the weapons. Kisses them all good-bye. (ll. 87f.)	• like a loving mother
• An AUROCHS bursts through the window and leaps onstage. MISS BATHSHEBA leaps into its arms. (ll. 96f.)	• rising tension; self-sacrifice ➔ climax
• The AUROCHS carries MISS BATHSHEBA off. (l. 100)	• the children are left behind – are helpless – their protective "shield" is gone

4. The given scene depicts an unusual combination of fairy tale elements (Long, long ago, when we all ..., ll. 14f.) and very realistic elements of an apocalyptic disaster (ll. 39f., ll. 48f.). Try to find examples from the text and say whether the scene can be interpreted as a fairy tale*.
Example: (ll. 5f.) glacier breaking loose ... ➔ global warming; melting ice caps ... (ll. 20f.) stupid cavemen ... ➔ ignorant people ...

For example:
This scene contains many fairy tale-like elements and can thus be interpreted as a kind of fairy tale. Most strikingly, the scene is a lesson in how to survive an apocalypse. Ms Bathsheba's lesson in survival is like the moral lesson of many fairy tales: One must be brave and strong in the face of adversity in order to overcome it. Also like in fairy tales, Ms Bathsheba is a heroine who saves the day. Like the cavemen, she sacrifices herself in order to save the children (ll. 96ff.). Moreover, the scene contains several magical, unexplained elements, which are a typical feature of fairy tales, such as lemons and grits falling from the sky (ll. 10, 39, etc.)... and extinct creatures suddenly appearing (ll. 48f., 96f.), ... etc.

SOLUTIONS ACTIVITIES

5. Not only Ms Bathsheba's lesson is like a fairy tale, the entire scene is mysterious, magic and unreal. On the one hand her "lesson" is extremely scary and shocking, on the other hand, Ms Bathsheba encourages and consoles (= trösten) the children.

a) In a first step, discuss whether or not you consider these to be useful pedagogic principles and

For example:

- I think Ms Bathsheba's lesson is one of the most important and valuable lesson someone can learn in life: that children are cared for, and that there are people who are willing to sacrifice themselves so that they can live. This lesson will make the children feel comforted, confident and protected their whole lives. ... She accomplishes this by...
- In my opinion, the lesson does not have much practical value. The teacher does not make clear how the children are supposed to defend themselves with lemons, eggs and flowers. ...
- ...

b) compare your findings to the lecture "The Uses of Enchantment" by Bruno Bettelheim (p. 101).

For example:

Ms Bathsheba's lesson	"The Uses of Enchantment"
Two very short lessons are presented: the story of the cavemen and the aurochs and the survival scenario with the warm beer.	It is characteristic of fairy tales to **state an existential dilemma briefly and pointedly**. This permits the child to come to grips with the problem in its most essential form... (ll. 1–4)
Ms Bathsheba drives the point home that the children are loved and cared for, even before they were born, and that she herself will take care of them (ll. 34ff., 85f.).	The fairy tale, by contrast, takes these **existential anxieties and dilemmas** very seriously and addresses itself directly to them: the **need to be loved** and **the fear that one is thought worthless**; the love of life and the fear of death. (ll. 15–19)
scrappy kids; bottom of the food chain ➔ kids are vulnerable and lack protection from families, community Ms Bathsheba teaches the kids not to be afraid and how to survive the apocalypse.	Today children **no longer grow up in the security of an extended family**, or of a **well-integrated community**. Therefore, even more than at the times fairy tales were invented, it is important to provide the modern child with images of **heroes who have to go into the world all by themselves** and who, although originally ignorant of the ultimate things, **find secure places in the world** by following their right way with **deep inner confidence.** (l. 30ff.)
Ms Bathsheba tells the children that "there are presents flying at you from every corner of the universe" (ll. 78f.).	The fate of these heroes convinces the child that, like them, he may feel outcast and **abandoned** in the world, groping in the dark, but, like them, in the course of his life he will be **guided step by step, and given help when it is needed**. (ll. 43ff.)

6. Against the background of your findings in task 5, have a look at the painting "Oh Well" (p. 92) again. Compare the catchphrases given here to the pieces of advice Ms Bathsheba gives to the children. Which do you consider to be the better alternative? Discuss.

Oh well ...	Ms Bathsheba ...
• Oh well, ... • That's the way it goes ...	• When in a disastrous situation, focus on enjoying a last cold beer (ll. 53ff.) ➔ live in the moment, focus on the positive
• It is what it is ...	• "Don't be scairt. Miss Bathsheba is gonna teach y'all how to live through it" (ll. 46f.)
• What can you do? • What will be will be.	• "they were going to do something about it" (l. 25)
• Don't get your hopes up.	• "You gonna survive!" (l. 69) ➔ hope
• Shit happens.	• "Apocalypse. Mercy. Aurochs. Grace. ... And there are presents flying at you from every corner of the universe. Look. Pay attention." (ll. 76, 78f.) ➔ focus on the positive
• Nothing ever changes.	• "And the cavemen couldn't do nothing about it ..." (ll. 20f.)/"they were going to do something about it" (l. 25) ➔ cavemen made a change, killed the aurochs
• Just learn to live with it ...	• "And the cavemen couldn't do nothing about it ..." (ll. 20f.)

SOLUTIONS GRAMMAR/LANGUAGE

7. **After school, Hushpuppy tells his dad about the unusual lesson. Use indirect speech and remember to backshift the tenses. Additionally, think about appropriate introductory verbs and phrases. Example: Ms Bathsheba explained to us that long ago, when people had lived in caves, the world had been swarming with ...**

→ Focus on Grammar, Tenses, p. 305
→ Focus on Grammar, Indirect Speech, p. 298

For example:
Mrs Bathsheba explained to us that long ago when people had lived in caves the world had been swarming with aurochs. Then she welcomed us to the end of the world. That was really scary. She said that the aurochs had been big and hungry and had eaten babies. The perfect breakfast for an aurochs had been a juicy little cave baby, she told us. Then she added that the aurochs had gobbled the babies right in front of their parents and they had not been able to anything about it because they had been too stupid and too small.
But next Mrs Bathsheba pointed out that finally the cavemen had started to fight for their babies because they had loved them. She went on to say that the cavemen had taken weapons and had waged a brutal war on the aurochs and had finally defeated and killed them.
Finally Mrs Bathsheba said that that was the last lesson and we all heard scary noises from outside the classroom. She told us that all of us would survive if we paid attention to her and did as she said. Then she gave us weapons out of a bucket in order to defend ourselves with lemons, eggs, grits and flowers. Then she kissed us all good-bye and leapt into the arms of the aurochs that burst through the classroom window.

Lucy Alibar, Benh Zeitlin

Beasts of the Southern Wild (pp. 102–105)

About the authors	Lucy Alibar lived in relative obscurity, making it pay-check to pay-check and working three jobs until her screenplay, *Beasts of the Southern Wild*, was picked up by the Sundance Institute. Born and raised in rural Florida, she moved to New York before making it big with her Academy Award winning screenplay. Behn Zeitlin is an American filmmaker, composer, and animator. Born to a pair of writers in New York City, it was not until the release of *Beasts of the Southern Wild* at the Sundance Festival where he found fame.
About the text	The text is an excerpt from the screenplay *Beasts of the Southern Wild*. It is telling of the climactic meeting between Hushpuppy, the six-year old main character, and the mother aurochs right before Hushpuppy's father passes away.
Level	● ● ●
Additional material	Film CD-ROM, 5 + 6 Differenzierungsmaterial, p. 57 GaST: no. 4 Comprehension: no. 10

- Die **Awareness-Aufgabe** wird in **Partnerarbeit** erledigt. Nachdem die Schülerinnen und Schüler den Cartoon mithilfe der Leitfrage analysiert haben, schreiben sie ihre Antworten nach dem Muster „A child's imagination is ..." auf **Moderationskarten**, die an einer Moderationswand oder an der Pinnwand im Klassenzimmer aufgehängt werden. Im Anschluss daran lesen und diskutieren die Schülerinnen und Schüler die Definitionen ihrer Mitschüler. Am Ende der Beschäftigung mit dem Text kann unter der Leitfrage „Was this only a child's imagination?" noch einmal auf diese Definitionen rekurriert werden.
- **Aufgabe 2** wird nach den Anweisungen in der Aufgabenstellung durchgeführt. Dazu müssen den Schülerinnen und Schülern die notwendigen Materialien wie Tapetenrollen oder andere große Papierbögen, Schreibzeug, Stifte, Klebeband etc. zur Verfügung gestellt werden.

- **Aufgabe 3** kann als die den ersten Teil der Beschäftigung mit dem Text abschließende **Hausaufgabe** eingesetzt werden. Ggf. muss mit den Schülerinnen und Schülern im Vorfeld die angegebene **Focus on Skills-Seite** (SB, S. 288) besprochen werden.
- **Aufgabe 4** wird **individuell** bearbeitet. Die Ergebnisse werden im **Unterrichtsgespräch** diskutiert und auf **Folie** gesichert (s. Lösungsvorschlag unten).
- **Aufgabe 5** kann in **Einzel- oder Partnerarbeit** durchgeführt werden. Die Ergebnisse werden im **Unterrichtsgespräch** ausgetauscht und informell an der **Tafel** gesichert.
- Die Bearbeitung von **Aufgabe 6** kann in **Partnerarbeit** erfolgen. Im anschließenden Unterrichtsgespräch werden die Ergebnisse besprochen und folgendermaßen an der **Tafel** gesichert:

Alibar, Zeitlin, "Beasts of the Southern Wild"

Hushpuppy encountering the Aurochs	***Hushpuppy experiencing her father's death***
she can hear the Aurochs approaching	she knows that her father is dying ("I gotta take care of mine", l. 59)
all the others flee in terror, *she is probably terrified herself* *Hushpuppy refuses to run (l. 18)* *when facing the Aurochs, she does not flinch, even though she is very close to it (ll. 30ff.)*	 *she does not break down in tears when her father holds her for the last time and he dies (ll. 75ff.)*
→ Hushpuppy's encounter with the Aurochs ...	*is a metaphor for how she deals with her father's death.*

- Die folgende Aufgabe (Aufg. 7) kann in einem informellen **Unterrichtsgespräch** bearbeitet werden. Die Ergebnisse werden in wenigen Sätzen an der **Tafel** gesichert.
- Die Beschreibung des **Screenshots** (Aufg. 8) erfolgt in **Einzelarbeit**. Die Schülerinnen und Schüler notieren dazu Stichwörter, die sie in anschließenden **mündlichen Kurzvorträgen** elaborieren.
- **Aufgabe 9** kann als **Hausaufgabe** eingesetzt werden. Die Klasse wird in vier **Gruppen** eingeteilt, von denen jede eine der in der Aufgabenstellung angegebenen Varianten bearbeitet. In der Folgestunde werden Gruppen von vier Schülern gebildet, sodass in jeder Gruppe Aufgabenvariante a), b), c) und d) vertreten ist. Die Schülerinnen und Schüler tauschen ihre Ergebnisse in den Gruppen aus und besprechen sie.
- Zur Bearbeitung von **Aufgabe 10** muss sichergestellt sein, dass die Schülerinnen und Schüler Zugang zum **Internet** haben.
- **Aufgabe 11** kann in **Gruppen** bearbeitet werden, wobei die Rezensionen nach der gemeinsamen Lektüre der **Focus on Skills-Seiten** (SB, S. 256 und S. 279) individuell erstellt werden. Die Ergebnisse werden im **Plenum** vorgelesen und ggf. diskutiert.
- **Aufgabe 12** wird im gemeinsamen **Unterrichtsgespräch** bearbeitet.

SOLUTIONS AWARENESS

What does the cartoon below tell you about a child's imagination?

./.

SOLUTIONS COMPREHENSION

Webcode SNG-40175-006 @

1. Pre-reading:
Before you start reading the screenplay, watch the video featurette provided on the webcode and get an overview of the plot of the film.

./.

2. The scene at hand intertwines two different storylines:
- **the death of Hushpuppy's father Wink and**
- **Hushpuppy's ultimate confrontation with the Aurochs.**

Divide the class into groups and read the text. Then, work out storyboards on wallpaper that visualize the development of the plot and the interconnections (see example in SB, p. 104). Display the storyboards in class and compare and discuss them.
→ Focus on Facts, Screenplays and Storyboards, p. 249

Individual solutions

3. Write a summary of the story of about 150 words, using your findings from the storyboards.
→ Focus on Skills, Writing a Summary, p. 288

Five-year-old Hushpuppy lives with her dying father, Wink, in the Louisiana bayou. Hushpuppy and her three young friends are approaching the house where her father lies dying. They are being chased by four Aurochs – gigantic prehistoric creatures. While her friends run away screaming, Hushpuppy is brave and does not run. She stops on a bridge near the house, looks at her father as he watches her from the house and turns to face the Aurochs. She is face to face with one of the Aurochs but she remains calm, and the Aurochs become docile and lie down together. Hushpuppy then dismisses the Aurochs, saying that she now has to "take care of mine". The Aurochs get up and leave. She goes into the house where Wink lies dying in his bed. She approaches him and promises him she will not cry. The two embrace and Wink dies, but Hushpuppy stays strong. (150 words)

SOLUTIONS ANALYSIS

4. Closely examine the two paragraphs depicting Hushpuppy's confrontation with the Aurochs (ll. 27 – 53). Explain how Hushpuppy stands her ground.
→ Focus on Skills, Analysis of a Screenplay, p. 257

Aurochs	Hushpuppy	Hushpuppy's reaction
• a deafening stampede	• walks steadily forward	→ refusing to run → face ... determined
• bear down	• stands her ground	
• inconceivably large	• balls her fists	→ unafraid, courageous
• roars	• ---	
• inches away	• doesn't flinch	→ brave; fearless
• stops	• ---	
• snorts	• her hair is blown back	→ not afraid of physical closeness
• stares face to face	• raises her chin	→ defiance; courage
• sniffs	• ---	
• takes a step backwards	• stands her ground	→ courage
• sniffs		
• a loud snort (purr?)		
• lowers her head		
• eyes well with emotion		→ courage
• steps back		

Aurochs	Hushpuppy	Hushpuppy's reaction
• take a knee	• ferocious warrior	
• lies down	↓	→ affection; emotional closeness
• joyful, lazy repass		
• grunts		→ understanding → "You're my friend ..."
	• strange calm; a smile; peace and affection; sees Aurochs as her equal	
	• she can understand	

5. Illustrate what the Aurochs and Hushpuppy have in common.

Although the Aurochs and Hushpuppy are very different at first glance physically – Hushpuppy is a tiny girl and the Aurochs are massive (l. 9), boar-like creatures – they share some similar inner qualities. Both the Aurochs and Hushpuppy are strong and ferocious, but at the same time calm and unafraid. The Aurochs are physically large, strong and swift, but when they finally catch up to Hushpuppy, they become gentle and docile (cf. ll. 33ff.). Similarly, Hushpuppy has deep reserves of inner strength. She does not lose self-control or back down in the face of the Aurochs, but instead "balls her fists" (l. 30) and "doesn't flinch" (l. 34). Although the Aurochs are chasing her and she is surely frightened, she resists the urge to run and instead faces her fears head-on. She is described as a "ferocious warrior" (l. 46), and the Aurochs recognize and respect this as being like themselves (ll. 45f.). They are both described as being "children" (l. 53): Hushpuppy is literally a child, and the creatures are childlike in that they are simple and not malicious. The Aurochs lie down calmly, and Hushpuppy has a moment of calm and peace (ll. 47–53). (195 words)

(also cf. solution no. 4)

6. Interpret Hushpuppy's final thoughts (ll. 90 – 93) and correlate them to Ms Bathsheba's lesson about the pre-historic cavemen (p. 98).

Hushpuppy speculates that the scientists of the future will know about her and her father and how they lived in the Bathtub (ll. 90–93). This is similar to Ms Bathsheba's story about the cavemen and the Aurochs, in which she describes what the cavemen were like and how they sacrificed themselves to save their children (ll. 14–38). Ms Bathsheba emphasizes that the cavemen loved the children of today before they even knew them (ll. 35–38). Likewise, the children are learning the stories of ancient cavemen. This shows how the past, present and future are interconnected. This interconnectedness is also underlined by Hushpuppy's claim that the scientists of the future will know about her and her father's story.

7. Interpret the deeper symbolic meaning of Hushpuppy's encounter with the Aurochs and explain how it prepares her for her father's death and makes her strong and mature.

Hushpuppy's encounter with the Aurochs can be seen as a metaphor for how she deals with her father's death. She can hear the Aurochs approaching, and even though her friends flee in terror, screaming (ll. 15ff.), and she is probably terrified herself, Hushpuppy refuses to run (l. 18). Similarly, she knows that her father is dying ("I gotta take care of mine", l. 59). When facing the Aurochs, she does not flinch, even though she is mere inches away from a gigantic, terrifying beast (ll. 30ff.). She also does not break down in tears when her father holds her for the last time and he dies (ll. 75ff.). In both instances, Hushpuppy refuses to give in to fear, and instead looks at her fears head-on. By looking at scary situations instead of running away, her fears become less scary, and she is in control.

8. Look at the screenshot on p. 105. Describe it and compare it to the situation depicted in the text. Which aspects does it emphasize?
→ Focus on Skills, Analysis of Visuals, p. 262

(cf. solution no. 4)

SOLUTIONS ACTIVITIES

9. There is hardly any dialogue or direct speech in the given scene. Choose one of the options below and write an interior monologue that reflects one character's thoughts and emotions:
a) Hushpuppy encountering the Aurochs
b) the Aurochs when it is face to face with Hushpuppy
c) Hushpuppy when she is together with her dad
d) Wink while watching his daughter facing the Aurochs
Finally, read out your monologues in class and discuss the different perspectives taken.

./.

Webcode SNG-40175-006 @ **10. Do further research on the background of the film and its protagonists using the links provided on the webcode. Be prepared to give a short presentation about your character or topic.**

Individual answers

5 **11. Work with the scene *The Aurochs* on the CD-Rom and evaluate how the film renders the play and the screenplay. Write a critical review of about 250 words.**
→ Focus on Skills, Analysis of a Film Scene, p. 256
→ Focus on Skills, Writing a Comment and a Review, p. 279

Individual answers, e. g.:
This scene does an effective job of portraying the death of a young girl's father from her point of view. It does this by using various cinematic devices that make the scene exceptionally beautiful and emotional ...
... the use of swelling orchestral music → very moving atmosphere, suspense
... the exchanging of glances between Hushpuppy and Wink without words → suspense; understanding and closeness between father and daughter
... close-up of Wink watching Hushpuppy → disbelief, wonder
... shaky camera movements → creates a feeling of realness (stampeding Aurochs coming closer, Hushpuppy walking towards the shack)
... the contrast between the relative sizes Aurochs and Hushpuppy → emphasizes how small and brave Hushpuppy is
... Aurochs are fantasy creatures, yet totally realistic-looking
... close-up shot of the Aurochs' eye → gentleness, kindness, relief
... the scene falls into complete silence when Hushpuppy finally speaks → underlines the seriousness/solemnity of the situation
... camera follows Hushpuppy as she approaches the shack to show her point of view
... Hushpuppy feeds Wink and herself → symbolizes that she is now taking on the role of a caregiver, self-sufficiency
... gentle, tender music underlines the tender moment between father and daughter as Wink is dying
...
In sum, I found this scene to be very moving and tender. Its mixing of magical and real elements makes it an awe-inspiring fantasy, yet it is still relatable.

6 **12. After working with the excerpt from the *Making of* of *Beasts of the Southern Wild* discuss whether it is a good idea to disenchant the audience like this and bring them "back to reality".**

Individual answers, e. g.:

- This scene gives additional information that helps the viewer to appreciate not only the technical and artistic aspects of filmmaking, but also the director's intention and the main themes the movie is trying to convey. This helps the viewer to learn about the true message of the film ...

- I think it is better to let the viewer come to their own interpretation while watching the film. If you reveal the director's intention and meaning, it competes with the viewer's own personal reaction. Showing how the Aurochs were created makes the scene less magical ...

John Irving

Trying to Save Piggy Sneed (pp. 106–110)

About the author	John Irving is an American novelist and Academy Award winning screenwriter. After achieving worldwide success with his novel *The World According to Garp*, he has gone on to write nineteen more pieces of critically acclaimed writing, five of which have been made into films.
About the text	The text is the story *Trying to Save Piggy Sneed*. Piggy Sneed was a mentally handicapped man whom Irving knew when he was a child. The story itself takes place the night Sneed's farm burned down which coincidentally was the night Irving knew he wanted to become a writer.
Level	● ● ●
Additional material	Audio CD 1, 12 Differenzierungsmaterial, p. 66 GaST: no. 6, 11 Comprehension: no. 11

- Die **Awareness-Aufgabe** kann in **Kleingruppen** bearbeitet werden. Im Anschluss an die Bearbeitung werden die Gruppenergebnisse kurz im **Plenum** vorgestellt.
- Die Länge des Textes erfordert bei der Überprüfung des Hörverstehens ein hohes Maß an Konzentration. Daher kann der Text beim ersten Hördurchgang auch **zweigeteilt präsentiert** werden. Nach dem Anhören der ersten drei Tracks tauschen sich die Schülerinnen und Schüler kurz über den Inhalt und die Abschnittsüberschriften aus, danach folgt der zweite Teil der Präsentation des Textes mit der Diskussion der Ergebnisse. Diese können informell an der **Tafel** gesichert werden.
- Für die Bearbeitung der Detailfragen **reduzieren** die Schülerinnen und Schüler diese auf die wichtigsten Aspekte, sodass ihnen das Identifizieren der relevanten Informationen im Text keine Schwierigkeiten bereitet. Folgender **Heftaufschrieb** ist denkbar:

J. Irving,"Trying to Save Piggy Sneed"

1) *Piggy's outward appearance/living conditions*
2) *the Volunteer Fire Brigade*
3) *children's behaviour – Piggy*
4) *firefighters' reactions – fire + Piggy's death/disappearance*
5) *narrator's/his grandmother's explanations*

Die Ergebnisse werden im **Unterrichtsgespräch** ausgetauscht und **stichwortartig** an der **Tafel** gesichert. Alternativ dazu können die Schülerinnen und Schüler ihre Ergebnisse selbstständig mithilfe des Textes überprüfen. Dies kann in **Partnerarbeit** geschehen.

- **Aufgabe 3** kann in **Partnerarbeit** erledigt werden. Die Schülerinnen und Schüler füllen dazu eine **Tabelle** aus (s. Lösungsvorschlag unten). Die Ergebnisse werden gemeinsam besprochen und über **Folie** gesichert.
- **Aufgabe 4** wird im gemeinsamen **Unterrichtsgespräch** bearbeitet. Während den Schülerinnen und Schülern der Begriff „Ironie" geläufig sein dürfte, muss unter Umständen erläutert werden, was man unter „schwarzem Humor" versteht.
- Zur Bearbeitung von **Aufgabe 5** übernehmen die Schülerinnen und Schüler folgende **Tabelle** ins Heft. Bei in der rhetorischen Analyse von Texten ungeübten Lerngruppen kann die erste Spalte vorgegeben werden. Die Schülerinnen und Schüler müssen dann nur noch Beispiele suchen und deren Funktion erläutern. Im Vorfeld sollte die angegebene **Focus on Skills-Seite** (SB, S. 255) zur Kenntnis genommen werden. Die Sicherung der Ergebnisse erfolgt über **Folie**.

stylistic devices	**examples**	**function**
formal language register		
informal language register; simple/paratactic sentence structure		
choice of words		
choice of words		
choice of words		
emotive words		

- Vor der Bearbeitung von **Aufgabe 6** müssen die Begriffe *panoramic presentation* und *scenic presentation* geklärt werden. Kurzdefinitionen finden sich in der Übersicht über literarische Begriffe (**Focus on Skills**, S. 309). Die Aufgabe wird zunächst in **Partnerarbeit** bearbeitet. Im Anschluss an die Erarbeitungsphase werden die Ergebnisse im **Unterrichtsgespräch** gebündelt und in folgendem **Tafelbild** gesichert:

Modes of presentation

Trying to Save Piggy Sneed

↙ ↘

scenic presentation
- *how the children sneak up and scare Piggy (ll. 41–55)*
- *when the Fire Department Truck encounters Piggy on the road (ll. 87–104)*
- *the night the pig barn burned down (ll. 105–201)*
- *the author recollects a conversation with his grandmother (ll. 209-229)*

↓

description of specific incidents; use of dialogues, thoughts, specific actions covers only minutes or hours

panoramic presentation
- *why the narrator became a writer (ll. 1–4)*
- *Piggy: comes twice a week for many years (ll. 56f.)*
- *the narrator: he changes as he grows older: they learn more about Piggy Sneed, join the Volunteer Fire Department (ll. 68–86)*

↓

brief description and reflection of events that take place over a long period of time

↓

The author jumps back and forth between these modes of presentation to show the reader

particular, important events as they occurred … *and then reflect on them at a distance as an adult or to describe the passage of time in a short amount of text.*

- **Aufgabe 7** kann in **Partnerarbeit** bearbeitet werden. Ein Partner sucht Beispiele für direkte, der andere für indirekte Charakterisierungen. Die Ergebnisse werden in **Tabellen** eingetragen (s. Lösungsvorschlag unten). Die Diskussion und ggf. Korrektur der Ergebnisse erfolgt im Austausch mit einer weiteren Zweiergruppe. In Anschluss daran übernehmen die Schüler die Ergebnisse ihrer Partner.
- Die **Aufgaben 8 und 9** können alternativ als diesen Teil der Arbeit mit dem Text abschließende **Hausaufgabe** eingesetzt werden.
- **Aufgabe 10** wird anhand der Erläuterungen im Schülerbuch durchgeführt.
- In einer **Doppelstunde** zum Thema *Creative Writing* können die **Aufgaben 11 und 12** bearbeitet werden. Dabei bleibt es dem einzelnen Schüler überlassen, welche Aufgabe er auswählt. Die Präsentation der Ergebnisse erfolgt in einer **Milling Around Phase**, in der die Schülerinnen und Schüler im Klassenzimmer umhergehen und sich auf ein Signal des Lehrers bzw. der Lehrerin ihre Arbeiten gegenseitig vorlesen. Dieser Vorgang kann bis zu dreimal wiederholt werden.
- **Aufgabe 13** kann als abschließende **Hausaufgabe** erteilt werden.

SOLUTIONS AWARENESS

The protagonist of this memoir, Piggy Sneed, is a mentally retarded man who collects garbage and raises pigs to earn his living. Why do you think might an author choose somebody like this to write a story about? Speculate about possible reasons and a storyline.

Individual answers

unusual character, unique person, possibly an underdog/outcast character ...
stories about how this unusual person interacts with "normal" people; adventures with pigs ...

SOLUTIONS COMPREHENSION

CD 1 12

1. **In a first listening/reading, try to get a general understanding of the story and find a suitable headline for each track/part of the text.**
   1: The Front Street children and Piggy Sneed, the retarded garbage collector
   2: The Stratham Volunteer Fire Department
   3: The fire at Piggy Sneed's pig barn
   4: Speculations about Piggy Sneed's whereabouts (Aufenthaltsort)
   5: A writer's business

2. **Then, in a second listening/reading, take notes on the following aspects:**

   - **Piggy Sneed's outward appearance and his living conditions**
   He has certain piglike facial expressions and gestures; he squints his eyes; he has pink wrinkles in his neck; he has pale bristles around his jaw. As result of his mental retardation he cannot talk; he squeals or oinks like a pig.
   He lives together with his pigs that he raises on a small pig farm which consists of one single barn. He collects garbage.

   - **the Volunteer Fire Brigade and its members**
   They could be called for service and felt important. They liked the drill and the excitement.

   - **the behaviour of the Front Street children towards Piggy Sneed**
   They surprise him and leap out at him and squeal at him "Piggy! Piggy! .... Oink Wee!" which makes him panic and squeal back at the children.
   The children imagine Piggy was having a party with his pig friends; they were drinking and dancing together; one of the pigs was jealous and burned another pig's tail ...

   - **the firefighters' reaction to the fire and Piggy's death/disappearance**
   At Piggy's house, they encounter the biggest fire Stratham has ever seen: the sheds of the barn have burst from the heat, everything was on fire and manure from the pigs was everywhere. They decide to let the fire burn itself out because of the enormous heat.
   Afterwards, when Piggy cannot be found, they imagine Piggy is either staying in Florida or in Europe.

- **the narrator's and his grandmother's explanations.**

His bad conscience and the power of his imagination as a writer allowed him to save Piggy Sneed in his stories. His grandmother thinks her grandson just has a bad conscience and should have treated Piggy Sneed better when he was alive.

3. As you may have noticed while listening/reading, the first-person narrator gives additional personal comments on the situation described in each paragraph. Make some additional short notes on these comments and remarks.

quote/line(s)	meaning/what it tells about the narrator
(ll. 1 – 4) I think I have become a writer ...	**➔ reason/motivation for becoming a writer; memories of his grandmother ...**
(ll. 58 – 61) Now I would like to say ...	➔ narrator wishes he was more ashamed of what he did and that he had changed to become a kinder person, but he hasn't
(ll. 75ff.) I felt so superior to Stratham that it surprises me, now, that ...	➔ realizes that he was very arrogant towards his town
(l. 104) I suppose I heard my voice, too. (ll. 146f.) ... It may have been me.	➔ ashamed about how he behaved, reluctant to admit it to himself and the reader
(ll. 148–155) One reason I'm a writer ... I began my first story.	➔ even though he and the boys were behaving in bad taste, he realizes now that it was their way of coping with the situation; although he is ashamed, he feels sympathy; used humour and storytelling to cope with grief/regret

SOLUTIONS ANALYSIS

4. Examine the specific tone of the narration. Explain how the author uses (black) humour and irony when he describes the behaviour and reaction of the "Front Street children".
➔ Focus on Skills, Analysis of a Fictional Text, p. 255

The author makes frequent references to death that are rather shocking and paradoxical. He uses images of death/violence/terror in everyday descriptions, and uses a light-heartened tone or focuses on superficial matters when speaking about situations that are actually quite serious and gruesome. In other words, he uses the opposite tone that one would expect, given the subject matter, creating an undertone of irony. He also employs exaggerated and grotesque imagery to evoke humour.

- you would have to be dead to look worse than Piggy Sneed looked to us children on Front Street (ll. 8f.)
- When *he* got hungry (we imagined), he ate a pig. 'A whole pig, at once,' we used to say ... (ll. 33f.)
- ... as if we'd stuck him with the slaughtering knife ... as if he'd caught us trying to bleed him in his sleep (ll. 50ff.)
- When the terror passed, we couldn't wait for him to come again. He came twice a week. What a luxury! (ll. 55ff.)
- The night that Piggy Sneed's place burned, we Front Street children were imagining a larkish, if somewhat retarded spectacle ... (ll. 106–108)
- we were afraid the new paint, or the new tires, would blister in the heat. 'No point in wasting the water'... (ll. 132ff.)
- there would be less of a mess that way (ll. 139f.)

5. Analyse the use of particular stylistic devices and explain their function, e.g.
- **the language register and particular choice of words**
- **positive and negative emotive words in connection with a particular character.**

➔ Focus on Skills, Analysis of a Fictional Text, p. 255

stylistic devices	examples	function
formal language register	specifically (l. 2), possible exception (l. 6) absorbed, uniqueness (l. 20) proximity (l. 21) etc.	underlines author's adult voice as a writer ➔ more educated, thoughtful
informal language register simple/paratactic sentence structure	shit (l. 156) He just got sick of pigs (l. 162) Somehow pigs were easier. Maybe friendlier (l. 186) etc.	the Front Street children's simple manner of speaking; more childlike, naïve; simplicity, meanness, vulgarity
choice of words	Mr Sneed (l. 228) Piggy Sneed	grandmother uses formal, respectful from of address, while Front Street kids call him "Piggy" ➔ contrasts kindness of grandmother with mean kids
choice of words	jut (l. 22) rooting (l. 24) squinted, twitched (l. 25) snout, deep pink wrinkles (l. 26) bristles (l. 27) short, heavy, strong (l. 29) heaved, hurled (l. 30) grunted, squealed, oinked (ll. 38f.) panicked, lurching, mindlessly (l. 48)	describes Piggy Sneed's similarity to pigs; he is more animal/pig than human
choice of words	good manners, polite, kind, in heaven's name, kindness, more pity than vexation, patted my hand, dear	describes grandmother's kindness in contrast to the Front Street kids
emotive words	panicked (l. 48) slaughtering knife (l. 51) bleed him in his sleep (ll. 52f.) red-eyed screaming monster (l. 98) etc.	evokes pity for Piggy Sneed, underlines cruelty of the children's actions

6. Explain the different modes of presentation* that are used to emphasize the message of the text.
➔ Focus on Language, Literary Terms, p. 308

The author employs **scenic presentation** in order to describe how specific incidents took place. These are marked by the use of dialogue, thoughts, specific actions, etc. and cover a time period of minutes/hours:

- ll. 41–55: how the children would sneak up and scare Piggy Sneed
- ll. 87–104: incident that happened one night when the Fire Department truck encountered Piggy on the road and passed him
- ll. 105–201: the night the pig barn burned down
- ll. 209–229: the author recollects a conversation with his grandmother

He uses **panoramic presentation** to briefly describe and reflect on events that take place over a much longer period of time, i.e. years, in only a few sentences:

- ll. 1–4: why the narrator became a writer
- ll. 56f.: Piggy would come around twice a week over the course of many years
- ll. 68–86: the narrator tells how he changed as he grew older: they learned more about Piggy Sneed, joined the Volunteer Fire Department

➔ The author jumps back and forth between these modes of presentation to show the reader particular, important events as they occurred (scenic) and then reflect on them at a distance as an adult or to describe the passage of time in a short amount of text (panoramic).

7. Give examples of the use of direct and indirect characterization and explain their function and effect.
→ Focus on Skills, Characterization of a Figure in Literature, p. 264

direct characterization (examples)	function/effect
my grandmother was always polite and ... (l. 4)	the narrator's grandmother is a special person
His name was Piggy Sneed. He smelled worse than ... (ll. 5f.)	evoking a feeling of nausea
... he lived on a pig farm ... (l. 12)	evoking a feeling of disgust
... we children imagined ... (l. 17)	exaggeration
His face would jut ... (l. 22)	evoking pity and fun at the same time
... he couldn't talk ... (l. 35)	Piggy is helpless – at the children's mercy
... his language; he learned it from his friends (ll. 39f.)	Piggy is more pig than human
... the code of small towns is simple ... (ll. 61f.)	criticism of people's attitudes
... many forms of cruelty are ignored (ll. 62f.)	people are ignorant and cruel
It made us ... important. (l. 84)	the Front Street children feel important
Poor Piggy Sneed ... so drunk and foul as to be barely human ... (ll. 100f.)	evoking pity/sympathy
... we were in high spirits ... telling ... pig jokes (ll. 109f.)	brutality, ignorance
... I sympathized with our need to do this (l. 149)	understanding
... the hard time we gave him ... (l. 177)	bad conscience; remorse
... the helplessness of Piggy Sneed's human condition ... (ll. 220f.)	bad conscience of the narrator; sympathy; understanding

indirect characterization (examples)	function/effect
"A whole pig, at once", we used to say ... (ll. 33f.)	exaggeration; irony
We children ... would sneak up on him ... (l. 41)	cruelty; ignorance
We'd squeal at him ... (l. 46)	funny; showing the cruelty of children
When the terror passed, we couldn't wait for him to come again. (ll. 55ff.)	exaggeration; humour
... he was encouraged to be a pig ... (ll. 66f.)	reveals townspeople's intolerance, cruelty
... it gave us a status that only disasters can create for the young (ll. 85f.)	arrogance and cruelty of teenagers
... his stinking pick-up, blocking our importance ... (ll. 91f.)	irony; criticism
I distinctly hear us calling ... my voice, too. (ll. 102ff.)	criticism of brutal behaviour; narrator is ashamed of himself
... telling ... about how we imagined the fire was started ... (ll. 110f.)	cruelty
... we were afraid the new paint ... would blister ... 'No point in wasting the water ...' (ll. 132ff.)	cold-heartedness; cruelty of the teenagers and the captain
'Piggy, Piggy,' one of us called ... (l. 148)	cruelty; bad taste
... because everyone in the Stratham Volunteers began every sentence with the word 'shit'. (ll. 156f.)	ignorance; bad education; bad manners
'He's paid us back – that's clear ... ' (ll. 179f.)	dealing with the bad conscience
... pigs were easier ... maybe friendlier ... I added thinking of us all (ll. 186f.)	dealing with the bad conscience; criticism
... her kindness to Piggy Sneed ... in combination with the helplessness ... (ll. 119ff.)	expressing understanding; a bad conscience

8. As the narrator points out right at the beginning, this memoir provides the explanation why he has become a writer. Interpret the respective passages from the text and draw conclusions about the writer's intention and the message of the text.

The narrator describes the cruelty he and his friends repeatedly subjected Piggy Sneed to, e.g. sneaking up behind him and scaring him, running him off the road with the fire truck, taunting and making fun of him, especially at inappropriate times. In doing so, he clearly reveals that, looking back, he feels ashamed of his actions (ll. 41ff., 58ff., 104, 147). At the same time, he understands and sympathizes with his and his friends' bad behaviour because it is human nature to sometimes act badly and in "bad taste" (ll. 58–61, 148–151). At the time the events were unfolding, they do not have much of an effect on the narrator because he continues to act cruelly towards Piggy Sneed along with the other children

Piggy Sneed's death has a different effect on the narrator. He cannot accept Sneed's tragic death, so he uses his imagination to think up alternative, happier endings in which Piggy does not die a horrible death. It is the narrator's way of coping with the terrible situation (ll. 153ff.). He later explains to his grandmother how the incident of Piggy Sneed's death inspired him to write, but she sees through him and says that he is trying to clear his bad conscience (ll. 213–229). He feels especially bad about Sneed's death because of the cruel way he treated him as a child.

→ The writer's intention is to clear his bad conscience through storytelling and try and make sense of the tragic events and his cruel behaviour.

9. Choose *one* of these characters
a) Piggy Sneed,
b) the first-person narrator,
c) the Front Street children (as a group) and write a literary characterization of about 300 words.
→ Focus on Skills, Characterization of a Figure in Literature, p. 264

For example:
Piggy Sneed is a mentally retarded man living in the town of Stratham. He is the son of a mentally handicapped woman who was hit by a car (ll. 196ff.). He has the mental capacity of a small child and due to his mental handicap, either does not or cannot speak (ll. 35ff.). He works as a garbage collector driving a truck and also raises pigs for a living. He bears a physical resemblance to pigs: He has small red eyes, deep pink wrinkles in his neck and bristle-like hairs on his face. He is short, heavy and strong and makes pig-like squeals and noises (ll. 20–29). He lives together with his pigs in a barn with only a wood stove in one of the stalls for warmth (ll. 13ff.). As a result of these unhygienic living conditions, he smells extremely unpleasant. He is thus socially isolated and regularly falls prey to the cruelty of neighbourhood children, who heap scorn on and deride him. He is easily scared by the children and reacts in a panicked way, not seeming to remember the same trick even after it is pulled multiple times (l. 49). Piggy Sneed drinks quite a bit, and it is hinted that he may be an alcoholic because he also drives drunk. He eventually perishes one winter night when the barn burns down. (225 words)

10. Look at the photograph on p. 110 and
a) in a Round Robin activity, state your impressions of the man and his surroundings,
b) compare the message of the photograph and the impression the man makes on you to the text. State the differences and similarities.
→ Focus on Methods, Round Robin, p. 270
→ Focus on Skills, Analysis of Visuals, p. 262

a) The photo shows a middle-aged man sitting on a bed on a floral bedspread with his arms wrapped around a large pig in his lap. He is bald with white/grey curly hair on the sides of his head. The man is wearing workman's overalls and a dirty, worn out T-shirt. He is staring blankly at the camera with his mouth open. The pig is quite large and has dark bristles. The wallpaper is peeling and sooty and one can see an electrical socket and several plugs on the wall/floor.

b) **Similarities:**
- Brian's blank stare and open mouth suggest mental retardation, like Piggy Sneed.
- Both Brian and Piggy Sneed live in close proximity with their pig friend(s).
- Both Brian and Piggy live in rather unhygienic housing conditions.

Differences:

- Brian seems to live in a house with electricity and furniture, while Piggy Sneed lives in an actual pig barn.
- Brian has a pet pig, while Piggy Sneed makes his living caring for and slaughtering pigs.
- Brian seems more affectionate towards his pet pig because he is hugging it close, while we do not see Piggy Sneed actually interacting with his pigs.
- etc.

SOLUTIONS ACTIVITIES

11. Write a different ending of the story on your own.
→ Focus on Skills, Continuation of a Fictional Text, p. 277

Individual solutions

12. Throughout the story, we only get to know about the thoughts of the first-person narrator and some of the Front Street children. Now, put yourself in Piggy Sneed's position and imagine what he might have been thinking and feeling about his situation and being treated like this. You can choose between different text forms:
a) an interior monologue*
b) a dialogue* with his pigs
c) a dialogue* with the narrator's grandmother.
Present your monologues*/dialogues* in class and discuss and evaluate the different views taken.

Individual answers, for example:
Oh no, what's that? Oh, it's those darn kids! They scare me so bad! They are so mean! I hate it when they sneak up and scare me. Why are they calling me Piggy? That's not my real name. I remember what my mama used to call me … She was the only one who was ever nice to me … etc.

SOLUTIONS GRAMMAR/LANGUAGE

13. As is the custom after a person's death, the mourners try to find words of praise, and obituaries are composed to stress the good qualities of the deceased. Nevertheless they might hint "gently" at a person's shortcomings and trespasses. Imagine you have to find appropriate "last words" for Piggy Sneed from different perspectives expressing either grief or relief or anger or hope, etc. Write an obituary for Piggy Sneed. You can use the expressions in the vocab box on this page.
Example: Dear inhabitants of Front Street … our beloved neighbour Piggy Sneed has lost his life in a tragic accident … his unique character and …

For example:
Dear inhabitants of Front Street,
We have gathered to mourn the passing of our beloved neighbour Piggy Sneed who has lost his life in a tragic accident. His unique character and friendliness should be an example to all of us and we will greatly miss him. We never truly realized what a service he was to the whole city and his passing leaves us alone with our grief and sadness.
With deep regret we have to realize that we never were the friends and neighbours he wanted us to be. His only true friends and companions were his pigs that went with him through hell and back.
Let me express my deepest sympathy and let us all mark the occasion with a moment of silence … etc.

Sarah O'Connor

London's Rail Stations Still Attract Vulnerable Runaways (pp. 111–113)

About the author	Sarah O'Connor is a writer for the *Financial Times*. She has a blog on the *Financial Times* website in which she specializes in monetary supply.
About the text	The text explains, in minor detail, the situation of runaways using the rail systems to escape notice.
Level	●●○
Additional material	GaST: no. 8

- Die **Awareness-Aufgabe** wird in einem kurzen **Unterrichtsgespräch** bearbeitet.
- Für das Einüben von **Lesestrategien** (Aufg. 1 und 2) erscheint es sinnvoll, dass den Schülerinnen und Schülern der Text in **Kopie** vorliegt, damit sie ihn aktiv durch Unterstreichungen, Markierungen und Anmerkungen bearbeiten können.
  Die Aufgaben werden anhand der Angaben im Schülerbuch bearbeitet.
- **Aufgabe 3** kann in Partnerarbeit bearbeitet werden. Die Ergebnisse werden im Unterrichtsgespräch diskutiert und fließen in folgendes Tafelbild ein:

Railway Children

text	*effect on the reader*
two workers of Railway Children are shown at work (ll. 1–23)	*interesting, easy to read*
the charity is sponsored by the Financial Times (ll. 21f.)	*not necessarily objective, possibly used for public relation purposes*
the chief executive about Railway Children's work in Britain (ll. 24–29)	*the quotation is incomplete and therefore less convincing*
statistics (ll. 30–43)	*the data are not exact*
Louise's story (ll. 44–end)	*the story is incomplete, the reader is not told how Louise "is trying to get back on track"*

➔ *The article mentions convincing details but the overall impression is that of a lack of reliable information.*

- Die Recherche-Aufgaben (**Aufg. 4 und 5**) können in **Partnerarbeit** erledigt werden. Die Ergebnisse werden im **Unterrichtsgespräch** gebündelt und informell an der **Tafel** gesichert.
- **Aufgabe 6** kann in **Kleingruppen** erledigt werden. Die Schülerinnen und Schüler können die Ergebnisse ihrer Arbeit auf **Flipchartbögen** visualisieren und im **Plenum** kurz präsentieren. Alternativ dazu können die Flipchartbögen im Klassenzimmer ausgehängt und von der Klasse zur Kenntnis genommen werden. An die Präsentation der Ergebnisse schließt sich die **Diskussion** der Thematik im Plenum an.
- **Aufgabe 7** kann als **Hausaufgabe** erteilt werden. Zum Gebrauch des *simple present* sollten die Schülerinnen und Schüler einmal mehr auf das –s in der 3. Person Singular aufmerksam gemacht werden.

SOLUTIONS AWARENESS

Name some of the reasons that in your opinion induce teenagers to run away from home.

- abuse
- lack of Freedom
- dysfunctional family
- drug use
- lack of food at home
- unsafe home
- peer pressure from friends
- mental issues

SOLUTIONS COMPREHENSION

1.

Step 1: In a first reading, skim the text and try to understand the gist of the article. Take some notes on the most relevant information (who – what – where – when – why).

Step 2: Pair up with a partner and summarize the most relevant information to each other. Ask each other questions about the text to make sure you have understood everything correctly. Correct and/or add information that you consider to be important.

→ Focus on Skills, Reading Techniques, p. 247

Who: Runaway Children/Those trying to find runaways
What: Runaway children using rail stations as an escape
Where: Rail stations in the UK, mainly King's Cross in the article
When: Presently
Why: Children want to escape their home life and those trying to help are concerned for the runaways' well-being

2. In a second reading, scan the text for additional details and complete your notes.

The article also concerns children in East Africa and in India (ll. 22–23). The organizations that are mentioned try to help kids from these three areas but the article itself is focused in the King's Cross Station. There is also a small focus on an individual runaway named Louise (l. 57) who was not helped in the best way, but was helped all the same.

SOLUTIONS ANALYSIS

3. The article at hand informs about and promotes a charity organization sponsored by the paper itself (The Financial Times). Analyse the text and determine whether the article presents reliable information or whether it is biased and rather one-sided. Pay attention to the following aspects and stylistic devices, e. g.:

- **the composition and structure of the article (e. g. line of argument*, train of thought*)**
- **employment of factual information (numbers, facts, data, references, etc.)**
- **employment of human interest (evoking emotions, appealing to readers)**

→ Focus on Skills, Analysis of a Non-Fictional Text, p. 258

I did not find the article very well-written. The beginning of the article (ll. 1–23) was anecdotal and that was all well and good, but after that the waters become a little murkier. At ll. 21f., the reader finds that the charity in question is sponsored by the paper itself and it is around then the reader sees a strange line of structure. The quotation from the chief executive is a nice touch but then the quotation is lost when trying to conclude the thought. It ends in a summation by the author, not a fully quoted source (in addition, ll. 30–31 is slightly convoluted in the thought process).
This then transitions into statistics that, once again, start quite strongly but end with the line 'A similar proportion stayed away for more than four weeks' (ll. 35–36). This is data that is not fully represented by the article, making the statistic itself fall flat for the reader. Just as soon as these numbers begin, they end quite abruptly and go into another anecdote, this one concerning Louise (ll. 57ff.). This was another point where I was left wanting more because the very end of the article concludes with Louise 'trying to get back on track' (ll. 72–73) but does not describe at all what she is doing. Though the pun about railroad tracks is appreciated from my point of view, as an interested reader, I would like to know how Louise ended up after being 'helped' by the program.

Webcode SNG-40175-007 @

4. The second part of the article informs the reader about "New Horizon", a youth centre involved in the "Railway Children" project. Compare the information about "New Horizon" given in the text to the information given on the youth centre's homepage. The respective link is provided on the webcode.

The article is very short in the description of New Horizon. All it says is that the centre has started doing street work for the charity (ll. 49–50). The homepage does not give a lot about the connection to the Railway Children project but it does provide information on what the Youth Centre is up to, donation links, aid for the homeless, offering of facilities for the homeless, and classes for everyone.

This is provided on the detail page: Day centre for young homeless people. Benefits, housing, careers advice. Laundry/showers/clothes. Free lunch. IT, ESOL, literacy, numeracy, cookery, drama classes. Women only groups. Nurse. Mental health support. Resettlement support. Female sex worker project. Street outreach. Rough sleeper luggage store. Life skills support. Art, gym, sports. Volunteer project. Alcohol support.

Webcode SNG-40175-007 @ **5. Use the link provided on the webcode and examine the quality of the "Railway Children" homepage. Who do you consider to be the target group of the website? Do you think that it appeals to runaway children – the ones who would most need to be attracted by it?**

→ Focus on Skills, Research, p. 318

The quality of the website is fairly high though it appeals to adults. It has backing information on the Railway Children's ongoing projects. It also provides links to who the program is trying to reach out to, possible solutions, and the actual children they are helping or have helped. To me, the website seems to be calling out to those who are concerned with the children on a worldwide basis, not the children themselves. The program needs monetary donations and I believe it is the donors who the website is trying to reach out to.

SOLUTIONS ACTIVITIES

Webcode SNG-40175-007 @ **6. Helping runaway children is important but in some ways this only treats the symptoms whereas the underlying reasons often go unnoticed and remain unchanged. The recently published UNICEF report on "Child well-being in rich countries" found some striking differences between "child well-being" and "children's life satisfaction". Examine the data given in the report (on pp. 39 – 43, 53) as well as the bar chart on p. 96 (Child Deprivation Rates in Rich Countries). You can find the link to the report on the webcode. Try to answer the following questions:**

a) What possible reasons for children's and teenagers' dissatisfaction with their lives can you detect?

b) Can these data provide answers and explanations in the wider context of runaway children or teenage suicides? Discuss in class.

a) The biggest problem when coming to life satisfaction is on an interpersonal level. The level of satisfaction begins with interpersonal relationships, family and friends. If the child comes from a rough home life (alcohol abuse, physical abuse, drug abuse, poverty) then they, naturally, have a high rate of running away and eventually suicide. This can also transition in the peer-to-peer relationships. If a child is struggling with his or her peers then the feeling of needing to escape would be much greater while a person who feels that they do not have any true friendships would be the most likely type to commit suicide.

b) This data can find some correlation with the interpersonal relationship question, but the data can also be very flawed due to the self-reported nature of it. The vast majority of the data is correlative with each chart so one could rightfully assume, with the given data, that these relationships are partly to blame for runaways and suicides.

SOLUTIONS GRAMMAR/LANGUAGE

7. Choose one of the charts mentioned in the report above and turn the data and percentage figures into words and compare them. Be careful to use the correct words and phrases and simple present for your text.

Webcode SNG-40175-007 @ **Example: (UNICEF report, pp. 40 – 41)**

The comparison of child well-being and children's life satisfaction shows some striking disparities. Whereas German children rank sixth in well-being, the German children's own subjective assessments differ significantly, ranking only 22nd. These figures match the percentage figures on p. 41 ...

→ Focus on Grammar, Tenses, p. 305

→ Focus on Skills, Analysis of Statistical Data, p. 261

For example:

The comparison of child well-being and children's life-satisfaction shows some striking disparities. Whereas German children rank 6 in well-being, the German children's own subjective assessments differ significantly, ranking only 22nd. These figures partly match the figures on page 41 where Germany ranks 10 out of 28 countries, being 10 percentage points behind the leading Netherlands.

However, on average, about two thirds of the German children and teenagers consider their classmates kind and helpful and find it easy to talk to their mother and father. As in all of the other countries, German teenagers found it easier to talk to their mothers than to their fathers. In comparison, only 63.3 % of the British teenagers consider their classmates to be kind and helpful – this number is even lower in the United States: only 56.2 % of the teenagers think that their classmates are nice and helpful.
Most interestingly, the relative figures for the country ranking top in both charts, the Netherlands, seem to indicate that child well-being and teenagers' subjective assessments are connected with social well-being and close relationships.

Youth in Crisis – Broken Dreams and Lost Hopes

Generation Jobless (pp. 114–118)

About the text	The text is explaining the situation of the jobless youth who are also inactive in education. This jobless rate is not only effecting the poor countries in the world, but wealthy countries like Spain, France, and Italy are also afflicted by this phenomenon, with Germany and the United States being on the lower end of the spectrum. Though there are spots in many companies available, the prerequisites in experience and education are failing for many of the applicants.
Level	● ● ●
Additional material	Differenzierungsmaterial, p. 77 GaST: no. 7, 8, 9 Comprehension: no. 12

- Die **Awareness-Aufgabe** kann in einer kurzen einleitenden Sequenz bearbeitet werden.
- **Aufgabe 1** wird nach den Angaben im Schülerbuch durchgeführt. Die Ergebnisse können in einem kurzen **Unterrichtsgespräch** verglichen und ggf. korrigiert werden.
- Bei der Bearbeitung von **Aufgabe 2** müssen sich die Schülerinnen und Schüler noch einmal detailliert mit dem Text auseinandersetzen. Sie notieren sich die Ergebnisse ihrer Untersuchung in **Stichwörtern**. Der Austausch der Ergebnisse erfolgt im anschließenden **Unterrichtsgespräch**.
- **Aufgabe 3** wird in **Partnerarbeit** bearbeitet. Die Schüler füllen dazu eine **Tabelle** aus (s. Lösungsvorschlag unten). Die Ergebnissicherung erfolgt im Unterrichtsgespräch über **Folie**.
- Zur Bearbeitung von **Aufgabe 4** wird die in **Aufgabe 3** erstellte Tabelle um die Spalte „**Text**' erweitert und inhaltlich ergänzt. Die Aufgabe wird wiederum in **Partnerarbeit** erledigt. Die Ergebnisse werden mit einer weiteren Zweiergruppe ausgetauscht und besprochen.
- Die beiden Cartoons (**Aufg. 5**) werden in **Einzelarbeit** bearbeitet. Die Schülerinnen und Schüler wählen dazu eine der beiden Darstellungen aus und notieren vor dem Hintergrund der jeweiligen Aufgabenstellung **Stichwörter**, die sie im Anschluss zur Stärkung der **mündlichen Sprachkompetenz** in **Kurzvorträgen** elaborieren.
- Die in **Aufgabe 6** geforderte Diskussion kann als Vorbereitung zur Durchführung des Computerspiels (Aufg. 7) eingesetzt werden. In der sich dem Spiel anschließenden **Evaluation** kann noch einmal auf die Ergebnisse der Eingangsdiskussion rekurriert werden.
- Vor der Bearbeitung von **Aufgabe 8** sollte die entsprechende **Focus on Skills-Seite** (SB, S. 290) zur Kenntnis genommen werden.

SOLUTIONS AWARENESS

In a Think! Pare! Share! activity (→ FoM, p. 273) reflect on the title of the article: What are possible consequences of a "generation of jobless" young people?

./.

SOLUTIONS COMPREHENSION

1. Be prepared to read the article at least two times as it employs a lot of technical terms and expert language in connection with economic subjects and the labour market. In order to give you some additional help the article has already been subdivided into thematic units.
First, read the article on your own and make notes on the questions below.
After each paragraph, crosscheck your notes with a partner and make additions and/or corrections if necessary.

Paragraph 1:

- **Define the term "NEET".**
  a person who is "not in employment, education or training"

- **State the number of young people who are a) unemployed and b) "inactive".**
  75 million are unemployed
  almost 290 million (almost a quarter of the planet's youth) are neither working nor studying

- **What kind of jobs do young people have a) in rich countries, b) in poor countries, c) worldwide?**
  a) more than a third have temporary contracts
  b) one fifth are unpaid family labourers or work in the informal economy
  c) nearly half are outside the formal economy or contributing less productively than they could

- **What are the consequences for the countries concerned and the taxpayers?**
  heavy burdens on taxpayers to pay for welfare; economic loss due to unemployed youth in Europe in 2011 was $153 billion, more than 1% of GDP; lower growth today and in the future

Paragraph 2:

- **Which countries suffer most from youth joblessness?**
  rich world: Spain, France, Italy, Greece
  emerging world: Morocco, Egypt, other North African and Middle Eastern countries

- **Describe the mismatch between skills that young people have and those that are needed and required by employers.**
  in one study, only 43% of employers (in the US, Brazil, Britain, Germany, India, Mexico, Morocco, Saudi Arabia and Turkey) thought they could find enough skilled entry-level workers

- **Point out the most important reasons for this mismatch.**
  - poor basic education
  - lack of vocational education/apprenticeships/actual work experience
  - schools fail to teach needed technical skills

- **Why does Germany have low youth unemployment rates?**
  it has a long tradition of high-quality vocational education and apprenticeships

- **Which problems do young job seekers have to face in France and North Africa?**
  France: students do not get any real work experience at school
  North Africa: universities do not provide students with needed technical skills

Paragraph 3:

- **What are the youth unemployment rates in Britain?**
  ca. 1 million NEETs (11.5% of the labour force)

- **Which problems do young Britons have acquiring "work experience"?**
  only 8% of British employers offer training, and the opportunities have been declining over the past 15 years; only 7% of pupils receive mentoring from a local employer and only 19% had visited one

Paragraph 4:

- **Describe the interest that large companies are taking in training young people.**
  IBM is sponsoring a school in New York
  McDonald's has an ambitious new training scheme
  Indian IT company Infosys plans to train 45,000 new employees a year
  Americana Group lets trainees split their time between work and college

- **Which technological solutions help young people to gain "experience and skills on the job"?**
  "serious games" train young people virtually at a low cost
  - McDonald's uses video games to teach people how to use the till and interact with customers
  - Mozilla has created an "open badges" initiative to show off their programming skills

→ Focus on Skills, Reading Techniques, p. 247

SOLUTIONS ANALYSIS

2. Examine the reasons given for a) youth unemployment and b) "youth inactivity". Who – according to the article – is to blame for the situation and what needs to be done/changed to get young people into employment?

→ Focus on Skills, Analysis of a Non-Fictional Text, p. 258

./.

3. Analyse the bar chart on p. 116 and the line graph on p. 114 and state

- **which European countries show a significantly high percentage of young people who do not participate in education, work or training,**
- **which trends are obvious concerning the rise of youth unemployment over the last decade.**

→ Focus on Skills, Analysis of Statistical Data, p. 261

bar chart (NEET rate)	line graph (youth unemployment)
corresponding matching data:	**corresponding matching data:**
• Spain: 13 % NEETS	• significant rise since 2007 • Spain: rise from 10 % to 20 % → doubling of unemployment rate
• Greece: ca. 8 % NEETS	• drop from 10 % to ca. 5 % between 2000 and 2008 • significant rise in 2008 to more than 15 %
• France: ca. 6.5 % NEETS	• steady unemployment, ca. 7 % • rise in 2008 to ca. 10 %
• Germany: 4 % NEETS	• ca. 4.8 % unemployed young people
• USA: ca. 9 % NEETS	• ca. 9 % unemployed young people
differences:	**differences:**
• Greece: ca. 8 % NEETS (in 2013)	• ca. 15 % youth unemployment (in 2013)
• Spain: ca. 13 % NEETS (in 2013)	• ca. 20 % youth unemployment (in 2013)
• Britain/UK: ca. 9.5 % NEETS	• ca. 12 % unemployed young people

4. Relate your findings from task 3 to the information given in the article and illustrate the corresponding facts and data.

./.

5. Describe the cartoons below and explain
a) which view on "vocational training" is taken in cartoon no. 1,
b) how cartoon no. 2 interprets the "mismatch between the skills young people offer and skills that employers need" (ll. 42 ff.).
→ Focus on Skills, Analysis of Visuals, p. 262

a) Cartoon no. 1 shows a classroom of university or possibly high school students and a teacher standing at the front of the room at the chalkboard. The teacher, wearing a tie and sh rt sleeves, is pointing at a list of items on the board and giving a lecture to prepare the students for life after graduation. The list of items consists of many government benefits for the unemployed/poor, and the teacher explains that the students will need to know how to fill out these government forms in order to receive these benefits after graduation. The students look baffled because they expected to find work after graduation and earn their own money.
The caption "The New Normal" shows that it has becoming totally common for graduates to not find work and to have to receive government benefits. Instead of preparing graduates for actual work and the labour force by teaching them practical skills, the teacher/school is teaching students how to survive unemployment because it is clear that there are not enough jobs available anyway.

b) Cartoon no. 2 consists of two panels. In the first panel, we see a recent university graduate wearing a mortarboard and robe talking to a bald man wearing a tie and glasses. The young man is applying for a job, and the boss is reviewing the candidate's credentials. He informs the graduate that he is not as qualified as the other candidate: He has a Master's degree, but all the other applicants have PhDs. In the second panel, it is revealed that the graduate was applying for a job at McDonald's and that he will try to find a job at Burger King next.
This picks up on the mismatch between candidates' skills and what employers need. Work in the fast food industry is considered low-skilled work and is not competitive, but the applicant is still comparatively underqualified. It shows that even highly educated individuals are having a hard time finding a job because they lack the specific skills employers need. As a result, even people with Master's and doctoral degrees are having to take on low-skilled jobs in order to make money.

SOLUTIONS ACTIVITIES

6. One solution put forward to get young people into a kind of vocational education is "Serious Games" (ll. 99 ff.). Discuss whether (or not) the use of "competitive video games" (l. 102) can be useful and substitute for real "experience on the job" and for vocational training that is mentored by experts. Find arguments for and against this "solution".

For example:
- Could be useful for highly mechanical/digital/technical/computer-based jobs, since video game interface would be quite similar to actual work.
- Less useful for e.g. service industry jobs, manual labour, hands-on skills that cannot be simulated digitally, jobs that require one-on-one communication ...
- Someone else could complete the training to gain a qualification for someone else dishonestly.
- Some people learn better by doing or listening.
- etc.

Webcode SNG-40175-008 @ **7. Play a "serious game" yourself and try the "Collapsus" animation which deals with the energy crisis and its effects on young people. The webcode provides the links to the website and further information. Afterwards, share your experiences with the game in class and discuss whether games like this one can help to train and educate young people for "real life".**

Individual answers

8. You are upset about the appalling situation. Together with a partner, write a letter to your local city council or mayor in which you demand changes and an improvement of vocational education and training on the job.
→ Focus on Skills, Writing a Letter to the Editor, p. 290

Martin Mustermann
Gartenweg 1
54327 Köln
Germany

Mayor Nicolas Schmidt
Gartenweg 2
54327 Köln
Germany

20 May 2014

Dear Mayor Schmidt,

I am writing about the serious situation of youth unemployment. I am very concerned about the rising number of unemployed young people who ...
According to a recent Economist article, many young people are ...
This trend has negative consequences for taxpayers as well ...
We desperately need more on-the-job training opportunities in order to ...
Please keep in mind that ...

Thank you for your consideration.

Yours sincerely,

Martin Mustermann

Hillary Clinton

Remarks on Youth (pp. 118–119)

About the text	The text is a recording of a speech given by Hillary Rodham Clinton to a group of Tunisian youth. The speech was given after a revolution to overthrow an autocratic regime and was concerning the place of young people in both Tunisia and throughout the world.
Level	●●○
Additional material	Audio CD 2,1 GaST: no. 7, 9, 24 Comprehension: no. 13

- Die Awareness-Aufgabe wird in einem kurzen Unterrichtsgespräch bearbeitet.
- Die Comprehension-Aufgaben (Aufg. 1–4) werden nach den Angaben im Schülerbuch durchgeführt.
- Aufgabe 5 kann im Unterrichtsgespräch behandelt werden. Die Ergebnisse werden informell an der Tafel gesichert.
- Nach dem Ansehen des Mitschnitts der Rede von Hillary Clinton diskutieren die Schülerinnen und Schüler ihre Eindrücke (Aufg. 6). Die Ergebnisse der Diskussion werden in folgendem Tafelbild festgehalten:

Hillary Clinton as a speaker

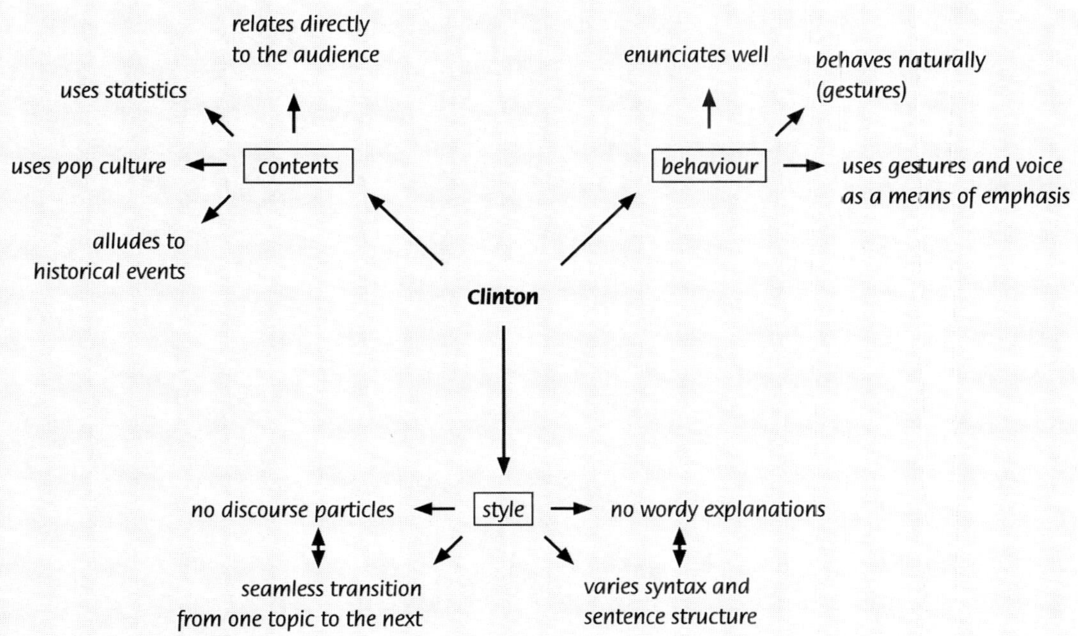

- **Aufgabe 7** wird im **Unterrichtsgespräch** bearbeitet.
- Bei der Bearbeitung von **Aufgabe 8** können **Moderationskarten** eingesetzt werden, auf denen die Schülerinnen und Schüler mögliche Fragen an Hillary Clinton verzeichnen. Diese Karten werden eingesammelt und thematisch geordnet an der **Tafel** oder auf einer **Moderationswand** angebracht. Danach werden die **Themenbereiche** festgelegt, aus denen die Fragen kommen. Die Auswahl der thematisierten Aspekte wird im Anschluss diskutiert.

SOLUTIONS AWARENESS

On February 25, 2012, then U.S. Secretary of State, Hillary Rodham Clinton, engaged with young Tunisians in a Town Hall in Tunis. In 2011, in the so-called "Arab Spring", a revolution in several Northern African countries resulted in the overthrow of the autocratic regime and the first free democratic elections were held in the country. In Tunisia, ca. 40.2 % of the population is younger than 25 (cf. Germany: ca. 24.1 %). Against this background, what might be interesting issues and topics for young people to talk about there – especially when they are speaking with an American (female) politician?

The future of young people in the world would be the obvious first choice. Americans in general have a much easier road to economic freedom when compared to someone in a place like Tunisia. In addition to that, immediately after an Arab autocracy, women would be put in a strange light and seeing a high-powered politician like Clinton as a speaker would be something that would bring about quite a bit of conversation.

SOLUTIONS COMPREHENSION

CD 2 (1) **1. Listen to Hillary Clinton's speech for a first time and try to get the gist of her message to Tunisian youth. Jot down some notes on aspects you consider most relevant.**

- Young people started the change in Tunisia
- Rights and Dignity of Humans cannot be denied forever
- Young people are optimistic, courageous, dynamic, and innovative throughout the world
- Young people can help rebuild economy, build democracy, fight oppression
- Needs and concerns of the young have been marginalized for too long, they are ignored
- There is a youth bulge, 3 billion people under the age of 30
- Insufficient wages for young people
- The global economy connects everyone but the global marketplace is still moving

- Young people combine technology of service
- Family ties are dwindling and are leaving young people behind for criminals and extremists to pick up
- Young people want peace, prosperity, and dignity — same as everyone
- Expand English language training because it has become the language of commerce
- Internet communication is mainly English
- Social networking can help bring down regimes, expose corruption, and encourage good government, going hand in hand with freedom
- Social networks enable and empower
- New democracies are difficult to build

2. Exchange your findings with a partner and clarify your results.

Individual answers

3. Now listen to the speech a second time. Before listening, divide the class into seven groups, each group focusing on a different aspect of the speech:
- **the special role and importance of young people and their empowerment in today's society**
- **challenges, problems and the type of ignorance young people have to cope with**
- **unemployment and poverty**
- **loss of family and community and its consequences**
- **action taken to support and empower young people by the USA**
- **the relevance of the English language and education in general**
- **social media and networks.**

- Young people are courageous, dynamic, innovative – they have the power to topple oppressive regimes and build stronger societies.
- Young people are ignored, at many times forgotten due to their youth. With the youth bulge occurring, there are too many young people throughout the world to be completely supported; many will be left behind without change.
- The youth bulge is a large part of unemployment, even those with graduate degrees struggle finding employment because the job market believes that these young people are not prepared for the field.
- Family ties are dwindling and are leaving young people behind for criminals and extremists to pick up.
- The USA is trying to train many emerging democracies in English and commerce, networking and other technological advancements that the previous regime may have kept from the public.
- English is becoming the language of commerce and of the internet. Though there are obviously many types of communication in both business and over the internet, English has become the dominant form and as such is being taught more and more.
- Social media and social networks have become a tool for power. Social networking can help bring down regimes, expose corruption, and encourage good government, going hand in hand with freedom.

4. After a third listening, complete your notes.
→ Focus on Skills, Listening Comprehension, p. 244

Individual answers

SOLUTIONS ANALYSIS

5. Examine Hillary Clinton's attempt to encourage her young listeners and strengthen their self-confidence. Find examples from the speech and explain their effect.

When speaking about the youth bulge, Clinton explains that if people empower the young, then the world as a whole will be better off, if we try to overlook the young then it will be a disaster. She then goes on to compare the young people to everyone from other generations. Because of this, she is showing the young people that they are no different than generations prior. That is one of the most encouraging things that she can do, comparing them to those who have already advanced.

She does this by another way when encouraging this specific group of Tunisians when speaking about democracy. By telling them of the struggles of the United States when their democracy was just newly conceived, she is connecting an established power's process to what the new Tunisian government is just about to undertake. The effect that both of these instances can have is that it will give the young Tunisians confidence in what they are doing.

Webcode SNG-40175-009 @ **6. Examine Hillary Clinton's abilities as a speaker. How does she try to bring across her message to the audience? Is she able to hold her audience's attention? In order to get a better impression of her oratory competence, you can watch her speech in the video provided on the webcode.**

→ Focus on Skills, Analysis of a Political Speech, p. 260

- she makes her points relate to the audience directly (young people in the audience and all points are concerning young people, in Tunisia and all points relate back to the young people in Tunisia)
- enunciates well (never stutters and always slows her speech in order to make sure she is understood, "Rights and dignity should never be overlooked by an oppressive regime")
- brings in statistics (youth bulge, 3 billion under the age of thirty)
- hand gestures are not overdone and used appropriately (staying within the invisible box and counting points on fingers to emphasize)
- no discourse particles ('like' or 'um' etc.)
- brings attention with certain gestures of the hands and then changes tone and inflection of her voice to emphasize different pieces of the speech (using the word free brings up the volume)
- uses pop culture (Facebook and Social Media)
- transitions from one topic to the next seamlessly (social networking to toppling corrupt regimes)
- does not get overly wordy (explains youth bulge only through a number as opposed to going into excessive detail)
- alludes to historical events (civil war, abolition)
- changes syntax and sentences structure (long sentences transition to short)

SOLUTIONS ACTIVITIES

7. Evaluate the concluding part of Hillary Clinton's speech. What picture does she draw of the USA and how does this match up with the hopes and dreams of the young Tunisians?

She is explaining how the United States struggled for a great many years in becoming a democracy. The civil war, slavery, all sorts of war; democracies are not easy to build, especially at first. The Tunisians can take this as a sign that, although they are just starting, democracy is at hand and they too can become a strong nation throughout the world.

8. After Hillary Clinton's speech the students were given the opportunity to ask questions and discuss matters with the Secretary of State. What questions do you think they asked her?

The young people might ask what opportunities they should take advantage of with this new type of government or what different types of projects would be most beneficial to the new system. They may ask questions concerning the power of social networking and what they can do to keep their newfound government in check. Young females may ask what the best strategies are to get into politics and be successful. All questions about democratic process would be fair game along with anything related to economic policy, diversity, and generational differences.

Christopher Dickey

Kill Zone (pp. 119–123)

About the text	The article here is describing the ludicrous amount of gun violence in the United States. Beginning with an anecdote of Tyquran Horton, the article paints a picture of urban city areas that are rife with guns and gun violence. *Kill Zone* goes on to explain that although 82 % of gun owners in America are white, 72 % of gun related homicide is caused by black or Hispanic gun holders.
Level	● ● ○
Additional material	GaST: no. 2, 8, 24 Comprehension: no. 14

- Die meisten Schülerinnen und Schüler werden keine Mühe haben, sich zur Mitgliedschaft in einer Clique zu äußern (**Awareness-Aufgabe**), wenn es jedoch darum geht, Stellung zur Zugehörigkeit zu einer (Jugend-)Bande zu nehmen, ist die Gefahr gegeben, dass auf Klischees, die man aus Büchern, dem Fernsehen, Filmen oder dem Internet kennt, zurückgegriffen wird. Ist dies der Fall, muss der Lehrer bzw. die Lehrerin in die Diskussion eingreifen und die Klasse für diese Problematik sensibilisieren.
- Die **Comprehension-Aufgabe (Aufg. 1)** wird nach den Anweisungen im Schülerbuch durchgeführt.
- **Aufgabe 2** wird in **Einzelarbeit** erledigt. Die Schülerinnen und Schüler machen sich während des Zuschauens **Notizen**, die sie für die anschließende Diskussion im Klassenverband nutzen.
- **Aufgabe 3** kann in **Einzel- oder Partnerarbeit** bearbeitet werden. Die Ergebnisse werden im Anschluss an die Erarbeitungsphase im **Unterrichtsgespräch** diskutiert und in folgendem **Tafelbild** gesichert:

C. Dickey, "Kill Zone"

the author

for guns
possible in rural America:
less violence
guns make people feel more secure
police want more gun freedom
guns ownership is justified in rural areas

against guns
description of the negative side of guns
(Tyquran's story)
the violence of guns

⇩

Guns should be allowed in the country ... *but not in big cities.*

- Die Bearbeitung von **Aufgabe 4** erfolgt **individuell**. Die Schülerinnen und Schüler notieren sich **Stichwörter**, die sie in mündlichen **Kurzvorträgen** elaborieren.
- Für die in **Aufgabe 5** geforderte Recherche und die Vorbereitung der Präsentationen sind zwei bis drei Einzelstunden zu veranschlagen. Für die Präsentationen werden je nach Größe der Lerngruppe zwei bis drei Einzelstunden benötigt.
- Aufgabe 6 kann als abschließende **Hausaufgabe** eingesetzt werden.

SOLUTIONS AWARENESS

Of course, young people like to meet each other and hang out together and have fun. However, being together in a group of peers can have many different facettes. What do you consider to be the difference between a clique and a "gang"?

Cliques are groups of like-minded individuals who, although they may have a superiority complex, are non-violent. 'Gangs' are, in my opinion, groups of people who are willing to resort to very violent measures to protect their members and their 'turf'. Cliques in general do not have designated areas where they are in 'control' while these gangs do and they will engage in both scare tactics and violence to keep other gangs away.

SOLUTIONS COMPREHENSION

1. In a Group Puzzle activity, divide the class into four groups, each group working with one section of the text.
Step 1: Read the sections on your own and try to get a general understanding.
Step 2: In your group, ask questions about anything that is unclear.
Step 3: In your group, tell each other the gist of your section.
Step 4: Then, after a second reading, try to answer the following questions in your groups:

Section 1:
- **Which members of Tyquran's family were killed in street violence?**
- **Give an outline of the respective circumstances of the killings.**
- **Describe Tyquran's personal experiences with gun violence and the police in his neighbourhood.**

Section 2:
- **What are Tyquran's dreams and plans for the future?**
- **Point out how Tyquran views the work and behaviour of the police.**
- **In what way does the family remember Tyquran's mother?**

Section 3:
- **Describe the overall atmosphere in many American cities during summertime.**
- **Outline the horrifying results of gang violence in Los Angeles County, Chicago and New York.**
- **State what – according to the author – the "great American tragedy of our time" is.**

Section 4:
- **Which kind of letters are sent to New York City's Mayor and to the President?**
- **Outline the statistical data given on gun owners and gun-homicide victims.**
- **Describe people's attitude towards guns in rural areas and small towns and how the police react to the subject.**

Following this, the groups remix and inform each other about their results.
→ Focus on Methods, Group Puzzle, p. 271

Section 1: Two uncles and his mother
- Uncle 1, mugging, someone wanted his coat; Uncle 2, an argument turned violent; Mother, a gang member began firing shots wildly into a crowd while Tyquran's mother protected her children by covering them with her body (ll. 1–18).
- Obviously, gun violence is a bad situation with Tyquran. Having three family members killed and seeing all the gang violence in his neighbourhood make for a sour taste when it comes to guns (ll. 1–18). The police in his neighbourhood dress in street clothes and drive unmarked cars. Being in a high-crime neighbourhood, the police officers often stop black kids and frisk them for weapons, making the police officers come across as villains in the neighbourhood (ll. 38–44).

Section 2: Tyquran wants to escape the neighbourhood and go to college (ll. 28–29)
- Tyquran is terrified of the police. After hearing stories of their brutality and the strange tactics they take in order to find weapons, it is natural to be scared (ll. 45–51).
- They have a large framed photograph of her with the words "In Loving Memory of a Daughter, Sister, Mother & Community Hero." (ll. 52–55)

Section 3: According to the article, summer is the killing season in American cities (l. 57). With rising temperatures and tempers, people are out on the streets with young men taunting, hunting, and shooting at one another.
- LA, 450 gangs, 45,000 members, half of all murders are gang-related, 414 deaths; Chicago, 12 shootings and one death in the last weekend, 435 deaths last year; NYC, 26 people shot with seven deaths in one weekend, 223 deaths in one year (ll. 67–83, 106–109).
- The great American tragedy of our time is that we fail to recognize the difference between the embattled city streets which are considered the gunland while the backwoods and country areas, though full of guns, are wildly different places (ll. 91–94).

Section 4: Letters have been sent with poison in them to the President and the Mayor, with phrases like 'If you take my guns then wait until you see what I'll do to you' in them (ll. 100–104).

- 82 percent of gun owners are white and most are outside metropolitan areas but 72 percent of gun-related homicide victims are black or Hispanic, both living and dying in city areas (ll. 113–117).
- People in rural areas feel more secure with their guns than without them. It is a matter of security. 59 percent of rural households have guns and local police officers in those areas favour less gun control as opposed to more (ll. 123–134).

Webcode SNG-40175-010 @ **2. Tyquran Horton from Brooklyn is not the only African American teenager who is a victim of gun violence and shootings. Watch the video provided on the webcode and get informed about a private organization which tries to help teenagers and victims of gun violence, gang criminality and shootings in Chicago's South Side.**

SOLUTIONS ANALYSIS

3. Find out whether or not the author takes sides in his article. In order to do so, examine and pay particular attention to these stylistic and rhetorical devices:

- **language: e.g. keywords, phrases, choice of words, word fields, language register, etc.**
- **rhetoric: e.g. use of patterns of solidarity and identification, key symbols, personal remarks, climax, enumerations, factual information vs. human interest, etc.**

→ Focus on Skills, Analysis of a Non-Fictional Text, p. 258
→ Focus on Language, Literary Terms, p. 308

In this particular article, it is difficult to make out which side the author intends to take. After the rather emotional beginning to this essay (the piece of Tyquran and his family) in which Dickey uses descriptive language to truly bring out the negative side of guns (ll. 15–18, 22–24, 46–49). The most emotive of these being 'Moments later she died, her blood spread out across the sidewalk like a Rorschach of urban violence'.
This type of writing continues along through much of the remaining sections 2, 3, and 4. Negative connotations about guns are strewn about these sections, most of them referring back to Tyquran and the excessive violence guns bring into cities (ll. 52–55, 57, 71–83, 105–117). Tyquran's quote asking 'why should the United States have guns in the first place', the beginning of 3 'Summer is the killing season in America', the relentless statistics concerning the violence – it all paints a very negative picture.
This pattern changes however when Dickey begins to refer to the rural American areas. Much less violence, guns making the owner more secure, and a police force that wants more gun freedom (ll. 113–134) – all make this sound like guns are not a big issue in the rural areas. With that knowledge, I would say that Dickey's position is trying to rid the cities of their weapons and only allow those outside metropolitan areas to be gun owners.

4. Analyse the bar chart below and the bar chart on p. 120 and explain which aspects they add to the author's thesis of the "irreconcilable divide" (ll. 118 – 124) that separates the pro- and anti-gun population.
→ Focus on Skills, Analysis of Statistical Data, p. 261

The chart on page 120 shows that cities have the least percentage of guns by household and that the rural areas have the most households owning guns (suburban, naturally fitting in between). The chart on page 122 shows that cities are in a much high favour for limiting the gun ownership while rural are at a 2–1 ratio in favour of protecting owners' rights. That knowledge combined with the article's message about gun violence within the city and the lack thereof in the rural areas shows the drastic differences in ownership. Those who want more control are more susceptible to the violent nature of the gun owners in cities while those in rural areas, who do not see a lot of violence, want to keep their guns. This is the major divide. The people trying to limit gun ownership do not understand where rural gun owners are coming from and vice versa. Rural gun owners do not see the problems of the cities and cannot possibly comprehend the amount of violence concerning gun ownership in urban settings.

SOLUTIONS ACTIVITIES

Webcode SNG-40175-010

5. On February 26, 2012, 17-year-old African-American high school student Trayvon Martin was fatally shot by George Zimmerman, a man of mixed-race Hispanic background, who volunteered as a neighbourhood watch coordinator in a gated community in Sanford, Florida. Although Zimmerman was initially accused of murder, the (all-white) jury's verdict finally was "not guilty" – which led to nationwide demonstrations and protests and sparked off a new debate about racism and racial injustice. In groups, do research on Trayvon Martin and his death, using the links provided on the webcode and work out presentations on the case.
→ Focus on Skills, Presentations, p. 276

On the night of February 26, 2012, in Sanford, Florida, United States, George Zimmerman fatally shot Trayvon Martin, a 17-year-old African American high school student. George Zimmerman, a 28-year-old mixed-race Hispanic, was the neighbourhood watch coordinator for the gated community where Martin was temporarily staying and where the shooting took place. According to Zimmerman's subsequent testimony, Zimmerman shot Martin, who was unarmed, during an altercation between the two. Responding to an earlier call from Zimmerman, police arrived on the scene within two minutes of the shooting. Zimmerman was taken into custody, treated for head injuries, then questioned for five hours. The police chief said that Zimmerman was released because there was no evidence to refute Zimmerman's claim of having acted in self-defense, and that under Florida's Stand Your Ground statute (In the United States, stand-your-ground-law states that a person may justifiably use force in self-defense without an obligation to retreat first. Under these legal concepts, a person is justified in using deadly force in certain situations and the "stand your ground" law would be a defense or immunity to criminal charges and civil suit), the police were prohibited by law from making an arrest. The police chief also said that Zimmerman had had a right to defend himself with lethal force. As news of the case spread, thousands of protesters across the country called for Zimmerman's arrest and a full investigation. Six weeks after the shooting, amid widespread, intense, and in some cases misleading media coverage, Zimmerman was charged with murder by a special prosecutor appointed by Governor Rick Scott.

Zimmerman's trial began on June 10, 2013, in Sanford. On July 13, 2013, a jury acquitted him of second-degree murder and of manslaughter charges leading to more protests concerning racial profiling, the stand-your-ground-law, and gun rights. The racial question was the most outspoken of the protests due to the all-white jury, a history of racial profiling, and George Zimmerman's (although Hispanic genetically) physical appearance as a white man. The racial injustice of a seventeen year old black man being gunned down by a 'white' neighbourhood watchman hit the newstands like wildfire and demonstrations spread throughout the United States with a great fervour and these protests were only intensified after the trial had concluded with an acquittal.

6. Following the presentations on the Trayvon Martin case, write a letter to the editor in response to Christopher Dickey's article.
→ Focus on Skills, Writing a Letter to the Editor, p. 290

Dear Editor,
I enjoyed the Christopher Dickey article entitled Kill Zone. It was well-researched with backing statistics and a poignant underlying story (Tyquran Horton and his family). I could not help but to agree with many of Dickey's points when concerning urban gun-violence. The obvious connection I made to the article was the Trayvon Martin case. The parties involved were a black teenager and a twenty-eight year old Hispanic man, living in a metropolitan area of Florida, with the prior dying from a gunshot wound inflicted by the latter. Dickey's statistics about the racial divide and the violence within cities really hit home when speaking about the Martin case and I would like to applaud Dickey on bring up a lesser known case and using the information he had at hand to really get into the true problem in America; gun violence against minorities in cities. Dickey explains how rural areas are not a big issue when it comes to gun-ownership and violence and he also makes it clear that minorities are not the root cause of the difficulties; it is the city, the socioeconomic differences, and the urban setting of gangs and access to illegal guns that become the problem.
The one thing that I would advise is making sure that people also know that there are quite a few unregistered weapons that gangs use and that, although the chart shows that 28 % of urban households own guns, that does not take into account the illegally obtained weapons that many gang-involved people carry. It may skew the data slightly. In any case however, I think putting this article on display was a great choice and I believe that Dickey did a sensational job to not make the problem about race.

Sincerely,
Gun-owning Reader

Moms Demand Action on Gun Laws (pp. 123–125)

About the text	The 'text' here is mostly a visual representation of the fairly ridiculous standards in a couple of American laws. All three images depict one child holding a seemingly innocent item that is outlawed in the United States or in American schools and then another child holding an assault weapon. The caption explains why the innocent item is banned while the title piece states 'One child is holding something that's been banned in America to protect them. Guess which one.'
Level	● ○ ○
Additional material	GaST: no. 2, 20, 27

- Die Awareness-Aufgabe wird nach den Angaben im Schülerbuch durchgeführt.
- Aufgabe 1 wird in Gruppen zu sechs Teilnehmern bearbeitet, wobei je zwei Schülerinnen und Schüler ein Bild bearbeiten. Im Anschluss an die Erarbeitungsphase tauschen die Schüler ihre Ergebnisse innerhalb der Gruppen aus und füllen gemeinsam folgende Tabelle, die sie in ihre Hefte übernehmen, aus:

Moms Demand Action on Gun Laws

stylistic devices	examples	function
- two children: a boy and a girl - the boy is holding a Kinder chocolate egg - the girl is holding a gun - the children look very serious	One child is holding something that's been banned in America to protect them. Guess which one. We won't sell Kinder chocolate eggs in the interest of child safety. Why not assault weapons?	- two children - one holding a toy - one holding a gun - both looking very serious - the first part of the caption explains that one item has been banned in the U.S. to protect children - the reader is asked to tell which one - the second part explains why the toy in question is banned in the U.S. ➔ There is an element of surprise which makes the reader think about the issue because one would automatically assume the gun to be banned and not the seemingly harmless toy.
- two boys - one boy is holding an inflatable rubber ball - the other boy is holding a gun - the boys look very serious	One child is holding something that's been banned in America to protect them. Guess which one. We ban the game dodge ball because it's viewed as being too violent. Why not assault weapons?	
- two girls - one girl is holding a copy of "Little Red Riding Hood" - the other girl is holding a gun - the girls look very serious	One child is holding something that's been banned in America to protect them. Guess which one. We keep "Little Red Riding Hood" out of schools because of the bottle of wine in her basket. Why not assault weapons?	

Die Ergebnissicherung erfolgt in einem kurzen Unterrichtsgespräch über **Folie**. Alternativ dazu füllen die Schüler die Tabelle auf Folie aus und präsentieren ihre Ergebnisse.

- Bei der Bearbeitung von **Aufgabe 2** in **Einzel- oder Partnerarbeit** werden die Ergebnisse in eine Tabelle (s. Lösungsvorschlag unten) eingetragen. Die Sicherung erfolgt im **Unterrichtsgespräch** über **Folie**.
- Die im Rahmen der Bearbeitung von **Aufgabe 3** entworfenen Briefe werden im Klassenzimmer ausgehängt und im Rahmen eines **Museumsrundgangs** von der Klasse zur Kenntnis genommen und diskutiert.
- Bei der Bearbeitung von **Aufgabe 4** müssen eine Doppelstunde für das Erstellen der Präsentationen und eine weitere für die Präsentationen veranschlagt werden. Den Schülerinnen und Schülern muss Moderationsmaterial zur Verfügung gestellt werden. Darüber hinaus muss der Zugang zu PCs und dem Internet gewährleistet sein.

SOLUTIONS AWARENESS

"Moms Demand Action", a collective of mothers calling for gun law reform, has launched a print and television advertising campaign focused on children in school. In a Round Robin activity (➔ FoM, p. 270), state your first impression of this idea/campaign.

The images here are very attention capturing. Seeing a very young child holding an assault weapon is very disconcerting and then putting that child next to the 'banned' items that are seemingly innocent is a genius marketing strategy that will definitely make people look.

SOLUTIONS COMPREHENSION

1. **One day after the Sandy Hook massacre, on December 15, 2012, Shannon Watts, a 42-year-old mother of five children from Indianapolis, Indiana, founded "Moms Demand Action" (MDA) on Facebook. The initiative immediately gained tens of thousands of followers and has launched several anti-gun advertising campaigns since.**
   Take a look at the adverts and describe them in detail taking into consideration
   a) pictorial and
   b) textual elements in order to identify the message of the adverts.

➔ Focus on Skills, Analysis of Visuals, p. 262

All three images depict one child holding a seemingly innocent item that is outlawed in the United States or in American schools and then another child holding an assault weapon. The caption explains why the innocent item is banned while the title piece states 'One child is holding something that's been banned in America to protect them. Guess which one.'

- In **picture 1**, the innocent item is a candy egg that was banned in the United States because it has a toy embedded inside. This, by rule of the Food and Drug Administration, is against American law and is therefore banned. The egg being considered 'dangerous' when in comparison to the assault weapon is rather silly.
- In **picture 2**, the innocent item is an inflatable rubber ball used to play dodgeball. Due to injuries in gym class, dodgeball was banned in the United States after being dubbed 'too violent', an awkward thought when compared to the violent capabilities of a completely legal assault weapon.
- **Picture 3** shows a copy of 'Little Red Riding Hood' (not the Brothers Grimm version) which was banned in schools for showing a bottle of wine in her basket. The thought here was that showing the bottle of wine would lead children to imbibing alcohol. When put next to an assault weapon, the question one should ask when using the same logic, "Should not an assault weapon be banned then, because that will lead to killing?"

All three images use the phrase 'One child is holding something that's been banned in America to protect them. Guess which one.' This is because the seemingly obvious choice of which should be banned would be the gun, but in the United States, the other objects are against the law.

SOLUTIONS ANALYSIS

2. Relate the message of the adverts to the article "Kill Zone" by Christopher Dickey and explain what they have in common. The links on the webcode provide you with further information on "Moms Demand Action" and their campaigns.

Webcode SNG-40175-011 @

The adverts are comparable to the article because of the availability of guns in the United States. The advertisements are depictions of a readily available gun, completely legal, and an illegal object that does not make a lot of sense in comparison. In Dickey's article, he begins with the world of Tyquran Horton, a child, who sees guns constantly. Weapons are part of the boy's world and are something that he has grown accustomed to being around (l. 19).

Seeing how the police officers are required by their superiors to stop a boy of Tyquran's age, it is obvious that underage people have the ability to obtain weapons (ll. 38–51). This then transitions to Tyquran asking the same question as the adverts, "Why should the United States have guns in the first place (ll. 55–56)?"

Kill Zone	Moms Demand Action
Young people have access to weapons.	children holding assault weapons
Tyquran's question, 'Why should the US have guns in the first place?'	why assault weapons are not banned but these innocent items are
relates killing to young people in schools	shows children in schools with weapons
Guns are used for 'protection'.	Banning these items for protection but allowing assault weapons is rather ironic.
Weapons are part of city children's lives.	The children look comfortable holding the weapons.
Tyquran's grandmother says that the kids are given guns at a young age to make them into killing machines.	The comfortable way the children are holding the weapons make them seem like they are the children the grandmother speaks of.
Minorities are the ones hurt by the weapons while white people are less inclined for the damage and are more secure with weapons.	All of the photos depict a Caucasian child holding the weapon next to a minority, those minorities are at risk to be injured while the white kids are looking more secure.

SOLUTIONS ACTIVITIES

3. Together with a partner, write an Internet blog in response to the advertising campaign "Moms Demand Action". State what you like or dislike about it and make suggestions for further/different campaigns.

➔ Focus on Skills, Writing a Letter to the Editor, p. 290

Guys Against Guns (Blog)

Alright guys, haven't written anything for a little while but I saw some advertisements that definitely caught my eye, definitely attention grabbing for anyone who wants more gun control!
All three of the Moms Demand Action images depict one child holding a seemingly innocent item that is outlawed in the United States or in American schools and then another child holding an assault weapon. The caption explains why the innocent item is banned while the title piece states 'One child is holding something that's been banned in America to protect them. Guess which one.' The advertising strategy here is genius. What type of person wouldn't be a little shocked to see an 8–10-year old holding an AK-47 next to a kid holding a chocolate egg?
That shock and awe factor has to be one of the things I like most about the image. The two wildly different items held by two very similar people make for a great look into the backwards nature of America's gun control laws. How would Little Red Riding Hood be a banned item when a military grade assault rifle is not? The stoic faces, the comfortable nature in which the kids look like they are holding the gun, the setting of each photoshoot; it is all perfect for a great ad.
There is one minor detail that could be pulled out a little bit and that is the clarification words. They are a little small for the text to be explaining the scene and I would rather see that a bit larger so as an onlooker could get a further grasp of what is being depicted. I would think Moms Demand Action could keep going with adverts like this. The United States has some very silly laws. In Indiana it is illegal for a monkey to smoke a cigarette, horses cannot be kept in bathtubs in South Carolina, in Boulder, Colorado, a person cannot leave a couch outside a porch; yet, assault weapons are still perfectly legal. Using the ridiculous laws that some of the States have would be a perfect way to keep this advertising campaign going.

4. In groups, think about other campaigns to reduce (gun) violence in schools, school buses, etc. Design and create posters, websites or blogs that demand action to be taken. Afterwards, display your results in class and discuss their various messages.

Other campaigns all relating to end gun violence:
- Brady Campaign
- Not One More Campaign
- Everytown for Gun Safety
- Stop Handgun Violence Organization

One such way would be to design a poster with kids in a school bunkered down behind upturned desks and broken chalkboards, all of them holding a weapon, maybe one pulling the pin out of a grenade, and then have the text 'When did school become a warzone?'.
Doing something like this would keep the shock value of kids holding weapons and then also relate what is happening with gun violence to the world tragedy that is war.

Common Grounds and Cultural Clashes?! – Living Together in the 21st Century

TM[1]	SB[2]	Author: Title of text	Type of text	Topic	Competences	Audio CD	Film CD-ROM	GaST[3]	Diff[4]	Comp[5]
Start-up Activities										
182	128	Applying for U.S. Citizenship	cartoon	people of various professions queuing for US citizenship	• analysing a cartoon • preparing and acting out a role play					
182	129	The Global Village Project	online article, visual	a film about a project providing young survivors of war with an education and social services	• analysing the contents of a text • preparing and giving a presentation			no. 17, 24		
Are You with Us? – Cultural Clashes and Common Grounds										
184	130	Eric Bogosian: subUrbia	play, book cover, cartoon	three Americans talking about immigrants and the countries they are from their lack of knowledge of other countries and their prejudices	• interpreting stage directions • listening comprehension • analysing the contents and language of a play • writing a characterization • analysing a cartoon • creative writing • grammar: tenses and indirect speech, working with vocabulary	CD 2, 2			84	no. 15
192	135	Marike Frick: Tanz mit mir	German newspaper interview, cartoon	interview from *Zeit* newspaper about different ways of expressing oneself in different cultures	• mediating a text • analysing a text • writing and acting out a role play • grammar: gerunds and infinitives			no. 17		

1 TM = page in Teachers' Manual
2 SB = page in Students' Book
3 GaST = material in Grammar and Skills Trainer
4 Diff = page in Differenzierungsmaterial
5 Comp = material in Comprehension: Reading – Listening – Viewing

TM[1]	SB[2]	Author: Title of text	Type of text	Topic	Competences	Audio CD	Film CD-ROM	GaST[3]	Diff[4]	Comp[5]
195	137	David Cameron: Speech on the Government's Immigration Policy	political speech, visual, cartoon	Prime Minister David Cameron about various aspects of immigration visual: cultural kaleidoscope cartoon: immigrants queuing to be permitted into the country	• listening comprehension • analysing a documentary video • analysing visuals • preparing and carrying out a hot seat activity • creative writing • grammar/ language: formal and informal English	CD 2, 3		no. 25	93	no. 16
202	144	Marilyn Chin: How I Got That Name – An Essay on Assimilation	poem, photo	a Chinese immigrant talks about her family and their attempts to become Americans	• listening/reading comprehension • analysing a poem • analysing a photo • doing Internet research • creative writing	CD 2, 4			104	
Let's Come Together?! – Migrants, Minorities, Majorities										
206	146	David Cameron: The Doctrine of Multiculturalism Has Failed	political speech	the failure of multiculturalism and its reasons extremism as one possible consequence possible solutions	• discussing a text			no. 25		
207	147	Sunny Hundal: Multiculturalism Has Won the Day. Let's Move On	newspaper article	Britain as a multicultural society the positive response of the British population	• reading comprehension • analysing texts • creative writing • grammar: reported speech				112	
207	148	Khola Hasan: Mr. Cameron, British Multiculturalism Is Doing Fine	newspaper article	British multiculturalism as a positive experience problems and chances of a multicultural Britain	• see above					
215	151	Fareed Zakaria: Broken and Obsolete	magazine article, cartoon, statistics	the USA as an immigration country compared to others immigration and assimilation	• analysing the contents and language of a text • analysing statistics • planning a campaign					

TM[1]	SB[2]	Author: Title of text	Type of text	Topic	Competences	Audio CD	Film CD-ROM	GaST[3]	Diff[4]	Comp[5]
220	153	Sandra Cisneros: No Speak English	short story, magazine cover	the situation of a Latina who has followed her husband to the USA she does not speak English and is not at all integrated into society	• analysing the contents and style of a text • creative writing • grammar: adverbs and adverbials					no. 17
	156	Great Britain: Immigration and Minorities	Focus on Facts							
	158	The United States: Immigration and Minorities	Focus on Facts					no. 25		
226	159	Jhumpa Lahiri: The Namesake	novel, film, film stills	a teenage boy growing up between two cultures the search for one's identity	• analysing the contents and style of a fictional text • describing and analysing a visual • characterizing a figure in literature • analysing a film scene		7	no. 1		no. 18
	163	Thematic Vocabulary	Focus on Vocab							

Start-up (pp. 128–129)

About the artist	Pat Bagley is a liberal American editorial cartoonist and journalist for *The Salt Lake Tribune* in Salt Lake City, Utah, and an author and illustrator of several books.	---
About the picture **About the project**	The cartoon is showing Uncle Sam accepting immigrants into the states while a representative for the republican party sees them only as more votes for the democratic party.	The Global Village Project provides female refugees from war-torn countries with a school to better support them in their displacement to the United States. With over 35,000 refugees displaced a year, the school hopes to provide them with a longstanding voice.
Level	● ● ○	● ● ○
Additional Material	---	GaST: no. 17, 24

- Zur Bearbeitung von **Aufgabe 1 können folgende Internetadressen** von Nutzen sein:
  www.migrationpolicy.org/article/frequently-requested-statistics-immigrants-and-immigration-united-states-1
  immigrationinamerica.org/603–immigration-waves.html
  www.migrationpolicy.org/article/frequently-requested-statistics-immigrants-and-immigration-united-states
- Die Schülerinnen und Schüler analysieren den Cartoon gemeinsam und notieren sich **Stichwörter**, die sie in **mündlichen Kurzvorträgen** über den Cartoon bündeln.

- **Aufgabe 2** kann in **Gruppen** zu 4–6 Schülerinnen und Schülern erledigt werden. Die eine Hälfte der Gruppe erstellt **Rollenkarten für Vertreter der Einwanderungsbehörde, die andere Hälfte erstellt Karten für die Einwanderer. Danach wird das Rollenspiel zunächst in den Gruppen durchgeführt. Während dieser Phase hat der Lehrer bzw. die Lehrerin die Möglichkeit, sich verschiedene Dialoge anzuhören und einzelne für eine Präsentation im Plenum auszuwählen.**
- **Aufgabe 3** wird nach der **individuellen Lektüre** des Textes im **Unterrichtsgespräch** bearbeitet. Die Ergebnisse der Diskussion können in einem informellen **Tafelanschrieb** gesichert werden.
- Für die Erarbeitung der Präsentationen (**Aufgabe 4**) müssen die entsprechenden Materialien zur Verfügung gestellt werden. Für die Gruppenarbeit ist eine Doppelstunde, für die Präsentationen eine weitere Doppelstunde zu veranschlagen.

SOLUTIONS START-UP ACTIVITIES

1. Together with a partner, first get some background information and read the info box, then describe the cartoon. What kind of immigrants are applying for U. S. citizenship and how do the "authorities" react to them?

The cartoon depicts Uncle Sam (Initials U.S., is a common national person fication of the American government that, according to legend, came into use during the war of 1812 and was supposedly named for Samuel Wilson, a meat-packer from New York) speaking with an elephant in a suit (representing the Republican Party) about the immigrants coming into the United States. One immigrant is holding a science book along with a backup signaling that she intends to go to university while the others are holding objects that are stereotypes when concerning illegal immigrants (gardening tools, cooking pans, children, fruit picking bag, cleaning supplies. Uncle Sam is saying that these people are working hard for their citizenship, which is true considering their employment options, while the elephant sees them only as donkeys, symbol of the democrats, which would give the Democratic Party more votes in any election. Uncle Sam, symbol of American freedom, does not see the problem while the elephant only sees the implications brought on by bringing in more poor people for the democratic vote.

2. Imagine: Some of you are the immigrants and some are the "authorities" shown in the cartoon. Think about a) a strategy and arguments that might convince the immigration authorities to accept you as a legal citizen and b) questions you would ask to get information from the immigrants.

Act out role plays in class.

a) Need to escape the drug cartel's abuse of the poor in Mexico, intent to attend university, intent to immigrate legally, capabilities in the work force
b) How they gained access to the country, what they do for a living, how many children they have and if they too are in the States, intended employment/line of study, previous criminal activity, familial ties in the States

3. Read the information given about the objectives (*Ziele*) and plans of the *Global Village School*. What is the project's long-term goal?

The long-term goal of the *Global Village School* is to raise awareness of the children displaced by war, and to show that these children are not beyond our borders but have become new US citizens capable of helping build the country's future (ll. 45–48).The hope is, that through the film and by working together, the young women of the *Global Village School* will become a unified voice for all refugee children that are relocated to the US.

4. In groups, prepare presentations on the work of the *Global Village School* and watch the documentary film provided on the webcode. Give presentations in class and, additionally, compile hand-outs or posters providing further details and information on the school.

Webcode SNG-40175-012 @

→ Focus on Skills, Presentations, p. 276

- People from war-torn countries like Thailand, Uganda, Congo, etc. move away due to war.
- They do not have clothes, shelter, food, etc.
- These girls are all teenagers, coming from war, and have to deal with both their present and past.
- The school ensures no one is lost in subjects, allows for specific activities and learning opportunities.

- Special care is given to those who have just arrived and tutors knowledgeable in the language of the student are brought in to help ease transition.
- Some teachers come from refugee school backgrounds.
- Atlanta Presbyterian Church gave them the building and a grant was given by Atlanta Charter Schools.
- Some children have lost their parents.
- Arrive at the school around 8:30 AM and just talk for half an hour to make sure people are doing well.
- Writing, social studies, math, reading, and science; these are the classes offered – Fridays have art class instead of science.
- The Geneva Convention which comprised four treaties, and three additional protocols, that establish the standards of international law for the humanitarian treatment of war, allows for people to become refugees depending upon a criteria.
- Some people do not know how to use elevators or bathrooms, they do not know a lot of very normal things in the United States.
- Enrolling students in normal schools is of high priority for Global Village.
- It was difficult for the girls in normal high schools because students would beat them up and blame things on them.
- The film also depicts areas in foreign countries that hold refugee camps.

Are You with Us? – Cultural Clashes and Common Grounds

Eric Bogosian

subUrbia (pp. 130–134)

About the author	Eric Bogosian is an American actor, playwright, monologuist, and novelist. He is well-known for his plays *Talk Radio* and *subUrbia* along with numerous one-man shows. Bogosian has performed on Broadway and has won three Obie Awards for his solo shows. As a Guggenheim Fellow, he is considered one of the most exceptional creative artists in the field of theatre.
About the text	The text here is concerning three friends talking about another person who is in a convenience store. The convenience store worker is an Indian immigrant while the three friends are speaking about the man's right to be in the United States.
Level	● ● ●
Additional material	Audio CD 2, 2 Differenzierungsmaterial, p. 84 Comprehension: no. 15

- Bei der Bearbeitung der **Awareness-Aufgabe** können die Schülerinnen und Schüler dazu aufgefordert werden, ihre Ideen auf Blätter zu schreiben, die im Klassenzimmer aufgehängt werden. Am Ende der Besprechung des Auszugs kann dann auf diese Blätter rekurriert werden, um herauszufinden, wie viel des tatsächlichen Handlungsverlaufs die Schülerinnen und Schüler korrekt antizipiert haben.
- **Aufgabe 1** kann in **Partnerarbeit** bearbeitet werden. Die Ergebnisse werden mit einer anderen Zweiergruppe verglichen und diskutiert. Um zu vermeiden, dass die Schülerinnen und Schüler bereits hier Teile des Textes lesen, der in der folgenden Aufgabe zunächst nur über Hörverstehen zur Kenntnis genommen werden soll, erscheint es sinnvoll, die dem ersten Akt vorangestellte Bühnenanweisung entweder in **Kopie** oder auf **Folie** zu präsentieren.
- **Aufgabe 2** wird anhand der Anweisungen im Schülerbuch bearbeitet.
- **Aufgabe 3** kann wiederum in **Partnerarbeit** erledigt werden. Die Ergebnissicherung erfolgt im **Unterrichtsgespräch** über **Folie**.

- Nachdem die Materialien des **Webcodes** präsentiert wurden (**Aufg. 4**), erhalten die Schülerinnen und Schüler den Auftrag, sich individuell **Stichwörter** zur Aufgabenstellung zu notieren.
- Die Ergebnisse dieser Arbeitsphase werden im Unterrichtsgespräch diskutiert und gebündelt. Die Sicherung erfolgt über **Tafelanschrieb**:

American Culture and Patriotism

The Pledge of Allegiance
one nation ... with liberty and justice for all

The Star-Spangled Banner
- *American military triumph*
- *"land of the free, home of the brave"*

America the Beautiful
- *natural beauty of the land*
- *God's will*
- *freedom/liberty*

↘ ↓ ↙

recurring values
- *brotherhood*
- *equality*
- *freedom/liberty*
- *oneness*

↕

Tim and Buff think Nazeer has no right to learn the Pledge of Allegiance because he is a foreigner and therefore inferior to Americans.

- **Aufgabe 5** wird zunächst **individuell** gelöst. Ggf. muss im Vorfeld der Begriff *Language Register* erläutert werden. Dies kann mithilfe der angegebenen **Focus on Language-Seite** (SB, S. 315) geschehen. Die Ergebnisse der Textuntersuchung werden im **Unterrichtsgespräch** gebündelt und in Form einer **Tabelle** (s. Lösungsvorschlag S. 189) auf **Folie** gesichert. Um die Zeit der Heftübernahme zu sparen, kann die Folie im Anschluss für die Klasse kopiert werden.
- **Aufgabe 6** kann als den ersten Teil der Beschäftigung mit dem Text abschließende **Hausaufgabe** erteilt werden.
- Der Vergleich der drei Werke (**Aufg. 7**) wird in **Gruppen** zu vier Schülerinnen und Schülern durchgeführt. Jeweils zwei Schüler beschäftigen sich mit einer Teilaufgabe. Im Anschluss an die Erarbeitungsphase werden die Ergebnisse innerhalb der Gruppen erläutert und diskutiert. Jeweils ein Vertreter der Gruppen präsentiert die Gruppenergebnisse im Plenum. Der Lehrer bzw. die Lehrerin bündelt die Ergebnisse und sichert sie in folgendem **Tafelbild**:

"Juicy and Delicious", "subUrbia", "Beasts of the Southern Wild" – a comparison

Juicy and Delicious	subUrbia		Beasts of the Southern Wild
end of the world scenario		*the possibility to learn from history*	
Miss Bathsheba: *people need to start thinking of the universe as a whole;* *it is important to care for others*	*Jeff:* *people have to know about other parts of the world*	*Jeff:* *people will be unaware of and uninterested in what happened before them*	*Hushpuppy:* *scientists of the future will find out about her way of life;* *this will teach them valuable lessons*

- **Aufgabe 8** wird in **Partnerarbeit** nach den Angaben im Schülerbuch bearbeitet.
- Nach der Erarbeitung des Dialogs (**Aufg. 9**) erhalten die Schülerinnen und Schüler Zeit, eine Präsentation einzustudieren. Die Dialoge werden in **Gruppen** zu sechs Schülerinnen und Schülern vorgeführt. Während dieser Phase hat der Lehrer bzw. die Lehrerin die Gelegenheit, sich einzelne Schülerarbeiten anzuhören und sie zu kommentieren.
- Alternativ zu Aufgabe 9 kann **Aufgabe 10** bearbeitet werden. Für die Kreativphase ist eine Doppelstunde, für die Präsentation der Ergebnisse eine weitere Doppelstunde anzusetzen.
- **Aufgabe 11** wird im Unterrichtsgespräch durchgeführt. Die Ergebnisse werden informell an der **Tafel** gesichert.
- Vor der Bearbeitung von **Aufgabe 12** sollten die angegebenen **Focus on Grammar-Seiten** (SB, S. 305 und S. 298) besprochen werden. Beim Gebrauch des *Simple Present* für die Zusammenfassung sollte auf das **3rd person -s** hingewiesen werden. Zu einem möglichen **Tafelanschrieb** für die indirekte Rede vgl. LB, S. 51.
- **Aufgabe 13** kann als **Hausaufgabe** erteilt werden.

SOLUTIONS AWARENESS

The given scene takes place in a multicultural suburban city in the USA. What do the items on the cover of this version of the play (on the opposite page) tell you about "life in a suburb"? Anticipate what the play might be about and what kind of characters the playwright has created.

The playbook cover is a cartoon-like illustration full of bright colours. It looks a lot like a comic book or an advertisement. One can see a large piece of pizza with splashing tomato sauce being shot by a revolver. There is also a doughnut with coloured sprinkles, a green bottle pouring out beer and the underside of a beverage can. There is also a small, blue, Smurf-like figure wearing a striped pointed cap. These are all popular commercial products found all over the US.
The play might deal with consumer culture, superficiality, American values, sameness in suburban life ...

SOLUTIONS COMPREHENSION

1. Read the stage directions given at the beginning of the scene and imagine the arrangement of the stage (e.g. scenery, props, furniture, decoration, lighting, sounds, etc.). Sketch out a rough draft of the stage and compare and discuss your various ideas in class.
→ Focus on Facts, Drama and Theatre, p. 254

Individual answers, for example:
- pay phone, bench, ice machine
- gap pumps
- trash can
- flyers/posters/stickers on the wall ("God bless America", "God bless our troops"...)
- spotlight on the bench
- an American flag
- sounds of nearby cars, traffic, honking, people walking by ...
- etc.

2. Before listening, divide the class into groups of three students each and distribute the three protagonists of the scene within your group. Take notes on your chosen character and follow the steps below.

CD 2 2

Step 1: In a first listening/reading, collect general information that is given about the characters (w-questions).

Tim Mitchum is a twenty-one-year-old American man. He is a former air force veteran who has served in a number of different countries, including India, the Philippines, Sri Lanka and Iraq (ll. 44ff., 61ff.). Tim is good friends with fellow-Americans Buff and Jeff and together they are spending their time talking outside the suburban neighbourhood convenience store (in which the Pakistani Nazeer "Norman" Chaudry, 24, and his sister Pakeesa, 20, work) eating pizza and Oreos, typical American snack foods. The area is obviously multicultural. Buff Macleod is about twenty years old. He is on rollerblades, balancing a boom-box. Jeff Gallagher is about twenty years old and is simply dressed with messy hair. They are having an animated discussion, frequently using strong language.

Step 2:
Copy the grid below and listen to/read the scene a second time. Make notes on your chosen character and his attitudes to the respective topic.

	Nazeer Chaudry	the Third World	world politics
Tim	• ... crack his dot head ... • moron • he has no right • give him a one-way ticket back to greaseball land	• third-world shit • smell like you wiped your ass ... • people are dog-eating greaseballs • soak [our clothes] in gasoline just to kill the bugs • they're all the same ... sub-human	• the gooks do it to themselves • fucking chaos on a stick • the Cos used to give us that shit
Buff	• I caught him practicing the Pledge of Allegiance ... • I know better than he does • ... isn't that guy from Arabia ... • You're not a gook if you're from Arabia	• Gooks are like Chinese and shit.	• ... you're getting me all upset ... • Total waste ... • at least there's Oreos
Jeff	• The guy is just nervous. • Stranger in a strange land. • Of course he has a right. • He's trying to improve his situation. • He's from a third-world country. I respect him for that. • He's a human being. • He wants to be like us.	• India and Saudi Arabia aren't even the same continents ... • pizza could feed a family ... • ... that slice ... could be the difference between life and death ...	• The American Empire. • Everyone should get upset. • Nothing ever fucking changes ... • ... generations of suckers will try to figure out ... they will all be fuck of shit. • It's all so fucking futile! • There's a world outside this fucking tar pit of stupidity. • Let's play in the mud with our iPods ... • It's the end of the world ... no ideas, no hope, no future.

Step 3: After a third listening/reading, complete your notes.
Tip: If you still have some "blanks" in your grid and need further help and information, you can form "expert teams" in your class which only consist of students who focused on the same character. After exchanging your findings and completing your notes, go back to your initial group (see diagram, SB, p. 132).

Step 4: Finally, the students in each group exchange their findings and results on all the characters in the scene and complete the grid.
→ Focus on Skills, Reading Techniques, p. 247
→ Focus on Skills, Listening Comprehension, p. 244

SOLUTIONS ANALYSIS

3. In a first step, juxtapose (*gegenüberstellen*) what the characters reveal about "the American way":

	"The American Way"	characters' views and attitudes
Tim	• ... crack his dot head ... • ... neo-fascist ... • ... he has no right • ... third world shit ... • ... those places smell like you wiped your ass ... • ... the people are dog-eating greaseballs ... • ... give him ... a one-way ticket back to greaseball land. • ... Goa ... gasoline to kill the bugs ... get the shits for a week. • The Cos used to give us that shit • ... they're ... sub-human ...	→ racist → prejudiced → excluding others → looks down on other cultures → fascist
Buff	• The Pledge of Allegiance ... invisible ... • I know better ... • Gooks are like Chinese and shit ... • Total waste. • ... at least there's Oreos ...	→ patriotic but ignorant; uneducated → prejudiced → racist → child-like; naïve; reproducing advertising slogans
Jeff	• ... stranger in a strange land ... • ... liberty ... indivisible ... • Of course he has a right. • He's trying to improve his situation. • That's the American way. • He's from ... I respect him for that. • He's a human being. • It's my duty as a human being ... • Iraq .. Darfur ... Haiti ... tar pit ... the end of the world • Let's play with our iPods ...	→ understanding → American values and goals → individual achievement and improvement → multiculturalism → respect → responsibility → criticism of military actions ... war ... → criticism of consumption ... banal entertainment ...

In a further step, explain what these views express/imply about the characters' views and attitudes on immigration and foreigners.
→ Focus on Skills, Analysis of a Fictional Text, p. 255

Webcode SNG-40175-013 @

4. Use the material provided on the webcode and try to give a definition of "the American Way", i. e. the American culture and patriotism. Compare and contrast Tim's and Buff's understanding of "one nation under God" to the ideas of liberty and justice for all and the patriot dream as described in the materials provided on the webcode.

the Pledge of Allegiance → one nation ... with liberty and justice for all
the Star-Spangled Banner → emphasizes American military triumph, "land of the free, home of the brave"
America the Beautiful → emphasizes natural beauty of the land, God's will, freedom/liberty
recurring values: brotherhood, equality, freedom/liberty, oneness

Tim and Buff refer to the American Pledge of Allegiance. They claim that Nazeer (and immigrants in general) "has no right" (l. 30) to learn and say it because he is not a "real" American. Ironically, Buff scoffs at Nazeer's attempts to learn it – presumably to pass the test to become a naturalized American citizen – but cannot recite it properly himself, even though he is a "real" American (ll. 23–26). Tim claims that foreigners are fundamentally inferior to Americans and therefore do not deserve the same treatment as the superior Americans (ll. 53ff., 64f.). This contradicts the Pledge of Allegiance's message of America as "one nation" and "with liberty and justice **for all**".

5. Examine the characters' use of language and their language register and explain how it supports the message of the scene (play).

→ Focus on Language, The Language Register of English, p. 315

character	example from the text	characters' views and attitudes – explanation
Tim	• crack his dot head • moron • shove 'em up your ass • spare me ... shit • I've seen ..., man. • greaseball ... • shit • ass ... • I gotta ... • get back to base ... get the shits ... • ... fucking ... • Goans ... Schmoans ... • bullshit	→ slang, offensive language → taboo words → informal English → vulgarity → lack of education and manners → ignorance
Buff	• Boning up for ... • ... one nation under God, invisible ... • But like ... • ... some shit like that ... • gooks • Yo, homey ... • ... coagulated ... chocolaty ... delicious ...	→ informal language → wrong adjective (indivisible) → slang → offensive taboo words → some Standard English words/advertising language ... → limited education → advertising language/knowledge
Jeff	• It's gotta be hard. • He's trying to improve ... • ... indivisible ... not invisible ... • ... screwed up 'cause we fuck them up ... • ... Hitler was greasing the Jews ... You're bumming me up ... ever fucking ... those suckers ... • ... this tar pit of stupidity ... • void	→ informal English → Standard English → education → slang, taboo words → slang, taboo words → metaphorical language → formal → flexible use of different language registers → more educated and critical; knowledge of history

6. Based on the information you collected in the grid and the previous tasks, write a coherent characterization of your chosen character in about 200 – 250 words.

→ Focus on Skills, Characterization of a Figure in Literature, p. 264

Tip: Do not forget to back up your findings with quotes from the scene.

For example:
Tim Mitchum is a twenty-one year old American man. He is a former air force veteran who has served in many different countries, including India, the Philippines, Sri Lanka and Iraq (ll. 44ff., 61ff.). Despite his extensive travels, Tim holds very negative and scornful stereotypes about foreigners in general. He uses racial slurs, such as dot head (l. 13), gook (l. 53), and greaseball (l. 38), which reveals his biased and stereotyped way of thinking. He also regularly uses violent and vulgar language and obscenities (ll. 14f., 36ff.).

He has no sympathy with the situation of third-world citizens and is very judgemental, claiming that they "did it to themselves" (l. 53), and considers them all to be exactly the same and "sub-human" (ll. 61–65). He is also extremely contemptuous towards foreigners in his own neighbourhood, shouting slurs and prejudiced insults at a local Indian man who is obviously not doing Tim any harm. Tim is good friends with Buff and Jeff and spends his time outside the neighbourhood convenience store eating pizza and Oreos, typical American snack foods. He rejects his friend Jeff's more understanding and tolerant view, refusing to acknowledge America's role in the Third World. (197 words)

7. Analyse Jeff's final statement about "the world outside the tar pit of stupidity" (ll. 101 f.) and his view of the "end of the world" and correlate it with the excerpts from
a) Lucy Alibar's play "Juicy and Delicious" (pp. 97 ff.) and
b) the screenplay version of Lucy Alibar's play, "Beasts of the Southern Wild" (pp. 102 f.).
→ Focus on Skills, Analysis of a Screenplay, p. 257

a) Both excerpts depict end of the world scenarios. In *Juicy and Delicious*, Miss Bathsheba points out that "the universe is coming unrendered. Things are dying ain't supposed to die" (ll. 43f.). This implies that people need to start caring about the universe as a whole, not just their own small part of it. Miss Bathsheba also tells the children about the importance of caring for people they haven't even met yet (ll. 35f.) and being sweet and taking care of one another (ll. 91f.). In a similar way, Jeff calls for people to start caring about other parts of the world by ironically saying that they should all just ignore it and "play in the mud with [their] iPods" (ll. 102f.). What he really means is that people should pay attention to other parts of the world outside of their own "tar pit" (l. 101) and start "giving a shit", i.e. caring, even though he thinks that the situation is hopeless.

b) There is a striking parallel between the excerpts with regard to history and whether or not subsequent generations will learn from earlier ones. In *Beasts of the Southern Wild*, Hushpuppy asserts that "When I die, the scientists of the future, they gonna find it all. They gonna know, once there was a Hushpuppy, and she lived with her Daddy in the Bathtub" (ll. 90ff.). In other words, Hushpuppy's story will be of interest to future generations and can help them and teach them valuable lessons. In contrast, Jeff claims that in fifty or a hundred years or more, people will be unaware of what happened before them: "they won't even know we were ever here" (ll. 86f.). He underlines the futility of learning and improving over time because people refuse to take an interest and care about what happened before. Thus, his outlook is much more pessimistic than Hushpuppy's.

8. Together with a partner, analyse the cartoon (p. 134):
a) Describe the pictorial elements first.
b) Examine the caption and visualize the implied correlations in a diagram (e.g. SB, p. 133).
c) Identify the message of the cartoon and relate it to the given scene from the play "subUrbia".
→ Focus on Skills, Analysis of Visuals, p. 262

a) The cartoon shows four children, each of a different race, holding hands in a circle. Each child is staring at the next child in a counterclockwise direction and giving him/her a dirty look. An African American boy with curly hair and wearing a striped shirt is sneering at a white girl with blonde pigtails on his left. She, in turn, is glaring at an Asian girl with straight hair wearing jeans, who is baring her teeth at a Hispanic girl wearing a pleated skirt and a blouse with fluffy sleeves.

b) Individual answers

c) The cartoon shows that the different racial groups have preconceived notions about each other regarding their relative similarities and differences to other groups, but these claims are completely wrong. In fact, they are the complete opposite of what each group thinks about the other. It shows that it is impossible to generalize about entire races. Since the groups have such varying and contradictory ideas about each other, they probably have much more in common than they think.

In the same vein, Jeff is able to sympathize and empathize with someone of a different race – Nazeer, a young Indian man. Jeff speculates that "it's gotta be hard" to be an immigrant (l. 21). He also states that he respects Nazeer for trying to improve his situation (ll. 31ff.). Unlike Jeff, and like the children in the cartoon, Tim makes sweeping generalizations about his own race versus people from third world countries, such as India and Iraq. He claims that Americans are inherently superior to Asians, saying that "They're all the same. Sub-human" (ll. 64f.).

SOLUTIONS ACTIVITIES

9. Throughout the scene Nazeer Chaudry and his sister Pakeesa have overheard the conversation of the three young men hanging out in front of their convenience store. Together with a partner, collect ideas about what they might have been thinking about the three young Americans and their behaviour and write a dialogue that reflects their thoughts and feelings. Afterwards, act out your dialogues in class.

Individual answers

Nazeer: Those boys! Don't they know we can hear them talking about me? Such ignorance! I'd like to have them arrested for loitering.
Pakeesa: Don't, Nazeer! It will only make things worse! Just ignore them.
... etc.

10. In groups, develop ideas about how the scene might go on. Sketch out a storyline and write dialogues/ monologues, etc. Do not forget to employ stage directions. Finally, act out your additional scenes in class and discuss the respective rendering.
→ Focus on Skills, Continuation of a Fictional Text, p. 277

Individual answers

11. Comment on and discuss Jeff's statement that "he [Nazeer] wants to be like us" (l. 43). What exactly does he mean – and do you think that this is true?

When Jeff claims that Nazeer wants to be like him and his friends (l. 43), he means that Nazeer wants to become an American citizen and lead a "typical American" life. Nazeer wants to live according to fundamental American principles and values, such as liberty, freedom, etc. He also wants the chance to run his business and become successful, i.e. live the American Dream: make a better life for himself (ll. 31f.), earn his own money, make a living, have a family, house, material possessions, etc.
On the other hand, Nazeer is obviously very different from the three American boys: He is quiet, well-behaved, employed, and ambitious, while the three boys (especially Tim and Buff) are ignorant, crude, loud and racist. Buff seems more interested in Oreo cookies than serious social issues (ll. 94ff.). It is clear that Nazeer is not striving to become "more like them" in this sense – i.e. more materialistic, crude and ignorant.

SOLUTIONS GRAMMAR/LANGUAGE

12. Summarize the given scene. Be careful to use the correct tense and indirect speech to report what the characters say. Additionally, transform the scene into appropriate English and avoid informal and slang expressions.
→ Focus on Grammar, Tenses, pp. 305 ff.
→ Focus on Grammar, Indirect Speech, pp. 298 f.

For example:
The given scene from Eric Bogosian's play *subUrbia* is taken from the first act and takes place in a multicultural suburban area in a city in the USA. Three young Americans, Tim Mitchum, Buff Macleod and Jeff Gallagher, are standing in front of a convenience store that is owned and run by a Pakistani immigrant, Nazeer Chaudry, and his sister Pakeesa.
Tim and Buff appear to be very prejudiced and are upset about the presence of Nazeer Chaudry and his sister. They call him offensive names and mock him in a very rude and offensive way and threaten to attack him. Tim claims to have seen the world and explains that people like Nazeer are from smelly and dirty places where people eat dogs. He hates political correctness and finally claims that these foreigners are sub-human. Buff shares Tim's views and is very prejudiced and offensive as well. In contrast, Jeff seems to understand Nazeer's situation and contradicts Tim's and Buff's insulting statements. He also corrects Buff's mistakes when citing the Pledge of Allegiance. Jeff explains to Buff and Tim that improving one's situation is the American way and that he respects Nazeer for his thrift and ambition. Additionally, he shows that he is critical of people's stupidity and ignorance and their endless consumption of useless things, especially as there are so many serious problems in the world that should be tackled.

13. Make clusters to express Nazeer's mixed feelings about his situation. Use your dictionary for help (examples: see SB, p. 134).

- Cluster 'positive feelings': hopeful, relieved, confident, expectant, trusting, optimistic, whole-hearted, cheerful, etc.
- Cluster 'negative feelings': disappointed, appalled, annoyed, displeased, disturbed, miserable, depressed, unhappy, etc.
- Cluster 'ambivalent feelings': homesick, ambivalent, hesitant, sorrowful, unstable, ashamed, doubtful, indecisive, etc.

Marike Frick

Tanz mit mir (pp. 135–137)

About the author	Marike Frick is a German journalist. Her articles have been published in *DIE ZEIT*, *Brigitte WOMAN*, and *Geolino*. She has published several texts on the topic of intercultural relation(ship)s.
About the text	"Tanz mit mir" is an interview with intercultural trainer Gary Thomas. Thomas talks about potential difficulties in intercultural relations and he describes some typical traps. He gives advice on how to avoid embarrassment especially in more formal situations such as business meetings.
Level	● ● ○
Additional Material	GaST: no. 17

- Die **Awareness-Aufgabe** kann in **Kleingruppen** durchgeführt werden.
- Die Gruppenergebnisse werden im **Plenum** kurz vorgestellt und miteinander verglichen.
- Zur Bearbeitung von **Aufgabe 1** wird der Text in **Kopie** ausgeteilt, damit die Schülerinnen und Schüler die Passagen markieren können, die ins Englische übertragen werden sollen. Ggf. muss vor der Bearbeitung die angegebene **Focus on Skills-Seite** (SB, S. 265) besprochen werden. Die Aufgabe kann zunächst in **Partnerarbeit** bearbeitet werden. Die Schülerinnen und Schüler wählen vor dem Hintergrund der Aufgabenstellung die Inhalte aus, die ins Englische übertragen werden sollen. Die Mediation selbst wird in **Einzelarbeit** durchgeführt.
- Die inhaltliche Besprechung der Schülerarbeiten kann im **Plenum** stattfinden, eine sprachliche Korrektur muss individuell erfolgen.
- **Aufgabe 2** wird im **Unterrichtsgespräch** erledigt. Die Ergebnisse können informell an der **Tafel** gesichert werden.
- **Aufgabe 3** wird anhand der Erläuterungen im Schülerbuch durchgeführt.
- Um sicherzustellen, dass alle drei Situationen bearbeitet werden, kann der Lehrer bzw. die Lehrerin den einzelnen Gruppen die von ihnen zu bearbeitende Situation zuweisen.
- Die Grammatik-Aufgabe (**Aufg. 4**) kann als abschließende **Hausaufgabe** eingesetzt werden.

SOLUTIONS AWARENESS

Look at the cartoon below and state which "multicultural problem" is depicted there. Discuss what the man could reply to ease the embarrassing situation.

The cartoon highlights the differences between Arab and 'Western' marital practices. Whereas in Western culture it is the rule to be married to only one partner (at a time), there are societies in which polygamy is the norm: It is legally possible for men to be married to more than one wife.

The man could be honest and explain his blunder but he could also try to avoid a possibly awkward situation by pretending that he actually said 'Frauen', not 'Frau'. He could also offer to provide more presents so that all of the man's wives receive a gift box. He might even decide to use a trick and refer the question back to his counterpart by explaining that the Arab man should give the present to the woman whose birthday comes up next.

SOLUTIONS COMPREHENSION

1. Mediate the interview with Gary Thomas who works as intercultural trainer and is CEO of the Deutsche Gesellschaft für Interkulturelle Trainingsqualität and point out:
- **why making judgments rashly can be problematic**
- **the differences in the way of criticizing somebody between Germans and Britons**
- **what can be done when somebody "beats around the bush" and avoids giving concrete answers**
- **possible misunderstandings in communication between Italians and Germans**
- **how Indians avoid saying "No" in a direct way.**

→ Focus on Skills, Mediation, p. 265

Generalizations and sweeping, often rash judgements can be a problem in a multicultural context because one assumes that one's own normality is the sole criterion. It is better to observe the situation and the behaviour of others first, then one is in a better position to direct proceedings.
When it comes to criticizing someone, Germans are often very direct, whereas the British use indirect, polite formulations in an attempt, as they see it, not to offend anyone and to protect the relationship. The Germans are, for their part, not particularly worried that straight talk could jeopardize a relationship.
If someone beats around the bush and finds it difficult to articulate a clear point of criticism or give a clear answer, then you can try to make them become more specific by for example asking: "Help me, please. What exactly do you mean?" Relationship-oriented cultures usually respond well to such an appeal.
In Italy hierarchy and bella figura play a big role. The Italian always wants to look good, to cut a good figure. Germans often try to pin things down. The Italian negotiating partner might agree to something but then it turns out that he or she was not authorized to make the decision in question.
Indians try to avoid saying "No" because they do not want to jeopardize the relationship. They might say "Yes, we will see" or "Yes, we will try" or even just "Yes" but often this is just their way of saying "No".

SOLUTIONS ANALYSIS

2. Examine and explain why people from different cultures
- **use more paraphrases and ornate (*blumig*) formulations**
- **want to come to the point directly**
- **consider it to be important to create and keep up a certain pretence of their status**
- **cannot say "No".**

→ Focus on Skills, Analysis of a Non-Fictional Text, p. 258

People from different cultures (like the British) use more paraphrases and ornate formulations because they do not want to be too direct. They use indirect formulations to protect the relationship and to avoid offending the person they are dealing with.
Many people, like, for example, most Germans, Austrians and Dutch, like to come to the point directly. They are more task-oriented and less relationship-oriented. They do not waste time beating around the bush but like to come straight to the point. They are less worried that this could jeopardize a relationship.
Some people, such as the Italians, consider it important to create and keep up a certain pretence of their status because they want to be well-received and to look good in the eyes of others. They do not want to lose face.
There are certain cultural groups that have difficulty saying "No" directly – Indians for example. They cannot say "No" because they do not want to jeopardize or in any way endanger the status of the relationship.

SOLUTIONS ACTIVITIES

3. When visiting a foreign country, there can be lots of pitfalls (*Fallstricke*) and you can get into difficult or embarrassing situations. In groups of 3 – 4 students, work out role plays and think about strategies and appropriate formulations to avoid and prepare for the above-mentioned difficulties. Here are some examples of difficult situations, along with useful phrases to start off with. Of course, you can think up further situations yourselves. Afterwards, perform the role plays in class and discuss your strategies.

Situation 1: At mealtime
You have been invited for a meal and are being served way too much food ... which you do not particularly like ...

You: Excuse me, I'm afraid I can't eat the Kung Pao chicken. You see, it has peanuts on it and I am fairly allergic to them.
Host: Oh no! I didn't even think of that. I am so sorry about that.
You: Would it be a problem if I had something else, maybe just the chicken and the rice that has not touched any peanuts. I'd love some of that.
Host: Absolutely, I will see what I can cook up for you.
You: Would you mind if I taste a little, just to be sure it doesn't have any peanut residue on it too? Maybe see if it needs salt?

Situation 2: Breaking something at your host's home/in a shop
Your host loves collectibles of any kind and they are everywhere in his/her home ... unfortunately, you hit a little glass figurine ... Or: While shopping in a souvenir store you overlooked a small table and broke something ...

You: Excuse me, can I talk to you for a moment?
Host: Of course.
You: I'm really sorry but I need to tell you I have had a bit of a problem with your glass figurine of the Yellow Submarine.
Host: Oh no, well, what happened?
You: I'm not sure how, but as I was telling a story, I ended up knocking the figurine to the floor. It shattered ...
Host: That's terrible!
You: I know, I promise I will pay for it. I don't know how it happened but I know I need to take responsibility for it.
Host: Well thank you for the offer, but honestly, I just picked that up at the market for no more than five Euros. It's not that big of a deal so you need not worry about it.

Situation 3: Meeting somebody at a disco and chatting her/him up
You are visiting a disco with your hosts and meet a really nice boy/girl who you want to get to know and become friends with ...

You: Hi, I don't think I've seen you around here before. Are you new to town or just to the disco?
New Person: Yeah, actually I just moved here about a month ago, haven't really had the chance to go out a whole lot so I decided to take advantage of my chance.
You: Well, that's pretty cool. Want to get a drink with me? I can tell you a little bit about the area.
New Person: That sounds like a good plan to me.
You: I feel like you would get along great with my group of friends. Let's go over and sit with them for a little bit and I'll grab drinks from the waitress. Sound good?
New Person: Sounds good!

SOLUTIONS GRAMMAR/LANGUAGE

4. In order to improve your style, use gerunds and/or infinitive constructions whenever possible.
Example: Judging people in a very direct way can be offensive ...
Focusing entirely on your own culture can appear very judgmental ...
→ Focus on Grammar, Infinitive With/Without "To" and the Gerund, p. 300

- **Judging** people in a very direct way can be offensive.
- **Focusing** entirely on your own culture can appear very judgmental.
- **Accepting** only your own culture as the measure of normality seems to be narrow-minded.
- Germans **love to make** direct statements and suggestions.
- Many cultures use indirect formulations in order **to be** more polite and **protect** the relationship.
- Germans tend **to feel** uncomfortable with wordy indirect explanations because they consider this to be **beating** about the bush.
- **Misinterpreting** somebody's vague statement as approval can **lead** to serious misunderstandings.
- Distinctly **saying** "yes" or "no" may **pose** a problem for people from certain countries.
- etc.

David Cameron

Speech on the Government's Immigration Policy (pp. 137–143)

About the speaker	David Cameron is the current prime minister of the United Kingdom. He was elected in 2010 and is a member of the Conservative Party. He was elected to Parliament in 2001 and became the leader of the Conservative Party in 2005.
About the text	The speech outlines Cameron's plan to reduce immigration to the UK.
Level	● ● ●
Additional material	Audio CD 2, 3 Differenzierungsmaterial, p. 93 GaST: no. 25 Comprehension: no. 16

- Als Vorbereitung der umfangreichen Hörverstehensaufgabe (Aufg. 1) sollten die Schülerinnen und Schüler einen Antwortbogen vorbereiten, in den sie die Ergebnisse des Hördurchgangs eintragen können. Ein solcher Bogen könnte folgendermaßen aussehen:

David Cameron, Speech on the Government's Immigration Policy

Topic	Speech
immigration: *motivation for reform* *mistakes of the past* *political goals*	
benefits of immigration	
pressures on communities, schools, housing, healthcare	
measures to be taken by Cameron	
– *arguments against critics of immigration control* – *examples of immigration* – *different ways of entering Britain*	
Do migrant workers take jobs from British? *How is welfare system abused?*	
– *how to cut immigration* – *immigration policy in the future*	

- Die **Aufgaben 1 und 2** werden anhand der Anleitungen im Schülerbuch durchgeführt.
- Die Ergebnisse können im Anschluss an die Bearbeitungsphase von den Schülerinnen und Schülern **individuell** anhand des Textes im Schülerbuch **korrigiert** bzw. **ergänzt** werden.
- **Aufgabe 3** kann in **Gruppen** zu drei oder vier Schülerinnen und Schülern erledigt werden. Die verschiedenen thematischen Aspekte werden unter den Gruppenmitgliedern aufgeteilt, was die Bearbeitung der Aufgaben erleichtert. Die Ergebnisse werden innerhalb der Gruppen ausgetauscht und von einem Gruppenmitglied schriftlich fixiert. Dieses trägt die Gruppenergebnisse im **Plenum** vor. Dort werden sie kurz diskutiert und ggf. informell an der Tafel gesichert.
- Für das in **Aufgabe 4** geforderte **Ranking** werden die Inhalte des Kaleidoskops auf **Moderationskarten** übertragen. Die Karten werden an der **Tafel** oder auf einer **Moderationswand** fixiert. Vor dem Ranking werden die Karten diskutiert. Weniger wichtige Aspekte werden aussortiert und neue werden ggf. angefügt. Danach erhalten die Schülerinnen und Schüler pro Person eine bestimmte Anzahl von **Klebepunkten**, die sie an denjenigen Karten anbringen, die sie vor dem Hintergrund einer der beiden Fragestellungen (a) oder b)) für wichtig halten. Anhand der Anzahl der Klebepunkte wird das Ranking vorgenommen. Dieses wird im Unterrichtsgespräch diskutiert und kommentiert. Eine individuelle **Verschriftlichung** des Ergebnisses auf der Grundlage der abschließenden Diskussion ist möglich.

- **Aufgabe 5** kann zur Stärkung der mündlichen Sprachkompetenz in Form von auf **Stichwörtern** basierenden **Kurzvorträgen** erledigt werden. Alternativ dazu kann diese Aufgabe als **Hausaufgabe** erteilt werden. In diesem Fall sind die Ergebnisse der Analyse schriftlich zu fixieren.
- Um die Vorbereitungszeit für den **Hot Seat** (**Aufg. 6**) zu verkürzen, kann die Erstellung der Rollenprofile ebenfalls zu Hause erfolgen. Dabei muss im Vorfeld geklärt werden, welche Schülerinnen und Schüler die Rolle des Premierministers und welche die übrigen Rollen übernehmen.
- **Aufgabe 7** kann in **Partnerarbeit** bearbeitet werden, wobei die Vorbereitungen für den Artikel (Recherche, Materialsammlung) gemeinsam erledigt werden können, die schriftliche Ausarbeitung muss jedoch individuell erfolgen. Im Vorfeld sollte die angegebene **Focus on Facts-Seite** (SB, S. 250) zur Kenntnis genommen werden. Die fertigen Texte werden als **Wandzeitung** im Klassenzimmer ausgehängt und können so von den Schülerinnen und Schülern gelesen und diskutiert werden.
- Zur Bearbeitung von **Aufgabe 8** sollte den Schülerinnen und Schülern ein **einsprachiges Wörterbuch** zur Verfügung stehen. Zusätzlich können sie den Auftrag erhalten, die in der Aufgabenstellung vorkommenden unbekannten Vokabeln nachzuschlagen und in ihr Vokabelverzeichnis aufzunehmen.

SOLUTIONS AWARENESS

Prime Minister David Cameron is a member of the Conservative Party, which is known for its criticism of the Labour Party's state multiculturalism. What do you expect David Cameron to say about immigration in general and what might he criticize about Britain's multicultural society in particular?

general: there should be less immigration, British jobs should be protected ...

Britain's multicultural society: need to integrate/assimilate, too many social/ethnic/racial clashes due to high migrant population, UK's borders are too open ...

SOLUTIONS COMPREHENSION

CD 2 3 **1. Listen to the speech given by Prime Minister David Cameron. In a first listening, take notes on:**

1	• **his motivation for reforming the immigration policy:** listening to concerns of British people during the election campaign about high levels of immigration • **the mistakes made in the past by the previous government:** politicians talked tough but did nothing; inflamed the debate: Labour Ministers promoted the idea that concerns about immigration were racist; Ministers made promises to reduce immigration but did not follow through • **his political goals concerning immigration:** wants immigration to no longer be a central political issue; wants to put an end to public anxiety about immigration and extremist parties; wants to implement effective policy that allows good immigration but not mass immigration
2	• **what Cameron considers to be the benefits of immigration:** skilled workers benefit the country: hospital workers, teachers and professors, entrepreneurs; add richness to local life: charities, financial services, fashion, food, music
3	• **what pressures immigration poses on communities, schools, housing, healthcare:** pressures on schools, housing and healthcare have been "serious"; in some communities, significant numbers of newcomers cannot speak English and/or are not willing to integrate, causing discomfort and disjointedness
4	• **what measures Cameron and his government plan to take during their legislative period:** reduce net migration to where it was in the 1980s and 90s; introduce a cap on non-EU immigration; stop illegal immigration; effectively deal with the asylum system

5	• **Cameron's arguments against critics of immigration control:** critics' arguments and Cameron's counterarguments: three major arguments are wrong: 1: legal immigration is impossible to control because the UK is in the EU ➔ the numbers of immigrants are much higher from outside the EU, and this can be more easily controlled; they have shown that an immigration cap works; 2: it is impossible to control illegal immigration ➔ (Cameron does not elaborate on this point); 3: immigration will always be high because immigrants do jobs the British will not do ➔ (see #6 below) • **his examples of immigration from EU and non-EU nations:** EU immigration is only a small proportion of overall immigration; in the year up to June 2010, only 27,000 EU nationals immigrated to the UK; since the EU opened up to include eastern Europe in 2004, over one million immigrants from these countries came to the UK; in the year up to June 2010, 198,000 non-EU immigrants entered the country • **the different ways immigrants enter Britain:** employment; marriage or joining family; student visa
6	• **whether migrant workers are taking jobs from British workers:** of all the 2.5 million new workers in the economy since 1997, 75 % are foreign; not the case that foreigners are taking British jobs; there are not a fixed number of jobs; immigrants also create wealth and new jobs • **how weak points in the state's welfare system are abused:** British welfare system pays people not to work; foreigners are taking on the jobs instead
7	• **Cameron's conclusion of how to effectively cut immigration:** all different avenues of entry must be dealt with at the same time, both legal and illegal • **the general immigration policy of the British government in the future**: UK will be open to the best and brightest foreigners and those who are being persecuted, but controlled and only within the limits of what the country can manage

➔ **Focus on Skills, Listening Comprehension, p. 244**

SOLUTIONS ANALYSIS

2. Before listening to the speech a second time, divide the class into four groups, each group focusing on a different stylistic and rhetorical aspect of the speech:

1	• **language (e.g. keywords, phrases, choice of words, language register, etc.)**
2	• **grammar (e.g. sentence structure, use of grammatical tenses/conditional sentences, imperatives, etc.)**
3	• **rhetoric (e.g. rhetorical questions, use of contrast/antithesis, key symbols, slogans, grammatical persons, etc.)**
4	• **manner of speaking/voice (volume, tempo, intonation, etc.)**

1	**language**
key words, key phrases	• immigration (ll. 11, 16, etc.), politicians (ll. 13, 24, etc.), government (ll. 5, 27, etc.), debate (ll. 17, 25, etc.), controlling immigration (ll. 21, 36), benefit (ll. 58, 270), pressures on communities (ll. 77, 79, 81), real integration (l. 89), commitment (l. 106), European Union (ll. 120, 130, etc.), net migration (ll. 107, 132, 133, etc.), restrict (l. 142), cap (ll. 112, 154, 159), bogus (ll. 196, 206), simultaneously (ll. 220f., 222), labour market (l. 264), control (ll. 21, 36, 102, etc.)
choice of words	• positive connotations: sensibly (l. 25), reasonably (l. 26), fair-minded (l. 54), honest (l. 55), benefited immeasurably (l. 58), caring (l. 61), inspiring (l. 64), welcome (l. 71), genuine (l. 167), loving (l. 167), clear-headed (l. 269), strengthens (l. 277), enhances (l. 277), best and brightest (l. 291) • negative connotations: fed up (l. 13), soft touch (l. 22), racist (l. 31), hell-bent (l. 32), extremist (l. 38), discomfort (l. 97), disjointedness (ll. 97f.), bullied (l. 173), threatened (l. 173), sham (l. 178), bogus (ll. 196, 206), exploiting (ll. 229f.), eye-wateringly high (ll. 249f.)

1	language
language register	• <u>formal register/expert language</u>: assertion(s) (ll. 17f., 20), substantive arguments (l. 18), unalloyed (l. 20), burnishing (ll. 32f.), credentials (l. 33), transitional controls (l. 141), etc. • <u>informal register/colloquial words:</u> fed up (l. 13), soft touch (l. 22), stamp it out (l. 177), chat down the pub (l. 88), go home (ll. 213f.), playing the system (l. 229), stuck on welfare (ll. 250f.), etc. ➔ switching back and forth gives the speech balance: Cameron comes across as formal, serious and credible but the speech is easy enough for anyone to understand

2	grammar
sentence structure	• <u>paratactical syntax:</u> We recognise that – and we welcome it (l. 71); Each part of that argument is wrong (l. 127); It is wrong, full stop (l. 176); But this isn't the end of the story (l. 186); No ifs. No buts (l. 295); etc. ➔ simple, easy for the listener to follow; emphasizes the directness and simplicity of Cameron's plan
grammatical tenses	• <u>present continuous:</u> people from Uganda ... caring for our sick; teachers ... inspiring our young people; entrepreneurs ... adding to the local economy ... playing a part in local life (ll. 60–67), We are controlling legal immigration ... (l. 111), We are clamping down ... (l. 113), we are getting to grips with ... (ll. 114f.) • <u>will-future:</u> transitional controls will be put in place ... (ll. 144f.), these proposals will cut the number of student visas ... (ll. 216ff.) • <u>simple past:</u> I heard loud and clear on the doorstep ... (ll. 3f.), We said back then that ... (ll. 141f.), That's a promise we made ... (l. 296) • <u>active voice:</u> immigrants make a huge contribution to Britain (l. 70); we placed interim limits on the number of visas ... (ll. 160ff.)
use of conditional sentences	• if and when new countries join the European Union, transitional controls will be put in place (ll. 143ff.) • if people come over here to study, they should be studying not working (ll. 211f.) • if one hundred migrant workers come into the country, they don't simply displace job opportunities for a hundred British citizens (ll. 258ff.) • if we take the steps set out today ... then levels of immigration can return to where they were in the 1980s and 90s (ll. 282ff.)
imperatives	• Go into any hospital ... Go into schools and universities ... Go to almost any high street ... (ll. 60–65)

3	rhetoric
rhetorical questions	• The others? (l. 200) ➔ used as a framing device; Cameron goes on to answer his own question
contrast/ antithesis	• I believe that the role of politicians is to cut through the extremes of this debate ... The last government, **in contrast**, actually helped to inflame the debate. (ll. 24ff.) • **On the one hand**, there were Labour Ministers who closed down discussion ... **On the other**, there were Ministers hell-bent on ... (ll. 29ff.) • time for a new approach – one which opens up debate, **not** closes it down; where politicians don't just talk, **but** actually act. (ll. 50ff.)
key symbols	• the doorstep (l. 9) ➔ the place where Cameron met and spoke with concerned British citizens • immigration debate as a fire ➔ inflaming debate (ll. 27f.), starving extremist parties of the oxygen of public anxiety (ll. 45ff.) • the balloon that gets bigger at the other end when squeezed (ll. 224ff.) ➔ demonstrates the necessity of controlling all avenues of immigration at the same time
slogans	• good immigration, not mass immigration (ll. 48f.) • we are leaving no stone unturned (ll. 273f.) • No ifs. No buts. (l. 295)

3	rhetoric
grammatical persons	• **I:** I want them to feel they can be honest ... Here's what I think. I can see why this argument is made. ➔ Cameron is personally engaged with the topic and has strong opinions • **We/us/our:** We've all heard them. We recognise that – and we welcome it ... we are on track to meet that aim ... This is the figure we can more easily control ... ➔ creates solidarity between Cameron, his party, and the British people • **They/them:** they take up vacancies that are available, but they also come and create wealth and new jobs ➔ refers to immigrants
simile	• controlling immigration by clamping down on one route alone is "like squeezing a balloon ... Push down work visas and the number of student visas will shoot up. Clamp down on student visas and family visas will spring up" (ll. 223ff.) ➔ helps the listener to visualize the problem; emphasizes the importance of controlling all avenues of immigration at the same time

4	manner of speaking/voice
volume	• loud and clear
emphasized phrases	• Cameron speaks rather emphatically throughout entire speech • inflame the debate (ll. 27f.) • burnishing their hard-line credentials (ll. 32f.) • talking tough ... doing (ll. 33f.) • I remember when immigration wasn't a central political issue (ll. 42f.) • get the policy right (l. 48) • good immigration, not mass immigration (ll. 48f.) • the whole system was out of control (l. 204) • eye-wateringly high (ll. 249f.)
tempo	• conversational, easy to follow
intonation	• overall: energetic and with a sense of urgency • mocking tone of voice: "immigrants coming over here and taking our jobs" (ll. 254f.) ➔ Cameron is enacting the voice of ignorant immigration opponents; he makes it clear that he disagrees with this argument

Following this, the groups remix and inform each other about their results.
➔ Focus on Methods, Group Puzzle, p. 271
➔ Focus on Skills, Analysis of a Political Speech, p. 260

Webcode SNG-40175-014

3. In your groups, watch the short documentary video on UK immigration and race relations "Where Are We Headed" which is provided on the webcode. Take notes on what is depicted about:

- **the "uncomfortable topic" of immigration in Britain today**
  growing unrest and conflict after decades of mass immigration and multicultural life
- **the problem (mass) immigration poses for the British society**
  overcrowding, too few jobs, housing, schools; immigration cap is needed
- **people's changed view on immigration and immigrants in Britain**
  due to economic downturn
- **the role of the political parties**
  proposing harsher immigration rules as a solution; pressure to solve immigration issues
- **the function of "scape-goating"**
  blaming immigrants for various problems (e.g. unemployment) as a way to divert attention away from one's own inability to solve problems

- **(Asian) views on immigration and the British immigration policy**
  big talk pre-election, but parties all very similar; not just a UK problem because migrants are working all over the globe; first generation of immigrants contributed enormously to economy

- **the situation in Birmingham (economy, immigrants' views, white people's views)**
  long history of hosting immigrants, largest non-white population outside London; race riots 30 years ago; peaceful multiculturalism; some gang activity, but mostly peaceful, people keep to themselves; economic decline, factories closing (Cadbury); rise in white unemployment ➔ more people think immigration is a problem

- **the fear of terrorism and Muslims (Islamophobia)**
  students at Islamic Society at University College London under constant surveillance after former member attempted to blow up a plane; racial stereotyping; petition to remove Assed Baig, student of Pakistani descent and born in UK, as president of student union, due to his race/religion, racist accusations; death of young black man, institutionalized racism

- **where Britain is heading when it comes to the issue of immigration**
  heading towards more isolationism; government will need to be in control, but should not stop immigration; people need to trust each other, live together

First, exchange your results in class, then relate your findings to David Cameron's view on immigration and discuss the differences and common grounds of the views taken.

both documentary and Cameron mention:
- limited number of jobs, housing, school places (ll. 79f.)
- politicians scapegoating, refusing to take effective action (ll. 27ff.)
- people in Birmingham keep to themselves; Cameron underlines need for common social experiences (ll. 82ff.)
- etc.

differences:
- Cameron goes into much greater detail about e.g. the various ways immigrants enter the country, what specific steps he wants to take to cap immigration, etc.
- Cameron does not mention terrorism or Islamophobia specifically.
- etc.

4. Examine the "Cultural Kaleidoscope" (SB, p. 142) and explain the various cultural markers and items. Discuss a possible ranking of these markers in class:
- **Which ones do you consider to be more or less a) dominant and influential or b) relevant and effective in everyday life?**
- **Which further markers would you like to add – which items are possibly redundant?**

Individual answers

5. Skilled migrants are attracted and welcomed by many nations. Describe and analyse the cartoon on the opposite page and relate the view taken on migration to David Cameron's speech and his views on the matter.

➔ Focus on Skills, Analysis of Visuals, p. 262

The cartoon shows a line of skilled workers of various ethnicities standing in a queue waiting to enter the country. The workers are: a scientist carrying a microscope, a construction worker, a professor/academic, a surgeon, a genetic scientist/engineer carrying a two-headed sheep, a scientist in a hazardous materials suit carrying a test tube, a doctor, and finally a cricket player. A woman is rushing towards the cricket player and ushering him to the front of the queue, implying that he and his profession are a higher priority than the other people standing in line. This is presented as being rather ridiculous/backwards, since the other workers are highly trained and educated and will help improve society and people's lives, whereas the cricket player's profession only has entertainment value. Nonetheless, it is common for sport teams to import talented players from abroad and pay them very high salaries.

David Cameron mentions valued skilled immigrant workers and their contribution to Great Britain in his speech. He emphasizes that the UK "will always be open to the best and brightest from around the world" (ll. 291f.). He mentions hospital workers, teachers and professors (all represented in the cartoon) and entrepreneurs (not represented in the cartoon) (ll. 58–72). He does not mention sport players at all, perhaps precisely because their contribution to British society is questionable.

SOLUTIONS ACTIVITIES

6. Imagine you are
- **a representative of a British political party (for or against immigration),**
- **a representative of an NGO (non-governmental organisation) supporting immigration,**
- **an immigrant trying to stay and work in Britain who listened to the PM's speech and who has now been given the opportunity to ask David Cameron some (critical) questions.**

Put the Prime Minister in the Hot Seat and interview him about the government's immigration policy.
- **Before you start, work out a set of questions you want to ask.**
- **Try to corner the PM by referring to the statements he made in his speech.**
- **Do not ask questions that can simply be answered with "yes" or "no".**

→ Focus on Language, Conversation and Discussion, p. 266
→ Focus on Methods, Hot Seat, p. 270

For example:
- representative of a British political party (for or against immigration): If fewer immigrants are admitted into the UK, how will you close the gaps in the labour market, considering the large number of British citizens on welfare who refuse to work?
- representative of an NGO supporting immigration: What concrete evidence do you have that suggests the UK can handle tens of thousands of new immigrants per year, but not hundreds of thousands? What is this number based on?
- immigrant trying to stay and work in Britain: How do you define "the best and the brightest"?

7. As a journalist, you are asked to write about the PM's speech and the subsequent interview. Write a cover story that depicts the relevant issues. You can be a journalist from
- **a quality newspaper,**
- **a tabloid,**
- **an online newspaper that takes the view of an NGO, e.g. Amnesty International.**

→ Focus on Facts, The Press, p. 250

Individual answers

SOLUTIONS GRAMMAR/LANGUAGE

8. In (political) rhetoric the use of figurative language helps to make a speech more appealing and vivid. However, sometimes it is important to decode these images in order to see through the political strategy and understand the underlying motivation. Transform the following phrases and figurative expressions into everyday English:
- **mass immigration is an unalloyed good (ll. 20f.)**
- **burnishing ... hard-line credentials (ll. 32f.)**
- **the oxygen of public anxiety (ll. 45f.)**
- **good immigration (ll. 48f.)**
- **real communities are bound by common experience (l. 84)**
- **targeting bogus colleges (l. 206)**
- **... we've had persistently eye-wateringly high numbers of British born people stuck on welfare (ll. 249ff.)**
- **a sober, comprehensive and effective plan to cut immigration (ll. 266f.)**
- **No ifs. No buts. (l. 295)**

- assertion that mass immigration is an unalloyed good (ll. 20f.) → mass immigration seems to be something valuable but in fact it is not
- burnishing ... hard-line credentials (ll. 32f.) → to present yourself as a political hardliner
- the oxygen of public anxiety (ll. 45f.) → the power and the fuel that public fear provides
- good immigration (ll. 48f.) → less/reduced immigration

- real communities are bound by common experience (l. 84) → a real community consists of people that share the same experiences and (cultural) background
- targeting bogus colleges (l. 206) → to eliminate false colleges
- we've had persistently eye-wateringly high numbers of British born people stuck on welfare ... (ll. 249ff.) → the number of native Britons who had to live on welfare was, sadly, enormously high

Marilyn Chin

How I Got That Name – An Essay on Assimilation (pp. 144–145)

About the author	Marilyn Chin is an American award-winning poet whose family immigrated to the US from Hong Kong. Her poems mainly deal with Asian-American feminism and coming to terms with a bicultural identity.
About the text	This excerpt from a poem details the speaker's immigration to the U.S. from China with her family in the 1950s and their subsequent life in their new home country.
Level	● ● ●
Additional material	Audio CD 2, 4 Differenzierungsmaterial, p. 104

- Zur Bearbeitung von **Aufgabe 1** kann neben den zahlreichen **Bildbänden** und **Biografien**, die es über Marilyn Monroe gibt, die entsprechende **Wikipedia**-Seite und die offizielle Website von Marilyn Monroe (www.marilynmonroe.com) von Nutzen sein. Die Schülerinnen und Schüler können die recherchierten Informationen in Partner- oder Gruppenarbeit aufarbeiten und auf **Plakaten** präsentieren.
- Die Hör- bzw. Leseverstehensaufgaben (**Aufg. 2 bis 4**) werden anhand der Angaben im Schülerbuch durchgeführt. Zur Sicherung der Ergebnisse kann nach deren Austausch mit einem Partner der Text (SB, S. 144) herangezogen werden.
- Aufgabe 5 kann in **Einzelarbeit** erledigt werden. Die Ergebnisse werden im **Plenum** diskutiert und in **Tabellenform** (s. Lösungsvorschlag unten) auf **Folie** gesichert. Die Folie kann im Anschluss für die Lerngruppe **kopiert** werden.
- **Aufgabe 6 kann im Unterrichtsgespräch** bearbeitet werden. Die Sicherung der Ergebnisse erfolgt per **Tafelanschrieb:**

Marilyn Mei Ling Chin

Marilyn, the American movie star, wearing Chinese clothes

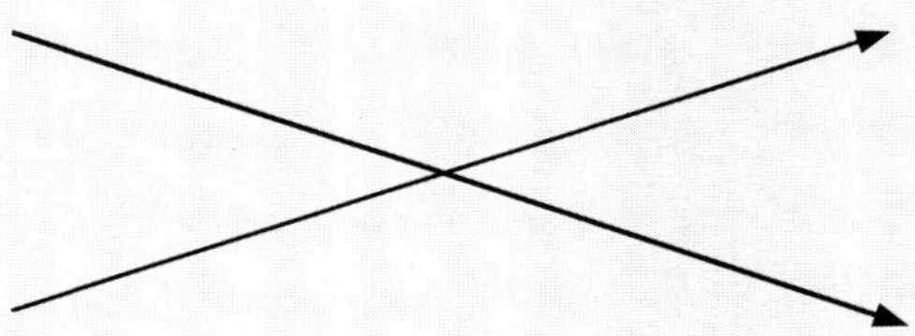

assimilation – Mei Ling's mother?

Mei Ling Chin, the daughter of Chinese immigrants, "wearing" an American identity

- Vor der Bearbeitung von **Aufgabe 7** sollte die Bedeutung der literarischen Form des **Essays** erläutert werden. Dies kann mithilfe der entsprechenden Focus on **Language-Seite** (SB, S. 311) geschehen. Die Aufgabe kann im **Unterrichtsgespräch** bearbeitet werden. Ein abschließender informeller Tafelanschrieb zur Sicherung der Ergebnisse ist möglich.
- Bei der Bearbeitung von **Aufgabe 8** erhalten die Schülerinnen und Schüler den Auftrag, ihre Definitionen nach dem Muster „Assimilation means ..." zu formulieren. Die Definitionen werden auf **Moderationskarten** geschrieben und an einer Moderationswand angebracht. Im anschließenden **Unterrichtsgespräch**

wird auf die verschiedenen in den Definitionen genannten thematischen Aspekte eingegangen. Die Moderationskarten können anhand dieser Aspekte geordnet werden.

- Die Ergebnisse der in **Gruppen- oder Partnerarbeit** durchgeführten Recherche (**Aufg. 9**) können in Form von **Kurzvorträgen** präsentiert werden.
- Neben dem Webcode können folgende Internetseiten hilfreich sein:
  www.immigrationdirect.comn/?r=ga-cpc-imm_world-immigration_usa
  www.uscis.gov/
- **Aufgabe 10** wird anhand der Angaben im Schülerbuch durchgeführt.

SOLUTIONS AWARENESS

The picture shows a statue of the famous American actress Marilyn Monroe, dressed in Chinese clothes. What do her body language, facial expression and the way she is dressed express?

This statue of Marilyn Monroe is typical of images of the "real" Marilyn: She is depicted as a sexy woman. Her body language is relaxed and friendly, with one hand raised as if in greeting, and she is smiling broadly in a flirty way. Her clothing has typical Chinese detailing and is bright red, which is usually considered an attention-getting colour. Striking is that her outfit is skin-tight, emphasizing her breasts, waist, hips and even her pubic bone.

SOLUTIONS COMPREHENSION

@ **1. Before listening/reading, do research on the American actress Marilyn Monroe, her biography and her untimely death.**

Individual answers

CD 2 4 **2. In a first listening/reading, try to get a general understanding about**
- **where and when the speaker's first name was changed into Marilyn**
- **what the speaker thinks about the actress Marilyn Monroe.**

- The speaker's original name was Mei Ling, but her father was obsessed with Marilyn Monroe, so when the family moved to the U.S. he renamed his daughter after her (ll. 11 – 12).
- This 'renaming' took place in the late 1950s near Angel Island. This is an island in San Francisco Bay in the United States (ll. 8 – 10).
- The phrase the speaker uses is 'tragic' when speaking about Marilyn Monroe (l. 18). The reference to Monroe being swollen with Gin and Nembutal is no doubt an allusion to her overdose and death. The speaker would think this is tragic because Marilyn Monroe had the world at her fingertips. She was considered beyond beautiful. She was rich and famous, one of the most influential people in all the world, and she overdosed. This is the tragic nature of Monroe's death and, although the speaker calls to mind the lust of which men had for Monroe (l. 15), the actress had a way with people that could have changed a great deal around the world.

3. In a second listening/reading, pay attention to details and try to answer these questions:
- **Why was the speaker, Marilyn Mei Chin, named after the American actress?**
- **What does the poem reveal about the family's immigration to the United States?**
- **How does the family make a living?**

→ Focus on Skills, Listening Comprehension, p. 244

- Marilyn Mei Chin's father was obsessed with the actress Marilyn Monroe. He changed (transliterated) her name from "Mei Ling" to Marilyn when the family immigrated to the US (ll. 6 – 12).
- The family immigrated to the US sometime in the late 1950s and arrived at Angel Island (ll. 8 – 10). It is not explicitly stated where the family originates from, though the poem mentions Hong Kong (l. 26). The speaker was just a baby at the time (l. 17), and the father was a "paper son" (l. 9), i.e. he obtained fake/illegal papers claiming he and his family had relatives in the US and therefore had the right to enter the country (footnote no. 4).
- The father of the family earns money illegally through gambling and crime (l. 27). He buys a chain of restaurants using "bootlegged Gucci cash" (ll. 28 – 30). However, he is not very successful: he only

"dithers" in these different ventures (l. 25). Meanwhile, the mother stays at home in the kitchen and takes care of the children (ll. 23f.). (173 words)

4. After a third listening, complete your notes and compare them with a partner.

Individual answers

SOLUTIONS ANALYSIS

5. Analyse the poetic devices* that are employed to describe the life of a first generation Chinese immigrant family in the USA.

→ Focus on Skills, Analysis of Poetry and Lyrics, p. 259

Quote	line(s)	poetic/ rhetorical device	effect
bombshell blonde	11	alliteration	emphasizes speaker's father's lustful obsession
tomcat in Hong Kong trash	26	metaphor	describes father: shady, wild character, not to be tamed or trusted
paper son petty thug joints Piss River Gucci cash	9 27 28 29 30	slang/vulgar language	creates atmosphere of poor social background, crime jargon, "street talk"
nice, devout bright, industrious	32 33	positive connotations/irony	used ironically to reveal the illusion of the "perfect" family
Oh how I love the resoluteness of that first person singular followed by that stalwart indicative of "be", without the uncertain i-n-g of "becoming".	2 – 6	comparison/ juxtaposition	underlines speaker's disdain for striving towards identity (becoming instead of being) and having to work to assimilate
filial piety	34	high/formal register	used ironically, since speaker obviously did not truly respect her father
sublime ignorance	23	paradox	describes mother's no-win situation: she could be happy and ignorant, or learn the truth about her husband's illegal jobs

6. Explain in what way the photo on page 144 reflects the position Marilyn Mei Ling Chin is in. In what way is her mother's life different?

The photo shows a statue of a hybrid Marilyn: Marilyn the American is seen in Chinese clothes. The speaker is in the opposite situation: a Chinese girl in American, i. e. in American clothes, and a mix of the two cultures. The speaker's mother does not assimilate as much as her daughter:

- she cannot pronounce the "r", which implies she probably does not learn English or cannot speak it very well (l. 20)
- she is confined to the kitchen and raising the children (ll. 23 – 24)
- is sublimely ignorant of her husband's activities (l. 23), while her daughter Marilyn is aware of the situation

7. Although the text is only an excerpt from a longer poem, try to figure out why it is called "an essay on assimilation".

Although the text is a poem, it is also an essay because the speaker is sharing her views on assimilation based on her personal opinion and own experiences.

8. After reading the text, work together with your partner on a definition of the term "assimilation".

Assimilation means adapting to a new culture so that one can cope with everyday life with the natives of that culture. This can include:

- learning the local language
- taking part in local customs
- learning and adhering to new sets of rules and etiquette
- adapting one's appearance (e.g. fashion, hairstyle, ...)
- taking part in local traditions and celebrations
- sharing one's native culture with the new culture

SOLUTIONS ACTIVITIES

Webcode SNG-40175-015 @

9. In order to become a legal citizen of the United States, you need a document that is commonly known as the "Green Card". Use the links given on the webcode and do further research about what is required to legally immigrate to the US.

Individual work

10. A haiku is a brief Japanese poem reduced to 17 syllables and three lines. Its traditional structure is:
1st line: an observation of nature/a situation/a person (5 syllables)
2nd line: a reflection on that observation (7 syllables)
3rd line: a conclusive statement (5 syllables)

In groups, write haikus from the perspective of the Chinese immigrants as well as from the American perspective. Display your haikus in class.

Individual answers

ADDITIONAL TASK

Imagine you are the speaker of the poem and you are writing your autobiography. Use the information from the poem to write one chapter (200 – 250 words). Think of a suitable title.

New name – new person?
My family immigrated to the USA in the 1950s. I was born in China but we came to the USA when I was still a small baby. My family was hoping to live a better life in America so my father forged his immigration papers and we were admitted into the country. Shortly before we arrived in San Francisco my father changed my Chinese name of "Mei Ling" to "Marilyn". This was not just an attempt at transliterating my Chinese name into an English one. He also called me Marilyn because he was obsessed by the beautiful blonde actress. My mother cannot speak English very well and she has never managed to pronounce the "r" so she calls me "number one female offshoot". My mother never really arrived in America, so she stays in the house most of the time, where she is content to be a mother and a housewife. My father reached his goals in life in a way: he owns a number of Chinese restaurants which he financed with money from small crimes. Still, he is a respected member of the Asian community.

Let's Come Together?! – Migrants, Minorities, Majorities

David Cameron

The Doctrine of Multiculturalism Has Failed (p. 146)

About the speaker	David Cameron is the Prime Minister of the United Kingdom, First Lord of the Treasury, Minister for the Civil Service and Leader of the British Conservative Party. After graduating from Brasenose College at Oxford, he ran through the conservative party hierarchy from researcher to special adviser then to media company Carlton followed by a stint in Parliament before being elected as a leader of the Conservative Party.
About the text	The text in question here is Cameron speaking about multiculturalism in the UK. Multiculturalism is a doctrine in which those with different cultures try to live in separate areas with separate lives. Cameron is speaking on how this doctrine has failed, which is both a bad and a good thing. The goal was to try and force Muslims and followers of Islam to become more integrated in society and lead separate religious lives. This came as a problem because some of these people turn to radicalization and some extremist ideology. That is naturally the bad side of the coin while he also believes that people need to work together to build a stronger society and he also believes that instead of different cultures being separated, people can come together as members of one society.
Level	● ● ○
Additional material	GaST: no. 25

- Aufgrund der Länge des Ausgangstextes und der vorgeschlagenen Arbeitsform sind für die Awareness-Aufgabe mindestens 30 Minuten Arbeitszeit zu veranschlagen. Um Zeit einzusparen, kann der Text in häuslicher Lektüre vorbereitet werden.

SOLUTIONS AWARENESS

In a polarizing speech on radicalization and Islamic extremism at a Security Conference in Munich on 5 February 2011, Prime Minister David Cameron stated that "state multiculturalism" had failed. Read the snippet from Cameron's speech below and identify its message. In a 4–Corners activity (➔ FoM, p. 273), reflect on Cameron's thoughts and clarify to what extent you share his view.

Cameron is speaking on how the doctrine of multiculturalism has failed, which is both a bad and a good thing. The goal was to try and force Muslims and followers of Islam to become more integrated in society by leading separate religious lives. This came as a problem because some of these people turn to radicalization and some extremist ideology. That is naturally the bad side of the coin while he also believes that people need to work together to build a stronger society and he also believes that instead of different cultures being separated, people can come together as members of one society.

Cameron is not remiss in saying that there are negative aspects of trying to separate Islam believers from the mainstream. This does have a chance of young Muslims turning towards extremist views (ll. 29–31) but his latter point is much more telling for how he feels about the doctrine. By saying that people need to see themselves more as 'Londoners' or 'Berliners' (ll. 53–54) as opposed to only identifying as a Hindu or a Muslim or a Christian, then people become part of a multicultural community or society instead of being separated by their cultures in the way the doctrine would have done.

1. Sunny Hundal

Multiculturalism Has Won the Day. Let's Move On

2. Khola Hasan

Mr. Cameron, British Multiculturalism Is Doing Fine (pp. 147–150)

About the authors	Sunny Hundal is a British journalist, blogger and an academic. Born in London to Sikh parents of Indian origin, Hundal has a degree in Economics from Brunel University. He is best-known as the founder and editor of the centre-left group blog Liberal Conspiracy.	Khola Hasan is a writer, broadcaster and public speaker. After writing a book at age 17, she moved on to become a director for Albatross Consultancy Limited. Also a broadcaster for television and radio, she is a regular contributor for Radio 4's 'Beyond Belief' series of programmes, and a debate that she took part in 2005 with Irshad Manji on the subject of Women in Islam later won the Sony Gold prize for Best Speech programme. She also took part in one of the renowned Doha Debates on the issue of equality for women.
About the texts	Hundal's article explains how much of the UK believe and accepts the premise of Great Britain as a multicultural state.	This essay is a response to David Cameron's "Multiculturalism is Dead" speech and the response is saying that multiculturalism is alive and well, that it worked. Hasan does say that there are some issues but multiculturalism is thriving all the same.
Level	● ● ●	● ● ●
Additional material	Differenzierungsmaterial, p. 112	---

- Die **Leseverstehensaufgaben** (**Aufg. 1 bis 3**) werden anhand der Erläuterungen im Schülerbuch durchgeführt. Für die Bearbeitung der Texte ist es hilfreich, diese in **Kopie** auszuteilen, damit die Schülerinnen und Schüler Unterstreichungen und Annotationen anbringen können.
  Vor der Bearbeitung der Texte sollten die angegebenen **Focus on Skills-Seiten** (SB, S. 247, S. 276 und S. 258) zur Kenntnis genommen werden.
  Alternativ zum Vorschlag in der Aufgabenstellung kann die Klasse je nach Größe in 4 bis 6 Gruppen eingeteilt werden, von denen jeweils zwei bzw. drei einen Text bearbeiten. Die Ergebnisse werden unter je zwei Gruppen ausgetauscht, die unterschiedliche Texte bearbeitet haben.
- Für die Bearbeitung von **Aufgabe 4** wird die Klasse in zwei **Gruppen** eingeteilt, die sich mit dem Vergleich eines der beiden Texte mit dem von David Cameron beschäftigen. Die Ergebnisse werden im **Unterrichtsgespräch** diskutiert und in folgendem **Tafelbild** gesichert:

The Issue of Multiculturalism

Hundal, "Multiculturalism Has Won the Day"

- multiple, repeated negative references to conservative politicians, media
- reference to statistics on British public's views on multiculturalism

➔ more political article, overall message: scolding right-wing politicians for their fearmongering surrounding the subject of immigration

➔ reflects **The Guardian's** liberal political views

Hasan, "Mr. Cameron, British Multiculturalism Is Doing Fine"

- mostly anecdotal stories/examples
- no numbers, facts, statistics
- call to encourage British people to seek out more multicultural contact in everyday life
- descriptive

➔ less political (apart from the headline): more focussed on day-to-day life, experiences with food, clothing, school, neighbours, strangers, etc.

➔ typical "opinion piece"
➔ human interest story typical of Daily Star

- pro-multiculturalism sentiment
- discuss ongoing problems with immigration/multiculturalism that still need to be solved
- written in reaction to Cameron's speech …

↕

David Cammeron, "The Doctrine of Multiculturalism Has Failed"

- **Aufgabe 5** wird im **Unterrichtsgespräch** erledigt, die Ergebnisse können informell an der **Tafel** gesichert werden.
- **Aufgabe 6** wird nach der gemeinsamen Lektüre der **Focus on Skills-Seite** (SB, S. 290) **individuell** bearbeitet. Im Anschluss an die Erarbeitungsphase tauschen die Schülerinnen und Schüler die Ergebnisse in einer **Milling Around Activity** aus. Dabei gehen die Schüler im Zimmer umher und auf ein Zeichen des Lehrers bzw. der Lehrerin suchen sie sich einen Partner oder eine Partnerin und lesen sich gegenseitig ihre Briefe vor. Dieser Vorgang kann bis zu dreimal wiederholt werden. Während der Präsentationsphase hat der Lehrer bzw. die Lehrerin die Möglichkeit, einzelne Arbeiten zur Kenntnis zu nehmen und sie inhaltlich und sprachlich zu korrigieren.
- **Aufgabe 7** kann als **Hausaufgabe** eingesetzt werden. Ggf. sollte im Vorfeld auf die Bildung der indirekten Rede im Englischen eingegangen werden. Dies kann mithilfe der **Focus on Grammar-Seite** (SB, S. 298) geschehen. Zu einem möglichen **Tafelanschrieb** vgl. LB, S. 51.

SOLUTIONS COMPREHENSION

1. The two articles above (SB, pp. 147–149), published by well-known British quality and popular newspapers, present different views on multiculturalism and (partly) react to David Cameron's Munich speech of 2011.
Before reading, divide the class into two groups, with each group working with one of the articles and doing the respective tasks. Here are some methodical tips on how to work in your teams:

Step 1: Read the article individually first.

- **Take notes on words, phrases, names, etc. you do not understand.**
- **Take notes on keywords, numbers, facts, etc. that you consider to be important.**

1:
Individual answers

2:
yarmulke (l. 17): a skullcap worn in public by Orthodox Jewish men or during prayer by other Jewish men
rogan tosh (l. 25): Indian mutton
saag paneer (ll. 25): Saag paneer is a classic Indian dish of cooked spinach studded with cubes of fried paneercheese.
shalwar kameez (l. 43): a pair of light, loose, pleated trousers tapering to a tight fit around the ankles, worn by women from South Asia, typically with a kameez
biryani (ll. 44f.): an Indian dish made with highly seasoned rice and meat, fish, or vegetables
bhangra (l. 47): a type of popular music combining Punjabi folk traditions with Western pop music

Step 2: In your group, ask each other questions about anything you did not understand.

- **If necessary, use a dictionary for help.**
- **Correct and/or add ideas and information to your notes you think are relevant.**

1:
Individual answers

2:
Most of the things I did not understand had to do with clothing and food. I could put together what the words were by cues in the sentence but to find out exactly what they all were I had to look them up. See above.

Step 3: Read the article again and complete your notes.

Individual answers

2. While reading, focus and take notes on these aspects:

1: Sunny Hundal

1	• **public opinion about multiculturalism in the UK today** 90% of all Britons agree that Britain has become a multicultural country, and 70% are in favour of this development • **the way Britons interact with different cultures and ethnicities** Britons have interacted positively with ethnic minorities, watching them contribute to the UK in areas such as sport, business and academia • **direct and indirect reactions to David Cameron's 2011 speech in Munich** his speech did not appeal to most voters, even to Conservatives • **the new challenges relating to race relations and ethnicity** exploitation of eastern Europeans; securing higher wages for immigrant workers; amnesty for undocumented immigrants; rising anti-Semitism and Islamophobia • **the changes Britain has undergone since the 1970s** ethnic minority voters are still turned off by remarks made by Tories • **the (changed) relationship between British society and (rightwing) politicians** British society no longer buys into the politicians' fearmongering regarding the dangers of immigration and multiculturalism

2	• **multiculturalism in everyday situations** author's example of meeting a man and discussing various issues at a subway station; people meeting, smiling, doing business and communicating with perfect strangers of different cultures • **the role of the English language** English absorbs new foreign words = sign of its confidence in multiculturalism • **British Asians today** second-generation British Asians can switch between languages and religious and cultural codes with ease • **the problem of self-segregation** people choose to leave a neighbourhood when it grows more ethnically diverse (= white flight) • **radicalization of young Muslims** no result of not liking British identity, but in reaction to British foreign policy throughout history that killed Muslims; needs to be discussed more openly • **the difference between Muslims and extremists** Muslims: enjoy, contribute to the wealth and success of the country; pay taxes; active in medical and legal professions; dream of playing cricket for England's team; worry about their children's education; live happy and productive lives extremists: rely on a fear of the other to promote hatred

2: Khola Hasan

1	• **public opinion about multiculturalism in the UK today** If Hasan's article is any indication, then the public opinion is favourable of multiculturalism. She believes it is working. • **the way Britons interact with different cultures and ethnicities** The way Hasan interacts with the Jewish man on the train is very civil and non-judgmental. • **direct and indirect reactions to David Cameron's 2011 speech in Munich** Hasan directly comments on Cameron's speech with disagreement and seeing the interactions between Hasan and the Jewish man would be an indirect disagreement. Seeing the two interact in a civil and happy way would be that personified disagreement. • **the new challenges relating to race relations and ethnicity** With all the different cultures coming together in the UK, there can be minor problems such as differences in dress and food or much larger problems involving racism and hate crimes. Hate groups like the Ku Klux Klan and the Aryan Brotherhood may arise. • **the changes Britain has undergone since the 1970s** (not mentioned) • **the (changed) relationship between British society and (rightwing) politicians** Throughout history, foreign policies have resulted in innocent Muslims being killed as collateral damage. This has obviously strained relationships between multicultural Britons and the conservative party. Over the past few years, the relationship has gotten better, but the foreign policies still need work.

2	• **multiculturalism in everyday situations** The everyday situation depicted in this article was the meeting on the subway line (ll. 1–12). Hasan met with a Hebrew man and spoke to him about the "Jews of Islam". • **the role of the English language** English has become the language in which many different cultures can communicate. Hasan describes how the English language has 'embraced new words with ease' (ll. 22–23). • **British Asians today** British Asians are 'able to switch between Asian and English cultures, between different religious and cultural codes, with fluidity' (ll. 39–41). They are also comfortable in traditional Asian carb or blues and skirts. Hasan is saying that British Asians have mastered the cultural shift. • **the problem of self-segregation** The problems of self-segregation include: migration of long-term neighbourhood residents as they become racially mixed, high poverty, racism, high unemployment. • **radicalization of young Muslims** This is not due to a dislike of British values or identity, it is due to British foreign policies throughout history. Foreign policies have resulted in innocent Muslims being killed as collateral damage. Radical Muslim speakers put emphasis on these illegal wars and the deaths of Muslim civilians. • **the difference between Muslims and extremists** Muslims enjoy and contribute to the wealth and success of Great Britain. They pay taxes, are active in medical and legal professions, and worry about their children's education – the same as any British person. Extremists rely on a fear of the other to promote their hatred.

→ Focus on Skills, Reading Techniques, p. 247

Finally, the groups should present their results to the whole class and be prepared to give a short presentation on their article.

→ Focus on Skills, Presentations, p. 276

Individual answers

SOLUTIONS ANALYSIS

All groups:

3. Examine the line of argument* in your article and show how the examples given as well as factual information underline the respective message.

→ Focus on Skills, Analysis of a Non-Fictional Text, p. 258

1: Sunny Hundal

- reference to "Rivers of Blood", Enoch Powell speech → greater context of changing attitudes towards multiculturalism; Britons feel more strongly favourable towards multiculturalism today
- factual information, numbers: results of survey → back up the author's first claim
- three lessons to be learned:
  - 1: reference to Cameron's speech = did not appeal to the public → people are less swayed by the press, politicians, most swayed by their own experiences
  - 2: call to writers, activists, and academics to focus on new challenges rather than rehashing the old question of multiculturalist society; list of specific new issues related to immigration → underlines the need to focus on more practical matters
  - 3: politicians can no longer afford to alienate the public with harsh attacks on immigrants/culture → times have changed
- final thoughts: references to right-wing politicians/media of the past and present whose fearmongering no longer influences voters → cumulative evidence that anti-multiculturalism sentiment will not work

2: Khola Hasan

Khola Hasan begins with an anecdote that illustrates how multiculturalism has not failed. She, a Muslim woman wearing her traditional Islamic garb, was sitting in a subway where a Jewish man walked up to her

and began to discuss a book she was reading (ll. 1–12). This begins the line of argument which Hasan only continues to back up.
Though she does not use numerical data and statistics, Hasan uses real life stories and examples to show that multiculturalism is thriving. She brings about what people wear (yarmulke, headscarf, sari, skirt, jeans, shalwar kameez, etc., ll. 17–18, 42–43) and how no matter what people look like, others will still communicate with them. She then gives the example of what children learn in school about religious figures (Guru Nanak, Jesus, Buddha, l. 19) as a clear indication that religious barriers are being broken by the education system in the UK. This feeling is only reiterated when concerning the food people eat in the UK, whether it be biryani or chips (ll. 44f.).
Hasan does make it clear that multiculturalism is not perfect saying there are issues of 'extremism and radicalization' along with 'self-segregation' and a host of economic issues. She concludes by stating that is not a dislike of British values but a dislike of the history of foreign policies against Muslim-majority nations and that radicals thrive on that history. Her final point is an argument that more multiculturalism would allow for this history to be fought by one nation, a multicultural Britain (ll. 60–75).

- personal anecdote ➔ illustrates positive benefits of interacting with people from other cultures
- examples of multiculturalism in everyday life in the UK: clothing, learning about religion in schools, the English language ➔ positive benefits, relatable situations for everyday people
- description of second-generation Asian immigrants as bilinguists who navigate easily between cultures ➔ creates harmonious picture, no tension or pressure to choose between the cultures; peaceful coexistence
- addresses issues of self-segregation, extremism, Islamophobia ➔ underlines that there are still issues surrounding multiculturalism that need to be solved

4. Compare the messages of the different articles to David Cameron's speech on the failure of multiculturalism and try to detect similarities and differences. Bear in mind that the newspapers have a different background and (political) focus.
➔ Focus on Facts, The Press, p. 250

1: Sunny Hundal
multiple, repeated negative references to conservative politicians, media; reference to statistics on British public's views on multiculturalism
➔ more political article, overall sentiment/message/addressee = scolding right-wing politicians for their fearmongering surrounding the subject of immigration
➔ reflects *The Guardian's* liberal political views

2: Khola Hasan

Idea	Cameron	Hasan
multiculturalism	failed, has encouraged separate cultures to lead separate lives	working and needs more, people live together in a way that allows for a multicultural society
extremists	large problem, multiculturalism is the root cause because extremists bond together over separation	large problem, caused by a history of negative foreign policies
separation of lives	people live separate lives based on the culture, creating a segregation	though there is self-segregation, an integration of cultures has occurred with dress, food, and education
the build of stronger societies	needed, less passive tolerance and more liberalism	needed, people can become a stronger society through more acceptance of other cultures
identity	people need to identify themselves through individual cultures but also through their cities, a Londoner, a Berliner, etc.	embrace individual cultures in the mainstream and become more accepting of identities as individuals
point of separation	culture differences	historical foreign policies

mostly anecdotal stories/examples; no numbers, facts, statistics; descriptive; call to encourage British people to seek out more multicultural contact in everyday life
➔ typical "opinion piece", human interest story, typical of *Daily Star*
➔ less political (apart from the headline); more focussed on day-to-day life, experiences with food, clothing, school, neighbours, strangers, etc.

articles 1 and 2, compared with Cameron speech:
- pro-multiculturalism sentiment
- discuss ongoing problems with immigration/multiculturalism that still need to be solved
- written in reaction to Cameron's speech ...

5. Discuss the (critical) views taken on multicultural Britain and the UK immigration figures against the background of the problems of youth unemployment and the kind of flexibility required as presented and discussed in the texts "EU Migration to Germany – *Sprechen Sie Job?*" (SB, pp. 80f.) and "Generation Jobless" (SB, pp. 114f.).

1: Sunny Hundal
For example:
- In light of high youth unemployment, young people and immigrants are competing for jobs ...
- It is unacceptable to have so many NEETs and yet let in high numbers of immigrants.
- Due to high youth unemployment throughout the EU, young, qualified workers must remain flexible to go where the jobs are. The host countries must welcome them and accept multiculturalism as a normal part of life ...
- The UK has the (dis)advantage of having English as its language, which attracts even more immigrant workers ...

2: Khola Hasan
Though Hasan does not take very critical views on multicultural Britain, there is a couple of points that hit home with the other articles.
The most obvious connection relates to Hasan speaking on the English language, how it is a connective unit for many people. She says that 'the speaker can switch languages with ease, depending upon context and audience' (ll. 36–38). This feeling is relayed in the article 'EU Migration' when saying 'language has replaced work visas as the main barrier to mobility' (ll. 36–37). By using that phrasing, one can see the importance of language throughout the UK and the EU as a whole. Knowing that language is an important step in both the workplace of the EU and the multicultural status of the UK because it creates a professional and interpersonal connection between two parties in which they can interact. With English becoming the dominant profession language and with different cultures embracing English as a language, both the workplace and the social settings of the UK are becoming multicultural.
Something Hasan does not take into account is the number of immigrants from other cultures taking jobs from the British people. In the 'Generation Jobless' article, the statistic of unemployed British youth is at 11.5 percent (l. 77). This is a part of the multicultural UK that may come across as a negative to many Britons. As different cultures begin to integrate into the workforce, many young Britons may lose chances for employment.

SOLUTIONS ACTIVITIES

6. **You are a student who wants to study in the UK and has to overcome many obstacles to get a student visa. Choose one of the articles and, in response to Cameron's speech, write a letter to the editor in which you express your view of a multicultural society and explain why obtaining access to a foreign country in order to study or work there is important today.**

→ Focus on Skills, Writing a Letter to the Editor, p. 290.

1: Sunny Hundal

Dear Sir or Madam,

I am writing in response to Sunny Hundal's recent article, *Multiculturalism Has Won the Day. Let's Move On*. As a German student who has been trying very hard to obtain a visa to study in the UK, I share the author's view that ...
I would also like to comment on the argument that ... In today's global economy, it is essential that ...
etc.

Yours faithfully,

A.B.

2: Khola Hasan

Dear Editor,

I've read Khola Hasan's article in response to the David Cameron's speech on multiculturalism. I would have to say I agree much more with Ms. Hasan than the Prime Minister. As someone who has overcome many obstacles in getting a student visa to study in the UK, I would say that a multicultural society is a must in today's day and age. Coming from the United States, I can understand the fear of extremism and radicalization, but I am also part of a melting pot of cultures here in the States. I know the good that can happen through meeting people from different cultures and I know how important it is to become familiar with foreign countries in order to become comfortable with people from all different walks of life. People fear what they do not understand, so obtaining knowledge of the unknown would be the easiest way to eclipse that fear.

Sincerely,

Moving from America

SOLUTIONS GRAMMAR/LANGUAGE

7. Report the excerpt from Cameron's speech (p. 146) to a friend who has not had the opportunity of listening to/reading it. Use reported speech and pay attention to the tenses (backshift!) and the pronouns. Additionally, think about appropriate introductory verbs and phrases. The vocab box gives you some verbs as a start off.

Example: David Cameron criticized that they had allowed the weakening of their collective identity. He stated that under the doctrine of ...

→ Focus on Grammar, Indirect Speech, pp. 298 f.

For example:

David Cameron criticized that they had allowed the weakening of their collective identity. He stated that under the doctrine of state multiculturalism they had encouraged different cultures to live separate lives ...

He pointed out that they had failed to provide a vision of society to which different cultures felt they wanted to belong. He stated that they had even tolerated segregated communities behaving in ways that ran counter to their values. He explained that when a white person held objectionable views – racism, for example – they rightly condemned them. Cameron stated that on the contrary, when equally unacceptable views or practices had come from someone who wasn't white, they had been too cautious and fearful to stand up to them.

He insisted that they had to build stronger societies and identities at home and needed a lot less of the passive tolerance of recent years ...

He explained that a passively tolerant society would say to its citizens that as long as they obey the law they would be left alone. Cameron pointed out that society should stand neutral between different values. But he demanded that a genuinely liberal country should do much more.

He demanded that a genuinely liberal country should believe in certain values and should actively promote these. Cameron referred to freedom of ...

He stated that these values defined them as a society and that belonging to this society required belief in these values. He called for the forming of a common purpose by having the people come together and work together ... He claimed it would also help build a stronger pride in local identity so people felt free to say yes, I am ...

Fareed Zakaria

Broken and Obsolete (pp. 151 – 153)

About the author	Fareed Zakaria is an Indian-American journalist and author. From 2000 to 2010, he was a columnist for *Newsweek* and editor of *Newsweek International*. In 2010, he became editor-at-large of *Time*. He is the host of CNN's *Fareed Zakaria GPS*. He is also a frequent commentator and author about issues related to international relations, trade, and American foreign policy.
About the text	This text is about the immigrant nature of the United States. Once the forerunner in immigration, the USA has fallen behind the like of Great Britain, Canada, Australia, Singapore, China, and India. Zakaria is examining how this has happened and what should be done.
Level	● ● ○

- Die **Awareness-Aufgabe** kann in **Gruppen** bearbeitet werden. Im Anschluss an die Erarbeitungsphase erläutert ein Gruppensprecher in wenigen Sätzen das Ergebnis der jeweiligen Gruppe.
- Die **Comprehension-Aufgaben 1 und 2** können im **Unterrichtsgespräch** bearbeitet werden. Um Zeit zu sparen, kann Aufgabe 2 **arbeitsteilig** erledigt werden, d.h., eine Hälfte der Klasse beschäftigt sich mit Aufgabenteil a), die andere mit Aufgabenteil b).
- Die Ergebnisse werden in folgendem **Tafelbild** gesichert:

The USA as an immigration country

the USA	*Canada*
– *other countries have improved the American immigration system* – *others recruit more talents and are more attractive* – *foreign born US graduates cannot obtain work visas and so move elsewhere* – *tougher enforcement of immigration law* – *lack of reform*	– *recruits talents* – *considers the country's need* – *visas can be obtained before being offered a job* – *technical skills add points to the visas*
↓	↓
The USA has lost its status as the world's leading immigrant society.	*Canada receives talented workers who fill the needs of the country and can still regulate the influx of immigrants.*

problem for the USA:
- *the transition to Canada easier and more beneficial*
- *many top graduates cannot get work visas and so go home or go to other countries*

- **Aufgabe 3** kann ebenfalls im **Plenum** besprochen werden, die Ergebnisse können informell an der **Tafel** gesichert werden.
- **Aufgabe 4** wird in **Partnerarbeit** erledigt. Vor der Bearbeitung der Aufgabe sollte die **Focus on Skills-Seite** (SB, S. 258) besprochen werden.

Die Schülerinnen und Schüler füllen eine **Tabelle** aus: s. Lösungsvorschlag, 217 f.

Es ist darauf zu achten, dass beide Partner den Heftaufschrieb übernehmen. Die Ergebnissicherung erfolgt im **Unterrichtsgespräch** über **Folie**.

- Die Bearbeitung von **Aufgabe 5** kann im **Unterrichtsgespräch** erfolgen. Die Ergebnisse werden informell an der **Tafel** gesichert.
- **Aufgabe 6** wird in **Partnerarbeit** bearbeitet, wobei die Partner die Statistik gemeinsam analysieren und die Ergebnisse in **Stichwörtern** festhalten. Diese können Grundlage für eine individuelle Ausarbeitung in einen **mündlichen Kurzvortrag** oder alternativ dazu für eine individuelle **schriftliche Ausarbeitung** sein.
- Für die Bearbeitung von **Aufgabe 7** müssen den Schülerinnen und Schülern entsprechende Materialien zur Verfügung gestellt werden. Der Zugang zu Computerarbeitsplätzen erscheint ebenfalls sinnvoll.
- Für die Erarbeitung der Kampagne sind drei bis vier Einzelstunden, für die Präsentation der Ergebnisse eine Doppelstunde zu veranschlagen.

SOLUTIONS AWARENESS

The two cartoons (SB, pp. 152 f.) can be understood as "before and after" snapshots of the relationship between the USA and Mexican immigrants in the past and today. Describe the caricatures and speculate on which one is the "before" and which one the "after" snapshot. Give reasons for your decision.
→ Focus on Skills, Analysis of Visuals, p. 262

The first cartoon (p. 152) has a caricature of Uncle Sam asking for Mexico's poor and tired, a slogan engraved in the Statue of Liberty as a welcoming for European immigrants to New York. Behind Uncle Sam is clearly a stereotypical caricature of a Mexican immigrant who is working in the USA but is on strike, signaled by his sign 'Huelga' meaning strike. The second cartoon (p. 153) shows a Mexican man looking at himself in the mirror and seeing the image of Uncle Sam, signifying that he belongs in the United States.

I would speculate that the cartoon on p. 153 is the before snapshot, a Mexican-American seeing himself as a patriot amongst patriots before he lands in America. The Hispanic man is very proud to be considered an American in the United States. That is where the second cartoon becomes the after snapshot. After entering the United States and receiving the rights that American citizens enjoy, the migrant worker then goes on strike while the United States just brings in more Mexicans to fill the gap in workers. Once he is lured into the country by the promises of citizenship, the Hispanic man does not want to be exploited for cheap labour and, as a new and legal citizen, he has the right to go on strike to obtain what is fair.

SOLUTIONS COMPREHENSION

1. Specify why the USA has lost its status as the world's leading immigrant society.
2. Describe the consequences of Canada's immigration policy
a) for the Canadian economy and scientific research and
b) for the U.S. economy and American science-related job openings.

1. There are multiple reasons: Other countries have started using the United States' system of immigration and have made the system better, other countries now recruit more talents and provide better compensation, foreign born US graduates cannot obtain work visas and so move elsewhere, higher enforcement on immigration especially concerning Mexico, lack of reform on these issues
2. a) The immigration policy is focused around recruiting talents and the country's needs (ll. 20–22). Individuals can also apply for their own work visas which allow for them to obtain the visas before being offered a job and if they have technical skills then there are points added to the visas. The 'consequences' for Canada are all good. They receive talented workers who fill the needs of the country while still being able to regulate who comes in (ll. 24–26).
b) This proves to be a problem for the United States. As more and more skilled workers find the transition to Canada easier and more beneficial, the process in the United States is becoming more difficult. Many top graduates cannot get work visas because of the process and head home (ll. 40–43). Because of this strategy, those trained in science-related fields head home or to countries where obtaining work visas is easier.

3. Point out what has happened to net Mexican immigration to the USA.

The net migration status between the USA and Mexico is now at zero or, possibly, the number going back to Mexico is greater than those coming in. This has happened due to the higher enforcement along the US/Mexico border and the decline in Mexican fertility rates which is caused by poor education and slim opportunities in Mexico (ll. 56–66).

SOLUTIONS ANALYSIS

4. Analyse the use and function of rhetorical devices employed in the article, paying particular attention to:
- **the train of thought*/argumentative structure**
- **the use of contrast/antithesis***
- **the choice of words**
- **the employment of pronouns.**

→ Focus on Skills, Analysis of a Non-Fictional Text, p. 258

rhetorical device	use/function
train of thought	• the US has historically been a great immigrant society • the US is not as exceptional as it was (explanation of how Canada, Australia, a few European countries have surpassed the United States) • statistics to back Zakaria's notion that the United States is on the decline • Americans 'do not do immigration better than everyone else any more, they do assimilation better than anyone' ➔ the reader feels positive ➔ the article provides a hope for the American future
contrast	• different immigration systems: the USA used to accept anyone, no filter for those who could actually help the economy Canada and the new USA/Mexico net Migration ➔ examples and counterpoints for everything the author says ➔ provides the reader with knowledge of both sides of the argument, United States and foreign nations
choice of words: • **USA words** • **other nations**	 • USA: words with negative connotations: not exceptional, lessening, struggling, problem, national suicide, economic weakness, striking decline, breakdown • other nations: words with positive connotations: big boost, recruiting talent, awards, results, best and brightest ➔ this changes in the last paragraph about the United States (assimilation) ➔ words change with tone: better, magically, drive, dedication, patriotism, renew
pronouns	• no use of pronouns when talking about countries • use of pronouns when referring to talented immigrants

5. **Find evidence in the text for the author's criticism of a) U.S. politics in general, b) U.S. immigration policy in particular.**

- **Train of thought**: Zakaria begins his article with fairly accepted notion that the United States has historically been a great immigrant society. He then turns that thought on its head by stating that the US is not as exceptional as it was (ll. 1–9). The train of thought then shifts to an explanation of how Canada and Australia, along with a few European countries, have all but surpassed the United States in terms of immigration. This is used as a hook to get the reader's attention before going into an explanatory state of the argument.
  In the next few paragraphs (ll. 20–66) statistics are used to back Zakaria's notion that the United States is on the decline. This technique is obviously used to prove a point. Bringing about statistics from Canada's immigration strategy and the problems within the US/Mexico immigration, Zakaria provides information that the reader can use to establish the argument's theme.
  The train of thought takes a big turn in the last paragraph however (ll. 73–88). By saying that Americans 'do not do immigration better than everyone else any more, they do assimilation better than anyone'. This is a strange way to end the argument but it leaves the reader feeling positive and provides a hope for the American future.
- **Contrast**: The main points of contrast are within the immigration systems. The USA used to accept anyone and everyone with no filter for those who could actually help the economy. This is contrasted in two ways; one with Canada, and two with the new USA/Mexico net migration. Canada filters their foreign workers through recruiting and incentives while the United States still has no way of attracting the great employees and keeping those less talented from entering the States (ll. 10–47). There is also the contrast with the net migration of Mexico. Formerly, the US did not have a lot of enforcement at the border and Mexico had high fertility rates. This is the exact opposite now (ll. 48–66). Using contrast allows for examples and counterpoints for everything Zakaria says. It provides the reader with knowledge of both sides of the argument, United States and foreign nations.

- **Choice of words**: In much of the article, when referring to the United States, Zakaria is using a negative connotation while using a positive when referring to other nations' immigration systems (see below for specific lines/references).
  USA words: not exceptional, lessening, struggling, problem, national suicide, economic weakness, striking decline, breakdown (ll. 7–8, 9, 38, 45, 47, 63, 64, 68)
  Other nations: big boost, recruiting talent, awards, results, best and brightest (ll. 18, 20, 24, 27, 48–49)
  This then changes in that last paragraph about the United States. The words change with the tone when Zakaria switches to assimilation. Using words like: better, magically, drive, dedication, patriotism, renew (ll. 76, 79, 81 85, 87)
- **Pronouns**: This portion of word choice is of particular interest. Zakaria usually does not refer to any of the nations in the pronoun form due to the multiple countries that are being used as examples. Where he does use a lot of pronouns is when referring to the talented immigrants. 'They', 'those people', 'them'; these words are seen a lot in reference to foreign workers and by using these pronouns in reference to one group throughout allows for less
  a) 'The US is not as exceptional as it once was' (ll. 7–8), 'This trend might be partly a product of tougher enforcement, but it is most likely caused by economic weakness' (ll. 61–63), 'metaphor for the breakdown of political process' (ll. 67–69)
  b) 'Immigration advantage is lessening' (ll. 8–9), 'American companies are struggling to fill 3.7 million job opening' (ll. 37–39), 'The US's current approach is "national suicide"' (ll. 46–47), 'The failure of immigration reform is ...' (ll. 67f.)
  These instances show that Zakaria is very aware of failings in general American politics but is hitting hard on the failings of immigration. He is especially aware that the immigration policy is affecting the national politics as a whole and, if fixed, would be beneficial to the country.

6. Analyse the data given in the bar chart above and compare it with the demographic developments depicted in the article. What possible changes and differences are evident?
→ Focus on Skills, Analysis of Statistical Data, p. 261

The data shows that the white non-Hispanic subset of US population will decline by percentage while the other three types of 'race' will grow. The major change that I can see is that Zakaria is mistaken when he says there is a negative net migration and a major decline in Mexican fertility (ll. 53–66). This projection on the chart shows that the Hispanic subset will have the largest growth which would imply that those 'facts' are not entirely factual from Zakaria.
The growth in these pieces of population cannot be simply thrown into a fertility rate discussion but there must be some migration to the United States from these sets of people, especially those with Hispanic origin.

SOLUTIONS ACTIVITIES

7. Finally, the U.S. government has realized the disastrous effect of their restrictive immigration policy on economy and science. You and your team have been hired to work out a campaign that attracts young people worldwide, especially in Europe, to migrate to the USA. Think about the opportunities, offers and chances the country can offer on the one hand and the skills, education, experience, etc. which the economy and research require. Work out an online/a magazine advert, flyers, brochures, TV spots, etc. to reach out to young people internationally. Then display your campaign items in class and discuss their design and effectiveness.
→ Focus on Skills, Creating an Advert, p. 278

College Recruit to Professional
Just like the college recruiting process for American sports, now top universities are recruiting the top foreign talent and then sending them to the pros! After the Supreme Court recently changed rulings on work visas, all foreign students going through American graduate schools will now be awarded permanent work visas in order to keep the top students within the United States. Universities will be in constant touch with Fortune 500 companies from around the states so that those companies will be able to recruit these students and keep the American economy strong!

Sandra Cisneros

No Speak English (pp. 153–155)

About the author	Sandra Cisneros is an American writer best known for her acclaimed first novel *The House on Mango Street* (1984) and her subsequent short story collection *Woman Hollering Creek and Other Stories* (1991).
About the text	"No Speak English" is told by an unnamed narrator and is the story about a large Hispanic woman, Mamacita, and her entrance into the United States. The kids make fun of her and she struggles with her new surroundings as she does not know the language. Mamacita stays in her apartment all the time, listening to Spanish songs while her baby boy is learning English through the television.
Level	● ○ ○
Additional material	Comprehension: no. 17

- Zur Bearbeitung der **Awareness-Aufgabe** wird die Klasse in zwei Hälften aufgeteilt, die nach dem Muster „My picture shows ..." jeweils eine der beiden Fotografien beschreiben. Nach der Erarbeitung der Beschreibungen schließen sich zwei Schülerinnen und Schüler zusammen, die unterschiedliche Bilder bearbeitet haben, und lesen sich gegenseitig ihre Ergebnisse vor. Dieser Vorgang kann bis zu dreimal wiederholt werden.
- Die **Comprehension-Aufgaben 1** bis 2 können **individuell** bearbeitet werden. Die Schülerinnen und Schüler erhalten den Auftrag, die ersten beiden Aufgaben in kurzen, zusammenhängenden **Texten** zu bearbeiten. Diese werden im **Plenum** vorgelesen und ggf. diskutiert.
- Die **Aufgaben 3 und 4** werden ebenfalls **individuell** erledigt, wobei die Schülerinnen und Schüler lediglich **Stichwörter** notieren. Die Ergebnisse werden im Anschluss an die Erarbeitung im **Unterrichtsgespräch** diskutiert und in folgendem **Tafelbild** gesichert:

Mamacita's life in the new country

Mamacita's life

- *stays at home nearly all the time*
- *cannot communicate with other people*
- *she sits at home and sings songs in her native tongue*
- *while she thinks back on her home in Mexico*
- *lives a lonely and reclusive life*

↓

consequences of her isolation

for herself	*for the relationship with her husband*	*for the relationship with her little boy*
does not belong in her new place cannot develop any new relationships	*strained, he wants her to learn English*	*tumultuous because he learns English*
↓	↓	↓
becomes an outcast in her new world	*begin to argue, she cries constantly*	*she will not be able to communicate with him*

- **Aufgabe 5** wird im **Unterrichtsgespräch** bearbeitet. Im Vorfeld sollten die verschiedenen **Erzählperspektiven** besprochen werden. Dies kann mithilfe der **Focus on Language-Seite** (SB, S. 309) geschehen. Dazu kann folgender **Tafelanschrieb** erstellt werden:

The narrative perspective of a story

narrator	***explanation***
omniscient narrator	*knows everything*
third-person narrator	*stands outside the story, describes events in the 3rd person*
first-person narrator	*character in the story, limited point of view*
witness/observer narrator	*character in the story* *(protagonist or minor character)*
objective/reliable	*can be trusted by the reader*
subjective/unreliable	*cannot be trusted by the reader*

Die Ergebnisse der Beschäftigung mit der Aufgabe selbst werden folgendermaßen an der **Tafel** gesichert:

The narrative perspective of a story

narrator	***example***
first-person narrator	– *the personal pronoun "I"*

third-person narrator	– *telling the story of someone else*
	– *expresses sadness and empathy towards Mamacita:*
	  – *she is afraid*
	  – *she is homesick*
	  – *she is sad*
	– *feels sad connection to Mamacita:*
	  – *'and then I think she cries. I would'*
	  – *'And then to break her heart forever, the baby boy … starts to sing the Pepsi commercial …'*

→ *The story is generally told from a first-person narrator but changes to the perspective of a third-person narrator at crucial points.*

- **Aufgabe 6** wird im **Unterrichtsgespräch** bearbeitet.
- **Aufgabe 7** kann zunächst in **Partnerarbeit** erledigt werden, im Anschluss an die Erarbeitung werden die Ergebnisse im **Plenum** diskutiert und informell an der **Tafel** gesichert.
- Für die Bearbeitung von **Aufgabe 8** bietet sich die Sozialform der **Gruppenarbeit** an. Jeweils die gleiche Anzahl von Gruppen bearbeiten Aufgabenteil a) bzw. Aufgabenteil b). In einem nächsten Schritt werden neue Gruppen gebildet, die sich aus zwei Mitgliedern, die Aufgabenteil a) bearbeitet haben, und zwei Mitgliedern, die Aufgabenteil b) bearbeitet haben, zusammensetzen. In diesen Gruppen werden die verschiedenen Ergebnisse ausgetauscht. Es ist darauf zu achten, dass alle Schülerinnen und Schüler die Ergebnisse ihrer Beschäftigung mit dem Text schriftlich fixieren. Dies kann in Stichwörtern geschehen.
- Die beiden kreativen Schreibaufgaben **(Aufg. 9 und 10)** können alternativ erledigt werden, wobei es den Schülerinnen und Schülern überlassen bleibt, welche Aufgaben sie zur Bearbeitung auswählen.
- **Aufgabe 11** kann als **Hausaufgabe** eingesetzt werden. Im Vorfeld kann die entsprechende **Focus on Grammar-Seite** (SB, S. 293) besprochen werden. Folgender **Tafelanschrieb** ist hier möglich:

Adverbs

<u>use:</u>

adverbs quantify or modify
- *verbs*
- *adjectives*
- *adverbs*
- *phrases*

<u>kinds of adverbs:</u>

- *adverbs of manner*
- *adverbs of frequency*
- *adverbs of degree*
- *adverbs of time*
- *adverbs of place*

} *formed from adjectives, s.b.*

<u>formation:</u>

attachment of –ly to the adjective
- *easy – easily*
- *simple – simply*
- *whole – wholly*
- *friendly – in a friendly way*
- *automatic – automatically*

<u>adverb and adjective with the same form:</u>

- *daily, hourly, weekly, monthly, yearly, early, likely, fast, long, far, straight, low*

<u>adjectives and adverbs with different meanings:</u>

adj.	same meaning	adv.	different meaning	adv.
right		right		rightly – zurecht
hard		hard		hardly – kaum
fair		fair		fairly – ziemlich
deep		deep		deeply – zutiefst
pretty		pretty		prettily – ziemlich
high		high		highly – höchst
late		late		lately – in letzter Zeit
most		most		mostly – meistens
short		short		shortly – in Kürze

<u>comparison of adverbs:</u>

adverbs of time and place: attachment of -er, -est
adverbs ending in –ly: more, most

SOLUTIONS AWARENESS

Which image of a "Latina", i.e. a Latin American or Hispanic woman, do the covers on page 154 convey? You can use the vocab box (SB, p. 154) for help.

The images on the magazine covers convey an idea of the 'sexy Latina'. Both women are 'posing in a sexy posture' while 'looking directly into the viewer's eyes'. The way the magazines have the women dress brings attention to the women's 'deep necklines and substantial cleavage' by 'wrapping' them tightly in a way that 'highlights the female shape'. The 'sleeveless' dress is 'draped around the body' so it can show the attractive nature of Latina women.

SOLUTIONS COMPREHENSION

1. Describe the arrival of *Mamacita* in the USA.

Mamacita comes out of a taxi to the apartment and her bulbous frame makes it rather difficult for her to get out. To get her out 'the man had to pull, the taxicab driver had to push' (ll. 12–13). Once out of the taxi, she is described like this: 'huge, enormous, beautiful to look at, from the salmon-pink feather on the tip of her hat down to the little rosebuds of her toes' (ll. 14–16). Singing songs of her homeland and crying a lot, Mamacita stays in the apartment and argues with the man, all the while not learning English.

2. How does *Mamacita* communicate?

People believe she is afraid to speak English because she only knows eight words; *'He not here, No speak English,* and *Holy smokes'* (ll. 23–27). Inside the apartment she speaks to her husband in Spanish though that frustrates him because he wants her to learn English (ll. 54–55).

3. Point out what her life is like in the new country.

Mamacita stays at home nearly all the time. Unable to communicate with other people, she sits at home and sings songs in her native tongue while she thinks back on her home in Mexico (ll. 35–49). It is a rather lonely and reclusive life now that she cannot communicate.

4. What are the consequences of her isolation
a) for herself,
b) for the relationship with her husband,
c) for the relationship with her little boy?

a) She does not belong in her new place. Without a friend in the world, she cannot develop any new relationships and with a refusal to learn English she becomes an outcast in her new world.
b) Her relationship with her husband is strained because he wants her to learn English (ll. 54–55). They begin to argue and she cries constantly.
c) The relationship with her little boy becomes tumultuous because he learns English. With that fact, she will not be able to communicate full with him.

SOLUTIONS ANALYSIS

5. Identify the narrative perspective* and examine the narrator's stance on *Mamacita's* stay in the USA. Give evidence from the text that proves your findings.
→ Focus on Skills, Analysis of a Fictional Text, p. 255

Though it is being told technically in a first-person perspective (the narrator using the personal pronoun "I"), it is a little grey area because the narrator is telling the story of someone else, making the majority a close third-person perspective. The narrator is telling the story with some sadness and empathy towards Mamacita's situation. There are many minor moments when this empathy comes into play (knowing she is afraid, speaking on homesickness, calling her sad, ll. 24, 40, 52) but there are two in particular to call attention to. When the narrator says, 'and then I think she cries. I would', the reader can see that the narrator can feel some sort of sad connection to Mamacita. The other point is when the narrator speaks about the little boy (ll. 60–66). 'And then to break her heart forever, the baby boy ... starts to sing the Pepsi commercial he heard on TV.' This shows the narrator truly does empathize with Mamacita's plight in the new world.

6. How do you interpret *Mamacita's* repeatedly asking her husband *¿Cuándo?*

Cuándo, meaning "when", can be used in several different ways in this sense. The most obvious to the situation would be asking, 'when can we go home?' Mamacita really wants to return to Mexico but her husband makes vehemently clear that they are already home. Other possible interpretations would be 'when can we speak Spanish' or 'when will I learn English'.

7. Analyse the stylistic devices* that create both the satirical/ironic and the melancholic/sentimental character of the excerpt from the episodic novel.

- **use of contrast/choice of words:** fat/beautiful (ll. 14–15): This is an ironic sequence of statements because an explanation of an enormous woman would usually not signal beauty. It begins to put a question mark on what people perceive as beauty.
- the pink house (ll. 43–49): This is another point of irony establishing differences in cultures. Most people in the United States would not consider a bright pink house to be a beautiful thing. Mamacita is longing for her pink home.
- singing songs (ll. 35–42): This is a melancholic/sentimental piece of the character. 'Sitting all day by the window listening to Spanish radio' sounds fairly melancholic, but the sentimental nature of her wanting to hear familiar sounds complicates the character.
- Pepsi commercial (ll. 60–66): Though Mamacita's character is not directly affiliated with the Pepsi commercial, her pleas to her son to 'no speak English' is very melancholic. She is trying not to learn and bubbles into tears with the fact that her son is learning English. This is still a sentimental thought however as she wants to keep her son close to his native land with the native language.

8. Interpret the ending of the excerpt:
a) Why does the baby boy's singing the Pepsi commercial "break her heart forever" (l. 60)?
b) What does the baby boy's way of learning English demonstrate about the culture of the family's new "home"?

a) This 'breaks her heart forever' because she knows that English will become the boy's dominant language. With that knowledge, Mamacita knows she will not be able to communicate with him as fully as if his dominant language was Spanish. This is a new culture from what she is used to in Mexico. The television can provide a fair deal of education in the United States, especially concerning the language.
b) The culture of the new home will be English first. This is so the family will fit in with the new surroundings of the home and because the little boy already knows some English, he is already becoming acclimated to this new area whereas Mamacita is not. This is a brand new culture for her where the television is providing education and estranging them from their original, rich culture in Mexico. There is enormous influence given by the TV and commercials in a way that highlights the new American culture; capitalism and the incessant need for new items.

SOLUTIONS ACTIVITIES

9. *Mamacita's* husband does not know what to do about the desperate situation. Finally, he decides to write a letter to the "agony aunt" of a local American newspaper and asks for help. Together with a partner, first write the man's letter and in a second step, write the agony aunt's response. What kind of advice might she give to him? Afterwards, read out your letters in class.
→ **Focus on Facts, The Press, p. 250**

Dear Agony Aunt,

I moved to the United States a few months ago and just got the chance to bring my wife and child over. We have a little apartment down town that is really a great home but she isn't really giving the new area a chance. She speaks very little English and all but refuses to learn sitting up in the apartment listening to the local Spanish Radio show and wallowing in her own pity. I have tried to get her out of the apartment but she just won't come out and see what this new place has to offer. It really hit her hard last week when my son began to sing along with a commercial in English because she knew she couldn't understand my son's new language. What can I do?

Sincerely,

The New Guy

Dear New Guy,

I'm glad to hear that you have adjusted well to the States and your writing is very good as English can be a difficult language to master. Keep that in mind when it comes to your wife. It will take a lot of time for her to get used to this new place, this new world. It is very different and she will start taking baby steps at first; a trip to the market, maybe to the gas station to grab band aids or something – but it will get better. Try to help her with the language, especially when your son starts using it more and more. Help her to understand what your son is saying because she will want to do that. After she understands your son, then she will begin to learn more and more.

Sincerely,

Agony Aunt

10. Choose one of the characters, *Mamacita* or her husband, and write an interior monologue* that describes their feelings about
a) the new home,
b) *Mamacita's* homesickness,
c) the frustration about being unable to communicate (properly).

Mamacita:
It's really not too bad, it's just different. I miss hearing my wind chimes in the tree outside our house in Mexico, the way the sun shined off the pink adobe and the warmth both outside and in, even the little neighbour boys running around with the footballs and kicking them into the siding. This place is just different. I don't know anyone and no one speaks my language.
If I could just go back to Mexico and speak to Rosa about everything that has happened, I'd be happy. I really want someone other than my husband to talk to but I don't know how to say anything. The language is hard. Words sound the same but things don't mean the same. Letters don't make the same sounds all the time and it just makes me wish I had someone to talk to.

Husband:
I just don't understand why she doesn't like it. We have a great opportunity here. This is America! We have a home and beds and food and a job. We have everything we need to get started on a new life away from the cartels and the poverty. I understand why she misses our house but it was dangerous for our boy. I know she misses her friends but if she could just walk outside and talk to someone then she might get over it quicker but she just sits up in the apartment and listens to the Spanish radio, not helpful.
Honestly, if she just turned on an English speaking station then she might be able to communicate with someone around here but she's too stubborn. She needs to learn. She needs to be able to speak to people in the United States, especially our son. He's already picked up a few words and if she could even learn from him then she would be fine.

SOLUTIONS GRAMMAR/LANGUAGE

11. The neighbours are chatting about *Mamacita* **and her family. Based on the information given in the short story, imagine what they might be saying and gossiping. Use adverbs and adverbials to "flesh out" the gossip and make it more vital and chatty. Together with a partner, work out dialogues and read them out in class.**
Example:
Neighbour A: Before that terribly fat woman arrived, the man was awfully nice and handsome ...
Neighbour B: Oh, dear, and the day she arrived, when she was wearing these ridiculously pink shoes ...,
→ Focus on Grammar, Adjectives and Adverbs, p. 292

Neighbour A: Before that terribly fat woman arrived, the man was awfully nice and handsome ...
Neighbour B: Oh, wasn't he though? Always worked hard and he already has the language. He's the type of immigrant that we all need around these parts. Incessant worker and truly motivated; he's a great man.
Neighbour A: Right? Not like that lady.
Neighbour B: Oh, dear, and the day she arrived, when she was wearing these ridiculously pink shoes ...
Neighbour A: Oh and that silly hat, how hysterical did that look?
Neighbour B: The huge high heel and the weirdly purple suitcases, disgusting!
Neighbour A: Yep, and if she wasn't blubbering all the time up in that apartment then maybe she could actually learn a thing or two about the language.
Neighbour B: But she won't. She'll just sit up there, curled up in the fetal position, tears streaming down like a waterfall, and cry about how unfair her life is outside of Mexico.
Neighbour A: Yeah, some people.

Jhumpa Lahiri

The Namesake (pp. 159–162)

About the author	Jhumpa Lahiri ['dZu:mpA lA'hi:ri] is an Indian-American author. She has written two collections of short stories and one full-length novel, *The Namesake* (2003).
About the text	This excerpt depicts a day in the life of Gogol, an American-born teenager of Bengali descent, on his fourteenth birthday. The novel covers Gogol's life from birth to young adulthood.
Level	●●○
Additional material	Film CD-ROM, 7 GaST: no. 1 Comprehension: no. 18

- Bei der Durchführung der **Gruppenarbeit** (Aufg. 1) sollte darauf geachtet werden, dass die Schülerinnen und Schüler die eigenen und die in der zweiten Phase vorgestellten Ergebnisse der anderen Gruppen stichwortartig in **informellen Mitschrieben** festhalten.
- Aufgabe 2 kann im **Unterrichtsgespräch** bearbeitet werden. Die Ergebnisse können informell an der **Tafel** gesichert werden.
- Aufgabe 3 kann arbeitsteilig erledigt werden, d. h., eine Hälfte der Klasse konzentriert sich auf Ashoke, während sich die andere Hälfte mit Gogol beschäftigt. Die Ergebnisse können in folgendem **Tafelbild** festgehalten werden:

Ashoke	**Gogol**
traditional	*polite*
conservative	*impatient*
caring	*assimilated*
older	*modern*
old-fashioned	*ungrateful*
disappointed	*disinterested*
accomodating	*lazy*
tolerant	*enthusiastic*
awkward	*frustrated*
out of place	*young*
proud	

- Aufgabe 4 wird als diese Sequenz abschließende **Hausaufgabe** erteilt.

- Vor der Bearbeitung von Aufgabe 5 sollten sich die Schülerinnen und Schüler mit der relevanten **Fachterminologie** vertraut machen. Dies kann mithilfe der entsprechenden **Focus on Skills-Seite** (SB, S. 255) geschehen.
- Aufgabe 6 kann in **Gruppen** bearbeitet werden. Die Ergebnisse der Untersuchung werden von einem Gruppenmitglied dokumentiert und im Plenum präsentiert.

SOLUTIONS AWARENESS

Gogol Ganguli, born in the USA as the eldest son of Bengali parents, is torn between two very different lifestyles. On the one hand, he is a typical 14-year-old American teenager; on the other hand, his family is trying to maintain their Bengali tradition. Thus, Gogol constantly has to cross borders and is struggling hard to find his own identity. What are possible conflicts that can arise in a migrant family like this one?

There are often conflicts between the parents, who grew up in a foreign culture and who may not have assimilated very much into the new culture, and the children, who feel more at home in the new culture. When the parents impose their own traditional values on the children, it can be very hard.

SOLUTIONS COMPREHENSION

1. Form four groups, with each working on a different task. Read the excerpt from the novel and collect information about:

a) how Gogol's birthday is celebrated by his friends/by his family

Friends: Gogol invites his friends over from school. They eat pizzas, watch a baseball game on TV and play Ping-Pong. This party is more grown-up than his previous birthdays, which involved more youthful elements (cake, balloons, hot dogs, ice cream ...). One of his friends gives him the Beatles *White Album* as a present. The party is a traditional American birthday party.

Family: Gogol's family's celebration is a Bengali party. His parents' Bengali friends are invited, and it is much more extravagant than the "American" party, with lots of traditional homemade food, including Gogol's personal favourite dishes, and lots of presents (ll. 10 – 31).

b) Gogol's attitudes and behaviour

- is not really interested in his father's gift (ll. 63 ff.), but says "thank you" (ll. 67, 123) and tries to appear interested (ll. 73 – 74), so he is basically polite towards his father
- is becoming lazy about speaking Bengali, and prefers to speak English, and otherwise acts more American than Bengali (wears shoes in the house, uses a fork, wears typical American clothes) (ll. 68 – 71, 87 f.)
- is more interested in the *White Album* than classical Indian music (ll. 33 ff., 146 ff.)
- is sometimes annoyed by his father (ll. 184 f.)
- does not like his name (ll. 100 ff.)

c) Ashoke

- does not often enter his son's room (l. 43)
- has a small potbelly and his hair is starting to go gray (ll. 43 – 46)
- has never given his son a special birthday gift just from him (ll. 46 ff.)
- is eager for his son to like and appreciate his gift of Gogol's short stories (ll. 58 – 62, 73 – 74)
- has no photos of his life before he came to America (ll. 137 ff.)
- feels a special kinship with Gogol the writer because they both spent most of their lives outside their home country (ll. 148 f.)
- was involved in a horrific accident (ll. 165 ff.)

d) the special gift Ashoke gives his son as a birthday present.

- a book: *The Short Stories of Nikolai Gogol* (l. 56)
- was especially ordered by Ashoke, rare copy (ll. 60 ff.)
- contains a drawing of the author (ll. 75 ff.)
- written by Ashoke's favourite author, but Gogol (the son) is not interested (ll. 100 ff.)
- Ashoke reread the stories before giving the book to his son (ll. 144 ff.)
- the book has a special meaning for Ashoke, but he is not ready to tell Gogol about it yet (ll. 173ff.)

Following this, the groups have to remix, with each group consisting of at least one member from all the other groups (see diagram, SB, p. 162). In this new group, each member informs the others about the results of the initial group.

→ Focus on Methods, Group Puzzle, p. 271

Individual solutions

2. Describe the film still on p. 160 in detail and relate your findings to the text. Which attributes of the respective cultures are striking? Discuss in class.

The men in the picture are wearing typical western-style clothes: Gogol, on the far left, is wearing a sports T-shirt, khaki trousers and running shoes. The other young man is dressed more formally, wearing a white dress shirt, black trousers, and leather dress shoes. The women are both wearing tradition Indian-style clothing. The woman on the left is wearing a black and red outfit, with a long skirt that reaches the ground and a long scarf made from Indian-style prints. Her red tank top is less traditional, however, because it is also typical of western fashion. The woman on the far right is wearing a traditional green, gold and blue sari. Both women have a small red dot on their forehead.

SOLUTIONS ANALYSIS

3. Based on the information you have already collected, try to find as many adjectives as you possibly can to characterize both Ashoke and Gogol.

Zur Lösung s. Tabelle in den Unterrichtshinweisen, LB, S. 227.

4. Then, formulate an entire characterization, using these adjectives and the information from your group work.

→ Focus on Skills, Characterization of a Figure in Literature, p. 264

Ashoke is a traditional older Bengali man who came to the United States to live as a young man. He continues to live in the Bengali tradition with his wife and their two children. He tends to be rather conservative and old-fashioned, preferring to eat Bengali food, to listen to Bengali music and to speak Bengali with his family. Because he is proud of his heritage, he sometimes feels disappointed in the fact that his son is more interested in American than Bengali culture, and his interactions with him are often awkward as a result of this. Nevertheless, he is accommodating and tolerant towards his son's preferences, and he is overall a caring father.

Gogol is an American 14-year-old boy of Bengali descent who lives with his parents and sister. Despite his Bengali background, he prefers a more modern, American lifestyle, and is often impatient and frustrated with his parents' foreign ways. He is very enthusiastic about western music and fashion, and disinterested in Bengali music and his father's literary passion.

5. Examine the narrative techniques* employed by the author and explain how they help to make the gap between the generations and the cultures visible.

→ Focus on Skills, Analysis of a Fictional Text, p. 255

The **third-person omniscient narrator** is able to reveal the innermost thoughts of both Gogol *and* Ashoke. This helps the reader to gain deeper perspective into both generations and cultures. For example, the narrator reveals that Gogol would have preferred another birthday present even though Gogol does not say this out loud or visibly show his disappointment to his father (ll. 64 ff.). Later, the point of view shifts to Ashoke, where we learn that he has memories of a horrific accident which he is not yet ready to share with his son (ll. 165 ff.).

SOLUTIONS ACTIVITIES

6. Work with the corresponding film scene *The Graduation Present* on the CD-ROM and notice which cinematic devices are used to capture the atmosphere of the novel.

- cutting shots in the beginning underline chaotic atmosphere; when Gogol is interrupted by his father, camera shot is stationary to emphasize an "end to the fun"
- loud rock music emphasizes Gogol's feeling of being interrupted by his father, and his father's feeling of interrupting his son; symbolizes that father and son are communicating poorly
- camera angle, shot from the point of view so that we can see Gogol's annoyed face when he is turned away from his father
- over-the-shoulder shots when father and son are sitting down having a conversation emulates their respective points of view

The Global Village – The World in a Nutshell?!

TM[1]	SB[2]	Author: Title of text	Type of text	Topic	Competences	Audio CD	Film CD-ROM	GaST[3]	Diff[4]	Comp[5]
Start-up Activities										
233	166	David J. Smith, Shelagh Armstrong: If the World Were a Village	children's book, visual	statistics about world population reduction of these numbers to those of a small village life in this village	• analysing a text • creative writing					
233	167	Living in the Global Community	cartoon	the countries of origin of everyday items	• analysing a visual					
Message in a Bottle? – Plastic, Pollution & Progress										
236	168	Greenpeace: The Trash Vortex	photo, online article, documentary, role cards, visual, cartoon	the problem of plastic waste for the eco-systems of the oceans	• reading/listening comprehension • analysing the contents and language of a text • preparing and giving a presentation • analysing a visual • holding a discussion • grammar: the simple present, the passive voice, indirect speech, adjectives	CD 2, 5		no. 3, 14	120	
	173	Plastics	Focus on Facts					no. 3, 14		
	174	Environmental and Ecological Movements	Focus on Facts							

[1] TM = page in Teachers' Manual
[2] SB = page in Students' Book
[3] GaST = material in Grammar and Skills Trainer
[4] Diff = page in Differenzierungsmaterial
[5] Comp = material in Comprehension: Reading – Listening – Viewing

TM[1]	SB[2]	Author: Title of text	Type of text	Topic	Competences	Audio CD	Film CD-ROM	GaST[3]	Diff[4]	Comp[5]
242	175	Clemens Höges: The Children of Sodom and Gomorrah – How Europe's Discarded Computers Are Poisoning Africa's Kids	magazine article, photo	electronic trash from industrial countries is sent to Africa how it is used there its benefits and dangers	• analysing the contents and style of a text • analysing a visual • doing Internet research • preparing and giving a presentation • creating material for a campaign • grammar: expert language and everyday English				131	no. 19
Getting Active & Being Responsible										
248	179	Lenny Kravitz: What Did I Do with My Life?	song	the speaker of the poem/ lyrics is asking himself questions about what he did with his life	• analysing the contents and rhyme scheme of lyrics • creative writing	CD 2, 6		no. 12, 19		
249	180	Katrin Zeug: Mit Biodiesel zur Party	German newspaper article, photo	new concepts for music festivals as incentives for an ecological lifestyle	• mediating a text • carrying out an interview • doing Internet research • analysing a text • holding a discussion • grammar: working with vocabulary			no. 15		
253	183	Global Giving – The Girl Effect	Internet website, visuals	a charity creating opportunities for girls and their families issues girls from disadvan-taged backgrounds are confront-ed with	• analysing visuals • analysing a video • creating a video clip • grammar: if-clauses			no. 16		
257	185	Malala Yousafzai: Speech at the United Nations	honorary address	Malala Yousafzai's address to the United Nations on human rights and the effects of war, extremism and the importance of women's rights and education	• listening comprehension • analysing a video clip • doing Internet research • writing a comment • grammar: simple present and indirect speech	CD 2, 7				no. 20

TM[1]	SB[2]	Author: Title of text	Type of text	Topic	Competences	Audio CD	Film CD-ROM	GaST[3]	Diff[4]	Comp[5]
262	187	HOKISA – Homes for Kids in South Africa	report, photos	the life and experiences of a young boy in an African township	• analysing the contents and form of a text • characterizing a person • writing a letter of application • creative writing					no. 21
267	190	Derek Markham: Recycled Orchestra Turns Trash Into Music	Internet article, photos	the story of the Landfill Harmonic orchestra, a project which supports young people by showing them how to play music on recycled instruments	• analysing a video • analysing the contents and language of a text • creative writing					
	193	Technology, Progress & Responsibility in a Global World	Focus on Facts					no. 14		
Fashion, Fabrics & Fabs – How Expensive is Cheap Fashion?										
271	194	Hasnain Kazim, Nils Klawitter, Wieland Wagner: The High Human Price of Cheap T-Shirts	magazine article, photos, statistics	the collapse of a factory building in Dhaka, Bangladesh corruption in the Bangladeshi construction sector as a reason for illegal and unsafe building the responsibility of western clothes companies attempts to improve the situation	• analysing visuals • analysing statistics • generating a mind map • scanning a text • giving a presentation • analysing the contents and style of a text • carrying out a hot seat discussion • creative writing • grammar: working with vocabulary			no. 20, 26	136	
276	200	How Expensive Is Cheap Fashion? – The Best Eco-Fashion Brands and Eco-Criteria	photo page	eco-fashion	• describing visuals • making a ranking • working with vocab • analysing the style of a text • doing Internet research • preparing a fashion show			no. 20		

TM[1]	SB[2]	Author: Title of text	Type of text	Topic	Competences	Audio CD	Film CD-ROM	GaST[3]	Diff[4]	Comp[5]
279	202	Made in Germany: Eco-Fashion – Save the Planet and Look Good	Internet report, cartoons	eco-fashion as an attractive commodity	• listening comprehension • analysing a visual • doing Internet research • viewing comprehension • doing a project • grammar: adjectives and adverbials	CD 2, 8				no. 22
282	204	Brita Belli: The Eco-Fashion Revolution – You Are What You Wear	Internet article, photos, visual	eco-fashion: designers, companies, customers	• analysing a text • describing and analysing visuals • doing Internet research • creative writing				148	no. 23
	207	Thematic Vocabulary	Focus on Vocab							

Start-up (pp. 166–167)

About the authors	David J. Smith is a Canadian writer for children. His book *If the World Were a Village: A Book About the World's People*, illustrated by Shelagh Armstrong, has won a number of awards. Shelagh Armstrong is a Canadian illustrator, and was the recipient of the 1985 Will Davies award for excellence in illustration.	
About the text **About the cartoon**	The text here is an excerpt of a children's book in which the author condenses the entire population into 100 people, a ratio of 67 million represented by each individual.	The cartoon shows three friends having lunch/coffee together at the airport preparing for a departure and has labels showing where all their items came from, which coincidentally is eleven different countries which implies the topic of globalisation.
Level	●●○	●○○

- **Aufgabe 1** kann zur Stärkung der **mündlichen Sprachkompetenz** eingesetzt werden. Die Schülerinnen und Schüler werden dazu aufgefordert, das dem Kinderbuch zugrunde liegende Konzept in einem kurzen **Statement** zusammenzufassen.
- Aufgabe 2 wird gemeinsam im **Unterrichtsgespräch** bearbeitet. Die Ergebnisse fließen in folgendes **Tafelbild** ein:

Food in the global village

food

vegetables | *bread* | *animals (produce food; source of food)*

no shortage of food

↕

50 people: no reliable source of food; hungry some/all of the time
16 people: severely undernourished
34 people: always have enough to eat

- Die Gruppen (**Aufg. 3**) erarbeiten jeweils ein weiteres Kapitel, das sie als Text ausformulieren. Ein Schüler bzw. eine Schülerin pro Gruppe fixiert den Text schriftlich. Im Anschluss an die Erarbeitung werden die Texte im Klassenzimmer ausgehängt und im Rahmen eines **Museumsrundgangs** zur Kenntnis genommen und diskutiert. Gelungene Texte können für die ganze Lerngruppe kopiert werden.
- **Aufgabe 4** wird nach den Angaben im Schülerbuch bearbeitet.
- **Aufgabe 5** kann zunächst in **Partnerarbeit** erledigt werden. Die Schülerinnen und Schüler notieren sich **Stichwörter** zur Beschreibung und Interpretation des Cartoons. Die anschließende **schriftliche Ausarbeitung** erfolgt **individuell**, ggf. in **häuslicher Arbeit**.

SOLUTIONS START-UP ACTIVITIES

1. Describe the underlying concept of the children's book "If the World Were a Village".

The author condenses the entire population into 100 people, a ratio of 67 million represented by each individual. By doing this, he can highlight the unfair dispersal of food and wealth in the greater world by showing it through the lens of a small village.

Having a smaller number allows for the author to do two things; relay it easier to children and amplify the impact of the ratios. Dropping the numbers down make things more manageable for children to understand. Kids will not be able to drop 6.6 billion into manageable numbers while changing it to 100 makes things much more simple. Saying that only thirty-four out of one hundred people are always well-fed (ll. 45f.) has a lot more impact than saying 2.2 billion have enough to eat.

2. What does the second paragraph reveal about the variety and supply of food in the "global village"?

The market (ll. 25ff.) is a place where people go to purchase food. With that ideological stance, it would stand to reason that only those with money can buy food at this 'market'. In addition to that, the reference to the 'tables' would connote that only those with money to take from the table and put it on their own will be fed, leaving the 'scraps' for those less fortunate.

These numbers also show that there is no shortage of food in the global village (ll. 38ff.). With animals outnumbering humans by a wide margin, everyone in the global village could – and should – be fed. Putting this to the larger scale, the real world, that would mean that the worldwide problem of hunger should not need to exist though with over half of the world/village it happens (much of Africa, India, some Middle Eastern and Central American countries etc.). The choice of food shows the most common food choices of people throughout the world, but, with that being said, it also shows that the traditional third-world dishes are not part of the 'normal' food choices because they do not have enough food to eat in the real world. All of the food choices come from established first world areas for the most part (though the author does not take into account fish as it is not a domestic animal).

3. In groups, think about further "chapters" of the book and continue the story about the "global village". Here are some ideas: nationalities, languages, money and possessions, schooling ... the village in the future ...

All of the continuing chapters would most likely follow along with the theme established in the first two: use of the ratio highlighting the injustice of the greater world.

Nationalities: Chinese 'villagers' along with Indians would make up about 33 villagers while a country like the United States would have less than five percent of the population and Germany would have barely over one villager. Some of these nationalities (American vs. Middle Eastern, black vs. white etc.) may cause problems with various inhabitants in the way racism and foreign policies cause issues between nations in the greater world.

Languages: Mandarin, Spanish, English and Hindi would be the most widely spoken languages but there would still be a smattering of other languages heard around the village (French, Portuguese, German, Arabic, etc.) and many of the other inhabitants would not be able to communicate with one another through spoken word.

Money: All of Europe and the United States/Canada make up around 15 % of the world population but these countries hold around 54 % of all the wealth in the world. That would equate with fifteen villagers having over half of the money/possessions in the global village while the African villagers (making up around 11 % of the world population) would own less than 1 % of the village's wealth.

Schooling: Once again, European countries alongside the United States and Canada will have the majority of the education while at the same time the female villagers as a whole will get less of an opportunity than their male counterparts.

Future Village: The future is fairly grey for the village. With onl. 100 people, it would be very likely that nationalities would mix and these separations in the present would cease to exist in a couple generations. If that would be the case, then a domino effect (one change changes everything) would come into being and many of the problems above would be removed simply by mixing nationalities. People would learn to speak a common tongue, the wealth would be given to nearly everyone due to the change in nationalities, schooling would follow suit; it would be better in the long run but, as for the greater world, a mix of nationalities would be a much harder sell than in a small village of 100 people.

4. In a Placemat Activity (→ FoM, p. 271), first reflect on the statement by Upton Sinclair, then share your thoughts with your class.

Upton Sinclair's quote is rather poignant when considering the way the wealth is distributed in the world today. Yes, many men are behind bars and the things they want to obtain are outside but for many more men, nearly the entirety of the third-world, they live outside and free but the wealth and desirable items are kept away from these people. While countries hoard the wealth of the world (European nations, United States, Canada, China) other countries are kept on the exterior of this 'Garden of Eden'. All the wealth and likable things are kept to a select few, while many more remain outside this garden, living free, but still locked away from these things.

5. Describe the cartoon above: What impression is given of the "global village"? Detect elements that are "global" and elements that belong to the "village".
→ Focus on Skills, Analysis of Visuals, p. 262

The cartoon shows three friends having lunch/coffee together at an airport (most likely departing to another country) and has labels showing where all their items came from, which coincidentally is eleven different countries. The global elements would be the items of communication that would be unneeded in a village setting (i.e. phone, iPod, television) and wrapped food (chocolate bar and taco meal). Those items, in a village of one hundred people, would be superfluous. Items like the clothes would probably be made inside the village and so would items like backpacks along with the produce (coffee) in the farms and fields. The technological advancements would be all but useless in a village of one hundred while clothes and readily available food would be necessities. It would be unlikely that people would sell wrapped chocolate and drive-thru taco meals but what would be more appropriate is fresh fruit, vegetables, and meat.

Message in a Bottle? – Plastic, Pollution & Progress

Greenpeace

The Trash Vortex (pp. 168–172)

About the author	**Greenpeace** is a non-governmental environmental organization with offices in over forty countries and with an international coordinating body in Amsterdam, the Netherlands. Greenpeace states its goal is to "ensure the ability of the Earth to nurture life in all its diversity" and focuses its campaigning on worldwide issues such as global warming, deforestation, overfishing, commercial whaling, genetic engineering, and anti-nuclear issues. It uses direct action, lobbying and research to achieve its goals.
About the text	The text at hand is describing the trash flow of environmentally hazardous plastics in the pacific ocean. They collect in currents and the North Pacific sub-tropical gyre that circulates these materials into a giant island of trash that is the equivalent of the size of Texas.
Level	● ● ●
Additional material	• Audio CD 2, 5 • Differenzierungsmaterial, p. 120 • GaST: no. 3, 14

- Die **Awareness-Aufgabe** wird nach den Angaben im Schülerbuch bearbeitet.
- **Aufgabe 1** kann als Übung zur Stärkung des **mündlichen Ausdrucksvermögens** eingesetzt werden. Die Schülerinnen und Schüler analysieren das Foto und notieren sich dabei **Stichwörter**. Diese bilden die Grundlage eines **mündlichen Kurzvortrags**.
- Die **Aufgaben 2 und 3** werden nach den Angaben im Schülerbuch erledigt. Zur Bearbeitung der Aufgaben sollten zwei verschiedene Räume zur Verfügung stehen, einer für die Gruppe, die den Text im Schülerbuch bearbeitet, ein anderer für die Gruppe, die den Hörtext bearbeitet.
- Vor der Bearbeitung von **Aufgabe 4** werden die entsprechenden **Focus on Facts-Seiten** (SB, S. 258 und S. 261) zur Kenntnis genommen. Die Ergebnisse der Beschäftigung mit der Aufgabe werden entweder auf Flipchartbögen mithilfe von Moderationskarten visualisiert und präsentiert oder von einem Gruppensprecher in einem mündlichen Vortrag erläutert. In letzterem Fall werden die Ergebnisse aller Gruppen in einem kurzen Gespräch im **Plenum** gebündelt und in folgendem **Tafelbild** gesichert:

The Trash Vortex

- *100 million tonnes of plastic produced each year (ll. 3f.)*

↓

- *10 % of this plastic each year ends up in the sea (l. 5)*

↓

- *larger plastic items break down into smaller pieces over time (ll. 18ff.)*

↓

- *they are joined by small manufactured plastic pellets lost/dumped into the sea (ll. 23ff.)*

↓

- *they wash up on beaches or accumulate in the middle of the sea (ll. 29ff.)*

↓

- *they are eaten by seabirds and other animals (ll. 45ff.)*

↓

- *over a million seabirds and 100,000 marine mammals and sea turtles die each year (ll. 52ff.)*

↓

gigantic soup of trash

- Für die Bearbeitung von **Aufgabe 5** wird die Klasse in drei **Gruppen** unterteilt. Jede dieser Gruppen bearbeitet einen der in der Aufgabenstellung vorgeschlagenen Teilaspekte (Step 1). Die Ergebnisse werden im **Unterrichtsgespräch** gesammelt und auf **Folie** gesichert (s. Lösungsvorschlag unten). Step 2 wird im Unterrichtsgespräch besprochen.
- **Aufgabe 5** wird anhand der Angaben im Schülerbuch bearbeitet.
- **Aufgabe 7** kann als den ersten Teil der Beschäftigung mit dem Text abschließende **Hausaufgabe** eingesetzt werden.
- **Aufgabe 8** wird zu Hause vorbereitet. Die Schülerinnen und Schüler erstellen Listen, die im Unterrichtsgespräch vorgestellt und diskutiert werden.
- Bei großen Lerngruppen kann die Klasse zur Bearbeitung von **Aufgabe 9** in zwei **Gruppen** eingeteilt werden, sodass ein Teil mithilfe der vorgeschlagenen Rollen das Meeting durchführt, der andere Teil beobachtet das Meeting und gibt den Teilnehmern ein persönliches **Feedback**. Dazu wird folgender **Feedbackbogen** ausgefüllt. Die einzelnen Kategorien müssen im Vorfeld erläutert werden.

Feedback for: ____________________

aspect	**++**	**+**	**+/0**	**0/-**	**-**	**- -**
contents						
communication skills						
vocabulary						
grammar						
additional aspects						

- Alternativ dazu können die einzelnen Rollen doppelt besetzt werden, dazu werden noch zwei **Diskussionsleiter** und zwei **Protokollführer** eingesetzt, die den Verlauf und die Ergebnisse der Diskussion festhalten. Die Protokolle werden im Anschluss an die Diskussion den Schülerinnen und Schülern zur Verfügung gestellt und dienen als Grundlage für die Bearbeitung von Aufgabe 10.
- Im Vorfeld der Bearbeitung von **Aufgabe 10** sollten die angegebenen **Focus on Grammar-Seiten** (SB, S. 305, S. 303, S. 292ff. und S. 298f.) erläutert werden.

SOLUTIONS AWARENESS

It is hard to imagine the modern world without plastics ... cars, computers, cell phones, kitchen utensils, textiles ... even food ... made of or wrapped in plastic are part of everyday life and plastic appears to be irreplaceable. In a Pyramid Discussion (→ FoM, p. 272), exchange your views on whether plastics are a blessing or rather a curse of life today.

For example:

advantages: convenience, some plastic food containers are reusable, sturdy, lightweight, low cost ...
disadvantages: made from dangerous chemicals, difficult to recycle, non-biodegradable ...

SOLUTIONS COMPREHENSION

1. Before reading or listening to one of the texts, have a closer look at the photo above the text. Describe the photo using the words and phrases from the vocab box. Then relate the photo to the title of this chapter – what is its "message in a bottle"?
→ Focus on Skills, Analysis of Visuals, p. 262

The photo shows the carcass of an albatross. Most of its body has decayed and all that is left is its dishevelled plumage and skeleton. We can see that its intestines were full of small plastic items, such as husks, bottle caps and other scrap plastic. This surely was the cause of the animal's death.

A message in a bottle is usually a cry for help or a request to be rescued sent by someone who is stranded on a deserted island after a shipwreck. In this case, however, the plastic bottles (and other plastics) are causing animals to die. People need to respond to the alarming "message" that can be read in the bottlecaps in the bird's carcass: Plastic is destroying the environment, and the environment needs saving.

2. **Divide the class into groups of 3 – 4 students each. The groups have a choice here:**
a) you can either read the Greenpeace text about the Pacific Trash Vortex or
CD 2 5 **b) you can listen to the Planet100 audio text on the same topic.**
Whatever material you choose, take notes while reading/listening and try to answer the questions/tasks below.

Be careful: not all the questions refer to both materials – thus you cannot answer all the questions/tasks at once.

	Greenpeace text	Planet 100 audio
• What is the meaning of the term "Pacific Trash Vortex"?	(ll. 33–43)	huge soup of trash in Pacific Ocean
• Where does all the trash come from?	ships and platforms (20%), rest from land (ll. 5f.)	land (80%), sea vessels and oil platforms (20%); mostly developed world
• What kind of garbage is discarded into the ocean?	plastic toys, plastic textiles, polystyrene packaging and polyurethane foam pieces, fishing net, traffic cones, etc. (ll. 7ff.)	90% plastic, "Chinese-made crap"
• Point out a) the visible signs of the problem of the floating trash vortex	larger pieces of trash (ll. 16f.)	Chris Jordan's photos of albatross
b) the even more dangerous invisible problems of the trash vortex	small, broken-down pieces, pellets (ll. 18ff.)	---
• State why "marine tumbleweeds" are a serious problem.	they accumulate in huge quantities (ll. 27ff.)	---
• How and where does the trash vortex move – or float?	areas where winds and currents are weak (ll. 31f.) North Pacific sub-tropical gyre; clockwise in slow spiral (ll. 33ff.)	Eastern garbage patch between HI and CA, Western garbage patch between HI and Japan
• Which dangers and risks does the trash pose to seabirds and other marine animals?	over a million sea-birds, one hundred thousand marine mammals and sea turtles killed each year (eating, getting caught in plastic) (ll. 52f.) small jelly-fish like creatures are harmed (ll. 56ff.)	kills millions of animals and birds every year
• Is there any solution to the problem?	---	stop buying plastic items; carry own grocery bags instead of using plastic bags; recycle

→ **Focus on Skills, Reading Techniques, p. 247**
→ **Focus on Skills, Listening Comprehension, p. 244**

3. **After completing your notes, the different groups remix (see diagram, SB, p. 170) and exchange their findings. Have in mind that the materials provide slightly different information and details and add further information to your notes if necessary.**

./.

SOLUTIONS ANALYSIS

4. In your groups, explain in what way the different components of the problem add up and finally result in this "gigantic soup of trash". Find evidence from the text and, additionally, use the graphic on p. 172 to explain this phenomenon.

→ Focus on Skills, Analysis of a Non-Fictional Text, p. 258
→ Focus on Skills, Analysis of Statistical Data, p. 261

- 100 million tonnes of plastic are produced each year (ll. 3f.).
- 10 % of this plastic each year ends up in the sea (l. 5).
- Larger plastic items do not biodegrade, but rather break down into smaller pieces over time (ll. 16ff.).
- These tiny pieces are joined by small manufactured plastic pellets that are lost/dumped into the sea (ll. 23ff.).
- These pieces of plastic either wash up on beaches or accumulate in the middle of the sea, where they are kept in place by the wind and ocean currents (ll. 29ff.).
- The pieces of plastic are eaten by seabirds and other animals (ll. 45ff.).
- This leads to the death of over a million seabirds and 100,000 marine mammals and sea turtles each year (ll. 52ff.).

5. Step 1: Examine and analyse the stylistic devices* paying particular attention to
- **specialist vocab (expert language),**
- **word fields,**
- **positive and negative emotive words (in connection with a certain aspect).**

→ Focus on Skills, Analysis of a Non-Fictional Text, p. 258

device	example from the text	function/effect
specialist vocab		
• environment	• to float, current, subtropical convergence zone, resources, marine environment, subtropical gyre, plankton, marine mammals	→ underlines the competency, reliability of the given information; trustworthiness of the author
• technology	• seafaring vessel, to incinerate, durability, polythene, polystyrene, polyurethane	
• pollution	• the biggest landfill, plastic, trash vortex, garbage patch, discarding, to incinerate, disposal, plastic debris, accelerating, PVC, washed ashore, to degrade, mechanical abrasion, pellets, to accumulate, plastic filament	
wordfields		
• environment	• planet, Pacific, current, subtropical convergence zone, resources, animals, seabirds, marine environment, tide, natural materials, sub-tropical gyre, islands, beach, shore, plankton	→ emphasis on the enormous impact of garbage and pollution
• technology	• plastic, oil platforms, seafaring vessels, to incinerate, PVC, recycling, durability, stability, polythene, polystyrene, polyurethane, polypropylene, new plastics	→ emphasis on the impact of modern technology
• pollution	• trash, landfill, garbage, mess, to discard, to replace, crap, waste, debris, plastic toys, plastic bottles, plastic bags, waste stream, disposable, degrade, mechanical abrasion, pellets, plastic filament, plastic particles	

device	example from the text	function/effect
positive/negative emotive words • positive • negative	• special, huge, to commit to sth., major step, more ideas, dedicated volunteers, tiny jelly fish • trash, dubious, superlong, mess, Chinese-made crap, monster, killing, worse, toxic, waste stream, problem, expanded (packing), casually, much larger problem, weak, ill effects, dead, killed	→ fewer positive words → there is nothing positive about plastic ... → emphasises the danger and extension of the pollution

Step 2: Against the background of your previous findings and results categorize the type of text and relate it to the message Greenpeace wishes to convey to the readers.

→ Focus on Facts, Basic Types of Non-Fictional Texts, p. 246

feature	example from the text	message to the readers
appeal	• ... who is responsible for this mess? • Chinese-made crap ... • ... but did you know ...? • ... why do we care ...? • Check out Chris Gordon's photos ... • We need to start ... • Do we need all these ... toys ...? • Can we say no ...? • Can we commit ...? • Let us know ... leaving a comment ... • Take a walk along any beach ... • ... dedicated volunteers ... • ... animals ... mistake them for prey • ... a turtle ... over a thousand pieces of plastic ...	→ (indirect) appeal to feel responsible ... to take action ... → appeal to face reality → appeal to people's conscience → emotional appeal
entertainment	• Welcome to ... today's special episode ... • ... but did you know ...? • ... a superlong current ... • Chinese-made crap ... • ... it's no wonder ... • ... each of us tosses ... • ... we'll see you tomorrow ...	→ directly addressing the viewer → evoking his/her interest → casual/informal language to connect to the (young) viewer
description	• ... a huge soup of trash ... • ... washed ashore will be ... • These big items do not degrade ... smaller particles are joined ... • ... a single one litre bottle ... • ... dedicated volunteers ...	→ information about and description of the situation and amount of waste → description of the process for ordinary people
information	• ... the who-what-when-why-where and how of the Pacific Trash Vortex ... • ... the biggest landfill on the planet ... • 90 percent/80 percent/20 percent ... • ... the Eastern ... the Western garbage patch ... • US ... 5 percent ... 30 percent ... • ... millions of animals and birds ... • 185 pounds of plastic every year • graphic proof ... • 40 percent of the world's oceans ... • 100 million tons ... 10 percent ... 20 percent ... • ... six kilos of plastic for every kilo of ... plankton ...	→ introduction/overview/ clarity → factual information → visual proof (photo)

Webcode SNG-40175-017 @ **6. Use the links provided on the webcode to gain further background information on the problem. Afterwards, prepare 5-minute presentations and inform your class about your chosen topic.**
→ Focus on Skills, Presentations, p. 276
→ Focus on Facts, Plastics, p. 173

Individual answers, e.g.:

- The patch does not resemble a huge "floating island" on top of the water, but instead consists of tiny plastic particles that cannot always be seen by the naked eye.
- "The actual discovery of the patch was made by a racing boat captain, Charles Moore. Moore was sailing from Hawaii to California after competing in a yachting race. Crossing the North Pacific Subtropical Gyre, Moore and his crew noticed millions of pieces of plastic surrounding his ship."
- There is also a North Atlantic Gyre.
- etc.

7. Describe and analyse the cartoon depicting different stages in the development of mankind. Explain what perception of the world and man's responsibility is shown here.
→ Focus on Skills, Analysis of Visuals, p. 262

The first panel shows cavemen in loin cloths. They are using a bone and a wooden cudgel as primitive tools for digging. The second panel shows Greek/Roman philosophers during the period of Antiquity. They are wearing togas and standing in front of a building with pillars while having a debate. The third panel shows planet Earth from space, with stars and planets in the background and two space stations in orbit. The final panel shows a dump truck hauling and dumping garbage in a landfill. In the background a city skyline can be seen.

The cartoon is making a joke about this being the age of garbage ("garbAge"). The first three ages deal with positive, useful human developments that show the creativity and progress of humankind. The last panel presents a very negative perception of the current era as being wasteful and destructive to the environment. It shows that humans are responsible for creating waste and pollution and therefore also responsible for solving this problem.

SOLUTIONS ACTIVITIES

8. Examine your/your parents' home and environment: How many useful/necessary and redundant (*überflüssig*)/unnecessary items made of plastic can you detect? In class, discuss your findings and think about possible alternatives to using plastics in everyday life.

For example:

necessary items: laptop, computer mouse, cleaning products, shampoo bottles ...

unnecessary items: candy containers, toys and trinkets, pens, cosmetic packaging ...

alternatives to plastic: glass/metal/paper food/drink containers ...

9. Plastic trash can be a hazardous (dangerous) burden as well as a financial trap for a whole community – the problem therefore has to be taken care of. For this reason, the city has called for a meeting of politicians, experts on both environmental and recycling and reuse issues, local citizens, businessmen/-women and journalists.

a) Prepare rolecards and discuss the pros and cons, dangers and possible benefits of plastics (examples see SB, p. 171).

b) Act out the community meeting, using the notes you have prepared.

→ Focus on Language, Conversation and Discussion, p. 266
→ Focus on Methods, Panel Discussion, p. 270

./.

SOLUTIONS GRAMMAR/LANGUAGE

10. You are a journalist:

a) Write a cover story* about the community meeting and the discussed dangers of plastics in your community. Choose whether your story is factual and focuses on information or whether your story is sensational and wants to emotionalize the readers.

→ Focus on Facts, The Press, p. 250

Individual solutions

b) Write a feature story* about a family that is concerned about the effects of plastic in relation to their children but cannot afford expensive household utensils.

→ Focus on Facts, The Press, p. 250

Should children be exposed to plastics?

Susan Miller (35), Andrew Miller (37), their children Sammy (5) and Timothy (3) have made a decision: no more plastic houseware and plastic toys in their home! After Susan and Andrew Miller watched the Greenpeace documentary they realized what danger plastic items can pose for their health. Susan Miller, "Just to think that plastic particles can get into people's blood ... what a nightmare ... all the plastic toys my children are playing with every day ... we decided that our children should not be exposed to this toxic material."

"It's going to be hard to exchange their toys and buy healthy stuff instead ... ", says Andrew Miller. "And what will the future be like for our kids – all that plastic trash that we cannot recycle .... our kids will have to live in a world of trash one day ... what a nightmare ..." etc.

c) Write a comment* about the meeting organized by the city authorities and appeal to politicians and businessmen/- women to take action.

→ Focus on Skills, Writing a Comment and a Review, p. 279

Individual solutions

Employ the respective linguistic devices, e.g. the simple present, the passive voice, adjectives, indirect speech to quote the people, etc.

→ Focus on Grammar, Tenses, pp. 305ff.
→ Focus on Grammar, Passive, p. 303
→ Focus on Grammar, Adjectives and Adverbs, pp. 292ff.
→ Focus on Grammar, Indirect Speech, pp. 298f.

Clemens Höges

The Children of Sodom and Gomorrah – How Europe's Discarded Computers Are Poisoning Africa's Kids (pp. 175–178)

About the author	Clemens Höges is a German journalist and the head of foreign correspondents for *Spiegel* magazine. He is also the co-author of *Die letzte Reise: Der Fall Christoph Columbus* (2006).
About the text	This *Spiegel* article looks at the practice of developed countries dumping their old, unwanted electronics in the developing world. Here, a landfill in Ghana is presented where old electronics from the West are dumped, with devastating effects on the people who live in the area and the environment.
Level	● ● ●
Additional material	• Differenzierungsmaterial, p. 131 • Comprehension: no. 19

- Die Länge des Textes lässt eine **häusliche Vorbereitung** sinnvoll erscheinen. Neben der gründlichen Lektüre des Textes können auch die **Comprehension-Aufgaben** (Aufg. 1–4) als vorbereitende **Hausaufgabe** bearbeitet werden. Um den Umfang der Hausaufgabe auf ein machbares Maß zu beschränken, kann die Klasse in zwei Gruppen unterteilt werden, von denen jede zwei der vier Aufgaben erledigt. Alternativ dazu können die Schülerinnen und Schüler aufgefordert werden, alle Aufgaben zu bearbeiten, jedoch zwei davon in Stichwörtern und zwei in ausformulierten Texten. Die Auswahl der Aufgaben ist den Schülern überlassen.
- Aufgabe 5 wird zunächst in **Einzelarbeit** gelöst. Dazu wird die im Schülerbuch vorgeschlagene Tabelle ins Heft übertragen. Die Ergebnisse werden im **Unterrichtsgespräch** ausgetauscht und auf Folie gesichert.
- Aufgabe 6 kann in **Einzelarbeit** erledigt werden. Zur Stärkung **der mündlichen Sprachkompetenz** notieren die Schülerinnen und Schüler ihre Ergebnisse in Stichwörtern und arbeiten diese mündlich zu einem kurzen Vortrag aus.
- Zur Bearbeitung von Aufgabe 7 wird die im Schülerbuch vorgeschlagene Tabelle ins Heft übernommen und in Partnerarbeit ausgefüllt. Die Ergebnisse werden im **Unterrichtsgespräch** ausgetauscht und auf Folie gesichert.
- Für die Bearbeitung von Aufgabe 8 können den Schülerinnen und Schülern folgende **Internetadressen** an die Hand gegeben werden:
  www.basel.int/Home/tabid/2202/mctl/ViewDetails/EventModID/8295/EventID/44
  www.basel.int/Portals/4/Basel%20Convention/docs/text/BaselconventionText-e.
  legal.un.org/avl/ha/bcctmhwd/bcctmhwd.html
- Aufgabe 8 kann als **Hausaufgabe** eingesetzt werden.

SOLUTIONS AWARENESS

Over the years, sorting and selling electronic scrap has become a big business. Speculate about the reasons.

- People are buying more electronics and replacing them faster. – Electronic scrap contains valuable material that can be recycled.
- Electronics are not built to last very long.
- Electronics contain material that is harmful if not taken care of properly.
- There is a high demand for working/usable second-hand electronics.

SOLUTIONS COMPREHENSION

1. Outline the nightmarish situation at the waste dump near Accra.

The waste dump, full of old electronics, is completely polluted. There are several fires constantly burning plastics and old electronic devices, creating thick, poisonous smoke. The river is black and full of pollution and garbage. Poor young children, mostly boys, and young men scour through the waste, looking for valuable metals to sell. (ll. 13–43)

2. Point out the extent of the practice of discarding electronics globally and disposing of them in developing countries.

Electronics from developed countries are discarded in developing countries such as Ghana, Nigeria, Vietnam, India, China and the Philippines (ll. 44–48). According to the UN, up to 50 million tons of electronic waste is disposed of globally per year (ll. 59f.). The EPA estimates that 40 million computers are thrown away per year just in the US (ll. 72f.).

3. Define the international laws and directives that regulate waste disposal.

The Basel Convention is an international treaty from 1989 that prevents (in theory) developed countries from dumping their toxic waste in developing countries. 172 countries signed the treaty, but of those, the US, Afghanistan and Haiti did not ratify it [since the article was published, Afghanistan has ratified it] (ll. 64–70).

The EU later created similar directives that were signed by individual countries: WEEE (Waste Electrical and Electronic Equipment) and RoHS (Restriction of Hazardous Substances) (l. 74ff.). Germany has particularly strict laws concerning waste disposal, but they are not well enforced (ll. 78–81).

4. Describe how boys like Bismarck try to make a living with the electronic scrap.

The boys roam around the landfill looking through the discarded electronics for valuable metals (ll. 38–41). They break apart the devices using rocks and throw them onto fires which burn away the plastics leaving the valuable metals behind (ll. 52–54). There is a hierarchy at the landfill, and the young men in their mid-20s buy the metal from the younger children and then resell it to a foundry nearby. Those in the middle of the hierarchy who are about 18 years old fetch the electronics from scrap importers and bring them to the landfill; they either search through them to find metals themselves or sell them to the younger boys (ll. 99–120).

SOLUTIONS ANALYSIS

5. Illustrate and explain the impact of the dangerous chemicals and toxins in the area a) on the boys' health, b) on the environment and c) on humans in general.

	impact on ...		
chemicals toxins	**boy's health**	**environment**	**humans in general**
poisonous smoke	**➔ ...**	**➔ pollution of air**	**➔ painful to lungs**
Toxins	**➔ small physique**	**➔ pollution of air ...**	**➔ ...**
...			

a) on the boys' health: They breathe in the toxic fumes and heavy metals from burning the electronics (ll. 56f.); Kwami Ama's eyes are bright red and irritated from the smoke (ll. 125f.); his hands are full of scars from handling broken devices (ll. 127f.); his memory is failing, possibly due to toxic exposure (l. 134); it is difficult to completely assess the medium- and long-term effects, since only young people work at the dump and there are no studies, but it is clear that the children are very sick (ll. 180–188).

b) on the environment: The air is highly polluted from the smoke, and the river is black and filthy (ll. 13ff.). Highly toxic metals such as lead, cadmium and arsenic, plus dioxins, furans and polychlorinated biphenyls are leaking into the soil and water (ll. 142–145).

c) on humans in general: Being exposed to these various chemicals and toxins causes headaches and stomach cramps in the short-term. Prolonged exposure harms the nervous system, the kidneys, the blood and the brain. Exposure to lead in particular can shrink the brain and lower somebody's intelligence (ll. 146–151).

6. Describe the photo on p. 176 and compare its message to the headline of the article and the explanation given about the biblical cities of Sodom and Gomorrah. Explain the function of this reference to the Bible.
➔ Focus on Skills, Analysis of Visuals, p. 262

The photo shows a Ghanaian boy (about 13 years old) standing in the middle of a landfill. He is wearing a red and blue sports outfit and is either barefoot or wearing very flimsy flip-flop sandals. His eyes are closed and he is wearing a weak and grim expression on his face. He is holding a computer monitor high above his head, as if he is about to smash it on the ground to break it. The landfill is filled with broken and filthy electronic devices and other waste, and a white broken-down truck is located nearby. The sky is filled with thick, black and grey smoke from a large fire burning garbage in the background. The atmosphere is filthy and dismal.

The title *The Children of Sodom and Gomorrah* refers to Agbogbloshie being slowly destroyed by the toxic waste and the fires, just as God destroyed Sodom and Gomorrah with fire and brimstone because the people were sinful (ll. 6–11). However, in the case of developing countries, it is not God who is harming the citizens, but the West. The slum children are not being punished because they are evil or sinful; rather, they are victims of the West's carelessness with its waste. One might even say that it is the West that is being evil and sinful by dumping their old electronics abroad rather than disassembling and recycling them in a responsible way. The reference to the Bible draws up an image of suffering and destruction by fire that matches the photo, but it also alludes indirectly to morality and ethics.

7. Examine the style of the article: Which rhetorical and structural devices* are used to convey the appalling situation to the reader?

→ Focus on Skills, Analysis of a Non-Fictional Text, p. 258
→ Focus on Facts, Basic Types of Non-Fictional Texts, p. 246

	device	**example from the text**	**function**
rhetorical devices	**reference/allusion**	**Sodom and Gomorrha (ll. 6ff.)**	**→ reference to Bible/Old Testament** **→ emphasis on destruction**
	contrast/antithesis	**people in the West ... Africa (ll. 1ff.)**	→ This contrast between the 'Western World' and Africa is used to highlight the very different lives of the privileged in the West and those less fortunate in Africa in addition to showing how the western world's use of computers is harming the young African boys in their homeland.
		The computers of the rich are poisoning the children of the poor (ll. 57f.).	→ underlines the relationship and disparity between rich/poor, West/developing world
	descriptive language/negative emotive words	eke out a living (l. 3), poisoning (l. 5), plagued by toxins (ll. 9f.), Acrid, black smoke (l. 13), infernal fires (l. 21), vague, foggy (ll. 23f.), small, stooped (l. 35), steamrolled (l. 159), crumbling (l. 162), defective (l. 164), tatters (l. 166), etc.	→ creates a vivid picture of the dismal and appalling situation at the landfill as well as the Ghana Chemicals Control and Management Center
	descriptive language/positive emotive words	Kwami has a strong body and a round, honest face (ll. 124f.)	→ creates sympathy for those who are affected by the terrible situation; underlines the boy's innocence/portrays him as a victim
	inside perspective, description	Breathing in too deeply is painful to the lungs (ll. 21f.)	→ the author gives the reader a sense of what it actually feels like to be at the landfill
	portraits of individual boys	Bismarck (ll. 29–43) and Kwami Ama (ll. 123–131)	→ gives the reader a view into the daily lives of the boys that work in these dumps; the personal angle creates sympathy for their situation
	simile	The river ... is black and thick like used oil (l. 14)	→ creates a more vivid picture
structural devices	**introduction**	According to the Bible ... and he disappears again into smoke. (ll. 6–43)	→ The essay begins with a look into the biblical tale of Sodom and Gomorrah then transitions to conditions for the young Ghanaian, Bismarck. By structuring the essay with this type of introduction, the reader is granted the ability to see it through the lens of a familiar story (ll. 6ff., speaking of fire and brimstone raining down) and then compare the description of Ghana (ll. 9–24) and Bismarck's life (ll. 25–43) to the tale of Sodom and Gomorrah.

device		example from the text	function
structural devices	**main part**	The refuse of the Internet age ... can also cause cancer, among other things. (ll. 44–157)	➔ The main portion of this essay is concerning statistics. The paragraphs titled "The refuse of the Internet age", "A business worth millions", and "Shrinking the brain" are all about the statistical analysis of the refuse and of the outcomes of the business, both economically and physically. Because of all this data, the author structures it in a way that keeps the stats in the middle so the reader will be drawn in and let out with human interest points. There is also a structural ploy that drops Bismarck's story in between the analysis points to keep the reader interested in the plight of the Ghanaian boy.
	subheadings	'The refuse of the Internet Age' 'A business worth millions' 'A euro a day' 'Shrinking the brain' 'Why don't you halt the flow of junk?'	➔ The first subheading simply denotes what the trash flow into Ghana's Sodom and Gomorrah is made out of. The second highlights a reason why it is happening. People do not want to give up their cheap way of disposing of their refuse. The companies make more money by shipping it to Africa than by disposing of the refuse properly. The third subheading is a comment on Bismarck's lifestyle. He is doing all of this work and being subjected to the toxins and carcinogens for only a euro a day. The fourth section is a shout to what is happening to these children. It is a small phrase that clearly relays the dangers this lifestyle has. The fifth and final subheading is a question that is not directed at the companies, but to all those who even indirectly participate in the junking. It is a comment that is a plea for help. All of these subheadings do the job of telling what their respective sections are about and they do it in small phrases. By using these headings, the reader will have an idea of what each section is about and can more easily recall the information by the transitioning.

	device	example from the text	function
structural devices	**conclusion**	It's all moving faster and faster ... even without a study that it's disastrous. (ll. 158–188)	→ The concluding section of the essay goes back into a human interest vein so that the article comes full circle. It started with Bismarck, a child who is subjected to these chemicals and toxins, and ends with John Pwamang, a man trying to clean up those same chemicals. The author structured it this way to show all the sides of the problem; those affected, those causing, and those trying to stop it. In addition, ending with a plea for help calls to the reader to provide aid in the hope that anyone reading would be willing and able to help with this difficult problem.

SOLUTIONS ACTIVITIES

@ **8. Do research on the Basel Convention of 1989 and prepare a presentation in which you outline its basic objectives and guidelines. Try to find legal loopholes and discuss possibilities of closing them.**

- Full name: Basel Convention on the Control of Transboundary Movements of Hazardous Wastes and Their Disposal
- Afghanistan has since ratified it; now only the US and Haiti have not ratified it.
- Purpose: to reduce hazardous waste from being transported across national borders, especially from developed to less developed countries

Loopholes:
- allows export of hazardous waste to developing countries if it is to be recycled → many exporters claim that waste will be recycled, but instead just dump it in a developing country; attempts were made to close this loophole in 1995 with the Basel Ban Amendment, but not enough countries accepted it for it to take effect
- excludes the transportation of radioactive waste

To close the recycling loophole:
- The ban could also forbid materials from being moved abroad for recycling purposes.
- If it is to be allowed, exporters have to provide some kind of proof that the material is actually recycled properly; introduce mandatory inspections ...

SOLUTIONS GRAMMAR/LANGUAGE

9. Imagine you are a Greenpeace activist trying to explain the life-threatening impact of the chemicals on the boys and teenagers working in the junkyard. In groups, create material (posters, flyers, leaflets, etc.) that is comprehensible and visually clear. In a first step, paraphrase complicated expert language using everyday English. Use your dictionary for help.

Example:
carcinogenic → likely to cause cancer
dioxin → by-product of industrial processes, e.g. the production of plastics (PVC); highly poisonous; can cause cancer; can be inhaled or ingested through breastfeeding ...

- to discard → to get rid of sth. that you do not want or need any longer; to throw away
- heavy metals → a metal of a high relative atomic weight or density, e.g. lead; dangerous/poisonous substances; a chemical that can make you sick
- convention → an agreement between states

- to ratify → to make sth. (a treaty) officially valid; to sign and give consent to sth.; to make a new law/ rule
- directive → an official or authoritative instruction; a rule/announcement
- electrical appliance → electrical gadget, e. g. a computer, TV set, refrigerator, etc.
- chemical substance → a particular kind of chemical matter/material

Getting Active & Being Responsible

Lenny Kravitz

What Did I Do with My Life? (pp. 179–180)

About the author	Lenny Kravitz is an American singer-songwriter, instrumentalist and music producer. He is a four-time Grammy award winner and has released a total of nine studio albums. Some of his best known hits include *Are You Gonna Go My Way, Fly Away* and *American Woman*.
About the text	This song appeared on the *Baptism* album which was released in 2004.
Level	● ● ○
Additional material	• Audio CD 2, 6 • GaST: no. 12, 19

- Die bei der Bearbeitung der *Awareness*-Aufgabe gesammelten Ideen können dazu benutzt werden, vor der Präsentation des Liedes über dessen Inhalt zu spekulieren.
- Vor der Hörverstehens-Aufgabe sollten die Schülerinnen und Schüler die Arbeitsanweisungen mit entsprechendem Raum für ihre Notizen in ihre Hefte übertragen.
- Aufgabe 3 kann als abschließende **Hausaufgabe** eingesetzt werden.

SOLUTIONS AWARENESS

With respect to the question asked in the title: What have you done with your life so far?

Scholastic accomplishments, friendships, sports/music/arts/hobbies/talents ...

SOLUTIONS COMPREHENSION

CD 2 6 **1. Listen to the song and explain why the speaker asks himself so many questions. What kind of questions are they? What advice does the speaker give to his listeners?**
→ Focus on Skills, Listening Comprehension, p. 244

The singer seems to be looking back and reflecting on his life. Perhaps he is old and preparing to die, or has already died and is looking back at his life. He is trying to determine whether he had/has lived his life in a meaningful and righteous way. Alternatively, he may not be that old, but is simply questioning his life up until that point, possibly realizing that he has not lived meaningfully and has decided to make some changes.

The questions are about how the singer thinks he should have lived. Most are yes/no questions, and the 'correct' answer is 'yes'. However, the singer does not reveal the answer to his own questions.

He encourages the listeners to embrace life and live their lives in a self-determined way, and to live courageously (ll. 15 – 20, 29 – 34).

SOLUTIONS ANALYSIS

2. Examine the rhyming words. Which words are connected and emphasized?
→ Focus on Skills, Analysis of Poetry and Lyrics, p. 259

Throughout the verses, every second line is rhymed. In the first part, the same rhyme carries over four stanzas (right, fight, sight, might, light, bite, ll. 2 – 13). The chorus also has one rhyme (dance, chance, romance, ll. 16 – 20, 30 – 34), and there is a third rhyme in lines 23 – 27: heart, part, art.

SOLUTIONS ACTIVITIES

3. Imagine you are the poetic speaker: Give answers to the questions in the song.

- *Did I work on the battlefield?* – Although I was not an actual soldier, I have 'fought' for others. I performed volunteer work and donated money to help those who were less fortunate. I had strong beliefs about equality and fairness, and I voiced my opinions to others and tried to live my life according to those beliefs.
- *Did I do what I thought was right?* – When I was younger, I struggled to find what I thought was right. I was often swayed by peer pressure and went along with a group even when I was unsure of myself. For example, I bullied a girl and drank a lot of alcohol in order to fit in, even though I knew it wasn't a good idea. Other times, though, I did what I thought was right, like when I returned a wallet full of money to its owner instead of taking it for myself.
- etc.

Katrin Zeug

Mit Biodiesel zur Party (pp. 180 – 182)

About the author	Katrin Zeug, born in 1980, studied Psychology and Journalism in Hamburg and Lisbon and is now a free-lance journalist working mainly in the fields of psychology, the environment and social topics. She has worked for example for SPIEGEL, SPIEGEL ONLINE and DIE ZEIT. She is also a book author. She wrote this article for DIE ZEIT in May, 2013.
About the text	This text deals with Jacob Bilabel and his Green Music Initiative. It outlines his first experiences in the field at a party in the Plänterwald region of Berlin and goes on to describe the green motivation behind his work and his cooperation with the organizers of the Melt! festival. The music branch is a good instrument for bringing about social change in terms of saving energy and assuming responsibility for the environment because music festivals have a formative influence on young people.
Level	● ● ○
Additional material	• GaST: no. 15

- Die **Awareness-Aufgabe** wird in einem kurzen **Unterrichtsgespräch** erledigt.
- Zur Bearbeitung von **Aufgabe 1** wird der Text in **Kopie** ausgeteilt, damit die Schülerinnen und Schüler Unterstreichungen und Notizen anbringen können. Die Anweisungen der Aufgabenstellung können dahingehend erweitert werden, dass die Schülerinnen und Schüler aufgefordert werden, zunächst die Passagen im Text zu finden, die die in der Aufgabenstellung genannten Aspekte enthalten, und dazu dann passende Fragen zu formulieren.
- Um allen Schülerinnen und Schülern die Möglichkeit zu geben, ihr Interview durchzuführen, können die Interviews zunächst in **Gruppen** zu sechs Schülern durchgeführt werden. Der Lehrer bzw. die Lehrerin hat dabei die Möglichkeit, sich verschiedene Ergebnisse anzuhören und diese ggf. zu korrigieren. Im Anschluss an die **Präsentation** in Kleingruppen können einige gelungene Interviews im **Plenum** vorgestellt werden.

- Die **Aufgaben 2 und 3** werden in **Gruppen** bearbeitet. Die Ergebnisse werden in einem kurzen Vortrag präsentiert, wobei darauf zu achten ist, dass jedes Gruppenmitglied einen Teilaspekt der Aufgabenstellung präsentiert.
- **Aufgabe 4** wird nach den Angaben im Schülerbuch erledigt.
- Für die Bearbeitung von **Aufgabe 5** bietet sich die Sozialform der **Gruppenarbeit** (Gruppen zu sechs Schülern) an. Je zwei Schülerinnen und Schüler bearbeiten einen der genannten Themenbereiche und tauschen ihre Ergebnisse im Anschluss an die Erarbeitungsphase aus. Es ist darauf zu achten, dass am Ende der Bearbeitung alle Gruppenmitglieder alle Cluster ins Heft übertragen haben.
- Bei der Bearbeitung von **Aufgabe 6 können dieselben Gruppen wie zuvor zusammenarbeiten.**

SOLUTIONS AWARENESS

What do you like or dislike about music festivals?

LIKE	DISLIKE
• the music and musical acts are very entertaining • seeing many people gathered together who all love one specific type of music is a great thing • with like-minded interests in music, festivals are a great way to meet new people • music, by its nature, makes people happier • the large selection of acts to see	• some festivals devolve into rampant drug and alcohol use • in many festivals, rioting comes with the territory • the after effects of festivals (minor hearing loss, lethargy, sickness) • the mosh pits (when many people gathered for a band come into the center and push, shove, and punch one another for the sake of excitement) • not every band is one that you want to see

SOLUTIONS COMPREHENSION

1. Together with a partner, mediate the German newspaper article and turn it into an interview. Choose who wants to be the journalist/interviewer and who takes Jacob Bilabel's position. Be careful to ask the right questions and consider the following aspects and topics:

- **the atmosphere in Plänterwald**
- **Jacob Bilabel's experiment five years ago**
- **the reactions of the partygoers to Bilabel's experiment**
- **the ecologic principles of Bilabel's "Green Music Initiative"**
- **Bilabel's co-operation with the Melt! festival organizers**
- **the reasons why the music industry is the perfect hub for a green change**
- **experiences made in Denmark and England**

→ Focus on Skills, Mediation, p. 265
→ Focus on Skills, Writing an Interview, p. 285

Afterwards, act out your interviews in class and discuss the various results.

→ Focus on Skills, Writing an Interview, p. 285

Interviewer: Mr. Bilabel, your first Green Music Festival was in the Plänterwald forest area in Berlin. What was the atmosphere like?

Bilabel: It was very special – the sound of music wafting between the trees, people dancing barefoot in the grass, colourful feathers in their hair.

Interviewer: What was the main idea behind your experiment of a festival in the forest five years ago?

Bilabel: I wanted to see how people who are celebrating would react when they were inspired to think a bit about what was for them a new situation. It all worked out just as I had hoped it would. When the music stopped, everyone looked towards the DJ and he said to them: "If you want to dance, climb on the bikes!" Four bikes were beside the mixing desk, wired up to the music equipment and only by pedalling away could electricity be produced. Now people who frequently go to clubs to dance are looked upon as very egocentric but the moment the music stopped, people formed groups and cheered each other on. Some even called up their friends and asked them to come and help and join in the party.

Interviewer: So your experiment worked. What did this prove to you?

Bilabel: It proved that a green future must not be boring and dreary. Today my Green Music initiative advises event organizers on how best to bring together two states of mind that at first sight may seem very contrary: the egocentricity of the party-going types and a sense of ecological responsibility. We help them to work out their carbon footprint and to find suitable methods of saving energy.

Interviewer: For three years now you have worked together with the organizers of the Melt! festival.

Bilabel: Yes, with 20,000 visitors in three days, the result is mountains of garbage and carbon dioxide emission and electricity consumption on the scale of a small town. We organized a bike tour to the festival site, to encourage people to leave their cars at home. There were affordable train tickets. In future the stage will be operated with the help of solar energy. And we also improved the whole catering concept.

Interviewer: Why does the music industry lend itself to this kind of green change?

Bilabel: It is not just that it consumes so much energy and produces so much trash, it also serves well as a role model. A festival is a social experiment that has a great influence in different ways on young people.

Interviewer: What about the big festivals in Denmark and England?

Bilabel: At the Roskilde Festival in Denmark you are given a cold beer when you hand in a full bag of garbage. And at the Glastonbury Festival in England thousands of volunteers separate all the garbage. They even provide decomposable tent pegs made of potato starch.

SOLUTIONS ANALYSIS

Webcode SNG-40175-018 @ **2. Ecological music festivals have seemingly become very popular. Do further research on the Melt! festival by**
a) using the links provided on the webcode and
b) examining the quality of the festival's homepage.
→ Focus on Skills, Research, p. 318

The Melt! festival in Gräfenhainichen near Dessau in Germany has been in existence since 1995 and now attracts 20,000 visitors to a town of just over half this size. The site itself is called "Ferropolis" – the "city of iron" and is an open museum of huge, old industrial machines on what was formerly the site of a strip mining operation. Some of the links provided, for example Wikipedia, faz.net and vimeo, concentrate almost exclusively on the type of music played there and the artists and the bands involved in the festival while the festival homepage itself covers not just the aspects associated with the music involved but also a considerable range of points relating to the subjects of ecology, sustainability and cooperation with the Green Music Initiative. The aim here is to develop ideas and strategies that make it possible to combine the components of music and entertainment and fun and environmental protection. The festival homepage provides details of the measures it has taken to help protect the environment and to increase ecological awareness among the young people attending the event. The festival website is attractive and contains for example backstage interviews and impressions, main stage videos, and photos and information on many different subjects. It enables the user to get a good overall impression of the atmosphere at this unique festival site and of the activities that go on there.

SOLUTIONS ACTIVITIES

3. "Green Music Festivals" – Yes or no? In a Pyramid Discussion, reflect on and discuss possible pros and cons, advantages and disadvantages of this new trend.
→ Focus on Methods, Pyramid Discussion, p. 272
→ Focus on Language, Conversation and Discussion, p. 266

PROS
The music is great.
Dancing is great.
You can meet lots of other young people and have great fun. Festivals are a shared experience.
There is a large infusion of cash into the area.
Publicity for the area.
Exposure for new talent.
Festivals are part of a culture industry providing jobs for many.
Positive participation of the local community.
You can assume responsibility for environmental protection.

CONS
Hundreds of tons of waste are produced.
Problems with hygiene.
A lot of energy is consumed.
The people living in the immediate area have to put up with a lot of noise and general disturbance.
Accidents can happen.
Festivals are only about profit.
The area of the festival is overrun by strangers.
Drug problems can accompany the festival.
Young people can get into difficulties.
Danger of mass hysteria.
Organizational problems.
Dangers of infection.

SOLUTIONS GRAMMAR/LANGUAGE

4. Reactivate your knowledge and collect words, expressions and phrases in connection with the topics "ecology", "sustainability" and "environment". If necessary, use your dictionary for help and arrange your findings in clusters like these (examples, see SB, p. 182).

- **ecology:** recycling, climate change, greenhouse effect, carbon emission, waste disposal, etc.
- **sustainability:** renewable energies, biodegradable, organic farming, raw material, reduction of, etc.
- **environment:** recycling, solar energy, renewable energies, environmentally-friendly, etc.

5. Together with a partner, revise and improve your first draft of the mediated text above. Try to use connectives and adverbs and more formal language as well as further words and phrases from the vocab box and/or your dictionary for help.
→ Focus on Language, Connectives and Adverbs, p. 291
→ Focus on Language, The Language Register of English, p. 315

Individual solutions

Global Giving – The Girl Effect (pp. 183–185)

About the author	Before founding Global Giving, Mari Kuraishi and Dennis Whittle were heads of strategy and innovation at the World Bank. While in that post, they created the first-ever Innovation Marketplace for Bank staff in 1998, an internal competition in which Bank employees pitched their own ideas for fighting poverty worldwide. The winners received grants to make their ideas happen. The competition resulted in some of the most innovative ideas and effective programs in World Bank history.
About the text	The 'text' in question here is a series of three screenshots from the Global Giving website. The images show 1) a girl falling into a vortex while upside down. The black and white image of the girl is contrasted by the orange spiral and it provides a disorienting effect, 2) an image of horizontal and vertical, red and black lines that look like they are grabbing onto a small image of a girl in order to pull her into the large capital letters HIV and 3) the donation page where a confidently posed, African girl stands on an African landscape.
Level	● ○ ○
Additional Material	GaST: no. 16

- Die **Awareness-Aufgabe** kann um die Frage erweitert werden, wie die Schülerinnen und Schüler ihre eigene Position als Junge oder Mädchen in der Familie, in der Schule und in der Gesellschaft einschätzen.
- Die **Aufgaben 1 und 2 können in Partnerarbeit** erledigt werden. Die Ergebnisse werden im **Unterrichtsgespräch** ausgetauscht und in folgendem **Tafelanschrieb** gesichert:

The girl effect

threats and dangers: →	*happy ending:*
– *getting lost in the world of poverty and crime* – *being thrown about (physically or emotionally)* – *not knowing a way to escape* – *being pushed and pulled in every direction* – *being pulled down into more and more dangerous situations* – *being infected with HIV* – *being sexually assaulted* – *abusing drugs*	} *people donating money can help young women to live happy lives*

- **Aufgabe 3** wird in **Partnerarbeit** bearbeitet. Die Ergebnisse werden im **Plenum** diskutiert und informell an der Tafel gesichert.
- Für die Bearbeitung von **Aufgabe 4** wird die Klasse in **Gruppen** eingeteilt, die sich mit einer der beiden angegebenen Großkategorien beschäftigen. Innerhalb der Gruppen sollten die einzelnen Unteraspekte **arbeitsteilig** bearbeitet werden. Die Ergebnisse jeder Gruppe werden in Form einer **Tabelle** auf **Folie** gesichert. Die Folien werden im Anschluss an die Erarbeitung präsentiert. Gelungene und umfassende Folien können für die gesamte Lerngruppe kopiert werden.
- Vor der Bearbeitung von **Aufgabe 5** wird die angegebene **Focus on Facts-Seite** (SB, S. 249) besprochen. Zur Erarbeitung der Video Clips sollten zwei Doppelstunden, zur Präsentation sollte eine weitere Doppelstunde veranschlagt werden.
- **Aufgabe 6** wird in **häuslicher Arbeit** erledigt. Zu einem möglichen **Tafelanschrieb** zum Thema *conditional clauses* s. LB, S. 41.

SOLUTIONS AWARENESS

Global Giving is a non-profit charity fundraising website that gives social entrepreneurs and nonprofit organisations worldwide the opportunity to raise money. In 1997, World Bank executives Mari Kuraishi and Dennis Whittle were asked to help innovate ways to fight poverty and founded the "World Bank's Development Marketplace" which had enormous success. When participants asked for a real marketplace that was open all year and operated virtually, Mari Kuraishi and Dennis Whittle realized the brilliance of this innovative idea and launched Global Giving. One of Global Giving's initiatives is the "Girl Effect" which is aimed at creating opportunities for girls and their families and fighting poverty and HIV and providing them with microloans. Why do you think does Global Giving focus on girls – and not on boys? Discuss possible reasons.

Women and girls have long been considered expendable by many societies. In many countries where HIV and poverty are prevalent, women are much worse off than men due to high rape numbers and workplace biases that have longed plagued the female gender. Additionally, these girls are many times responsible for both income and the ability to run the household, all the while retaining a low social position. Global Giving focuses on girls because not many local organizations do in these types of areas. Maligned and abused, women do not have a place to turn to and Global Giving provides for them a chance for a better life.

SOLUTIONS COMPREHENSION

1. **Describe the screenshots No. 1 and 2 taken from the Global Giving homepage and state which possible threats and dangers for girls are visualized.**

1) A girl with pigtails in her hair falling into a vortex while upside down. The black and white image of the girl is contrasted by the orange spiral and it provides a disorienting effect, much like what the girl would feel being upside down. The possible dangers that are visualized in this graphic design would include: getting lost in the world of poverty and crime, being thrown about (physically or emotionally) by those involved in the world, not knowing a way to escape, being pushed and pulled in every direction, allowing your body to be tossed about like it was nothing more than a leaf in the wind, being pulled down into more and more dangerous situations.

2) An image of horizontal and vertical, red and black lines that look like they are grabbing or to a small image of a girl in order to pull her into the large capital letters HIV. The girl also looks rather lost while she is holding on to what looks like a child. The most obvious danger here is that possibility of HIV. Men in poor and HIV riddled worlds are more likely to act out a sexual assault and pass on HIV. These types of people will grab and pull, do whatever they must for sexual gratification, including the spreading of HIV. In addition to the possible sexual assault angle, the spread of HIV through the sharing of needles. Drug abuse is common in poverty stricken communities and the sharing of needles contributes mightily to the spread of HIV. This is visualized in the image through the crisscross of lines, looking as if they are filled with blood like veins, making the whole thing seem rather threatening.

2. **Screenshot No. 3 shows the end of the short video clip "The Girl Effect." What kind of solution or "happy ending" does it employ?**

3) The donation page shows the silhouette of a confidently posed African girl (seeing as she has African style braids in her hair) standing on an African landscape. The screenshot is also dosed in harmonious and warm colours to allow the viewer a sense of accomplishment. The connotation that it brings up is that by donating, giving time and money to this organization, people can help these girls escape poverty, rape, drug abuse, and HIV with just a small donation. By providing the organization with monetary assets, a person can truly help these young women have a happy ending.

Webcode SNG-40175-019 @

3. **Watch the video clip "The Girl Effect" which is provided on the webcode. Give an outline of the**
   a) visual/pictorial elements and
   b) the textual elements of the video clip.

a) The visual elements start with a small, faceless girl (signifying that it could be any young girl) who is said to be twelve. This girl then 'ages' to 14 and marries, becomes pregnant at 15, then sells her body at 16 and contracts HIV. The pictorial elements throughout this sequence include: adding size to the girl (pregnancy), adding a small yellow coloured child (the baby) and then is chased by long black arms that turn red (selling body and contracting HIV). The girl then goes through a hypothetical situation in which she receives the proper education and ages without marrying. She girl then starts walking through doors (signaling a generational shift) as she has more of the yellow children who then age through the same process of walking through doors, showing how education can keep young girls healthy and out of poverty.

b) The textual elements follow the same storyline as the picture elements. As each image changes, words appear in a way that leads the viewer to the next word and the next image, following the storyline through both visuals and text.

SOLUTIONS ANALYSIS

4. Together with a partner, examine the cinematic devices* employed in the video clip and explain their function and effect on the viewer. Focus on the following aspects and take notes:
- **narrative techniques (setting, plot, suspense, characters, body language, communication)**
- **cinematic devices (camera operations, animations, visual symbols, colours, music/sound, special effects).**

→ Focus on Skills, Analysis of a Film Scene, p. 256

If necessary, watch the video clip a second time. Afterwards, exchange your findings with your partner and compare your notes.

- **Narrative techniques:**
  Setting: There is no true setting in the clip. This is because the situation can happen anywhere there is poverty and can happen to any young girl.
  Plot: The plot follows a chronological timeline of a young girl's probable life when living in poverty and then reverses it by adding in a hypothetical education which changes the outcome.
  Characters: These are all faceless so that there is an 'everyman' trait about them, any girl could be in the situation.
  Body language: In the first sequence, the downcast look of the girl and almost fearful running show that the situation is not an enviable one but, when the education hypothetical is added, the confidence appears and the girl's head is almost always looking up.
  Communication: This is done mostly through running text which gives the viewer a faster paced read as the text moves along with the visual story.

- **Cinematic devices:**
  Camera Operations: The camera moves along using tracking shots with the girl and the text (also continuously pans right). This too provides a faster pace to the story and keeps a viewer focused on the movement. The camera also changes in distance, using long shots and close-ups depending upon the moment (either focus on the girl or focusing on her surroundings).
  Animation: This obviously runs throughout the clip. By animating it, the viewer cannot put a face to the girl and can therefore assume that this lifestyle could happen to anyone.
  Visual symbols: The most noticeable symbols used are the whirlwind, the reaching arms, and the opening doors. The vortex can symbolize getting lost in the world of poverty and crime, being thrown about (physically or emotionally) by those involved in the world, not knowing a way to escape, being pushed and pulled in every direction, allowing your body to be tossed about like it was nothing more than a leaf in the wind, being pulled down into more and more dangerous situations. The reaching arms can signify the men in poor and HIV riddled worlds are more likely to act out a sexual assault and pass on HIV as the girl's body is being sold. These types of people will grab and pull, do whatever they must for sexual gratification, including the spreading of HIV. In addition to the possible sexual assault angle, the spread of HIV through the sharing of needles. Drug abuse is common in poverty stricken communities and the sharing of needles contributes mightily to the spread of HIV. This is visualized in the image through the crisscross of lines, looking as if they are filled with blood like veins. Then, the girl starts walking through doors (signaling a generational shift) as she has more of the yellow children who then age through the same process of walking through doors, showing how education can keep young girls out of poverty.
  Colours: Most of the story is told in orange and black. These two colours are very contrasting which, I believe, would signify the two completely different worlds of those living in poverty and those who are fully educated and have a comfortable life. There is also a change in colour when HIV comes into the equation as red lines signal the blood transfers of the disease.

Music: The music sounds hopeful, almost happy throughout the entire clip. I would assume this has to do with the hope for education.
Special effects: The special effects go along with the animation portion (the vortex, the reaching arms, and the opening doors).

SOLUTIONS ACTIVITIES

5. Your team is asked to create a video clip on boys.

Step 1: In a first brainstorming, collect ideas: Which topics and issues in connection with boys in developing countries need to be addressed (e. g. child labour, child soldiers, etc.).

Step 2: Think about a possible title and coherent plot of your video clip and develop a (first) storyline.

Step 3: Sketch out a rough draft on how to visualize your story (e. g. using stick figures (Strichmännchen), freeze frames (Standbilder), etc.).

Step 4: Connect textual and visual elements and think about additional music/sound effects or a speaker.

Finally, present your "video clips" in class and discuss and evaluate them.

→ Focus on Facts, Screenplays and Storyboards, p. 249

Step 1:	Child labour, child soldiers, poverty, racism, gangs, human trafficking
Step 2:	The Lost Boys: Using the framing of the lost boys from the Peter Pan tale (boys who never learned to grow up). I would connect this lack of knowledge to the way child soldiers are taught how to live. The only thing they know is how to kill, but when recovered from these terrible places, the people trying to rehabilitate the boys will teach them again how to live in normal societies.
Step 3:	Stick figures holding guns showing them shooting friends and family then ultimately switching to the figures holding books and speaking with friends outside lockers.
Step 4:	Textual elements would first tell how the lost boys of Peter Pan never grew up. This would then shift to child soldiers never learning how to live outside of war and never gained education. Statistics about soldiers would have to be added, especially life expectancy, and then a shift to the kids with books and how education can save them would end it.

SOLUTIONS GRAMMAR/LANGUAGE

6. Write about possible dangers as well as opportunities connected with the video clip "The Girl Effect". Use different types of if-clauses (types I, II and III) to express which of the risks and chances are more or less likely to happen or come true. Say what should have been/should be done differently in the life of a girl. Example: If the girls were not married off at the age of 14, they could go to school.

→ Focus on Grammar, Conditional Sentences (If-Clauses), p. 296

For example:
- If the girls were not married off at the age of 14, they could go to school. (type II)
- If a girl living in poverty turns twelve years old, her future is out of her control. (type I)
- If the girl had not had to sell her body, she would not have contracted and spread HIV. (type III)
- If you rewind the clock of the girl's life to 12, you can see that there is another solution other than that of marrying her off. (type I)
- If the girl visits a doctor regularly and stays in school, she will be able to use her education to earn a living. (type I)
- If she did not get an education, she would be dependent on somebody else. (type II)
- If the girl got an education and was able to support herself, she could marry when she felt ready and could have healthy children. (type II)
- etc.

Malala Yousafzai

Speech at the United Nations (pp. 185–187)

About the author	Malala Yousafzai is a Pakistani school pupil and education activist from the town of Mingora in the Swat District of Pakistan's northwestern Khyber Pakhtunkhwa province. She is known for her activism for rights to education and for women, especially in the Swat Valley, where the Taliban had at times banned girls from attending school. In earl. 2009, at the age of 11–12, Yousafzai wrote a blog under a pseudonym for the BBC detailing her life under Taliban rule, their attempts to take control of the valley, and her views on promoting education for 22 girls. Due to her activism, a Taliban member boarded a bus, asked for Malala by name, and shot her in the head and shoulder. In 29 April 2013 issue of *Time* magazine, Yousafzai was featured on the magazine's front cover and as one of „The 100 Most Influential People in the World". She was the winner of Pakistan's first National Youth Peace Prize. Although Yousafzai was widely tipped to win the Nobel Peace Prize, it was awarded to the Organisation for the Prohibition of Chemical Weapons.
About the text	This is a recording of a speech Malala Yousafzai gave in front of the United Nations. Much of the speech deals with the right of every child to have an education but she also speaks on the influence of extremist and terrorist organizations and then also on the power that each person has to influence the world.
Level	● ● ○
Additional material	• Audio CD 2, 7 • Comprehension: no. 20

- Die bei der Bearbeitung der **Awareness-Aufgabe** angestellten Spekulationen über den Inhalt der Rede können auf **Moderationskarten** geschrieben und auf einer Moderationswand oder Pinnwand aufgehängt werden. Nach der Besprechung des Textes kann zum Abgleich noch einmal darauf rekurriert werden.
- Die **Hörverstehensaufgaben** (**Aufg. 1 und 2**) werden nach den Angaben im Schülerbuch erledigt. Zur Bearbeitung von Aufgabe 2 wird den Schülerinnen und Schülern folgendes **Arbeitsblatt** ausgeteilt:

Malala Yousafzai's Speech at the United Nations

topic	***further details***
her expression of thanks to various people	
speaking up for human rights	
the Taliban attack on her and how she feels about it today	
her non-violent role models	
the reasons why the Taliban kill students and women	
the teachings of Islam	
the effects of war and extremism on children, men and women	
The importance of women's rights and girl's education	
Her goals for taking action directed to *– governments* *– developed nations* *– communities* *– women around the world*	
her future goals	
the victims of poverty, injustice and intolerance	
the Education First initiative and the power of books and pens	

- Vor dem Hören des Textes markieren die Schülerinnen und Schüler die wichtigsten Stichwörter pro Aspekt.
- **Aufgabe 3** wird nach den Angaben im Schülerbuch bearbeitet.
- Nach der Durchführung des **Gruppenpuzzles** (**Aufg. 4**) sichern die Stammgruppen ihre Ergebnisse auf **Folie** und präsentieren sie. Gelungene Arbeiten können für die gesamte Klasse kopiert werden.
- Die Ergebnisse der Bearbeitung von **Aufgabe 5** werden jeweils von einem Gruppenmitglied in **Stichwörtern** notiert. Der Austausch der Ergebnisse erfolgt im **Plenum** und wird in **Tabellenform** an der Tafel oder auf Folie gesichert (s. Lösungsvorschlag unten).
- Die **Aufgaben 6 und 7** können alternativ als **Hausaufgabe** eingesetzt werden. Zur Bearbeitung von Aufgabe 7 werden die entsprechenden **Focus on Skills-** bzw. **Focus on Grammar-Seiten** (SB, S. 288, S. 305, S. 298) besprochen.

SOLUTIONS AWARENESS

Malala Yousafzai (born Jul. 12, 1997) is a Pakistani school girl who, in 2009, wrote a blog under a pseudonym for the BBC about her life under Taliban rule and her opinion of promoting education for girls. On 9 October 2012, she was shot in the head in an assassination attempt by Taliban gunmen while returning home on a school bus. After a time of intensive medical treatment and rehabilitation in the U. K., she was awarded Pakistan's first National Youth Peace Prize. On her 16th birthday, 12 Jul. 2013, which was officially named "Malala Day" by the United Nations, she held a speech at the United Nations to promote and demand worldwide access to education for everybody. Speculate on the topics and issues Malala Yousafzai might have addressed in her speech. What do you expect her to say in order to motivate people to stand up for children's rights in general and girls' rights in particular?

The two most prevalent issues that she would most likely speak on would be fearmongering and women's education. She is obviously a proponent for women's rights and education due to her past so that would more than likely be the first issue raised. The other topic that would have to be brought up is about the fear tactics used by the Taliban. Their tyrannical ways and treatment towards women would be a topic in the speech most definitely, especially with Malala's personal incident in which she was shot by a Taliban member. She would motivate people through her own story. The Taliban came after her as an individual yet she survived and has thrived, becoming a symbol for peace and for women's rights in Pakistan and the Taliban influenced world as a whole.

SOLUTIONS COMPREHENSION

CD 2 7 **1. Malala Yousafzai's address to the U. N. can be subdivided into seven parts. Following this sequence, listen to the speech for a first time and try to get a general understanding of the topics she mentions.**

1. thank you section
2. activism and human rights
3. Taliban attack
4. the fear of the Taliban and misuse of the religion
5. effects of war
6. importance of women and their education
7. goals and closing comments

2. In a second listening, take notes on what Malala says about:

1	• **her expressions of thanks *(Danksagungen)* to various people** President of the General Assembly, Gordon Brown, respected elder, brothers and sisters, honourable people, and a special thank you to God and everyone who has prayed for her, the children, nurses and doctors
2	• **speaking up for human rights** 100s of activists do this all the time, struggling for the goal, people need to speak up for those without a voice, everyone has right to dignity and peace, right to education
3	• **the Taliban attack on her and how she feels about it today** They thought the attack would silence them but instead it rose a thousand voices, making Malala stronger, strength, fervour and courage were born, ambitions and hopes remain the same, she is not looking for revenge but for education for everyone. • **her non-violent role models** Martin Luther King, Mandela, Gandhi, Mother Theresa, and her parents
4	• **the reasons why the Taliban kill students and women** reasons: fear of knowledge and education, fear of women and their voices, they fear the unknown • **the teachings of Islam** Islam: a religion of peace, each child has a duty to education
5	• **the effects of war and extremism on children, men and women** child labour, destruction of schools, domestic labour, early age marriage, poverty, ignorance and racism, deprivation of basic rights

6	• **the importance of women's rights and girls' education**
	They are suffering the most. Women used to ask men to stand up for the women's rights. That has to change. Women need to become independent and fight for themselves, they need to speak up.
	• **her calls for taking action directed to:**
	  • **governments**
	  Change policies to protect women and children. Ensure education for every child. Fight terrorism and protect children.
	  • **developed nations**
	  Support expansion of education in developing worlds.
	  • **communities**
	  Be tolerant, accept colour, religion, gender, caste, etc.
	  • **women around the world**
	  Be brave. Embrace strength within and realize potential.

7	• **her future goals** Change the world through a united cause in global education, empower those through knowledge and unity. • **the victims of poverty, injustice and intolerance** Millions are not in school, millions are in poverty, millions are terrorized. • **the Education First initiative and the power of books and pens.** These are our most powerful weapons, education is the only solution.

→ Focus on Skills, Listening Comprehension, p. 244

3. Form groups of 3 – 4 students each and exchange your listening results. Crosscheck your notes and make additions and corrections if necessary.

./.

SOLUTIONS ANALYSIS

4. Before listening to the speech a third time, divide the class into four groups, with each group dealing with a different rhetoric and stylistic aspect of the speech:

1	• **language (e.g. keywords, phrases, choice of words, word fields, language register, etc.)** **keywords/phrases/choice:** extremism, Taliban, terrorism, etc. All have negative connotations and bring a lot of baggage by using them. That is Malala's goal because she has personal experience with all of these things and the negative nature in which she experienced them is brought out fully in her treatment of the words. Thousands of people have been killed by the terrorists. I am just one injury. **language register:** enunciation is very clear here and as such the register is strong when speaking to an assembly of national leaders 'In the name of God, the most beneficient, the most merciful …' all of this is very clear
2	• **grammar (e.g. sentence structure, use of grammatical tenses, imperatives, conditional sentences, etc.)** The diverse treatment of sentence structure allows for the audience to understand the train of thought easier. If one uses the same length of sentence all the time, the speech would be hard to follow or easy to forget. (Short sentences fail to keep people interested and make the argument hard to follow, continuously using long sentences makes people forget the idea and forces a loss of focus.) 'Today it is an honour for me to be speaking again after such a long time, being here with such honourable people is a great moment in my life. I don't know where to begin. I don't know who all to thank. But most of all, thank you to God.' The changes in lengths and structures all for an easy-to-follow speech. Tenses change quite a bit. When telling about her past and of what she has seen, Malala obviously uses the past tense. But when calling to attention what needs to be done, the future tense is used. 'Thousands have been killed' … 'courage was born' … changes to 'we will speak up …', 'we will change …' Imperatives are used when Malala is trying to get governments, other nations, and other women etc. to do things to make education more attainable. This use makes for the audience to want to help. 'World leaders change strategic policies to protect women's and children's rights, governments ensure education, developed nations support the developing …' 'If I had a gun and saw the Talib who shot me ..' (use of conditional sentence) is a very poignant moment in the speech, showing her compassion and forgiveness through a hypothetical situation.
3	• **rhetoric (e.g. metaphors, anaphora, parallelism, use of contrast/antithesis, climax, grammatical persons, etc.)** Contrasting the plight of women and the need of education with the Taliban's treatment of women and the fear they have concerning education creates a strong point. Use of anaphora (repeating phrases) hammers in points that she tries to make (e.g. millions of people …, women need …). 'Today is the day of every man, every woman, every boy, and every girl …' That is one use of anaphora. Getting to her climactic point brings back information she has already spoken on earlier in the speech and that reiteration brings her entire speech to a head, allowing for the audience to recollect her previous points in addition to understanding the major details of the entirety. 'Importance of pens and books …'
4	• **manner of speaking/voice (e.g. volume, tempo, intonation, dialect, etc.)** Dialect is not something that she can change on the fly, but a native Pakistani provides more ethos when she relays her experiences with the Taliban. (Victims sounds like wictims, back sounds like baghck.) Malala's volume changes drastically when getting to her climactic points. Her volume raises when speaking about her main points and this allows for the audience to grasp more fully what she is trying to say. Intonation, much like her volume, changes when she is trying to make a strong point. By dropping her tone, she sounds more serious and as such is taken more seriously. Reference directly to the moment when she is speaking on the 'Talib who shot her', her tone drops and volume rises dramatically.

Webcode SNG-40175-020 @ **In order to get a better impression of the atmosphere of the speech at the U. N. you can listen to the speech and watch the video provided on the webcode. Following this, the groups remix and inform each other about their results.**
→ Focus on Skills, Analysis of a Political Speech, p. 260
→ Focus on Method, Group Puzzle, p. 271

By watching the video, one can see the members of the UN are impressed by Malala's courage and by her story, even going as far as taking pictures of her during her speech. Everyone in the room seems to be enthralled by what Malala is saying and she makes sure that eye contact is made with many people around the room, reciprocating that level of focus right back to those in the room.

It was surprising to see so many youth delegates at the UN, and out of these, nearly all were young girls (less surprising due to the nature of the speech about young women). With that knowledge, it was not surprising at all to see the level of concentration in the room.

5. **In your groups, compare the message of Malala's speech to the video clip "The Girl Effect" (pp. 183f.). What do both initiatives have in common – what differences can you detect?**

The main comparison one could make concerning the video clip and Malala's speech would be their insistence on education as the most important piece. Both stress how important education is and how it can change a young girl's life. They also stress how it is key that girls be allowed to live their lives without marriage until later in life.

Some big differences include the stress on HIV in *The Girl Effect* and then the stress on the Taliban (also extremists and terrorists) in Malala's speech. *The Girl Effect* stresses HIV because their goal is to liberate girls from poverty and in Africa poverty usually comes with HIV. Malala however has a history with the Taliban (being shot) and as such has been profoundly affected by their role in Pakistan.

	Malala speech	**The Girl Effect**
similarities	• stress on the education of women as a right • focus is on young girls • stresses men (Taliban) as a danger	• stresses education for women as a saving grace • focus is on young girls • stresses men (people participating in prostitution and underage marriage) as a danger
differences	• stresses gun violence • focused in the Middle East • personal history with the violence	• stresses dangers of HIV • focused in Africa • impersonal through a website

SOLUTIONS ACTIVITIES

@ 6. **Do research on Malala Yousafzai's Internet blog (www.malala-yousafzai.com) and write a comment or a letter to her, responding to her U. N. speech and initiatives.**
→ Focus on Skills, Writing a Comment and a Review, p. 279

Dear Malala,
I want to congratulate you. I want to congratulate you not just for the numerous awards you have earned and received, but I want to congratulate you on becoming the symbol you have become. By just being yourself, you have given hope to millions of people, given them the power to stand up for themselves and all those who are maligned by less than suitable conditions. Everything that you have been through is a testament to your bravery and your resolve as a person to do what is right. Your courage has become a beacon of hope and an inspiration, not only to young women throughout the world, but to everyone, man, woman, and child alike. I urge you to continue your speeches on the right to education and I hope you do not stop until every single child enjoys that right.
Thank you,
Andrew

SOLUTIONS GRAMMAR/LANGUAGE

7. **Write a summary of Malala's speech of about 150 words. Use the simple present as predominant grammatical tense and indirect speech to report essential statements. Do not forget to write an introductory sentence that answers the w-questions.**
Example: In her speech at the United Nations on 12 Jul. 2013, Malala Yousafzai, a 16-year-old Pakistani, emphasizes the importance of human rights, such as ...

→ Focus on Skills, Writing a Summary, p. 288
→ Focus on Grammar, Tenses, pp. 305ff.
→ Focus on Grammar, Indirect Speech, pp. 298f.

In her speech at the United Nations on 12 Jul. 2013, Malala Yousafzai, a 16-year-old Pakistani, emphasizes the importance of human rights, such as living in peace, being treated equally and with dignity as well as the right to be educated. Malala describes how she was shot in the head by a Taliban but was able to forgive him because her role models are people like Gandhi, Martin Luther King or Nelson Mandela with their philosophy of non-violence. In the following she emphasizes the importance of education and knowledge as a means of creating a democratic society. Thus she deduces that the education of children and of girls in particular is of the utmost importance in the fight against terrorism and violence. She demands the protection of women's and children's rights and compulsory education for every child all over the world. Concluding, she appeals to the people of the world to stand together and fight poverty, injustice and ignorance and states that education is the only solution to the world's problems. (169 words)

HOKISA – Homes for Kids in South Africa (pp. 187–190)

About the text	This excerpt is written from the point of view of an eleven-year-old South African boy, Sive Maholwana. He talks about life as an orphan with HIV/Aids in Masiphumelele township, meeting tourists from abroad, school and his HOKISA home. HOKISA is an acronym for Homes for Kids in South Africa.
Level	● ○ ○
Additional material	• Comprehension: no. 21

- Um eine allzu oberflächliche Diskussion der Aids-Problematik zu vermeiden, sollten die Schülerinnen und Schüler zur Vorbereitung der Bearbeitung der Awareness-Aufgabe das Thema **recherchieren**. Folgende **Internetadressen können ihnen dazu an die Hand gegeben werden:**
  www.aids-stiftung.de/
  www.aidsmap.com/
  www.who.int/hiv/en/
- Aufgabe 1 kann in **Partnerarbeit** bearbeitet werden. Die Ergebnisse werden in einem anschließenden **Unterrichtsgespräch** gebündelt.
- Die Aufgaben 2–4 können **arbeitsteilig** erledigt werden. Die Ergebnisse können in folgendes **Tafelbild** einfließen:

HOKISA – Homes for Kids in South Africa

Life in a township
people suffer from:
hunger, violence, HIV/Aids, slums, poor housing, overcrowded, poverty, crime, theft

Sive's idea of life in foreign countries
- *there are Tsotsis in Berlin and New York, too*
- *some other countries have snow*
- *tourists fly on planes*
- *southern and northern hemispheres have different seasons*

Sive's life in HOSIKA
- *can go to school*
- *has a supportive family network*
- *is offered medical help*
- *has an adopted dad, Perry*

Sive
- *has a positive outlook on the future*
- *is hopeful and enthusiastic*
- *has plans for the future*

- Aufgabe 5 kann in **Partnerarbeit** erledigt werden. Die Ergebnisse werden im Unterrichtsgespräch ausgetauscht.
- Aufgabe 6 kann ebenfalls in **Partnerarbeit** bearbeitet werden, wobei sich ein Partner auf Sive, der andere auf seinen HOKISA-Vater konzentriert. Die Ergebnisse werden in einer **Tabelle** (s.u.) gesammelt, wobei darauf zu achten ist, dass jeder Partner die Tabelle ins Heft übernimmt. Ein kurzes **Unterrichtsgespräch** schließt die Beschäftigung mit dieser Aufgabe ab.

Sive and his HOSIKA-dad

Sive	his dad
eleven-year-old orphan	Perry
lives at HOKISA	close relationship with Sive
probably suffering from or affected by Aids/HIV	Sive can talk about everything with him
does not know who his father is; does not mention his mother (has most likely died of Aids)	respects Sive
attends school every day	accomplished cook
very curious about the world	gay
trying to find out information; trying to understand something new	
likes to meet and speak with foreign tourists who visit his township	
best friend: Lolo	
learning to play the guitar	

- Aufgabe 7 wird im **Unterrichtsgespräch** bearbeitet. Die Ergebnisse werden informell an der **Tafel** gesichert.
- Die kreativen Schreibaufgaben 8–10 können als die Beschäftigung mit dem Thema abschließende **Hausaufgabe** eingesetzt werden. Dabei kann den Schülerinnen eine der drei Aufgaben zur Wahl gestellt werden. Will man sichergehen, dass alle drei Aufgaben bearbeitet werden, so kann man die Klasse in drei Gruppen teilen, von denen je eine Aufgabe erledigt wird. In der Folgestunde können die Ergebnisse im Klassenzimmer ausgehängt und von der Lerngruppe im Rahmen eines **Museumsrundgangs** zur Kenntnis genommen und diskutiert werden.

SOLUTIONS AWARENESS

In class, gather information about HIV/Aids and the dangers and problems connected with it.

For example:
- Human Immunodeficiency Virus (HIV) causes → Acquired Immunodeficiency Syndrome (Aids)
- attacks the body's immune system, making it difficult to fight off infections
- spread via bodily fluids (unprotected sex, blood contact through contaminated needles) or from mother to baby
- no cure for these viruses, but can be treated
- origins in Africa in the earl. 20th century; originally found in primates (chimpanzees, monkeys) and later transferred to humans
- in the 1980s in the US HIV/Aids were considered "gay diseases" due to rapid spread within the gay community
- people with HIV/Aids are often stigmatized
- huge numbers of orphaned children, especially in Africa
- sub-Saharan Africa has the greatest number of cases
- South Africa has the largest HIV-positive population in the world

SOLUTIONS COMPREHENSION

1. Describe the boy in the blue jacket (p. 188) and speculate on the symbolic meaning of the jacket.
→ Focus on Skills, Analysis of Visuals, p. 262

The picture shows a full-body shot of a young African boy, perhaps between 7 and 10 years old, looking pensively/defiantly/confidently into the camera. He is barefoot and bare-legged and wearing a brown newsboy cap. He is standing on some wooden logs in front of a plain beige building and is wearing a hugely oversized blue jacket and crossing his arms in a defensive/confident/defiant manner.
- The jacket might symbolize poverty: The boy cannot afford a jacket that fits him.
- Perhaps it is a sort of "security blanket" from a departed older relative.
- The boy may be cold/in need of protection/shelter.
- It may symbolize that the boy has to take on an adult role, e.g. because he is an orphan. ...

2. Present the social and economic situation inhabitants of townships often find themselves in.

Townships suffer from problems of hunger, violence, Aids/HIV, slums/poor housing, overcrowding, poverty, crime and theft (ll. 3–9, 37–44).

3. Point out what the narrator – Sive – knows about foreign countries and what he understands or does not understand about them.

what Sive knows/understands	what Sive does not understand
• there are Tsotsis (= criminals/thieves) in Berlin and New York, not just where he lives in South Africa (ll. 44ff.) • some other countries have snow (ll. 49f.)	• how airplanes that foreign tourists fly on work; why planes do not crash even though they are so big (ll. 51ff.) • that the southern and northern hemispheres have different seasons (ll. 55ff.)

4. Describe Sive's life in HOKISA and his outlook on the future.

Sive probably has HIV or Aids because he has to take regular blood tests and pills (ll. 94f.). The township where he lives is very crowded and poor with some crime, but life in HOKISA offers him schooling and a supportive family network and medical care. He does not know his father (ll. 89ff.), and his mother is not mentioned, so she may be dead. He goes to school every day with fifty children, and he is proud of this and seems to enjoy it (ll. 62ff.). He has an adopted dad, Perry, with whom he has a close relationship (ll. 92ff.). Despite the hardships, Sive has a positive outlook on the future and is hopeful and enthusiastic. He makes plans and has goals of learning more about the world, learning to play the guitar and opening a restaurant (ll. 96ff.).

Webcode SNG-40175-021 @ **5. Find out more about HOKISA and use the links provided on the webcode.**

For example:
- main foreign donors are Germany, the Netherlands, the US, the UK, Scotland and Ireland
- non-profit NGO
- founded by Karin Chubb, then a South African senior lecturer at the University of the Western Cape, and Dr. Lutz van Dijk, a Dutch-German writer
- the royalties/profits from van Dijk's books go to support HOKISA
- extra fun activities/visits/parties for the children: horseback riding, sports day, German Navy visit, World Cup 2010 ...
- cares for up to twenty children

SOLUTIONS ANALYSIS

6. Characterize Sive and his HOKISA-dad.
→ Focus on Skills, Characterization of a Figure in Literature, p. 264

Sive is an eleven-year-old orphan who lives at HOKISA, a home for orphaned children suffering from or affected by Aids/HIV in Masiphumelele, a township outside of Cape Town, South Africa. Sive does not know who his father is (l. 89) and does not mention his mother, so she has most likely died of Aids. He attends school every day with fifty other children (ll. 62ff.) and is very curious about the world (ll. 47ff.). He is quite persistent when trying to find out information or trying to understand something new (ll. 51ff., 87ff.). He especially likes to meet and speak with foreign tourists who visit his township and learn new things about where they are from (ll. 49f., 55ff.). He has a vivid imagination and likes to think about how his life could have been/could be different (ll. 87ff.). His best friend is named Lolo and he is learning to play the guitar.
Sive's adopted "HOKISA-dad" is named Perry. He and Sive have a close relationship, and Sive feels he can ask Perry anything. Perry talks to Sive with respect and does not often tell him e.g. that he is too young or stupid to know something. Perry is an accomplished cook and a gay man (ll. 97–110).

7. Analyse the narrative technique* that is employed here and explain whether Sive's way of talking about his life is typical of a twelve-year-old child.
→ Focus on Skills, Analysis of a Fictional Text, p. 255

The text employs a **first-person narrator**: Sive. He shares his **very limited view of the world**, since he is only eleven years old (almost twelve) and has not travelled outside of his township. This helps the reader to see the world from Sive's point of view.
- "I don't know that many townships" (ll. 24f.)
- "I will be twelve soon, so I'm already quite old" (ll. 19f.) → underlines the high death rates/low life expectancy in South Africa due to the Aids epidemic; twelve is already considered "old"
- "I still don't quite understand that ..." (ll. 57f.)

Sive also **speaks directly to the reader** from the pages of the book. This helps the reader to form a more direct connection with Sive.
- "Do you have cities that are named ...?" (ll. 29ff.)
- "Just start to walk around, or turn the pages of this book. (...) This picture shows me looking at you ..." (ll. 67ff.)
- "And worst of all – we can't get to know you!" (l. 78)

Features of typical eleven-year-old speech:
- simple vocabulary: "stuff like that" (l. 107)
- informal/colloquial register/manner of speaking: "That's a cool name, isn't it?" (l. 29)
- paratactical sentence structure: "If not, no problem. Maybe even better." (ll. 2f.)

SOLUTIONS ACTIVITIES

8. You want to spend a year in South Africa doing volunteer work.
a) What would you do to prepare yourself for such a task?
b) Write a letter of application to HOKISA showing that not only do you have good intentions but you are also well prepared and can offer something that might really help the children.

→ Focus on Skills, Writing a CV and a Letter of Application, p. 289

a) **For example:** Get first aid training; volunteer at a local hospital with HIV/Aids patients/sick children; learn about South African culture/language/customs; read books/articles about South Africa/volunteer work/HIV/Aids; take course on childhood development/childcare ...

b)
Dear Sir or Madam,
I would like to apply to volunteer at HOKISA in Masiphumelele township for one year starting September 2014 or as agreed. ...
I have already gathered some experience working with children/hospital patients/first aid/social work/teaching. ... I have a very friendly, outgoing personality and have excellent rapport with children. ...
I am very eager to work in South Africa because ... interested in new experiences/languages/Africa/Aids epidemic/education/cultural exchange/want to work for Doctors Without Borders someday ...
Yours faithfully,
Sarah Martin

Webcode SNG-40175-021 @ **9. Ayakha – the boy in the blue jacket – does not want to tell anything about himself in the book. What might his story be? Try to anticipate what his story has to do with his oversized jacket. Then, compare your ideas to the text provided on the webcode.**

Gist of the text:
Ayakha arrives at HOKISA as a very weak, sickly baby with his teenaged, HIV-infected mother. His mother has nowhere for them to live so she leaves baby Ayakha at HOKISA while she travels to visit a friend to see if they can live with her. His mother does not return and baby Ayakha becomes dangerously ill, but survives. The adults at HOKISA try to contact the mother, but cannot find her. Several years later, when Ayakha is eight, one of his teachers tracks down Ayakha's mother, who is very ill but begins to visit him regularly, but she dies soon after. Ayakha's adopted grandfather, with whom he has a close relationship, breaks the news to Ayakha, who is deeply saddened by the news. One month later, his adopted grandfather has to leave for a trip to Europe, and Ayakha, who fears another possible loss of someone close to him, has terrible separation anxiety. To comfort Ayakha, his adopted grandfather leaves him his blue jacket for Ayakha to sleep in while he is away. This helps Ayakha to be strong and not cry like he did when his mother died.

10. Write a letter to Sive telling him
a) what you learned about his life and
b) what you learned about life in South African townships that you did not know before and
c) what unanswered questions you have that he might be able to answer.

Dear Sive,

I very much enjoyed reading about your life at HOKISA in Masiphumelele township. I found it very interesting that ... (name of township/curious about foreign countries/meeting tourists/HOKISA-dad/school/dreams of restaurant/playing guitar ...)
I never knew that ... (orphans/HIV/Aids/crime/Tsotsis/poverty/gay ...)
How do people at HOKISA/in South Africa deal with the stigma of HIV/Aids? What kind of food would you serve at your restaurant? What do you want to be when you grow up? What else would you like to know about life in Germany? ...

Hope to hear from you soon!
Mark

Derek Markham

Recycled Orchestra Turns Trash Into Music (pp. 190–192)

About the author	Derek Markham is a New Mexico based writer that focuses on Green Movements and natural living.
About the text	The text is concerning Paraguayan music teacher who turned objects in the Cateura landfill into working musical instruments. He then took kids off the gang infested streets and taught them how to play these instruments, forming a Recycled Orchestra. Now the Recycled Orchestra has been turned into a social movement that is affecting places as far as Haiti and Kenya where people turn trash into music.
Level	● ● ○

- Die Ergebnisse der Awareness-Aufgabe werden auf Moderationskarten geschrieben und an einer Moderationswand oder Pinnwand gesammelt. Die Schülerinnen und Schüler nehmen die Karten zur Kenntnis und kommen darüber miteinander ins Gespräch.
- Die Eindrücke, die die Schülerinnen und Schüler beim Ansehen des Videos gewonnen haben (**Aufg. 1**), werden in einem kurzen Unterrichtsgespräch gebündelt.
- **Aufgabe 2** wird in **Einzelarbeit** bearbeitet. Die Ergebnisse werden im **Unterrichtsgespräch** diskutiert und in folgendem **Tafelbild** gesichert:

> ***The residents of Cateura***
>
> <u>*living conditions*</u>
>
> - *people live on top of a landfill*
> - *they sort through trash for a living*
> - *poverty leads to crime, gangs, drugs, violence*
>
> *There is little hope for a better future.*

- Die **Aufgaben 3 und 4** werden zusammen in **Gruppen** bearbeitet. Die Schülerinnen und Schüler übertragen die in der Aufgabenstellung vorgegebenen Aspekte auf **Moderationskarten** und ergänzen die fehlenden Schritte ebenfalls auf Moderationskarten. Diese werden dann auf Papierbögen angebracht, die im Plenum präsentiert werden.
- **Aufgabe 5** kann in **Partnerarbeit** erledigt werden. Die Schülerinnen und Schüler übernehmen die vorgegebene **Tabelle** und ergänzen sie. Die Ergebnissicherung erfolgt im Unterrichtsgespräch über **Folie** (s. Lösungsvorschlag unten).
- Vor der Bearbeitung von **Aufgabe 6** sollte die **Focus on Skills-Seite** (SB, S. 258) besprochen werden. Die Aufgabe kann in **Einzel- oder Partnerarbeit** bearbeitet werden. Die Ergebnisse werden von den Schülerinnen und Schülern zunächst **stichwortartig** festgehalten und danach im **Unterrichtsgespräch** ausgetauscht und diskutiert. Die Sicherung der Ergebnisse erfolgt in einem informellen **Tafelanschrieb**.
- Nach der Lektüre der **Focus on Facts-Seite** (SB, S. 250) entscheiden sich die Schülerinnen und Schüler für eine der zur Auswahl stehenden Textsorten und bearbeiten die Aufgabe. Die Ergebnisse werden in einem **Double Circle** ausgetauscht.

SOLUTIONS AWARENESS

Discuss the statements below (SB, p. 190) in class and try to find your own "definition" of the power and effect of music.

All of these statements directly relate music to change for the better. Hendrix believes that music is the only thing that can truly change things. In some cases, that is true. Bob Marley was an activist and his music changed quite a lot in his life and even more after his death.

Billy Joel's quote equates music with healing. Many songs resonate with millions of people. They have helped people through depression and sadness and, in a way, have become a healing factor.

Christian Nestell Bovee's comment is incredibly telling. In all cultures, music is an integral part of their lives. All humans yearn for food, shelter, and clothing; all cultures yearn for music.

Definition: Music permeates through every culture and through every person. It has become a part of life that is needed to keep moving. It is to the ears what oxygen is to the lungs.

SOLUTIONS COMPREHENSION

Webcode SNG-40175-022 @

1. **Before reading the Internet article, watch the short video about the Landfill Harmonic orchestra using the link provided on the webcode. State your first impression of the orchestra's members, their environment – and their music, of course.**

   Members: They look like normal kids, just trying to find an outlet for their creativity. They are excited to create music and to perform.

   Environment: It truly does look like they live on top of a landfill. Trash and mud are everywhere and it looks like they walk over trash wherever they go.

   Music: It sounds exactly like a normal instrument orchestra is playing classical music. One may be able to hear less quality if the person is a music expert but to an average listener I could find no real difference.

2. **After reading the article, describe the living conditions of the Cateura residents.**

   "In Cateura, Paraguay, residents essentially live on top of a landfill, and many of them make their living by sorting through the trash in order to find items to sell or refurbish. Poverty keeps kids at risk there from its handmaidens of crime, gangs, drugs, and violence, and hope is not an easy thing to come by" (ll. 8–13). The community as whole is living in trash and poverty, because of this, living conditions are bleak along with the high crime rate.

3. **Give an outline of how the orchestra came into being and what transformation it has brought about at Cateura (diagram, see SB, p. 192).**

   The orchestra came into being when a passionate music teacher began offering classes and quickly had more students than available instruments (ll. 14–16). To combat this, the teacher met with a garbage picker and luthier who could help him create recycled instruments. With the help from the entire community, an entire orchestra was formed, helping not only to relieve the streets from trash but also possible crime (ll. 20–31).

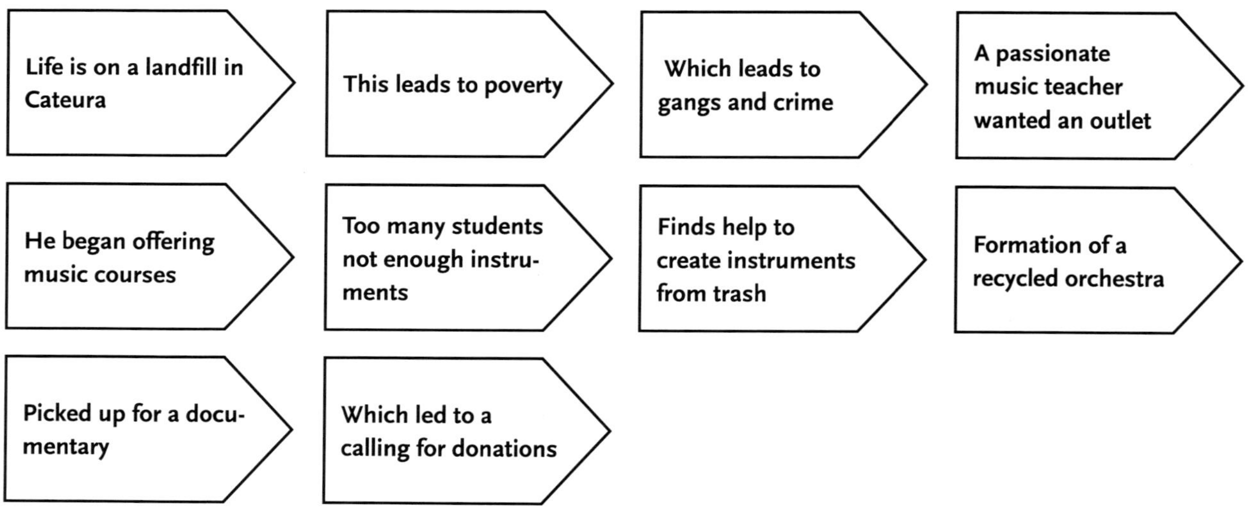

4. Which further aims has the orchestra in mind?

The orchestra has plans to further their movement into other nations. With help from Kickstarter, the program has already raised over $50,000 and intends to keep making recycled instruments for children in countries like Haiti and Kenya (ll. 44–72).

SOLUTIONS ANALYSIS

5. Examine and categorize the type of text by paying particular attention to typical linguistic, rhetorical and stylistic devices.

→ Focus on Skills, Basic Types of Non-Fictional Texts, p. 246

devices		example from the text	reference to type/category of text
linguistic	word fields	→ creativity, passion inspiration (ll. 1ff.) → poverty, despair, struggle (l. 4)	→ human interest/emotions → narrative device used to elaborate an idea
	dramatic language	→ transformed into beautiful music (ll. 40–41) → brought hope and inspiration to many (ll. 30–31) →transformation into precious human beings (l. 43)	→ all of these are narrative devices used in order to evoke an emotional reaction
	evaluating language	→ reference to Kickstarter (ll. 47f.) → speak volumes about the human spirit (ll. 71f.) → thanks to the work (ll. 35f.)	→ philanthropic text is used as a direct call to the intended audience, those willing to donate money for philanthropic reasons
rhetorical	positive emotive words	→ unique and inspiring (ll. 6f.) → hope and inspiration (ll. 30f.) → potential for transformation → transformed into beautiful sounding musical instruments (ll. 41f.)	→ all narrative techniques to bring about a positive connotation
	emotional appeal	→ heartfelt story (l. 32) → poverty and despair (l. 4) → brought hope and inspiration to many (ll. 30–31)	→ emotions
	pattern of solidarity	→ When I first saw (l. 68) → That's where you come in (l. 46) → You can also help by donating (l. 58)	→ plural first person and second person usage allows for human interest in togetherness

devices		example from the text	reference to type/category of text
further stylistic devices	alliteration	→trash transformed (ll. 40ff.)	→ narrative technique
	climax	→ transformation of precious human beings (ll. 42–43) → fundraising information (ll. 44–67) → 'speaks volumes about the human spirit and the incredible effects of a great teacher' (ll. 71ff.)	→ human emotion → human interest/philanthropy to end paragraphs on a high note
	enumeration	→ handmaidens of crime, gangs, drugs, and violence, and hope is not an easy thing to come by	→ accumulation of baggage
	contrast	→ beginning with harsh reality of Cateura and ending with the positive nature of the orchestra	→ narrative technique used to highlight difference between the two worlds of Cateura
type of text	→ predominantly narrative with elements of description		

6. Analyse the author's stance on the Landfill Harmonic orchestra taking into consideration the type of text, the stylistic devices and the medium the text was published in.
→ Focus on Skills, Analysis of a Non-Fictional Text, p. 258

It is fairly evident that the author believes the Landfill Harmonic orchestra to be a great thing. By beginning with the negative reality of Cateura (ll. 4–13) and the shifting immediately to Favio Chávez's great influence (ll. 14–31), the author allows for a dramatic shift in connotation in language and images. Using phrases like 'but when a passionate teacher ...', 'the Recycled Orchestra has brought hope ...', 'This heartfelt story ...', 'Bring witness to the transformation ...' (ll. 14, 29f., 32, 42) the author shows his hand in agreement with what the orchestra is doing. This is shown further from ll. 44–67 when the author is asking for donations for the project. If the author did not stand in union with the Orchestra's idea, then there is no way he would be asking for donations.

SOLUTIONS ACTIVITIES

7. Together with a partner, transform the article into a different type of text, e.g. a feature story*, a factual text, a diary entry or a tabloid front page editorial.
→ Focus on Facts, The Press, p. 250

Dear Diary,

I just cannot tell you how thankful I am for everything Mr Chávez has done for me. Without the orchestra, I am sure that I would have ended up further in the slums, either with drugs or dead, and I know that playing this instrument saved me from that fate.

Listening to classical music at grandma's house, I have a predilection towards the orchestra's music and I had always wanted to become a cellist after listening to Yo-Yo Ma so many times before. I am just glad that Mr Chávez formed the orchestra to give me a chance. I mean, I know I'm not playing a million-dollar instrument but I would argue that this oil-can and set of strings is worth even more than the most artfully crafted instrument in this world.

Fashion, Fabrics & Fabs – How Expensive is Cheap Fashion?

Hasnain Kazim, Nils Klawitter, Wieland Wagner

The High Human Price of Cheap T-Shirts (pp. 194–199)

About the author	Hasnain Kazim is a German journalist. He is a winner of the CNN Journalist Award in 2009. Nils Klawitter is a German writer for *Spiegel* Online. Wieland Wagner is a German journalist and correspondent to *Spiegel*.
About the text	This article is about a disaster that occurred when a high rise in Bangladesh occurred in 2013. The high rise was five floors higher than deemed safe and, when cracks were seen in foundation walls, five floors of sweatshops that produced cheap clothing declined to allow their workers a day off. The offices of a bank on one of the lower floors were cleared out due to the safety issues and the day after the cracks were seen the entire building collapsed resulting in hundreds of deaths from those working in the sweat-shops.
Level	● ● ●
Additional material	• Differenzierungsmaterial, p. 136 • GaST: no. 20, 26

- Die **Awareness-Aufgabe** wird nach den Angaben im Schülerbuch bearbeitet.
- Die Ergebnisse der Bearbeitung von **Aufgabe 1 können entweder auf Folie** oder auf **Flipchartbögen** präsentiert werden, wobei die Folienpräsentation die weniger zeitintensive Variante ist.
- **Aufgabe 2** wird wie im Schülerbuch angegeben bearbeitet.
- Nach der Lektüre der angegebenen **Focus on Skills-Seite** (SB, S. 258) wird **Aufgabe 3** in **Partnerarbeit** bearbeitet. Die Schülerinnen und Schüler notieren sich **Stichwörter**, die sie im anschließenden **Unterrichtsgespräch** diskutieren. Die Sicherung der Ergebnisse erfolgt über **Tafelanschrieb**.
- Das Ergebnis der Bearbeitung von **Aufgabe 4**, die im **Plenum** besprochen wird, wird an die **Tabelle** angefügt.

The High Human Price of Cheap T-Shirts – line of argument

section	*line of argument*
1	– *basic facts* – *personal, human perspective* – *description of carnage and suffering*
2	– *the incident within the greater context* – *background information (political corruption, specifics about the building, ongoing construction)* – *reference to similar incident in 2005* – *political connections of buildings' owners, corruption*
3	– *further examples of corruption, illegal building permits* – *background info: lack of factory inspectors, unannounced inspections* – *false claims that the building was safe* – *background info: competition with China leads to added pressure to produce*
4	– *background info: Bangladeshi producers needed to produce at all costs or risk losing business* – *list of European suppliers/retailers who bought clothes from the collapsed factory* – *Primark's ethical trading promise and code of conduct*
5	– *description of attempts to improve the situation (Clean Clothes Campaign)* – *further horrific description of the scene at the collapsed factory*

➔ *The text has*
- *narrative elements: personal, human touch*
- *expository elements: details of what happened, background information.*

- **Aufgabe 5** kann in Gruppen bearbeitet werden, wobei der Lehrer bzw. die Lehrerin darauf achten muss, dass die Schülerinnen und Schüler die Diskussion durchgehend in der Fremdsprache führen.
- Bei großen Lerngruppen können die Rollen für den **Hot Seat** (**Aufg. 6**) gedoppelt werden. Alternativ dazu kann die Klasse in zwei Gruppen geteilt und die Hot Seat Diskussion zweimal durchgeführt werden. Dabei können die jeweils nicht gerade an der Diskussion teilnehmenden Schülerinnen und Schüler in der Zwischenzeit **Aufgabe 8** bearbeiten.
- Die Ergebnisse der kreativen Schreibaufgabe (**Aufg. 7**) werden im Klassenzimmer ausgehängt und im Rahmen eines **Museumsrundgangs** zur Kenntnis genommen und diskutiert.
- **Aufgabe 8** kann als **Hausaufgabe** eingesetzt werden.

SOLUTIONS AWARENESS

Before reading the article, carry out the following activities:

Step 1: Take a close look at the headline of the article and, in groups, take notes on your associations with the implied topics. Compile mind maps of the aspects that come to your mind (example, see SB, p. 194). Display your mind maps in class and discuss possible connections between the various aspects.

Example:

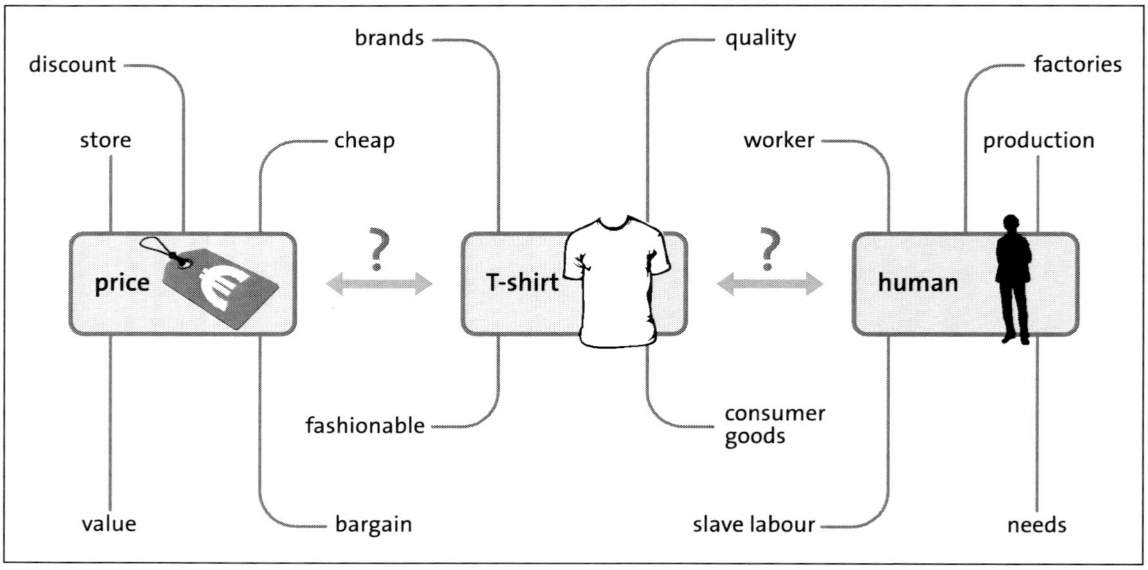

Step 2: Following this, formulate questions about the topic of the headline:
... 10 things I want to know about ...

Example:
- **How come T-shirts can be produced and sold at such low prices?**
- **Why are ...?**
- Who makes my T-shirts?
- How much money do factory workers make?
- ...

Step 3: In your groups, write down your expectations relating to the information given in the article on slips of paper.

Example:
- **I expect to find a story about workers in sweatshops in ...**
- **I expect to get background information about German retail companies ...**
- I expect to find out which companies treat/pay their workers well/poorly.
- I expect to find out more about the chain of production for textile goods.
- ...

Afterwards, display the slips of paper on a wall/blackboard – you will need them again later on.

SOLUTIONS COMPREHENSION

1. Form groups of five students each and look at the photographs on p. 195 and p. 196 as well as on the graph on p. 199:
a) Describe the photographs.
b) Specify the information given in the map/graph (p. 199).
Then, collect all the information and deduce what actually happened in Bangladesh and which role German retail companies play in the production and trade of cheap textiles.

a) Photo 1 shows an overview shot of masses of people gathering in a square. There are several multistory buildings nearby. One of the buildings has collapsed and is lying in a heap of rubble. A couple of the buildings that are still standing nearby are under construction, as can be seen from the iron scaffolding and unfinished walls/roofs.

Photo 2 shows a line of people in a building. They look shaken and are searching for the bodies of their missing loved ones and relatives. There is a line of corpses covered in cloth waiting to be identified.

b) The map shows the German companies that were formerly connected with the factories in the collapsed building in Rana Plaza in Bangladesh. These include NKD, C&A, G. Güldenpfennig, and Kik. It also shows the value of all textile imports. Germany imports 9.8€ billion worth of textiles from China, 2.2€ billion from southeast Asia, 3.0f.om Bangladesh, 1.5f.om India, 0.7f.om Pakistan and 3.9f.om Turkey.

2. The magazine article itself consists of five sections, each one focusing on a different aspect of the topic. Accordingly, form five groups, with each group dealing with one section and performing the respective tasks below.

Step 1:
Each of the groups should compile one part of a mind map whose branches and sub-branches are to be written on single sheets of paper that will later be assembled on the blackboard to create a full picture and one complete mind map (example, see SB, p. 198).
→ Focus on Skills, Presentations, p. 276

Scan the text and take notes on:

- **Jamil's and Rezaul's experiences and memories**

Jamil heard voices from people trapped under the building: pleading, praying, screaming, whimpering, begging for water, reciting prayers; he helped bring food and water to some who could be reached.
Rezaul saw a woman whose leg was pinned down by a pillar. Her face was bloody and she begged him to free her, he tried to get her help, but could not find any.

- **the rescue of people and workers from the collapsed building**

3,000 people were inside when the building collapsed; more than 380 bodies have been found, hundreds are still missing; chance of finding survivors is getting smaller; very hot conditions, stench of decomposing flesh, chaos, grief

- **the role of Bangladeshi politicians**

culture of corruption, illegal construction permits, lax safety standards in factories

- **the reasons for the collapse of the factory building**

owner added three more stories without a permit and was adding a fourth when building collapsed

- **further disasters in connection with textile factories producing for German retailers**

2005 collapse of Spectrum Sweater building in Savar killed 64 people; producer for German retailers including KarstadtQuelle and Steilman

- **corruption in Bangladesh and its consequences**

in both cases the owners of the collapsed buildings had political connections to obtain illegal permits and avoid punishment

- **the consequences of the competition between China and Bangladesh**

high pressure on Bangladeshi factories to keep up production so as not to lose business to China, making owners desperate to continue production despite unsafe working conditions

- **the goals of the "Clean Clothes Campaign" and international reactions and commitments to it**

improve safety standards for factory workers, ensure decent wages, introduce unannounced inspections, make German companies accountable for human rights abuses by its suppliers;
mixed reactions: H&M, C&A and Kik did not agree, but Calvin Klein, Tommy Hilfiger and Tchibo want to take part

Step 2:
The groups should present their part of the mind map to the whole class and be prepared to give a short presentation on their topic/part of the text.

./.

SOLUTIONS ANALYSIS

3. Examine the line of argument* in each section and show how examples and factual information underline the scandalous situation.

➔ Focus on Skills, Analysis of a Non-Fictional Text, p. 258

1:
- First sentence gives most basic facts on the event (w-questions).
- Story gives personal, human perspective on disaster: two eyewitnesses describe what they saw and heard at the site after the collapse; horrific description of carnage and suffering.

2:
- The bigger picture of how this incident fits into the greater context ➔ "nothing has changed"
- Background information on political corruption, specifics about the building and ongoing construction. ➔ People knew it was unsafe, but demanded workers to continue anyway.
- Reference to similar incident in 2005 ➔ shows how we have not learned or changed
- Description of known political connections of buildings' owners, corruption ➔ no consequences for human rights violations that lead to many deaths

3:
- Further examples of corruption, illegal building permits
- Background info: lack of factory inspectors, unannounced inspections
- False claims that the building was safe ➔ exposes lies
- Background info: competition with China leads to added pressure to produce ➔ profit no. 1 priority

4:
- Background info: Bangladeshi producers needed to produce at all costs or risk losing business
- Lists of European suppliers/retailers who bought clothes from the collapsed factory ➔ underlines the connection/complacency of the Western retailers/customers
- Primark's ethical trading promise and code of conduct ➔ not upheld, untrue claims

5:
- Description of attempts to improve the situation (Clean Clothes Campaign) ➔ possible solution
- Ends with a further horrific description of the scene at the collapsed factory ➔ consequence of not improving the human rights situation, underlines urgency to solve problem

4. Against the background of your previous findings, categorize the type of text by identifying and explaining its specific features.

➔ Focus on Facts, Basic Types of Non-Fictional Texts, p. 246

The article contains narrative and expository elements. In particular, the descriptions of the scene at Rana Plaza give the text a personal, human touch, and are therefore a feature of a **narrative** text. The eyewitness reports evoke readers' sympathy and show how individuals are affected by the tragedy (e.g. Rezaul's story of meeting the woman whose leg was crushed by a cement pillar). The description of the extreme heat and the stench in the air as described at the end of the article let the reader know what it is like at the scene. At the same time, the article contains many **expository** elements: It focuses not only on what exactly happened at the building collapse site, but also gives a lot of background information to show the complex situation that led to the tragedy (political corruption, global competition, etc.). It shows the reasons behind the collapse and offers a possible, logical solution in the form of the Clean Clothes Campaign.

SOLUTIONS ACTIVITIES

5. Take a look at the slips of paper you took notes on when completing Step 3 in the Awareness task. Compare your "before reading expectations" with your state of information now. Start like this:
Example:

- **I expected and/but I found ...**
- **I was surprised to read/see that ...**

→ Focus on Language, Conversation and Discussion, p. 266

Individual answers

6. In order to further investigate the international entanglements that have finally led to the disaster in Bangladesh, put some of the responsible people on the Hot Seat:
a) a representative of a German/Irish/American retail chain or
b) a Bangladeshi politician or
c) Mohammed Sohel Rana, the owner of the building.
Prepare rolecards and try to identify with your respective role beforehand.

→ Focus on Methods, Hot Seat, p. 270

./.

7. In groups, rewrite (parts of) the magazine article and turn it into
a) a feature story,
b) the front cover of a tabloid,
c) an online article published by a human rights organization or
d) an online statement published by one of the German/Irish/American retail companies in order to polish up their battered image.
Display and discuss your articles in class.

→ Focus on Facts, The Press, p. 250

Individual answers

SOLUTIONS GRAMMAR/LANGUAGE

8. Collect the most relevant technical terms and phrases from the text and formulate equivalent everyday explanations. Use your dictionary and/or the Focus on Vocabulary pages in your Students' Book.
Example:

- **basic safety standards → e.g. wearing safety glasses, dusk masks, ear plugs, etc.**
- **regulatory authorities → public administration responsible for example for public health, safety, etc.**

- basic safety standards → e.g. wearing safety glasses, dusk masks, ear plugs, etc.
- regulatory authorities → a public administration responsible for public health, safety, etc.
- to bring sb. to justice → to put sb. on trial for their mistakes and criminal doings
- to issue a permit → to give sb. written permission which allows him/her to do sth.
- backroom deals → inofficial and often illegal deals which are made at a secret place
- state authorities → official bodies run by the state/government
- the public sector → governmental and public organizations or corporations
- the insurance was inadequate → the money the insurance would pay in case of an accident etc. was much too low; the insurance coverage was too low
- code of conduct → a set of rules and regulations that tells people how they are expected to behave in a certain situation
- etc.

How Expensive Is Cheap Fashion? – The Best Eco-Fashion Brands and Eco-Criteria (pp. 200–202)

About the text	The text explains various kinds of eco-fashion. It elaborates on the different ways garments are made and how they differ from conventionally-made clothing. Photographs of popular eco-clothing brands and designers are pictured at right.
Level	● ○ ○
Additional material	● GaSt: no. 20

- Zur Einstimmung auf das folgende Thema können die Schülerinnen und Schüler zunächst dazu aufgefordert werden, die **Waschzettel** der Kleidung, die sie tragen, zu lesen, um festzustellen, aus welchen **Materialien** sie gefertigt ist und wo sie hergestellt wurde. Eine solche kurze Umfrage in der Klasse wird vermutlich ergeben, dass viele Kleidungsstücke aus **Chemiefasern** in sogenannten **Billiglohnländern** in der dritten Welt hergestellt wurden. Von dieser Aktivität kann auf die Diskussion der in der Awareness-Aufgabe gestellten Fragen übergeleitet werden.
- Aufgabe 1 kann im Unterrichtsgespräch bearbeitet werden.
- Die Ergebnisse der Bearbeitung von Aufgabe 2 können als **Tabelle** gesichert werden. Aufgrund des inhaltlichen Umfangs empfiehlt sich eine Sicherung auf **Folie**, die dann für alle kopiert werden kann.

Protecting the environment

Vegetarian/ animal free	Community based	Craft/ artisan	Custom-made or tailor-made	Fair trade	Organic	Recycled	Vintage/ second-hand
– *protects the animals and saves resources which would have been used to feed and raise those animals*	– *producers are less likely to pollute or be wasteful because they are living and working in the same place*	– *uses less machinery/ fossil fuels and energy*	– *garments are more likely to be kept and worn longer than thrown away and replaced quickly; tailors use less machinery/ fossil fuels*	– *more sustainable production uses less energy/ resources than if producers move to different locations and build a new factory, for example* – *specifically promotes environmental protection*	– *no pesticides or toxic materials used* – *good for environment and growers*	– *saves old clothes from the landfill* – *uses fewer new raw materials/ resources*	– *saves old clothes from the landfill; uses fewer new raw materials/ resources* – *less trendy: broadens society's ideas about acceptability of wearing older styles* – *creating less demand for the latest trends*

- Die Ergebnisse der Bearbeitung von Aufgabe 3 können gegebenenfalls ins **Vokabelheft übertragen und gelernt werden. Weiterhin erhalten die Schülerinnen und Schüler den Auftrag, zwei der acht Abschnitte in** Alltagssprache umzuformulieren, z. B.:

  Vegetarian/animal free: Products made without leather, fur or animal skin, for example shoes or bags made from rubber rather than animal skin.

  Recycled: Through recycling new pieces of clothing can be made from the cloth of old clothes.
- An diese Übung kann sich eine Untersuchung des **Stils**, d. h. der Funktion und Wirkung des Gebrauchs von **Fachausdrücken**, wie sie in Aufgabe 4 gefordert wird, anschließen.
- Neben den angegebenen **Internetadressen** (Aufg. 5) können die Schülerinnen und Schüler auch die **Internetseiten** der auf S. 200 genannten Designer aufrufen und als Einstimmung auf Aufgabe 6 eine persönliche **„eco-collection“** zusammenstellen.
- Aufgabe 6 wird nach den Angaben im Schülerbuch bearbeitet.

SOLUTIONS AWARENESS

Eco-fashion is a generic term that can mean many things. In general, it refers to all fashion products that have been created in such a way as to contribute to a healthier and more equal world. What kind of clothes do you like and what do you associate with "eco-fashion"?

For example:
- I like trendy clothes from H&M because ...
- Eco-fashion is more expensive but better quality than a lot of mass-produced fashion ...

SOLUTIONS COMPREHENSION

1. **Look at the pictures: Do these garments look "eco" to you? What do you like/dislike about these looks? Discuss in class.**

   Individual answers

2. **Point out in what way the criteria listed above help to protect the environment. Which of these criteria do you consider more – or less – important? Make a ranking.**

   (rankings will vary)
   - **Vegetarian/animal free**: protects the animals and saves resources which would have been used to feed and raise those animals
   - **Community based**: producers are less likely to pollute or be wasteful because they are living and working in the same place
   - **Craft/artisan**: uses less machinery/fossil fuels and energy
   - **Custom-made or tailor-made**: garments are more likely to be kept and worn longer than thrown away and replaced quickly; tailors use less machinery/fossil fuels
   - **Fair trade**: more sustainable production uses less energy/resources than if producers move to different locations and build a new factory, for example; specifically promotes environmental protection
   - **Organic**: no pesticides or toxic materials used; good for environment and growers
   - **Recycled**: saves old clothes from the landfill; uses fewer new raw materials/resources
   - **Vintage/second-hand**: saves old clothes from the landfill; uses fewer new raw materials/resources; less trendy: broadens society's ideas about acceptability of wearing older styles, creating less demand for the latest trends

SOLUTIONS ANALYSIS

3. **Which technical terms* (expert language) are employed in the text? Use your dictionary and find everyday expressions that are equivalent to these terms.**

   (equivalent terms in italics)

fashion	environment/recycling	technology/industry/production	economy/fair trade
to craft *to make* **embroidery** *fancy stitching* **tailor-made** *made to order* **fabric** *cloth, material* **demi-couture** *specially made* **vintage** *second-hand, used* **garment** *piece of clothing*	**to preserve** *to keep, maintain, save* **disposable** *able to be thrown away, unnecessary* **environmental** *green, having to do with nature* **protection** *care, safety, safe-keeping* **pesticides** *poison* **toxic** *harmful, poisonous*	**animal tissue** *leather, fur, skin* **artisan skills** *crafting/craft* **custom-made** *made to order, special order* **producers** *makers* **constructed** *made*	**social equality** *public/common fairness* **economic security** *safe job, financial safety* **certification** *passing a test* **disadvantaged** *poor* **perpetuation** *continuing, doing the same thing*

4. **Explain the function and effect of the technical terms. Talk about why it is (not) necessary to employ expert language in certain texts.**

Technical terms are used when dealing with a very specific topic or field to describe specialized processes, concepts, or objects. They are necessary when dealing with specialty areas because they need to use the same terminology. This shows that a text has been well researched and is therefore credible. On the other hand, some texts are meant for audiences who have no prior knowledge about highly specialized areas. In this case, it would be better to use everyday language so that the reader can better understand, or the author should at least explain the technical terms that are used.

SOLUTIONS ACTIVITIES

Webcode SNG-40175-023 @

5. **Do further research on cool eco-fashion brands and trends, using the links provided on the webcode.**

Squidoo: Trashion (a portmanteau of "trash" and "fashion") is a term for art, jewelry, fashion and objects for the home created from used, thrown-out, found and repurposed elements. Squidoo itself puts on fashion shows and 'this is where art, fashion, sustainability and activism meet and have a big party'. The materials used in these shows may vary. Some may recycle clothes/textiles and items such as buttons, zippers and so on from donated, damaged or otherwise discarded pieces of clothing.

Marie Claire is an international monthly magazine for women. First published in France, various editions are published in many countries and languages. The United States edition focuses on women around the world and several worldwide issues, including eco-fashion.

Sustainability Technology Education Project (STEP) focuses on informing people about the harmful nature of textiles and how they should be recycled to cease the damage.

SNIPE is a German company that specializes in recycling shoes.

Kings of Indigo make quality denim jeans in the American style with a Japanese eye for detail using sustainable technology of today, making these jeans a recycled product.

IKA BABEL is a sustainable jewelry label for women who embrace life with an ecological awareness, a contemporary attitude, and a consciousness of their individual worth. The philosophy of IKA BABEL is to distinguish itself by fashioning new uses for materials and their details to create a trailblazing jewelry line that prides itself in its wearability and comfort.

6. In groups, develop new clothing that is made from recycled base products and then plan and perform a fashion show to present and promote your clothing and designs. Your base products may be worn T-shirts, dresses, shoes, knitted material, etc. or unusual starting products like plastic bags, newspapers, cans, etc. One basic condition you have to fulfil is that you do not use any new products/materials – everything has to be recycled material. Your final presentation of the product should include
a) a fashion show to present the product(s),
Webcode SNG-40175-023 @ **b) a brochure/handout/flyer that informs consumers about your product and your basic ideas,**
c) a final rounding off in which the audience can ask questions.
Decide who in your group will be the model(s) and who will be the presenter.

Individual answers

7. Now, after having designed and produced vintage or second-hand clothing yourself, evaluate the whole process. Usually second-hand clothes are cheaper than new ones. Would you buy recycled or second-hand clothes yourself – and pay more? Do you think that new clothes should be more expensive than recycled ones? Discuss in class.
→ Focus on Language, Conversation and Discussion, p. 266

I would not be willing to pay more for recycled clothing. Because it has already been worn, the fabric might be thin or worn which means that it might have or get holes soon. The colour might be faded or the hems might be frayed. This means that you might not be able to wear the clothing for as long as you would a new garment. On the other hand, a lot of second-hand clothing has only been worn once, or not at all. I think it is OK to pay more money for clothes that are still in good condition, but not as much as clothing that has never been worn.

Made in Germany: Eco-Fashion – Save the Planet and Look Good (pp. 202–203)

About the cartoonist	Gerhard Haderer is an award-winning Austrian cartoonist and caricaturist. He is a regular contributor to the German magazine *Stern*.
About the text	The audio piece looks at the Dutch eco-clothing label Kuyichi and explores the question of why eco-clothing is becoming more popular, as well as what consumers are looking for when they buy clothing in general.
Level	● ● ○
Additional material	• Audio CD 2, 8 • Comprehension: no. 22

- Die **Awareness-Aufgabe** kann in einem kurzen Unterrichtsgespräch bearbeitet werden.
- Vor dem ersten Hördurchgang (Aufg. 1) erhalten die Schülerinnen und Schüler den Auftrag, die wichtigsten Wörter in den angegebenen Fragen zu **unterstreichen**, damit sie sich beim Hören auf die entsprechenden **Schlüsselbegriffe** konzentrieren können. Dazu werden ihnen die Fragen in **Kopie** ausgeteilt.
- Aufgabe 2 schließt sich an die Bearbeitung von Aufgabe 1 an.
- Aufgabe 3 wird zunächst in **Einzelarbeit** in **Stichwörtern** bearbeitet. Diese dienen als Grundlage für die **mündlichen Kurzvorträge**, in denen die Schülerinnen und Schüler den Cartoon beschreiben.
- Aufgabe 4 kann ebenfalls in **Einzelarbeit** erledigt werden. Die Ergebnisse werden im **Unterrichtsgespräch** gesammelt und informell an der **Tafel** gesichert.
- Aufgabe 5 kann zunächst in **Partnerarbeit** bearbeitet werden. In dieser ersten Bearbeitungsphase notieren die Schülerinnen und Schüler ihre Ergebnisse in **Stichwörtern**. Diese werden in einem zweiten Schritt individuell in kurzen Texten **schriftlich ausformuliert**.
- Aufgabe 6 wird nach den Angaben im Schülerbuch erledigt.

- Aufgabe 7 wird zunächst **individuell** bearbeitet. Die Präsentation der Ergebnisse kann, wie in der Aufgabenstellung vorgeschlagen, im Plenum oder aber im Rahmen eines **Milling Around** geschehen. Dazu werden die Schülerinnen und Schüler aufgefordert, im Klassenzimmer umherzugehen und auf ein Signal hin die Ergebnisse mit dem Nächststehenden auszutauschen. Dies kann zweimal wiederholt werden. Der Lehrer bzw. die Lehrerin hat die Möglichkeit, sich verschiedene Kurzvorträge anzuhören und ggf. zu korrigieren.
- Das in Aufgabe 8 vorgeschlagene Projekt kann als eine die Beschäftigung mit dem Text begleitende **Wochenaufgabe** erteilt werden, die die Schülerinnen und Schüler selbstständig erledigen.
- Vor der Beschäftigung mit Aufgabe 9 sollte mit der Klasse die angegebene **Focus on Grammar-Seite** (SB, S. 292ff.) durchgesprochen werden.

SOLUTIONS AWARENESS

Berlin has become a centre of fashion in Germany over the years. Environmentally-friendly clothes are in fashion, especially the Dutch label Kuyichi, which sells and promotes "style-conscious" fashion that combines individual style with eco-friendliness and environmental consciousness. Speculate on the term "ethical fashion": What might the name refer to?

- working conditions of the producers, e.g. no sweatshops, living wages ...
- vegan materials, no animals harmed/killed
- no pesticides/harmful dyes etc. used to produce raw materials, cloth ...
- etc.

SOLUTIONS COMPREHENSION

CD 2 8 **1. Listen to the report on German eco-fashion and take notes on these questions (see below).**
→ Focus on Skills, Listening Comprehension, p. 244

- **What – aside from being "green" – makes eco-fashion interesting to customers?**
  - the design, having an attractive or unique look, good fit, looking good from behind (especially for women)
- **What is the Kuyichi manager's understanding of being "style-conscious"?**
  - the primary aspect is that clothing looks and feels good and is of good quality; the secondary aspect is the "green" factor: being conscious of ethical, organic, fair-trade factors
- **What makes people today more interested in ecology?**
  - shoppers are becoming increasingly aware/conscious of their ecological impact and growing more critical about what they buy
- **Why is "transparency" particularly important – according to the organization MADE-BY?**
  - customers want to know what they are buying and what kind of environmental and social impact their purchases are making; by getting good ratings in these areas, companies can improve their images and attract customers
- **To what extent are retail stores interested in green fashion?**
  - A green label, Kuyichi, is being sold in Berlin's Galeries Lafayette, but it is located at the back of the store. = There is some interest in green fashion, but it is still not in top demand.

2. Listen to the report a second time and complete your notes.

Individual solutions

3. Describe the cartoon (SB, p. 202) and state how it relates to the topic of "green fashion".

The cartoon shows a sales assistant standing at a cash register helping a customer. The saleswoman is enthusiastically holding a green high heeled shoe and explaining to the customer that the eco-friendly Italian shoe can be eaten with pasta sauce. The customer looks shocked and disgusted.

"Green" fashion products should be as **natural** as possible and **biodegradable**. The cartoon carries this aspect to the extreme: The shoe is so natural that it can be eaten, and no **waste product** will remain once it is no longer worn.

SOLUTIONS ANALYSIS

4. Examine the rhetorical devices* used by the reporter and explain how they underline the uniqueness and popularity of eco-fashion.
→ Focus on Skills, Analysis of a Non-Fictional Text, p. 258

alliteration: **f**ashion **f**ollows other rules → grabs the listener's attention

youthful register/choice of words/positive connotations: chic, relaxed, trendy, of-the-moment, crazy, hot, young, hip, fantastic → underlines traits that fashion has/needs to have in order to be popular

unexpected connotations/choice of words: "presenting an image that's **worthy** and **down-to-earth** don't have a chance with Kuyichi's manager ... It would be bad for business." → Seems like a paradox at first: "worthy" and "down-to-earth" seem like positive marketing traits one usually associates with "eco", but here the importance of trendiness/style is underlined further.

rhetorical questions: But are any of them interested in knowing under what conditions their clothes have been made? But are customers interested in green fashion? So, is eco-fashion going to be the next big trend? → Reporter goes on to answer these questions, helps to emphasize and structure the main points of the report.

direct quotes by boutique owner, consumer, Kuyichi's manager, Made-By: gives the direct, insider story of what is currently happening in the eco-fashion industry; personal opinions/voices draw the listener in

M **5. Taking a closer look at the cartoon by Gerhard Haderer (SB, p. 203): Explain how it ridicules "fashion" and "style". What kind of "style consciousness" is presented and mocked here?**
→ Focus on Skills, Analysis of Visuals, p. 262

The couple in the cartoon are depicted as being completely over-the-top. They are so "stylish" and extravagant that they look ridiculous. They are overwhelmed by their oversized fur coats. The fur is contrasted with their exotic-looking pet Afghan hound, and it is ironic that pet owners would wear fur, which is cruel to animals. The dog is looking at the woman's coat, and one can see the actual heads of several minks in the coat upon close inspection, which is a rather jarring image that evokes sympathy for the minks. Their jewellery is very sparkly and their leather shoes and boots are very shiny. The man is leaning in an exaggeratedly relaxed fashion against a luxury car. Most striking about the cartoon is the fact that the people are invisible; only their clothing, hair, jewellery and glasses give their bodies shape. This implies that they are hollow, empty and completely superficial. They are obsessed with fashion and style, but lack personality, character and morals.

SOLUTIONS ACTIVITIES

Webcode SNG-40175-024 @ **6. Use the link provided on the webcode and do research on the organization MADE-BY. Prepare and give a short presentation about the goals and activities of the organization.**
→ Focus on Skills, Presentations, p. 276

- European not-for-profit organization that is trying to improve environmental and social conditions within the fashion industry → sustainable fashion
- 22 partner brands, including Kuyichi (as of December 2013)
- larger, well-known brands (e.g. Tommy Hilfiger, Galeria Kaufhof, Otto, Gucci) have taken part in Level 1 and 2 consultancy packages
- consultancy packages: Educating brands on certain sustainability aspects (e.g. various materials, textile workers ...), helping them to improve their sustainability, according to each brand's needs
- "Scorecard" system rates various aspects of a brand's sustainability over time; shows progress
- Track&Trace: "As of 31 December, 2012, 'Track&Trace' is no longer available on the MADE-BY website. Brands are either managing the system themselves, or they are implementing an alternative traceability system. Please contact the brands directly if you would like more information."
- etc.

Webcode SNG-40175-024 @ **7. Watch the interview with British fashion icon Vivienne Westwood and tell your class about her understanding of eco-fashion.**

Buy fewer, better-quality items; be creative with items you already own, improvise; take an active part in creating a look, do not simply consume; do not overwash clothes in order to prolong their lifespan; choose only clothing items that you truly love ...

Webcode SNG-40175-024 @ **8. Do a project on the working conditions of textile workers in Bangladesh. The link on the webcode provides you with further material.**

- workers make clothes for stores such as Asda, Tesco, Primark
- sweatshop workers work up to 80 hours/week for 900 Taka/6.50£, often locked into the factories, forced to do unpaid overtime, no sick or holiday pay
- terrible living conditions, often no running water or sanitation
- President of the National Garment Workers Federation, Amin Amirul Haque
- War on Want: UK organization that fights international poverty

SOLUTIONS GRAMMAR/LANGUAGE

9. Take a close look at the Haderer cartoon again (SB, p. 203). Imagine the couple is talking about their understanding of being "style conscious" and describing their way of life and the things that matter to them. Employ as many adjectives, adverbs and adverbials as possible to make their statements more vivid. Your text can be exaggerated, funny or satirical like the cartoon.
Example: Honey, this absolutely breathtaking fur coat is so adorable ... and you look so incredibly stylish ...

→ Focus on Grammar, Adjectives and Adverbs, pp. 292ff.

- Honey, this absolutely breathtaking fur coat is so adorable ... and you look so incredibly stylish in it.
- Yes, darling, I bet Justine and Calvin will be green with envy when they see it. I'm so glad that we were able to get you those shiny patent-leather boots – they match your luxurious coat perfectly and give you that sexy appearance.
- Don't you think that I should get that gorgeous silk scarf – wouldn't it be perfect with my mink coat? And it also matches the sophisticated blue of the Mercedes ...
- etc.

Brita Belli

The Eco-Fashion Revolution – You Are What You Wear (pp. 204–206)

About the author	Brita Belli is an American writer and the editor of *E – The Environmental Magazine*. She is also the author of *The Complete Idiot's Guide to Renewable Energy for Your Home* (2009). Her writing focuses on environmental issues, her material has appeared in many books and periodicals. She has a blog which reports "green" sports stories (playitgreen.com).
About the text	The following article was published in *E – The Environmental Magazine*. This American magazine reports on a wide range of environmental issues, with a focus on how individual readers can make a difference in saving the planet.
Level	● ● ●
Additional material	• Differenzierungsmaterial, p. 148 • Comprehension. no. 23

- Als **vorbereitende Hausaufgabe** erhalten die Schülerinnen und Schüler den Auftrag, ihren Kleiderschrank durchzusehen und festzustellen, welche Kleider sie im vergangenen Jahr gekauft haben, ob sie bestimmte Marken bevorzugen, welches diese Marken sind und welche Art von Markenartikeln sie besitzen. Informationen zu diesen Fragen sollten **stichwortartig** in der Fremdsprache notiert werden. Die *Awareness*-Aufgabe kann in **Kleingruppen** diskutiert werden und im Anschluss daran können die Ergebnisse in Form einer kleinen **Statistik** präsentiert werden.

- Wegen des Umfangs des Aufgabenapparates können Aufgaben 2 und 3 **arbeitsteilig** erledigt werden, d. h., die Klasse wird in zwei **Gruppen** unterteilt, von denen eine Aufgabe 2 und eine zweite Aufgabe 3 bearbeitet. Die Ergebnisse werden im Plenum vorgetragen und besprochen.
- Ebenso kann bei den Aufgaben 4 und 5 verfahren werden.
- Aufgabe 6 wird im Unterrichtsgespräch bearbeitet.
- Bei der Bearbeitung von Aufgabe 7 ist es wichtig, dass die Schülerinnen und Schüler das **Wortspiel** mit dem Begriff „fashion victim" erkennen und verstehen. Unter Umständen ist es daher sinnvoll, diesen Begriff im Vorfeld zu definieren. Die Ergebnisse der Bearbeitung von Aufgabe 7 können in folgendes **Tafelbild** münden:

Fashion victims

particular about clothes
obsessed with clothes
buys latest trend
↓
fashion victims
↓
made victim by fashion industry
exploited by fashion industry

→ ***consumer awareness*** →

socially responsible
production standards
no disposable clothes
↓
no more fashion victims
↓
fewer factories
less exploitation

- Die in Aufgabe 8 geforderte Präsentation kann als Abschluss dieser Unterrichtssequenz dienen. Eine Organisation in **Kleingruppen** erscheint hier sinnvoll.
- Aufgaben 10 und 11 können als **Ergebnissicherung** von Aufgabe 9 eingesetzt werden. Da es sich bei beiden um **kreative Schreibaufträge** mit ähnlichem Inhalt handelt, können sie den Schülerinnen und Schülern zur Wahl gestellt werden.
- Die Ergebnisse der Internetrecherche (Aufgabe 12) sollten in Form von **Plakaten** o. Ä. gesichert werden.
- Aufgabe 13 kann als abschließende **Hausaufgabe** gestellt werden.

SOLUTIONS AWARENESS

Are you always up-to-date with the latest in style? Do you wait impatiently for next season's hot looks? Would you not be seen dead in anything less than designer brands? If yes, you may be a fashion victim. How important are fashion trends or designer brands to you?

I have no interest in brand names whatsoever; I am more concerned with what the clothing looks like/its quality than the name on the label ...
Or:
I like to shop at certain stores because I know that they have trendy clothing that is good quality. It is much easier to stay with brands that I know and like because it makes it easier and faster to find things I want to wear. It is important for me to look good and feel comfortable, so I tend to stick with certain brands ...

SOLUTIONS COMPREHENSION

1. First of all, make a list, then explain the differences between "disposable" and "ethical" clothing.

disposable clothing	ethical clothing
• discarded quickly (often after only one season)	• trans-seasonal, kept and worn for many years
• no special meaning for wearer	• cherished by wearer
• cheap (shoppers can buy so many clothes they need a whole shopping cart to carry them, l. 116)	• more expensive
• easy to find, found in stores everywhere	• found only in select, higher-end stores
• made with pesticides and chemicals	• organic, made without pesticides
• producers often live in extreme poverty	• farmers earn more money, are healthier, and have a better-quality life

2. **What, according to Edun, is the idea behind "trade not aid"?**

The idea is to try to help African cotton farmers become more self-sufficient by securing their place in the global cotton market so they are better able to earn a good living. Instead of being given charity money, farmers are able to support themselves with farming and rise out of poverty. Organic farming further improves farmers' lives by omitting the harmful pesticides which harm their health (ll. 14 – 20).

3. **Outline why consumers are tempted to buy clothes they can dispose of easily. How should their attitude towards clothes change and how can the mainstream be informed about ethical fashion?**

Consumers buy disposable clothing because they are most likely to buy clothing that is very cheap (ll. 45f.) and currently trendy. Instead, consumers should only buy something because they really love an item and will wear it for a long time (ll. 46ff.). They should also take more of an interest in where and how the materials were grown and the living conditions of the farmers/workers (ll. 54ff.). The mainstream can be informed of these factors with the help of "government-regulated labeling" so that whenever they look at an item, they will be reminded that their purchase has consequences and also whether a particular item meets certain social and environmental standards (ll. 106ff.).

SOLUTIONS ANALYSIS

4. **Examine in what ways shopping, i. e. consumption, is connected with politics.**

First of all, consumers' shopping habits can have a huge effect on the politics of production as demand dictates what will be produced (or not) (ll. 31f., 66f.). Second, someone's political beliefs and social background often influence where a person shops and what that person buys because the items/stores will be more in line with that person's political beliefs. Organic clothing lines tend to be sold at stores where customers spend more money, meaning that the customers probably have more money in general and may tend to be better-educated than the average consumer. In turn, they may understand and care more about the environmental and social issues behind their purchases (ll. 109ff.).

5. **Give reasons for the assumption that "government-regulated labelling" (ll. 106f.) forces companies to take (more) responsibility for what and how they produce.**

Labelling would make all consumers aware that their clothing has environmental and social implications (many consumers are not aware of this). As more consumers become aware of these implications, they will probably want to support brands with higher standards. As a result, clothes with higher standards will probably be rewarded with more sales, while brands with poorer standards will suffer. In order to not lose sales, companies will try to meet higher standards to promote their brand image and sales (ll. 83 – 86, ll. 104ff.).

6. **Explain the statement "We don't eat clothing" (l. 80). Do you think that clothing, bags or fragrances should be subject to the same quality standards as food? What would be the consequences?**

Organic food has become important to many people because they do not want to eat harmful pesticides and chemicals. However, many people do not realize that some clothes are chemically treated and can therefore directly affect our personal health, too. Therefore, fewer consumers are interested in buying organic clothes. They are more interested in price, trends, appearance, etc. I think higher standards would be a good idea in theory. Advantages would include better health, fewer allergies, and more environmental benefits for everyone. ... However, products would also cost a lot more, so it is not a very realistic solution. Most people still want to buy cheap items and would not be willing to pay more for items like bags. ...

7. **Take a close look at the cover page taken from the brochure of the NGO War on Want and reconsider the term "fashion victim" from this perspective. Against this background, interpret the message of the Katharine Hamnett T-shirt (SB, p. 204).**

Usually the term "fashion victim" refers to someone who is extremely particular about and obsessed with the clothes they wear. A fashion victim buys all the latest trends.

Here, the term "fashion victim" is turned around to mean someone who is literally victimized/exploited by the fashion industry. The workers look like they live in the developing world and have sad, serious expressions on their faces and are working busily. Some of the workers are very young girls/children. They are probably earning very little money and living in poverty. The fashion workers are being exploited and live hopeless, miserable lives.

Hamnett's T-shirt "no more fashion victims" thus calls for more socially-responsible production standards to stop the victimization/exploitation of factory workers. Moreover, if there were no "fashion victims" in the usual sense, and people did not buy so much disposable clothing and buy into every seasonal trend, there would be less demand for cheap, disposable clothes. As a result, production would slow and there would be fewer factories and less exploitation.

SOLUTIONS ACTIVITIES

@ **8. Patagonia is a designer of (organic cotton) clothing and gear, e.g. sportswear. Do research on Patagonia's website and prepare a short presentation about their understanding of ethical fashion: www.patagonia.com**

- CR = corporate responsibility: company takes responsibility for their impact on customers, employees, communities and the environment
- implemented third-party audits to ensure good, humane working conditions for factory workers
- openly publish their list of factories for transparency
- uses 'green' materials: organic cotton, recycled polyester, hemp, chlorine-free wool and recycled nylon

@ **9. In groups, discuss the "vita" of a piece of clothing/an accessory that you wear daily, e.g. a T-shirt, a jacket, a pullover, a pair of jeans or a pair of shoes/boots, etc. and draw its "life cycle". Think about its origin (the plant, the animal ...) and the manufacturing process in the country of its production as well as the product's "journey" to the shop where you bought it until it finally made its way into your wardrobe. What will its future be? This website provides a glossary of textile manufacturing: en.wikipedia/org/wiki/Textile_manufacturing_terminology**

Pair of jeans
- cotton grown in Uganda with pesticides under poor worker conditions
- cotton shipped to a Chinese factory where it was processed into denim cloth
- cloth made into jeans in Bangladesh by child workers
- jeans transported via airplane to H&M distributor
- truck to local H&M store
- jeans bought by me and worn for only one year before they are no longer in fashion
- put into charity bin
- taken back to Africa and worn by a cotton farmer living in poverty

10. Write a formal curriculum vitae (CV) in which you introduce yourself. You are a) a woollen pullover, b) a pair of jeans or c) a pair of leather shoes/boots.
→ Focus on Skills, Writing a CV and a Letter of Application, p. 289

For example:

Name	Levi's Jeans
Address	Gartenweg 20 54327 Cologne
Telephone No.	......
Nationality	American
Date/Place of Birth	17 Jul. 2012, China
Profile	High-quality, classic blue jeans which offer good looks, durability, and comfort
Experience	Never been purchased. Three weeks' experience in being tried on by dozens of men in store dressing room.
Background	Made of cotton farmed in Uganda (harvest 2012) Assembled in factory in ...

11. The tale your jeans/your sneakers have to tell ... Write an imaginary diary entry. Having almost reached the end of your life, you remember where you came from. Think of Africa ... or India ... the weather ... your journey across the ocean ... the factory where you were manufactured ... the person who bought you ... how you were treated ... You can write about funny/exciting/sad experiences. Use stream of consciousness* as the point of view to portray the memories and events.

Dear Diary,

As I lay here in a plastic sack with other old clothes in a charity bin, I think back on my life when I was just a little cotton plant in the fields of Uganda ... It seems so long ago and far away from this tiny German village, and I am sad that I was only in Günther's life for such a short time ...

@ **12. Why is "product-labelling" of textiles/clothing so important? Do research on the Internet and find out about toxic or hazardous substances that are used in the production of textiles and shoes.**

Labelling is important so that the consumers know the conditions under which a product was produced and purchase according to their beliefs/values. This makes companies accountable for how they choose to make their products. Consumers might also want to avoid certain substances in the clothing itself due to allergies, sensitivities or for general health reasons.

Examples of toxic substances used to manufacture clothing/materials:
- pesticides
- insecticides
- fungicides

In clothing (during production):
- bleach
- formaldehyde
- certain dyes
- heavy metals
- caustic soda
- sulfuric acid
- disinfectants
- ...

13. Imagine that textiles or shoes/bags were labelled like ready-made food. What information should the consumer be given? Examine the labels of products that you have at home and design a label for a fashion product of your choice. The information should be tagged to the product like the washing instructions.

Individual answers

ADDITIONAL TASK

Start an ethical fashion campaign at your school and design a website in which you
a) inform your fellow students about "eco-fashion" and "ethical fashion"
b) promote the idea of "slow fashion" and
c) start a swap meet and/or second-hand store for clothes.

Individual answers

Virtual Communities and Social Networks – Living in the Digital Age

TM[1]	SB[2]	Author: Title of text	Type of text	Topic	Competences	Audio CD	Film CD-ROM	GaST[3]	Diff[4]	Comp[5]
Start-up Activities										
290	210	Blue Man Group: GiPad	photo	the digital lifestyle – parody and reality	• analysing a visual • analysing video clips					
290	211	Digital Lifestyle	cartoon, statistics	s.a.	• analysing a visual • analysing statistics			no. 10		
It's a Digital World – Connections & Disconnections										
292	212	Matt Richtel: Wasting Time Is New Divide in Digital Era	newspaper article, statistics, cartoons	the digital divide the attempts to bridge this divide the need to teach students how to sensibly use comput-ers the conse-quences of unrestricted use of computers by students	• analysing the contents of a text • analysing the author's stance • mediating statistical data • grammar: if-clauses, adverbs, the future			no. 10		no. 24
292	216	Mehr Lehm	German newspaper article, photo	different toys reflecting the different ways of life and the different chances in the future of children in industrial and in third world countries	• mediating a text					

[1] TM = page in Teachers' Manual
[2] SB = page in Students' Book
[3] GaST = material in Grammar and Skills Trainer
[4] Diff = page in Differenzierungsmaterial
[5] Comp = material in Comprehension: Reading – Listening – Viewing

TM[1]	SB[2]	Author: Title of text	Type of text	Topic	Competences	Audio CD	Film CD-ROM	GaST[3]	Diff[4]	Comp[5]
297	217	Tablet Teachers – Digital Education in Kenya	magazine article, photo	the introduction of tablet computers in a school in a Kenyan slum as a way to meet the higher demands for places at schools due to the higher number of students the consequences for the IT sector the ensuing question of the quality of education	• analysing the contents and style of a text • analysing a visual • preparing and acting out a panel discussion • creative writing • grammar: registers of English					
303	220	Vivian Yee: A School Distanced from Technology Faces Its Intrusion	newspaper article, photo	a school in an area without access to the Internet offering programs to bring its students closer to nature the problems and challenges the school will be faced with when access to the Internet will be available students experiencing and cherishing a lifestyle without the possibility to constantly use the Internet	• analysing a text • carrying out a project and evaluating it • grammar: if-clauses				153	
	223	Key Qualifications and Soft Skills	Focus on Facts					no. 17, 21		
306	224	Robert Waugh: TXT BAD 4 UR BRAIN? Text Messaging Can Dent Your Reading Abilities Say Scientists	newspaper article, cartoon	the way frequent text messaging influences people's reading and speaking skills	• analysing a text • analysing a visual • holding a discussion • grammar: pronunciation			no. 10		no. 25
	226	The Media	Focus on Facts					no. 10		

TM[1]	SB[2]	Author: Title of text	Type of text	Topic	Competences	Audio CD	Film CD-ROM	GaST[3]	Diff[4]	Comp[5]
Chat Room or Conference Room? – Meeting People in Formal and Informal Situations										
309	227	James Poniewozik: Serial Killing	magazine article, visual	violence on TV the relationship between violence on TV and the murder rates in a country fear as a reason why violence on TV is appreciated by audiences	• analysing the contents and tone of a text • preparing and holding a panel discussion • grammar: adjectives, adverbs and adverbials				160	
313	230	Spaces and Spectres – Living Multimedia-Based	cartoon strips	cartoons about how TV influences people's lives and their perception of reality	• analysing cartoons • holding a pyramid discussion			no. 10		
316	232	Chat Rooms – Opportunities and Risks	cartoon, statistics, screenshot, visual	pros and cons of social networking	• analysing a visual • discussing a given topic • mediating a video • analysing statistical data • creating cartoons • doing Internet research			no. 10		
320	235	Charlie Rose: Exclusive Interview with Facebook Leadership Mark Zuckerberg and Sheryl Sandberg	Interviews	Mark Zuckerberg and Sherly Sandberg: their relationship their education the history of facebook	• listening comprehension • analysing a text • holding a discussion • preparing and carrying out an interview • grammar: indirect speech	CD 2, 9				no. 26
Sending You an SMS ... – Youth Culture & Digital Lifestyle										
323	237	Adam Sorensen: Cats, Bears and Bacon. How to Build a Web-Comic Phenomenon	magazine article, cartoon strip	online comics compared to traditional ones which are published in newspapers and magazines new ways of publishing comics web comics and art simplicity as a characteristic of web comics	• analysing a text • analysing a visual • creating cartoons				166	

TM[1]	SB[2]	Author: Title of text	Type of text	Topic	Competences	Audio CD	Film CD-ROM	GaST[3]	Diff[4]	Comp[5]
325	239	Rosemary Bennett: Why Facebook Friends Click When They Meet in the Flesh	newspaper article, cartoon	a comparison between online and "real" relationships	• analysing a text • analysing a visual			no. 17		no. 27
	240	Thematic Vocabulary	Focus on Vocab							

Start-up (pp. 210–211)

About the artists	The Blue Man Group is an organization founded in 1987 by Chris Wink, Matt Goldman and Phil Stanton. The organization produces theatrical shows and concerts featuring experimental music (with an emphasis on percussion), comedy and multimedia.	---
About the performance **About the visuals**	The GiPad shows three members of the Blue Man Group performing in front of three giant iPads. Each one has an app that does something to make a new digital self and the three different devices, along with the performers, interact.	The cartoon shows two young women standing at a corner close to a disco. They are focusing on the social messaging through the phone as opposed to the personal interaction and physical contact in the disco. The "Digital Lifestyle" statistics depict relevant figures in connection with the everyday use of mobile phones.
Level	● ○ ○	● ● ○
Additional material	---	• GaST: no. 10

- **Aufgabe 1** kann in **Gruppenarbeit** bearbeitet werden. Die Schülerinnen und Schüler beschreiben das Foto gemeinsam und führen die geforderte Diskussion in den Gruppen durch. Danach kann jeweils ein Sprecher bzw. eine Sprecherin pro Gruppe die Ergebnisse der Diskussionen in einem kurzen **Statement** zusammenfassen.
- **Aufgabe 2** wird zunächst in **Partnerarbeit** bearbeitet. Die Ergebnisse werden im **Unterrichtsgespräch** ausgetauscht und in folgendem **Tafelanschrieb** gesichert:

Advantages of the GiPad

- *Digi-Mirror: no change, real world person looking into a computer*
- *Digi-Tizer: makes person completely digital, puts person into digital form*
- *Digi-Enhancer: changes user for the 'better', gives them enhancing objects*

→ the Blue Man show are parodying the way people live their digital lives:
  - *one lives separate from the digital*
  - *one becomes the digital self*
  - *one makes a different version of himself*

→ all three facets of the digital (s.a.) world are collected

- Die Ergebnisse der Gruppenarbeit (**Aufg. 3**) werden jeweils auf **Folie** festgehalten und von einem Gruppensprecher bzw. einer Gruppensprecherin präsentiert.

- Die in **Aufgabe 4** vorgeschlagene Diskussion wird im **Plenum** durchgeführt. Die Sicherung der Ergebnisse erfolgt über **Folie** in Form einer **Tabelle** (s. Lösungsvorschlag unten).
- **Aufgabe 5** kann als **Hausaufgabe** eingesetzt werden.

SOLUTIONS START-UP ACTIVITIES

1. Describe the photo showing the "Blue Men" performing the Gipad (Giant iPad) parody. Discuss the connections between the visual and the title of the unit.

The photo shows the three members of the Blue Man Group performing in front of a giant iPhone. The 'GiPad' behind them is calling into a customer service group to help the Blue Man Group with their digital device. This visual connects with the title "Virtual Communities and Social Networks – Living in the Digital Age" because the Blue Man Group is using an iPad, something that has become its own community. Users are all connected through their iPads and iPhones and are constantly connected to their social networks (Facebook, Twitter, Instagram, Pinterest, etc.). Due to the iPad becoming such a 'giant' influence, the digital age will forever be connected through the devices.

Webcode SNG-40175-025 @ **2. Together with a partner, watch the various video clips of the GiPad Apple parody provided on the webcode. Which "advantages" do the different GiPads (Digi-Mirror, Digi-Tizer and Digi-Enhancer) offer? What is your general impression of the Blue Man show?**

The 'advantages' that the separate GiPads offer are as follows: The Digi-Mirror allows for no change whatsoever at the digital level, a simple reflection on screen so one can see himself without change (a real world person looking into a computer); the Digi-Tizer makes the person completely digital when stepping behind it, putting the person into a digital form (much like social media today), the Digi-Enhancer changes the user for the 'better' by giving them enhancing objects like maracas or Spanish festive wear, this is how some people use the digital world, to create a better version of him/herself because you can really be anyone on the internet. My impression of the Blue Man show is that they are parodying the way people live their digital lives. One lives separate from the digital, one becomes the digital self, and one makes a different version of himself; that way all three facets of the digital world are collected.

M **3. In a group, examine the digital lifestyle of juveniles as depicted in the graph *Digital Lifestyle* (p. 211) and show whether such a lifestyle is potentially addictive.**

The average teen receives over 3,000 texts in a month and at all times, especially at meals. Almost seventy percent of teens are receiving 'phantom rings', rings that they feel but are not actually happening, false alarms. These teens also spend a great deal of time playing on apps, especially angry birds.

This lifestyle is obviously addictive if people cannot even put their phones down to have a decent meal. In addition to that, the false alarms show that teens are so connected to their phones that they imagine a vibration or a ring.

4. Discuss the pros and cons of "the digital lifestyle" as well as possible dangers it poses.

pros	cons	possible dangers
always connected	dependence on digital devices	lack of knowledge/intelligence due to overuse
keep up with news	lacks physical connection to people	no interpersonal skills and/or relationships
quick alerts to threats	phones and computers can be tracked	people and/or agencies can find a person with ease
easy access to harmless fun	no need for books or imaginative thinking to create fun	lack of reading skills and critical thinking ability

5. Describe the cartoon on page 211 and state what view it takes on the possible consequences of the "digital lifestyle".

→ Focus on Skills, Analysis of Visuals, p. 262

The cartoon shows two women standing around a corner close to a disco. One of them has just received an SMS and she is now showing it to her friend. Her friend is now looking at the display and both are focusing on social messaging through the phone as opposed to the genuine, interpersonal, physical contact that takes place in the disco in the background. This illustrates the consequence of partaking in the 'digital lifestyle' too much. To really bring home this point, one of the women states that her boyfriend has just ended their relationship by means of a text message. Her friend responds: "Well, at least it was a very long SMS!" Even intimately emotional messages are now often not delivered personally but by impersonal digital means.

It's a Digital World – Connections & Disconnections

Matt Richtel

Wasting Time Is New Divide in Digital Era

and

Mehr Lehm (pp. 212–216)

About the author	Matt Richtel is an American writer and journalist for *The New York Times*. He was awarded the 2010 Pulitzer Prize for National Reporting for a series on distracted driving.	---
About the text	The text is an article concerning the overuse of technology by children, specifically in lower income families, and the time-wasting gap between those in higher socioeconomic classes and those in the lower sections.	"Mehr Lehm" is a short text published in 2012 in DIE ZEIT with an accompanying photograph about children in a refugee camp in Malawi who, in contrast to their counterparts in wealthy countries, do not possess cameras, but who make cameras out of clay with which they then take imaginary photos.
Level	● ● ○	● ○ ○
Additional material	• GaST: no. 10 • Comprehension: no. 24	---

- Die **Awareness-Aufgabe** wird in **Gruppenarbeit** durchgeführt, wobei jede Gruppe eine bestimmte Anzahl von **Moderationskarten** erhält, auf der sie ihre Ideen verzeichnet. Die Moderationskarten werden an der Tafel geordnet und diskutiert.
- **Aufgabe 1** wird im **Unterrichtsgespräch** erörtert.
- **Aufgabe 2** wird zunächst **individuell** bearbeitet. Die Ergebnisse werden im **Unterrichtsgespräch** diskutiert und in folgendem **Tafelanschrieb** gesichert:

M. Richtel, "Wasting Time Is New Divide in Digital Era"

the new digital divide

↓

the digital literacy corps

- *teach productive use of computers to parents, students, and job seekers*
- *send literacy trainers to schools, Boys and Girls Clubs, League of United Latin American Citizens, NAACP, etc.*
- *teach basic keyboard and word processing use*
- *teach parents the use of filters*

- **Aufgabe 3** wird im **Unterrichtsgespräch** bearbeitet. Die Ergebnisse werden informell an der **Tafel** gesichert.
- Zur Bearbeitung von **Aufgabe 4** wird die Klasse in drei gleich große **Gruppen** eingeteilt. Die Schülerinnen und Schüler bearbeiten **individuell** eine Person pro Gruppe. Danach treffen sich je ein Schüler bzw. eine Schülerin aus den drei Großgruppen und tauschen ihre Ergebnisse aus.
- **Aufgabe 5** wird in **Partnerarbeit** erledigt. Die Schülerinnen und Schüler legen dazu eine **Tabelle** an (s.u.), in die sie die Ergebnisse ihrer Bearbeitung des Textes eintragen. Die Sicherung erfolgt im **Unterrichtsgespräch**.

M. Richtel, "Wasting Time Is New Divide in Digital Era"

choice of words	positive/negative examples	factual information
'time-wasting gap' 'growing cause for concern' 'mirrors and magnifies existing problems' 'We failed to account …' 'meaningful content creation is miniscule' → negatively connoted words; concern about less wealthy children who are locked into place due to their lack of education in technological fields	*positive examples: The Ross family: rewarded their children because of good grades and then supervised the access to their computers negative examples: Markiy Cook: uses the devices for games, videos, and social networking; bad grades, poor family, probably staying the same Alejandro Zamora: 'Facebook Freak'; mother not literate in technology; too connected to social media and not focusing on how to fix the problems*	*statistics: divide very problematic to poorer/less educated families; children spent on average 90 minutes more per day exposed to media than children from high socioeconomic families; 2013, these children spent 11.5 hours each day exposed to digital media, in 1999 the average was only 4.67 hours; digital devices used for pure entertainment more than for education*

→ author's stance on the new divide: things need to be changed.

- Zur Bearbeitung von **Aufgabe 6** werden die Schülerinnen und Schüler aufgefordert, ihre Definitionen nach dem Schema „Digital literacy means …" zu formulieren und im **Plenum** vorzustellen. Die Ergebnisse können ggf. diskutiert werden.
- Zur Bearbeitung von **Aufgabe 7** wird der Text in **Kopie** ausgeteilt, damit ihn die Schülerinnen und Schüler für die **Mediation** bearbeiten können. Die Schülerinnen und Schüler besprechen zunächst in **Partnerarbeit**, welche Textpassagen vor dem Hintergrund der Aufgabenstellung für die Mediation relevant sind. Die Mediation wird in **Einzelarbeit** durchgeführt. Dazu sollten den Schülerinnen und Schüler **einsprachige Wörterbücher** zur Verfügung stehen. Anschließend wird im **Plenum** zunächst besprochen, welche inhaltlichen Aspekte für die Mediation wichtig sind. Danach werden einzelne Arbeiten vorgelesen und korrigiert.
- **Aufgabe 8** wird in **Einzelarbeit** erledigt, die Ergebnisse werden im **Unterrichtsgespräch** ausgetauscht.
- **Aufgabe 9** kann als **Hausaufgabe** eingesetzt werden.
- **Aufgabe 10** wird im **Plenum** bearbeitet, die Ergebnisse können in einem informellen **Tafelanschrieb** gesichert werden.
- Nach der gemeinsamen Besprechung der if-clauses anhand der entsprechenden **Focus on Grammar-Seite** (SB, S. 296) werden die Bedingungssätze in **Partnerarbeit** formuliert und auf **Moderationskarten** geschrieben. Die Karten werden an der Tafel oder auf einer Moderationswand gesammelt. Im Anschluss daran werden einzelne ausgewählte Karten im Plenum beispielhaft korrigiert. Danach erhalten die Schülerinnen

und Schüler ihre Karten zurück und korrigieren diese selbst, wobei der Lehrer bzw. die Lehrerin für Fragen zur Verfügung steht.

- **Aufgabe 12** kann nach der Besprechung der **Focus on Grammar-Seiten** (SB, S. 292ff. und S. 305ff.) als **Hausaufgabe** erteilt werden.

SOLUTIONS AWARENESS

What do you consider to be a good age for children to learn about computers and social networking? What most important "lessons" should they learn? Collect ideas in class.

A few years ago, I would have said that learning about computers would not have been necessary until age ten-twelve, but now that has all changed. The younger a child can learn about computers and everything they can do, the better they will be in this day and age. Learning about computers early will open doors for a child later in life if the boy/girl kept learning more and more over the maturation due to the high use of computers in all facets of business, science, communication, and nearly every other profession.

Social networking on the other hand is a different story. Once a child gets to high school/secondary education I could see a use of social networking simply for the sake of staying in touch with friends and family members and then college social networking paves way for professional networking in the future. Before high school, kids are usually with their friends every day in primary school and have no real need of a social networking app, site, or technology.

SOLUTIONS COMPREHENSION

1. Define the term "time-wasting gap" (l. 15).

Children in poorer families are spending considerably more time than children from more well-off families using their television and gadgets to watch shows and videos, play games and connect on social networking sites. This is the time-wasting gap that researchers believe is more related to the monitoring ability of the parents than the way children use technology (ll. 10–18).

2. Describe the various tasks of the "digital literacy corps" (ll. 28f.).

- teach productive use of computers to parents, students, and job seekers (ll. 30–32)
- send literacy trainers to schools, Boys and Girls Clubs, League of United Latin American Citizens, NAACP, etc. (ll. 33–40)
- teach basic keyboard and word processing use, teach parents the use of filters (ll. 42–45)

3. Point out which problems are "magnified" because of the "new" digital divide, according to the Kaiser study.

It magnifies the existing problem of technology being used solely for entertainment purposes as opposed to education. Children from parents who do not have a college degree spent on average 90 minutes more per day exposed to media than children from high socioeconomic families (ll. 60–73). In 2013, these children spent 11.5 hours each day exposed to digital media whereas in 1999 the average was only 4.67 hours (ll. 75–79). The reality is that these digital devices are used for pure entertainment more so than for education (ll. 89–92).

4. Outline the examples given in the article of Markiy Cook, Alejandro Zamora, the Ross family in Boston.

Markiy Cook	Alejandro Zamora	the Ross family
• 12-year-old boy • African-American • 2 laptops, Xbox 360, Wii, and a phone • mostly uses them for Facebook, Youtube, and video games • GPA barely over a 1.0 • ll. 100–115	• 13-year-old boy • Hispanic • 'Facebook Freak' • did not use computer for homework • mother was clueless on Youtube • ll. 120–128	• 15-year-old girls • African-American • 2 laptops • used for homework and music research • grandmother is strict about computer use • ll. 135–160

SOLUTIONS ANALYSIS

5. Analyse the author's stance on the "new divide" and the use of digital media today. Focus on:
- **his particular choice of words in connection with (the lack of) "media literacy",**
- **positive and negative examples given in the article,**
- **factual information on the matter.**

→ Focus on Skills, Analysis of a Non-Fictional Text, p. 258

I would argue that the author's stance on the new divide is that it needs to be changed. This is an informative essay on the subject with connotations leaning towards the negative when concerning the divide at hand.

Choice of words: 'Time-wasting gap', 'growing cause for concern', 'mirrors and magnifies existing problems', 'We failed to account ...', 'meaningful content creation is miniscule' (ll. 15, 26, 61, 67, 90f.)
All of these are negatively connoted in a way that shows Richtel's view on the divide. It is not that he is antitechnology, just that he is concerned about the less wealthy children being locked into place due to their lack of education in technological fields.

Positive examples: The Ross family; they rewarded their children because of good grades and then supervised the access to their computers, making sure they were not wasting time on their technological devices (ll. 135–156).

Negative examples: Markiy Cook: he uses the devices for games, videos, and social networking. His grades are suffering and his family is tight on money, making it unlikely he will break the trend (ll. 100–119). Alejandro Zamora: he is a 'Facebook Freak' with a mother who is not literate in technology. She said that 'he would have a tantrum' if it was not working, making it obvious that is is too connected to social media and not focusing on how to fix the problems (ll. 120–128).

Statistics/Factual information: Richtel uses statistics showing that the divide is very problematic to poorer families. Children from parents who do not have a college degree spent on average 90 minutes more per day exposed to media than children from high socioeconomic families (ll. 60–73). In 2013, these children spent 11.5 hours each day exposed to digital media whereas in 1999 the average was only 4.67 hours (ll. 75–79). The reality is that these digital devices are used for pure entertainment more so than for education (ll. 89–92).

6. Explain the term "digital literacy". Which skills and what kind of knowledge does it imply?

Digital literacy is the ability to find, evaluate, utilize, share, and create content using information technologies and the Internet (Cornell University). These skills include but are not limited to: word processing, spreadsheet technology, search engines, website creation/management, coding, computer video use etc. (ll. 43–45, productive use of the computer, l. 31).The knowledge does not have to be all-encompassing and all-knowing. Saying one is digitally 'literate' implies that there is a working knowledge base that one can pull from to use some of these technologies.

M **7. Mediate the text taken from a German newspaper (SB, p. 216) and explain the difference between children from industrialized and developing countries with regard to their way of dealing with digital cameras.**

→ Focus on Skills, Mediation, p. 265

This short text from *DIE ZEIT* deals with poor children from a refugee camp in the third world country of Malawi, who in contrast to their counterparts in wealthy industrialized countries, be they from the West or the East, play with sham cameras that they have made themselves out of clay. The children from prosperous countries have their very own digital cameras. The poor children from developing countries have nothing but they have here plenty of clay.

Children in wealthy countries start taking photos at a very early age. They record what they briefly see in front of their display. The children in Malawi take their clay and form a camera and take photos of things that cannot be recorded, that are the products of their imagination. It would be preposterous and going too far to perceive the children from Malawi as being happy as a result and the children of the affluent society as being impoverished but what one could wish would be a little less clay for one group and a little more clay for the other.

8. Take a closer look at the two cartoons on p. 215 in the Students' Book and explain their message. Which effects of "the digital era" do they make fun of?
→ Focus on Skills, Analysis of Visuals, p. 262

Cartoon 1: This shows a toddler wearing a diaper playing on a computer keyboard. The 'game' is placing everyday toy blocks on top of one another for a score, in this case building a gate by pushing the keys. The message behind this is that children are starting too early with their technologies. Instead of developing motor skills with tactile objects, the infant is playing a game on a computer that would hinder that development. The cartoon is making fun of young children owning computers.

Cartoon 2: This four picture cartoon shows a child complaining, bawling even, that he needs a bigger iPhone and smaller iPad. His father then switches the two objects and runs off indicating that the objects are basically the same thing at different sizes. The child then looks rather perplexed and is thinking about what actually happned. The cartoon is making fun of the fact that these objects are very similar, but, in the digital age, kids 'need' to have both types.

M

9. Mediate and examine the statistical data given in the bar chart (SB, p. 215) and
- **analyse the development of the use of phones in Germany,**
- **speculate on possible reasons for the rapid increase of cell phones in 2000,**
- **relate your results to the article at hand.**

→ Focus on Skills, Analysis of Statistical Data, p. 261

The bar chart on p. 215 illustrates in millions the number of cell phones in use in Germany since the start of normal operations in 1992 with the Motorola International 3200 up until the year 2013. Sales development in the first six years was slow but from 1999 to 2000 the number of mobile phones in use doubled from 23 million to 48 million. This was shortly after the introduction of the first BlackBerry device, an email pager, which proved very popular and was a great improvement. After that services got even better, the range of possibilities increased and things began to "snowball" and by 2006 the number of phones in use in Germany had doubled again to 97 million, when the first iPhone came on the market. This, too, led to an increase in connections to 107 million and after that, since 2008, the figure has remained fairly constant at around 113 million. The market seems now to be saturated. The Samsung Galaxy came out in 2013 and it remains to be seen if this will lead to any further change.

As access to these devices spread and as their range of technical possibilities improved, they also made a major contribution to the digital divide and the time-wasting gap. Proper and fast use of cell phones is also a key component of digital literacy.

SOLUTIONS ACTIVITIES

10. Discuss the rather critical views taken on digital media in the two texts (SB, pp. 212ff., p. 216) as well as in the cartoons. Does the (over-)use of digital gadgets really "spoil" children and distract them from what is really important in life?
→ Focus on Language, Conversation and Discussion, p. 266

Richtel: From what is said in this article, it would be hard to argue that these gadgets do not spoil children. Just relating to the margin between lower income and higher socioeconomic families (low income children use technology over an hour half more ll. 76–79) and with the given examples of addiction on the part of Markiy Cook and Alejandro Zamora (ll. 100–128) it is easy to see that these kids are struggling not only with academics and education, but also in their nuclear families.

Cartoon 1: Although created for its comedic value, the cartoon of the baby playing with building blocks using a keyboard is a commentary on how young children begin to use technology. At this age, I would not say that technology 'distracts' a child from what is important because a toddler would not be able to notice the important things regardless of the technology. It does however show that these kids are spoiled in the way they begin learning at such a young age, not having to use concrete materials but rather using digital devices, which, in the long run, may be beneficial in a world where technology reigns.

Cartoon 2: This cartoon definitely shows the spoiled side of children. The young boy is complaining, not about a lack of iPhone and iPad, but about having the wrong sizes. Years ago, iPhones and iPads did not even exist much less have different sizes to choose from. The boy in the cartoon is spoiled by the technology he has and seems distracted from the 'real' things in life (family, education, living friends – not digital ones).

Cartoon 3 (p. 211): This cartoon illustrates the contrast between the physical world of real contact and personal interaction (here: the disco) and the impersonal nature of the digital world and its devices. The point is really driven home when one of the women depicted shows her friend how her boyfriend has ended their relationship by sending a text message by cell phone to that effect. Even extremely personal messages are now often not delivered personally, eye to eye.

SOLUTIONS GRAMMAR/LANGUAGE

11. Think of the pros and cons of digital media and gadgets again. Make if-clauses (type I, II and III) and reflect on situations when for example a computer, a cell phone, etc. was of use for you and situations when it distracted you or even got you into trouble ...
Example:
- **If I hadn't used my new digital camera in the holidays, I couldn't have taken all the great photos. (type III)**
- **If I get the new iPad, I will be able to ...**

- If I had not used my new digital camera in the holiday, I could not have taken all the great photos. (type III)
- If I get the new iPad I will be able to download more useful apps. (type I)
- If you bought that new computer game as well, we could have lots of fun. (type II)
- If I had not played "Angry Birds" in the English lesson, I wouldn't have been thrown out. (type III)
- If we were not allowed to use the modern calculators in the Math exam, I would be in big trouble. (type II)
- etc.

12. Think about how mobile phones have changed over the years, and speculate on how they might continue to develop over the next 20 years. Present your ideas and predict how these developments will alter our social and work lives. Collect words and expressions (adverbs) to use in predictions and forecasts such as perhaps, maybe, eventually (*irgendwann, schließlich*) or this will have been achieved/developed/invented and use them in your answer.
→ Focus on Grammar, Adjectives and Adverbs, pp. 292ff.
→ Focus on Grammar, Tenses, pp. 305ff.

- Perhaps scientists will be able to design larger computers that will use less energy.
- Eventually scientists will develop computers that are smarter than man.
- Most likely methods will have been developed that prevent people from being spied at home.
- etc.

Tablet Teachers – Digital Education in Kenya (pp. 217–219)

About the author	*The Economist* is an English-language weekly newspaper owned by The Economist Newspaper Ltd and edited in offices in London. *The Economist* claims that it "is not a chronicle of economics". Rather, it aims "to take part in a severe contest between intelligence, which presses forward, and an unworthy, timid ignorance obstructing our progress".
About the text	The text here is about schools in Africa going digital. The company eLimu is running a pilot program giving schools in Kenya tablets and touch screen computers which, unlike in the United States, has led to high reading skills and paved the way for the Worldreader program to hand out Amazon Kindles to the kids of Kenya.
Level	● ● ○

- Die **Awareness-Aufgabe** kann um die Frage erweitert werden, wie sich die Schülerinnen und Schüler Schule ohne „richtige" Lehrer, dafür aber mit Tablet-Computern vorstellen.
- Die **Aufgaben 1–4** werden **arbeitsteilig** erledigt. Dazu wird die Klasse in vier Gruppen eingeteilt. Innerhalb dieser Gruppen werden die Aufgaben in **Einzel- oder Partnerarbeit** bearbeitet. Die Ergebnisse werden im **Plenum** besprochen und in folgendem **Tafelbild** gesichert:

Tablet Teachers – Digital Education in Kenya

digital education in Kenya
- *provides schools with tablets and e-readers*
- *attempts to disrupt traditional textbook vendors which are slow and expensive*
- *tablets: expensive at the first purchase, in the long run tablets cheaper than rebuying texts every year*
- *each tablet loaded with multimedia versions of the syllabus, used by 5 children at a time, teaches the basics of schooling*
- *Amaf school charges $10 per month which in turn is given in micropayments to eLimu through downloads*

↓

business as usual not working
- *schools in Africa: severely underfunded, poorly managed*
- *need of capable teaching solutions*
- *not enough money to buy books and to hire new teachers*
- *need of the tablet teaching solution*

← *Amazon and Intel*

Amazon:
- *digital education directly connected to the sales of Kindle*
- *adding features with African consumers in mind: new languages, talking e-books, long battery life*

Intel:
- *helping African governments buy entry level computers*
- *bringing companies together to form exam-prep tools*

↓

quality of digital education
- *results encouraging*
- *Ghana: reading skills increased*
- *Ethiopia: children accustomed to using tablets, have developed reading skills*
- *Amaf School: average marks in science increased from 58 to 73 out of 100 in a single term*

→ *Digital education is working in Africa, the quality is just as high if not higher than real teachers.*

- **Aufgabe 5** wird **individuell** bearbeitet. Die Ergebnisse werden in **Stichwörtern** festgehalten, die als Grundlage für **mündliche Kurzvorträge** genutzt werden.
- Die Ergebnisse der Bearbeitung von **Aufgabe 6** werden im **Plenum** diskutiert. Die Sicherung erfolgt in **Tabellenform** auf **Folie**.
- **Aufgabe 7** kann in **Partnerarbeit** bearbeitet werden. Die Schülerinnen und Schüler erhalten den Auftrag, die Ergebnisse in Form einer **Tabelle** (s. Lösungsvorschlag unten) festzuhalten. Die Sicherung erfolgt im **Unterrichtsgespräch**.
- **Aufgabe 8** wird ebenfalls in **Partnerarbeit** erledigt. Die Ergebnisse werden in Stichwörtern notiert und im anschließenden **Unterrichtsgespräch** diskutiert. Danach kann folgender **Tafelanschrieb** erstellt werden:

Digital Abilities/Capabilities

children with computers	*children without computers*
- *quick to learn how to handle computers* - *higher reading skills* - *higher marks in science*	- *use their imagination and manual skills to make toys* - *use their imagination as a substitute for the "real thing"*
Learning outcomes are improved but children are not encouraged to use their imagination.	*Children use their imagination but have no chance to form or improve their intellectual knowledge.*

- Zur Durchführung der in **Aufgabe 9** vorgeschlagenen **Podiumsdiskussion** erhalten die Schülerinnen und Schüler den Auftrag, Listen mit Argumenten für ihren jeweiligen Standpunkt zu erarbeiten.
- **Aufgabe 10** wird in **Partnerarbeit** erledigt. Die Ergebnisse werden im Klassenzimmer ausgehängt und im Rahmen eines **Museumsrundgangs** zur Kenntnis genommen und diskutiert.
- **Aufgabe 11** kann als abschließende **Hausaufgabe** eingesetzt werden.

SOLUTIONS AWARENESS

Tablet teachers instead of "real" teachers – what do you think about this idea?

Thought I do see the use in tablet teachers (access to many people all at the same time and no need to travel and such), I would still argue an in-class teaching lesson from a real person would be more beneficial. I may be speaking from a developed country's standpoint, but tablets provide too big of a distraction for children to be focused on the material. A 'real' teacher ensures the lesson be taught without interruption from the Internet or application.

SOLUTIONS COMPREHENSION

1. Give an outline of the pilot project at the Amaf School in Kenya run by eLimu.

- Provides the school with tablets and e-readers (ll. 14–16).
- It is an attempt to disrupt traditional textbook vendors which are slow and expensive (ll. 38–40).
- Though expensive at the first purchase, in the long run tablets are cheaper than rebuying texts every year (ll. 40–42).
- Each tablet is loaded with multimedia versions of the syllabus and then used, 5 children at a time, to teach them the basics of schooling (ll. 11–13).
- The Amaf school charges $10 per month which in turn is given in micropayments to eLimu through downloads (ll. 74–77).

2. Point out why "business [education] as usual is not working" (ll. 33f.) in Africa.

Being severely underfunded and poorly managed, schools in Africa are in need of capable teaching solutions. Without the cash flow necessary to buy books and to hire new teachers, the growing number of pupils was in need of the tablet teaching solution that has proven to work for the state schools of African nations (ll. 25–36).

3. State what makes digital education interesting for Amazon or Intel.

For Amazon, this venture into digital education is directly connected to the sales of their e-reader device, Kindle. Amazon is adding features with African consumers in mind; new languages, talking e-books, and long battery life included. This is due to the boom in digital education as African children are more interested in the e-readers (ll. 48–56).

Intel is helping African governments buy entry level computers and bringing companies together to form exam-prep tools which have become hugely popular (ll. 57–69).

4. **What do the results reveal about the quality of digital education so far?**

Early results are encouraging. Reading skills in Ghana have dramatically increased amongst 350 children who had been given e-readers by Worldreader. In Ethiopia, even in the absence of teachers, children have become accustomed to using tablets and have developed reading skills. At the Amaf School, average marks in science have increased from 57 to 73 out of 100 in a single term. This reveals that digital education is working in Africa and that the quality is just as high if not higher than real teachers (ll. 78–91).

5. **Describe the photo on page 217: What impression do the children make on you?**
→ Focus on Skills, Analysis of Visuals, p. 262

The photo shows a large group of African children sitting at a bunch of computers, all of the children completely enthralled by what is going on in front of them on the screen. Though the room looks crowded, the atmosphere does seem to imply aggressive learning with a fun spin (look to the faces of the kids for their learning constitution while the bright colours add in a fun flavour for the environment). That being said, the impression I receive from the kids is that they are invested in learning about the computers and invested in their general education as well. Their focused looks portray them in a way that make them seem mesmerized by the on-screen activities. The body language presented in the photo would lead to an assumption that the kids are pulled into their learning due to the way they are sitting closely to the computer and making sure they understand the information

SOLUTIONS ANALYSIS

6. **The article was published in *The Economist*, a British weekly publication targeted at highly educated readers, businesspeople, influential executives and policy-makers. The magazine itself claims to be supportive of free trade, globalization, free immigration, etc. Together with a partner, examine the style of the article and the author's line of argument*. How do these stylistic means and further devices (e.g. language, choice of words, etc.) relate to the target readership?**
→ Focus on Skills, Analysis of a Non-Fictional Text, p. 258
→ Focus on Facts, Basic Types of Non-Fictional Texts, p. 246
→ Focus on Facts, The Press, p. 250

This is an expository text. Complicated facts are presented in a matter-of-fact way through the lens of the school children in Kenya. Using an antithetical approach, the author compares the status of the children before and after tablets as well as contrasting the development of those outside of the Amaf School (ll. 1–24). The line of argument follows a before-eLimu to after-eLimu route and then goes into the economic success of the program before returning to the benefits for the children (ll. 1–24, 70–91). That route is one of the ways that this is fitting of a publication like *The Economist*.

Many of the readers will hone in on the business aspect of this venture so it is a must-have for the article to contain something related to monetary gain while also giving enough backing detail as to why these educated people would aid the program. Both the style and tone are written in a matter-of-fact way (statistics, ll. 70–91, lack of emotive words) that allows for the information and storyline of the kids to interact on paper without causing a mishmash of ideas. Without slang or overly technical terms clouding up, the formal nature (statistics/only concrete ideas/lack of abstract) of the storytelling puts the educated reader at ease with all that is happening in the article.

7. **Compare the article at hand to the text "Wasting Time is New Divide in Digital Era" (pp. 212ff.), which claims that children from less well-off and lower educated families are having difficulties in gaining "computer literacy". Explain the similarities and differences between American (African-American, Hispanic) and African children with regard to their "digital abilities/capabilities".**

In the United States, these children from less well-off and lower educated families use the digital technology as a way to connect socially and engage in entertaining ways whereas the African children are using the technology to better their lives by learning to read and trying to understand the workings of the computer.

	Americans	Africans
reading on computer	although Americans do read quite a bit on their computers, much of this is because of social networking and not an attempt to better educate themselves (Markiy Cook, Alejandro Zamora, ll. 100–128)	African children are focusing on the reading aspect of the computer in order to better their lives (l. 80)
entertainment on computer	even from the more well-educated socioeconomic class the gadgets are mainly used for entertainment, and that's over an hour and a half less time per day then the less educated children (ll. 80–85)	for many of these African children, the line between entertainment and education is thin ... it is a grey area between which is which (see photo)
social networking	most of the American children use the gadgets for social networking (see Markiy Cook and Alejandro Zamora, ll. 100–128)	social networking, from the article, is not even mentioned as a factor much less a large scale problem
educational use	though some Americans do use their technology for research and education (ll. 138–141), many more use the devices for entertainment and social networking (ll. 13–14)	the article here is showing that the devices are used almost exclusively for education

8. Compare the photo on page 217 and the article at hand to the German text and the photo on page 216. Are the African children who are using computers at school at risk of losing their imagination? Explain the different views taken in the two articles.

→ Focus on Skills, Analysis of a Non-Fictional Text, p. 258

Are the views taken in the two articles really so different? "Tablet Teachers – Digital Education in Kenya" makes the main point that pupils in Africa are profiting from going digital. They have improved their skills and their results in a variety of fields. They take easily to using tablets and other digital devices. They discover things themselves and are motivated to improve their status. And the little boy in Malawi with his camera of clay is no different. He, too, wanted to improve his position and he, too, put his imagination to good use. Both photographs are a testimony to a healthy sense of intellectual curiosity, combined with a sense of inventiveness and the will to get on in life. Neither of these groups of children are in danger of losing their imagination. What is really different is the material position of both groups of children. The lucky pupils in Kenya have been given a chance that the boys from Malawi have not.

SOLUTIONS ACTIVITIES

9. Act out a Panel Discussion and discuss the advantages and disadvantages or possible threats/dangers of focusing on digital learning. Possible groups could be:

- **representative from eLimu/One Laptop Per Child**
- **representatives from Amazon, Intel and further technology giants**
- **concerned parents who fear that their children will be totally westernized and might fall prey to online manipulation**
- **enthusiastic parents who hope that their children will obtain access to profound and modern education**
- **teachers who fear that they will be made redundant and unemployed soon**
- **educators/psychologists who recommend to be more careful and critical about digital learning because children can easily be manipulated and even abused**

→ Focus on Methods, Panel Discussion, p. 270
→ Focus on Language, Conversation and Discussion, p. 266

eLimu rep, concerned parents, enthusiastic parents:

eLimu rep: There is a big advantage to be gained here due to the computers. Not only can your children learn reading and computer skills, but they can also be more prepared for the future of the world through use of these technologies.

Concerned parent: Yes, I agree that the technology could help them in the future, but it could also harm them in the present. Access to the Internet is a gateway for manipulation and these computers could possibly lead to our loss of culture.

Enthusiastic parent: Oh, that is not a big deal. Most of these computers have parental locks to keep children outside of chatrooms and other places where these kids can be manipulated.

Rep: That's true. We make sure to monitor where each device is going over the Internet and can assure that no dangerous websites or chatrooms can be entered by the child.

Concerned parent: That is helpful I suppose. But what can you say about our culture? These computers are very western and we have a rich culture that can be lost by the connectivity.

Enthusiast: Our culture will always stay our culture. Just because we are connected to the rest of the world does not mean we will lose it.

Concerned: But there is that risk we take. The more we westernize the less African we become. Like Johannesburg before, it could happen and it could end poorly.

Rep: There is that risk but I can assure you that you can tailor your syllabus to keep African culture alive and well. There is no set curriculum with our methods so you can keep African history a major portion of that.

Concerned: I see. I am still not comfortable with the idea but it cannot hurt to try.

Enthusiast: I agree! We have to start the program quickly to keep our children ahead of the pack.

Rep: I will talk to my supervisor then and try to get things moving quickly.

10. Put yourself in the position of an African teenager and write a letter to the editor* in response to the article. You can choose between these versions:
a) the use of a tablet computer/access to learning and the Internet provided you with the chance of a lifetime; it even enabled you to graduate and study at a university ...
b) the use of a tablet computer and access to the Internet was such a tempting experience for you that you got distracted from learning and were even lured to buy things online; you and your family ended up with a lot of debts ...

→ Focus on Skills, Writing a Letter to the Editor, p. 290

Dear editor,

I want to say that the article entitled 'Tablet Teachers – Digital Education in Kenya' hit very close to home. I went through the Amaf School and was taught using tablets. It provided me with the chance to learn at a quickened rate, not held back by a teacher trying to please everyone, and enabled me the opportunity to study things that interested me. I am currently enrolled in University in Cape Town and I know that I would not have had the chance if not for the use of those tablets. I just wanted to say thank you for highlighting such a wonderful programme.

Sincerely,
University Bound

SOLUTIONS GRAMMAR/LANGUAGE

11. Transform the following expert terms and phrases into everyday English. If necessary, use your dictionary for help.

- **touch screen** → a computer screen that you touch to get information, buy sth. etc.
- **multimedia** → using a combination of pictures, sound and words, esp. in computers and software
- **mobile operator** → a company that provides services for people in order to use their mobile devices
- **e-reader** → a small electronic device with a screen that allows you to read books in an electronic form
- **application** → a computer programme or piece of software that is designed for a particular purpose that you can download onto a mobile phone or other mobile device
- **digital education** → teaching people how to handle digital devices such as computers and software, etc.
- **download** → the process of copying or moving programmes or information into a computer's memory, esp. from the Internet or a larger computer
- **telecom carrier** → a company that provides telecommunication services
- **digital tool** → e.g. a software that you use on your computer
- **entry-level computer** → the cheapest or simplest version of a particular product or service

Vivian Yee

A School Distanced from Technology Faces Its Intrusion (pp. 220–222)

About the author	Vivian Yee is a writer for the *New York Times*. She specializes in local Brooklyn news but has a focus on Northeast United States.
About the text	This text highlights a school in Vermont that goes (nearly) completely without technology. Instead, the Mountain School focuses on natural skills (navigation and directional skills, farming, environmental science, animal science, etc.). The article is concerned over the possible input of a cellphone tower in the area and the possibility of the Mountain School losing its most endearing feature: lack of technology.
Level	● ● ●
Additional material	Differenzierungsmaterial, p. 153

- Die Awareness-Aufgabe kann um die Frage erweitert werden, welche Regelungen an der eigenen Schule für die Nutzung der zur Diskussion stehenden Medien gelten und ob diese Regelungen sinnvoll und ausreichend sind bzw. welche Chancen und Gefahren von diesen Medien an einer Schule ausgehen.
- Die Comprehension-Aufgaben (Aufg. 1–4) werden in Gruppenarbeit erledigt. Die Gruppenarbeit kann arbeitsteilig organisiert werden, d.h., jeder Schüler bearbeitet eine Aufgabe. Die Gruppen erhalten den Auftrag, ihre Ergebnisse auf Folie zu visualisieren und zu präsentieren.
- Aufgabe 5 wird in Partnerarbeit bearbeitet. Die Ergebnisse werden mit einer weiteren Zweiergruppe ausgetauscht.
- Aufgabe 6 wird individuell erledigt, die Ergebnisse werden im Unterrichtsgespräch ausgetauscht und informell an der Tafel gesichert.
- Aufgabe 7 wird nach den Aufgaben im Schülerbuch bearbeitet.
- Vor der Bearbeitung von Aufgabe 8 kann die Bildung der Konditionalsätze wiederholt werden (Focus on Grammar, SB, S. 296; zu einem möglichen Tafelanschrieb s. LHB, S. 41).
- Die Ergebnisse werden im Anschluss an die Erarbeitungsphase vorgelesen und gemeinsam in der Klasse korrigiert.

SOLUTIONS AWARENESS

School without Internet, DVDs, computers, cell phones, iPads ...? Discuss whether (or not) you would want to go to a school like this.

Individual answers

SOLUTIONS COMPREHENSION

1. **Describe the surroundings of the Mountain School in New Hampshire.**

   rural: chicken coop, wooden buildings, potato patch, llama, periphery of civilization, nearby mountain ...

2. **What kind of "lessons" do students have there – and what is the school's mission?**

   lessons: solo camping trips for quiet reflection, orienteering skills without GPS, English, environmental science, caring for farm animals, chopping wood, reading Robert Frost

   mission: encouraging collaborative learning and shared work; to make students think more carefully about their use of technology

3. **Give an outline of the technology policy which students, teachers and alumni are discussing.**

   possible ban on technology on campus (mobile phones); draft policy: students must hand over their phones to the faculty upon arrival and get them back for off-campus trips, and request them back after a month

4. **How do the students experience being "off-line"?**

   At first they miss it, but after a while they get used to it and use their computers mostly for schoolwork and only infrequently for things like Facebook, music downloads, etc. Their focus shifts more to their immediate surroundings, and it becomes a welcome relief. Students look down on people who are overly attached to their laptops and phones.

SOLUTIONS ANALYSIS

5. **Go through the text again and make a list of the various classes students have at the Mountain School. In a second step, together with a partner, match corresponding skills and capabilities students acquire from these lessons and activities. Copy the grid below and complete it.**

classes and activities	*acquired skills and competences*
– *taking care of chickens*	→ *social skills; to take on responsibility*
– *digging potatoes*	→ *manual skills*
– *taking care of animals (e.g. a llama)*	→ *focus on relevant things in life*
– *taking solo camping trips for reflection*	→ *being self-sufficient*
– *practice orienteering skills without GPS*	→ *being (more) independent*
– *environmental science classes*	→ *teamwork*
– *chopping wood*	→ *sharing experiences*
– *reading Robert Frost*	→ *preserving values*
– *engaging with the rural setting and one another*	→ *focus on the things in front of you*
– *doing collaborative learning/shared work*	→ *careful use of technology*
– *looking at the stars*	

6. **Explain Smith's concluding sentence: "The idea is not to be going back in time where things were better but where the richness of every day is defined by the food you eat, the company you keep, the work you do." (II. 109 – 112) Which skills and competences with regard to the students' future life as adults do they acquire?**

→ Focus on Facts, Key Qualifications and Soft Skills, p. 223

- **not to be going back in time where things were better ...**
  - no mobile phones, Internet, computers = less/more primitive technology → "no technology" is not the point
  - not about romanticizing the past, "traditional" values ...

... but where the richness of every day is defined by

- **the food you eat ...**
  - growing food, interacting with nature (plants and animals, the soil, the weather ...), cooking one's own meals instead of buying pre-packaged food

skills and competences: growing, eating and preparing nourishing food; learning about nature, animals and gardening

- **the company you keep ...**
  - students focus on peers and people around them, not "virtual" friends and people far away via the Internet

skills and competences: face-to-face communication, engaging with people, getting along with people in person, making new friends

- **the work you do ...**
  - tangible work (e.g. working with the land, with one's hands), as opposed to virtual/electronic work on a computer

skills and competences: better focus on the present, physical world; patience, less distraction; living in the moment

SOLUTIONS ACTIVITIES

7. In an experiment, "simplify your life" and eliminate digital technology and gadgets that are not strictly necessary in everyday life.

- **Step 1: If you want, you can make a ranking first, placing items in a range from "absolutely necessary" to "totally redundant" (see grid in SB, on p. 222).**
- **Step 2: In your groups copy the grid on posters or wallpaper and complete your ranking system. Then display your grids in class.**
- **Step 3: In class, evaluate the activity and discuss and/or negotiate your rankings.**

→ Focus on Skills, Conversation and Discussion, p. 266

ranking	gadget/device	purpose/reason
absolutely necessary	cell phones	emergency calls
	GPS device	navigation
	Internet	looking up information, communication
partly necessary	digital camera	taking photos
	Facebook, Twitter, etc.	social networking
	TV	news, entertainment
dispensable	tablet	surfing the Internet
	e-reader	reading electronic books, documents
totally redundant	video games	pure entertainment

SOLUTIONS GRAMMAR/LANGUAGE

8. **Turn your notes from task 7 into coherent sentences and explain what would happen if you did not have a certain digital/technical gadget or tool. Use if-clauses (type I, II and III) for your sentence.**
   Example:
   - **If I wasn't able/allowed to listen to my mp3-player, I would ...**
   - **If I hadn't been able to use my cell phone after the accident, I would have ...**

→ Focus on Grammar, Conditional Sentences (If-Clauses), p. 296

- If I was not able/allowed to listen to my mp3-player, I would ...
- If I had not been able to use my cell phone after the accident, I would have ...
- If we are not allowed to watch the new sitcom on TV, it will be a boring evening.
- If the school cannot afford to buy the new e-books, the parents will be very angry.
- If the school did not have high-speed Internet, we could not check our Facebook pages.
- etc.

Rob Waugh

TXT BAD 4 UR BRAIN? Text Messaging Can Dent Your Reading Abilities Say Scientists (pp. 224–225)

About the author	Rob Waugh [wa:] is a freelance journalist for *Mail on Sunday, Yahoo!* and other publications. He specializes in writing about technology, science and space.
About the text	This newspaper article presents findings from a study which suggests that reading traditional print media helps people's reading skills, while heavy texting is associated with reading problems.
Level	● ● ○
Additional material	• GaSt: no. 10 • Comprehension: no. 25

- Das in der Awareness-Aufgabe geforderte Ranking kann in Gruppen mithilfe von Moderationskarten durchgeführt werden. Hierzu erhält jede Gruppe eine bestimmte Anzahl von Karten (von der Anzahl der zu beschriftenden Karten hängt die Dauer der Unterrichtsphase ab), auf denen die Gruppenmitglieder die Vorteile des SMS-Schreibens verzeichnen. Die Schüler sollten darauf hingewiesen werden, dass auf jede Karte nur ein Stichwort geschrieben wird und dass die Begriffe so groß geschrieben werden, dass sie auch aus einiger Entfernung noch gut lesbar sind. Nach dem Beschriften werden die Karten gesammelt und zunächst doppelte oder ähnliche Begriffe aussortiert. Danach einigt sich die Gruppe auf die Reihenfolge, in der die Karten auf einen Flipchartbogen geklebt werden. Die Gruppenergebnisse werden im Plenum vorgestellt und diskutiert.
- Die Ergebnisse der Bearbeitung der Aufgaben 1 und 2 können stichwortartig notiert und danach in der Klasse diskutiert werden.
- Aufgabe 3 kann als kurze Schreibübung eingesetzt werden. Dabei verfasst jeder Schüler bzw. jede Schülerin auf einer Moderationskarte eine Definition nach dem Muster „Textism is ...". Die Ergebnisse werden auf einem Flipchartbogen, einer Moderationswand oder einer Wandzeitung gesammelt und im losen Klassenverband zur Kenntnis genommen und diskutiert.
- Aufgabe 4 wird nach einer individuellen Erarbeitung in Unterrichtsgespräch erledigt.
- Aufgabe 5 wird individuell bearbeitet, die Ergebnisse werden im Klassenverband diskutiert. Sie können in einem Tafelbild gesichert werden:

> **Rob Waugh, TXT BAD 4 UR BRAIN?**
>
> *point of view:*
>
> *The author is critical of texting.*
> → *text messaging may stunt reading skills (l. 1)*
> → *heavy texters are less able to understand new words (ll. 4f.)*
> → *heavy texters are less willing to accept new words (l. 5)*
> → *text messaging is constrained and not creative (ll. 10ff.)*
> → *text messaging is limited to small groups of peers (l. 15)*
> → *text messaging is subject to rigid rules (l. 22)*
> → *the number of words used is limited (ll. 23f.)*
> → *new or unknown words are rejected (ll. 31ff.)*
>
> *message of the text:*
> *People who text frequently are less able and willing to read, understand and use new or uncommon words.*

- Bei dem in Aufgabe 6 geforderten Vergleich der Aussagen des Textes und der Karikatur wird auf die in Aufgabe 5 erarbeiteten Ergebnisse zurückgegriffen. Nach der in Einzel- oder Partnerarbeit durchgeführten Analyse der Karikatur wird deren Gesamtaussage der des Textes gegenübergestellt. Die Schülerinnen und Schüler erhalten in einer anschließenden Diskussion die Möglichkeit, für eine der beiden Haltungen Stellung zu beziehen. Diese Diskussion kann um die in Aufgabe 7 vorgeschlagene Thematik erweitert werden.
- Aufgabe 8 wird in **häuslicher Arbeit** erledigt.

SOLUTIONS AWARENESS

What do you consider to be the advantages of text messaging? Discuss in class and make a ranking.

- cheaper than calling someone on a mobile phone
- can be done silently (during a film, lecture, while other people are talking)
- messages can be written very quickly and easily

Rankings will vary.

SOLUTIONS COMPREHENSION

1. Present the positive effects of reading print media.

- makes people more comfortable accepting and understanding new words (ll. 6ff.)
- exposes people to variety and creativity in language (ll. 12f.)

2. What possible dangers does text messaging pose for people, according to the text?

- text messaging may stunt reading skills (l. 1)
- heavy texters are less able/willing to understand/accept/learn new words (ll. 25f.) compared to people who read more traditional print media

3. Define the meaning of "textism".

Textisms are words that are commonly used in texting language. These include unusual spellings, abbreviations and acronyms, such as LOL, that are generally recognized by all texters (ll. 37ff.).

SOLUTIONS ANALYSIS

4. Examine the reliability of the statements and information given in the article. Reactivate your knowledge of newspapers and their characteristics and compare them to the *Daily Mail* article.

→ Focus on Facts, The Press, p. 250

- source: Daily Mail → tabloid newspaper known for sensationalist articles
- eye-catching title grabs the reader's attention
- short length of article

- one-sided reporting: only one source of study, Joan Lee of Calgary University (l. 11)
- no explanations about the study's sample size, numbers, reliability, statistical significance, etc.
- The only other person quoted is UK's poet laureate, Carole Ann Duffy, but her statement – that texting and poetry are similar – is simply an opinion and neither confirms nor refutes the main argument of the article (ll. 18–20).

→ less reliable article; more information/evidence is needed

5. Specify and analyse the point of view that is taken in the article and determine its message.
→ Focus on Skills, Analysis of a Non-Fictional Text, p. 258

The article's message is that texting hinders people's reading skills and that heavy texters are less able and willing to understand and accept unknown words than people who read more traditional print media. It draws on one particular study, by Joan Lee of Calgary University, who did a study with these results (ll. 9ff.). The article refers to previous assumptions and studies that claimed text messaging encouraged creativity and unconstrained language, but shows that these turned out to be false (ll. 10f.).

6. In what way does the cartoon on page 224 present the problem? Compare its message to the conclusions made in the article.
→ Focus on Skills, Analysis of Visuals, p. 262

The cartoon shows a first grade classroom. The teacher is teaching the children how to write, explaining that writing is like texting except that in writing one must use all of the letters in each word. The implication here is that the children have started school already knowing how to text, but not how to write, which is impossible and illogical.

The main message of the cartoon coincides with that of the article, namely that texting interferes with reading/writing skills. The children in the classroom do not accept or recognize the real words on the blackboard because they only know textisms (ll. 37ff.).

SOLUTIONS ACTIVITIES

7. In class, discuss the views presented in the article and relate them to your own experiences. Do you have difficulties with reading (longer) texts and spelling – if so, what do you consider to be the reasons for this?

Individual answers

SOLUTIONS GRAMMAR/LANGUAGE

Webcode SNG-40175-026 @

8. Reactivate your knowledge of British pronunciation and phonetic symbols. In a Think! Pair! Share! activity find out how to pronounce the words in the list (see SB, p. 225). Then, read them aloud to your partner. Check the reference pages in your dictionary for help.
→ Focus on Methods, Think! Pair! Share!, p. 273
Additionally, you can cross-check your pronunciation with a spoken dictionary on the Internet.
After doing the exercise, discuss whether the (printed) phonetic spelling is still necessary or whether new (audio) media are a better alternative.

ˈædmərəbl admirable	**ˌædvənˈteɪdʒəs** advantageous	**blæksplɔɪˈteɪʃn** blacksploitation
tʃɑ:dʒ charge	**ˌjʊərəˈpi:ən** European	**ˌgləʊbəlaɪˈzeɪʃn** globalisation
ˌɪntəˈrʌpʃn interruption	**ˈdʒu:vənaɪl** juvenile	**ˌlaɪəˈbɪləti** liability
ˈlɒdʒɪkl logical	**pəˈtɪkjələli** particularly	**ˈpɒpjələ(r)** popular
ˌri:lækˈseɪʃn relaxation	**rɪˈtaɪə(r)** retire	**ˌteliкəˌmju:nɪˈkeɪʃnz** telecommunications
ˈteliʃɒpɪŋ teleshopping	**ʌnˈfɔ:tʃənətli** unfortunately	**dʌmˈfaʊndɪd** dumbfounded

Chat Room or Conference Room? – Meeting People in Formal and Informal Situations

James Poniewozik

Serial Killing (pp. 227–229)

About the author	James Poniewozik is an American journalist and television critic. He writes *Time*'s *Tuned In* column and has a blog with the same name. He contributed to publications such as *The New York Times Book Review*, *Fortune*, and *Rolling Stone*. From 1997 to 1999, he was the media critic and editor of the media section at Salon.com.
About the text	The text is about violence on television. Is there too much? Is it too extreme? Is it dumb violence or exceptionally intelligent violence? Poniewozik is writing about the types of violence and why it is on TV in such great volume.
Level	● ● ●
Additional material	● Differenzierungsmaterial, p. 160

- Die **Awareness-Aufgabe** wird in einem kurzen **Unterrichtsgespräch** erledigt.
- Die **Aufgaben 1 und 2** werden **individuell** bearbeitet. Die Ergebnisse werden im **Plenum** ausgetauscht und in folgendem **Tafelanschrieb** gesichert:

J. Poniewozik, "Serial Killing"

violence on TV

extreme:
hacking off a finger,
feeding it to a dog

mindful:
serious themes
misogyny, morality,
mortality

mindless:
s. examples given in
the box above the text

Violence on TV isn't mere entertainment and collective fear governs people.

- **Aufgabe 3** wird in **Gruppenarbeit** erledigt. Die Gruppen halten ihre Ergebnisse auf **Folie** fest und präsentieren sie anschließend im Plenum.
- **Aufgabe 4** wird **individuell** bearbeitet. Die Ergebnisse werden im Unterrichtsgespräch diskutiert.
- Vor der Bearbeitung von **Aufgabe 5** sollten die angegebenen **Focus on Skills-** und **Focus on Language-Seiten** besprochen werden. Danach wird die Klasse in fünf **Gruppen** eingeteilt, die jeweils einen in der Aufgabenstellung aufgelisteten Aspekt bearbeiten. Die Arbeit innerhalb der Gruppen erfolgt **individuell** oder in **Partnerarbeit**. Die Ergebnisse werden im **Plenum** gesammelt und auf **Folie** gesichert. Die Folie kann im Anschluss für die gesamte Lerngruppe kopiert werden.
- **Aufgabe 6** wird in **Partnerarbeit** bearbeitet. Die Schülerinnen und Schüler halten ihre Ergebnisse in einer **Tabelle** (s. Lösungsvorschlag S. 311f.) fest. Die Besprechung erfolgt im Plenum, wobei die Schülerinnen und Schüler ihre Tabellen ggf. ergänzen bzw. korrigieren.
- Vor der in **Aufgabe 7** vorgeschlagenen **Podiumsdiskussion** sollten die angegebenen **Focus on Skills-Seiten** (SB, S. 270 und S. 266) besprochen werden. Für die Vorbereitung der Diskussion sollte eine Doppelstunde, für die Durchführung eine Einzelstunde veranschlagt werden.
- **Aufgabe 8** wird in **Partnerarbeit** erledigt. Die Ergebnisse werden im Klassenzimmer ausgehängt und von der Klasse zur Kenntnis genommen und gemeinsam korrigiert.

SOLUTIONS AWARENESS

Look at the visual (SB, p. 227) depicting "Six Ways to Die on TV" and discuss which "categories of violence" they could be related to, e. g. torture, murder, accident, etc. Can you think of further "categories" of how death, killing or violence in general are presented on TV?

- Game of Thrones: torture
- True Blood: accident
- Fringe: accident? murder?
- Boardwalk Empire: torture
- Spartacus: torture, murder
- Sons of Anarchy: murder

- other categories of violence: heroic/justified violence ("the bad guy deserves it"); medical drama and sickness/death; natural disasters; monsters, vampires, zombies ...

SOLUTIONS COMPREHENSION

1. **Point out the different "qualities" of violence the writer refers to in the introductory part (ll. 3ff.).**

   - extreme: hacking off a finger and feeding it to a dog
   - mindless: the examples given in the box above the text
   - mindful: serious themes → misogyny, morality, mortality

2. **Which conclusions does the writer draw concerning the societal effect of violence on TV?**

   1) this is not mere entertainment (ll. 28f.)
   2) collective fear governs people

3. **Present the reasons/explanations put forward as motivating the "mainstream" to watch violent TV shows or series.**

   1) feel-good escapism
   2) entertainment
   3) dreams
   4) fear

4. **Give an outline of the development of and changes in TV violence from "Grandma's entertainment of the 1920s" to the TV dramas of today.**

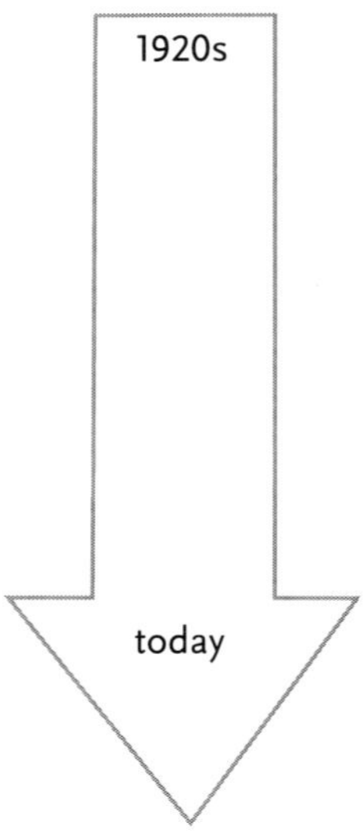

1920s:
- "cowboys and Indians" → white men = good guys, Indians = bad guys
- less explicit violence, little actual blood shown ...
- formulaic, predictable plots
- explicit gore and gratuitous violence

today:
- more explicit violence: blood, gore, shocking scenes
- complex stories, moral ambiguity, anti-heros
- more diversity/political correctness (racial minorities no longer always "the bad guys")

SOLUTIONS ANALYSIS

5. Examine and analyse the particular tone* of the article and explain how it supports the message the writer wishes to convey. Focus particularly on:

- **positive/negative emotive words that are used to (indirectly) evaluate sb./sth., e.g. "self-parodically extreme" (ll. 2f.), a negative evaluation ...**

frequent use of **negative emotive words** underline the author's negative stance towards excessive violence and killing on TV:
drowning (l. 5), dumb, mindless (l. 6), exhausting (l. 10), bloody (l. 18), bleakest (ll. 33f.), relentless struggle (l. 36), executioner (l. 37), pile of skulls (l. 40), brutal (l. 41)

the use of **positive emotive words** underlines the author's positive stance towards aspects of entertainment other than violence: daring, rich (l. 43), complex, thoughtful (l. 51)

- **the use of pronouns employed to relate to the reader**

you/your (ll. 16, 20, 35) ➔ directly calling on the reader for action, putting the reader on the spot
we/us (ll. 13, 21, 31) ➔ solidarity with readership

- **the use of (rhetorical) questions and answers as a means of persuasion**

Does TV make people kill? (l. 15)
... you have to ask why countries like Britain and Japan ... (ll. 16ff.)
➔ author thinks the answer is NO
... ask why we sit down for these grim bedtime stories ... (ll. 20ff.)
Why has TV-drama become so reflexively brutal? (l. 41)
➔ author goes on to explore the answers to these questions, which are not immediately obvious

- **the use of contrast/antithesis in order to emphasize certain differences or contradictions**
- dumb, mindless violence = smart, mindful violence ➔ emphasizes the different kinds of violence
- feel-good escapism = bleakest stuff ➔ contradiction between expectation and reality of what people want
- dreams = piles of skulls ➔ contradiction
- becomes so ... brutal = become so good ➔ shows have a lot of positive points besides all their violent content

- **structural devices* that guide the reader and focus on certain aspects**

title: "Serial killing" ➔ pun (TV show = serial)
paragraphs deal with different aspects of violence and TV:
ll. 1–10: the types of violence on TV today
ll. 11–40: relationship between TV violence and the viewer's actions, dreams
ll. 41–57: explanation of why shows have become more violent recently

➔ Focus on Skills, Analysis of a Non-Fictional Text, p. 258
➔ Focus on Language, Literary Terms, p. 308

6. Compare David Simon's statement that "[i]t would be 'ridiculous' to say the violence of the show inspires real murder" (ll. 26ff.) to Christopher Dickey's article "Kill Zone" (pp. 119ff.).

examples from the "Kill Zone"	connection to statement
• "He dresses for the street and he posts YouTube videos of himself playing a bad-ass comedian." (ll. 30ff.)	• typical teenager, more interested in entertaining than violence
• "Summer is killing season ... young men who might have been in school are out in the streets ... shooting at each other." (ll. 57ff.)	• Especially male teenagers may turn to violence out of boredom.
• "collateral damage ... [is] inevitable ..." (ll. 61f.)	• Innocent people are victimized as well.

examples from the "Kill Zone"	connection to statement
• "... 82 percent of the nation's gun owners are white ... but 72 percent of gun-homicide victims are black or Hispanic ..." (ll. 113ff.)	• Interestingly, the protagonists of most of the series that the article mentions are white.
• "... they use rifles and guns for hunting, skeet shooting, target practice." (ll. 125f.)	• Rifles and guns are often used responsibly for hunting and sport.
• "In rural America, 50 percent of the households own guns ..." (ll. 128f.)	• In rural areas where people are more isolated, people feel the need to protect themselves with guns.

SOLUTIONS ACTIVITIES

7. "... it's national consensus ... the visual rendering of the collective fear that governs us." (ll. 29ff.) "Contrary to the idea that the masses want feel-good escapism, the bleakest stuff dominates the mainstream." (ll. 32ff.)
In class, act out a Panel Discussion on the assumption (*Vermutung*) that people do not want to "feel good" but want to be "scared and shocked" by TV shows and series.

→ Focus on Methods, Panel Discussion, p. 270
→ Focus on Language, Conversation and Discussion, p. 266

People want to ...	
... feel good	**... be scared and shocked**
• feel-good escapism from problems ...	• thrill in contrast to boring everyday life
• relaxation	• when people watch terrible/shocking things on TV, their life seems better in comparison → gratitude
• laughter has many health/mood benefits → comedies make people feel better	• scary and shocking TV is more interesting/ engages the mind more, thus offering a more effective distraction → better escape
• people empathize with the characters on TV, so watching something scary/shocking leads to negative feelings	• viewers feel greater happiness/relief when they watch something scary/suspenseful and there is a happy ending
• when people watch happy characters on TV, they also feel happy	
• "light" entertainment is easier to watch, helps viewer to relax	

SOLUTIONS GRAMMAR/LANGUAGE

8. Use the information on TV shows or series given in the visual on page 227 or in the article at hand or, alternatively, choose a similar film yourself and rewrite the synopsis of the respective content. Use adjectives, adverbs and adverbials to "flesh out" your description and change the sentence structure whenever necessary.
Example:
Fringe: At a dark cemetery, a brutal, bloodthirsty villain was crushed to death slowly ...

→ Focus on Grammar, Adjectives and Adverbs, pp. 292ff.

Afterwards, read out your "bloody" texts and discuss them.
Tip: Before formulating sentences, collect words and phrases on the matter and sort them in clusters.

For example:

At a dark cemetery, a brutal, bloodthirsty villain was crushed to death slowly while coughing up disgustingly slimy blood ...

Lonely vampire Roman met a gruesome and shocking end in his coffin by being courageously impaled by a brave knight with his own stake ... etc.

Spaces and Spectres – Living Multimedia-Based (pp. 230–232)

About the author	Bill Watterson is an American cartoonist and the creator of the comic strip *Calvin and Hobbes*. The cartoon was featured in American newspapers from 1985 until 1995.
About the text	This cartoon features an imaginative young boy, Calvin, and his mother and father. Calvin's best friend, Hobbes, is a stuffed toy tiger (not featured here). These three cartoons deal with TV-based media.
Level	● ● ○
Additional material	• GaSt: no. 10

- Die Awareness-Aufgabe wird nach den Angaben im Schülerbuch bearbeitet.
- Die Präsentation der **Gruppenergebnisse** (Aufgabe 1) kann auf **Folie** erfolgen. Alle bzw. die wichtigsten Folien können im Anschluss für die ganze Lerngruppe kopiert werden.
- Die Untersuchung der **Stilebenen** kann ihren Abschluss finden, indem die Schülerinnen und Schüler dazu aufgefordert werden, sich zu überlegen, weshalb und in welcher Situation bestimmte Sprecher ein bestimmtes **Register** verwenden. Dabei wird deutlich werden, dass die Figuren in Alltagssituationen die entsprechende Sprache verwenden; wenn es jedoch darum geht, bestimmte Dinge auszudrücken, die nicht zum Alltag gehören, verwenden sie ein entsprechendes, der jeweiligen Redesituation angemessenes Register. Die Ergebnisse können in folgendes **Tafelbild** münden:

The use of certain registers

cartoon/explanation	***formal style***	***colloquial style***
cartoon 1	*romantic scene on TV*	*Calvin talking to himself*
explanation 1	*characters use the style of romantic novels*	*Calvin uses his everyday language*
cartoon 2	*Calvin's mom talking to Calvin and his dad*	*Calvin and his Dad talking*
explanation 2	*she imitates the scientific language of psychiatrists talking about adolescent fantasies*	*they use their everyday language*
cartoon 3	*Calvin's dad expressing his indignation about certain techniques on TV*	*Calvin's mom and dad talking*
explanation 3	*he imitates the scientific language of literary critics*	*they use their everyday language*
→ The characters use their everyday language when they speak as themselves; when they speak in a different situation (cf. the actors in a romantic movie) or adopt another persona (cf. a doctor, a literary critic) they assimilate their language accordingly.		

Die **Validität** dieses Ergebnisses kann mit den Schülerinnen und Schülern diskutiert werden. Dabei wird sich herausstellen, dass auch sie in bestimmten Situationen ein bestimmtes Register verwenden (Umgangssprache mit der Familie und den Freunden, formalere Sprache bei Referaten in der Schule etc.).

- Aufgabe 3 wird im Unterrichtsgespräch bearbeitet.
- Aufgaben 4 und 5 können in **Partnerarbeit** erledigt werden. Die Ergebnisse können an entsprechender Stelle auf von der Lehrerin bzw. dem Lehrer erstellte **Kopien** der drei Cartoons eingetragen werden.
- Der Bearbeitung von Aufgabe 6 sollte eine kurze Wiederholung der Grundregeln zur Formulierung der indirekten Rede vorangestellt werden. Dies kann mithilfe der angegebenen **Focus on Grammar-Seite** geschehen und in folgendem **Tafelanschrieb** gesichert werden:

Indirect Speech

Backshifting:

direct speech	indirect speech
present tense	past tense
past tense	past perfect
present perfect	past perfect
past perfect	past perfect
will-future	would + infinitive
going to-future	was/were going to
can	could
may	might

→ If the introductory verb is in the past tense you have to backshift.
→ The aspect of the verb is not changed.
→ The word order in indirect questions is s-v-o.
→ Indirect questions are introduced by a question word or if/whether.
→ Indirect commands use to **tell sb. to/not to** + verb.
→ Pronouns and adverbials of time and place have to be changed according to the situation of the speaker.

SOLUTIONS AWARENESS

In a Placemat activity (→ FoM, p. 271), first reflect on what kind of media you frequently use and whether you use these for fun or for work, then discuss your experiences with your group. In class, work out a ranking of the various media you use according to the frequency of use.

For example:
Internet, radio, TV, movies, magazines, books ...

(Rankings will vary.)

SOLUTIONS COMPREHENSION

1. Form groups of 3 – 4 students, with each group dealing with one of the cartoons.
a) State in your own words what the comic strip is about.
Cartoon 1 criticizes sexual content on TV as well as violence/murder/immorality and how this affects children.
Cartoon 2 deals with advertisements and the unrealistic images and messages they send to consumers.
Cartoon 3 criticizes the exploitation of people's personal tragedy and grief for entertainment purposes.

b) Describe the arrangement of the pictorial elements.
Present and exchange your results in class.
1: Calvin is sick in bed watching TV. The reader cannot see what is on the screen, but can read what the characters are saying: They are having an affair and kissing, and plan to murder their real spouses.
2: Calvin is watching TV in the living room, and the TV is jumping into the air, suggesting that it is very loud and obnoxious. Calvin's dad walks by, and Calvin suggests that he (his dad) and his mom aren't cool because they don't act/live/look like the people in the commercials. Finally, Calvin's dad pretends to believe the commercial too, and his mom "explains" that it is unrealistic.
3: Calvin's dad is watching another "jumping", loud, obnoxious TV. We cannot see the screen or hear what is being said, but Calvin's dad describes what is going on, namely that the programme is focusing intently on someone's pain in a very obvious, exploitative way, which he finds disgusting and hard to look at.

SOLUTIONS ANALYSIS

2. Examine who is speaking and what register and terminology is used in each of the cartoons.
➔ Focus on Language, The Language Register of English, p. 315

1: The TV characters are using a rather "high" style similar to that of cheap romance novels (ravishing, skimpy negligee, spouses). In the last panel, Calvin uses an everyday register to reflect on what he's watching.
2: Calvin and his dad use an everyday, casual register (hey dad, how come, yeah, you guys), while Calvin's mom uses a higher, formal register to underline her sarcastic tone (adolescent, require).
3: Calvin's dad uses a very high, formal register (anguish, violation, assault, human dignity ...), but he and his wife use everyday language in the last panel when he switches from a commentary/critique to just talking about what he is doing at that moment.

3. Specify what the cartoons criticize in particular, and say what the message is.
➔ Focus on Skills, Analysis of Visuals, p. 262

1: Criticizes sex and immorality on TV as entertainment. Children especially should not watch such rubbish, but they are attracted to and interested in it nonetheless.
2: Criticizes false advertising. People should not be persuaded by unrealistic commercials or think that buying/using products will make them younger/cooler/more popular.
3: Criticizes using real-life tragedy as entertainment. It implies that watching this kind of programming is a waste of time and not worth watching.

4. Comment on whether the cartoonist really hits the nail on the head and successfully conveys the message to the reader.

Individual answers

Are there aspects of the broadcasting media that are not mentioned?
The amount of time that people spend watching TV/getting addicted to TV ...
Cultural obsession with mediocre/lowbrow programming, e.g. reality TV, celebrity gossip ...

SOLUTIONS ACTIVITIES

5. Pyramid discussion – The quality of the broadcasting media
Step 1: Each student writes down a short (!) statement, an opinion or a suggestion for improvement on a piece of paper and fixes it to the board.
Step 2: Silently read the statements individually, and then decide on which ones you agree or disagree with.
Step 3: Now make a ranking of the statements, according to how much you agree or disagree with them. Reduce the list to the five to ten statements you agree with the most.
Step 4: Together with a partner, repeat step 3, and find 5 statements that both of you agree with.
Step 5: Find another pair and form a group of 4, in which you again repeat step 3. Finally, your group should reach a compromise and agree on 5 statements along with a ranking for them.
Step 6: Each group fixes their selection to the board. Now, together with the whole class, discuss and evaluate your choices and preferences.
➔ Focus on Language, Conversation and Discussion, p. 266

Individual answers

SOLUTIONS GRAMMAR/LANGUAGE

6. Transform the speech bubbles into indirect speech.
Example:
Mary's lover told her that she looked ravishing in that skimpy negligee.
Mary asked whether ...
➔ Focus on Grammar, Indirect Speech, pp. 298f.

- Mary's lover told her that she looked ravishing in that skimpy negligee.
- Mary asked whether he wished they were married.
- He replied that they were married – just not to each other.
- Mary suggested they murder their spouses and told him she had to have him.
- He called Mary a sick animal and said he loved it when she talked that way.
- Calvin said that he learnt more when he stayed at home and watched TV than he did at school.
- Calvin told his dad to watch the commercial.
- He asked his dad why he did not drive a cool sports car like the man in the commercial.
- His dad replied that the car cost $40,000.
- Calvin was impressed by the woman in the commercial and asked his dad why his mom did not dress like that.
- Calvin's dad teasingly asked his wife why she does not dress like that.
- Calvin's mom answered that her husband's fantasies were adolescent and required an adolescent model with implants.
- Calvin suggested that his parents needed to drink more beer.

ADDITIONAL TASK

Design cartoons yourself in which you mock (criticize/describe) the behaviour of people when it comes to watching TV.

Individual answers

Chat Rooms – Opportunities and Risks (pp. 232–234)

About the author	---
About the text	The following lesson includes a cartoon and a table of statistics, both concerning Internet communication. The subjective cartoon conveys a message about problems people may face when using the Internet, and the statistics offer an objective look at some recent trends regarding widespread Internet use.
Level	● ○ ○
Additional material	• GaST: no. 10

- Die *Awareness*-Aufgabe wird bei den Schülerinnen und Schülern auf breites Interesse stoßen, da die meisten von ihnen in **Chatrooms** organisiert sind. Gleiches gilt für den zur Diskussion stehenden Cartoon, da es unter Jugendlichen durchaus üblich ist, sich in Chatrooms für andere Personen (anderes Alter, anderer Wohnort, anderer Name etc.) auszugeben. Eine Diskussion des Sinns bzw. Unsinns von Chatrooms, die man unter solchen Voraussetzungen benutzt, kann sich anschließen.
- Aufgabe 1 wird individuell bearbeitet.
- Die **Ergebnisse** der Bearbeitung von Aufgabe 2 können in Form einer **Tabelle** (s. Lösungsvorschlag S. 317) gesichert werden.
- Aufgabe 3 wird in **Einzelarbeit** erledigt. Im Anschluss werden einige Arbeiten vorgelesen und korrigiert.
- Aufgabe 4 wird in **Partnerarbeit** bearbeitet, die Ergebnisse werden in **Stichwörtern** festgehalten und dienen als Grundlage für eine informelle Diskussion des Themas im Plenum.
- Aufgabe 5 wird nach den Angaben im Schülerbuch bearbeitet.
- Die Brisanz des Themas **„Cyberbullying"** erfordert eine sorgfältige **Begleitung** der Beschäftigung mit Aufgabe 6 **durch den Lehrer bzw. die Lehrerin**.
- Aufgabe 7 wird nach den Angaben im Schülerbuch bearbeitet. Im Anschluss an die Diskussion in den Gruppen trägt jeweils ein Gruppensprecher bzw. eine Gruppensprecherin die **Ergebnisse** der Diskussion in den Gruppen im Plenum vor.
- Die in Aufgabe 8 geforderte Diskussion wird nach der **individuellen Erarbeitung** im Klassenverband durchgeführt. Die Ergebnisse werden informell an der **Tafel** gesichert.
- Die Aufgaben 9 und 10 können alternativ als **Hausaufgabe** eingesetzt werden. Bei der Bearbeitung von Aufgabe 9 erhalten die Schülerinnen und Schüler den Auftrag, zur **Umwälzung** der zu lernenden Ausdrücke zu jedem Ausdruck einen **Beispielsatz** zu formulieren.

SOLUTIONS AWARENESS

Social-networking websites have become enormously popular and offer global platforms to millions of people to communicate and interact with each other. Along with the many opportunities those networks offer, there are certain uncontrollable risks that many people underestimate. Share your experiences and discuss the pros and cons of chat rooms in class.

For example:

Pros: Meeting new people with similar interests, new friendships, access to good information ...

Cons: Fighting and vulgarity, Internet predators, waste of time, becoming addictive ...

SOLUTIONS COMPREHENSION

1. **Describe the cartoon on page 232 and point out what problems it is hinting at.**
→ Focus on Skills, Analysis of Visuals, p. 262

The cartoon shows a woman and a man chatting to each other online. Both are rather unattractive and sitting in their underwear in dirty, shabby surroundings. The woman claims to be a model while the man says that he is a sexy male dancer and races speed boats, which implies that he is quite wealthy as well as attractive. Obviously, they are both lying. The heading "Honesty on the Internet" is thus meant ironically. It implies that you cannot believe everything you read on the Internet, because it is possible to lie and change one's online identity.

2. **Make a list of the advantages and disadvantages of Internet communication.**

advantages	disadvantages
• convenience (access from home, work, school ...) • anonymity may encourage shy people to reach out and make contact/seek information they need • free access to information, easier to find people with same interests • ...	• children exposed to dangerous contacts/images (paedophiles/pornography ...) • anonymity makes it difficult to know with whom one is really communicating • exposure to false/unreliable information • impersonal, not as satisfying as "real" face-to-face contact • ...

SOLUTIONS ANALYSIS

Webcode SNG-40175-027 @

3. **Watch the video "Wo ist Klaus?" which is provided on the webcode and mediate it. Explain in what ways it demonstrates the risks of communicating on the Internet.**

A car brakes violently in front of a house and four obviously radical right-wing men, one of them restraining a pit bull terrier, ring the doorbell. It is the house of the family of Dr. Vogel. They introduce themselves and ask the mother if her son is at home. She answers that he is up in his room and they march up to see him. Another car pulls up. The bell rings again and a mixed group of men and women, clearly working in the sex trade, stand at the door. "Is Klausi there?" "Yes, he's upstairs." "Then we'll go up and try out a new position." "Yes, great" responds the mother. And off they go upstairs. Same procedure yet again and a gun-shooting action hero blasts down the door and sprays bullets through the entrance area and the living-room before asking: "Is Klaus there?" He, too, is sent upstairs. The door now opens, an older man wearing glasses, sneaks in and addresses the little daughter, who is standing there holding a little toy hare. "You have a lovely hare. Come, I'll show you a real hare." He takes hold of her hand and walks away out through the open door with her, the mother looking on. After that the following words appear on the screen: "In real life you would protect your children. Then do the same on the Internet."

Klaus clearly has had access to right-wing political sites, to pornographic sites and to violent sites on the Internet, without his parents in any way interfering or supervising what he is doing. The house is literally open-door. Anyone can come in, if you let them. The message is clear. Parents must not permit their children to access sites of this nature on the Internet. Parents must protect their children.

Particularly disturbing is the possibility that paedophiles can establish contact with vulnerable children, without the knowledge of the parents, and can even manage to arrange to meet them in person.

The video is very effective and demonstrates very clearly the risks that exist for children when it comes to unsupervised use of the Internet on their part.

4. Compare the risks and opportunities of Internet communication with the rising number of users as indicated in the table. What do you think are the reasons for the rapidly growing number of users?

- Internet tools and technology are becoming cheaper and easier to use, so more people have more access to the Internet (smart phones, net books, Wi-Fi ...).
- Convenience: much information is nowadays only available online, and/or it takes too long to obtain information via telephone, "snail mail", etc.
- Networking sites like Facebook and Twitter allow users to communicate directly with politicians, celebrities, and other famous people, as well as with a person's regular friends, family, and work contacts.

SOLUTIONS ACTIVITIES

5. In a group, create your own cartoons on social-networking and Internet security and display them in class.

Individual answers

6. 15-year-old Canadian Amanda Todd committed suicide on 10 October 2012 after she was cyberbullied, blackmailed and stalked by a suspected paedophile. Weeks before her death, she posted her story to YouTube and tried to explain her situation and the reasons for her behaviour. Do further research on Amanda Todd's story using the links provided on the webcode and watch her YouTube video which she posted on 7 September 2012.
Find out a) why she was cyber-bullied
and b) how she tried to handle the situation.

Webcode SNG-40175-027 @

a) Amanda was bullied because an unknown stranger had talked her into posing for a revealing picture in front of her webcam. This picture was distributed to her friends and family. Despite her changing schools and eventually cities, these pictures would reappear wherever she went.

b) Amanda first tried to relocate and move on. As this proved impossible when the revealing picture reappeared, she grew increasingly isolated. Experiences with drugs and alcohol, cutting, and psychological problems followed. Finally, she entered a short-term relationship with a man who had been in a relationship at the time, possibly out of desperation and isolation. When this episode became known, the bullying intensified yet again and so did her psychological problems leading to attempted suicide and later suicide.

7. In a group, get an overview and understanding of the Safebook figure on page 234 and discuss
- **the suggestions made about how to stay safe on the Internet,**
- **whether these pieces of advice would have helped Amanda Todd,**
- **possible further aspects and recommendations that are not mentioned in the figure.**

- The image suggests multiple ways to stay safe on the Internet. These include: thinking before you post, only connect with friends, be kind to others, don't share passwords, and keep settings private.
- The main piece of advice that could and would have helped Amanda Todd is the tip to only connect with friends, meaning real friends and not those met through Facebook.
- One thing that the figure should make clear is that whatever is put on the Internet can be found. That being said, the 'Think Before You Post' should include a warning against any nude, scandalous, or sexually explicit images.

8. In contrast to Amanda Todd's heartbreaking video message, the cartoon on page 232 treats the dangers of chat rooms and communication on the Internet in a humorous way.
Which of these two approaches do you consider to be a) a more effective way of getting the message to the public and b) a more appropriate way of dealing with this serious problem?
Discuss your views in class.

Individual answers

SOLUTIONS GRAMMAR/LANGUAGE

9. Fill in the missing prepositions below: If necessary, check your dictionary.

- **to be connected ______ a wireless network**
- **PC users can log ______ to the network**
- **to upload a program ______ the computer**
- **to download information ______ one's PC**
- **to save one's files ______ a hard disc**
- **to do a search ______ a topic ______ the Internet**
- **a chat room is a forum ______ debating a topic online**
- **to back a file ______ onto a CD**

- to be connected **to** a wireless network
- PC users can log **on** to the network
- to upload a program **to** the computer
- to download information **to** one's PC
- to save one's files **on/onto** a hard disc
- to do a search **on/for** a topic **on** the Internet
- a chat room is a forum **for** debating a topic online
- to back a file **up** onto a CD

10. In groups, write a short guide on how to use chat rooms safely. Your recommendations and tips should be clear but polite – use modal auxiliaries.
Example: You should not write sensitive personal data on your website.
→ Focus on Grammar, Modal Auxiliaries, p. 301

- You should not write sensitive personal data on your website.
- You must not share your personal life with somebody whom you do not know.
- You can make friends with people in chat rooms.
- You can share experiences about holidays or hobbies with people you contact in chat rooms.
- You could ask your friends about their experiences with certain chat rooms and social websites before using them yourself.

ADDITIONAL TASKS

11. Write a short statement (3 – 5 sentences) on the opportunities and risks of the Internet. Use the vocabulary on p. 232 (Tips on vocab).

It is very easy to communicate with somebody on the Internet and to reach a great number of people because most people have Internet access nowadays. It is much easier to contact them via the Internet than it is to ring them up or write a letter. It's great to see photos of people who you haven't met for some time on one of the social networks. But there is also the danger of some people misusing these things. So, one should be careful when one publishes photos on the Internet. They might attract criminals and paedophiles.

Charlie Rose

Exclusive Interview with Facebook Leadership Mark Zuckerberg and Sheryl Sandberg (pp. 235–236)

About the author	Charlie Rose is an American television talk show host and journalist. Since 1991, he has hosted *Charlie Rose*, an interview show distributed nationally by PBS since 1993. He has also co-anchored *CBS This Morning* since 2012.
About the text	The audio text is an interview with Mark Zuckerberg and Cheryl Sandberg. The interview asks about the professional relationship between the two and also the new business strategies that Facebook is employing.
Level	● ● ○
Additional material	• Audio CD 2, 9 • Comprehension: no. 26

- Die **Awareness-Aufgabe** wird im **Unterrichtsgespräch** bearbeitet.
- **Aufgabe 1** wird nach den ausführlichen Erläuterungen im Schülerbuch bearbeitet.
- Die Bearbeitung von **Aufgabe 2** findet zunächst in **Partnerarbeit** statt. Die Ergebnisse werden im Plenum diskutiert und in Form einer **Tabelle** (s. Lösungsvorschlag S. 321f.) über **Folie** gesichert.
- **Aufgabe 3** kann in **Einzelarbeit** bearbeitet werden, die Ergebnisse werden im gemeinsamen Gespräch gebündelt und informell an der **Tafel** gesichert.
- Die Ergebnisse der in **Aufgabe 4** vorgeschlagenen Diskussion können informell an der **Tafel** festgehalten werden.
- Vor dem durchzuführenden Interview (**Aufg. 5**) erhalten die Schülerinnen und Schüler Zeit, sich Fragen und Antworten auszudenken. Dabei sollten sie lediglich **Stichwörter** notieren, die sie dann zur Stärkung der mündlichen Sprachkompetenz im Laufe des Interviews elaborieren. Die Interviews können zunächst in den Zweiergruppen durchgeführt werden. Während dieser Zeit kann der Lehrer bzw. die Lehrerin einzelne Interviewpassagen anhören und ggf. verbessern. Im Anschluss an diese Phase können einige Interviews im Plenum vorgestellt werden.
- Im Vorfeld der Bearbeitung von **Aufgabe 6** können im Plenum redeeinleitende Verben gesammelt werden, auf die die Schülerinnen und Schüler dann zurückgreifen können.

SOLUTIONS AWARENESS

In a Placemat activity (→ FoM, p. 271), reflect on and share your experiences with Facebook. Did you really find "friends" or have you also met "foes" (enemies)?

I personally have not met any enemies on Facebook but have connected with quite a few friends, even some that I did not know before Facebook. Going to college for the first time, I did not really know anyone at the university and Facebook became a very useful tool to meet new people in a new place.

SOLUTIONS COMPREHENSION

CD 2, 9

1. **The interview has already been subdivided for you – but be prepared to listen to the excerpt from the interview at least two times and take notes while listening.**
   Step 1: In a first listening, get an overall impression of the interview and try to understand the gist of what is said.
   Step 2: In a second listening, focus on relevant information and make notes on these aspects:

1	• **Mark Zuckerberg's and Sheryl Sandberg's personal and professional background** Zuckerberg went through the Ivy League before starting Facebook with his friends wile Sheryl Sandberg previously worked for the search engine company Google.
2	• **how the two got to know each other** • **what they have in common** Someone mentioned to Zuckerberg that Sandberg would be a good fit for Facebook and he recruited her to the team. They both wanted to build something to 'fundamentally change who people are and how they interact.'
3	• **why *Time Magazine* named Mark Zuckerberg Person of the Year in 2010** • **numbers and factual information given about Facebook users** 'In less than seven years, Mark Zuckerberg wired together a twelfth of humanity on a social network, creating an entity almost twice as large as the United States. If Facebook were a country, it would be the third largest in the world ... It has merged with all of human life, a permanent fact that we have entered the Facebook age' ... 800 million users
4	• **Facebook's mission** • **opportunities Facebook offers to its users** The mission is to make the world more open and connected. 'People can express new things about themselves and the world, they can learn about events and products, it just opens up a lot of doors.'
5	• **how Facebook got started** • **Zuckerberg's/Facebook's first aims and goals** It started in his dorm-room and they thought there was going to be something like this, a big social network, but it started as just a little college community social network and blossomed. The first goal was to just connect the University but then became connecting more and more people.
6	• **Facebook's idea of social networking** • **the importance of friends** Social networking is supposed to grow not only number of friends but also connections between products and businesses. All things become better when you are doing it with friends. Speaking about products like pizzas or going to the movies, these are better with friends.
7	• **the wisdom of crowds versus the wisdom of friends** • **the reasons why people use Facebook.** The wisdom of crowds is about links and getting from place to place whereas the wisdom of friends is a connection between real people not just pages on the web. People have a core desire to express who they are.

Step 3: If necessary, listen to the interview a third time to complete your notes.

→ Focus on Skills, Listening Comprehension, p. 244

Webcode SNG-40175-028 @ **Tip: In order to get a more complex understanding and impression of the interview, you can also watch the video provided on the webcode.**

SOLUTIONS ANALYSIS

2. Analyse Mark Zuckerberg's and Sheryl Sandberg's explanations and line of argument* when describing the purpose and the advantages of Facebook, e.g. in order to distinguish Facebook from Google. Pay particular attention to their choice of words in connection with the respective company.

Example:

- **Facebook** → connecting people/humanity
  → the social fabric of American life ...
- **Google** → anonymity
  → ...

→ Focus on Skills, Analysis of a Non-Fictional Text, p. 258

Facebook	Google
"Make things open and connected" (Fourth Minute)	"Anonymity" (Eighth Minute)
"social fabric of American life" (Rose's description in the Third Minute)	"links to other places" (Eighth Minute)
"grows other companies because other companies grow due to other friends" (Fifth Minute)	"non-social" (Eighth Minute)
"wisdom of friends" (Seventh Minute)	"wisdom of crowds" (Seventh Minute)

3. Mark Zuckerberg claims that Facebook's mission is "to make the world more open and connected", yet at the same time he talks about "new products" like movies or music that are launched through Facebook. Examine and explain the company's strategy of conveying the impression that Facebook is just about making friends – and making people forget that Facebook is a company that wants to make profit – and that it is a business giant with an annual revenue of $5.1 billion (in 2012).

"At its purest form, Facebook is supposed to be a way for friends to connect." It was originally designed as a social media site. People could post to 'walls' and send them photos and messages if they were friends on Facebook. This was long before all the movies had their own pages and the companies tried for everyone to 'like' them; it was just for social connection. Over the last decade however, this changed from social network to a "complete worldwide phenomenon in which outside companies could peddle their products to great success". The impression that Facebook started with is still what stands at the website's core, but over the years it has changed into this multi-billion dollar business giant. People do not realize that the business side is extremely prevalent on every page that every person opens up. They still see their friends posting to their walls and sending messages and photos to one another. This makes Facebook look like it is simply there to make more friends.

SOLUTIONS ACTIVITIES

4. Discuss Sheryl Sandberg's statement that "the social web can't exist until you are your real self online" and relate it to the material about "Chat Rooms" on pages 232ff. In the light of the discussion about cyberbullying and Internet safety – additionally discuss Facebook's slogan "Connect with friends and the world around you".

→ Focus on Language, Conversation and Discussion, p. 266

Through Facebook, most people show their real selves on the profiles and connect with their real friends. But for every real self out there, there is a chance of an anonymous cyberbully trying to take advantage of those real people. When Facebook says 'Connect with friends and the world around you', the company is expecting the user to only connect with people he/she actually knows, their real friends, and then connect with pages related to nationally recognized artists, companies, brands, and icons. Chat rooms outside of Facebook allow for countless anonymous people, many predators looking for young children to exploit, a chance to connect with other nameless people. Chat rooms allow for complete strangers to communicate which leads to unsafe Internet conditions.

5. What would *you* like to ask Mark Zuckerberg and Sheryl Sandberg? Together with a partner, collect ideas on how to continue the interview and make up further questions and answers.
Tip: Be careful not to ask questions that can simply be answered with "yes" or "no".
Afterwards, act out your interviews in class.

→ Focus on Language, Conversation and Discussion, p. 266
→ Focus on Skills, Writing an Interview, p. 285

Further questions:

- How has having Sheryl here, as part of the Facebook team, really helped push Facebook further with its technology?
- What plans do you and Sheryl have in the future to possibly prevent bullying or stalking through Facebook?
- Is there a way to ensure privacy?
- People complain about the adverts along the margin.
- What is the plan concerning those?
- What are your plans going forward, to try to reach 1 billion people?

SOLUTIONS GRAMMAR/LANGUAGE

6. Together with a partner, turn Mark Zuckerberg's and Sheryl Sandberg's statements and explanations into indirect speech. Be careful to vary your formulations in the introductory sentence and pay attention to the tenses (a backshift!).
Example: Mark Zuckerberg explained that somebody he really respected had pointed Sheryl out to him as someone who could be ... for him at Facebook.

→ Focus on Grammar, Indirect Speech, pp. 298f.

- Mark Zuckerberg explained that somebody he really respected had pointed Sheryl out to him as someone who could be .... for him at Facebook.
- He emphasized that he had a lot of respect looking at what she had built at Google ... and the lessons she had learned ...
- Mark Zuckerberg said that he wanted to spend more time learning from Sheryl.
- Sheryl Sandberg expressed that they had spent most of the time talking about what they both cared about and what had motivated them.
- She pointed out that she had been able to see from Mark what he really had wanted to build ...
- Mark Zuckerberg stated that the mission of Facebook was to make the world more open and connected in a way that had not been possible before.
- He explained that he was really proud of having made 800 million people use Facebook every month ...
- Zuckerberg referred to Facebook as a way of shaping the broader web and explained that it offered the possibility for people to tap into their friends in the future.
- He explained that subscribers liked to do things together with friends instead of doing things on their own.
- Sheryl Sandberg concluded that this was the wisdom of crowds compared to the wisdom of friends.
- She stated that the information web still existed but that the evolution of the social web was about the fact that people could be online as themselves and have the desire to express themselves online while connected to others.

Sending You an SMS ... – Youth Culture & Digital Lifestyle

Adam Sorensen

Cats, Bears and Bacon. How to Build a Web-Comic Phenomenon (pp. 237–238)

About the author	Adam Sorensen is an associate editor at TIME Magazine.
About the text	The text is about successful web-comics. Sorensen describes a couple of the more successful ones and then tries to explain the things they have in common with one another and that major aspect is simplicity.
Level	● ● ●
Additional material	• Differenzierungsmaterial, p. 166

- Die **Awareness-Aufgabe** wird zunächst in **Partnerarbeit** bearbeitet, danach werden die Ergebnisse im Plenum diskutiert.
- Die Comprehension-Aufgaben (**Aufg. 1–4**) können **individuell** oder in **Partnerarbeit** bearbeitet werden. Die Schülerinnen und Schüler erhalten den Auftrag, die Aufgaben 1 und 2 in **zusammenhängenden Texten** und die Aufgaben 3 und 4 in **Stichwörtern** zu lösen. Die Ergebnisse werden im Plenum vorgelesen und besprochen. Die Sicherung der Ergebnisse der Aufgaben 3 und 4 erfolgt per **Tafelanschrieb**.

Inman as a cartoonist
↓
launch of Oatmeal in 2009
↓
creation of a website
↓
immediate success:
a few million visitors every month
↓
first book ***5 Very Good Reasons to Punch a Dolphin in the Mouth (and Other Useful Guides)***

cartoon
↙ *simplicity*
↓ *endearing stick figures; science jokes*
↘ *an amazing comedic feat*

- **Aufgabe 5** kann als die direkte Beschäftigung mit dem Text abschließende **Hausaufgabe** eingesetzt werden. Die Schülerinnen und Schüler erhalten den Auftrag, ihre Ergebnisse auf DIN-A3-Blättern festzuhalten, die dann im Klassenzimmer ausgehängt werden und im Rahmen eines **Museumsrundgangs** zur Kenntnis genommen und diskutiert werden.
- **Aufgabe 6** kann in Zusammenarbeit mit dem **Kunstunterricht** bearbeitet werden.

SOLUTIONS AWARENESS

Online comic strips have become increasingly popular and successful over the last years. Have a look at the xkcd comic strip on page 238 and discuss
a) in what way it differs from comics published in newspapers or books,
b) which "modern" topic of everyday life the comic highlights and mocks.

a) very nondescript, generic-looking stick figures without faces; very rudimentary drawings → text/content/story is more important than the visuals/particular characters/art

b) eBay/online auctions/shopping

SOLUTIONS COMPREHENSION

1. **Give an outline of Inman's online comic series "The Oatmeal" and further popular online comics.**
   - The Oatmeal: an illustrated guide to everyday life; with random animals and scientific facts; no plot; charismatic characters; obsession with science, cats and video games
   - Xkcd: obsession with science, cats and video games; stick figures and science jokes
   - Dinosaur Comics: clip art of three chatting dinosaurs

2. **What induced the National Cartoonists Society to recognize online cartoons and comics?**
   - use of viral power for social action, raising millions of dollars online for many causes; starting charities; funding a museum

3. **Point out Inman's development as a cartoonist.**
   - launch of Oatmeal in 2009; creation of a website; immediate success: a few million visitors every month; first book *5 Very Good Reasons to Punch a Dolphin in the Mouth (and Other Useful Guides)*

4. **State the relevant elements that make comics appealing to people and guarantee a reliable source of income for the cartoonist.**
   - simplicity
   - endearing stick figures; science jokes
   - an amazing comedic feat

SOLUTIONS ANALYSIS

Webcode SNG-40175-029 @ **5. Use the links provided on the webcode and take a closer look at further xkcd strips and the Oatmeal or Ryan North's Dinosaur Comics. Choose one or two that you like best and compare them to cartoons of your choice in the Students' Book, e.g. Calvin & Hobbes, Peanuts, etc. Examine in what way these "typical" cartoons differ from the online comics – and what they have in common. Afterwards, present your cartoons in class and discuss your results.**

Individual answers, e.g.:

- Some online comics may contain more adult/mature content that is not suitable for children (swear words, vulgarity, sexual or violent content ...). Traditional comics printed in the newspaper are more heavily censored than privately published online comics.
- Online comics tend to contain more inside references to nerd/online culture (Internet memes, science, bacon, *Star Wars*, etc.), while traditional comics tend to focus on everyday/family life.
- etc.

SOLUTIONS ACTIVITIES

6. In groups, draw cartoons yourself or create cartoon-like collages on a topic of your choice, e.g. online shopping, the fun and risks of cell phones, etc. Your cartoons can be critical, funny, telling a little story, etc. Display your cartoons and collages in class and discuss their various messages.

Individual solutions

Rosemary Bennett

Why Facebook Friends Click When They Meet in the Flesh (p. 239)

About the author	Rosemary Bennett is a writer for the *UK Times*. She joined Reuters as a financial markets reporter in 1994 and became its political correspondent in 1997. She moved to the *Financial Times* in 1999 and then to *The Times* where she was Deputy Political Editor for five years. She became Social Affairs Correspondent in 2007. Her areas of special interest are adoption, welfare reform and the annual *Times* charity appeal, which she runs.
About the text	The text is comparing friend interaction between those who only use text communication and those who meet in the flesh. The main difference is that those meeting in the flesh were found to be quite a bit happier than those only using social media.
Level	● ● ○
Additional material	• GaSt: no. 17 • Comprehension: no. 27

- Die **Awareness-Aufgabe** wird im Unterrichtsgespräch bearbeitet.
- **Aufgabe 1** wird **individuell** gelöst. Die Ergebnisse werden anschließend diskutiert und an der **Tafel** gesichert.

Different kinds of relationships

studies	*online relationships*	*real relationships*
1)	*no substitute for meeting face to face*	*deeper relationships*
	fewer friends	*more friends*
2)	*no difference*	
3)	*laugh 50 % less*	*laugh 50 % more*

- **Aufgabe 2** wird im **Unterrichtsgespräch** erledigt.
- **Aufgabe 3** bearbeiten die Schülerinnen und Schüler in **Einzelarbeit**. Die Ergebnisse werden in **Stichwörtern** notiert und dienen als Grundlage für mündliche **Kurzvorträge**.
- **Aufgabe 4** kann als abschließende **Hausaufgabe** eingesetzt werden.

SOLUTIONS AWARENESS

What makes Facebook so fascinating for millions of "friends"? Discuss.

It is an easy way to keep connected with thousands of people. For many, Facebook allows for those to stay in touch with people hundreds and thousands of miles away by seeing what they are up to through status updates, photos, and messages. This fascinates people because without Facebook, many friends would be lost without some type of connection.

SOLUTIONS COMPREHENSION

1. Outline the important results of the different research studies conducted by Dr. Sam Roberts.

Chatting to friends on social media is no substitute for meeting face to face (ll. 1–3). Face-to-face meetings make for deeper relationships (ll. 4–5). Heavy Facebook users have fewer friends than those who use it less often (ll. 16–18). Another study found no difference (ll. 21–24). The final study showed that those who meet face to face laugh 50 % more than those who only use textual communication (ll. 25–29).

SOLUTIONS ANALYSIS

2. Explain why the research results on social networking were so surprising.
→ Focus on Skills, Analysis of a Non-Fictional Text, p. 258

The most surprising aspect of the study was concerning the laughing. With nearly fifty per cent more of these individual's time laughing, that shows that people who use social media less have happier lives than those who are always wired (ll. 25–29). Another surprising trait was the different answers the different studies came up with. This first study showed that heavy users have less relationships while the second study showed no difference at all (ll. 16–24). The different outcomes of the studies are then shown in a new light when considering laughing as a factor and attempts to quantify happiness through laughing (ll. 25–29). These differences were surprising and frustrating because there is no concrete answer as to the question of whether or not Facebook hinders interpersonal relationships.

3. Which view does the cartoon take on social networking?

The cartoon is criticizing how people 'spend time' with their friends online. It is supposed to be a social commentary that is against the overuse of social media. The mother in the background of the cartoon telling the child to 'Not come home late' is ironic because he will be home the entire time "On Facebook with his friends". He is not leaving to go have fun with his friends in a face-to-face meeting but rather staying home and looking at a computer screen. In direct relation to the article, this cartoon is showing someone with 'relationships' through the Internet but it does not show the depth of those relationships.

4. Contrast the findings of Dr Robert's research to the aims and opportunities that Mark Zuckerberg and Sheryl Sandberg explain in the interview with Charlie Rose (pp. 235f.). What are the striking differences?

Zuckerberg and Sandberg are attempting to provide more people with a connection to the rest of the world through Facebook. They believe that Facebook allows for people to find more friends through social media and that the connectedness of the website is beneficial to the greater world. Zuckerberg also explains how Facebook has become a little more business oriented in the last few years as the website connects not only people to people but also to businesses, artists, and brand names. Everything about Facebook is supposed to show how it is a useful connecting device to all who use it. Dr Robert's findings however point another way. The overall gist of the research explains that people are much happier with in-the-flesh meetings. Even though social media does help people stay in touch, those who use social media do not feel as close to their friends as people who meet face to face (ll. 12–20). Zuckerberg and Sandberg believe relationships can be built through the Internet while Dr Robert's findings point another way, that these relationships will not be as happy as those who meet face to face (ll. 25–32).